New Learning Solutions

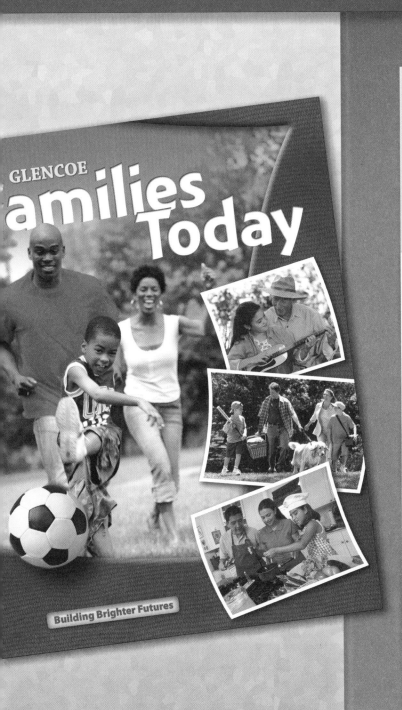

GLENCOE
amilies
Today

Building Brighter Futures

Improve Academic Performance

- National Academic Standards
- Academic Vocabulary
- Reading Guides
- Writing Tips and Activities
- Math and Science in Action
- Standardized Test Practice

Connect to the Real World

- Real-Life Scenarios & Problem Solving
- Independent Living
- Life Skills Checklists
- Financial Literacy

Hands-On Learning

- Leadership and Management Skills Support FCCLA
- Career Spotlights
- Unit Thematic Projects

Online Resources

- Online Student Edition
- Graphic Organizers
- Evaluation Rubrics
- Glossary/Spanish Glosario

 Log on to the *Families Today* Online Learning Center at **glencoe.com**

GLENCOE
Families Today

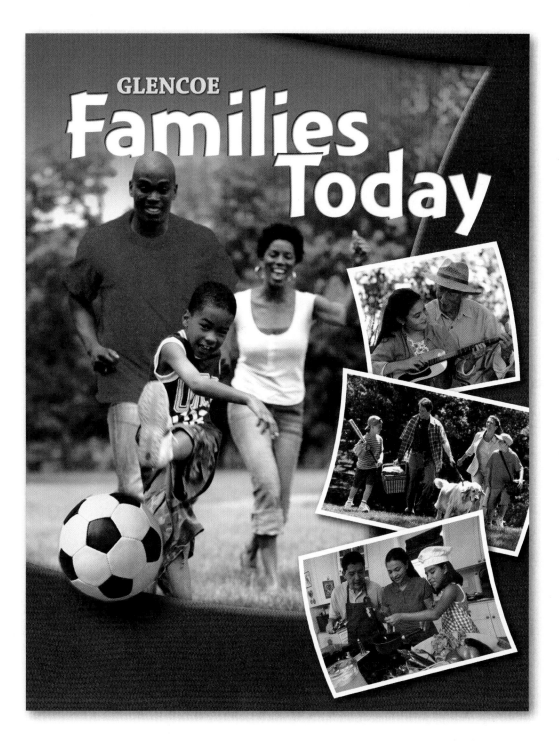

Connie R. Sasse

McGraw Hill Glencoe

The McGraw·Hill Companies

Copyright © 2009 by The McGraw-Hill Companies, Inc. All rights reserved. No part of this publication may be reproduced or distributed in any form or by any means, or stored in a database or retrieval system, without prior written permission of The McGraw-Hill Companies, Inc., including, but not limited to, network storage or transmission, or broadcast for distance learning.

Printed in the United States of America.

Send all inquiries to:
Glencoe/McGraw-Hill
21600 Oxnard Street, Suite 500
Woodland Hills, CA 91367

ISBN: 978-0-07-880662-9   (Student Edition)
MHID: 0-07-880662-3   (Student Edition)
ISBN: 978-0-07-888356-9   (Teacher Wraparound Edition)
MHID: 0-07-888356-3   (Teacher Wraparound Edition)

2 3 4 5 6 7 8 9   043/079   13 12 11 10 09 08

Author and Reviewers

Meet Our Author

Connie R. Sasse

Connie R. Sasse, CFCS, is an author and editor in the field of Family and Consumer Sciences. She is a long time member of Phi Upsilon Omicron Honor Society, AAFCS, and various state and local professional associations. She is a past president of the Kansas City Business Professionals in Family and Consumer Sciences. Connie has bachelor's and master's degrees in Home Economics Education from the University of Illinois. She did further graduate work at Texas Tech University and is a former home economics teacher and supervisor of student teachers. She is currently employed in the financial services industry.

Educational Reviewers

We wish to acknowledge the contributions of the following reviewers:

Sabrina Bennett, M.Ed., CFCS
Madison County High School
Danielsville, Georgia

Linda Brown
Sanderson High School
Raleigh, North Carolina

Nelda Clay, M.Ed., CFCS
Houston County High School
Warner Robins, Georgia

Kathryn Cox
Enloe Magnet High School
Raleigh, North Carolina

Lisa Kelley, M.S.
Monticello High School
Monticello, Arkansas

Tammy Lamparter
Smyrna High School
Smyrna, Tennessee

Sharon Ledgerwood, M.S.
Moore High School
Moore, Oklahoma

MaryJayne Lunsford
Miami Senior High School
Miami, Florida

Phoebe McGuire
James Monroe High School
Lindside, West Virginia

Vicki Pollard, M.A.
Palmetto High School
Williamston, South Carolina

Jill Tolleson
Lake Hamilton Junior High
Pearcy, Arkansas

Margaret Trione
Daphne High School
Daphne, Alabama

Patti Anne Tubbs, M.Ed.
Pierce Middle School
Merrillville, Indiana

Rhonda Wills, M.Ed.
Springfield Public Schools
Springfield, Missouri

Darlene Yoquelet, M.S., CFCS
Sachse High School
Sachse, Texas

Technical Reviewers

Joyce Armstrong, Ph.D.
Texas Woman's University
Denton, Texas

Steven Hamon, Ph.D.
The Antioch Group, Inc.
Peoria, Illinois

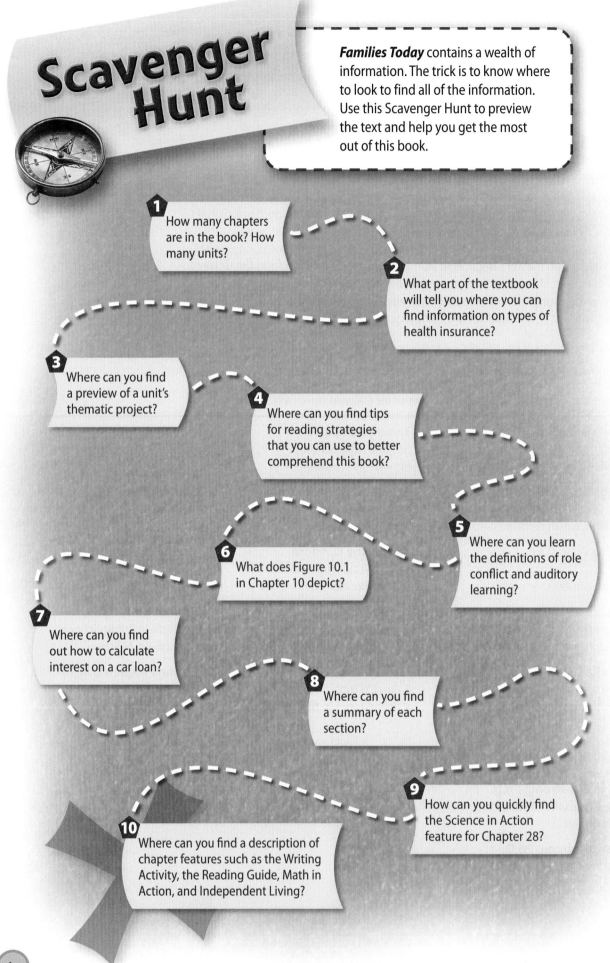

Scavenger Hunt

Families Today contains a wealth of information. The trick is to know where to look to find all of the information. Use this Scavenger Hunt to preview the text and help you get the most out of this book.

1 How many chapters are in the book? How many units?

2 What part of the textbook will tell you where you can find information on types of health insurance?

3 Where can you find a preview of a unit's thematic project?

4 Where can you find tips for reading strategies that you can use to better comprehend this book?

5 Where can you learn the definitions of role conflict and auditory learning?

6 What does Figure 10.1 in Chapter 10 depict?

7 Where can you find out how to calculate interest on a car loan?

8 Where can you find a summary of each section?

9 How can you quickly find the Science in Action feature for Chapter 28?

10 Where can you find a description of chapter features such as the Writing Activity, the Reading Guide, Math in Action, and Independent Living?

Table of Contents

FOCUS ON **Reading Strategies**
In each section, look for these reading strategies:

- Before You Read
- Graphic Organizer
- As You Read
- Reading Check
- After You Read

Table of Contents

Table of Contents

FOCUS ON

Academic Success
To help you succeed in your
classes and on tests, look
for these academic skills:

- Reading Guides
- Writing Tips
- Math Concepts and Hints
- Financial Literacy
- Science in Action

Table of Contents

FOCUS ON Visuals
Images help you learn key ideas. Answer the questions for all:

• Unit and Chapter Openers
• Photos and Captions
• Figures and Tables

Table of Contents

Table of Contents

Table of Contents

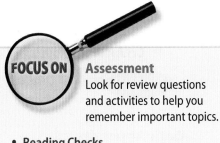

FOCUS ON Assessment
Look for review questions
and activities to help you
remember important topics.

- Reading Checks
- Section Reviews
- Chapter Reviews
- Unit Thematic Projects

Table of Contents

Unit 8 Forming Your Own Family 564

FOCUS ON Online Resources
Look for the online icon  and
go to the book's Online Learning
Center at **glencoe.com** for:

- Graphic Organizers
- Evaluation Rubrics
- Career Resources
- Worksheets
- Additional Activities

Academic Skills for Life!

How much do you think an apartment will cost? Do you know how to plan a personal budget? These academic features will help you succeed in school, on tests, and with life!

Math in Action

Science in Action

Financial Literacy

Features Table of Contents

What Would You Do?

Put yourself in someone else's shoes and use what you know to offer advice about real-world problems. Be thoughtful and give your informed opinion.

Real Life

Check Out These Life Skills!

When is the best time to exercise? How can I get more done in a day? How should I approach a difficult conversation? Use these handy checklists to find out!

Life Skills CHECKLIST

Features Table of Contents

Are You Prepared for Life After School?

Do you know how to prepare your own meals? How will you furnish your dorm room or first apartment? What is the best way to find a new job? Get ready to handle your independence with self-confidence!

INDEPENDENT Living

HOW TO...

What Do You Want to Be?

What career options are open to you? What skills will you need to succeed in your career? See what career steps these professionals took to reach their goals.

CAREER SPOTLIGHT

To the Student

Begin the Unit

Discover the World of Families

Successful readers first set a purpose for reading. *Families Today* teaches skills you need to build successful relationships at home, at school, at work, and in your community. Think about why you are reading this book. Use the Unit Opener to help you set a reading purpose and understand what you will learn in each unit. Consider how you might be able to use what you learn in your own life.

Read the Chapter Titles to find out what the topics will be.

Preview the Thematic Project at the end of the unit. A preview lets you know what is to come. Use the preview to think about how what you are learning applies to the project.

Unit 8

Forming Your Own Family

Chapter 29 **Choosing Marriage**
Chapter 30 **Build a Strong Marriage**
Chapter 31 **The Parenting Question**
Chapter 32 **Skillful Parenting**

Unit

Thematic Project Preview
Build Successful Relationships

After completing this unit, you will learn that using teamwork skills can help people in relationships make big decisions. In your unit thematic project, you can show how these skills build successful relationships.

My Journal

Decision Making Write a journal entry about one of the topics below. This will help you prepare for the unit project at the end of the unit.
* Identify the big decisions people in relationships have to make.
* Describe how people can use teamwork skills to make decisions together.
* State how you would use teamwork skills to make a difficult decision.

564

Explore the Photo
Forming a family can be exciting and fun when you take the proper steps to prepare. *What are some ways you can think of to help form a happy family?*

565

Practice Your Writing in a personal journal. Your writing will help you prepare for the project at the end of the unit.

Use the Photo to Predict what the unit will be about. Answer the question to help focus on unit topics

Close the Unit

What Did You Learn About Families?

Every unit ends with a Thematic Project that lets you explore an important issue from the unit. To complete each project, you will make decisions, do research, connect to your community, create a report, and present your project.

Read the Project Assignment and numbered steps. The assignment explains what you will need to do.

Follow the Project Checklist to make sure that you have done everything you need to complete your thematic project.

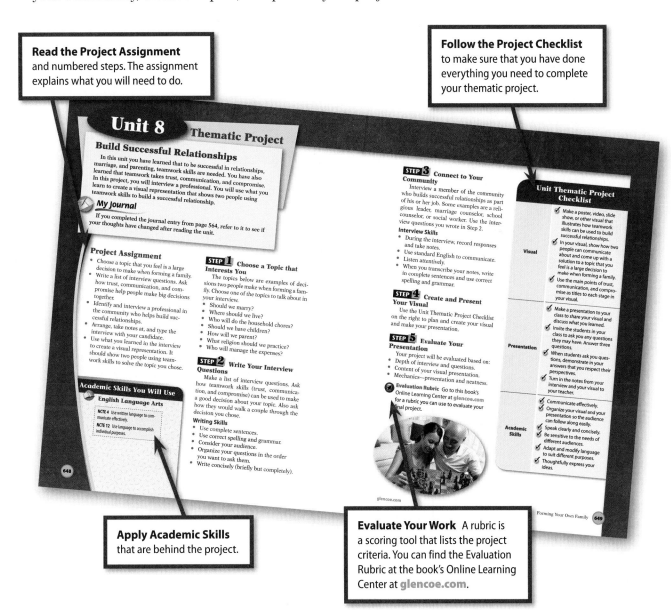

Apply Academic Skills that are behind the project.

Evaluate Your Work A rubric is a scoring tool that lists the project criteria. You can find the Evaluation Rubric at the book's Online Learning Center at **glencoe.com**.

To the Student

Begin the Chapter

What Is the Chapter All About?

Use the activities in the opener to help you connect what you already know to chapter topics. Think about the people, places, and events in your own life. Are there any similarities with those in your textbook?

Read the Chapter Objectives to preview the key ideas you will learn. Keep these in mind as you read the chapter.

CHAPTER 29

Choosing Marriage

Section 29.1
The Engagement

Section 29.2
Making Wedding Plans

▶ *Explore the Photo*
Finding the right person to marry is just as important as being the right person. *What can a person do to be the right person?*

566

Chapter Objectives

After completing this chapter, you will be able to:
- **Describe** the purposes of an engagement period.
- **Determine** when breaking an engagement is a wise choice.
- **Explain** the societal significance of weddings.
- **Identify** contracts and customs connected to weddings.
- **Suggest** ways to plan a successful wedding.

Writing Activity ✏ Descriptive Paragraph

Commitment People show commitment when they are true to their word and their values. You can show commitment to:
- A strong family.
- An education.
- Friends.
- A job.
- The environment.

Write a descriptive paragraph about one thing to which you are committed. Include specific actions you can do to strengthen your commitment.

Writing Tips To write a descriptive paragraph, follow these steps:
1. Decide what mood you want to create in the paragraph.
2. Write a strong topic sentence.
3. Orient the reader by presenting details in a logical order.
4. Select precise transition words.

Chapter 29 Choosing Marriage **567**

Strengthen Your Writing Skills
Use the writing tips to continue to develop your writing.

Explore the Photo to jump-start your thinking about the chapter's main topics.

Review the Chapter

Make Sure You Know and Understand the Concepts

Review what you learned in the chapter and see how this learning applies to your other subjects and other real-world situations.

Review Vocabulary and Key Concepts to check your recall of important ideas.

Critical Thinking takes your knowledge of the chapter further. If you have difficulty answering these questions, go back and reread the related parts of the chapter.

Apply Real-World Skills to situations that you might find in your day-to-day life.

Find More Activities Online at this book's Online Learning Center at **glencoe.com**.

Read the Chapter Summary to review the most important ideas that you should have learned in this chapter.

Practice Academic Skills and connect what you learned to your knowledge of language arts, math, science, and social studies.

Succeed on Tests with test-taking tips and practice questions.

CHAPTER 29 Review and Applications

CHAPTER SUMMARY

Section 29.1
The Engagement

Couples can use the engagement period to prepare for marriage. If a couple learns more about each other, they are less likely to have problems in their marriage. An engaged couple needs to see themselves as a team. The engagement period gives the couple's family and friends time to accept and adjust to their upcoming marriage. Many couples seek counseling before marriage. This can help ensure they are making the right decision. Wedding plans can be called off during the engagement period if a person has serious doubts.

Section 29.2
Making Wedding Plans

Weddings are important to society as well as to individuals. Marriage is a legal contract with certain rights and restrictions. A couple may make other contracts such as prenuptial agreements to cover personal concerns. Engaged couples can choose between a civil or religious wedding ceremony. There are also many customs they can include in their wedding. These customs can be regional, ethnic, or family traditions. When a couple takes time to plan for the wedding, the celebration can be less stressful.

Content and Academic Vocabulary Review

1. Use each of these content and academic vocabulary words in a sentence.
   Content Vocabulary
   ◊ engagement (p. 569)
   ◊ premarital counseling (p. 572)
   ◊ contract (p. 575)
   ◊ custom (p. 575)
   ◊ prenuptial agreement (p. 576)

   Academic Vocabulary
   ■ affect (p. 569)
   ■ trait (p. 572)
   ■ valid (p. 576)
   ■ require (p. 576)

Review Key Concepts

2. **Describe** the purposes of an engagement period.
3. **Determine** when breaking an engagement is a wise choice.
4. **Explain** the societal significance of weddings.
5. **Identify** contracts and customs connected to weddings.
6. **Suggest** ways to plan a successful wedding.

Critical Thinking

7. **Predict** Do you think people treat each other differently before marriage than they do after? How can a person prepare for this?
8. **Analyze** The bride traditionally receives more attention than the groom in wedding preparations. Why do you think this is? What change, if any, would you make in this custom?
9. **Explain** Which do you think is better, a simple wedding or an elaborate one? Give reasons for your choice.

CHAPTER 29 Review and Applications

Real-World Skills

Problem-Solving Skills

10. **Make Decisions** Jalen and Lakisha have been engaged for six months. Jalen began to notice differences in their values, so he told Lakisha he was unsure if he wanted to get married. She said that difference can make relationships interesting. What can Jalen and Lakisha do to be sure they want to get married?

Interpersonal and Collaborative Skills

11. **Work in Teams** Follow your teacher's instructions for working in teams. Research and compile a list of tasks that need to be done before a wedding. Research the order in which each task should be completed. Create a timeline that can help a bride and groom schedule their tasks. Share your list and timeline with your class.

12. **Discuss an Issue** Follow your teacher's instructions to form into groups. Discuss this statement: Marriage can survive on love alone, because loving partners put their relationship first. Have a discussion with all group members contributing to the discussion.

Family & Community Connections

15. **Interview Married Couples** Interview a married couple about their experiences being in a marriage. Ask them questions about how they met, what traits they looked for in a spouse, and what they expected marriage to be like. Share your findings with your class in an oral report.

16. **Research** Most communities offer resources that help couples prepare for marriage. Research where engaged couples can get marriage advice in your community. Share any materials you found with your class.

NET Connection

17. **Marriage Requirements** Go to this book's Online Learning Center at glencoe.com to find **Web Links** for **Marriage Documents**. List where in your state you can find legal documents you will need to marry.

Technology Applications

12. **Create a Spreadsheet** Imagine you are planning a wedding. There are many things you have to buy. You want to record the type of purchase as well as how much each purchase costs. Use spreadsheet software to create a document that lists all your wedding purchases and their costs.

Financial Literacy Skills

13. **Determine Your Financial Situation** Knowing your financial situation can help you and your partner plan for the future. Start by making a list of your possible finances: savings, monthly income, monthly expenses, and debts. Use a notebook or other document to categorize your expenses over a set period of time, such as a week or a month.

Additional Activities For additional activities, go to this book's Online Learning Center through glencoe.com.

Academic Skills

Mathematics

18. **Calculate Average Reception Costs** Most couples have a reception after their wedding ceremony to celebrate the marriage. Reception costs often include the catering, band, linens, and renting a hall. Most Americans spend about 48% of their wedding budget on the reception. If you have a wedding budget of $20,000, how much money will you need to cover the cost of the reception?

Math Concept **Multiply Decimals by Whole Numbers** A percent is a ratio that compares a number to 100. To multiply with percentages:

Starting Hint: You can rewrite the percent (48%) as a fraction with a denominator of 100. Convert the fraction to a decimal. Multiply this decimal by the number ($20,000). Remember to put the decimal point in the correct place.

For math help, go to the Math Appendix at the back of the book.

NCTM Number and Operations Understand numbers, ways of representing numbers, relationships among numbers, and number systems.

English Language Arts

19. **Write a Thank You Letter** Imagine you just got married. Your family helped you with a lot of the wedding preparations. You would like to send a letter thanking your family for making your wedding day special. Draft a letter to thank them. Include details stating what you really appreciated. Share your thank you letter with the class.

NCTE 5 Use different writing process elements to communicate effectively.

Social Studies

20. **Research Values** Research another culture's system of values. If possible, interview someone who grew up in that culture. Name and describe the values in that culture. Explain how those values affect weddings and marriage in that culture. Share your findings with the class in a five-minute oral report.

NCSS I.c Apply an understanding of culture as an integrated whole that explains the functions and interactions of traditions, beliefs and values, and behavior patterns.

STANDARDIZED TEST PRACTICE

MULTIPLE CHOICE
Read the following paragraph. Then read the question below the paragraph. Read the answer choices and choose the best answer to fill in the blank. Write your answer on a separate sheet of paper.

21. Lena's parents had premarital counseling and they have been married over 30 years. As a result, Lena is biased towards seeing a premarital counselor before she marries. In this sentence, the word *biased* means

a. running diagonally across the weave of a fabric
b. a distortion of a set of statistical data
c. voltage applied across an electronic

Test-Taking Tip In a multiple choice test, read the question before you read the answer choices. Try to answer the question before you read the answer choices. This way, the answer choices will not throw you off.

582 Unit 8 Forming Your Own Family

glencoe.com

To the Student

Prepare with Reading Guides and Study Tools

Use the reading guide at the beginning of each section to preview what you will learn in the section. See if you can predict events or outcomes by using clues and information that you already know.

Predict Before You Read what the section will be about.

Check Vocabulary lists for words you do not know. You can look them up in the glossary before you read the section.

Look for Academic Standards throughout the text. You can apply what you learn to other subjects.

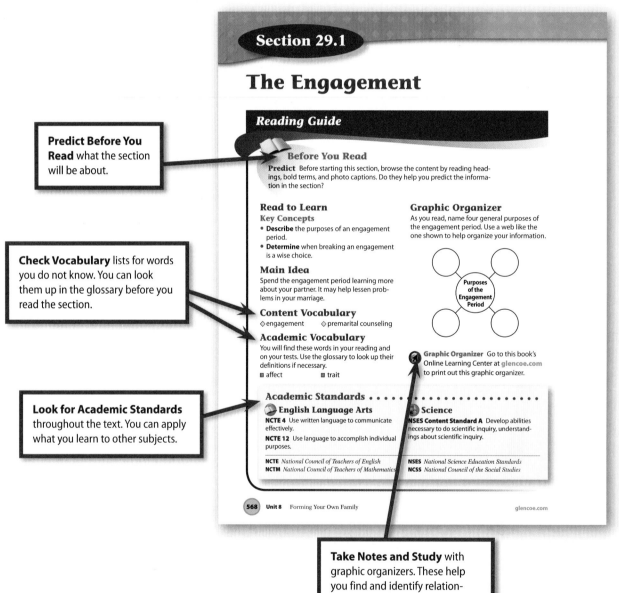

Section 29.1

The Engagement

Reading Guide

Before You Read

Predict Before starting this section, browse the content by reading headings, bold terms, and photo captions. Do they help you predict the information in the section?

Read to Learn
Key Concepts
- **Describe** the purposes of an engagement period.
- **Determine** when breaking an engagement is a wise choice.

Main Idea
Spend the engagement period learning more about your partner. It may help lessen problems in your marriage.

Content Vocabulary
◇ engagement   ◇ premarital counseling

Academic Vocabulary
You will find these words in your reading and on your tests. Use the glossary to look up their definitions if necessary.
▪ affect   ▪ trait

Graphic Organizer
As you read, name four general purposes of the engagement period. Use a web like the one shown to help organize your information.

Purposes of the Engagement Period

Graphic Organizer Go to this book's Online Learning Center at glencoe.com to print out this graphic organizer.

Academic Standards . . . . .
English Language Arts
NCTE 4 Use written language to communicate effectively.
NCTE 12 Use language to accomplish individual purposes.

Science
NSES Content Standard A Develop abilities necessary to do scientific inquiry, understandings about scientific inquiry.

NCTE *National Council of Teachers of English*
NCTM *National Council of Teachers of Mathematics*

NSES *National Science Education Standards*
NCSS *National Council of the Social Studies*

568 **Unit 8** Forming Your Own Family

glencoe.com

Take Notes and Study with graphic organizers. These help you find and identify relationships in the information you read.

Review the Section

Check Your Comprehension with Self-Assessments

After you read, use the section closer to check your understanding. Make sure that you can answer the questions in your own words before moving on in the text.

Broken Engagements

When a couple gets engaged, a marriage usually follows. However, about one-third of all engagements are broken before marriage. Many of these are broken with good reason.

As their engagement proceeds, some couples find that they are not ready to make the needed sacrifices and compromises for marriage. Some couples have conflicting traits and values that may be too difficult to overcome.

As people grow and have different experiences, it may cause strain on a relationship. Annessa and Lamar got engaged just before Annessa enlisted in the navy. Six months later Annessa came home. She had changed so much that she seemed like a stranger to Lamar. He, too, had made new friends and found new interests. When couples like Annessa and Lamar no longer have much in common, they may rethink their engagement. The lack of parental approval ends some engagements as well.

Breaking an engagement can be a painful experience. Both partners may grieve for the loss of an important relationship. They may feel a sense of failure. Explaining the situation to family and friends can be awkward. Breaking the ties is easier if the couple can act with dignity and treat each other with respect.

Even though a broken engagement is hard, it is not as difficult as a troubled marriage or a divorce. Marriage is meant to be a lifetime commitment. It should only happen when both partners know they can live happily with the decision.

Verify Your Understanding of key concepts in the section.

Section 29.1   After You Read

Review Key Concepts

1. **Name** four ways the engagement period prepares you for marriage.
2. **Explain** at least two reasons why a couple would consider breaking their engagement.

Practice Academic Skills

Practice Academic Skills with these cross-curricular activities.

English Language Arts

3. Imagine that you are engaged. List and define five characteristics or qualities that you would want in your marriage partner. Give an example of how he or she could demonstrate each of those qualities in your marriage.

4. If you are engaged, you and your partner may get marriage advice from a premarital counselor. Brainstorm some ways you and your partner may differ. Then write down two questions you might ask a premarital counselor before you got married.

> **NCTE 4** Use written language to communicate effectively.

> **NCTE 12** Use language to accomplish individual purposes.

Check Your Answers Check your answers at this book's Online Learning Center through **glencoe.com**.

Chapter 29 Choosing Marriage **573**

glencoe.com

Check Your Answers online at this book's Online Learning Center at **glencoe.com**.

To the Student

As You Read | Use Reading Strategies and Visuals to Study Effectively

In addition to the reading guide at the beginning of each section, there are lots of reading strategies to help you comprehend the text.

Keep a Vocabulary Journal Write down vocabulary words then find definitions in the text and in the glossary at the back of the book.

Connect what you already know to the new ideas you learn as you read.

Examine Visuals to reinforce content. Answer the questions so you can better discuss topics in the section.

Skim the Headings to help identify the main idea and supporting details.

Reading Checks let you pause to respond to what you have read.

Purposes of Engagement

Before marriage, most people go through an **engagement**. An engagement is a promise or intention to marry. At this stage, couples may be ready for the commitment and responsibilities of marriage. The engagement period is a time to prepare for the wedding.

During this time, couples may buy a wedding dress and change their names on their bank accounts. These tasks may be necessary, but the wedding day is not the only thing couples prepare for during their engagement. More importantly, the engagement period is a time to prepare for marriage. It lets couples address issues that may affect, or influence, the success of their marriage. This is a time of transition that leads to the joining of two lives into one future.

Learn About Each Other

Couples should use their engagement time to make sure they really know each other. It is good to know and be comfortable with aspects of the other's life such as their family goals, spending patterns, cleanliness habits, and food preferences. If they do this, there tend to be fewer surprises that can lead to problems during marriage. Some experts say the engagement should last six to twelve months. This allows enough time for this discovery process.

Identify Differences

During an engagement, a couple can identify and deal with differences. They can then decide if the difference will enhance or weaken their relationship. What effect do you think the following differences may have on a marriage?

- Tia likes fast food. Scott is a vegetarian.
- Martha wants to have two children once she and Glen have secure jobs. Glen wants to have four children, beginning right away.
- Tanya wants to live in a small town and Barry likes the city.
- Marcus does not like to be around a large group of people and Tabitha loves to go to big parties.

Only the couple can determine if their differences will threaten the success of their marriage. Relationships are successful when each partner knows his or her values and expectations.

Vocabulary
You can find definitions in the glossary at the back of this book.

As You Read
Connect Do you know any married couples? How long was their engagement period?

Look Closely
Spend time together to learn about your differences. What are some differences couples may have?

Chapter 29 Choosing Mar... 569

...t **premarital counseling** before ...marital counseling is when couples ...ed professionals before marriage. ...unseling helps couples focus on ...rrying. It lets them address questions...tionship. Couples may be asked: ...u fall in love? Was it quick and ...id it occur slowly for reasons ...d?

...your partner's most endearing ...g quality? Is it long-lasting? ...as appealing in the future? ...er reveal your weaknesses, ...each other? Are you both ...?

...ally helps show potential trouble ...it helps when a couple knows how they disagree on certain topics. It lets them handle their problems better and often resolve them before marriage.

There are other resources in the community that can help engaged couples. Religious organizations, social service agencies, and other educational groups may have classes or information on marriage issues.

The engagement period is an important step before marriage. It lets couples gain a deeper understanding of themselves and their relationship. This insight can help build an enduring marriage.

Reading Check **Summarize** How can seeking advice from a premarital counselor be beneficial for engaged couples?

Get Help
Many couples seek professional advice before marriage. Where can you find a premarital counselor in your community?

572 Unit 8 Forming Your Own Family

glencoe.com

To the Student

Study with Features

Skills You Can Really Use at School and in Life!

As you read, look for feature boxes throughout each chapter. These features build skills that relate to other academic subjects and prepare you for life on your own.

Make Math Simple You use math everyday—even if it is just counting money to buy a drink at your campus store. See how to use starting hints to break down math problems and solve them step by step.

Math in Action

Cost of Going Out to Eat

Dining out can be more convenient than making meals at home. It can also be more expensive. Compare the costs of dining out and eating at home. Use these steps:

1. List two meals you would typically eat when you go out.
2. Contact two restaurants and ask the cost of the meals you have listed.
3. List the ingredients for making the same food items at home.
4. Go to a grocery store and find prices for the ingredients you have listed.

Math Concept **Multi-Step Problems** When solving problems with more than one step, think through each step first.

Starting Hint: Calculate the average cost of dining out. Then total the cost of the ingredients for eating in. Subtract the smaller number from the larger number and determine which is more economical.

Building Academic Skills Go to this book's Online Learning Center through glencoe.com to complete a worksheet for this activity.

NCTM Problem Solving Apply and adapt a variety of appropriate strategies to solve problems.

Math For math help, go to the Math Appendix at the back of the book.

Science in Action

Scientific Method

Making sound decisions is important in order to solve problems and build a strong family life. Some of these decisions may include where to live or when to have children. Use the following steps to make a decision using the scientific method.

1. Define the question to be answered.
2. Form a hypothesis or possible answer.
3. Experiment. Collect and examine data.
4. Form a conclusion.

Building Academic Skills Go to this book's Online Learning Center through glencoe.com to complete a worksheet for this activity.

NSES Content Standard A Develop abilities necessary to do scientific inquiry, understandings about scientific inquiry.

Learn the Secrets of Science The secret is that it can be easy! You can use scientific principles and concepts in your everyday activities. Investigate and analyze the world around you with these basic skills.

Real Life — Family Living Careers

As you study families, take a look at the related career fields, such as those in the Human Services. Many careers let you work with families and provide services for them.

To be a success you will need good interpersonal skills and a concern for others. You can learn a lot about careers in family life if you do a little bit of research. Some examples of careers in the Human Services include:

- Child Care
- Counseling
- Health Care
- Social Services
- Personal Care Services
- Consumer Services

Problem-Solving Aiden is an outgoing, energetic student. He has a talent for inspiring and organizing others. He was the main motivation behind the senior class blood donation drive. Aiden thinks a career working with families would be rewarding. He wonders if he has the patience for a job in counseling, child care, or social services. He is not sure how to decide which career would be best. What advice would you give Aiden?

Solve Real-World Problems You will encounter disagreements or conflicts with your friends and family. Read about real problems and tell how you would resolve the issues.

To the Student

Features (continued)

Financial Literacy

Giving Back to Your Community

Together Ramon and Lupe earn about $80,000 per year. Giving back to the community is an important value to Ramon and Lupe, so they set aside 10% of their earnings to give to nonprofit organizations, such as rescue missions and literacy projects. Determine how much money they donate to nonprofits each year.

Math Concept **Multiplying by Percents** To compute how much money Ramon and Lupe give to nonprofits each year, multiply the amount they earn by the percentage they give away:

annual salary × percent donated = annual amount donated.

Starting Hint: To multiply by a percent you must change the percent to a decimal by moving the decimal point two places to the left. In this problem, 10% becomes 10, which you will multiply by 80,000.

Math For math help, go to the Math Appendix at the back of the book.

NCTM Number and Operations Compute fluently and make reasonable estimates.

Life Skills CHECKLIST

Communication Skills

Positive Discussions Your discussions will be positive and productive if you:

✓ Treat everyone with respect.
✓ Encourage others to share their ideas.
✓ Compliment others on their good ideas.
✓ Keep an open mind to other points of view.
✓ Share your thoughts and feelings.
✓ Consider how others feel.
✓ Be tactful.

Keep Your Life in Check! Simple checklists give you a quick reference to help navigate life issues. Show your strong character with these easy-to-remember tips about communication, leadership, management, and thinking skills.

Your Money Matters! Learn the basics of personal finance to help you make the most out of your money. Build a budget, compare costs, and find the best deals.

Get Ready for Life on Your Own Being on your own can be fun, but independence can bring many new challenges. Discover how to make new friends, plan a celebration, cook for others, or handle stress effectively. You will develop strong strategies to handle new situations.

INDEPENDENT Living

HOW TO Handle Stress

Being a teen is stressful. You have to juggle homework, family, friends, dating, and after-school activities. You may also be handling other stressful situations, such as parental divorce and peer pressure. Too much stress can take a toll on your emotional and physical health. Follow these guidelines to manage your stress:

1. **Exercise regularly.** It is a good idea to be physically active at least 60 minutes each day. Take a walk, swim some laps, or ride your bike.
2. **Eat for your health.** Eat regular meals instead of eating on the run or indulging in junk food. When you are in a hurry, reach for fruit, yogurt, and other healthy foods.
3. **Get plenty of sleep.** When you are well rested, you are better able to tackle what life throws at you. In addition, sleep gives your body a chance to recover from stress.
4. **Prioritize your activities.** Avoid overbooking yourself. Make sure that the things you choose to do are those that have the highest priority.
5. **Talk it out.** Talk about your problems with an adult or trusted friend. Sometimes letting out your fears or frustrations can reduce your stress level.

Take Action You may be putting pressure on yourself to be perfect. Of course, no one is perfect, but that can be hard to remember when your stress level is high. On a piece of paper, write down a promise to accept yourself at your best, not at a level of perfection you cannot achieve. Sign and date the promise, and keep it somewhere visible.

Career Options | Think About Your Future

What do you want to be? Get profiles of real-world workers to understand more about your career options. Think about what skills you would need to explore various career paths.

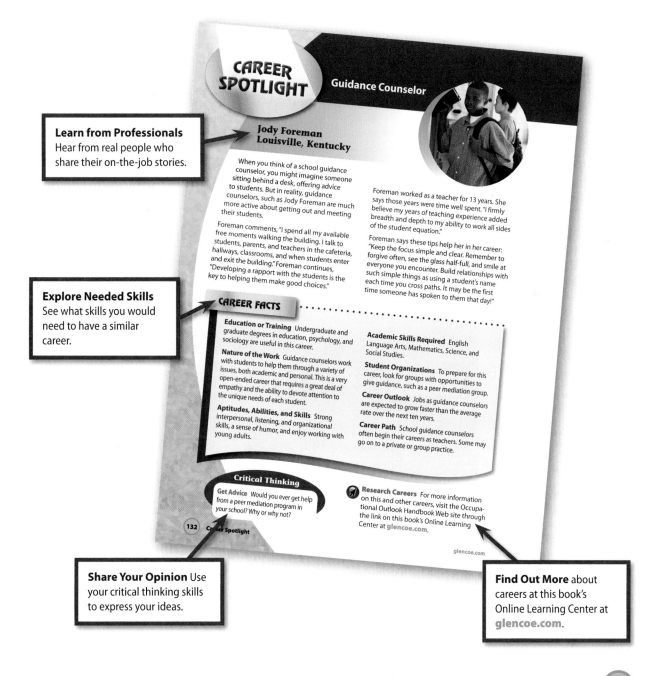

Learn from Professionals Hear from real people who share their on-the-job stories.

Explore Needed Skills See what skills you would need to have a similar career.

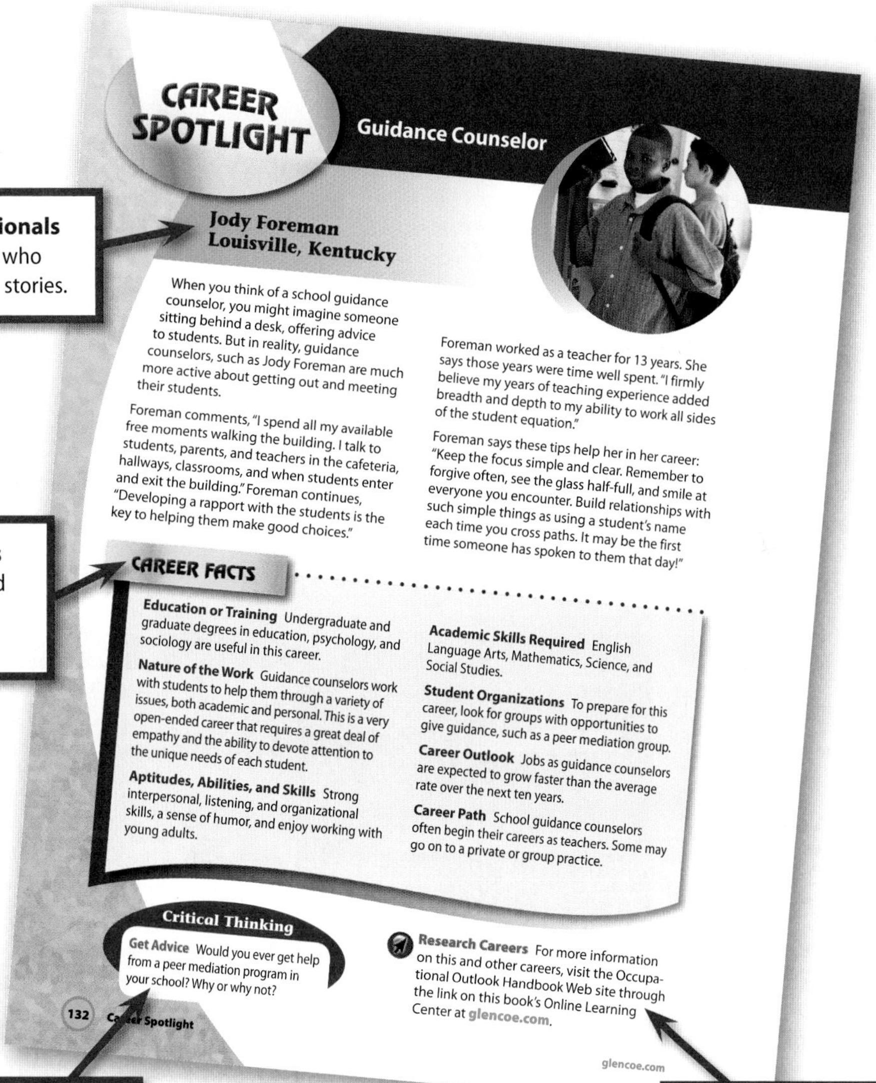

CAREER SPOTLIGHT

Guidance Counselor

Jody Foreman
Louisville, Kentucky

When you think of a school guidance counselor, you might imagine someone sitting behind a desk, offering advice to students. But in reality, guidance counselors, such as Jody Foreman are much more active about getting out and meeting their students.

Foreman comments, "I spend all my available free moments walking the building. I talk to students, parents, and teachers in the cafeteria, hallways, classrooms, and when students enter and exit the building." Foreman continues, "Developing a rapport with the students is the key to helping them make good choices."

Foreman worked as a teacher for 13 years. She says those years were time well spent. "I firmly believe my years of teaching experience added breadth and depth to my ability to work all sides of the student equation."

Foreman says these tips help her in her career: "Keep the focus simple and clear. Remember to forgive often, see the glass half-full, and smile at everyone you encounter. Build relationships with such simple things as using a student's name each time you cross paths. It may be the first time someone has spoken to them that day!"

CAREER FACTS

Education or Training Undergraduate and graduate degrees in education, psychology, and sociology are useful in this career.

Nature of the Work Guidance counselors work with students to help them through a variety of issues, both academic and personal. This is a very open-ended career that requires a great deal of empathy and the ability to devote attention to the unique needs of each student.

Aptitudes, Abilities, and Skills Strong interpersonal, listening, and organizational skills, a sense of humor, and enjoy working with young adults.

Academic Skills Required English Language Arts, Mathematics, Science, and Social Studies.

Student Organizations To prepare for this career, look for groups with opportunities to give guidance, such as a peer mediation group.

Career Outlook Jobs as guidance counselors are expected to grow faster than the average rate over the next ten years.

Career Path School guidance counselors often begin their careers as teachers. Some may go on to a private or group practice.

Critical Thinking

Get Advice Would you ever get help from a peer mediation program in your school? Why or why not?

Research Careers For more information on this and other careers, visit the Occupational Outlook Handbook Web site through the link on this book's Online Learning Center at glencoe.com.

132 Career Spotlight

glencoe.com

Share Your Opinion Use your critical thinking skills to express your ideas.

Find Out More about careers at this book's Online Learning Center at **glencoe.com**.

To the Student

Online Learning Center

Use the Internet to Extend Your Learning

Follow these steps to access the textbook resources at the *Families Today* Online Learning Center.

Online Learning Center Icon Look for this icon throughout the text that directs you to the book's Online Learning Center for more activities and information.

Graphic Organizer Go to this book's Online Learning Center at **glencoe.com** to print out this graphic organizer.

Step 1
Go to **glencoe.com**.

Step 2
Select **your state** from the pull-down menu.

Step 3
Select **Student/Parent**.

Step 4
Select **Family & Consumer Sciences**.

Step 5
Click **ENTER**.

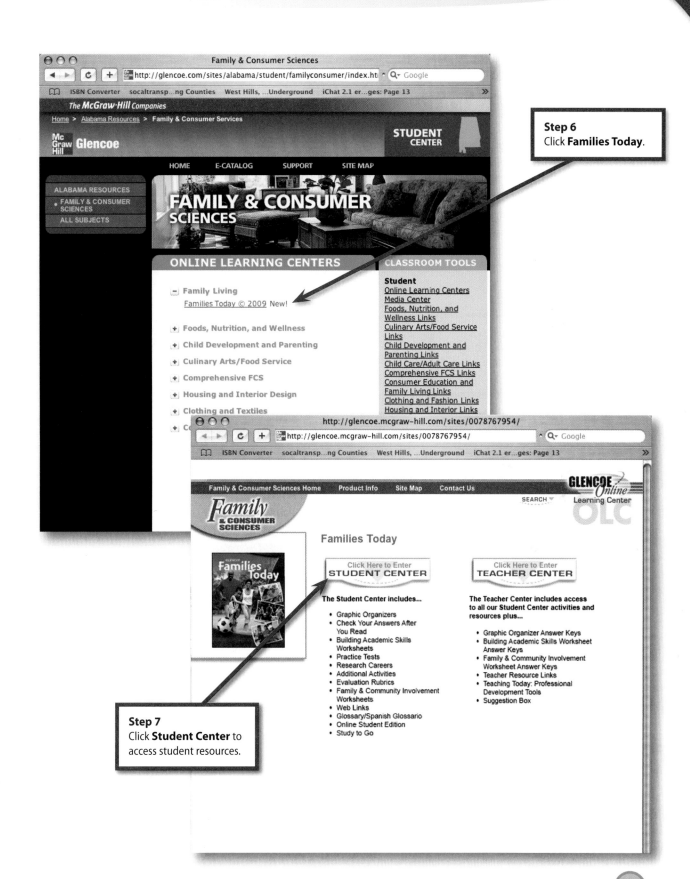

Step 6
Click **Families Today**.

Step 7
Click **Student Center** to access student resources.

Prepare for Academic Success!

By improving your academic skills, you improve your ability to learn and achieve success now and in the future. It also improves your chances of landing a high-skill, high-wage job. The features and assessments in *Families Today* provide many opportunities for you to strengthen your academic skills.

Academic Standards Look for this box throughout the text to know what academic skills you are learning.

NCTM Number and Operations Understand numbers, ways of representing numbers, relationships among numbers, and number systems.

National English Language Arts Standards

To help incorporate literacy skills (reading, writing, listening, and speaking) into *Families Today*, each section contains a listing of the language arts skills covered. These skills have been developed into standards by the *National Council of Teachers of English and International Reading Association*.

- Read texts to acquire new information.
- Read literature to build an understanding of the human experience.
- Apply strategies to interpret texts.
- Use written language to communicate effectively.
- Use different writing process elements to communicate effectively.
- Conduct research and gather, evaluate, and synthesize data to communicate discoveries.
- Use information resources to gather information and create and communicate knowledge.
- Develop an understanding of diversity in language use across cultures.
- Participate as members of literacy communities.
- Use language to accomplish individual purposes.

National Academic Standards

National Math Standards

You also have opportunities to practice math skills indicated by standards developed by the *National Council of Teachers of Mathematics*.

- Algebra
- Data Analysis and Probability
- Geometry
- Measurement
- Number and Operation
- Problem Solving

National Science Standards

The *National Science Education Standards* outline these science skills that you can practice in this text.

- Science as Inquiry
- Physical Science
- Life Science
- Earth and Space Science
- Science and Technology
- Science in Personal and Social Perspectives
- History and Nature of Science

National Social Studies Standards

The *National Council for the Social Studies* is another organization that provides standards to help guide your studies. Activities in this text relate to these standards.

- Culture
- Time, Continuity, and Change
- People, Places, and Environments
- Individual Development and Identity
- Individuals, Groups, and Institutions
- Power, Authority, and Governance
- Production, Distribution, and Consumption
- Science, Technology, and Society
- Global Connections
- Civic Ideals and Practices

Reading Skills Handbook

▶ Reading: What's in It for You?

What role does reading play in your life? The possibilities are countless. Are you on a sports team? Perhaps you like to read about the latest news and statistics in sports or find out about new training techniques. Are you looking for a part-time job? You might be looking for advice about résumé writing, interview techniques, or information about a company. Are you enrolled in an English class, an algebra class, or a business class? Then your assignments require a lot of reading.

Improving or Fine-Tuning Your Reading Skills Will:

- ◆ Improve your grades.
- ◆ Allow you to read faster and more efficiently.
- ◆ Improve your study skills.
- ◆ Help you remember more information accurately.
- ◆ Improve your writing.

▶ The Reading Process

Good reading skills build on one another, overlap, and spiral around in much the same way that a winding staircase goes around and around while leading you to a higher place. This handbook is designed to help you find and use the tools you will need **before, during,** and **after** reading.

Strategies You Can Use

- ◆ Identify, understand, and learn new words.
- ◆ Understand why you read.
- ◆ Take a quick look at the whole text.
- ◆ Try to predict what you are about to read.

- ◆ Take breaks while you read and ask yourself questions about the text.
- ◆ Take notes.
- ◆ Keep thinking about what will come next.
- ◆ Summarize.

▶ Vocabulary Development

Word identification and vocabulary skills are the building blocks of the reading and the writing process. By learning to use a variety of strategies to build your word skills and vocabulary, you will become a stronger reader.

Use Context to Determine Meaning

The best way to expand and extend your vocabulary is to read widely, listen carefully, and participate in a rich variety of discussions. When reading on your own, though, you can often figure out the meanings of new words by looking at their **context,** the other words and sentences that surround them.

Tips for Using Context

Look for clues like these:

◆ A synonym or an explanation of the unknown word in the sentence:
  Elise's shop specialized in millinery, or hats for women.
◆ A reference to what the word is or is not like:
  An archaeologist, like a historian, deals with the past.
◆ A general topic associated with the word:
  The cooking teacher discussed the best way to braise meat.
◆ A description or action associated with the word:
  He used the shovel to dig up the garden.

Predict a Possible Meaning

Another way to determine the meaning of a word is to take the word apart. If you understand the meaning of the **base,** or **root,** part of a word, and also know the meanings of key syllables added either to the beginning or end of the base word, you can usually figure out what the word means.

Word Origins Since Latin, Greek, and Anglo-Saxon roots are the basis for much of our English vocabulary, having some background in languages can be a useful vocabulary tool. For example, *astronomy* comes from the Greek root *astro,* which means "relating to the stars." *Stellar* also has a meaning referring to stars, but its origin is Latin. Knowing root words in other languages can help you determine meanings, derivations, and spellings in English.

Prefixes and Suffixes A prefix is a word part that can be added to the beginning of a word. For example, the prefix *semi* means "half" or "partial," so *semicircle* means "half a circle." A suffix is a word part that can be added to the end of a word. Adding a suffix often changes a word from one part of speech to another.

Using Dictionaries A dictionary provides the meaning or meanings of a word. Look at the sample dictionary entry on the next page to see what other information it provides.

Thesauruses and Specialized Reference Books A thesaurus provides synonyms and often antonyms. It is a useful tool to expand your vocabulary. Remember to check the exact definition of the listed words in a dictionary before you use a thesaurus. Specialized dictionaries such as *Barron's Dictionary of Business Terms* or *Black's Law Dictionary* list terms and expressions that are not commonly included in a general dictionary. You can also use online dictionaries.

Glossaries Many textbooks and technical works contain condensed dictionaries that provide an alphabetical listing of words used in the text and their specific definitions.

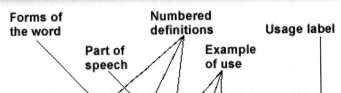

Dictionary Entry

Forms of the word

Part of speech

Numbered definitions

Example of use

Usage label

help (help) **helped** or (archaic) **holp**, **helped** or (archaic) **hol-pen**, **help-ing**. *v.t.* **1.** to provide with support, as in the performance of a task; be of service to: *He helped his brother paint the room.* ▲ also used elliptically with a preposition or adverb: *He helped the old woman up the stairs.* **2.** to enable (someone or something) to accomplish a goal or achieve a desired effect: *The coach's advice helped the team to win.* **3.** to provide with sustenance or relief, as in time of need or distress; succor: *The Red Cross helped the flood victims.* **4.** to promote or contribute to; further. *The medication helped his recovery.* **5.** to be useful or profitable to; be of advantage to: *It might help you if you read the book.* **6.** to improve or remedy: *Nothing really helped his sinus condition.* **7.** to prevent; stop: *I can't help his rudeness.* **8.** to refrain from; avoid: *I couldn't help smiling when I heard the story.* **9.** to wait on or serve (often with to): *The clerk helped us. The hostess helped him to the dessert.* **10. cannot help but.** *Informal* cannot but. **11. so help me (God).** oath of affirmation. **12. to help oneself to.** to take or appropriate: *The thief helped himself to all the jewels.* —*v.i.* to provide support, as in the performance of a task; be of service. —*n.* **1.** act of providing support, service, or sustenance. **2.** source of support, service, or sustenance. **3.** person or group of persons hired to work for another or others. **4.** means of improving, remedying, or preventing. [Old English *helpan* to aid, succor, benefit.] **Syn.** *v.t.* **1. Help, aid, assist** mean to support in a useful way. Help is the most common word and means to give support in response to a known or expressed need or for a definite purpose: *Everyone helped to make the school fair a success.* **Aid** means to give relief in times of distress or difficulty: *It is the duty of rich nations to aid the poor.* **Assist** means to serve another person in the performance of his task in a secondary capacity: *The secretary assists the officer by taking care of his corresponding.*

Idioms

Origin (etymology)

Synonyms

Recognize Word Meanings Across Subjects Have you learned a new word in one class and then noticed it in your reading for other subjects? The word might not mean exactly the same thing in each class, but you can use the meaning you already know to help you understand what it means in another subject area. For example:

Math Each digit represents a different place **value**.

Health Your **values** can guide you in making healthful decisions.

Economics The **value** of a product is measured in its cost.

▶ Understanding What You Read

Reading comprehension means understanding—deriving meaning from—what you have read. Using a variety of strategies can help you improve your comprehension and make reading more interesting and more fun.

Read for a Reason

To get the greatest benefit from your reading, **establish a purpose for reading.** In school, you have many reasons for reading, such as:

- to learn and understand new information.
- to find specific information.
- to review before a test.
- to complete an assignment.
- to prepare (research) before you write.

As your reading skills improve, you will notice that you apply different strategies to fit the different purposes for reading. For example, if you are reading for entertainment, you might read quickly, but if you read to gather information or follow directions, you might read more slowly, take notes, construct a graphic organizer, or reread sections of text.

Draw on Personal Background

Drawing on personal background may also be called activating prior knowledge. Before you start reading a text, ask yourself questions like these:

- What have I heard or read about this topic?
- Do I have any personal experience relating to this topic?

Using a K-W-L Chart A K-W-L chart is a good device for organizing information you gather before, during, and after reading. In the first column, list what you already **know,** then list what you **want** to know in the middle column. Use the third column when you review and assess what you **learned.** You can also add more columns to record places where you found information and places where you can look for more information.

K (What I already know)	W (What I want to know)	L (What I have learned)

Adjust Your Reading Speed Your reading speed is a key factor in how well you understand what you are reading. You will need to adjust your speed depending on your reading purpose.

Scanning means running your eyes quickly over the material to look for words or phrases. Scan when you need a specific piece of information.

Skimming means reading a passage quickly to find its main idea or to get an overview. Skim a text when you preview to determine what the material is about.

Reading for detail involves careful reading while paying attention to text structure and monitoring your understanding. Read for detail when you are learning concepts, following complicated directions, or preparing to analyze a text.

▶ Techniques to Understand and Remember What You Read

Preview

Before beginning a selection, it is helpful to **preview** what you are about to read.

> **Previewing Strategies**
>
> ◆ Read the title, headings, and subheadings of the selection.
> ◆ Look at the illustrations and notice how the text is organized.
> ◆ Skim the selection: Take a glance at the whole thing.
> ◆ Decide what the main idea might be.
> ◆ Predict what a selection will be about.

Predict

Have you ever read a mystery, decided who committed the crime, and then changed your mind as more clues were revealed? You were adjusting your predictions. Did you smile when you found out that you guessed who committed the crime? You were verifying your predictions.

As you read, take educated guesses about story events and outcomes; that is, **make predictions** before and during reading. This will help you focus your attention on the text and it will improve your understanding.

Determine the Main Idea

When you look for the **main idea**, you are looking for the most important statement in a text. Depending on what kind of text you are reading, the main idea can be located at the very beginning (news stories in newspaper or a magazine) or at the end (scientific research document). Ask yourself the following questions:

- What is each sentence about?
- Is there one sentence that is more important than all the others?
- What idea do details support or point out?

Taking Notes

Cornell Note-Taking System: There are many methods for note taking. The **Cornell Note-Taking System** is a well-known method that can help you organize what you read. To the right is a note-taking activity based on the Cornell Note-Taking System.

Graphic organizers: Using a graphic organizer to retell content in a visual representation will help you remember and retain content. You might make a **chart** or **diagram,** organizing what you have read. Here are some examples of graphic organizers:

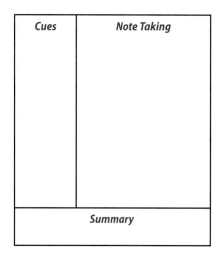

Venn diagrams When mapping out a compare-and-contrast text structure, you can use a Venn diagram. The outer portions of the circles will show how two characters, ideas, or items contrast, or are different, and the overlapping part will compare two things, or show how they are similar.

Flow charts To help you track the sequence of events, or cause and effect, use a flow chart. Arrange ideas or events in their logical, sequential order. Then draw arrows between your ideas to indicate how one idea or event flows into another.

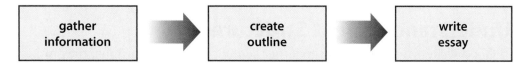

Visualize

Try to form a mental picture of scenes, characters, and events as you read. Use the details and descriptions the author gives you. If you can **visualize** what you read, it will be more interesting and you will remember it better.

Question

Ask yourself questions about the text while you read. Ask yourself about the importance of the sentences, how they relate to one another, if you understand what you just read, and what you think is going to come next.

Clarify

If you feel you do not understand meaning (through questioning), try these techniques:

> **What to Do When You Do Not Understand**
>
> ◆ Reread confusing parts of the text.
> ◆ Diagram (chart) relationships between chunks of text, ideas, and sentences.
> ◆ Look up unfamiliar words.
> ◆ Talk out the text to yourself.
> ◆ Read the passage once more.

Review

Take time to stop and review what you have read. Use your note-taking tools (graphic organizers or Cornell notes charts). Also, review and consider your K-W-L chart.

Monitor Your Comprehension

Continue to check your understanding by using the following two strategies:

Summarize Pause and tell yourself the main ideas of the text and the key supporting details. Try to answer the following questions: Who? What? When? Where? Why? How?

Paraphrase Pause, close the book, and try to retell what you have just read in your own words. It might help to pretend you are explaining the text to someone who has not read it and does not know the material.

▶ Understanding Text Structure

Good writers do not just put together sentences and paragraphs, they organize their writing with a specific purpose in mind. That organization is called text structure. When you understand and follow the structure of a text, it is easier to remember the information you are reading. There are many ways text may be structured. Watch for **signal words**. They will help you follow the text's organization (also, remember to use these techniques when you write).

Compare and Contrast

This structure shows similarities and differences between people, things, and ideas. This is often used to demonstrate that things that seem alike are really different, or vice versa.

Signal words: similarly, more, less, on the one hand / on the other hand, in contrast, but, however

Cause and Effect

Writers use the cause-and-effect structure to explore the reasons for something happening and to examine the results or consequences of events.

Signal words: so, because, as a result, therefore, for the following reasons

Problem and Solution

When they organize text around the question "how?" writers state a problem and suggest solutions.

Signal words: how, help, problem, obstruction, overcome, difficulty, need, attempt, have to, must

Sequence

Sequencing tells you in which order to consider thoughts or facts. Examples of sequencing are:

Chronological order refers to the order in which events take place.

Signal words: first, next, then, finally

Spatial order describes the organization of things in space (to describe a room, for example).

Signal words: above, below, behind, next to

Order of importance lists things or thoughts from the most important to the least important (or the other way around).

Signal words: principal, central, main, important, fundamental

▶ Reading for Meaning

It is important to think about what you are reading to get the most information out of a text, to understand the consequences of what the text says, to remember the content, and to form your own opinion about what the content means.

Interpret

Interpreting is asking yourself, "What is the writer really saying?" and then using what you already know to answer that question.

Infer

Writers do not always state exactly everything they want you to understand. By providing clues and details, they sometimes imply certain information. An **inference** involves using your reason and experience to develop the idea on your own, based on what an author implies or suggests. What is most important when drawing inferences is to be sure that you have accurately based your guesses on supporting details from the text. If you cannot point to a place in the selection to help back up your inference, you may need to rethink your guess.

Draw Conclusions

A conclusion is a general statement you can make and explain with reasoning, or with supporting details from a text. If you read a story describing a sport where five players bounce a ball and throw it through a high hoop, you may conclude that the sport is basketball.

Analyze

To understand persuasive nonfiction (a text that discusses facts and opinions to arrive at a conclusion), you need to analyze statements and examples to see if they support the main idea. To understand an informational text (a text, such as a textbook, that gives you information, not opinions), you need to keep track of how the ideas are organized to find the main points.

Hint: Use your graphic organizers and notes charts.

Distinguish Facts and Opinions

This is one of the most important reading skills you can learn. A fact is a statement that can be proven. An opinion is what the writer believes. A writer may support opinions with facts, but an opinion cannot be proven. For example:

Fact: California produces fruit and other agricultural products.

Opinion: California produces the best fruit and other agricultural products.

Evaluate

Would you take seriously an article on nuclear fission if you knew it was written by a comedic actor? If you need to rely on accurate information, you need to find out who wrote what you are reading and why. Where did the writer get information? Is the information one-sided? Can you verify the information?

▶ Reading for Research

You will need to **read actively** in order to research a topic. You might also need to generate an interesting, relevant, and researchable **question** on your own and locate appropriate print and nonprint information from a wide variety of sources. Then you will need to **categorize** that information, evaluate it, and **organize** it in a new way in order to produce a research project for a specific audience. Finally, **draw conclusions** about your original research question. These conclusions may lead you to other areas for further inquiry.

Locate Appropriate Print and Nonprint Information

In your research, try to use a variety of sources. Because different sources present information in different ways, your research project will be more interesting and balanced when you read a variety of sources.

Literature and Textbooks These texts include any book used as a basis for instruction or a source of information.

Book Indices A book index, or a bibliography, is an alphabetical listing of books. Some book indices list books on specific subjects; others are more general. Other indices list a variety of topics or resources.

Periodicals Magazines and journals are issued at regular intervals, such as weekly or monthly. One way to locate information in magazines is to use the Readers' Guide to Periodical Literature. This guide is available in print form in most libraries.

Technical Manuals A manual is a guide or handbook intended to give instruction on how to perform a task or operate something. A vehicle owner's manual might give information on how to operate and service a car.

Reference Books Reference books include encyclopedias and almanacs, and are used to locate specific pieces of information.

Electronic Encyclopedias, Databases, and the Internet There are many ways to locate extensive information using your computer. Infotrac, for instance, acts as an online reader's guide. CD encyclopedias can provide easy access to all subjects.

Organize and Convert Information

As you gather information from different sources, taking careful notes, you will need to think about how to **synthesize** the information, that is, convert it into a unified whole, as well as how to change it into a form your audience will easily understand and that will meet your assignment guidelines.

1. First, ask yourself what you want your audience to know.
2. Then, think about a pattern of organization, a structure that will best show your main ideas. You might ask yourself the following questions:
   - When comparing items or ideas, what graphic aids can I use?
   - When showing the reasons something happened and the effects of certain actions, what text structure would be best?
   - How can I briefly and clearly show important information to my audience?
   - Would an illustration or even a cartoon help to make a certain point?

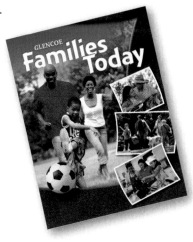

How to Use Technology

Introduction

Technology affects your life in almost every way, both at home and at work. Computers can do wonderful things. They are a path to the libraries of the world. They enhance and enrich your life. You can find the answers to many of your questions on the Internet, often as quickly as the click of your mouse. However, they can also be misused. Knowing some simple guidelines will help you use technology in a safe and secure way.

Practice Safe Surfing!

The Internet can also be a dangerous place. Although there are many Web sites you can freely and safely visit, many others are ones you want to avoid. Before you sign on to any site or visit a chat room, there are several things to consider:

- **Know to whom you are giving the information.** Check that the URL in your browser matches the domain you intended to visit and that you have not been redirected to another site.

- **Never give personal information of any sort** to someone you meet on a Web site or in a chat room, including your name, gender, age, or contact information.

- **Think about why you are giving the information.** For example, if a parent orders something online to be delivered, he or she will need to give an address. But you should never give out your social security number, your birth date, or your mother's maiden name without adult consent.

- **Check with a parent or other trusted adult** if you are still unsure whether it is safe to give the information.

Tips for Using the Internet for Research

The Internet is probably the single most important tool for research since the public library. There is so much information to access on the Internet that it can be difficult to know where to begin.

A good place to start is with a search engine, such as Google. Google is an automated piece of software that "crawls" the Web looking for information. By typing your topic into the search bar, the search engine looks for sites that contain the words you type. You may get many more sites than you are looking for. Here are some ways to get better results:

To get the best results when conducting a search online, be sure to spell all your search words correctly.

- ✧ **Place quotes around your topic,** for example, "sports medicine." This will allow you to find the sites where that exact phrase appears.

- ✧ **Use NEAR.** Typing "sports NEAR medicine" will return sites that contain both words and have the two words close to each other.

- ✧ **Exclude unwanted results.** Simply use a minus sign to indicate the words you do not want, for example, "sports medicine" – baseball.

- ✧ **Watch out for advertisements.** If you are using Google, know that the links on the right-hand side of the page, or sometimes at the top in color, are paid links. They may or may not be worth exploring.

- ✧ **Check for relevance.** Google displays a few lines of text from each page and shows your search phrase in bold. Check to see if it is appropriate for your work.

- ✧ **Look for news.** After you have entered your search phrase and have looked at the results, click on a *News* link on the page. This will show you recent stories about your topic.

- ✧ **Try again!** If you have made an extensive search and not found what you want, start a new search with a different set of words.

- ✧ **Check other sources.** Combine your Internet search with traditional research methods, such as books and magazines.

How to Use Technology

How to Evaluate Web Sites

Even though there is a ton of information available online, much of this information can be deceptive and misleading and often incorrect. The books in your library and classroom have been evaluated by scholars and experts. There is no such oversight on the Web. Learning to evaluate Web sites will make you a more savvy surfer and enable you to gather the information you need quickly and easily. When you are trying to decide whether a Web site provides trustworthy information, consider the following:

◈ **First, ask, "Who is the author?"** Once you have the name of the author, do a quick Web search to see what else the author has written. Search online for books he or she has written. This information will help you consider whether the person is credible.

◈ **Look at the group offering the information.** Be wary if they are trying to sell a product or service. Look for impartial organizations to provide unbiased information.

◈ **Look for Web sites that provide sources for each of their facts,** just as you do when you write a term paper. Also look for clues that the information was written by someone knowledgeable. Spelling and grammatical errors are warning signs that the information may not be accurate.

◈ **Check for the date the article was written and when it was last updated.** The more recent the article, the more likely it will be accurate.

◈ **Finally, when using information from a Web site, treat it as you would treat print information.** Anyone can post information on a Web site. Never use information that you cannot verify with another source.

Plagiarism

Using your computer in an ethical manner is simple if you follow certain guidelines. Plagiarism is the act of taking someone else's ideas and passing them off as your own. It does not matter if it is just one or two phrases or an entire paper. Be on guard against falling into the trap of cutting and pasting. This makes plagiarism all too easy.

It is acceptable to quote sources in your work, but you must make sure to identify those sources and give them proper credit. Also, some Web sites do not allow you to quote from them. Be sure to check each site or resource you are quoting to make sure you are allowed to use the material. Remember to cite your sources properly.

Copyright

A copyright protects someone who creates an original work. This can be a single sentence, a book, a play, a piece of music. If you create it, you are the owner. Copyright protection is provided by the Copyright Act of 1976, a federal statute.

If you want to use a portion of a copyrighted work in your own work, you need to obtain permission from the copyright holder. That might be a publisher of a book, an author, or an organization or an estate. Most publishers are willing to grant permission to individuals for educational purposes. If you want to reproduce information you found on the Web, contact the Webmaster or author of the article to request permission.

Once a work's copyright has expired, anywhere from 28 to 67 years from the date of creation, it is considered to be in the public domain and anyone can reprint it as he or she pleases. Remember the following tips:

✧ **What is copyrighted?** Original work published after March of 1989 is copyrighted, whether it says so or not.

✧ **Can I copy from the Internet?** Copying information from the Internet is a serious breach of copyright. Check the site's *Terms of Use* to see what you can and cannot do.

✧ **Can I edit copyrighted work?** You cannot change copyrighted material, that is, make "derivative works" based on existing material.

Student Organizations & FCCLA

What Is a Student Organization?

A student organization is a group or association of students that is formed around activities, such as:

- Family and Consumer Sciences
- Student government
- Community service
- Social clubs
- Honor societies
- Multicultural alliances
- Technology education
- Artists and performers
- Politics
- Sports teams
- Professional career development

A student organization is usually required to follow a set of rules and regulations that apply equally to all student organizations at a particular school.

Why Should You Get Involved?

Being an active part of a student organization opens a variety of experiences to you. Many student clubs are part of a national network of students and professionals, which provides the chance to connect to a wider variety of students and opportunities.

What's in It for You?

Participation in student organizations can contribute to a more enriching learning experience. Here are some ways you can benefit:

- Gain leadership qualities and skills that make you more marketable to employers and universities.
- Demonstrate the ability to appreciate someone else's point of view.
- Interact with professionals to learn about their different industries.
- Explore your creative interests, share ideas, and collaborate with others.
- Take risks, build confidence, and grow creatively.
- Learn valuable skills while speaking or performing in front of an audience.
- Make a difference in your life and the lives of those around you.
- Learn the importance of civic responsibility and involvement.
- Build relationships with instructors, advisors, students, and other members of the community who share similar backgrounds/world views.

Find and Join a Student Organization!

Take a close look at the organizations offered at your school or within your community. Are there any organizations that interest you? Talk to your teachers, guidance counselors, or a parent or guardian. Usually posters or flyers for a variety of clubs and groups can be found on your school's Message Board or Web site. Try to locate more information about the organizations that meet your needs. Then think about how these organizations can help you gain valuable skills you can use at school, at work, and in your community.

What Is FCCLA?

Family, Career and Community Leaders of America (FCCLA) is a national career and technical student organization for students in Family and Consumer Sciences. Involvement in FCCLA offers members the opportunity to develop life skills, expand their leadership potential, and explore careers. FCCLA lets you make a difference in your family, your career, and your community. Involvement offers members the opportunity to expand their leadership potential and develop skills for life—planning, goal setting, problem solving, decision making, character development, interpersonal communication, and career.

STAR Events Program

STAR Events (Students Taking Action with Recognition) are competitive events in which members are recognized for proficiency and achievement in chapter and individual projects, leadership skills, and occupational preparation. FCCLA provides opportunities for you to participate at local, state, and national levels.

What Are the Purposes of FCCLA?

1. Provide opportunities for personal development and preparation for adult life.
2. Strengthen the function of the family as a basic unit of society.
3. Encourage democracy through cooperative action in the home and community.
4. Encourage individual and group involvement in helping achieve global cooperation and harmony.
5. Promote greater understanding between youth and adults.
6. Provide opportunities for making decisions and for assuming responsibilities.
7. Prepare for the multiple roles of men and women in today's society.
8. Promote family and consumer sciences and related occupations.

Unit 1

The Family Foundation

Unit

Thematic Project Preview
Give Back to Society

After completing this unit, you will learn that strong families make society stronger. In your unit thematic project, you can show how contributing to society not only makes society stronger, but it also strengthens your relationships with members of your family.

My Journal

Taking Responsibility Write a journal entry about one of the topics below. This will help you prepare for the unit project at the end of the unit.

- A type of community service that interests you.
- The different ways strong families can make society stronger.
- What your community would be like if no one did volunteer work.

3

CHAPTER 1

Families, Society, and You

Section 1.1
The Need for Strong Families

Section 1.2
Why Study Families?

 Explore the Photo
Families add value and structure to individual lives and to society. *As you learn more about families, what new appreciation do you think you will have toward your own family?*

Chapter Objectives

After completing this chapter, you will be able to:

- **Identify** the functions of the family.
- **Explain** how families and society affect each other.
- **Describe** ways that families can take responsibility for being strong.
- **Identify** skills that contribute to strong family life.
- **Summarize** how studying families could help you in the future.

Writing Activity — Freewriting

Responsibility Responsible people make families stronger. Their behavior leads others to trust and count on them. Responsible people back up their words with actions. If something goes wrong, they will take charge. They admit it when they make a mistake. You can show responsibility by:

- Caring for your younger siblings.
- Doing assigned chores promptly.
- Completing school assignments on time.

Write about a time or event when you, or someone you know, showed responsibility.

Writing Tips To freewrite effectively, follow these steps:

1. Let your thoughts run free and simply begin writing whatever comes to mind.
2. Write without stopping to reread, rephrase, or rethink what you are saying.
3. Set a definite time limit.

The Need for Strong Families

Reading Guide

Before You Read

Preview Read the Key Concepts. Write one or two sentences predicting what the section will be about.

Read to Learn

Key Concepts

- **Identify** the functions of the family.
- **Explain** how families and society affect each other.
- **Describe** ways that families can take responsibility for being strong.

Main Idea

The family serves many functions for its members. Families and society affect each other in many ways. Society is strong when the families in it are strong.

Content Vocabulary

◇ family
◇ function
◇ dysfunctional
◇ society
◇ community

Academic Vocabulary

You will find these words in your reading and on your tests. Use the glossary to look up their definitions if necessary.

■ gain　　　　　■ array

Graphic Organizer

As you read, name three ways that society affects families. Use a chart like the one shown to help organize your information.

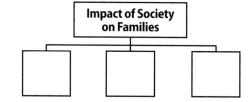

 Graphic Organizer Go to this book's Online Learning Center at **glencoe.com** to print out this graphic organizer.

Academic Standards . . . .

 English Language Arts

NCTE 4 Use written language to communicate effectively.

NCTE 5 Use different writing process elements to communicate effectively.

 Mathematics

NCTM Number and Operations Understand the meanings of operations and how they relate to one another.

NCTE *National Council of Teachers of English*
NCTM *National Council of Teachers of Mathematics*

NSES *National Science Education Standards*
NCSS *National Council of the Social Studies*

Functions of the Family

When asked to name what means the most to them, many people say, "My family." The U.S. government defines a **family** as a group of two or more people who live together. These people are related by birth, marriage, or adoption.

Why are families so important? Families provide a **function**, or purpose, to their members. These functions are also the responsibilities of family life. Have you ever thought about what families provide? The functions of the family include:

- Love and affection
- Economic support
- Security
- Procreation
- Protection
- Guidance
- Education
- Socialization
- Teaching values
- Recreation

For example, families help their members learn what to expect in life. This is part of the education function of families. People who know what to expect are more likely to be successful at school, at work, and in the community.

How the functions are carried out in the family has changed over the years. These functions may be handled differently in the future than they are today. However, these functions are basic actions needed for a healthy family life. They have remained constant over the years and exist in many societies.

Sometimes families do not carry out their functions. They are called **dysfunctional** families. Members of these families may have to work harder than others do to meet certain needs. However, a dysfunctional family may still meet some of its functions. The family can use their strengths to solve problems. There are community and government programs that can help dysfunctional families.

As you learn more about families, you will learn more about the functions of families. You will gain new insights into what it means to be a family. There are also many different kinds of families. Learning about these families may help you see the value in the similarities and differences between families.

Vocabulary

You can find definitions in the glossary at the back of this book.

As You Read

Connect What are some of the functions of your family?

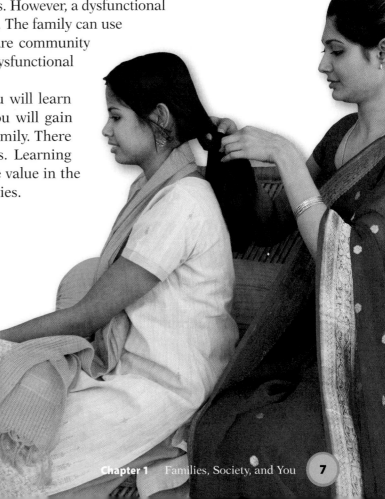

Family Functions

Love and support are the foundations of strong family relationships. *How can you show love for each member of your family?*

Interest on a Car Loan

Your family needs to buy a car. Together you decide that you will need a $5,000 loan to buy the car. The best loan you can find is a three-year loan at an interest rate of 6%. If you take this loan, how much money will you pay in interest?

Math Concept **Simple Interest** The formula to find simple interest is $I = p \times r \times t$.

I is the amount of the interest
p is the principal
r is the interest rate
t is time

Multiply the principal, rate, and time together to calculate the interest.

Starting Hint: The principal is the $5,000 amount you are borrowing. The interest rate is 6%, and the time of the loan is three years.

 For math help, go to the Math Appendix at the back of the book.

NCTM Number and Operations Understand the meanings of operations and how they relate to one another.

The Family: The Basic Unit of Society

The basic unit that makes up society is the family. **Society** is a group of people who have developed patterns of relationships from being around one another. These people often live in a community. A **community** is the common area where different people live. Each community or society is made up of many families. Families are vital to the health of society.

Society can be seen at many levels. Your family may live in a neighborhood, which is a small society. The city or state you live in is another larger level of society. Your country or nation is another even larger level. Families affect every part and level of society. Families often have the most impact on the community closest to them. It takes more work and effort to have an influence on the larger society.

If you unravel a rope, you see that single strands are woven to form a whole. A single strand is easy to cut or break. When the strands are woven, the rope is strong. In much the same way, people, families, and society support each other. When families and society work together, each is stronger.

✓ **Reading Check** **Explain** What is the basic unit of society?

Society and Families

You have learned that families can affect the larger society. For example, when Juan's family worked at a city clean-up day, they helped make the community better for all. It is important to know that parts of society also affect families. For example, when a road is closed for repair by the government, family members may have to change how they get to school or work. In big ways and small ways, you and your family are linked to your community.

Family Law

Laws of all types have an effect on families. Laws that deal with taxes and interest rates influence how much money families have to spend. Some laws are passed to set up programs for people who are poor, out of work, or need help.

Local, state, and national laws can also affect the education of children. Public schools are created and run based on local or state rules. National Social Security laws have an impact on older family members.

Laws can include all parts of family life. Some set up the rules for marriage and divorce. Child support laws make sure that parents support their children after a divorce.

Some laws relate to specific problems in family life. There are laws that deal with child, spouse, and elder abuse. Children who get in legal trouble are dealt with under special laws for juveniles.

Lawmakers are not the only ones responsible for laws. Public pressure can change and create laws as well. Society is stronger when people express their opinions and take an interest in the legal process. Stay informed by reading and listening to the news. You can share your ideas with others and work together to create change. Letters and phone calls to lawmakers can make a difference. When you are old enough to vote, be sure to cast your ballot in local and national elections.

The Business World

Businesses are also concerned about strong families. Families and businesses affect each other. When workers have problems at home, their work often suffers, too. Stress at work affects how workers relate to each other. It can also affect how workers relate to others in their families.

When businesses have policies that help with family needs, it often leads to success. Parents may have a hard time taking care of the needs of their children while working. If employers can be flexible, it can make it easier for working parents to meet their children's needs. When employers create helpful family policies, both sides **gain**, or profit. Home life is better, and people are happier. This makes more effective workers.

Community Involvement

Many groups have been formed to help families with their concerns. The following are examples of groups that help families:
- Social agencies offer a wide **array**, or range, of services. These can be for money issues, illness, or troubled relationships.
- Religious groups and spiritual leaders work to support families.
- Education is another example of how the community helps families. Schools help young people achieve success in life. They also handle discipline problems, provide meals, and give guidance. Schools educate students to be good workers and citizens as well.
- Police and the courts enforce the laws that help families.
- Communities have parks and activities for people who live there.

✓ **Reading Check**) **Identify** What are three aspects of society that directly impact families?

Society Cares
Schools are an example of how society helps families. *How has your school helped your family?*

The Family's Responsibility

Society works in many ways to help families with their needs. The resources society provides, such as education and law enforcement, help build strong families. However, families need to take an active role as well. Society cannot do it all.

Taking Responsibility

Families can find their strengths and build on them. If they take on more responsibility, families can relieve some of the pressure on society. They can help themselves as well as help others in the community. Families that grow strong can also help society grow stronger.

Family Strengths

Families have many good qualities, or strengths, that work for them. They communicate by listening and sharing feelings. Family members support each other. They spend time together, both working and playing. They care. These are some of the traits of strong families.

Describing strong families may not be easy. There is no magic line that is crossed when a family becomes strong. Each family has different

INDEPENDENT Living

HOW TO Spend Time with Your Family

Most of today's families are very busy. Families can no longer assume that they will always have time together. Many have started to set aside specific family time. Follow these guidelines to help your family spend more time together:

1. **Make chores fun.** When you do chores with another family member, make it fun by listening to music.
2. **Use time wisely.** If you take the time to talk to your family while riding in the car or waiting in line, you may learn more about them.
3. **Volunteer as a family.** Look for volunteer activities that you can do as a family. Some examples include collecting for a food drive, helping at a walkathon, or visiting residents of a nursing home.
4. **Create individual bonds.** Special bonds can be formed when siblings spend time together. This can also happen when you share time with only one parent.
5. **Make family a priority.** You have to make time to be with your family, even if it means giving up other activities.

Take Action Follow your teacher's instructions to form small groups. List specific ways that families can make more time to be together. Try to think of different ideas to fit different family situations.

strengths and weaknesses. No family is perfect. They can each find ways to improve upon their strengths and weaknesses.

A family's strength is not measured by how well it provides, how much money it makes, or what material items it owns. Instead, it is measured by how well the family works together. It is measured by the support family members give each other. A family that works to build their strengths can become strong.

Strong Families are Healthy Families

Sometimes, strong families are described as healthy families. These are the families that meet the needs of their members to the best of their ability. They see the strengths they have and those they still need. Then they work to build them. When problems arise, large or small, they look for ways to cope and try to find answers. They are willing to ask for help from outside the family if needed.

Society needs strong families. When families work well, they can act as a buffer against many of life's problems. Their strengths join with those of other families to make society strong, too.

Sometimes, people forget to look for the good in their family. It is important for family members to try to focus on the strengths in their family. They may appreciate their family more. This can also help encourage the family to continue to work together on strengths and weaknesses.

Section 1.1 — After You Read

Review Key Concepts

1. **Name** at least four functions of a family.
2. **List** at least two ways that society is directly linked to families.
3. **Explain** why families have to take responsibility for building their strengths.

Practice Academic Skills

English Language Arts

4. Select one of the functions of the family. Decide how this function relates to strong families. Write two paragraphs explaining how a family could meet this function and why the function is important in building a strong family.

> **NCTE 4** Use written language to communicate effectively.

5. Imagine that your local city changed its bus schedules. This means you cannot get to your after-school job on time. Write a paragraph explaining why the schedule change is a problem for you. Suggest actions you can take to help you get to work on time.

> **NCTE 5** Use different writing process elements to communicate effectively.

Check Your Answers Check your answers at this book's Online Learning Center through **glencoe.com**.

Why Study Families?

Reading Guide

Before You Read

Preview Look at the photos in this section and read their captions. Write one or two sentences predicting what the section will be about.

Read to Learn
Key Concepts

* **Identify** skills that contribute to strong family life.
* **Summarize** how studying families could help you in the future.

Main Idea

Interpersonal skills help people build strong families. You can use what you learn about families in your life now and in the future.

Content Vocabulary

◇ interpersonal
◇ communication
◇ management
◇ conflict resolution

 Graphic Organizer Go to this book's Online Learning Center at **glencoe.com** to print out this graphic organizer.

Academic Vocabulary

You will find these words in your reading and on your tests. Use the glossary to look up their definitions if necessary.

■ confront   ■ vital

Graphic Organizer

As you read, list four skills that are important in a strong family and explain how each can strengthen family life. Use a chart like the one shown to help organize your information.

Skills	How They Strengthen Family Life

Academic Standards . . . .

 English Language Arts

NCTE 4 Use written language to communicate effectively.

NCTE 12 Use language to accomplish individual purposes.

NCTE *National Council of Teachers of English*
NCTM *National Council of Teachers of Mathematics*

NSES *National Science Education Standards*
NCSS *National Council of the Social Studies*

Interpersonal Skills

There are many skills needed to build a strong family. These are called interpersonal skills. **Interpersonal** means occurring between people. Interpersonal skills help people get along better. Good relationships and strong families depend on these types of interpersonal skills:

- **Communication Skills** Good communication skills can help families solve problems. **Communication** is the process of sending and receiving messages. Misunderstandings can be avoided when ideas and feelings are clear. Learning to communicate well can help people build strong families.
- **Problem-Solving and Decision-Making Skills** Learning to make sound decisions is an important skill. Careful choices are needed when you face problems. Families must decide how to raise children, how to spend time, and how to relate to each other. These skills make life go more smoothly in the family.
- **Management Skills** The ability to manage is also a needed skill. **Management** is using what you have to get what you want. Learning to manage well helps bring order to family life. Sound family finances and well-run household schedules depend on this skill.
- **Conflict Resolution Skills** Arguments will happen and people need good conflict resolution skills to settle them. **Conflict resolution** is a way to solve disagreements. Conflict can get out of hand when people react with their feelings rather than thinking about solutions. Good conflict resolution skills help family members get along better with each other.

As you study the family, you will learn about all of these skills and others. You will see why they are important to families. You will also discover ways to put them to use in your life.

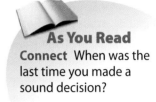

Vocabulary
You can find definitions in the glossary at the back of this book.

As You Read
Connect When was the last time you made a sound decision?

Build Your Skills
Your words, actions, and attitudes are all forms of communication. *How can you improve communication with your family?*

Strengthen Your Family Now

As you study families, you can learn to make the family you live in stronger. You may know teens who struggle to get along with their parents, or who argue with their siblings. All teens want a smoother family life, but they need tools to help them.

Learning about family life will increase your knowledge about what happens in relationships, both inside and outside the family. Using what you learn, you can strengthen your own family. The power of your family now depends, in part, on you. Your actions can make a difference.

Few families are problem-free. Having problems is a part of life. Even strong families have problems, but they develop ways to manage and solve their problems. What do families need to help them solve their problems? They need to know:

- The family comes first.
- Every family member contributes to the family.
- Change is possible.
- Problems can be solved.
- How to solve problems.
- Where to get help.

Families today have many challenges. Some are more complicated than others. Work schedules may have to be balanced with family time. Families may face money problems, illness, death, drug problems, abuse, or crime. Many families **confront**, or face, the challenges of divorce and remarriage. The world is changing, and advances in science and technology help create new ways of living. All of these affect families. By studying families, you will learn the knowledge and skills that you need to be successful in life.

✓ **Reading Check** **Explain** Why are interpersonal skills important?

Look to the Future

Studying the family can give you a foundation for what lies ahead. You may form a family in the future. If you do, you will have the ability to make it what you want it to be.

Learn About Yourself

What you learn about families can also give you a better understanding of yourself. The skills you build will help strengthen your family now and in the future. You will find out what kind of person you are and what you want and need to be. As you study families, you will see the **vital**, or important, link between families and their members. You may find ways to strengthen that link in your own life.

Put Your Knowledge to Use

When you are on your own you will be able to take what you have learned and use that knowledge. In a sense the family is a mini-version of the world. In the family, you learn skills to get along with other people. The more you understand about relationships in the family, the better equipped you are to make them work.

The knowledge and skills you gain in studying the family will help you have better relationships in the larger world. You will be able to take all that you have learned about relationships and use that knowledge when you are on your own.

For example, Luke's family had strong listening and communication skills. These helped his family solve problems together. When Luke started his new job, he found many ways to put the skills he learned in his family to use. When there was a problem at his office, he was able to communicate with coworkers. This helped Luke and his coworkers solve the problem together.

Real Life — Family Living Careers

As you study families, take a look at the related career fields, such as those in the Human Services. Many careers let you work with families and provide services for them.

To be a success you will need good interpersonal skills and a concern for others. You can learn a lot about careers in family life if you do a little bit of research. Some examples of careers in the Human Services include:

- Child Care
- Social Services
- Counseling
- Personal Care Services
- Health Care
- Consumer Services

Problem-Solving

Aiden is an outgoing, energetic student. He has a talent for inspiring and organizing others. He was the main motivation behind the senior class blood donation drive. Aiden thinks a career working with families would be rewarding. He wonders if he has the patience for a job in counseling, child care, or social services. He is not sure how to decide which career would be best. What advice would you give Aiden?

As you grow older, you look forward to adult life. You can make your future family what you want it to be. If you learn now what a family needs to be strong, you can use that knowledge when you build a family of your own. You will know what can go wrong and how to react so that problems do not get bigger or go on a long time. You can prevent many mistakes from happening. With foresight, skills, and knowledge, you can shape your future family life.

For example, imagine that your family spends one night each week together. You all help out with dinner and the clean up. Then your family plays a game or watches a movie together. If this is something you enjoy in your current family, you may want to include this in your future family.

Working with Families

As you study the family, you may find that your interest goes beyond your personal life. Some people choose careers that let them work with families. They may help people through law, medicine, or social work. Others work in education or personal care.

Public policies and laws that affect families interest some people. They may want to work in government or law enforcement. Some people become volunteers who give their time to provide services for families. There are many opportunities to volunteer in every community.

Working with families to build strong people, strong relationships, and a strong society can be rewarding. It can make you a better person and the world a better place in which to live.

Section 1.2 After You Read

Review Key Concepts

1. **Identify** four interpersonal skills needed for strong families.

2. **List** two ways you can use what you learn in this class in your future.

Practice Academic Skills

English Language Arts

3. Think about a time when you and a member of your family communicated well. Try to remember how that communication made you feel. Did it bring you closer? Were you able to share your thoughts more easily than before? Write a one-page paper that describes how that communication strengthened the bond between you and that member of the family.

> **NCTE 12** Use language to accomplish individual purposes.

4. Brainstorm a list of strengths your family has. For example, does your family work together to solve problems? Do they listen patiently when you have something important to say? Identify one strength that is your favorite, or that you feel the strongest about. Write a paragraph that explains why this strength is important in family life.

> **NCTE 4** Use written language to communicate effectively.

Check Your Answers Check your answers at this book's Online Learning Center through **glencoe.com**.

CHAPTER SUMMARY

Section 1.1
The Need for Strong Families

The family fills many functions for its members. The family is the basic unit of society. Families and society affect each other. Strong families help build a strong society. Laws, the business world, and community groups can affect families. Society needs strong families, but family members must also take responsibility for staying strong and healthy. When families recognize their strengths, it may be easier to solve their problems.

Section 1.2
Why Study Families?

Studying the family can bring many benefits. It gives you a chance to learn new skills, such as interpersonal, problem-solving, and management skills. Using the skills will help you strengthen your family now. They are also useful outside of the family, such as in the workplace and at school. You can use the skills in your own future family. If you really enjoy helping others, you may be interested in the many careers that are related to family life.

Content and Academic Vocabulary Review

1. Use each of these content and academic vocabulary words in a sentence.

Content Vocabulary
◇ family (p. 7)
◇ function (p. 7)
◇ dysfunctional (p. 7)
◇ society (p. 8)
◇ community (p. 8)
◇ interpersonal (p. 13)
◇ communication (p. 13)
◇ management (p. 13)
◇ conflict resolution (p. 13)

Academic Vocabulary
■ gain (p. 9)
■ array (p. 9)
■ confront (p. 14)
■ vital (p. 15)

Review Key Concepts

2. Identify the functions of the family.
3. Explain how families and society affect each other.
4. Describe ways that families can take responsibility for being strong.
5. Identify skills that contribute to strong family life.
6. Summarize how studying families could help you in the future.

Critical Thinking

7. Cause and Effect Do family problems cause problems in society, or do problems in society cause problems in the family? Explain your answer.
8. Predict Results What would some of the results be if a family does not work together to solve problems?
9. Draw Conclusions Why might focusing on family strengths be more important than focusing on weaknesses?

Real-World Skills

Problem-Solving Skills

10. Make a Plan Over the years, Tina's family has grown apart. Her three older brothers live in different states. She rarely sees them. Tina would like to be closer to her brothers. Write a list of things Tina could do to help rebuild her ties with her brothers.

Technology Applications

11. Create a Presentation Imagine you have been asked to create a public service advertisement for your school's television network. Develop a presentation that explains why strong families are needed for a strong society. Include illustrations that show the link between strength in families and society.

Interpersonal Skills

12. Show Leadership Jim is not looking forward to the next holiday family gathering. His mother and aunt do not get along. His younger cousin follows him around and annoys him. Write a list of things that Jim could do to show leadership in his family to help make the holiday fun.

Research Skills

13. Evaluate a Law Choose a law that affects families. Write two paragraphs that answer these questions: What is the purpose of the law, in terms of family life, you have chosen? Has the law done what it was designed to do? Has the law had a positive effect on families? Why or why not?

14. Discuss an Issue Follow your teacher's instructions to form into groups. In your group, discuss and define what makes a family. Read your definition to the class. As a class, discuss: How are the definitions alike and unlike?

15. Help Other Families With your classmates, arrange to provide child care at an elementary school during parent-teacher conferences. This will let parents meet teachers without worrying about child care or taking children to the conferences. Write a one-page report about how your group made the arrangements and your thoughts on the outcome.

16. Identify Careers Identify three careers in your community that are related to working with families. Write a paragraph to describe each career and how people in these careers strengthen families.

17. Student Organizations There are student organizations in your community such as Family, Career and Community Leaders of America (FCCLA) that help build strong families. Go to this book's Online Learning Center at **glencoe.com** to find **Web Links** for **Student Organizations**. Make a table with the organizations and how to contact them.

Additional Activities For additional activities, go to this book's Online Learning Center through **glencoe.com**.

Academic Skills

Mathematics

18. Calculate the Cost You are going to make dinner tonight for your family. You want to buy dessert for the dinner on your way home from school. Your neighborhood bakery makes bread, cakes, cookies, and pies. At the end of the day, the prices of all the leftover products are reduced by 75%. You are able to buy a pie at the end of the day for 87¢. What was the regular price of the pie?

 Algebra: Equations Using the information given in the problem, you can write an algebraic equation and find the solution. Let x stand for the regular price of the pie.

Starting Hint: First, multiply 75% by 100 to make the percent a decimal. Then, multiply 75% by the regular price of the pie (x). That is equal to what the pie sells for at the end of the day (87¢).

Math For math help, go to the Math Appendix at the back of the book.

> **NCTM Algebra** Represent and analyze mathematical situations and structures using algebraic symbols.

English Language Arts

19. Write a Letter Find a current local law that affects families. Write a letter to the head of your local government, for example, the mayor. Explain how you think a current local law that affects families could be improved. Explain your reasoning for the change. Or, if you think the law has helped families, explain why you think it should be continued.

> **NCTE 5** Use different writing process elements to communicate effectively.

Social Studies

20. Research Family Life Research what family life is like in another society. Look for information about how the families in that society fulfill their functions. Write a report about your findings. Compare how functions are fulfilled in that society to how they are fulfilled in your society. What conclusions can you draw?

> **NCSS I.a** Analyze and explain the ways groups, societies, and cultures address human needs and concerns.

STANDARDIZED TEST PRACTICE

MULTIPLE CHOICE
Read the sentence. Then read the question below the sentence. Read the answer choices and choose the best answer to fill in the blank.

> **Test-Taking Tip** In a multiple-choice test, the answers are usually specific and precise. Read the question first and carefully. Then read all the answer choices. Eliminate answers that you know are incorrect.

21. People may work in careers related to family life because they enjoy being in an *environment* that allows them to help others.

In this sentence, the word *environment* means _____.
a. one's surroundings
b. an apartment or house
c. ecology and temperature
d. envelopment

CHAPTER 2

Families Make a Difference

Section 2.1
Families Meet Many Needs

Section 2.2
Families Teach Values

Explore the Photo
Family members help meet each other's needs and teach each other values. *How is this older brother helping meet the needs of his younger siblings?*

Chapter Objectives

After completing this chapter, you will be able to:

- **Identify** the difference between needs and wants.
- **Determine** the ways emotional support affects the family and its members.
- **Describe** how families meet physical needs.
- **Explain** how social skills are learned.
- **Describe** how families can contribute to mental growth.
- **Analyze** how your values and value system are related.
- **Summarize** how values are learned.

Writing Activity

Prewriting

Helpfulness A helpful person shows regard for others by offering service, assistance, or emotional support. You can be helpful by:

- Helping your brothers and sisters do their homework so they can do well in school.
- Fixing dinner or setting the table to help a parent on a busy night.
- Volunteering to do chores and other tasks for grandparents or older relatives who need help.

Imagine that you need to write a one-page essay about ways you can be helpful to your family. Before you can write the essay, you should do a prewriting activity. This will help your essay be more organized.

Writing Tips To prewrite effectively, follow these steps:

1. Freewrite or collect ideas from other sources.
2. List ideas and see how they relate to each other.
3. Create a web to narrow the topic.

Families Meet Many Needs

Reading Guide

Before You Read

Preview Choose a content or academic vocabulary word that is new to you. When you find it in the text, write down the definition.

Read to Learn

Key Concepts

- **Identify** the difference between needs and wants.
- **Determine** the ways emotional support affects the family and its members.
- **Describe** how families meet physical needs.
- **Explain** how social skills are learned.
- **Describe** how families contribute to mental growth.

Main Idea

Everyone's emotional, physical, social, and mental needs are first met in the family.

Content Vocabulary

◇ need
◇ want
◇ emotion
◇ emotional support
◇ support system
◇ family bond
◇ personality
◇ socialization
◇ independence

Academic Vocabulary

You will find these words in your reading and on your tests. Use the glossary to look up their definitions if necessary.

- ■ distinguish
- ■ characteristic

Graphic Organizer

As you read, find four things children learn through socialization. Use a web like the one shown to help organize your information.

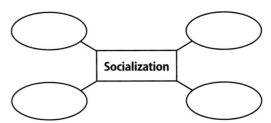

Socialization

 Graphic Organizer Go to this book's Online Learning Center at **glencoe.com** to print out this graphic organizer.

Academic Standards . . . .

English Language Arts

NCTE 4 Use written language to communicate effectively.

NCTE 12 Use language to accomplish individual purposes.

Mathematics

NCTM Number and Operations Compute fluently and make reasonable estimates.

NCTE *National Council of Teachers of English*
NCTM *National Council of Teachers of Mathematics*

NSES *National Science Education Standards*
NCSS *National Council of the Social Studies*

Family Needs and Wants

What do people need to become happy and useful members of society? One of the strongest influences is the family. Families are the support structure that takes care of people. They supply what members need to grow and develop. They give support to family members throughout life.

A **need** is something that is required for a person's survival and growth. Families fulfill needs that are emotional, physical, social, and mental. How well these needs are filled affects how people grow and develop. People feel good about themselves when their needs are fulfilled. How people relate to others can also be affected by how well their needs are met.

The first place most babies get their needs met is in the family. As children grow, society starts to meet more of their needs. For example, school can help meet children's physical, mental, and social needs.

Basic needs remain the same throughout life. How needs are filled however, may be different at different ages. Social needs for a baby may be filled by parents who cuddle and play. Older adults may meet social needs by spending time with friends or working on community projects. The family may be more important in meeting needs at some ages than at others.

Family needs are different from family wants. A **want** is something that is desired but not essential. The people in your family need food to survive. Food is a need. If you have a craving for ice cream, however, that is a want. Although your life might be better with ice cream, you can survive without it.

Both needs and wants affect family behavior. A need that is not met commands attention and effort until it is filled. After several hours without eating, for example, a baby needs food. A want that is not met may cause families to work together and plan. A family that wants a new computer might find ways to save for one. Families must decide what steps to take to get the things they need, and choose the wants that they will meet.

 **Vocabulary**

You can find definitions in the glossary at the back of this book.

 **As You Read**

Connect What are some examples of your family's needs and wants?

◀◀ *Wants and Needs* Families and members of families have wants and needs. This family has decided to spend time together. *Do you consider family togetherness a family want or a family need?*

It is important for families to be able to **distinguish**, or tell the difference, between their needs and wants. For example, a new computer will not solve the problems of a family that has grown apart. New things are not what count the most in family life. They are wants rather than needs. A family that has grown apart should focus on meeting the need of bringing the family back together. Perhaps after that has been accomplished, they can start to set goals for meeting their wants.

When you understand the needs and wants of your family, you can plan for the future. You and your family can set goals for how to meet the family's needs and wants. Helping your family understand what their real needs are, and then working as a team to meet those needs, is part of being a family.

✓ **Reading Check** **Define** What is a need?

Emotional Support

An **emotion** is a feeling you have in response to thoughts, remarks, and events. Each person in a family feels many different emotions. That is normal. Emotions affect how people act. They may cause people to act in positive or hurtful ways. One key to success in life is to manage your emotions in order to create positive actions.

Emotional support is the actions people take to meet the emotional needs of others. When families meet each other's emotional needs, they create a support system. A **support system** is a group of family and friends who are available to provide support when needed. When people receive support from their families, there are many positive outcomes. The support a family offers can help its members enjoy the good times. Support also provides strength to get through the hard times.

▶ *Showing Emotional Support*
With the right words and actions, you can support your family and friends. *How do you feel when someone shows you emotional support?*

When you say things or do things that make someone feel good, you help that person's emotional health. Being positive and making positive comments are useful because it helps others feel good and be positive themselves. Listening to someone who is trying to solve a problem is helpful. When you listen to another person's concerns, you give support.

The Time for Support

It is easier to give support when life is going well. Sharing good feelings like love and joy is fun. Family members offer recognition, pride, and warmth when good things happen.

When people are tense or unhappy, it can be harder to support others. People need support the most during difficult times. Problems are more manageable if you do not have to deal with them alone. Family members are often the first people to be there to provide support when something goes wrong.

Emotionally supportive families offer shelter from the outside world. It often feels good to get away from the pressures and duties of work and school. Even when dealing with the day-to-day problems, families can provide a safe place to be.

Create Family Bonds

Giving emotional support to family members can help build family bonds that can lead to long-term success. A **family bond** is a strong feeling of connection that unites a family in a committed relationship. As other people come and go, family ties remain. A sense of belonging exists in a strong family. Nurturing your family can build family bonds and lead to a support system that lasts a life time.

In a strong family, members accept and love each other without conditions. This does not mean that you will always get along with other family members. It means that underneath the day-to-day challenges in life, there is love and affection.

Providing emotional support is a two-way street. One person cannot always give support while someone else always receives it. Closeness in a family depends, in part, on people being able to do both. Adults need support as much as children and teens do.

Taking the First Step

You can show emotional support in many ways. Even when time is limited, you can find ways to show you care. Think about what you do in your family. By taking the first step, you can be the one who gets the cycle of support going. You will see that good feelings come with giving support as well as getting it.

Financial Literacy

Giving Back to Your Community

Together Ramon and Lupe earn about $80,000 per year. Giving back to the community is an important value to Ramon and Lupe, so they set aside 10% of their earnings to give to nonprofit organizations, such as rescue missions and literacy projects. Determine how much money they donate to nonprofits each year.

Math Concept **Multiplying by Percents**
To compute how much money Ramon and Lupe give to nonprofits each year, multiply the amount they earn by the percentage they give away:
annual salary × percent donated = annual amount donated.

Starting Hint: To multiply by a percent you must change the percent to a decimal by moving the decimal point two places to the left. In this problem, 10% becomes .10, which you will multiply by 80,000.

 For math help, go to the Math Appendix at the back of the book.

NCTM Number and Operations Compute fluently and make reasonable estimates.

Family and Personality

Personalities are shaped in the family. Your **personality** is made up of all the characteristics that make you unique. A **characteristic** about you is a distinguishing trait or quality. For example, friends say that Soo-Ling loves to have fun, and she is outgoing and caring. These characteristics are part of her personality.

Personality is formed in many ways. The family, however, is a very strong influence. Personality traits developed or learned in the early years are often kept for life. With emotional support from the family, people are more apt to have personality traits that help them to be successful in life. This is one reason why emotional support is important in family life.

✓ **Reading Check** **Explain** What is emotional support?

Physical Needs

A physical need is one that your body must have to work properly. People need food, sleep, shelter, and clothing to survive. For the most part, these needs are met in the family.

Providing these basic physical needs can be a struggle for some families. Most families do the best they can. It is important that family members value the care and the effort that is given by the other people in their family. What they have or do not have then seems less important.

As a rule, some family members have jobs so that they can earn money for what the family needs. When jobs are not possible, some families seek outside help. This may be through friends, relatives, or government programs.

▶▶ *Personality Traits*
Personality is formed early in life.
What is one of your favorite characteristics about your personality?

INDEPENDENT Living

HOW TO | Meet Special Needs

People come in all shapes and sizes. People also have a wide range of abilities. You may know someone who is not able to see, hear, or move around as well as you can. Follow these guidelines to assist people with special needs:

1. **Limited Mobility** People who cannot move around well need safe, wide pathways. Rearrange furniture and use ramps to help people in walkers or wheelchairs move around more easily.
2. **Visual Impairment** Use bright indoor lighting, large digital clocks, and items labeled in large print to help people who do not see well.
3. **Hearing Impairment** People with hearing impairments can use devices that make lamps flash when a doorbell rings. Phones can be amplified to make calls louder and clearer. A teletypewriter (TTY) lets people with hearing impairments communicate on the telephone by typing on a keyboard.
4. **Limited Strength** People with weakness in their arms and hands can use easy-to-grip handles on doorknobs. Keep kitchen counters clear of small appliances so that objects can be slid on the counter surface instead of lifted.

Take Action Make one change to your home that will make it more accessible to people with disabilities. After one week, describe the differences the change made in your routines.

Protecting Family Members

Physical needs include more than just food and shelter. Family members also protect each other. The family works to keep its members safe from harm. For example, families install smoke detectors in homes to warn family members if there is a fire.

Health care is another example of protection. Simple health care is often done at home, where minor illnesses and injuries are treated. Family members go to doctors and other health care workers if they need more help. Vaccinations protect people from diseases. Regular check-ups for babies assure parents that their children are healthy.

Families protect in other ways, too. Caring families set rules. These help protect children and other family members from danger or situations that they may not be able to handle. For example, children should not be allowed to touch a hot stove or walk in the street. Just like with younger children, rules set for teens are made to protect them. Rules about curfews, for instance, are made to keep teens safe. Remembering this makes following rules easier.

✓ Reading Check **Explain** Why is protection part of a person's physical needs?

Social Skills

Families help their members learn social skills. These skills include learning how to relate to others and how to get along with others in society. **Socialization** is the process of learning social skills. This process provides the tools a person needs in order to participate within their society.

Many small lessons are part of the process of learning social skills. People generally learn these lessons as children. As they grow older, however, they may continue to learn certain aspects of these lessons. Here are some of the lessons learned through socialization:

- **How to get along with others.** Learning to share a toy may have been one of your early lessons in getting along with others. Learning to work with others when you played games was another. People need to learn these lessons early. Many learn them from their older family members. They make it easier to relate to others later in life.

- **What actions are acceptable where you live.** In the family, people learn social rules. These rules help people know what actions are right and wrong in the area where they live. To do well in society, people need to know what is expected. Then they will be able to act accordingly.

- **How to be independent. Independence** is the ability to take care of yourself. There are two early lessons about independence that are learned early. They are learning how to put on your own clothes and how to cross the street alone. As a teen, you are learning how to make choices that are in your best interest. You want to manage well on your own.

- **What responsibilities you have to your world.** Responsibilities are first learned when children clean up and help others in small ways. These lessons are then broadened to include the world outside the family. Concern for issues such as having a clean neighborhood and preventing crime begin in the family. Families should look beyond their own interests. They can instill community spirit in their members.

When families prepare family members for life, getting along with others is easier. Family members can then relate to other people outside of the family. They find that socialization helps them fit well into the world around them.

Families Help
Responsibility begins at home. *Where does it go from there?*

✓ **Reading Check** **Identify** What is the process of learning social skills called?

Mental Growth

Throughout life, people develop their minds. They not only gain knowledge, but they learn to improve their thinking skills. Over time, wisdom comes in the form of good sense and insight. Families contribute to the mental growth of all members, but their impact on children is vital.

The family is a child's first teacher. Many of your first lessons in life were learned from members of your family. With a good start, children have a better chance of doing well in school and throughout life. Children learn by playing.

If you have younger brothers or sisters, you may have helped them grow mentally. All family members can help in this area. For example, you can play with and talk to siblings when they are younger, and then read to them as they grow older. Talking and playing with babies promotes development. Reading to toddlers and taking them for walks helps them learn about people and the world.

Families need to be involved in a child's schooling. Students are more apt to do well when adult family members are interested in education. Parents can help. They can support teachers in their efforts, check schoolwork, and go to special events.

People have many needs. These needs are met by families. The support a family provides impacts how individuals grow and develop. You can be a part of this by showing emotional support to your family.

Section 2.1 After You Read

Review Key Concepts

1. **Name** the four basic needs all people have.
2. **Describe** ways that families show emotional support.
3. **Explain** why physical needs are so important.
4. **Define** socialization.
5. **Identify** at which point in life people begin their mental development.

Practice Academic Skills

English Language Arts

6. It may not be easy to know what to say when providing emotional support. Write five sentences that show positive support for others. Some examples are, "Thanks for listening" or "I am glad you shared that with me."

   NCTE 4 Use written language to communicate effectively.

7. Think about a family event that you have attended. Identify the needs that were met during the event. Give a short oral report to the class, describing the event, listing the needs met, and explaining how the needs were met through the event.

   NCTE 12 Use language to accomplish individual purposes.

Check Your Answers Check your answers at this book's Online Learning Center through glencoe.com.

Families Teach Values

Reading Guide

Before You Read

What You Want to Know Write a list of what you want to know about how families teach values. As you read, write down the heads in this section that provide information.

Read to Learn

Key Concepts

- **Analyze** how your values and value system are related.
- **Summarize** how values are learned.

Main Idea

Values are beliefs and principles. They are based on ideas about what is right, good, and desirable. They are learned in the family and from society. What people do shows the values they hold.

Content Vocabulary

◇ values
◇ value system
◇ moral code

 Graphic Organizer Go to this book's Online Learning Center at glencoe.com to print out this graphic organizer.

Academic Vocabulary

You will find these words in your reading and on your tests. Use the glossary to look up their definitions if necessary.

◼ principle   ◼ controversy

Graphic Organizer

As you read, note the three ways that families teach values. Use a concept web like the one shown to help organize your information.

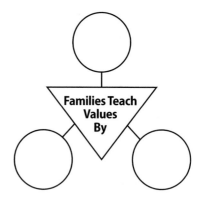

Families Teach Values By

Academic Standards •

 English Language Arts

NCTE 5 Use different writing process elements to communicate effectively.

NCTE 12 Use language to accomplish individual purposes.

NCTE *National Council of Teachers of English*
NCTM *National Council of Teachers of Mathematics*

NSES *National Science Education Standards*
NCSS *National Council of the Social Studies*

What Are Values?

As you look at the people you know, do you wonder what makes them act the way they do? Why they make certain choices? The answer has a lot to do with the values they hold.

Values are beliefs and principles. A belief is a state of mind in which trust is placed in some person or thing. A **principle** is a rule or code of conduct. Your values are based on ideas about what is right, good, and desirable. People and families decide which values they will hold. These values may vary from one person or family to another. The goals your family set for the future will often be based on you and your family's values.

The set of values that you have is called your **value system**. The choices you make about how you spend your time, energy, and money reflect your values. The words you choose and the nonverbal messages you send reveal your attitudes about what is important. You act according to what you believe. You may feel that some principles are worth standing up for, even fighting for. Others may not interest you at all. You adopt traits that you admire and believe are right for you. Together, these make up your value system.

Families have value systems as well. The adults in a family are the leaders in setting the family's value system. They teach others in the family what they think is important. The family value system affects all family members.

The Impact of Values

You will notice that some values have more impact than others. Some values are personal and apply to people. For example, some people value privacy and like to spend time alone. Others value companionship and want to be with people. Values like these often grow out of people's personalities.

Other values are held by society. These apply to all people and make life better. Core values include honesty, kindness, and social responsibility. Positive values guide choices and actions in favorable ways. Families often reinforce these core values of society. When societal values are upheld, life can be better for people and society and families are strengthened.

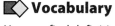 **Vocabulary**

You can find definitions in the glossary at the back of this book.

As You Read

Connect What set of values make up your value system?

▶ **Family Values**

Family values are what the members believe in and put into their actions. *What would you describe as a value held by this family?*

Common values are also shown in government documents and laws. The Declaration of Independence and the Constitution are based on values of freedom and equality. Laws that require children to go to school show the values of learning and education.

Another core value is that people are valuable and worthy of respect. This means that the way you treat others should reflect the way you want to be treated.

Personal beliefs about what is right and what is wrong become your **moral code** and guide your behavior. You can build your moral code once you have learned what you value.

✓ **Reading Check** **Explain** What is the difference between values and a value system?

Values Are Learned

Values are first learned within the family. Families help their members develop morally. They do this by teaching values that belong in a person's moral code.

Adults in a family need to express their values. This helps children grow up with a sense of what is right and good. Training in values gives people a feeling of security. Guiding principles are always there and ready for use. Children learn these values and may pass them along to their own children. Even when they do not adopt a value right away, they may do so later in life. Families teach values in these ways:

- **By Example** Older family members show their values to younger ones.
- **By Direct Teaching** Often lessons are taught by simply telling younger family members what is right.
- **By Religious Training** In many families, religion provides principles to live by. Religious teaching often focuses on core moral values.

Real Life — Value Emotional Support

Families show that they value each other when they give emotional support. How to show support is often taught by example. Exactly how it is shown depends on the values of the family. Here are some ways you can show emotional support to your family:

- Read and write letters or e-mails for an elderly relative who wants to keep in touch with friends.
- Bring a sibling or parent a special gift for no reason at all.
- Give frequent hugs to other family members.

- Send weekly e-mails to relatives who live far away.
- Say "I love you" to other family members.

Problem-Solving Karah will be the lead actress in the upcoming school play. She told her mother that she is nervous and she may forget her lines. Her mother said she would read the other actors' parts to help Karah get more practice before the play. How is Karah's mother showing that she values her family?

◀ **Influencing Your Values** Many people can influence your values. *Judging from this man's actions, how can this situation influence your values?*

Developing a Value System

Families provide the foundation for a value system. Many other influences also affect your thinking in both positive and negative ways. Friends can impact a person's values. This is especially true during the teen years. The values you learn from your friends may differ from the values you learned in your family.

Your values are tested in many ways. The media—movies, television, magazines, and newspapers—show all sorts of values. These are not all good ones. For example, smoking and drinking may be made to look appealing. Emphasis is placed on physical beauty and the way people dress. Violence may be a common theme. Your own good sense and a strong value system can help you see and resist bad influences.

There are many other influences that can affect your values. These can include people at school and in the community.

When Values Are Confusing

As you mature, you become more involved with people and events outside of your family. You will be more aware of how people's values can sometimes conflict. It is important to stay true to the core values in your moral code.

Some values can cause debate. Agreeing on a **controversy**, or a discussion where people have different views, is not easy. It may even be impossible. Families can be torn by conflicting values. There are some issues in society where differing values cause rifts and dispute.

Many issues are not clear cut. You may not be sure what is right. You may see reasons that support both sides of an issue. You may question why some people believe as they do when your beliefs are just the opposite.

Guidelines to Follow

As you build your value system, you need to be prepared to keep, defend, adjust, and strengthen your values. Good judgment will assist you. Turn to the values of people that you trust, such as your family, for guidance.

It pays to be cautious as you absorb other ideas into your thinking. When thinking about new issues, consider how your core values apply. When taking a position, be sure your reasoning is clear and logical.

There are guidelines, as shown in **Figure 2.1**, that you can use as you develop a value system. They will help you find core values that will serve you well throughout life.

Follow the Rules of Society The rules of society are based on values that respect life, property, and truth. Rules and laws are created by people who see that order is needed for progress. Thus, such acts as stealing and cheating are not allowed. Following laws and rules builds strength in society. It also makes you a stronger person.

People who follow the laws gain respect and opportunity in society. Laws, of course, are changed when necessary. Keep informed about issues so you know when laws need to be changed. Voting and writing to lawmakers can help bring about change.

Figure 2.1	Show Your Values

Use these guidelines to help you create a value system. *What is one way that you show your values?*

Choose What Is Right Take time to think if your decision is right or wrong.

Follow Rules Rules and laws help keep order in society.

Choose Right over Wrong Choices between right and wrong are not always clear. However, you will often know in your heart what is right. Before you make a choice between right and wrong, take time to think and ask yourself:

- Is it legal?
- Will it be harmful to me or anyone else?
- Will I regret it later?
- What is really best for you and others?

Learn from Others Watch what goes on around you. Learn from the mistakes and the successes of others. Knowing about the experiences of other people can help you strengthen your own values. Look at each source of information carefully to see if its influence is positive. Talk to an adult you trust such as a family member, teacher, or school counselor. The adult may be able to help you clarify your values.

Know What You Value Think about what is important to you. That will help you know clearly what your values are. If you know this, your values will be there when you need them.

Contribute to the Family Value System Your actions and words can strengthen the value system of your family. For example, imagine that one of your values is having family time. You can plan an evening of games and food with your family. The evening you plan can help promote family togetherness.

Learn from Others Notice what people around you value to see if you have the same values.

What Do You Value? Knowing your values can help you be successful in your life.

Help with Family Values Sharing your values with your family can strengthen your family value system.

Live Your Values

Values mean nothing without action. First you learn them. Then you live by them. For example, you are thoughtful when you pay attention to the feelings of others. You are honest only if you act that way, even when no one is watching. Your actions can show people your real values. You can also use your values to focus on others, not just yourself.

Your Actions Reflect Your Values

As you look at your value system, ask yourself if your actions match your beliefs. Do your words express what you value? If not, why? What can you do to act on important beliefs?

Your personal value system has many similarities with your family value system. Your actions reflect your values, just as a family's actions reflect the family's values. The same is true of the family value system. For instance, families who believe in togetherness, find ways to share time. A family may say they value cooperation. This is true if the members solve problems together. People who value education help younger family members learn. They encourage children to do well and stay in school.

A family value system can help the family make good decisions. It will only be as strong as family members make it. Families are responsible for teaching positive values. As a family member, you have to help put those values into action.

Section 2.2 — After You Read

Review Key Concepts

1. **Write** a sentence that defines values.
2. **Describe** in one or more paragraphs how families teach values.

Practice Academic Skills

English Language Arts

3. Think of a time when you held a value that one of your friends did not. For example, perhaps you value going to a younger sibling's sports event. Your friend thinks their homework is more important. Write a paragraph explaining your differences and what the effect was on your friendship.

> **NCTE 12** Use language to accomplish individual purposes.

4. Identify a value that is important to you in family life. Consider where that value came from. Did your family or people outside of your family teach you this value? Write a short story that shows where the value came from. Then continue the story to illustrate the impact the value has on a family and its members.

> **NCTE 5** Use different writing process elements to communicate effectively.

Check Your Answers Check your answers at this book's Online Learning Center through glencoe.com.

CHAPTER SUMMARY

Section 2.1
Families Meet Many Needs

People have basic needs. These are emotional, physical, social, and mental. Needs are necessary for survival while wants make life better. Needs are first met in the family. Emotional needs are filled when family members support each other. Emotional support builds family bonds and develops personality. Physical needs are important to keep families safe and healthy. Social skills are needed for socialization. Mental growth starts in the family and can be a lifelong process.

Section 2.2
Families Teach Values

Values are beliefs and principles. They define what people see as right and good. Values can affect every part of life. Values are learned first from the family. There are many other influences on values, some positive and some negative. The values a person holds make up a value system. A value system supports the family and society by helping a person know right from wrong. Living your values means making what you say and do match what you believe is good and right.

Content and Academic Vocabulary Review

1. Use each of these content and academic vocabulary words in a sentence.

Content Vocabulary
◇ need (p. 23)
◇ want (p. 23)
◇ emotion (p. 24)
◇ emotional support (p. 24)
◇ support system (p. 24)
◇ family bond (p. 25)
◇ personality (p. 26)
◇ socialization (p. 28)
◇ independence (p. 28)
◇ values (p. 31)
◇ value system (p. 31)
◇ moral code (p. 32)

Academic Vocabulary
■ distinguish (p. 24)
■ characteristic (p. 26)
■ principle (p. 31)
■ controversy (p. 33)

Review Key Concepts

2. Identify the difference between needs and wants.
3. Determine the ways emotional support affects the family and its members.
4. Describe how families meet physical needs.
5. Explain how social skills are learned.
6. Describe how families can contribute to mental growth.
7. Analyze how values and value system are related.
8. Summarize how values are learned.

Critical Thinking

9. Draw Conclusions Think about all of the needs a family meets. Which one do you think is most important? Why?
10. Predict What do you think might happen if you and a family member had different values? How might you get along together?

Real-World Skills

Problem-Solving Skills

11. Use Values to Prioritize Elena and her friends have tickets to a concert. Elena discovers that the concert is the night before her college entrance exam. Doing well on the exam is important. A high score will qualify her for financial aid. How will Elena's values affect her decision? What should Elena do?

Self-Management Skills

12. Personal Values Identify a value that you hold. Make a list of actions you can take and words and phrases you can use that show the value. Then write a paragraph that answers this question: In what settings and with what people would you show this value?

Financial Literacy Skills

13. Find Costs Research the costs for meeting the physical needs of a baby. Write a letter to your teacher that answers these questions: How much do diapers, baby clothes, and food cost? What does child care cost? How would knowing about the costs of having a baby help a couple plan more effectively?

Critical Thinking Skills

14. Conflicting Values Gary's friends are going to a movie that Gary knows his parents would not approve of. If he tells his parents his plans, he knows they will forbid him to go. He wants to go to the movie with his friends. What values are in conflict? Explain what Gary should do.

15. Observation Research Observe students in your school as they interact in the halls and at lunch. Write a report that describes what social skills are learned or put to use in this setting.

16. Media Analysis Locate an article about a person or event that reflects a value. Give a brief report to the class, describing the value and explaining how the value is shown in the article.

17. Plan an Activity Write a plan for an activity with a child that will help meet at least three basic needs. For example, a walk in the park meets: physical needs as you exercise; social needs as you talk together; mental needs as you talk to the child about nature; and emotional needs as you support and encourage the child to explore the park.

18. Evaluate a Web Site Values are reflected in Web sites. Go to this book's Online Learning Center at **glencoe.com** to find **Web Links** for **Popular Web Sites**. Choose one of the Web sites and identify values that are reflected in the content and design. Evaluate whether this site reflects any of the core values of society.

Additional Activities For additional activities, go to this book's Online Learning Center through **glencoe.com**.

Academic Skills

Mathematics

19. Calculate Ratios Volunteer work is an important value for many families. Some families spend part of their family time volunteering at places where they can help meet the needs of others. If your family set aside ten hours a week for family time, and two hours of that time for volunteering, what is the ratio of volunteer time to other family time?

Math Concept **Represent Ratios** A ratio is a comparison between two numbers that can be represented in different forms. The ratio *1:2* can also be expressed as *1 out of 2, 1 to 2,* or *½*. Usually, ratios are represented in their simplest form, also called lowest terms. For example, the simplest form of 2:4 is 1:2. In this case, both ratios represent *one half*.

Starting Hint: Begin by setting up this ratio as a fraction with two as the numerator and ten as the denominator. Your answer should be a fraction in simplest form, or lowest terms.

 For math help, go to the Math Appendix at the back of the book.

> **NCTM Number and Operations** Understand numbers, ways of representing numbers, relationships among numbers, and number systems.

English Language Arts

20. Analyze Write a one-page paper describing a time when your value system helped you make a difficult decision. Describe the decision you had to make and the choice you came to. Then, explain the values that affected your decision. Where did these values come from? Did your family's value system play a role in your decision? Determine whether you now think the decision was a good one, and whether you would use the same values again.

> **NCTE 5** Use different writing process elements to communicate effectively.

Social Studies

21. Understand History Read the Preamble to the Constitution of the United States. Notice the values displayed in the document. List at least three values promoted by the writers of this document. Follow your teacher's instructions to form into groups. Discuss with your classmates why the writers of the Declaration chose to stress these values. Write your findings in a two-paragraph response.

> **NCSS VI.c** Analyze and explain ideas and mechanisms to meet needs and wants of citizens, manage conflict, and establish order and security of a just society.

STANDARDIZED TEST PRACTICE

SHORT ANSWER
In a short answer question, write as neatly as possible. Use a separate sheet of paper to write your answers.

> **Test-Taking Tip** Put as much information into your answer as possible. Use easy-to-read, short sentences that define key words. Also give an example that explains your answer.

22. Write two or three sentences to answer each question.
  a. In what way is the self-esteem of family members affected by the family?
  b. What does it mean to "follow the rules of society"?

CHAPTER 3

Family Characteristics

Section 3.1

Family Structures

Section 3.2

Family Development

▶▶ Explore the Photo
All families are different. *What characteristics does your family have that make it different from others?*

Chapter Objectives

After completing this chapter, you will be able to:

- **Describe** various family structures.
- **Summarize** the qualities that make up a family's personality.
- **Compare** families in the media with those in real life.
- **Describe** the stages of family development common to many families.
- **Identify** exceptions to the typical pattern of family development.

Writing Activity Journal Entry

Trustworthiness When you trust someone, you believe that you will be accepted, believed, and supported by that person. The person who earns your trust is trustworthy. You can count on him or her to act with your best interests in mind. Families become stronger through trust. You can show trust in these ways:
- Follow the rules at home even when you are alone.
- Be honest with adults about where you will be and with whom.
- Obey traffic rules and speed limits when driving.
- Do not reveal confidential information told by a friend.
- Complete school assignments and jobs at work as expected.
Write a journal entry about how you are a trustworthy person.

Writing Tips To write a journal entry, follow these steps:
1. Date your entry.
2. Write about experiences, reactions, and observations.
3. Let one idea lead to another.

Family Structures

Reading Guide

Before You Read

Predict Before starting this section, browse the headings, bold terms, and photo captions to predict what this section is about.

Read to Learn

Key Concepts

- **Describe** various family structures.
- **Summarize** the qualities that make up a family's personality.
- **Compare** families in the media with those in real life.

Main Idea

Family structure is the form a family takes. Family personality is the traits that combine to make the family unique.

Content Vocabulary

◇ nuclear family
◇ single-parent family
◇ blended family
◇ extended family
◇ adoptive family
◇ legal guardian
◇ foster family
◇ interdependence
◇ dependent
◇ goal

Academic Vocabulary

You will find these words in your reading and on your tests. Use the glossary to look up their definitions if necessary.

■ minor
■ autocratic

Graphic Organizer

As you read, list and describe the nine structures that a family can have. Use a chart like the one shown to help organize your information.

Family Structure	Description
1._____	_____
2._____	_____

 Graphic Organizer Go to this book's Online Learning Center at **glencoe.com** to print out this graphic organizer.

Academic Standards . . . .

 English Language Arts

NCTE 2 Read literature to build an understanding of the human experience.

NCTE 5 Use different writing process elements to communicate effectively.

 Mathematics

NCTM Data Analysis and Probability Collect, organize, and display relevant data.

NCTM Number and Operations Understand numbers and ways of representing numbers.

NCTE *National Council of Teachers of English*
NCTM *National Council of Teachers of Mathematics*

NSES *National Science Education Standards*
NCSS *National Council of the Social Studies*

Family Structures

When you think of "family," what mental pictures come to mind? Families come in all shapes and sizes. The form a family takes is called a structure. The structure affects the way the family functions. Family structures change over time. People may move in and out of a family group. In recent years, the trend has been for families to include fewer members.

As you read about family structures, you will notice that families are as varied as the people in them. What truly counts is what happens inside the family. Within the family, people gain skills, strength, and knowledge to help them cope in society.

As You Read

Connect Think about the structure of your family.

Single People

Single people may live alone. Some share housing with a roommate or friends. Most maintain family bonds with parents, brothers and sisters, and other relatives. A single person who has no close family may turn to friends to fill the needs normally met by family members.

Single people often have freedoms that others do not have. Many come and go as they please. They do not have to coordinate with anyone else's schedule or needs. They have more time to devote to a career and interests. Many spend time with friends or helping in their community.

Family Images
Even when you live on your own, you are still part of a family structure. *How is this single person maintaining bonds with his family?*

Couples

Married couples are able to focus on each other. They rely and depend on their partners for support. Couples in committed relationships often form a close bond. Couples can also make time for other interests, friends, relatives, and community activities.

Income for a couple can also be a plus. With two people in the family, there can be two incomes. When there are two incomes in a family, expenses can be easier to manage and savings can grow. Couples earning two incomes may have more money for special activities and interests, such as travel.

One problem couples may have is career conflict when both partners have jobs. What if one of them is offered a job in another town? Will the other one stay behind, look for a new job, or quit working? These kinds of decisions are not easy to make.

Nuclear Families

◆ Vocabulary
You can find definitions in the glossary at the back of this book.

A **nuclear family** consists of a mother, father, and their children. In nuclear families, household as well as child-raising duties can be shared. Children in a nuclear family have both parents to provide love and support. They can learn firsthand what it means to be a mother and father. Parents can share the time they spend with their children. Parents in a nuclear family need to spend time together to keep their bond as a couple strong.

Single-Parent Families

A **single-parent family** is one parent and his or her children. Many single parents enjoy the one-on-one relationships they have with their children. It can be a challenge, however, to be a single parent. All the family duties must be handled by the single parent. Many single parents provide and manage all the income. They take care of all the chores and tasks. Finding the time and energy to do everything is not easy. Relatives, friends, and other people from the community may help out.

Single parents need to set aside special time for children. Giving them love and guidance builds the ties between the parent and the child. Children of single-parent families need to have contact with other adults, too. This helps them learn about both men and women. A grandparent or other people from the community can serve this purpose.

Blended Families

A **blended family** is a husband and wife, at least one of whom has children from a former relationship. A blended family can include the children of both spouses. It also may have children born to the couple.

Being part of a blended family is not always easy. Both adults and children have to make adjustments. With some extra effort, new routines and relationships can work. Living in a blended family calls for patience and insight.

Extended Families

An **extended family** includes relatives other than parents and **minor**, or smaller, children. Grandparents, aunts, uncles, and cousins are all part of the extended family. Some extended families live together.

Extended family members, regardless of where they live, can be a big help. Most relatives expect to be there for each other when they are needed. It is part of being a family.

Math in Action

Slice the Family Pie

Research the percentage of each type of family living in the same home in the U.S. Follow these steps to create a pie (or circle) graph to present your data:

1. Create a two-column table.
2. In the first column, list the different types of families.
3. In the second column, list the percentage of that type of family that exists in the U.S. (from your research).
4. Use the percentages in the second column to create your pie graph.

Math Concept **Creating Pie Graphs**
In a pie graph, there is a piece of pie for each topic represented in the graph. For this pie graph, you will create a piece of pie for each type of family.

Starting Hint: Be sure that when you add all of the percentages together, the total is 100%.

✈ Building Academic Skills
Go to this book's Online Learning Center through **glencoe.com** to complete a worksheet for this activity.

NCTM Data Analysis and Probability Collect, organize, and display relevant data.

 Math For math help, go to the Math Appendix at the back of the book.

An extended family can include a variety of personalities. For this reason, getting along with relatives may be a challenge at times. You may know families whose quarrels have kept them apart for years. Everyone loses when that happens. Working to keep the bonds close is worthwhile. Most people feel that nothing can replace family ties.

Adoptive Families

An **adoptive family** is a family with a child or children who are made part of the family through legal action. The child is not born to the parents. Instead, the parents have gone through a legal process to make the child a part of their family. The adopted child usually takes the family's last name. The child is protected by law. He or she has all the same rights that a child born to the family has.

When an infant is adopted, parents have to make many adjustments to their lifestyles. If the child who is adopted is older, the child has many adjustments to make, too. Parents need to be patient and understanding to help make the adopted child feel safe and secure.

Legal Guardians

Sometimes parents can no longer take care of their children. A relative or close friend of the family may wish to take care of the child. The courts can make this person a **legal guardian**. This means the person has financial and legal duties for the care of the child. The guardian acts as the child's parent. The child's last name does not change when this occurs.

Grandparents are sometimes named legal guardians. They may step in when parents have problems caring for children. Grandparents then have the legal right to care for children.

Foster Families

A **foster family** is a family that takes care of children on a short-term basis. Foster children may be waiting to be adopted. They may need a place to live while problems of their birth families are solved.

Foster parents are often licensed by the state. They are screened, or investigated by social workers and may be given special training to learn how to care for their foster children. They receive some money from the state to help pay the children's expenses. This amount often does not cover all the child's expenses. Foster parents act as parents while children live with them.

Foster Families
A foster family is a temporary way to provide care for children. *In what ways do you think being a foster parent is rewarding?*

The Cost to Rent

Families often decide where to live based on the amount of space they need and the amount of money they have to spend. If a two-bedroom apartment that rents for $750 in St. Louis rents for 250% of that price in Manhattan, what is the rent in Manhattan?

Math Concept **Percents Greater than 100** Percents greater than 100 represent values greater than one. They can be converted to mixed numbers or decimals greater than one.

Starting Hint: If 250% is changed to a decimal greater than one, it will look like 2.50. Multiply this decimal by the number ($750). Be sure the decimal point is in the correct place in your answer.

 For math help, go to the Math Appendix at the back of the book.

NCTM Number and Operations Understand numbers, ways of representing numbers, relationships among numbers, and number systems.

Foster parenting is rewarding for many people. It can be hard, however, if a child has many problems. Being attached to a child who will leave is a special concern for foster families. They must give love and be willing to let go when the time comes for the child to be adopted or go back to live with his or her birth family.

✓ **Reading Check** **Define** What is a family structure?

Family Personality

A family is like a puzzle with hundreds of pieces. Many different factors come together to make the whole. Each person brings special qualities to the group. The combination creates a unique result.

Just as you have a personality, a family does, too. The traits that combine to make a family unique give the family a personality. Family personalities are as different as they are complex. One of the ways that family personality is shown is in the atmosphere or feeling in the home. Another is how the family makes decisions.

There are other parts of family personality. What the family values and works for is important. Some families choose to spend money on their homes. Others may save extra money for vacations. Saving for their children's college education is the focus in other families. The way each family spends and saves reflects what is important to them.

Family Legacies, Traditions, and Rituals

Families have legacies, traditions, and rituals. These help cement the ties among family members. Legacies are something that has been handed down from previous family members. Family traditions vary. For example, one family may always go out for dinner on a member's birthday. In another, the person with the birthday chooses the menu and the family eats together at home. Family rituals vary but may include attending religious or cultural events with the family.

How Personality Affects Family Values

The personality of the family affects how the family fulfills its functions and needs. It has an impact on what family members learn and the values they hold. For example, a family that values education may have an intellectual personality. In a family like this, reading may be stressed as an important part of life. There may be many books in this household. To fit their personality, this family may spend evenings at home reading together.

Another family that values education may spend their time visiting museums and art galleries. They may go to national parks on vacation. They may choose to learn about all of the things they encounter wherever they go. These two examples show how families can fulfill a value for education in different ways. The family's personality may change if the structure of the family changes.

Family Atmosphere

After spending some time in a family's home, you become aware of the atmosphere of the household. Because people are all so different, family atmospheres are, too. The pace may be fast and loud, laid back and friendly, or formal and distant. You may be aware of the family atmosphere from simply being around the family. The atmosphere does not exist only within the family's home.

The Dawson family, for example, is loud. They laugh and they cry. Displays of love are common. Family members like to tease each other and have fun. Everyone is quick to show emotions. Quarrels are frequent but short. When quarrels are over, they are forgotten.

The Conner family is quiet. They talk a lot, but joking is not their style. They care, but do not hug or kiss each other much. Family members are more apt to show how they feel by helping each other. If differences of opinion take place, they are in the form of discussions, not quarrels. They settle arguments in a calm and rational way.

Your family may not be like either of these examples. Two families can feel loved and secure, yet their family atmospheres can differ. It depends on the traits of those in your family. In healthy families, the atmosphere allows family members to love one another and make the best of themselves and each other.

Family Boundaries

Another part of family personality is its boundaries. This is the line that divides a family from others. Sometimes the boundary is very tight. When family boundaries are strict, outsiders are not important in family life. These families do not have guests very often. The line between the family and others is strong.

Some families have looser boundaries. They accept others into their home and lives easily. Relationships with non-family members are part of family life. Children in this type of family may bring friends home without asking permission. Friends and neighbors may visit often and are always welcome. Anyone who is at home at mealtimes is invited to eat with the family. The boundaries between this family and others are weak and loose.

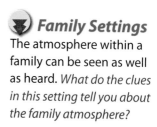

Family Settings
The atmosphere within a family can be seen as well as heard. *What do the clues in this setting tell you about the family atmosphere?*

Family Decision Making

A family's personality is linked to how it makes choices. Families make decisions in different ways. How they make decisions reflects, in part, how they relate to each other.

One Person Decides

In some families one person makes most of the decisions for the family. Choices about spending money, household routines, and chores are made by that person. Some minor choices may be made by others. The job of making major decisions is in one person's hands. This is the **autocratic** style of decision making.

Family Decisions
Families that operate democratically might decide on vacations as a group. *Does each person have an equal vote on every decision?*

Shared Decision Making

With the democratic style, decision making is shared. Choices are made by more than one person. Skills are taken into account when choosing who will take care of what. A family that makes decisions with this style may work together to set up a schedule of household duties to share. They take advantage of personal strengths and interests. This helps them decide how each person will help out.

In the democratic style, the thoughts and feelings of children are valued. This does not mean that children will get a vote in all matters. Parents need to use adult judgment. Their experience and knowledge help them make good choices. This is in the best interest of the whole family.

Interdependence

Families want members to become close. **Interdependence** is a feeling that family members can rely on each other. Knowing that you can rely on your family helps you to feel good about your family. Family members spend time together, sharing feelings and activities. They feel secure. Interdependence is closely tied to family commitment. When family members are interdependent, they become more committed to each other.

In families that are strong, interdependence is valued. Family members are close, but each person is still involved in the outside world. Members are empowered to make choices for themselves. They are free to explore relationships with others. The family provides a link to many opportunities and experiences.

Find a Balance

In healthy families, people rely on each other. Too much or too little reliance can be a problem. Achieving a balance between independence and dependence is the goal.

Dependent people rely too much on others. They may not be able to make decisions themselves. They want decisions made for them. They avoid taking action on their own. Too much dependence is confining.

When family members are too dependent, they do everything together. They are less aware of their own separate selves. They may shy away from the outside world. This increases their dependence on each other. In cases like these, children often do not learn to be independent and take care of themselves.

Some families have very independent members. This makes being close and maintaining family bonds a challenge. These families can miss out on the joys and pleasures of family life if they do not work together to maintain and nurture their relationships.

Strong families blend the best of dependence and independence. All members learn to stand by each other. At the same time, they learn to be active members of the outside world.

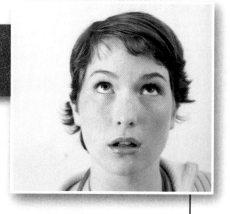

INDEPENDENT Living

HOW TO   Make Decisions

As you get older, you are responsible for making your own decisions. It is important to make these decisions wisely, as they will affect your future. Follow these guidelines to make sound decisions:

1. **Identify the decision you are making.** Write or state the decision as specifically as you can. Having a clear idea from the start will help you along the way.
2. **List your options and resources.** Knowing the resources that are available to you help you to make up your mind. For instance, if you are trying to decide among several after school activities, you need to know whether you have the interests, skills, and time for each option.
3. **Think through your options.** Once you have narrowed down your options, think about the possible results of each one. Be realistic and think about the pros and cons of each.
4. **Choose the best option.** If you are still having problems deciding, you may need to go back a step or two. You may need more facts. Let your goals and values guide your decision.
5. **Act on your decision.** Give your best effort, and know that you have thought carefully about your decision.

Take Action Give an example of how this process can be useful for making simple decisions, such as whether to subscribe to a certain magazine, or whether to pack a lunch or buy one at school.

Family Goals

All families, as well as individuals, have hopes and dreams. Many of these become goals that affect what goes on in the family. A **goal** is something you plan to achieve. You have to be willing to work for your goals. The goals that drive your family are likely different from those of other families. Each family's goals are linked to its personality.

Family goals are based on the unique values and needs of the family. Every day families take into account their values when they make decisions. Many of the decisions families make are casual. For example, a family might have a goal of spending an afternoon together. They may choose to have a picnic at a park, go shopping, or go to a movie. Different families make different choices. These choices are routine.

Other kinds of goals have greater impact. Will the family save money for a trip or a child's education? Will they spend free time working in their community or earning more income at a second job? Goals can be simple or complex. Goals that need careful planning and time to accomplish often have the most long-term impact.

Yuri's family, for example, would like to move to another part of the country. They want to live closer to his grandfather, who is ill and needs care and support. They are looking at ways that they could make the move happen. This is a goal that will have a major, long-term effect on the lives of all family members.

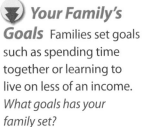

Your Family's Goals Families set goals such as spending time together or learning to live on less of an income. *What goals has your family set?*

✓ **Reading Check** **Explain** What is family personality?

Families and the Media

Many people's images of what a family should be like come from the media. You have seen families on television, in the movies, and maybe even in plays. The family structure and personality in these examples may seem ideal, or perfect. Family members seem to solve complex problems in minutes. The problems experienced by different types of families seem easy to solve.

A family in a movie, for example, might have a flawless holiday. The relatives, food, decorations, gifts, and sharing all happen without any problems. The messy kitchen, the overcooked turkey, and the tired cook may not be shown. Any issues that do arise are neatly resolved by the end of the story.

The media can influence your thinking more than you realize. What you see on the television or in the movies may begin to seem like the way real life is for other people. You may think your life and your family do not measure up. The personality of your family may seem dull or lacking in glamour.

Screenwriters aim to entertain you. They need a story line with an effective ending. Time puts limits on what they can do. In real life, the story line is long, complex, and sometimes involves routine decisions that are not exciting.

Real families are very different from media images. When you understand this, reality is easier to accept. Your family will probably not be like the ones in the movies. Real-life families have their strengths and weaknesses. The reality is that different does not mean better or worse. It simply means different.

Section 3.1   After You Read

Review Key Concepts

1. **Give** five examples of different family structures.
2. **Identify** at least three factors that make up a family's personality.
3. **Explain** if images of families in the media represent all families. Why or why not?

Practice Academic Skills

English Language Arts

4. Think about a book or story you have read where people live in a particular family structure. Identify the structure. Think about the ways the family structure helps or does not help members meet their needs. Write a short report summarizing your findings.

5. Think about your family's goals. How do those goals affect your family? Consider the goals of another family you know. How do their goals affect their family? Write your answers in two or more paragraphs.

NCTE 2 Read literature to build an understanding of the human experience.

NCTE 5 Use different writing process elements to communicate effectively.

Check Your Answers Check your answers at this book's Online Learning Center through glencoe.com.

Family Development

Reading Guide

Before You Read

Vocabulary To gain a better understanding of vocabulary, create a Vocabulary Journal. Divide a piece of paper into three columns: *Vocabulary*, *What is it?*, and *What else is it like?* Write down each word and answer the questions as you read the section.

Read to Learn
Key Concepts
- **Describe** the stages of family development common to many families.
- **Identify** exceptions to the typical pattern of family development.

Main Idea

Families go through common stages of development. These include starting as a couple, the parenting years, the middle years, and the retirement years. There are other patterns and variations to these stages.

Content Vocabulary
◇ development ◇ empty nest
◇ launching

 Graphic Organizer Go to this book's Online Learning Center at **glencoe.com** to print out this graphic organizer.

Academic Vocabulary
You will find these words in your reading and on your tests. Use the glossary to look up their definitions if necessary.
▪ cycle ▪ circumstance

Graphic Organizer

As you read, identify and describe the three parts of the parenting stage of family development. Use a chart like the one shown to help organize your information.

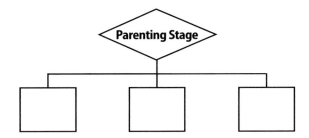

Academic Standards • • • • • • • • • • • • • • • • • • •
 English Language Arts

NCTE 5 Use different writing process elements to communicate effectively.

NCTE 12 Use language to accomplish individual purposes.

NCTE *National Council of Teachers of English*
NCTM *National Council of Teachers of Mathematics*

NSES *National Science Education Standards*
NCSS *National Council of the Social Studies*

Stages of Family Development

Social scientists describe a basic pattern of family development. **Development** is the process of growth and change over the course of life. Social scientists have applied this concept to families. They describe a basic pattern of growth and change in families. The pattern follows stages as a family moves from life as a couple, through the parenting years, and into the later years. This pattern is often called the family life **cycle**, or series of events. Not everyone labels each stage within the cycle the same way. The cycle is a general one and many exceptions exist.

The family life cycle represents a stable pattern that supports families. As families move through the life cycle, they are concerned about their needs and wants. In every stage, a family makes choices that affect members and their growth and development. People must be committed to each other and to the family itself.

◀▷ Vocabulary

You can find definitions in the glossary at the back of this book.

As You Read

Connect What parts of the life cycle has your extended family experienced?

Start as a Couple

The first stage of the family life cycle begins with a couple. Many couples find that having some time to spend without children is helpful. They can get to know each other better before another person shares life with them.

As a couple, two people learn to think and act as a team. Daily routines involve two people, not just one. They learn to rely on each other and yet be individuals. As they make plans, their ability to work together and communicate is tested. They are working to build a solid foundation for life.

People need time to adjust in their early years as partners because they come from different settings. They are moving into a new relationship with each other. A young couple must work out relationships with others, too. Each has an extended family. Learning how to get along with and include them may take some effort. The same is true of friends. Should a couple share former friends or make new ones together?

▶▶ Starting Out

Young couples are in the beginning stages of the family life cycle and have many decisions to make. *What decisions will affect the direction of their life together?*

How long couples stay in this stage depends on the couple. Some want to have children right away. Some never have children. Some couples choose not to have children. Other couples may not be able to have children for medical reasons. A couple may wait several years and then decide they are ready to have a baby.

Make Decisions Together

Couples face many choices in the first stage of the family life cycle. Decisions that were made alone before must now involve another person. Here are some of the things that couples have to consider:

- **Housing** Where to live is one of the first issues. How close should they live to other family members? Living too close may increase dependency. Living too far away may make it hard to maintain close family bonds. Because people are very mobile today, decisions on where to live may come up often.
- **Furnishings** Part of getting settled in a household involves getting all the furnishings and equipment needed to run a household. Doing so can be costly, especially if a couple has little money to start with. Some couples use items donated by family members. Others find bargains at garage sales and discount stores to help them get started. Couples also need to choose how to place their furniture and equipment in their home.
- **Education and Careers** Career plans are often a major concern at this stage of the family life cycle. Careers have a direct impact on finances. Choices about education and careers affect the family throughout the family life cycle.

More than One Stage A family can be in more than one stage of the family life cycle at the same time. *How is that true for this family?*

- **Money** How to manage money is an ongoing question first addressed in the couples stage. Many couples earn two incomes. Financial decisions that couples need to make include: Will they have separate checking and savings accounts or will they share accounts? Who will pay the bills? What purchases will they make? Will they have to ask permission from each other before spending money? As you can imagine, money can be a big source of problems. Decisions can be made by carefully considering the wishes of both people.
- **Children** A decision about having children should not be made lightly. When a couple decides to have children, they are choosing to move out of the couples stage of family development and into the parenting stage. Some couples do not have children, either by choice or by another **circumstance**, or event.

The Parenting Stage

A society needs children in order to survive. Families that follow the typical stages of family development fulfill this need. The family moves into the parent stage when children join the couple, whether by birth, adoption, foster care, or guardianship.

The parent stage of the family life cycle is about taking care of others. Parents need to have certain qualities to be good caregivers. They must be committed to their children. They should be patient and show kindness and caring. Children rely on parents to be dependable and trustworthy.

During the parent stage, families raise children to be productive, independent adults. This stage lasts until children are living on their own. It can be a long stage in the life of a family. It has three parts: the expanding years, the developing years, and the launching years.

The Expanding Family

The first part of the parent stage is the expanding years. New members are added to the family in this stage. While children are small, most families are very focused on home and family life. Young children need a great deal of time and attention from parents. Parents may feel tied down at times. It may be harder for couples to find the alone time they shared before having children.

Jason and Cassie, for example, used to enjoy many different activities together before they had children. They are still able to spend time together, but it is different than before. Now they do activities that their children can be a part of, such as going to the park, renting videos, and riding bikes. They love spending time as a family, but Cassie and Jason wish it was a little easier to find some time for the two of them.

Children can be a heavy financial burden. They have basic food and clothing needs that cost money. There are also medical, educational, and entertainment expenses to be met. If child care is needed, another expense is added to the budget. Families need to plan for these additional costs.

Life Skills CHECKLIST

Leadership Skills

Show Your Commitment
Your current family is most likely in the parenting stage of development. You can show your commitment in this stage if you:

✓ Support the goals of your family.

✓ Recognize that no family is perfect.

✓ Keep a positive attitude.

✓ Expect the best from others and yourself.

✓ Promote family traditions and rituals.

The Developing Family

As children grow older, the family moves into the developmental years. During this stage, children enter school. There are activities outside of the home.

Families with School-Age Children Family unity tends to peak when children are in elementary school. Parents' lives are less restricted than they were during the children's infancy and preschool years. Children can communicate well in this stage. They can contribute to family life by doing basic tasks and making simple decisions. These skills allow school-age children to feel that they play an important role in how their family functions.

Families with Teenagers As children grow into their teens, life becomes very different from the early years. Teens are getting ready to leave the family. They are learning the skills they will need to be independent. How much independence the teen needs is often a cause for debate.

While raising children, the family pace is often fast. Families have a limited amount of time to get everything done. People in the family can support each other by sharing duties and managing their time well. This will help prevent pressures from building. It can relieve stress if families accept that not every job can be accomplished or done perfectly.

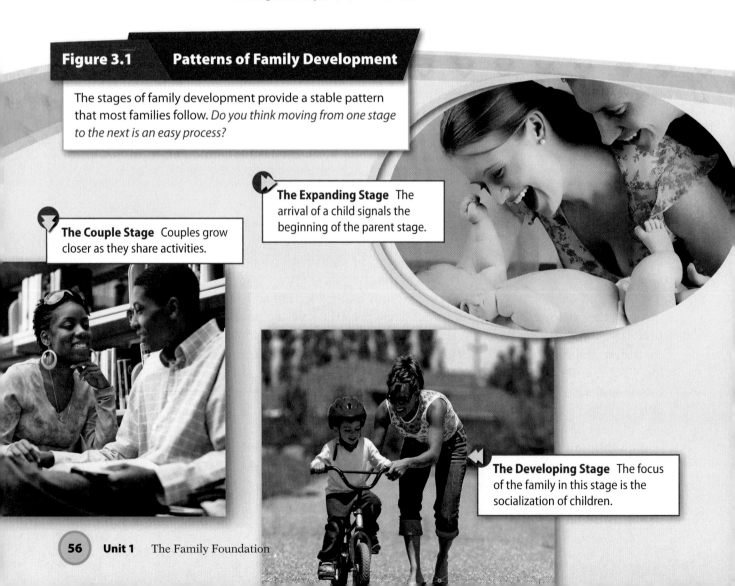

Figure 3.1   Patterns of Family Development

The stages of family development provide a stable pattern that most families follow. *Do you think moving from one stage to the next is an easy process?*

The Expanding Stage The arrival of a child signals the beginning of the parent stage.

The Couple Stage Couples grow closer as they share activities.

The Developing Stage The focus of the family in this stage is the socialization of children.

Launching

The end of the parenting stage is marked by the exit of children from the family home. During the **launching** process, children are sent out on their own, physically and financially. The latest trend in the launching stage of family life is that it lasts longer than usual. Children tend to be dependent on parents longer than they used to be. They may not earn enough to live on their own. They may also be attending school while living at home.

The parental stage also lengthens when adult children return home. Often the reasons are financial. The adult child may be saving money to buy a house. Some may be paying off a college loan. A divorced child may move back home, sometimes with his or her children. Many young adults live with their parents.

The Middle Years

When the children have grown up and left home, the family becomes a couple again. A new stage, the middle years, is entered. As the population ages, many people are finding added years during the middle years of life. **Figure 3.1** will help you understand the middle years and the basic pattern of family development.

The feelings of the middle years can be positive as well as negative. When a couple's children become adults and move out of the family home, the situation is called the **empty nest**. Having an empty nest leaves some parents feeling lost and without purpose. Other people love their newfound freedom after years of caring for children.

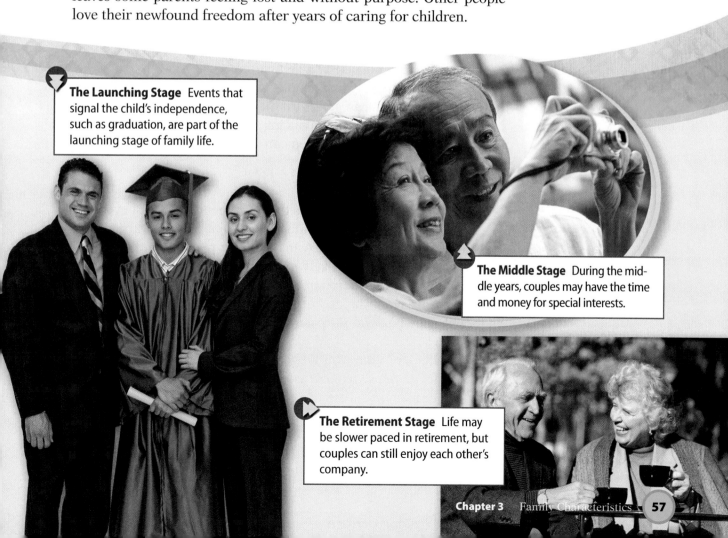

The Launching Stage Events that signal the child's independence, such as graduation, are part of the launching stage of family life.

The Middle Stage During the middle years, couples may have the time and money for special interests.

The Retirement Stage Life may be slower paced in retirement, but couples can still enjoy each other's company.

Becoming a grandparent is a special pleasure for many people who are in the middle years and later in life. They enjoy time spent with their grandchildren like a best friend and a parent. This special relationship can have many benefits for both the grandparents and the children. The relationship among grandparents and grandchildren can focus on fun rather than the duties of family life.

Sometimes grandparents take care of their grandchildren on a regular basis. Two common reasons for this are family problems and parents who are employed full time.

Problem-Solving

Lena needed to go back to work after her son was born. Her mother, Betty, was recently retired. Lena asked if she might take care of her baby while she was at work. Betty did not answer right away. What do you think Betty was considering before she answered? What do you think her answer would be?

The middle years stage of family development can be a time of questioning. Careers that have already peaked may feel less challenging. Most people work through these feelings by finding new goals and new purposes in life. They may change jobs or find a new career. Many find volunteer work meaningful. Others take time to enjoy or develop new hobbies. Couples may find they have less in common without children to focus on. They can work to renew the companionship and sharing that they enjoyed when they were starting out as a couple.

Income pressures often decrease during this stage. As people hit their career peaks, their incomes are often at an all-time high. Independent children are no longer an expense. Couples may have more money to travel, save for retirement, and spend on purchases they may not have been previously able to afford.

The middle years may find people caring for aging parents. Women have most often been caregivers for their parents. Men, however, also help with this family duty. Balancing personal needs with those of aging parents and grown children can be a challenge.

The Retirement Years

The final stage of family life is the retirement stage. Not everyone views retirement in the same way. Some people look forward to time for travel, hobbies, or to relax. If they have planned and saved for retirement, they are more likely to have positive feelings about it.

Other people fear retirement. They may wonder what they will do with themselves. The end of a career leaves some people feeling as though they have no purpose. Sometimes people have not saved enough, so lack of money is a major concern.

The retirement years can be good ones. People who feel fulfilled with the life they have led are usually prepared for their later years. They find simple pleasures and reflect on the past and share the wisdom that life has given them.

✓ **Reading Check** **Identify** What are some of the major choices couples make at the start of their lives as a couple together?

Other Patterns of Family Development

Not every family fits neatly into the stages of family development. There are many reasons why people follow different patterns. Some people do not marry. Some marriages end in divorce and single parenthood. Choosing not to have children is another pattern. Becoming a couple at an older age or raising a grandchild are two more patterns. The stages of development, despite these other patterns, explain the way many families' lives unfold.

Length of Time in Each Stage Varies

The stages of development may be different lengths for each family. One family may have two children, raise them to the teen years, and then have another child. The parent stage for this family is quite long. They may miss the middle years stage entirely. A family might have one child and a very short parent stage. The middle years stage would be long for them.

The stages may overlap in certain ways. For example, older parents may still have young children at home while they are retired. Two retired adults might marry. Grandparents may have children or grandchildren living with them.

In spite of the many variations, the basic patterns continue in society. Children grow up in families. They raise families of their own. It works for families and for society.

Section 3.2   After You Read

Review Key Concepts

1. **Describe** why it is helpful to break the family life cycle into stages of development.

2. **Explain** why the family life cycle does not describe every family's development.

Practice Academic Skills

English Language Arts

3. Write ten interview questions that you could use to interview an adult. The purpose of the questions is to determine the stage of family development the person's family is in and what the person sees as the pleasures and challenges of the stage. Your questions should reflect the purpose.

4. Imagine that you are part of a couple setting up your first home. Create a list of furnishings and equipment you might need. Then, identify possible low-cost ways you could obtain the items.

> **NCTE 5** Use different writing process elements to communicate effectively.

> **NCTE 12** Use language to accomplish individual purposes.

Check Your Answers Check your answers at this book's Online Learning Center through **glencoe.com**.

CAREER SPOTLIGHT

Adoption Coordinator

Ann Du Waldt
Glen Ellyn, Illinois

Ann Du Waldt, an adoption coordinator, feels the adoption of a child can be a beautiful process. It offers hope and possibility to both the parents unable to care for the child and the parents who want to. An adoption coordinator works to make it all happen.

"Having an interest in child welfare is important," says Du Waldt. "People who have been touched by adoption in some way are often drawn to the field."

Du Waldt says her work consists of helping the adoptive parents get through the application process. She also helps the birth families who have decided that adoption is right for them.

Du Waldt states, "I work with them to find the perfect family for their child. I also prepare them for the emotions involved in making an adoption plan and getting through the legal steps of the adoption."

The work is tough, but Du Waldt loves it. She explains, "I work with people who take the responsibility of parenting seriously, whether they are birth parents or adoptive parents. I get to see both sides of the story. I see the birth family's struggle in their decision to make an adoption plan. I also see the struggles that the adoptive parents, who are often dealing with infertility, go through."

CAREER FACTS

Education or Training A bachelor's degree is necessary; background in social work, sociology and psychology are helpful.

Nature of the Work Adoption coordinators work to facilitate the process and find the best possible home for the child.

Aptitudes, Abilities, and Skills Listening and communication skills, empathy with others, and a willingness to serve are all essential.

Academic Skills Required Language arts, math and social sciences are all helpful.

Student Organizations To prepare for this career, look for groups that are sensitive to peoples' needs and problems, such as a community service group.

Career Outlook Job opportunities for adoption coordinators are expected to grow faster than average over the next ten years.

Career Path Working as an adoption coordinator in a clinic may require an advanced degree in social work. Supervisory, administrative, and staff training positions usually require at least a master's degree.

Critical Thinking

Finding Homes Do you think finding a home for older children is harder than for babies? Why or why not?

 Research Careers For more information on this and other careers, visit the Occupational Outlook Handbook Web site through the link on this book's Online Learning Center at **glencoe.com**.

CHAPTER SUMMARY

Section 3.1
Family Structures

The form that family life takes is called the family structure. A family's personality is made up of traits that combine to make a family unique. It affects and is affected by many factors. These include family atmosphere, boundaries, decision making, and goals. It is important for families to be interdependent. There should be a balance of independence and dependence among each family member. Families shown in the media often have little to do with the lives of real families.

Section 3.2
Family Development

Most families go through predictable stages of family development. The family is started by a couple. When children are added, the couple moves to the parent stage. This includes the expanding stage, during which more children are added. The development stage is when children are growing up. The launching stage comes when children leave the home. The final two stages are the middle and retirement years. This pattern is general. There are many variations of these stages.

Content and Academic Vocabulary Review

1. Use each of these content and academic vocabulary words in a sentence.

Content Vocabulary
◇ nuclear family (p. 44)
◇ single-parent family (p. 44)
◇ blended family (p. 44)
◇ extended family (p. 44)
◇ adoptive family (p. 45)
◇ legal guardian (p. 45)
◇ foster family (p. 45)

◇ interdependence (p. 48)
◇ dependent (p. 49)
◇ goal (p. 50)
◇ development (p. 53)
◇ launching (p. 57)
◇ empty nest (p. 57)

Academic Vocabulary
■ minor (p. 44)
■ autocratic (p. 48)
■ cycle (p. 53)
■ circumstance (p. 55)

Review Key Concepts

2. Describe various family structures.
3. Summarize the qualities that make up a family's personality.
4. Compare families in the media with those in real life.
5. Describe the stages of family development common to many families.
6. Identify exceptions to the typical pattern of family development.

Critical Thinking

7. Distinguish How are nuclear and blended families similar and different?
8. Predict What might happen if one parent in a family prefers a democratic approach and the other an autocratic one? How could such situations be resolved?
9. Determine Which stage of family life do you think is the most difficult for people? Why? Which one do you think is the easiest? Why?

Real-World Skills

Problem-Solving Skills

10. Find Other Options Greg's grandfather is coming to live with his family. Greg has been told he must give up his room to his grandfather and share his brother's room. He and his brother do not get along very well, so Greg does not want to move in with him. What could Greg do?

Self-Management Skills

11. Make a Decision Patrick's father was a member of the Air Force, and he expects Patrick to enlist after high school. Patrick, however, is interested in becoming an apprentice electrician. Because his father is autocratic, Patrick is afraid he will not have a say in his career. What could Patrick do?

Financial Literacy Skills

12. Budget for Housing After the launching stage, a young adult must find new housing. Research what the options are in your community. How much would each option cost per month? If the person earned the minimum wage, could he or she afford any of the options?

Collaborative Skills

13. Media Analysis Follow your teacher's instructions to form into groups. Make a list of current television shows that show family life. For each, name the family structure and the stage of development the family is in. Is there a wide variety? If not, which are most popular? Why do you think this is?

14. Brainstorm With your classmates, brainstorm activities that a family could do together. List your suggestions. What stage of family development would each item be most suited? What type of family personality would each appeal to? How can these items help build family ties?

15. Research Investigate your community to learn about programs that are available to families in various stages of development. What activities are available for those in each stage? Who sponsors the programs? Is there a fee? Which of these activities might appeal to you as you create a family?

16. Community Groups Select a community group that supports families. If possible, visit a group meeting or visit their facility (if the group has one). Write a short report about the group and the kind of families or the family members it serves.

17. Family Calendar Families with teens often have busy schedules. Go to this book's Online Learning Center at **glencoe.com** to find **Web Links** for **Online Planning Tools**. Use the tool to make a calendar for your family for the next month. Schedule individual family members' events and a family event that suits your family's personality.

 Additional Activities For additional activities, go to this book's Online Learning Center through **glencoe.com**.

Academic Skills

 ### Mathematics

18. Represent Large Numbers Jana wants to know how many households in the United States do not have adopted children. In a recent year, the United States Census Bureau reported that there are approximately 111,100,000 households in the United States and 1,700,000 of those households have adopted children. How many households do not have adopted children?

Math Concept **Subtracting Large Numbers** When subtracting large numbers, it is sometimes easier to express the numbers as decimals. The number of households with adopted children can be changed to a decimal.

Starting Hint: You can rewrite 111,100,000 as 111.1 million. You can also rewrite 1,700,000 as 1.7 million. Make sure the decimal points are aligned before you subtract.

 For math help, go to the Math Appendix at the back of the book.

> **NCTM Number and Operations** Understand numbers, ways of representing numbers, relationships among numbers, and number systems.

 ### English Language Arts

19. Make a Bibliography One way children learn about life is from the books that are read to them. Go to a library or a book store and make a bibliography of at least five children's books. Choose books that relate to one of the following topics: a new baby in the family, adoption, divorce, blended family members, or grandparents. Include the name of the book and author, as well as each book's publisher and the year in which it was published.

> **NCTE 8** Use information resources to gather information and create and communicate knowledge.

 ### Social Studies

20. Geography Choose an extended family member who lives some distance from you. If you do not have a family member that lives far away, choose one of your friends. Use a map to plan a route to get to their home if you went by car. Use the map legend to find out how many miles the trip is.

> **NCSS III. b** Create, interpret, use, and synthesize information from various representations of the earth, such as maps.

STANDARDIZED TEST PRACTICE

TRUE/FALSE
Carefully read the statement. Pay attention to any key words. Also look for words like *always* or *never*. These mean the statement must be true *all* of the time or *none* of the time.

> **Test-Taking Tip** In a true/false question, you have a 50 percent chance of getting the correct answer, even if you are guessing. If you leave the question blank, you have no chance of getting it right.

21. Decide if the following statement is true or false.

All families use the democratic style to make family decisions.
a. True
b. False

CHAPTER 4

Families in a Changing World

Section 4.1

Society Affects Families

Section 4.2

Appreciate Diversity

▶▶ **Explore the Photo**

We all may look different from one another, but we are also similar in many ways. *In what ways do you think you are similar to this diverse group?*

Chapter Objectives

After completing this chapter, you will be able to:

- **Identify** trends in society that affect families.
- **Describe** changes in family structures.
- **Summarize** changes in the workplace that impact people and families.
- **Recognize** similarities and differences among cultures.
- **Explain** how families teach culture.
- **Evaluate** the importance of cultural pride.

Writing Activity

Write Using Details

A**daptability** An adaptable person makes the best of a situation. When you adapt your habits or priorities to fit changes, you have adaptability. You can show adaptability by:
- Doing the laundry when a parent has classes in the evening.
- Learning useful phrases from other common languages so that you can communicate and be friends with even more people.
- Changing weekend plans to be home when relatives visit.

Write a paragraph about a time when you were adaptable. Include specific details about how you showed adaptability.

Writing Tips To use details when describing something, follow these steps:
1. Choose details that will bring life to your description.
2. Use your senses to help you choose details.
3. Make sure all the sentences in the paragraph include details that support the main idea.

Society Affects Families

Reading Guide

Before You Read

Understanding Write down any questions you have while reading. Many of them will be answered as you continue. If they are not, you will have a list ready for your teacher when you finish.

Read to Learn
Key Concepts
- **Identify** trends in society that affect families.
- **Describe** changes in family structures.
- **Summarize** changes in the workplace that impact people and families.

Main Idea
Changes in society, the family, and the workplace can affect families.

Content Vocabulary
◇ trend
◇ environment
◇ service industry
◇ economy
◇ global economy

Academic Vocabulary
You will find these words in your reading and on your tests. Use the glossary to look up their definitions if necessary.
■ impact ■ efficiency

Graphic Organizer
As you read, list examples of changes that occur in society, the family, and the workplace. Use a chart like the one shown to help organize your information.

Society	Family	Workplace

 Graphic Organizer Go to this book's Online Learning Center at **glencoe.com** to print out this graphic organizer.

Academic Standards • • • • • • • • • • • • • •

 English Language Arts

NCTE 5 Use different writing process elements to communicate effectively.

NCTE 12 Use language to accomplish individual purposes.

 Mathematics

NCTM Data Analysis and Probability Select and use appropriate statistical methods to analyze data.

 Science

NSES Content Standard F Develop understanding of environmental quality.

NCTE *National Council of Teachers of English*
NCTM *National Council of Teachers of Mathematics*

NSES *National Science Education Standards*
NCSS *National Council of the Social Studies*

Changes in Society

Families today live in a world of rapid change. When looking at change, trends may appear. A **trend** is when a noticeable change takes place over time. Trends tell you what might happen in the future. You and your future family will need to be ready to face these changes. Many of today's changes directly **impact**, or affect, families.

The Aging Population

There are a larger number of older people today than in the past. People are living longer than they used to. This is due in part to better medical care. Another factor is improved nutrition and health. "Baby boomers" were born when birth rates increased after World War II. The older population is growing as the baby boomers age.

Lifelong Learning

Another trend is lifelong learning. Going to school is no longer just for the young. People of all ages attend college or take other training. Some want more education for a better job or a career change.

Learning is no longer tied to a time and place. In distance learning, people take classes through the Internet. They may be able to schedule their classes when they want.

Environmental Change

The **environment** is the conditions or circumstances that surround one. Society is concerned about changes in nature. The lack of fresh water in many parts of the world is troubling. Extreme weather conditions like hurricanes, tsunamis, tornadoes, and cyclones cause great damage. Many families are hurt or lose their homes when these storms hit.

When a family loses everything, all members are affected. The impact of loss can cause problems that may last a long time. Coping with the effects of environmental change is a challenge to all families.

> **Vocabulary**
> You can find definitions in the glossary at the back of this book.

> **As You Read**
> Connect What education or training are you interested in after high school?

> **Keep Learning**
> More older adults are going back to school to get an education than ever before. *How do you plan to continue your education throughout your life?*

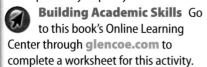
New Technology

New technology is exciting. It makes life easier. It entertains people. It increases **efficiency**, or effectiveness, at home and at work. Today, technology is changing faster than at any time in history.

Strong families find ways to use technology to strengthen their bonds. They make choices based on their values. They manage their resources so that technology is a tool to bring the family together.

✓ Reading Check **Define** What is a trend?

Changes Within the Family

There have been many changes in family life over the years. In pioneer days, life on the farm was hard labor. Families raised and prepared food, built homes, and made clothes. Families were large. Everyone helped to get the work done. During the 1800s many families moved to cities. Life in urban areas was not easy either. In some families, every member, even small children, had jobs.

Today's changes in society are different, but they still bring about changes in the family. One example is how family structures have changed.

- **Single People** The number of single-person households is growing. Waiting to marry at older ages adds to the number of singles. There is less social pressure to marry than in the past. More people remain single for life.
- **Couples** Couples make up a larger percent of households today than in the past. More couples postpone having children. They may have fewer of them or none at all. Because people live longer, there are more couples who have already launched their children.
- **Nuclear Families** In recent years, the number of nuclear families has decreased. Part of this is due to divorce. Some is because couples have fewer children. This means that the nuclear family stage of life is shorter. The increase in couples is related to the decrease in nuclear families.
- **Blended Families** The divorce rate has been going down in recent years. However, this has not created fewer blended families. Most divorced people with children remarry. That means that there are a large number of blended families.
- **Single-Parent Families** Divorce creates many single-parent families. The number of births to women who are not married also has grown. Although most single parents are women, many are men.

- **Extended Families** Many extended families are living together today. The number of adult children who live with parents is increasing. They may live with their parents alone or bring their children along, too. Older relatives may move in with younger ones. They may do this because they can share expenses and enjoy each other's company. Family members may also provide child care, or may need care themselves. When families do this, they take care of each other.

A growing number of households now have two or more wage earners. Many need two incomes to survive today. Some count on extra income from teens and extended family members in the home. Sometimes extended family members provide services such as child care. This may help families save on costs.

Many families struggle to make ends meet. Some are not able to buy homes of their own. The soaring cost of college means that families may not be able to pay for their children to go to school. Many people work very hard to pay for their own schooling. Some students pay for their educations with financial aid, student loans, and work income.

✓ **Reading Check** **Explain** Why is the number of couple families increasing?

Changes in the Workplace

Changes in society and the family affect the workplace. Similarly, changes in the workplace can also impact families and the society. Rapid change can be seen in the workplace. This change is often spurred by technology.

◀) **Work from Home**
People who work from home may find their workplace has become global rather than local. *In what ways would working at your home computer be global in nature?*

HOW TO Stay Safe on the Internet

Just like the world around you, the Internet has both people you want to know and people who should be avoided. These two groups can be harder to distinguish in the virtual world. Follow these guidelines to protect yourself when using the Internet:

1. **Get permission first.** Ask a trusted adult for permission when you use the Internet. Parents and guardians can often spot dangers that you may not see.
2. **Monitor discussion groups.** You may not be comfortable with the posters or topics in a certain group. If this happens, do not post messages or images to this group.
3. **Choose usernames thoughtfully.** Your username gives people a certain impression of you. What may people assume about Spacey Sally compared to Brainiac?
4. **Word messages carefully.** Write all your Internet communication (including e-mails, blogs, and instant messages) carefully. You do not want to give out private information about you and your family.
5. **Be alert to imposters.** Someone may say he or she likes the same music you do, but is not familiar with your favorite group. Another person may use teen slang in the wrong way. Tell a trusted adult if you have any doubts about anyone you talk to.

Take Action On a piece of paper, write a short message that may be sent to a teen or a chat room popular with teens. Exchange papers with a neighbor and discuss if there are any red flags or warning signs in the message and how you might handle them.

Technology and the Job Market

Special skills are needed for the jobs of today. Far fewer workers are needed for industrial jobs. New technology, such as computers, can do the tasks that people once did. Today, advances in technology are constantly and rapidly changing how people work. As companies increase their use of technology, the number of jobs will change.

You may hold jobs in the future that do not exist today. You may also have jobs that require training in new technology that you have not used before. Many people need retraining when jobs are changed, gone, or added. Others need new skills to reenter the workplace.

Service Industries

Most employed Americans now work in a **service industry**. This is a career that provides assistance to others for a fee. Service industry jobs often pay low wages. They may require workers to work at any time of the day or night.

Many services have resulted from changes in society. Online shopping, Web design, house cleaning, and food delivery are all service areas that have grown in recent years. Another example is that medical clinics can be found in drugstores.

A Global Workplace

The workplace has become global rather than local. This means that products and services are bought and produced by people and companies all over the world. Goods are made in one country and sold in another. People and companies from other countries may own businesses in your area. Decisions about work and jobs in your state may be made in another nation.

When you buy goods and services from other countries, you are participating in the global economy. An **economy** refers to the ways in which a group produces, distributes, and consumes its goods and services. A **global economy** refers to the ways in which the world's economics are linked. The global economy impacts the job market, or the demand for certain jobs, in each country.

The world continues to become smaller through improved communication and transportation. Modern technology will allow workers to perform many jobs from anywhere in the world. Links with other countries will continue to increase.

The global workplace has influenced families. Families are apt to live and work with people of all ethnic backgrounds as a result. Learning to understand and get along with different types of people is an important part of life.

Financial Literacy

Starting Salaries

Tran did an analysis of starting salaries for administrative assistants in his area. He called three schools and was quoted the following salaries: $32,000, $31,800, and $30,850. What is the average salary in his area?

Math Concept **Measures of Central Tendency** The mean, median, and mode are all measures of central tendency because they provide a summary of numerical data in one number. The mean is the same as the average.

Starting Hint: To find the mean, first add all of the values ($32,000, $31,800, and $30,850) together. Then divide the total of the values by the number of values in the set of data (3).

 For math help, go to the Math Appendix at the back of the book.

NCTM Data Analysis and Probability Select and use appropriate statistical methods to analyze data.

Section 4.1 After You Read

Review Key Concepts

1. **Explain** why identifying trends is important.
2. **Summarize** why there are more single people than in the past.
3. **Describe** how technology has caused changes in the workplace.

Practice Academic Skills

**English Language Arts**

4. You have been given information that shows a new trend. The trend is that there is a growing shortage of caregivers for the elderly. Write a report explaining the impact of this trend on families, business, and the government.

   NCTE 12 Use language to accomplish individual purposes.

5. Consider the types of technology your parents used when they were teenagers. Then think of the technology you use. Write a letter to a parent or guardian that compares the differences and similarities in technology between the two generations.

   NCTE 5 Use different writing process elements to communicate effectively.

Check Your Answers Check your answers at this book's Online Learning Center through **glencoe.com**.

Appreciate Diversity

Reading Guide

Before You Read

Create an Outline Use the section's heading titles to create an outline. Make the titles into Level 1 main ideas. Add supporting information to create Level 2, 3, and 4 details. Use the outline to predict what you are about to learn.

Read to Learn

Key Concepts
- **Recognize** similarities and differences among cultures.
- **Explain** how families teach culture.
- **Evaluate** the importance of cultural pride.

Main Idea

A culture is everything about a group of people, including their common traits and customs. Families teach and take pride in their culture.

Content Vocabulary

◇ culture
◇ diversity
◇ ethnic group
◇ empathy
◇ cultural heritage

Academic Vocabulary

You will find these words in your reading and on your tests. Use the glossary to look up their definitions if necessary.

■ influence   ■ source

Graphic Organizer

As you read, take notes on the ways that cultural diversity can be shown. Use a list like the one shown to help organize your information.

> **Cultural Diversity**
> • language
> • attitudes

 Graphic Organizer Go to this book's Online Learning Center at **glencoe.com** to print out this graphic organizer.

Academic Standards • • • • • • • • • • • • • • • • • • •

 English Language Arts

NCTE 4 Use written language to communicate effectively.

NCTE 9 Develop an understanding of diversity in language use across cultures.

NCTE *National Council of Teachers of English*
NCTM *National Council of Teachers of Mathematics*

NSES *National Science Education Standards*
NCSS *National Council of the Social Studies*

What Is Culture?

Everything that defines the identity of a specific group of people, including their common traits and customs, is called **culture**. Culture can be seen in what people believe as well as in how they act. Many things affect what a culture is like, including economic and geographic conditions, knowledge, art, and technology. As members of a society, people develop identity based on a culture that is shared by the group. This culture helps make the society strong. The more people participate in the culture, the stronger the society becomes.

Where Culture Comes From

Wherever people live, they learn what is customary in their culture. For example, the clothing people wear is based on the climate in their area. What people eat depends on what is available where they live. People need to know the rules of the society where they live. They learn to communicate so they can get along in that society. This often happens when children are socialized in the family. It helps them learn what society expects.

People who live together in a society figure out their own way of doing things. Patterns and beliefs are learned and carried on through the society's history. They are communicated to others through actions and words.

Culture Affects Family Life

Cultural patterns and beliefs have a direct effect on family life. Family members learn the customs and traits of their culture. A family takes on the patterns and ways of life that are common in its society. When a family knows about more than one culture, its life is richer. Family members can choose customs that fit their values.

Vocabulary

You can find definitions in the glossary at the back of this book.

As You Read

Connect In what ways has where you lived had an effect on your culture?

Real Life — Respecting Other Cultures

People sometimes lack respect for what they do not understand, including unfamiliar cultures. Respect for cultures can be learned and shown in many ways. Follow these steps to build respect for other cultures:

- Make friends with someone from another ethnic background.
- Give a child in your family a toy or book from another culture.
- Use positive language to talk about other cultures.
- Cook an ethnic dish for your family from a global foods cookbook.
- Watch television programs that teach about other cultures.

Problem-Solving Two students from another country are new to Tony's school. They are still learning English and have not made many friends yet. What can Tony do to help make them feel welcome?

Each culture also has a family system of some type. People may live together in different structures. Parents and children may have different roles. Families, however, are the basic unit of each society. Families around the world have the same functions. They help preserve their cultures and make their societies strong.

Cultural Diversity

Diversity is variety in the sense that people are all different in one way or another. It is important for people to learn about diversity and its **influence**, or power, over the family. When you sit down with your family to eat a meal, what kinds of food do you eat? The foods your family chooses to eat may express its diversity.

Some qualities that make each culture unique are their languages, attitudes, customs, and daily routines. Ethnic groups can also be different. An **ethnic group** is made up of people from the same race or nationality who share a culture.

When talking about cultures, it is easy to focus on how they differ. There are actually many similarities. People all around the world have the same basic needs, no matter where they live.

Diversity does not always have to be cultural. People are diverse in many ways, such as age, race, religion, gender, or ethnic group. Lifestyles and personality vary from person to person.

 **Reading Check** **Define** What is a culture?

Look Past Differences People may look different, but they all experience the same basic emotions. *How else are they similar?*

Families Teach Culture

Families are the main teachers of culture in any society. Each generation passes along what it has learned to the next. You may not know that you have learned the ways of a particular culture, but you have. Without teaching, people would not know what behaviors are and are not acceptable.

The boundaries between cultures today are not as distinct as they once were. People around the world have more chances and reasons to get together. They may travel and do business across cultures, communicate via the Internet, or move from one culture to another.

One of the important things families can teach is empathy. **Empathy** is the ability to put yourself in another person's situation. Empathy is needed when people judge others on cultural issues.

Sometimes people fear what they do not understand. A different culture may create such feelings in some people. Working to feel empathy for those who are different will improve relationships.

As people learn more about other societies, they understand them better. This can help as they meet and work with people from other cultures at home and on the job.

✓ **Reading Check** **Describe** Why are families the main teachers of culture?

Cultural Pride

Culture is a **source**, or cause, of pride for many families. Cultural pride includes self-respect and celebrating one's background. The cultural background is part of family history. For this reason, families want to save their cultures, not lose them.

Cultural Heritage

Many families take pride in teaching young members about their **cultural heritage**. This includes the beliefs, customs, and traits that have been important to their ethnic group. Their cultural heritage is often carefully saved within the family. Every family's heritage, no matter what it is, can be valued. It should never be a reason to look down on others. You can feel good about your own heritage and still value the heritage of others.

Families teach their own culture to their young members. They must also teach respect for other cultures as well. People of many backgrounds often live side by side. Society can be strong only when families understand and respect each other.

Section 4.2 After You Read

Review Key Concepts

1. **Explain** how people show their culture.
2. **Describe** why it is important that families teach empathy toward different cultures.
3. **Define** cultural heritage.

Practice Academic Skills

English Language Arts

4. Make a list of ways that a person could show empathy. Include at least one example from life at home, at school, and on the job.

5. When people of different cultures live together in a community, is it more important to blend the cultures or preserve them? Write a paragraph giving your answer to the question. Include at least two reasons for your answer.

NCTE 4 Use written language to communicate effectively.

NCTE 9 Develop an understanding of diversity in language use across cultures.

Check Your Answers Check your answers at this book's Online Learning Center through **glencoe.com**.

Robin Ryan
Seattle, Washington

Robin Ryan is a career counselor. She has appeared on more than 1,000 television and radio programs, including *Oprah* and *Dr. Phil*. People seek her help with resume writing, career coaching, and salary negotiation.

Ryan says her job involves working closely with clients. She helps them identify their skills and desires and pushes them toward the career that is right for them. She says that for this career, "You should be interested in helping people and advising them. It helps if you are curious about work and people's jobs."

She claims that good listening and communication skills are essential. She recommends working on the school newspaper. This can help to build real-world writing skills. She also suggests taking Introduction to Business classes to get an understanding of how the business world works.

Ryan enjoys being a career counselor. "I love my work—it's so much fun to help people find jobs and share in their happiness when they find a new position."

CAREER FACTS

Education or Training Many colleges offer undergraduate degrees in business, psychology or sociology. There are also Master's-level degrees that often specialize in Counselor Education.

Nature of the Work Career counselors explore and evaluate the client's education, training, work history, interests, skills, and personality traits. They also arrange for aptitude and achievement tests to assist the client in making career decisions.

Aptitudes, Abilities, and Skills Writing skills, public speaking, communication, and interpersonal skills.

Academic Skills Required English Language Arts can help with writing and speaking skills.

Student Organizations To prepare for this career, look for groups that advise people, such as peer counseling groups.

Career Outlook Employment of career counselors is expected to grow faster than the average over the next ten years.

Career Path Career counselors can become supervisors or administrators in their agencies. Some counselors move into research, consulting, or college teaching. They may also go into private or group practice.

Critical Thinking

Seek Guidance What factors may motivate a person to seek a career counselor?

 Research Careers For more information on this and other careers, visit the Occupational Outlook Handbook Web site through the link on this book's Online Learning Center through **glencoe.com**.

CHAPTER SUMMARY

 ### Section 4.1
Society Affects Families

There are many trends in society that affect the family. Some of these are the aging population, lifelong learning, environmental change, and new technology. There are changes in the structure of family life. Some family patterns are increasing while others are decreasing. The workplace is changing and developing different kinds of jobs. Service industries are growing and there is a more global workplace.

 ### Section 4.2
Appreciate Diversity

The world is made up of people from many cultures. Each culture has its own customs and traits that came about naturally. There are many likenesses among cultures. Two are that people must meet their basic needs and that families are the foundation of society. Still, there are cultural differences. Families teach their culture to their younger members. They often have a sense of cultural pride in their heritage.

Content and Academic Vocabulary Review

1. Use each of these content and academic vocabulary words in a sentence.

Content Vocabulary
◇ trend (p. 67)
◇ environment (p. 67)
◇ service industry (p. 70)
◇ economy (p. 71)
◇ global economy (p. 71)
◇ culture (p. 73)
◇ diversity (p. 74)
◇ ethnic group (p. 74)
◇ empathy (p. 74)
◇ cultural heritage (p. 75)

Academic Vocabulary
■ impact (p. 67)
■ efficiency (p. 68)
■ influence (p. 74)
■ source (p. 75)

Review Key Concepts

2. Identify trends in society that affect families.
3. Describe changes in family structures.
4. Summarize changes in the workplace that impact people and families.
5. Recognize similarities and differences among cultures.
6. Explain how families teach culture.
7. Evaluate the importance of cultural pride.

Critical Thinking

8. Evaluate Do you think change is stimulating or frustrating for people? Why?
9. Analyze Why do people often fear what they do not understand? What kinds of behavior might this cause?

Real-World Skills

Problem-Solving Skills

10. Make a Decision Ginny is worried about learning to use the new software her employer has bought. She loves her job. Ginny could find other work, but would not earn as much money. What should Ginny do?

Research Skills

11. Learn About a Culture Select a culture that is different from your own. Conduct research to learn more about this culture's family life, holidays, and schooling. Write a report on your findings.

Decision-Making Skills

12. Conflicting Schedules Neal will miss some school because of the holidays that his family celebrates. A math test is set for one day when he will be gone. It is important to his family that he observe their religious customs. What should Neal do?

Interpersonal Skills

13. Speaking Give a two-minute oral report on how a workplace would ideally handle diversity. Discuss how workers can show respect for people with cultural, gender, or age differences.

14. Interview Schedule an interview with a foreign exchange student or someone who grew up in another country. Write a list of questions to help you learn about the culture in that country. Be sure to ask what has been the biggest cultural difference he or she has observed. Write a report of your interview.

15. Ethnic Foods Visit a store that features ethnic groceries. Look at the foods displayed. Identify three that are similar to foods you eat and three that are unfamiliar. Choose an unfamiliar food that you might buy and prepare for your family. Ask a clerk for help. Give a short oral report to your classmates on what happened.

16. Technical Training Many people attend technical schools to learn more about computers and new technology. Conduct research to find out what programs are available in your area. Contact at least one program to find out what is offered. Write a one-page report of your findings.

17. Use a Search Engine Imagine that you are invited to the wedding of a friend from another country. You want to know what will happen at the wedding. Go to this book's Online Learning Center at **glencoe.com** to find **Web Links** for **Wedding Customs**. Write a report on your findings.

Additional Activities For additional activities, go to this book's Online Learning Center through **glencoe.com**.

Academic Skills

 Mathematics

18. Calculate Dimensions Tina has a new job at a department store. She has been asked to calculate the dimensions of some boxes. These will be used for the new line of kitchenware. The volume of the boxes can be no more than 1,800 cubic inches. To accommodate the products, the length must be 15 inches and the height 10 inches. What should the width of the boxes be?

Math Concept **Dimensions and Volume**
To calculate the volume of a three-dimensional figure use the formula: $V = l \times w \times h$. This formula means that Volume (V) equals length (l) times width (w) times height (h).

Starting Hint: Use the information that you have to create an equation for the volume of the box. Use w to represent the width: $V = 15 \times w \times 10$, solve for w.

 For math help, go to the Math Appendix at the back of the book.

> **NCTM Measurement** Apply appropriate techniques, tools, and formulas to determine measurements.

 English Language Arts

19. Write a Textbook Suppose you were a textbook writer in the past century. Research what life was like in a time you choose. Rewrite one of these parts of Section 4.1 as it might have appeared then: Changes in Society, Changes in the Family, or Changes in the Workplace. Remember to consider how that time was different from today.

> **NCTE 8** Use information resources to gather information and create and communicate knowledge.

 Social Studies

20. Community Action Imagine you are a business person or community leader. What could you do to help older people with these problems: lack of medical care; lack of housing suitable for seniors; reduced ability to read small print and signs; inability to drive; clothing that does not fit the shapes of aging bodies? Discuss the possibilities with your class.

> **NCSS IV.h** Work independently and cooperatively within groups and institutions to accomplish goals.

STANDARDIZED TEST PRACTICE

MULTIPLE CHOICE
Read the following question. Then read the answer choices and choose the best possible answer.

Test-Taking Tip Be sure to read the directions to see if you need to look for the *best answer* or the *correct answer*. If you are looking for the best answer, it is possible that there will be more than one correct answer to choose from.

21. According to this chapter, _____ is a trend affected by medical care.
a. global warming
b. increased rate of cancer survivors
c. the aging population
d. tobacco use among teenagers

Give Back to Society

In this unit you have learned about the foundation that makes up strong families. You have also learned that strong families make society stronger, and vice versa. In this project, you can volunteer with a member of your family for community service. You will use what you learn to create an illustrated story. The story will show how you and your family member did your part to make your community stronger.

My Journal

If you completed the journal entry from page 2, refer to it to see if your thoughts have changed after reading the unit.

Project Assignment

- Choose an area of community service that interests you.
- Research and make a list of opportunities for volunteering.
- Call your top choices and find out about types of volunteer opportunities.
- Ask one or more members of your family to join you when you volunteer.
- Organize a time and date to volunteer with your family member.
- Bring your camera or sketchbook, and a notebook to record your experience.
- Use what you learned during the community service to create an illustrated story.

Academic Skills You Will Use

English Language Arts

NCTE 5 Use different writing process elements to communicate effectively.

NCTE 7 Conduct research and gather, evaluate, and synthesize data to communicate discoveries.

STEP 1 Choose Community Service that Interests You

The suggestions below are examples of organizations or places that may need volunteers. Choose two groups. You can use these suggestions, or you can research your own area of interest.

- Food bank
- Animal shelter
- Literacy program
- Public radio station
- YMCA or YWCA
- Nursing home

STEP 2 Research Your Choices

Contact the organizations you selected and ask specific questions about types, dates, and locations of volunteer opportunities. This will help you narrow down which opportunity will work with your schedule.

Research Skills

- Perform research using a variety of resources.
- Gather specific information through interpersonal communication.
- Take notes on your research and write a summary of your findings.
- Use the information you gathered to narrow down your choices.

STEP 3 Connect to Your Community

Select one of the volunteer opportunities. Contact the organization to schedule the service. Ask a family member to join you. Ask for permission to bring a camera with you to document your experience.

Volunteer Skills
- Take initiative to complete tasks.
- Ask questions if you do not understand instructions.
- Make sure your family member is comfortable with his or her tasks.
- Use teamwork skills to get the job done.

STEP 4 Create and Present Your Illustrated Story

Use the Unit Thematic Project Checklist on the right to plan and create your illustrated story and make your presentation.

STEP 5 Evaluate Your Presentation

Your project will be evaluated based on:
- Extent of research conducted on volunteer opportunities.
- Structure and depth of illustrated story.
- Mechanics—presentation and neatness.

Evaluation Rubric Go to this book's Online Learning Center at **glencoe.com** for a rubric you can use to evaluate your final project.

Unit Thematic Project Checklist

Illustrated Story	✓ Create an illustrated story about your day of community service with a family member.
	✓ Illustrate your story by using photographs or your own drawings.
	✓ In your illustrated story, show what you learned by doing the service. This will include what you learned about how your relationship with the family member was affected and how volunteering strengthens society.
	✓ The beginning of your story will be researching the activity. Doing the volunteer work is the middle of your story. The way you felt when it was over and how you helped society will be the end of your story.
Presentation	✓ Make a presentation to your class to share your story and discuss what you learned.
	✓ Invite the students in your class to ask you any questions they may have. Answer three questions.
	✓ When students ask you questions, demonstrate in your answers that you respect their perspectives.
	✓ Turn in the summary of your research and your completed story to your teacher.
Academic Skills	✓ Organize your story so it has a beginning, middle, and end.
	✓ Speak clearly and concisely.
	✓ Use language that is easy to understand.
	✓ Tell your story so it holds your audience's attention.

Unit 2

Strengthen Your Relationships

Unit

Thematic Project Preview
Find a Role Model

After completing this unit, you will learn about the different roles you have in your relationships. In your unit thematic project, you can show how your role model displays a relationship skill that you admire.

My Journal

A Personality You Enjoy Write a journal entry about one of the topics below. This will help you prepare for the unit project at the end of the unit.

• Describe a person you respect.
• Make a list of the personality traits that you admire, either in yourself or someone else.
• Identify a person in your community who you would like to know better, and explain why.

Explore the Photo
There are many relationship skills that help make your ties to others stronger. *What helps you the most in getting along with your family?*

CHAPTER 5

Roles and Relationships

Section 5.1
The Importance of Relationships

Section 5.2
Examine Your Roles

 Explore the Photo

Family relationships are different from relationships with friends and coworkers. *In what ways is your relationship with your family different from that with your best friend?*

Chapter Objectives

After completing this chapter, you will be able to:

- **Identify** the qualities that help build healthy relationships.
- **Explain** how rewards and costs affect relationships.
- **Suggest** ways to improve relationships.
- **Describe** the purpose of roles and how they are learned.
- **Relate** role conflict to role expectations.

Writing Activity Paragraph Development

Loyalty People show loyalty when they are faithful to a cause or another person. People who are loyal do not let misunderstandings or pressure from others sway them. You can show loyalty by:

- Walking away when a group speaks unkindly about a friend.
- Taking care of a family member when they are sick.
- Making an effort to offer friends rides to school or work when their cars are being repaired.

Write a paragraph that describes a person who is loyal. Include specific details that make the person loyal.

Writing Tips To write an effective paragraph, follow these steps:

1. Write a topic sentence that clearly expresses the main idea of the paragraph.
2. Each sentence should have one or more details that support the main idea.
3. Make sure all of your sentences are linked clearly and logically to one another.

The Importance of Relationships

Reading Guide

Before You Read

Stay Engaged One way to stay engaged when reading is to turn each of the headings into a question, then read the section to find answers.

Read to Learn

Key Concepts

- **Identify** the qualities that help build healthy relationships.
- **Explain** how rewards and costs affect relationships.
- **Suggest** ways to improve relationships.

Main Idea

People have many qualities that help build and improve a healthy relationship.

Content Vocabulary

◇ relationship
◇ acquaintance
◇ mutuality
◇ trust
◇ self-disclosure
◇ rapport
◇ reward
◇ cost
◇ exploitation

Academic Vocabulary

You will find these words in your reading and on your tests. Use the glossary to look up their definitions if necessary.

■ voluntary　　　■ interaction

Graphic Organizer

As you read, identify six qualities of a healthy relationship. Use a concept map like the one shown to help organize your information.

Qualities in Healthy Relationships		

 Graphic Organizer Go to this book's Online Learning Center at **glencoe.com** to print out this graphic organizer.

Academic Standards . . . .

 English Language Arts

NCTE 4 Use written language to communicate effectively.

NCTE 6 Apply knowledge of language structure and conventions to discuss texts.

Science

NSES Content Standard C Develop an understanding of the interdependence of organisms.

NCTE *National Council of Teachers of English*
NCTM *National Council of Teachers of Mathematics*

NSES *National Science Education Standards*
NCSS *National Council of the Social Studies*

Build Your Relationships

Probably no part of life affects you more than a **relationship**. Relationships are your connections with other people. Learning about them and improving them is a worthwhile goal. They can serve major functions in your life. Healthy relationships:

- **Meet personal needs.** You feel taken care of, loved, and accepted.
- **Enrich life.** People share their feelings and new ideas.
- **Help you get things done.** What you achieve often depends on help and support from others.

Types of Relationships

Everyone has built-in relationships through the family. Few bonds are stronger or last longer than those among family members. Their value and influence can last a lifetime.

Most people also have relationships that extend beyond the family. They make friends, often with people of different ages and backgrounds. Some ties with friends are as strong as family bonds. Beyond family and friends are many casual relationships. A classmate may be your **acquaintance**. This is a person you know but are not close to.

Some relationships are **voluntary**. That is, you choose them. Friendships are voluntary. Other relationships, such as those with most family members and coworkers, are involuntary. They are not chosen.

Diversity in Relationships

You live in a society that blends all sorts of people. These people are old, young, and ethnically diverse. Exchanges with them can enrich your life and help prepare you for the future. Differences make people interesting. Having relationships with many people can make you more interesting.

What can you learn from people who are different from you? Older people can provide insights about life. Children can remind you of how exciting simple discoveries are. People from other cultures may share information about their food, music, clothing, or art.

◆ Vocabulary

You can find definitions in the glossary at the back of this book.

As You Read

Connect Think about what makes a good relationship and what makes a disappointing one.

▶ Connections with Others

Friendships with people who are different from you can be rewarding. *What qualities can diverse friends bring to your relationship?*

Healthy Relationships

Relationships are fulfilling and a source of growth. However, sometimes relationships can be disappointing and painful. No relationship is perfect. On the other hand, no relationship should bring only pain. To a great degree, relationships are what you make of them. There are several ways you can work to make your relationships healthy. For example, **Figure 5.1** shows how to create healthy relationships with your coworkers. The actions you take affect whether your relationships in and outside of work are fulfilling or painful.

Mutuality

A healthy relationship has **mutuality** (ˌmyü-chə-'wa-lə-tē). That is, both people contribute to the feelings and actions that support the relationship. They understand what they want from each other.

Mutuality is a balanced exchange between partners. The exchange does not always have to be equal. You might give more to a relationship one time. You might receive more at another. In close relationships, people are more willing to give without getting an instant return. Mutuality is shown and felt in many ways.

Figure 5.1   Healthy Relationships at Work

Employers value workers who can get along with others. The qualities that make healthy relationships are important on the job as well as in the family. *Which quality do you think is most important in relating to coworkers? Why?*

Trust Managers and workers have to trust each other to get the job done. If you say you will do something, do it.

Mutuality When you help others on the job, they will be more likely to help you.

Self-Disclosure Self-disclosure at work means making sure others know what you are doing. Then you can coordinate efforts

Trust

The belief that others will not reject, betray, or hurt you is called **trust**. Trust is needed in all relationships, both casual and close. Friends and family members trust each other to keep personal discussions private. Employers trust workers with equipment. In what other relationships do you see trust?

Self-Disclosure

The willingness to tell someone personal things about yourself is called **self-disclosure**. Sharing your feelings or thoughts with at least one other person is vital to good mental health.

The information you disclose says a lot about a relationship. People generally reveal the same type and amount of information as they receive. They tell more about themselves as the relationship deepens. People who are very close feel free to confide their hopes and sorrows. Trust strengthens when people self-disclose and honor confidences.

Rapport

Healthy relationships develop as people build **rapport** (ra-ˈpȯr). This is a feeling of ease with another person. Good rapport leads to more **interaction**, or doings between individuals. People are more apt to self-disclose when they feel rapport.

Empathy Show your support for others when they have problems at work.

Rapport Taking time to talk to others and get to know them helps build rapport. This improves working relationships.

Shared Interests Sharing interests helps build strong relationships in the workplace.

⬆ Build Relationships
Relationships often develop when people share an interest. *Would two teammates become close because they both enjoy football or because they spend time together?*

Empathy
When you have the ability to put yourself in another person's position, you show empathy. People who have empathy set aside their own ideas and opinions in order to understand someone else's point of view. These people are especially tuned in to feelings. They know when someone else is hurting and want to help.

Shared Interests
Suppose one teen likes skateboarding and biking, and another likes to read and listen to classical music. Can they form a close relationship? They might, although people who share at least some interests usually have a better chance. Shared interests can help form a strong base for building a relationship.

✓ **Reading Check**) **Define** What are relationships?

Relationship Rewards and Costs
Do you ever think about a person who used to be your good friend? Perhaps now you never think of them because you just drifted apart. You may wonder why some relationships endure and prosper while others slowly end. Experts who study relationships ask the same questions. What makes relationships last? What makes them end? One theory suggests that relationships survive based on rewards and costs.

A **reward** is what brings pleasure and satisfaction in a relationship. Some people look for material benefits that meet physical needs and wants. Others want emotional support, excitement, or love. A relationship is rewarding when people feel it meets their personal needs. A relationship that brings many rewards is often a healthy one.

A **cost** is the physical, mental, and emotional contributions you make to a relationship. Some costs are expected. All relationships cost time and energy. Money may also be a cost. For example, Kendall spent time, money, and energy to get the right birthday gift for his sister. Her pleasure was his reward.

Other costs may be painful. Madison's friends, for instance, promised to attend her cello recital. When they did not come, Madison was hurt. Her disappointment was a cost she paid in her friendship. Relationships with many costs tend to be unhealthy ones.

Relationships that have such qualities as mutuality, trust, self-disclosure, rapport, empathy, and shared interests are rewarding and usually last. A relationship that lacks these qualities is often short-lived. It has more costs than rewards.

Danger Signals in Relationships

Healthy relationships have certain traits. Unhealthy ones have danger signals. Staying alert for these signs can help you make repairs and improvements to your relationships. They may also tell you when it is time to end a relationship.

There is no doubt that a relationship thrives when it is satisfying. It suffers when it is not. When there is an uneven exchange of costs and rewards, a relationship weakens. Here are some examples of relationships with more costs than rewards.

- A worker may have a demanding, unreasonable manager. The poor relationship decreases satisfaction on the job.
- A friend may borrow money and never pay it back. This causes lack of trust and a weaker friendship.
- A group leader may make people who disagree feel unwelcome. This increases the mental cost of belonging to the group.

Some people make the effort and work to improve these situations. Others may choose to make the best of it. Some will make the decision to leave relationships that are too costly.

Think about the qualities of healthy relationships. You can see that problems with any of those qualities can signal trouble in the relationship. When needed qualities weaken, a relationship may not last. For example, if a couple stops trusting each other, they may not be able to communicate anymore. If two friends no longer have shared interests, it may be difficult to stay in touch. Both of these examples lead to less self-disclosure. As this happens, the relationship becomes less rewarding.

Exploitation

Some relationships can be damaged by something called **exploitation**. This is when one person uses another unfairly for personal benefit. How can you tell if someone is taking advantage of a relationship?

People who exploit others tend to be self-centered. They have little trust in others. An exploiter feels no guilt about failing to give equally in a relationship. The following are examples of exploitation.

- Showing no regard for people's feelings.
- Borrowing something without asking.
- Canceling plans at the last minute if something better comes up.

Science in Action

Relationships

Ecologists study relationships among organisms in a living community. There are some interesting similarities between relationships among organisms and relationships among people. Use the following information to discover some of these similarities.

1. Producers are organisms that produce food.
2. Consumers are organisms that get food from other organisms.
3. Organisms that depend on one another have symbiotic relationships. This means they live closely together.
4. Organisms that need the same things have competitive relationships. This means that when the needed resources are limited, the competition increases.

Building Academic Skills Go to this book's Online Learning Center through **glencoe.com** to complete a worksheet for this activity.

NSES Content Standard C Develop an understanding of the interdependence of organisms.

INDEPENDENT *Living*

HOW TO   Handle Unhealthy Relationships

Suppose your best friend keeps asking to borrow money, but has never paid you back. You are reluctant to start an argument with your friend, but your relationship with her is suffering. Follow these guidelines to keep your relationship healthy:

1. **Know what you want.** Identify the exact reasons for having the conversation. You may just want your money back, or you may want to stop feeling taken advantage of in general. Then, think of actions or behaviors that your friend does that make you feel the way you do.
2. **Prepare yourself.** Rehearse the conversation with another friend or adult. Have the other person role play with you so you can be prepared to defend your position.
3. **Speak with conviction.** Politely state exactly what you want. It will help the other person understand you clearly.
4. **Maintain strong body language.** Stand straight and keep eye contact to show determination and that you think this is important.
5. **Allow an acceptable compromise.** Decide in advance which habits you would be willing to change if your friend agrees to change hers.

Take Action Think of a situation in which a group of teens are making a decision, and one person is left out. Use the techniques here to demonstrate an assertive response from the teen who wants to be included. In class, discuss how this response maintains a healthy relationship with the rest of the group.

Walk Away

Ending any relationship, even an unhealthy one, may feel like defeat. It is hard to admit you were wrong about someone or something. Remember, though, that you can end voluntary relationships. You do not need people in your life who use, intimidate, or hurt you in some way. For example, you may have a friend that is negative about some of your teachers. If you enjoy thinking positively, this may be a difficult relationship for you to maintain. Walking away from a relationship that is not in your best interest is your responsibility. It is also your right.

Most family and work relationships are involuntary. As a result, people usually try to maintain them. Walking away from these relationships may be more difficult than voluntary ones. There are ways to repair unhealthy relationships. It may take time and effort from all people involved. A relationship that seems costly at first can bring some benefits once it is strengthened.

✓ **Reading Check** **Explain** What is a relationship cost?

Relationships with Others

Like everyone else, teens need healthy relationships in their lives. Sometimes building and keeping them is not easy. For instance, Hunter quit trying to make friends because his family moved so often. Always leaving friends behind was painful. Cal spent time at his computer instead of making friends. That seemed easier to him. Maureen was frustrated by relationships that were not satisfying. She wondered what she was doing wrong.

Skills You Will Need

Like these teens, you may wonder how to make quality relationships part of your life. You will learn helpful relationships skills that you can develop. These skills include knowing to communicate well, prevent and resolve conflicts, and reach out to others. Reading other books and magazine articles about relationships can help you understand more as well.

You can also benefit from the knowledge and experience of those around you. Learn from counselors and other adults. Watch people who get along well. What do they do to make their relationships work? Can you do the same?

Above all, learn to look beyond yourself. Relationships are most apt to thrive when you focus on others and their point of view. This will also help you develop mutuality, trust, self-disclosure, rapport, empathy, and perhaps even shared interests.

Life Skills CHECKLIST 93

Thinking Skills

Build Relationships As you think about your relationships, consider the qualities they have. Your relationships can be strong if you:

✓ Show your empathy for others' feelings.

✓ Develop shared interests with those you care for.

✓ Talk about yourself and ask others about themselves to promote mutual self-disclosure.

✓ Be someone whom others trust.

✓ Work for mutuality in your relationships.

Section 5.1 After You Read

Review Key Concepts

1. **Identify** three functions of relationships in a person's life.

2. **Explain** how rewards and costs affect the survival of a relationship.

3. **Describe** skills that can be learned to use in relationships with others.

Practice Academic Skills

English Language Arts

4. Write a paragraph that explains what might cause the rewards and costs in a relationship to become unbalanced. Give specific examples of individual rewards and costs. Write another paragraph that explains a person's options when rewards and costs are unbalanced. Should they continue the relationship or walk away?

    NCTE 4 Use written language to communicate effectively.

5. Create a poster that shows six qualities of a healthy relationship. How do you show these qualities in your relationships? List at least two examples under each quality.

    NCTE 6 Apply knowledge of language structure and conventions to discuss texts.

Check Your Answers Check your answers at this book's Online Learning Center through **glencoe.com**.

Examine Your Roles

Reading Guide

Before You Read

Prior Knowledge Look over the Key Concepts at the beginning of the section. Write down what you already know about each concept and what you want to find out by reading the section.

Read to Learn

Key Concepts

- **Describe** the purpose of roles and how they are learned.
- **Relate** role conflict to role expectations.

Main Idea

People fill many roles in life. Roles are learned from the family and others, such as role models.

Content Vocabulary

◇ role
◇ given role
◇ chosen role
◇ role model
◇ role expectation
◇ stereotype
◇ role conflict

 Graphic Organizer Go to this book's Online Learning Center at **glencoe.com** to print out this graphic organizer.

Academic Vocabulary

You will find these words in your reading and on your tests. Use the glossary to look up their definitions if necessary.

▪ effect   ▪ anticipate

Graphic Organizer

As you read, list various roles people have. Identify a role expectation that you associate with that role. Use a chart like the one shown to help organize your information.

Role	Role Expectation

Academic Standards . . . .

 English Language Arts

NCTE 4 Use written language to communicate effectively.

NCTE 12 Use language to accomplish individual purposes.

 Mathematics

NCTM Problem Solving Solve problems that arise in mathematics and in other contexts.

NCTE *National Council of Teachers of English*
NCTM *National Council of Teachers of Mathematics*

NSES *National Science Education Standards*
NCSS *National Council of the Social Studies*

Life's Many Roles

You may have noticed that people do not act the same way in every setting. People who study societies have noted the strong **effect**, or impact, of roles on behavior. A **role** is an expected pattern of behavior. It goes with a person's position in society.

No one has just one role. Each person has many. Roles help people know how to act in different situations. Do you act the same way with your friends as with your parents? The role of a friend is not the same as the role of a child. If you think about it, you will realize that you change your behavior to suit different situations. In other words, you take on different roles.

You may be surprised at all the roles you have. Family roles are probably most obvious. Within a family, a person can have several roles. Roles tend to change over the family life cycle. A woman, for instance, can be a wife, mother, daughter, grandmother, aunt, sister, and cousin.

Many other roles occur outside of the family. You are a student at school and may be an employee at a job. In society, you are a citizen and a consumer. You may be a friend to many people.

Given and Chosen Roles

Roles are either given or chosen. A **given role** is one that is automatically acquired. For example, at birth you became a son or daughter. If your parents have other children, you are a brother or sister. Your roles as a student and a citizen are also given roles.

A **chosen role** is one that is deliberately selected. People choose to marry and become husbands and wives. They may choose to become parents by having children. They become employees when they decide to take jobs.

Vocabulary

You can find definitions in the glossary at the back of this book.

As You Read

Connect What are some examples of roles you have chosen?

◀◀ **Your Role Models**
Observing good role models is one way to learn positive behavior. *Whom do you consider to be role models in your life?*

Calculate Pay

Esteban is deciding between two job offers. One pays $15.00 an hour for 40 hours a week. The other pays $17.50 an hour for 30 hours a week. Esteban wants to spend more time with his family, so he will probably choose the second job. If he does, how much less will he make each year?

Math Concept **Multi-Step Problems**
When solving problems with more than one step, think through the steps before you start.

Starting Hint: Calculate how much he will make in each job per year (52 weeks). After you have done that, calculate the difference in pay.

 Math For math help, go to the Math Appendix at the back of the book.

NCTM Problem Solving Solve problems that arise in mathematics and in other contexts.

Learn Your Roles

Like values, your knowledge of roles is mostly learned through examples and direct teaching. Families provide much of this information in a child's early years. Later on, other examples and influences can have an impact.

For example, the influence of technology can affect the roles people play. In the family, labor-saving devices can change how people fill their roles. At work, a paper-less work-flow system turns a file clerk into a person who inputs data.

Role Models

Observing others is a common way to learn a role. A person you learn behavior and attitudes from is called a **role model**. These people influence your thinking by giving you examples to copy.

Family members can serve as role models for relationships. Children, for instance, learn what it means to be a father or mother, a husband or wife, by watching the adults around them. They look to older siblings for examples of grown-up behavior. Children who see healthy relationships in the family learn to build healthy relationships with others.

Role models are also found outside the family. You may learn from a coworker how to soothe an angry customer. You may see how a neighbor volunteers their time to sweep the sidewalks of your neighborhood.

You, in turn, serve as a role model for others. Younger students may watch how you act at a school assembly or sports event. Children in your neighborhood will observe what you do. They may follow your example as you show your respect for neighbors and property.

Not all role models are good ones. Just as positive qualities can be mirrored, so too can negative ones. People must make good choices about what is worth imitating.

Role Expectations

As you learn about roles, you decide how you want to act in different situations. You also form ideas about what other people should be like. You know how they should behave. You **anticipate**, or give advanced thought to, certain behavior from a certain role. This is called a **role expectation**. In one sense, these are also relationship expectations.

Suppose two people meet who are filling specific roles. This could be teacher and student or manager and worker. They have a ready-made basis for knowing how they are supposed to act with each other. The role expectations in each case are well known and translate into a relationship expectation.

Stereotypes

Brett is over six feet tall. He wishes he had a dollar for every time someone asks him if he plays basketball. He does not. He does not even like the sport. Because of his height, however, people always assume that he plays a sport that many tall people play.

Brett is feeling the effects of a **stereotype**. Stereotypes are ideas about the qualities or behavior of a certain group of people. In this case, the stereotype people make about Brett is that tall people play basketball.

Stereotypes are about role expectations. They are ideas about people that often do not apply. Stereotypes may be linked to physical features, gender, or ethnic background.

Some stereotypes, such as the one made about Brett, can be annoying. Others can also be destructive. For example, two common stereotypes are that old men are grumpy and that an only child is spoiled. If you believe these, it can prevent you from seeing older adults and only children as they truly are. You may not be able to view people as individuals.

There are also stereotypes that people use to create humor. For example, some popular comedians create their routines around stereotypes. These are often related to their own gender or ethnicity. They believe that making a joke based on a stereotype helps make people laugh.

If you judge someone on the basis of a stereotype, you are likely to be wrong. If you go one step further and talk about or mistreat that person due to the stereotype, you are hurting them. Getting to know people is the only way to know what they are like. This will help you view them as individuals.

✓ **Reading Check** **Explain** What is the difference between given and chosen roles?

Real Life — Manage Household Chores

Role expectations often affect who does what chores. However, the more the chores are shared between family members, the faster they are completed. The following examples can help families manage chores.

- Make a list with your family of all the chores to be done.
- Work together to schedule daily jobs for each person. Assign jobs based on interest, not roles.
- Rotate jobs so no one always has the most boring ones.
- Volunteer to help other family members when they are busy. Doing this means you are more apt to get help when you are busy.
- Remember to pick up after yourself.

Problem-Solving Cleaning up after meals is Hannah's job. She is upset because her brother is excused from the household chores because he is a male. She has complained to her mother, who says, "Well, your father never does kitchen chores." What can Hannah do?

Role Conflict

People may have differing views of role expectations. This is called **role conflict**. Role conflict can occur any time that people disagree about roles. It can lead to arguments and bad feelings. For example, a manager feels that employees should work hard for their pay. A worker believes he or she needs to do the minimum required for his or her job. These two people are likely to have role conflict at work. Role conflict increases the costs in a relationship.

One reason role conflicts occur is that roles are learned from many different sources. The ideas about behavior that people learn at home may be different from those they see other places. When people form relationships, they will most likely need to discuss their role expectations. They may also need to talk about what sources those expectations came from.

Another reason that people view roles differently is that roles change gradually over time. As society changes, so do roles. Some people accept and promote new roles. Others prefer long-standing ones. This causes differences in points of view and disagreements.

Serious role conflicts may occur in life. When this happens, people need to examine what both sides expect. The differences can be resolved in some way. The first step is talking about role expectations. See how roles affect the beliefs and behavior of the people involved. Then work through the role conflict. This leads to understanding that improves relationships with others.

Section 5.2   After You Read

Review Key Concepts

1. **Explain** what roles are and how they impact a person and his or her relationships.
2. **Describe** role conflict and what solutions people can use to solve role conflict problems.

Practice Academic Skills

English Language Arts

3. Write a one-page essay that includes at least one role model you have in your life. Some examples may include a family member, a person in the community, or a celebrity. Include details of why this person is a role model for you.

   > **NCTE 4** Use written language to communicate effectively.

4. Write a job description for the role of family member. Include qualities that you believe family members should have to build strong family ties. Also provide any role expectations you have for that particular role.

   > **NCTE 12** Use language to accomplish individual purposes.

Check Your Answers Check your answers at this book's Online Learning Center through **glencoe.com**.

CHAPTER SUMMARY

 Section 5.1
The Importance of Relationships

Relationships are connections to others. A healthy relationship has qualities such as mutuality, trust, self-disclosure, rapport, empathy, and shared interests. It also has rewards and costs. Rewards are the satisfaction gained from relating to others. Costs are the energy spent on the relationship. There are danger signals in relationships that can warn you of weaknesses. There are ways to improve relationships.

 Section 5.2
Examine Your Roles

A person plays many roles in relationships. Some are given and some are chosen. Roles help people know how to act in different situations. People learn about roles from the family and from role models. Role expectations are ideas that people have about the behavior of someone in a certain role. A stereotype is a harmful kind of role expectation. Role conflict can occur when people have differing views of role expectations.

Content and Academic Vocabulary Review

1. Use each of these content and academic vocabulary words in a sentence.

Content Vocabulary
- ◇ relationship (p. 87)
- ◇ acquaintance (p. 87)
- ◇ mutuality (p. 88)
- ◇ trust (p. 89)
- ◇ self-disclosure (p. 89)
- ◇ rapport (p. 89)
- ◇ reward (p. 90)
- ◇ cost (p. 90)
- ◇ exploitation (p. 91)
- ◇ role (p. 95)
- ◇ given role (p. 95)
- ◇ chosen role (p. 95)
- ◇ role model (p. 96)
- ◇ role expectation (p. 96)
- ◇ stereotype (p. 97)
- ◇ role conflict (p. 98)

Academic Vocabulary
- ■ voluntary (p. 87)
- ■ interaction (p. 89)
- ■ effect (p. 95)
- ■ anticipate (p. 96)

Review Key Concepts

2. Identify the qualities that help build healthy relationships.
3. Explain how rewards and costs affect relationships.
4. Suggest ways to improve relationships.
5. Describe the purpose of roles and how they are learned.
6. Relate role conflict to role expectations.

Critical Thinking

7. Evaluate Dora thinks of Sean as her friend. He rarely talks to her unless he needs help with an assignment. He sometimes calls her at the last minute to go out. How would you evaluate their relationship? Explain your conclusions.
8. Analyze Suppose an actor who is famous for reckless behavior says, "I am not a role model. I have never wanted to be a role model." Does his saying this make it so? What may he really be saying?
9. Compare How are rapport and empathy similar? How are they different?

Real-World Skills

Interpersonal Skills

10. Analyze Behavior Think of the qualities of a healthy relationship that are described in this chapter. Write a paragraph that explains which you think is the most difficult to learn or develop and why. Also explain why you chose this quality.

Problem-Solving Skills

11. Face Stereotypes Vijay's friend told him about a neighbor who won a college scholarship. "She is really smart," his friend said, "but then, all those people are." Vijay stated that this was a stereotype. His friend said, "But it is a compliment." Write a script for how you think Vijay should respond to this statement.

Critical Thinking Skills

12. Evaluate a Theory This chapter described a theory that relationships are based on rewards and costs. Do you agree or disagree with this theory? Write a paragraph to explain your answer and the reasoning behind your answer.

Self-Management Skills

13. Role Conflict Amy and Lorie share a bedroom. Amy ends up cleaning Lorie's side of the room because she cannot bear to look at the mess. She gets annoyed because she knows Lorie now expects her to keep the room clean. Write a list of things Amy could do to try to improve the situation.

14. Discuss an Issue Follow your teacher's instructions to form into small groups. In your group, decide which quality of relationships is most important. Share your choice with your classmates. Did any of the groups choose the same quality? Write a summary of what you learned.

15. Conduct an Interview Interview a grandparent or someone of a similar age. Ask about their role expectations for marriage and family relationships. Write a letter to your teacher comparing their expectations to your own. How are your views alike and different?

16. Select Role Models Choose two people in your family or community that you think show the qualities of a positive role model. Write a short report describing the person. Identify the qualities that led you to choose the person.

17. Relationship Skills at Work Go to this book's Online Learning Center at glencoe.com to find **Web Links** for the **Occupational Outlook Handbook**. Find five jobs. Create a table with columns for the title of the job. Choose one quality of a good relationship that would be most important for each job and highlight it in the table.

 Additional Activities For additional activities, go to this book's Online Learning Center through glencoe.com.

Academic Skills

Mathematics

18. Calculate a Family Budget It is important for families to have a budget. This can often help them avoid money conflicts. Imagine you are making a family budget. You determine that your family's basic needs require 75 percent of your monthly income. The items you list as wants cost another 15 percent. Your monthly income is $2,000. How much are you spending on wants?

 Multiply Dollars by Percents A percent is a ratio that compares a number to 100. To multiply with percentages use the starting hint.

Starting Hint: You can rewrite the percent (15%) as a fraction. When doing this, 15 is the numerator and 100 is the denominator. Convert the fraction to a decimal. Multiply this decimal by the number ($2,000). Remember to put the decimal point in the correct place in your answer.

Math For math help, go to the Math Appendix at the back of the book.

> **NCTM Number and Operations** Understand numbers, ways of representing numbers, relationships among numbers, and number systems.

English Language Arts

19. Summarize Find an article, or recall one that you have read, in a newspaper or magazine about relationships or roles. Look for the important ideas in the article. For example, these may include certain roles family members take on or the relationship between coworkers. In your own words organize, summarize, and explain the information. Write a one-paragraph summary of the article.

> **NCTE 3** Apply strategies to interpret texts.

Social Studies

20. Research Roles Conduct research on how the roles and role expectations of family members have changed over time. This can include, but is not limited to, husbands, wives, parents, and children. While you are researching, look for what has caused these changes to occur. Create a time line of the roles and the expectations of the roles during each era you researched.

> **NCSS IV.b** Identify, describe, and express appreciation for the influence of various historical and contemporary cultures on an individual's daily life.

STANDARDIZED TEST PRACTICE

TIMED WRITING
Read the following prompt and respond in a two-page essay:

> **Test-Taking Tip** Use the essay prompt as a basis for your thesis statement to help you focus your essay and ensure that you address the essay prompt. For example, you might say, "People need positive relationships because . . ."

21. Define positive relationships and give several reasons why people need positive relationships. Illustrate your points with examples and details.

CHAPTER 6

Effective Communication Skills

Section 6.1
The Communication Process

Section 6.2
Skillful Communication

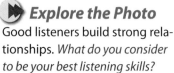 **Explore the Photo**
Good listeners build strong relationships. *What do you consider to be your best listening skills?*

Chapter Objectives

After completing this chapter, you will be able to:

- **Explain** the importance of communication in relationships.
- **List** the four elements that are needed for successful communication.
- **Identify** five effective listening and speaking skills.
- **Describe** three communication barriers and how to correct them.

Writing Activity   Autobiography

Tact Tact, or diplomacy, is the ability to say things in a way that will not hurt people's feelings. You can show tact by:

- Asking a parent calmly to talk about a subject that upsets you.
- Waiting to be alone to tell a friend unpleasant news.
- Setting an appointment with a teacher at a convenient time to talk about how to be a better student.
- Thanking someone who has asked for a date and explaining that just being friends would be more comfortable for now.

Write an autobiography about a time in your life when you showed tact, or someone you know showed tact to you. Include a clear description of how the example is a display of tact.

Writing Tips To write an autobiographical composition effectively, follow these steps:

1. Tell what happened.
2. Explain how you felt before and after the example.
3. Use details that make the example come to life for the reader.

The Communication Process

Reading Guide

Before You Read

Predict Before you read, browse the content by reading headings, bold terms, and photo captions to help you predict the information in this section.

Read to Learn
Key Concepts

- **Explain** the importance of communication in relationships.
- **List** the four elements that are needed for successful communication.

Main Idea

Communication is a two-step process of sending and receiving messages. It can be verbal or nonverbal. It requires participation and involves timing and the use of space.

Content Vocabulary

◇ ethics
◇ confidential
◇ communication channel
◇ verbal communication
◇ nonverbal communication

Academic Vocabulary

You will find these words in your reading and on your tests. Use the glossary to look up their definitions if necessary.

▪ process   ▪ dominate

Graphic Organizer

As you read, list the four elements of communication and describe each one. Use a web like the one shown to help organize your information.

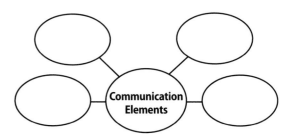

Communication Elements

 Graphic Organizer Go to this book's Online Learning Center at **glencoe.com** to print out this graphic organizer.

Academic Standards •

English Language Arts

NCTE 4 Use written language to communicate effectively.

NCTE 12 Use language to accomplish individual purposes.

NCTE *National Council of Teachers of English*
NCTM *National Council of Teachers of Mathematics*

NSES *National Science Education Standards*
NCSS *National Council of the Social Studies*

Communication with Others

Effective communication is the basis of every good relationship. Communication is a two-step **process**, or system. The first step is to create and send messages to others. The second step is to receive and process messages from others. People exchange information, ideas, and feelings as they communicate. It may sound simple. However, it involves a set of complex skills. People need to learn these skills to communicate well. They will use them in every part of their lives.

The Function of Communication

The main function of communication is to build relationships. They thrive on effective communication. This happens when people send and receive messages accurately. Communication is vital in all areas of life. It is important with family and friends. It is also needed at work and in the community. In any setting, communication helps people know what is happening. It lets them know what to do. Getting along with others would not happen without good communication. This is especially true in the family.

Ethical Communication

Ethics play a role in communication. **Ethics** are the principles of conduct that govern a group or society. Ethics are based on the core values of a society. Ethical communication is, above all, open and honest. People tell the truth. They do not hold back information that is needed. They use communication to help others, not harm them. Respect is shown through communication.

One part of ethics involves keeping some information **confidential**. This means there is a restriction on the flow of messages. For example, when your friends ask you to keep a secret, they are asking you to keep information confidential. Many workplaces also ask that company information stay confidential.

Vocabulary

You can find definitions in the glossary at the back of this book.

As You Read

Connect What words describe the methods you use to send and receive messages?

Keep Confidences When you confide in a friend, you are expressing your trust in that person. *In what other ways do you communicate in an open and honest relationship?*

Levels of Communication

There are levels of communication. For example, small talk is about everyday things such as the weather. As people develop rapport and trust, they will talk about more important issues such as careers and family life. They begin to disclose information that may mean a lot to them.

Communication Styles

People have different communication styles. This means they communicate differently. How they communicate is related to their personalities. What they express depends on their values, needs, and goals. Communication also differs based on how open or reserved a person is. All of these reflect a style of communicating with others.

To be a good communicator, you need to know how other people communicate. You may need to understand a person's communication style. The setting or context of a message may affect its meaning. There are cultural differences in communication. These can be important when dealing with people from another culture. Knowing what is appropriate is part of effective communication.

Sharing information, ideas, and feelings fosters understanding among people. It builds relationships. It helps maintain ties with others. Mastering the communication process takes time and practice. Being a good communicator means learning new skills. To communicate ethically, you need to use your values. They will help you be sensitive to the needs and values of others.

✓ **Reading Check** **Define** What is communication?

Elements of Communication

The communication process has four basic elements. These elements set the stage for communicating and lead to successful communication. When one or more are not in place, communication suffers. The four elements are communication channels, participation, timing, and the use of space.

Communication Channels

A **communication channel** is the way in which a message is passed. One of the main channels is **verbal communication**. This means spoken words. You communicate with speech more times than you can count every day. Speech, however, is only one way to share information. **Nonverbal communication** is communication without words. It can also be used to share thoughts and feelings.

Nonverbal communication takes many forms. Facial expressions, gestures, and posture all send messages. Nonverbal messages often add to the impact of verbal ones. For example, a smile and a handshake may make the message, "It is nice to meet you" more powerful.

Can You Hear Me Now? Technology has changed the way many of us communicate with each other. *How has new technology affected the way you communicate with others?*

Technology may reduce the nonverbal aspects of communication. This is because in many instances people cannot see each other's expressions or body language. There are few nonverbal clues in your communication when you:

- Write a note.
- Talk on the telephone.
- Use e-mail.
- Send an instant message.
- Receive a text message.

The words used, therefore, must be precise and to the point. When there are few or no nonverbal clues, it makes understanding harder. The words themselves must communicate the entire message.

Participation

How people participate in a discussion affects the quality of communication. The best communication happens when all those involved share in the exchange. There needs to be a balance in the give-and-take of ideas.

If you take part in small-group discussions at school, you may understand the importance of participation. One group member may try to **dominate**, or control, the session. In contrast, another may need to be urged to say something. Either way, ideas are missed. Communication works only when people are ready and willing to receive and return messages.

A lack of participation can also take place in the family. For example, a parent may be talking about something he or she thinks is important. A child may not be paying much attention to the conversation. This is not an exchange of messages. The parent is participating, but there is not a balance because the child is not listening.

Timing

True communication occurs when both the sender and the receiver focus on the exchange. Choosing the right time to send a message affects how well it is received. Suppose your parent or guardian has just been turned down for a raise at work. Is that a good time to ask if you can borrow money for a weekend trip?

Knowing when someone is ready and willing to listen to your message takes skill and sensitivity. By first saying, "How is it going?" or "Can I interrupt for a minute?" you can assess the other person's mood. You may get an answer both verbally and nonverbally. If either of these is not positive, you may want to wait for another time.

Use of Space

How space is used can affect communication. For instance, would you shout an apology across a crowded room? Something so personal requires a quieter setting. Talk tends to flow freely when family members sit around the kitchen or dining room table. Talk may lag when they are spread around the living room.

Have you ever talked with someone who seemed to be closing in on you? When you pulled back, the other person leaned closer. Communication is best when people are at ease with the space between them.

Physical viewpoint makes a difference, too. When you communicate with children, it helps to be down at their level of height. It works better than looking down from a position of power. Messages flow more freely when people feel they have equal status.

Section 6.1 After You Read

Review Key Concepts

1. **Describe** why ethical communication is important in communicating well.
2. **Explain** why the four communication elements are important.

Practice Academic Skills

English Language Arts

3. Write a paragraph describing how you could encourage everyone in a group to participate. Include at least two specific things you could do or say to bring everyone into the conversation.

4. Imagine that a friend has told you a secret. You believe your friend could be seriously hurt in the situation described. Would you tell an adult so your friend could be helped? Write a short essay explaining your answer. Discuss how confidentiality and ethical communication affected your answer.

NCTE 4 Use written language to communicate effectively.

NCTE 12 Use language to accomplish individual purposes.

Check Your Answers Check your answers at this book's Online Learning Center through glencoe.com.

Skillful Communication

Reading Guide

Before You Read

Understanding Write down questions while reading. Many of them will be answered as you read. If they are not, share the list with your teacher.

Read to Learn

Key Concepts

- **Identify** five effective listening and speaking skills.
- **Describe** three communication barriers and how to correct them.

Main Idea

Skills needed for effective communication include listening and speaking skills. There are barriers to communication that can be overcome.

Content Vocabulary

◇ listening
◇ passive listening
◇ active listening
◇ I-message
◇ feedback
◇ assertive

Academic Vocabulary

You will find these words in your reading and on your tests. Use the glossary to look up their definitions if necessary.

- aggression
- barrier

Graphic Organizer

As you read, look for skills and their sub skills needed for effective communication. Use a web like the one shown to help organize your information.

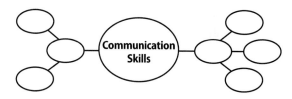

 Graphic Organizer Go to this book's Online Learning Center at **glencoe.com** to print out this graphic organizer.

Academic Standards • • • • • • • • • • • • • • • • •

 English Language Arts

NCTE 4 Use written language to communicate effectively.

NCTE 5 Use different writing process elements to communicate effectively.

 Mathematics

NCTM Data Analysis and Probability Understand and apply basic concepts of probability.

NCTE *National Council of Teachers of English*
NCTM *National Council of Teachers of Mathematics*

NSES *National Science Education Standards*
NCSS *National Council of the Social Studies*

Communication Skills

Learning communication skills can help you in many ways. These skills are needed to solve problems and make decisions. They are the basis for good relationships with others. They can help you feel good about yourself. You can also use communication skills to help others feel good.

When people live together, open communication is vital to getting along. It can help day-to-day life go more smoothly. Outside emotions, however, may get in the way. Staying calm may be hard as well. It is also difficult when family members take opposing views personally. It takes skill to communicate well.

Listening Skills

People spend many hours of their lives communicating. About one-half of that time is spent listening. Some people think hearing is the same as listening. Hearing is a physical response. **Listening** is a mental activity that lets you receive messages accurately. There are two kinds of listening skills. These are called passive listening and active listening.

As You Read

Connect What communication skills help you at school?

◇ Vocabulary

You can find definitions in the glossary at the back of this book.

INDEPENDENT Living

HOW TO   Be a Good Listener

When you are a good listener, you show respect for others. Follow these guidelines to be a good listener:

1. **Get rid of distractions.** It is difficult to listen to someone when the area around you is noisy. Turn off the television or radio. Focus and concentrate.
2. **Keep a positive attitude.** Know that the speaker has something meaningful to say. Look for ways to make the message useful.
3. **Stay open-minded.** It is important to listen even if you and the speaker disagree. If you judge ideas before they are spoken, you may miss important points. Listening gives you a chance to understand different points of view.
4. **Give nonverbal feedback.** Use body language to show you are listening. Make good eye contact. Nod or smile when you understand, and frown if you are confused. Responses like these can show the speaker that you are paying attention. They make the speaker feel comfortable sharing with you.
5. **Let the speaker finish talking.** You may be tempted to interrupt with your own thoughts. Let the speaker finish his or her thought. Otherwise, the speaker may feel like what he or she has to say is not important.

Take Action Tell a friend or family member about an interesting experience you had. Notice the other person's reactions. Do you feel like they are listening to you or do they seem distracted? How can you use the other person's responses to help you become a better listener?

Passive Listening

Passive listening is a response that invites the speaker to share feelings and ideas. The listener puts aside personal judgments. No questions are asked. Comments like "No kidding?" and "You said it!" show that the listener is focused on the speaker's words. The listener does not express any ideas, but encourages the speaker to talk more.

Active Listening

In **active listening** the listener works to understand the speaker's feelings and the message's true meaning. Active listeners use direct questions. They may restate the message they heard. These responses show that the listener hears and understands what is being said. They also encourage the speaker to keep talking.

Speaking Skills

Words are powerful. They can be used to help people but they can also be harmful. Care and self-control are needed to use them for positive communication.

I-Messages

An **I-message** is a message that accurately reflects what the speaker thinks, believes, and feels. They give facts to explain the speaker's reaction. They are called I-messages because the message starts with the word I. I-messages do not attack others. For example, "I was worried when you did not call me" is an I-message.

Messages that start with the word you are often the opposite of I-messages. These may be a direct attack on the person and their actions. These messages may blame the other person for the speaker's feelings. For example, "You make me so mad!" puts the blame for the anger on the other person.

I-messages are a good way to talk to someone when you are upset. Using them will help your message be less hurtful. If you are upset, it may be hard to use I-messages. Practicing self-control can help you state your feelings calmly. Venting your anger at someone rarely has a good outcome, even when the other person is at fault.

Feedback

Feedback is a way of checking out the meaning of messages. It is a response that shows whether a message was understood. It bridges the gap between listening and speaking.

Both a speaker and a listener may ask for feedback to make sure they agree on what was said. Listeners need to be sure they understand what the speaker has said. Speakers need feedback to know they have been understood. Active listening is one way to give feedback. If the listener restates the message, the speaker can tell that it was heard correctly.

Financial Literacy

Calculate Probabilities

Matt listened carefully and asked questions as his manager told him that there is a 50% probability that his salary will increase next year. There is also a 25% probability that his bonus will increase. What is the probability that both will increase?

 Probability of a Compound Event To calculate the probability that two independent events will both occur, multiply their probabilities.

Starting Hint: Multiply the two events' probabilities. For example, (50% $\times$ 25%). To make the problem easier, convert the percents into fractions. 50% becomes $\frac{1}{2}$ and 25% becomes $\frac{1}{4}$. Now multiply and represent your answer as either a fraction or a decimal.

Math For math help, go to the Math Appendix at the back of the book.

NCTM Data Analysis and Probability Understand and apply basic concepts of probability.

Many people have a hard time handling sensitive topics. In some families, death, divorce, and other personal subjects are off limits. Other families discuss them only with great difficulty. You can probably see why. Can you also see the problems that may arise when sensitive topics are not discussed?

Difficult subjects need careful treatment. It may be helpful to have more than two people when you are talking. You might open by talking about something similar that happened to a friend. Start with an I-message. It may be easier to start by writing your I-message.

Problem-Solving

Dawn wants to know more about her mother, who died when she was six. Dawn has tried to talk to her father, but he is uncomfortable talking about it, so she often ends up crying. What could Dawn do to improve communication about this difficult subject?

Assertiveness

When you are **assertive** (ə-'sər-tiv), you state your ideas and feelings firmly and positively. You are in charge of yourself. You can tell your ideas and let others express their opinions.

Being assertive is not rude. It differs from **aggression**, or force. Aggressive people push to have their own way. They often act hostile or use you-messages and threatening nonverbal messages.

✔ Reading Check **Contrast** What is the difference between hearing and listening?

Communication Barriers

With good communication skills, you can avoid many misunderstandings. Noticing a **barrier**, or factor, that makes communication harder is the first step. Seeing the problem allows you to do something about it. Some communication problems occur because people have different cultural backgrounds or different points of view. If music or the television are on, it can also interfere with communication.

One barrier is that people communicate in harmful ways. They may blame, interrupt, or start endless fights. Attacking someone's character is destructive. It is hard to move forward when faced with this kind of communication. By using positive skills, you can work to turn communication constructive.

Silence

Silence can be a nice break from talking. Some silences are comfortable. Others convey disinterest, boredom, or even hostility. Silence can also signal fear. Sharing feelings may be hard. In trying to find the right words, a person may fear saying something foolish. They may fear being laughed at. Communication on touchy subjects can be filled with awkward silences. When families have conflict, silence is the most common response of children.

Knowing the reason for the silence can help restart the flow of communication. If someone you know is silent, you can point this out. Depending on your relationship, you may say, "You are quiet. Is something bothering you?" You can also send supportive messages to encourage that person's trust. This will help the person feel comfortable sharing their feelings.

There may be times when silence indicates a serious problem, such as depression. It is important that you get a person to talk in this situation. Open communication may allow that person to get the help they need.

Mixed Messages

Sometimes different messages are sent over different channels at the same time. This is called a mixed message. In this type of message, the verbal and nonverbal messages do not match. For example, a person may say one thing, but their body language suggests something different. When a mixed message is sent, the nonverbal message generally reflects the sender's true feelings. A message that is expressed both verbally and nonverbally is much more convincing.

Thinking You Already Know

Mind reading is assuming you know what someone else is thinking. It often leads to wrong conclusions. Mind readers are sometimes too impatient to hear other people out. Mind reading can be a way to dominate a conversation and another person. People who know each other well may believe they can literally read each other's minds. To find out what someone thinks, pay attention. Ask questions and use feedback to learn what is really going on.

Section 6.2 — After You Read

Review Key Concepts

1. **Describe** why good communication skills are important.
2. **Identify** the first step in overcoming communication barriers.

Practice Academic Skills

**English Language Arts**

3. You have received an e-mail from a friend. The e-mail says a group of your friends is going to the movie on Friday night at 8:20 and that they will see you there. Write an e-mail to your friend asking for feedback to clarify the message.

> **NCTE 4** Use written language to communicate effectively.

4. List two communication skills. Give a specific example of how you might use each skill when you are on the job.

> **NCTE 5** Use different writing process elements to communicate effectively

Check Your Answers Check your answers at this book's Online Learning Center through **glencoe.com**.

Ginger Burr, AICI, CIP
Lynn, Massachusetts

For many people, there is a difference between the way they look and the way they wish to look. Making that difference go away is the job of image consultant Ginger Burr. She has spent more than two decades helping clients transform themselves into the person of their dreams.

Burr comments, "My clients come to me because they are frustrated about several things. This can include feelings about their body image or a lack of interest or knowledge about coordinating a wardrobe. Some may also feel overwhelmed when they enter a clothing store." She continues, "My job is to facilitate the process of helping them select clothing, makeup, accessories, and a hairstyle that they love."

Ginger says she relies heavily on intuition. This helps guide a client toward the choices that will complement their body shape, coloring, lifestyle, and personality.

Burr explains, "I am never bored. I have also been lucky enough to work with many of my clients over a long period of time, so I have had the pleasure of seeing them transform and blossom."

CAREER FACTS

Education or Training People skills and a creative eye are more important than the specific degree. For example, Ginger Burr's degree is in music. All graduate-level degrees, however, will provide an individual with the business and organizational skills needed for this career.

Nature of the Work Image consultants work with individuals on various aspects of their physical appearance, such as makeup, clothing, and hair style. They try to help them develop the look that they desire.

Aptitudes, Abilities, and Skills Writing skills, creative thinking, artistic ability, communication, interpersonal skills.

Academic Skills Required English Language Arts, Mathematics

Student Organizations To prepare for this career, look for groups that allow you to express your interest in apparel, such as a clothing or fashion club.

Career Outlook Jobs as appearance workers—which includes image consultants as well as barbers and cosmetologists—are expected to grow at an average pace over the next ten years.

Career Path Many image consultants are self-employed and build their practice on word-of-mouth marketing.

Critical Thinking

Business Sense Should image consultants understand business and marketing? Why or why not?

 Research Careers For more information on this and other careers, visit the Occupational Outlook Handbook Web site through the link on this book's Online Learning Center at **glencoe.com**.

CHAPTER SUMMARY

Section 6.1
The Communication Process

Communication is the two-step process of sending and receiving messages. It is the basis for all relationships. Using it ethically and keeping confidentiality builds trust between people. The two main channels are verbal and nonverbal. When everyone participates, the timing is good, and the use of space is considered, communication is better.

Section 6.2
Skillful Communication

Skillful communication means learning specific skills. Passive and active listening skills are used to understand messages received. I-messages, feedback, and being assertive can help spoken communication. Barriers to communication can be overcome. Common barriers include silence, mixed messages, and mind reading.

Content and Academic Vocabulary Review

1. Use each of these content and academic vocabulary words in a sentence.

Content Vocabulary
◇ ethics (p. 105)
◇ confidential (p. 105)
◇ communication channel (p. 106)
◇ verbal communication (p. 106)
◇ nonverbal communication (p. 106)
◇ listening (p. 110)
◇ passive listening (p. 111)
◇ active listening (p. 111)

◇ I-message (p. 111)
◇ feedback (p. 111)
◇ assertive (p. 112)

Academic Vocabulary
■ process (p. 105)
■ dominate (p. 107)
■ aggression (p. 112)
■ barrier (p. 112)

Review Key Concepts

2. Explain the importance of communication in relationships.
3. List the four elements that are needed for successful communication.
4. Identify five effective listening and speaking skills.
5. Describe three communication barriers and how to correct them.

Critical Thinking

6. Analyze When might verbal communication be the more effective channel of communication? When might nonverbal communication be better?
7. Extend Imagine that you are returning a portable DVD player you bought that does not work. Which communication skills could you use to your advantage when you do this?
8. Explain In your own words, explain the following quotation by Frank Tyger. "Be a good listener. Your ears will never get you in trouble."
9. Predict Identify two communications skills. Predict how you will use them in your future family life.

Real-World Skills

Interpersonal Skills

10. Give Feedback Imagine that you are in charge of a booth at a school fair. The person who is to sell the balloons seems unsure of what to do. Write a paragraph explaining what you could say to give and ask for feedback.

Communication Skills

11. I-Messages Write a list of ten I-messages you can use when someone disappoints you. Be sure that each I-message clearly states your feelings and positions. Review your I-messages to make sure that they do not cast blame on the other person.

Collaborative Skills

12. Evaluate Messages With a partner, speak this sentence in several ways: "You sure are a good friend." Try to show a different feeling each time. Write a paragraph about how people can express different messages with the same words.

Problem-Solving Skills

13. Social Skills Jada is talking to a friend who keeps looking away to see what is going on around them. Jada feels that her friend is not listening to her and she is getting frustrated. What should she do? Write a list of five suggestions.

14. Analyze Nonverbal Messages Recall a sporting event that you have seen. Many athletes show their feelings through their actions and use nonverbal signals to call plays. In a two-column table, explain ten nonverbal messages that you saw and what you think each meant. Put the messages in the first column and the meanings in the second column.

15. Family Communication Brainstorm with your family. Write down a list of ways you can communicate when you cannot speak to each other in person. Think of creative ways to use signs, symbols, and various technological devices.

16. On the Job Observe a worker in a service industry. What communication skills are used when serving customers? Does the worker use them effectively? Write a short report describing your observations and explaining why communication is an important job skill.

17. Confidentiality Agreements Businesses may require workers to sign confidentiality agreements. These state that workers will not reveal information they get while at work. Go to this book's Online Learning Center at **glencoe.com** to find **Web Links** for **Confidentiality Agreements**. Write a paragraph to summarize your findings.

Additional Activities For additional activities, go to this book's Online Learning Center through **glencoe.com**.

Academic Skills

 Mathematics

18. Communicate Income Rosa makes and sells costume jewelry. She needs to communicate her income during the first half of the year to her accountant. Her profits from January through June are listed below. Use this data to create a line graph to show her income over these six months.

Month	Income
January	$2,567
February	$3,445
March	$4,007
April	$4,975
May	$4,500
June	$4,789

 Line Graphs Line graphs are useful for displaying information about quantities that change over time.

Starting Hint: Put the months (January through June) along the horizontal axis and the dollar amounts in $500 increments along the vertical axis. Then plot the actual dollar (income) amounts and connect the plotted data.

 For math help, go to the Math Appendix at the back of the book.

NCTM Data Analysis and Probability Formulate questions that can be addressed with data and collect, organize, and display relevant data to answer them.

 English Language Arts

19. Literature Comparison Use the library to find a novel, magazine, or newspaper from a different time period. You can also recall something you have read previously. As you read, look for how written communication has changed over time. Note changes in word choice and differences in writing style. Write a one-page report on your findings.

NCTE 2 Read literature to build an understanding of the human experience.

 Social Studies

20. Cultural Differences Grant's family is hosting a Russian foreign-exchange student named Sergei. Sergei is very outgoing, and Grant wants to be his friend. Grant is often uncomfortable, however, because Sergei stands too close when they talk. If Grant takes a step back, Sergei moves closer to fill the gap. Grant does not want to offend Sergei. What should Grant do? Write a letter to Grant offering your advice for his problem.

NCSS I.f Interpret patterns of behavior reflecting values and attitudes that contribute or pose obstacles to cross-cultural understanding.

STANDARDIZED TEST PRACTICE

READING COMPREHENSION
Read the following passage. Then answer the question that follows.

Test-Taking Tip Read the passage carefully, identifying key statements as you go. Answer the question based only on what you just read in the passage, not based on your previous knowledge.

21. Interference, such as the television or a radio, can disrupt communication. People who want to communicate well try to eliminate interference first.

According to this passage, why do people who want to communicate well try to eliminate interference first? Write your answer on another piece of paper.

CHAPTER 7

Conflict Prevention

Section 7.1

Understand Conflict

Section 7.2

Deal with Conflict

▶▶ Explore the Photo

Resolving a conflict may require more than one approach. *What are some successful approaches you have used to resolve disagreements?*

Chapter Objectives

After completing this chapter, you will be able to:

- **Determine** what causes conflict.
- **Describe** tactics that are useful in resolving conflicts.
- **Recognize** ways to avoid conflict.
- **Identify** interpersonal skills that are useful in dealing with conflict.
- **Summarize** how people can be respectful of others during conflicts.
- **Explain** why setting a good example is important in conflict situations.

Writing Activity — Unified Paragraphs

Cooperation To cooperate is to work together. Cooperation helps prevent conflict. You can show cooperation when you:

- Do your fair share when involved in team projects.
- Volunteer to do extra chores to help keep the house clean.
- Cheerfully go along with the family's weekend plans even though other plans sound more fun.

Write two unified paragraphs about a time when a family member or friend's cooperation helped make your life a little easier. Include specific actions this person did to cooperate with you.

Writing Tips To write unified paragraphs, follow these steps:

1. Each paragraph should focus on one main idea.
2. Make sure all of the sentences in each paragraph support the main idea.
3. Use transition words—such as *because, also,* and *in addition*—to link the ideas in the paragraphs.

Understand Conflict

Reading Guide

Before You Read

What You Want to Know Write a list of what you want to know about understanding conflict. As you read, write down the headings in this section that provide that information.

Read to Learn

Key Concepts

- **Determine** what causes conflict.
- **Describe** tactics that are useful in resolving conflicts.
- **Recognize** ways to avoid conflict.

Main Idea

Conflict is a disagreement or struggle between two or more people. There are several tactics to use in resolving conflict. If possible, conflict should be prevented.

Content Vocabulary

◇ conflict
◇ power
◇ control
◇ negotiate
◇ compromise
◇ mediator

Academic Vocabulary

You will find these words in your reading and on your tests. Use the glossary to look up their definitions if necessary.

■ tactic ■ assume

Graphic Organizer

As you read, look for three types of conflict. Use a concept web like the one shown to help organize your information.

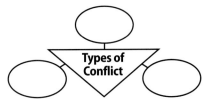

 Graphic Organizer Go to this book's Online Learning Center at **glencoe.com** to print out this graphic organizer.

Academic Standards . . . .

 English Language Arts

NCTE 4 Use written language to communicate effectively.

NCTE 7 Conduct research and gather, evaluate, and synthesize data to communicate discoveries.

 Mathematics

NCTM Number and Operations Understand numbers, ways of representing numbers, relationships among numbers, and number systems.

NCTE *National Council of Teachers of English*
NCTM *National Council of Teachers of Mathematics*

NSES *National Science Education Standards*
NCSS *National Council of the Social Studies*

Types of Conflict

Conflict is a disagreement or struggle between two or more people. It happens when one or more people try to prevent or interfere in some way with the actions of others. Conflict is part of any close relationship. In fact, the closer your relationship is, such as in your family, the more heated your conflicts can be. Conflicts also happen between friends, at school, and in the workplace. Conflict is not pleasant, but it does not have to be painful. It can be handled so that it strengthens a relationship.

You can learn to prevent or avoid conflict. In some settings, conflict seems impossible to avoid. When it does occur, it can be handled so there is a positive outcome. Conflict can be constructive. People who work together to solve a problem reach a better understanding of each other and are apt to be happier with the outcome.

Conflict can also be negative. In destructive conflict, people attack each other rather than the problem. They try to hurt each other. Destructive conflict is not healthy for a relationship.

The sources of specific conflicts vary. In general there tends to be three common causes of conflict:

* Situational conflict
* Personality differences
* Power struggles

Situational Conflict

Sometimes a specific situation gives rise to conflict. Situational conflict can occur in all kinds of relationships. It can also happen in any part of daily life. These conflicts may be intense. Fortunately, they are often short-lived.

Suppose three teens have to share a bathroom. As you may guess, this situation causes conflict. The teens cannot control the fact that they must share a bathroom. They can, however, control how they handle the situation. They can work to settle their disputes so all three are happy with the solution.

Personality Differences

Another way that conflict may arise is from differences in personalities. As you know, each person has a distinct personality. Their different combination of values and traits can enrich life. They can also, however, create conflict. If two siblings share a room, for example, and one likes to read and the other enjoys listening to music, a conflict may occur. This conflict is due to a difference in personality.

Vocabulary

You can find definitions in the glossary at the back of this book.

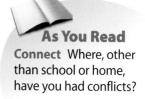

As You Read

Connect Where, other than school or home, have you had conflicts?

Resolving Conflicts Conflicts are a part of any relationship, including family relationships. *In what way have you resolved a conflict with a family member about doing chores?*

Conflicts caused by clashing personalities are often about small matters. One person's habits may get on another person's nerves. These small matters, however, may build into major battles.

Power Struggles

Power is the ability to influence another person. Power struggles occur when issues are important to both sides. Using power is one way people get others to agree to their terms.

A related issue is the desire or need for control. **Control** is the action of directing another person's behavior. When power is the cause of conflict, the desire for control may get in the way of a solution.

✓ **Reading Check** **Define** What is conflict?

Resolve Conflicts

The family is usually the first setting where children face conflict. They see how conflict is handled between other family members. They also learn attitudes and behaviors about conflict. As they grow older, children's attitudes and behaviors are also influenced by:

- The media, particularly television.
- Interactions with other children.
- Other experiences at school.

People handle conflict in different ways. This often depends on their personality and attitude. Some seem to enjoy it. Others try to prevent or avoid it. Still others work to manage it so that outcomes are positive.

The goal of conflict resolution is to solve problems without violence. People can do this if they learn how to correctly resolve conflicts. They can then solve their problems with nonviolent strategies at home, at work, at school, and in the community.

You can learn to settle differences constructively. Success comes with understanding a basic **tactic**, or method, for dealing with conflicts. These tactics include defining the problem, setting limits, negotiating, getting outside help, and following up. These are not always easy to do. The people in a conflict have to want to solve their problem in order to achieve a positive result.

Define the Problem

Constructive conflict resolution begins when parties agree on what they are arguing about. This step may seem unnecessary. It can, however, be the hardest step. People may not be able to put their feelings into words. They often **assume**, or guess, that they know what others are thinking. Putting thoughts into words sets the tone for a calm, orderly discussion.

During discussion, all points of disagreement should be exchanged. You may want to have a game plan. This could be a strategy to help the other person understand your position. To resolve the conflict, you also need to say things that acknowledge the other's point of view. This should be done in a respectful way, even if what they say is hard for you to understand.

Set Limits

To keep a discussion on track, parties need to set limits. They should agree on the points to be argued. Other issues and personal attacks are off limits. Bringing up old disagreements will not help solve today's problem. It will only turn the discussion destructive.

Negotiate

To **negotiate** is to deal or bargain with another person. When you settle conflicts with family and friends, you negotiate. During negotiation, people suggest possible solutions. They seek points of agreement. More suggestions can lead to more agreement. Gradually, the parties figure out a solution that is acceptable to all.

INDEPENDENT *Living*

HOW TO   Resolve a Conflict

Resolving a conflict with an important person in your life can lead to a stronger relationship. Follow these guidelines to resolve conflicts constructively:

1. **Define the problem.** Put into words why you are upset. Listen to the other person to find out why they are upset. It may be for a different reason from what you assume.
2. **Set limits.** Agree to discuss only the immediate problem. Do not bring up issues from the past. Make an effort to keep the argument from becoming personal.
3. **Negotiate.** Think of possible solutions to the problem. Listen to the solutions the other person suggests. This discussion should lead to a compromise that works for both of you.
4. **Get outside help.** You may not be able to resolve the conflict constructively. Find a person who is not involved to help you settle the argument. This person can be a teacher, parent, or peer whom you feel can be objective.
5. **Follow up.** When you have resolved the conflict, make sure the other person feels good about the solution. Checking in with each other from time to time can prevent future conflicts from occurring.

Take Action Imagine that you and your sibling both have use of the family car. You often have different plans to use the car on the same night, which leads to arguments. Ask a friend to play the part of your sibling, and role play the conflict, using the steps above.

Negotiation works when people are willing to compromise. **Compromise** means giving in on some points of disagreement and having your way on others. You give a little to get a little. The goal of negotiating and compromise is to achieve a "win-win" situation. This means that all parties feel as though they have received a fair deal. It satisfies their needs and concerns.

Negotiation is not always successful. Each side may be unwilling to give up something the other side wants. In the family or between friends, this may mean more conflict. Feelings may be hurt and relationships damaged.

Sometimes a solution fails because it does not really please everyone. One party may accept an agreement just to end the conflict or even try to make it work. Unless the terms satisfy everyone involved, however, the quarrel is apt to crop up again later.

Mediate a Conflict Sometimes it takes another person to help solve a conflict. *What are the advantages to bringing another person in to help solve a problem?*

Get Outside Help

Sometimes outside help is needed to resolve a conflict. A person who leads those in conflict to solutions is called a **mediator**. This person does not take sides in the dispute. Mediators can be informal, such as a friend. There are also formal, structured mediation programs. In these, the mediator follows a set procedure. This helps the parties understand each other. They can then negotiate, compromise, and solve their problem.

Communities have resources to help people with conflict. Some schools have peer mediation programs to handle conflict between students. The courts may sponsor classes for those who have problems with physical abuse. There are safe homes where people who are abused can go. Many companies give help when employees have problems with conflict issues.

Follow Up

The last step in resolving a conflict is to follow up. During follow up, solutions are put into action. Perhaps more importantly, bad feelings are dealt with and managed. Proper follow up includes feedback that lets each party evaluate if the conflict was resolved.

✓ **Reading Check** **Describe** Why is it important to set limits when resolving conflicts?

Avoid Conflict

A conflict that never develops is one you do not have to worry about. How do you avoid conflict? Here are some techniques that may help you.

- **Do not let others irritate you.** Recognize when someone is only looking for a reaction from you. Make sure the issue is worth quarreling over.
- **Focus on the positive.** When you focus on advantages, disadvantages can seem less bothersome.
- **Change the subject.** If you feel things get tense, lead the conversation in a different, less emotional direction.
- **Take a personal stand against serious, and especially physical, conflict.** Let others know that you are not going to resort to violence.
- **Do not be intimidated or provoked into fighting.** Show your strength by doing what you know is right, not what others may want.
- **Walk away.** You may realize the conflict is not worth fighting about. You can be proud and show self-confidence by calmly walking away.

These tips are not easy to follow. They require control of yourself and your emotions. Pride often gets in the way. In the long run, these techniques show your maturity. They will make your relationships with others more satisfying.

Section 7.1 After You Read

Review Key Concepts

1. **Identify** the three types of conflict.
2. **Describe** how conflicts can be resolved constructively.
3. **Explain** the qualities that are shown when a person walks away from a conflict.

Practice Academic Skills

English Language Arts

4. Conflicts may arise from disagreements. How can the process of resolving the conflict be considered constructive? Write a paragraph to answer this question.

5. Conduct research to find out what kind of training mediators need. What skills do they learn? How do they use these skills? Write an explanation describing what you found in your research. Include information about how mediators use their skills.

NCTE 4 Use written language to communicate effectively.

NCTE 7 Conduct research and gather, evaluate, and synthesize data to communicate discoveries.

Check Your Answers Check your answers at this book's Online Learning Center through glencoe.com.

Deal with Conflict

Reading Guide

Before You Read

Vocabulary To gain a better understanding of vocabulary, create a Vocabulary Journal. Divide a piece of paper into three columns. Label and fill in the columns: Vocabulary, What is it?, and What else is it like?

Read to Learn
Key Concepts
- **Identify** interpersonal skills that are useful in dealing with conflict.
- **Summarize** how people can be respectful of others during conflicts.
- **Explain** why setting a good example is important in conflict situations.

Main Idea
One way to deal with conflict is to use interpersonal skills to resolve it. It is important to show respect for others during conflict. People set a good example when they prevent or avoid conflict.

Content Vocabulary
◇ clarification
◇ competition
◇ vulnerable

Academic Vocabulary
You will find these words in your reading and on your tests. Use the glossary to look up their definitions if necessary.
■ frustration   ■ constructive

Graphic Organizer
As you read, identify communication skills and how they can be used to resolve conflicts. Use a chart like the one shown to help organize your information.

Communication Skills	Used in Conflict Resolution

 Graphic Organizer Go to this book's Online Learning Center at **glencoe.com** to print out this graphic organizer.

Academic Standards ● ● ● ● ● ● ● ● ● ● ● ● ● ● ●

 English Language Arts

NCTE 5 Use different writing process elements to communicate effectively.

NCTE 12 Use language to accomplish individual purposes.

NCTE *National Council of Teachers of English*
NCTM *National Council of Teachers of Mathematics*

NSES *National Science Education Standards*
NCSS *National Council of the Social Studies*

Apply Interpersonal Skills

As you know from experience, resolving disputes does not come naturally. People do not always have the skills needed to resolve conflict. They may understand the actions involved but not how to carry out those actions. When dealing with a conflict, you want to have good communication skills, self-control, teamwork, and be able to pick a good time to talk.

Communication Skills

People who handle conflict well use good communication skills. You do not have to wait for a conflict to practice these skills. If you work on them every day, in fact, you may encounter fewer conflicts. Conflicts cannot be settled without communication skills.

Listen

It is important to have good listening skills in order to resolve a conflict. This is also a time, however, when listening can be the most difficult. Have you ever been so upset that what someone said did not register in your mind? If you receive a negative message, you tend to get more upset and more negative. Listening effectively to an opposing view depends on several key skills.

Empathy During a disagreement, try to listen with empathy. If you appreciate the other person's position, you may solve the problem faster. Do not only think about your position and your hurt feelings. This makes it harder to work toward a solution.

Feedback A misunderstanding can get in the way of good communication. Give and accept feedback to help prevent misunderstandings. Ask questions and restate the other person's message to show that you are trying to understand. Others will appreciate your efforts.

Clarification Mixed messages show the sender's mixed emotions and can be confusing to the receiver. **Clarification** means to make clear. When you clarify, you find out what the message really is. Watch what you say and do to avoid sending mixed messages. State your feelings honestly. Make sure your body language matches your words.

📖 **As You Read**
Connect Think about the skills you have or will need to have to resolve conflicts.

◆ **Vocabulary**
You can find definitions in the glossary at the back of this book.

▶▶ *Careful Listening*
Listening is a communication skill that can help you in the classroom as well as in solving conflict. *How can careful listening help you understand someone else's point of view?*

Talk

Negotiation and compromise are not possible if parties do not talk to each other. They must keep communication going. Avoid giving the other person the silent treatment. It sends negative nonverbal messages and builds barriers. If no one is talking, no solution can be reached.

How both parties talk directly affects whether or not a conflict can be resolved. Avoid using you-messages. These messages cast blame. They often lead to the other person becoming defensive. In the end, they can destroy communication.

I-Messages It is important to use I-messages when resolving conflict. I-messages state what you want but avoid blame. When both sides use I-messages, those in conflict are more apt to stick to the issues. When talking, be assertive. If you are aggressive, you hurt your own cause. The best approach is to state your position calmly and clearly.

Show Self-Control

Resolving conflict is impossible without self-control. The more intense the conflict, the more self-control you need. Unfortunately, people tend to lose control when they need it most. Both emotions and physical reactions must be controlled. Focus calmly on the issue, not on the other person.

Emotional Control

Feeling annoyed is natural when someone gets between you and what you want. As conflict builds, annoyance can turn into hot emotions, such as anger and **frustration**, or disappointment. When this happens you may not be able to see the other person's position. Keeping emotions cool helps you stay calm. That lets you use reason and empathy. These are needed for working out problems between people. If the discussion gets heated, it is wise to call a time out. This is a short cooling-off period. Later, you can return and refocus on the problem.

Real Life   Let Go of Conflict

You will not always be able to change situations that cause conflict. So what do you do? You may need to let go of a quarrel or the pain you feel. A ceremony based on one of these ideas could help you put a conflict to rest:

- Let a seed cluster (such as a dandelion) represent the conflict and blow it away.
- Write the issues on balloons. Then pop them.
- Write the issues on paper and ceremoniously shred the paper.
- Write the issues on leaves and set the leaves adrift in a stream.

Letting go is not giving in to the problem. Instead, you are making a choice to accept peace of mind in situations you cannot change.

Problem-Solving Angie is hurt and angry. For the third time in a row, her father has cancelled their weekend together. Her father says he is working, but Angie does not believe him. What could Angie do to help herself learn to accept the situation?

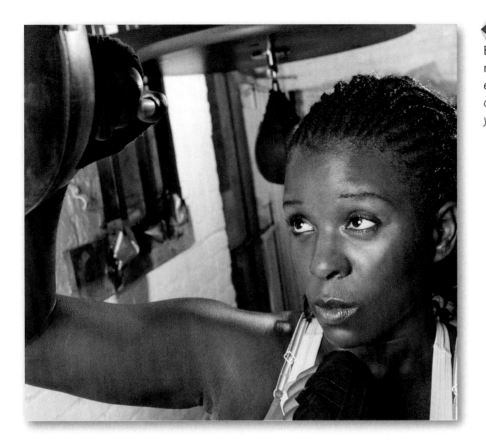

◀) Find an Outlet
Emotions that build up need an outlet such as exercise. *What physical outlets help you release your anger or frustration?*

Physical Reactions

Physical reactions are a poor means of solving problems. When children argue they may bully others, hit, kick, scream, and yell. People who never learn to control their physical impulses often react like children when conflict arises. Physical reactions can cause:

- Hurt feelings and, sometimes, people.
- Damaged or destroyed relationships.
- More violence.
- A conflict to remain unresolved.

Try a **constructive** outlet, or one that leads to improvement, when energy and emotional tension increase. Try activities such as taking a walk or a run, lifting weights, vacuuming the house, or washing a car. Clear your mind and body of frustration and tension. This can help restore positive energy for finding a solution.

Use Teamwork

Many people, unfortunately, feel they need to compete during a conflict because they want to win. A **competition** is a contest between rivals. People may feel they can win the argument only if the other side loses. The spirit of negotiation and compromise cannot survive with this us-versus-them thinking.

People who are successful in conflict resolution, realize that no side wins unless all sides win. They see that everyone is on the same team. The opponent is not the other party involved. It is the problem or conflict between the two parties. If people can work together as a team, they may find a solution that everyone can live with.

Choose the Right Time

Not every time is a good time for tackling a conflict. Choosing a good time is important. The right time is:

- **When all sides are in a proper frame of mind.** They have set aside other concerns to focus on the conflict. For example, meal-time and bedtime may not be good choices. Self-control is often more difficult when you are hungry or tired.
- **When all sides have enough time.** If you rush through a discussion, you may miss facts that you need in order to reach a satisfying outcome. Set a time to meet about the problem, if necessary.
- **When all sides are not distracted.** Choose a time when the person you want to talk to is not distracted. Distractions can include homework, chores, or the television.

✓ **Reading Check** **Explain** How can interpersonal skills help solve conflict?

Respect Others

Most people agree that everyone deserves respect. Others should be shown appreciation or esteem. In a heated debate, however, respect may be forgotten. It often becomes easy to belittle other people. You may say things that show disrespect for opinions that differ from yours. Emotions may cause you to lose self-control.

Respect is easier if you understand. Try to see people and situations as they are. You may be able to defuse a conflict by showing understanding. Ask yourself what you respect and value in the other person. Sometimes your respect can help you overlook issues that are not worth arguing about.

Use Respectful Language

The language used in an argument reflects the degree of respect each person feels for the other. Profanity and name calling show little respect. Such words raise the emotional level of the quarrel as well. They also reduce the chance of reaching a positive outcome.

◀◀ *Show Respect*
By resolving a conflict with a student after class, the teacher is showing respect and good timing. *How can you show good timing when resolving conflict?*

Have a Respectful Attitude

Treating others decently also shows respect. Conflict between parties who know each other well can be especially hurtful. Each side knows the areas where the other is most **vulnerable**, or able to be wounded. Respectful people do not abuse their closeness. They do not take advantage of this knowledge.

✓ **Reading Check** **Explain** Why is it difficult to show respect during conflict?

Set an Example

Some of the biggest trends in society start with a single, influential person. An actor might wear a certain type of sunglasses or utter a clever line in a movie. Millions of people may buy the same brand of sunglasses or repeat the actor's line.

You can be a trendsetter, too. Every time you resolve a conflict, you set an example. You serve as a role model for others. Younger siblings can learn by watching your methods. You may work with your peers to spread the practice of nonviolent conflict resolution.

Some conflicts can be prevented. Many conflicts can be resolved. If you practice your interpersonal skills, such as communication, self-control, teamwork, and being able to choose the right time, you can be successful when dealing with conflict. It is important to respect yourself and others during conflict. You can set an example for others of how to do this. Make a commitment to prevent conflict or to solve it constructively. This will improve the quality of life for you, your family, and friends.

Life Skills CHECKLIST

Management Skills

Deal with Conflict The next time you face a disagreement, check your approach to resolving conflict. You will be successful if you:

✓ Evaluate the importance of the issue to see if it is worth risking a damaged relationship.

✓ Understand the other person's point of view, even if you do not agree.

✓ Have all the facts about the conflict.

✓ Respond in a mature, grown-up way.

✓ See the humorous side of the situation.

✓ Suggest ways to compromise on the issue.

✓ Believe your actions will lead to a peaceful solution.

Section 7.2   After You Read

Review Key Concepts

1. **List** five communication skills that are especially important in resolving conflict.

2. **Describe** three ways to show respect for others.

3. **Explain** how you can set a positive example of conflict resolution.

Practice Academic Skills

English Language Arts

4. Write an article for the school newspaper about skills needed to resolve conflicts. Discuss how the skills could be used for the type of conflicts that are typical at your school. Include a sketch or a graphic organizer that illustrates aspects of effective conflict resolution.

5. Write a paragraph that explains the following statement: "A major part of self-control is mouth control." How does this apply to conflict resolution?

NCTE 5 Use different writing process elements to communicate effectively.

NCTE 12 Use language to accomplish individual purposes.

Check Your Answers Check your answers at this book's Online Learning Center through glencoe.com.

Guidance Counselor

Jody Foreman
Louisville, Kentucky

When you think of a school guidance counselor, you might imagine someone sitting behind a desk, offering advice to students. But in reality, guidance counselors, such as Jody Foreman are much more active about getting out and meeting their students.

Foreman comments, "I spend all my available free moments walking the building. I talk to students, parents, and teachers in the cafeteria, hallways, classrooms, and when students enter and exit the building." Foreman continues, "Developing a rapport with the students is the key to helping them make good choices."

Foreman worked as a teacher for 13 years. She says those years were time well spent. "I firmly believe my years of teaching experience added breadth and depth to my ability to work all sides of the student equation."

Foreman says these tips help her in her career: "Keep the focus simple and clear. Remember to forgive often, see the glass half-full, and smile at everyone you encounter. Build relationships with such simple things as using a student's name each time you cross paths. It may be the first time someone has spoken to them that day!"

CAREER FACTS

Education or Training Undergraduate and graduate degrees in education, psychology, and sociology are useful in this career.

Nature of the Work Guidance counselors work with students to help them through a variety of issues, both academic and personal. This is a very open-ended career that requires a great deal of empathy and the ability to devote attention to the unique needs of each student.

Aptitudes, Abilities, and Skills Strong interpersonal, listening, and organizational skills, a sense of humor, and enjoy working with young adults.

Academic Skills Required English Language Arts, Mathematics, Science, and Social Studies.

Student Organizations To prepare for this career, look for groups with opportunities to give guidance, such as a peer mediation group.

Career Outlook Jobs as guidance counselors are expected to grow faster than the average rate over the next ten years.

Career Path School guidance counselors often begin their careers as teachers. Some may go on to a private or group practice.

Critical Thinking

Get Advice Would you ever get help from a peer mediation program in your school? Why or why not?

 Research Careers For more information on this and other careers, visit the Occupational Outlook Handbook Web site through the link on this book's Online Learning Center at **glencoe.com**.

Section 7.1
Understand Conflict

Conflict is a disagreement or struggle between two or more people. It is created by situations, personality differences, or power struggles. Resolving conflict successfully requires several things. The problem must be defined before it can be solved. Limits need to be set on language and behavior to prevent direct attacks on each other. Negotiation and compromise help to reach a win-win solution. A mediator can be used if people cannot agree on their own. Follow up is needed to be sure the resolution was good for both people. If possible, people should work to prevent or avoid conflict.

Section 7.2
Deal with Conflict

There are many interpersonal skills needed to resolve conflict. Listening to the other person helps in understanding. Empathy, feedback, and clarification are often needed. It is important to talk to others about your feelings. I-messages help keep the discussion on the issue. Emotions and physical reactions should be kept under control. Using teamwork can be useful in resolving conflict. The timing needs to be right when dealing with conflict. During any conflict, respect is vital. The use of respectful language and attitudes helps work toward a solution. People can set an example for others in dealing successfully with conflict.

Content and Academic Vocabulary Review

1. Use each of these content and academic vocabulary words in a sentence.

Content Vocabulary
- ◇ conflict (p. 121)
- ◇ power (p. 122)
- ◇ control (p. 122)
- ◇ negotiate (p. 123)
- ◇ compromise (p. 124)
- ◇ mediator (p. 124)
- ◇ clarification (p. 127)
- ◇ competition (p. 129)
- ◇ vulnerable (p. 131)

Academic Vocabulary
- ■ tactic (p. 122)
- ■ assume (p. 122)
- ■ frustration (p. 128)
- ■ constructive (p. 129)

Review Key Concepts

2. Determine what causes conflict.

3. Describe tactics that are useful in resolving conflicts.

4. Recognize ways to avoid conflict.

5. Identify interpersonal skills that are useful in dealing with conflict.

6. Summarize how people can be respectful of others during conflicts.

7. Explain why setting a good example is important in conflict situations.

Critical Thinking

8. Draw Conclusions How can a competitive spirit sometimes be a barrier when trying to resolve a conflict?

9. Cause and Effect What factors could cause a small disagreement to become a large conflict?

Real-World Skills

Problem-Solving Skills

10. Make a Choice Kristy and Robert work part time at a drug store. Robert works hard when the store manager is watching, but hardly works the rest of the time. Kristy is frustrated. She wants to tell Robert what she thinks of him. Write a paragraph about what Kristy should do.

Communication Skills

12. Develop Skills When Alex and his girlfriend Tess have a disagreement, she becomes emotional. She cries and pouts, and he responds with silence. His refusal to talk makes her more upset and angry. Write a paragraph that explains what they could do to help solve their differences.

Technology Skills

11. Create a Presentation Use presentation software to prepare a presentation on dealing with conflict in the workplace. Include information on interpersonal skills that could be used to prevent, avoid, or resolve conflict. Show your presentation to your classmates.

Collaborative Skills

13. Evaluate Bring to class various comic strips that show conflicts. Follow your teacher's instructions to form into groups. With your group, evaluate the interpersonal skills shown in each of the comics. Suggest one skill that could help make the resolution constructive.

14. Create a Questionnaire Follow you teacher's instructions to form into groups. Create a questionnaire with your group. Design it to reveal how well a person handles conflict. Be sure to keep the questionnaires anonymous and exchange them with another group to try them out. Tally the results and share them with your classmates.

15. Observe For one week, observe conflicts in your school and neighborhood. Keep notes on your observations. Give a presentation to your class to describe what you noticed and took notes about. Share ideas and discuss solutions to the problems you saw.

16. Survey Survey your community to find resources available to help with conflict prevention and resolution. Answer these questions in your survey: What agencies deal with these issues? What kinds of programs are offered? How do people get into these programs? Are they required by the courts or voluntary? How might that affect their effectiveness?

17. Peer Mediation Programs Go to this book's Online Learning Center at **glencoe.com** to find **Web Links** for **Peer Mediation Programs**. What is their purpose? How are they set up? What is the result when they are used in high schools? Write a report on your findings.

Additional Activities For additional activities, go to this book's Online Learning Center through **glencoe.com**.

Academic Skills

 Mathematics

18. Calculate Weekly Pay Fran is a teenager who wants to get a job. She thinks that with school she will be able to work 15 hours a week. She expects 20% of her income to go to taxes. Create an inequality that represents the hourly wages Fran should expect to earn in order to end up with weekly take-home pay of $200.

Math Concept **Solve Inequalities** To solve an inequality, perform the same operations on both sides of the inequality for it to remain true. For example, if you add 5 to one side of the equation, you must add 5 to the other side.

Starting Hint: Using the variable *x* to represent the hourly wage, write an inequality to solve the problem. The total take-home pay ($200) will be on one side of the inequality. The hours worked times the variable wage (15x) minus the before-tax income (0.2 × 15x) will be on the other side. Solve for x, making sure to express the answer as an inequality.

 For math help, go to the Math Appendix at the back of the book.

> **NCTM Problem Solving** Apply and adapt a variety of appropriate strategies to solve problems.

 English Language Arts

19. Write a Dialogue Think of a topic that may cause a conflict. One example may include who should clean the dishes tonight. Write a dialogue that shows how a conflict such as this one can be resolved constructively. Use language that sounds real and appropriate to the people talking. Write with accurate grammar and spelling. Remember to use quotation marks appropriately.

> **NCTE 6** Apply knowledge of language structure and conventions to discuss texts.

 Social Studies

20. Research Conduct research to find examples of groups and agencies that help families resolve conflicts. Find one group that interests you the most. Look into the specific conflict resolution strategies the group uses. Do they discuss the importance of setting limits, negotiating, or getting outside help? Share what you learned with your classmates in a one-paragraph summary.

> **NCSS I.a** Analyze and explain the ways groups, societies, and cultures address human needs and concerns.

STANDARDIZED TEST PRACTICE

MULTIPLE CHOICE
Read the following question. Then read the answer choices and choose the best possible answer.

> **Test-Taking Tip** Be sure to read the entire question and all of the answers. To be true, all parts of a statement must be true.

21. Which of these statements is true?
   a. Needless conflict cannot be avoided.
   b. Conflict can have either constructive or destructive results.
   c. Defining the problem, setting limits, and following up are not important for successful conflict resolution.
   d. Teamwork is not a factor in finding lasting solutions to conflicts.

CHAPTER 8

Build Family Relationships

Section 8.1

Qualities of Strong Families

Section 8.2

Strengthen Family Relationships

 Explore the Photo

Families look forward to celebrating together. *In what ways do your family members celebrate and honor each other?*

Chapter Objectives

After completing this chapter, you will be able to:

- **Identify** the qualities and skills needed to build a strong family.
- **Explain** the importance of spending time together in the family.
- **Describe** a family system.
- **Suggest** ways that teens can improve relationships with parents or guardians.
- **Identify** ways that teens can build stronger ties with siblings.

Writing Activity Poem

Humor Humor is the ability to see the lighter side of a situation. It can help build relationships if you laugh with others, not at them. You can show a sense of humor when you:

- Frost a cake that flopped and serve it as volcano cake.
- Give a favorite baby sweater that shrank in the wash to the family dog to wear.
- Make a large name tag to wear to class after a teacher has repeatedly forgotten your name.

Write your own poem about how you have used humor recently. If you have trouble thinking of something, try freewriting to come up with an idea for your poem.

Writing Tips To write an effective poem, follow these steps:

1. Use poetic devices such as similes and metaphors. An example of a simile is "as cool as a cucumber." An example of a metaphor is "it is raining cats and dogs."
2. Decide whether rhyme or free verse will be more effective.
3. Use sensory details and clear language to convey your feelings.

Qualities of Strong Families

Reading Guide

Before You Read

Create an Outline Use the section's heading titles to create an outline. Make the titles into levels. Use the outline to predict what you will learn.

Read to Learn
Key Concepts
- **Identify** the qualities and skills needed to build a strong family.
- **Explain** the importance of spending time together in the family.

Main Idea
Families have certain qualities that make them strong, such as communication skills, respect, unity, and family traditions.

Content Vocabulary
◇ affirmation   ◇ tradition
◇ commitment

Academic Vocabulary
You will find these words in your reading and on your tests. Use the glossary to look up their definitions if necessary.
▪ stable   ▪ tact

Graphic Organizer
As you read, identify qualities of strong families. Use a concept map like the one shown to help organize your information.

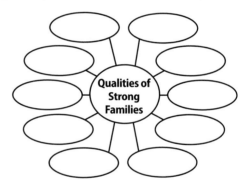

 Graphic Organizer Go to this book's Online Learning Center at **glencoe.com** to print out this graphic organizer.

Academic Standards

 English Language Arts
NCTE 4 Use written language to communicate effectively.
NCTE 5 Use different writing process elements to communicate effectively.

 Mathematics
NCTM Problem Solving Monitor and reflect on the process of problem solving.

NCTE *National Council of Teachers of English*
NCTM *National Council of Teachers of Mathematics*

NSES *National Science Education Standards*
NCSS *National Council of the Social Studies*

Strong Families

A strong family is comparable to a winning team. Both work to build the skills needed for success. Like a winning team, families have to learn skills and qualities, such as communication and commitment, to become strong.

Social scientists have long studied families. They have listed qualities and actions that strong families share. Not every family has every quality. The more they have, the better their chance of building strong family bonds.

Children learn how to relate to others from their experiences within the family. They learn the skills that support the families' strengths. These skills work for them as they move into the outside world. In strong families, members are apt to have good relationships with others outside of the family.

As you read about strong families, you may see some of the qualities of your family. You can build on those. You may also spot some weaknesses. Remember that any family can improve if the members want to. Strong families are found where people work together toward a goal.

Communication

Open communication is vital to any relationship in and outside the family. In the family it fills a need for closeness. It is a sign that family members are in touch with each other's feelings and lives. Good communication helps keep the family **stable**, or steady.

One common barrier to good family communication is the television. Some people can get wrapped up in the lives of fictional families. As a result, they may fail to interact with their own. The television can also cause people to have unrealistic expectations of what family life should be. Families should work to control barriers such as the television.

As You Read

Connect What qualities does your family have that contribute to its strengths?

Vocabulary

You can find definitions in the glossary at the back of this book.

◀) *Family Time*

Families can learn to control communication barriers such as the television. *How can your family enjoy time together while watching the television?*

Affirm Each Other

In strong families, people show their love clearly. They do this both verbally and nonverbally. Family members find many ways to show their good feelings toward each other. When you do this, you are giving **affirmation** (ˌa-fər-ˈmā-shən). This means you give positive input that helps others feel appreciated and supported.

Some people do not share their feelings directly. This may leave family members wondering how others feel about them. It is unrewarding when people have to guess whether others care about them. Most people want others to show or say how they feel.

Respect Each Other

Another mark of a strong family is respect for each other. Family members see that each person is different. They take pride in individual traits and abilities. They do not take advantage of anyone's shortcomings. Family members of all ages are respected.

Respect for others' opinions takes **tact**, or skill and grace when dealing with others. In a strong family, members are tactful and respect each other's opinions. Family members are able to draw their own conclusions. For example, Matthew has political views that differ from his parents'. They listen to his opinions. Matthew responds by trying to understand their point of view.

Everyone has a need for privacy at times. Each person needs a safe place for personal things and time to be alone. Strong families respect this need. They try to step back and make room for each other. This can happen even when living space is small.

▶▶ Learn to Trust
Children learn to trust at an early age when they find that their parents meet their needs. *Should you give someone a second chance if you have lost trust in them?*

Show Unity

Members of a strong family appreciate the many ways that they are united. They build unity and become a team. They share trust, beliefs, and responsibility. Unity takes work. Family members must find time to be together. Family activities help develop unity.

Demonstrate Commitment

A **commitment** is a pledge to support something of value. People who value the family are committed to it. They are willing to work together. They give up things for the benefit of the family unit. They take genuine interest in the happiness and welfare of each family member. Time and energy are invested in family activities. Families who are committed to each other tend to have fewer problems and less conflict.

Trust Each Other

Trust is important in the family. Family members must know they can count on each other. Children learn trust as infants when their parents supply what they need. Trust builds when parents are caring and true to their word. People who learn trust in the family tend to see the world as a safe place. They learn to rely on others.

Children, in turn, learn to be worthy of trust. Ten-year-old Gerard, for example, showed he could be trusted when he came home on time for lunch. His grandmother feels good about letting him play at his friend's house again. As he matures, Gerard will be given more freedom.

Learning to trust and be trustworthy is not always easy. Children and parents alike can and do make mistakes. Once trust is lost, it is very hard to regain. The best way to maintain trust is to be and act trustworthy. However, strong families believe in second chances. Members work to do better when they are given another chance to be trusted.

Share Values and Beliefs

Strong families share many values and beliefs. These may be ideas about education and politics. They may share religious beliefs and a moral code. A core of beliefs provides stability and a shared outlook on life. Shared values lead to shared activities. These can help build family ties.

A family may share a belief in an ideal beyond themselves. For example, Nathan's family believes in caring for nature. His mother runs a recycling program. His father is a science teacher who advocates for a clean environment. Family vacations are spent backpacking in national parks. Their deep sense of concern for nature brings the family together.

Math in Action

Family Vacations

A family vacation can be a good way to strengthen family relationships. Use these steps to complete a vacation budget.

1. Decide how many nights you will need to pay for lodging.

2. Determine how many times you will dine out.

3. Determine transportation costs.

4. Determine how much entertainment will cost.

Math Concept **Problem Solving**

When a math problem involves multiple steps, it is helpful to outline the information before you solve it. Make a list of the information you already have and the information you are investigating, then decide how to use the information to solve the problem.

Starting Hint: Add all of the individual costs (lodging, food, etc.) to find the total vacation budget.

 Building Academic Skills
Go to this book's Online Learning Center through **glencoe.com** to complete a worksheet for this activity.

NCTM Problem Solving Monitor and reflect on the process of problem solving.

 For math help, go to the Math Appendix at the back of the book.

Many families find strength in faith. Belief in a higher power can give families hope. It helps them remain positive about life. This can be especially helpful during troubled times. Families who participate in organized religion often make faith a part of their daily lives.

Build Strong Morals

Many families have a moral code. A moral code consists of principles of right and wrong. Strong families communicate this code clearly. Parents who agree on basic issues are more likely to teach morals. They discuss their beliefs. This helps parents support each other in what they teach to their children. Children are expected to respect the family moral code.

Act Responsibly

Strong families practice and teach responsibility. People learn to do the jobs that are expected of them. They do this without needing reminders or pressure from other members of the family. Family members also show responsibility by caring for each other and giving support. Each family member can act responsibly by doing a task that contributes to the smooth running of the home.

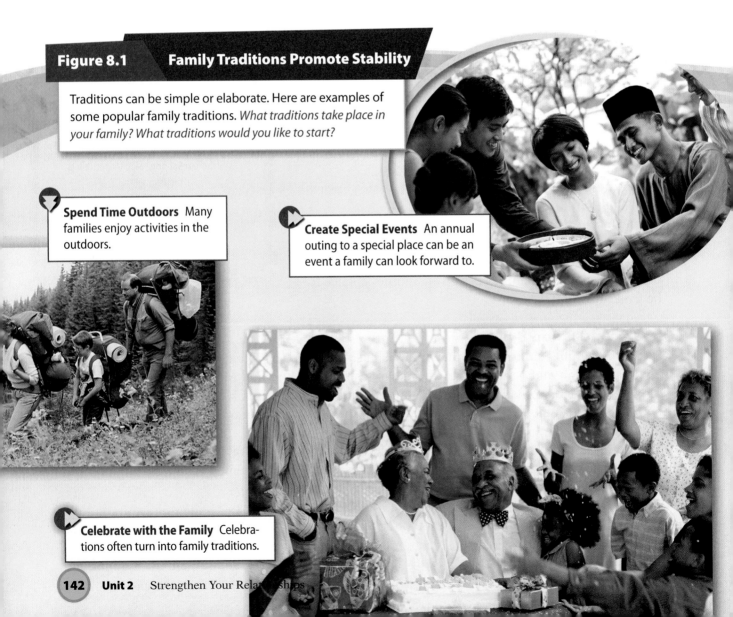

Figure 8.1   Family Traditions Promote Stability

Traditions can be simple or elaborate. Here are examples of some popular family traditions. *What traditions take place in your family? What traditions would you like to start?*

Spend Time Outdoors Many families enjoy activities in the outdoors.

Create Special Events An annual outing to a special place can be an event a family can look forward to.

Celebrate with the Family Celebrations often turn into family traditions.

Overcome Problems as a Team

All families have problems. Strong families figure out ways to approach and solve their problems together. They use good communication skills to spot a problem early. This is when the problem is the most manageable. They are committed enough to the family to work and even sacrifice for solutions.

When real trouble strikes, strong families pull together as a team. They know that they are stronger when they are together rather than apart. They trust in one another and in their shared beliefs. Sometimes problems may be beyond a family's ability to solve. If this happens, the family looks to outside resources for help.

✓ **Reading Check**) **Explain** What is an affirmation?

Spend Time Together

Can you feel close to people if you rarely spend time with them? When families spend time together, it is both a sign of family strength and a way to build it. Strong families have common interests and activities. When families participate in these activities together, it increases the traits that keep them strong. Families also share traditions, as shown in **Figure 8.1**. A **tradition** is a custom that is followed over time. Traditions help keep families together.

Help Around the House Certain chores that families complete together can also turn into family traditions.

Have Shared Hobbies A hobby or interest is an activity that promotes sharing and improves relationships.

Take Time to Travel Traveling with your family can create family traditions and memories that last a lifetime.

In many families, finding time for each other is a struggle. Jobs, school, volunteer work, and other activities cut into family time. These things are important because people need personal fulfillment.

Family members, however, also need to make a commitment to being with family. Sharing at least one leisure activity a week is a goal many strong families achieve. For example, a family may make the time to have a family night every Friday night. Another way families can spend time together is by sharing housework. Several members of the family can help each other out with chores. This can make cleaning up more fun.

Establish Traditions

Part of a family's time together can be spent creating traditions. These are often passed from one generation to another. They build family memories and enhance stability.

Traditions can be simple or complex. For example, a simple tradition may be a family having pizza for dinner every Sunday night. An annual block party for the neighborhood, however, takes more time and work. An event such as a block party, although complex, can promote a tradition for not only a family, but for the community as well.

Many families have traditions that are based on their cultural heritage. The traditions are one way that families teach their members about their culture. Children can learn how to prepare certain foods. The family may take part in a community cultural festival. They may observe rituals at home that have meaning in their culture. However they are observed, traditions are a part of the life of strong families.

Section 8.1 After You Read

Review Key Concepts

1. **Explain** why certain qualities are important in family life.
2. **Discuss** why families often find it hard to spend time together.

Practice Academic Skills

English Language Arts

3. Suppose your drama teacher has called a last-minute play practice. You were supposed to watch your sister after school. You arrange for your best friend to stay with your sister. You need to let your mother know about your plans. Write out how you will communicate this situation to your mother in a phone call.

> **NCTE 5** Use different writing process elements to communicate effectively.

4. Select one way that a family can show unity. Write a paragraph that explains why this contributes to family unity. Give details of what a family can do when they show unity this way.

> **NCTE 4** Use written language to communicate effectively.

Check Your Answers Check your answers at this book's Online Learning Center through glencoe.com.

Strengthen Family Relationships

Reading Guide

Before You Read

Stay Engaged One way to stay engaged when reading is to turn each of the headings into a question, then read the section to find the answers.

Read to Learn
Key Concepts
- **Describe** a family system.
- **Suggest** ways that teens can improve relationships with parents or guardians.
- **Identify** ways that teens can build stronger ties with siblings.

Main Idea
A family system is family members, with their roles and personalities, acting together. Good relationships with parents and siblings will strengthen the family system.

Content Vocabulary
◇ family system
◇ nurture
◇ sibling
◇ heredity
◇ subjective
◇ birth order

Academic Vocabulary
You will find these words in your reading and on your tests. Use the glossary to look up their definitions if necessary.
■ intrigued   ■ novice

Graphic Organizer
As you read, look for concerns that parents have. Use a chart like the one shown to help organize your information.

Parental Concerns
- _____ • _____
- _____ • _____

 Graphic Organizer Go to this book's Online Learning Center at **glencoe.com** to print out this graphic organizer.

Academic Standards •

 English Language Arts

NCTE 4 Use written language to communicate effectively.

NCTE 12 Use language to accomplish individual purposes.

 Mathematics

NCTM Number and Operations Understand the meanings of operations and how they relate to one another.

NCTE *National Council of Teachers of English*
NCTM *National Council of Teachers of Mathematics*
NSES *National Science Education Standards*
NCSS *National Council of the Social Studies*

The Family System

Vocabulary

You can find definitions in the glossary at the back of this book.

A **family system** is family members, with their roles and personalities, acting together. It is like a web that ties members to each other. What any person in the system does affects others. Suppose you come home humming cheerfully. You offer to make dinner when it is not your turn. What reactions can you expect from others? How might their reactions, in turn, affect you? In the family system, everything is connected. Every action by one person brings a reaction in others.

One goal of a family system is to nurture its members. To **nurture** means to help growth or development. In the web-like family system, nurturing is everyone's job. In strong families, each person nurtures all the others. In turn, each gets nurtured. This promotes the growth and development of all members.

As You Read

Connect What are some nurturing acts that you have witnessed in your family?

Getting along within the family system can be a challenge. When people make an effort, however, the family system functions well. Each person is important. The family system is only as strong as the people in it. When families support each member, the system itself grows stronger.

✓ **Reading Check** **Explain** What is a family system?

Relate to Parents

Most teens have one or more adults who fill the parent role. These adults may be parents, stepparents, or legal guardians. Whatever your situation, you can apply the principles about parents described here.

Most relationships between parents and teens are loving. Surveys of teens show that most get along well with their parents. They have strong relationships with them. In any close relationship, however, problems can occur. In order to keep relationships with parents strong, it can be helpful to try and understand your parents' point of view. It is also important to talk to your parents and respect the limits and rules they set.

◀ *Family Roles*
The many roles you have in your family system also include responsibilities. *What are some of the roles and responsibilities you have in your family?*

Understand Parents

Getting along with people is easier when you understand them. Many books have been written for parents on understanding teens. To make the relationship work well, teens must also understand their parents.

Show Empathy

To improve understanding, nothing works better than empathy. Try writing a job description for parenting. The job lasts for years. It has many duties. There is no salary. Most people are not taught how to parent. Parents are human. They want to do a good job. They do not want to make mistakes any more than you do. Putting yourself in a parent's shoes can help you understand them.

You have your own concerns and pressures in your life. Why should you bother to make an extra effort to get along with your parents? The answer is simple. You need each other. You will continue to do so, probably for a long time. Destructive patterns and habits become harder to break the longer they go on.

First steps are often the most difficult. What you do now may set the tone of your relationship with your parents for your entire adult life. A parent-teen relationship strengthens as mutual understanding grows. If you want your parents to be there for you, then you need to be there for them, too.

Parents' Concerns

As a teen, you may have many concerns about life. Parents also have plenty to think about. They may be concerned with many of the following issues.

- **Making a Living** Handling the pressures of work can be stressful, especially if the parent is unhappy with the job. In certain times, keeping a job can be a concern.
- **Providing for You** Most parents want to give children more than they had when they were children. They often would like to give more than they are able.
- **The Family Situation** Decisions about caring for older family members and other family problems are a parent's duty.
- **Health** Not everyone is in good health. Age may make parents a little slower or more tired than before.
- **The Future** Just like you, parents may worry about how they will manage as they get older.
- **You** Parents worry about whether they have taught you to make wise choices. You are a major part of their lives.

Many other concerns can also affect how a parent acts. Preoccupation or moodiness often has nothing to do with you. It helps to remember that parents have their own needs and ups and downs in life, just like you do.

Financial Literacy

Clothing Costs

Marc and his wife went shopping for new clothes for his upcoming job interview. They found the following on sale: a $140 suit at $35 off, a $232 briefcase at 25% off, and two pairs of socks that are $8.00 each. How much did Marc and his wife spend?

Math Concept Order of Operations

To solve an equation, you must use the correct order of operations. First, simplify within the parentheses. Multiply and divide from left to right, then add and subtract from left to right.

Starting Hint: Before solving this problem, write an expression using the correct symbols (remember that 25% off means that he paid 75% (0.75) of the price: ($140 − $35) + ($232 × 0.75) + (2 × $8). Solve using the correct order of operations.

 For math help, go to the Math Appendix at the back of the book.

NCTM Number and Operations Understand the meanings of operations and how they relate to one another.

Different Perspectives

Understanding parents also hinges on knowing what motivates them. They do not always see things the same way you do. Their experiences and backgrounds are different from yours.

Although it comes as a surprise to some teens, most parents do know some things. Just as you have knowledge that can be helpful to a young child, parents have experience and wisdom that can be helpful to you. When you ask for help or information, parents feel useful and special to you. When you respect their opinions as adults, they see that you are moving closer to adulthood yourself.

Talk to Parents

Teens want to be treated as adults. Parents, however, still see them as children. This is due in part to the fact that teens have known their parents only as adults, but parents have watched their children change dramatically. This can explain part of why parents treat and talk to teens as they do. Demanding adult treatment is not apt to improve matters. Show that you deserve to be treated as an adult.

INDEPENDENT Living

HOW TO Strengthen Relationships with Parents or Guardians

Taking small steps to build your relationships with your parents or guardians can benefit everyone involved for years to come. Follow these guidelines to strengthen your relationships with your parents or guardians:

1. **Get to know your parent or guardian.** Your parents or guardians were young once. They may have had experiences similar to yours. Getting to know your parents as people can take your relationship to a new level.
2. **Keep a positive attitude.** Making your voice neutral or positive, even when you do not like what is being said to you, can make your conversations easier.
3. **Take initiative.** If your parent has had a bad day, bring him or her a cup of tea, or make dinner without being asked. Small gestures like these go a long way towards building a healthy relationship.
4. **Be trustworthy.** Arrive home at the agreed upon time. Do an errand you promised to do. The more you can be trusted, the more privileges you will earn.
5. **Use humor.** If you feel that a conversation with a parent or guardian is not going well, use humor to lighten the situation and get the conversation back on track.

Take Action Write a letter to yourself from your parent's or guardian's point of view. How does it feel to stand in the other person's shoes? Does the change in point of view give you more understanding of your parent or guardian? Does it make you look at yourself in a different way?

Parents and teens often do not understand each other. By talking with each other, they can know each other better. The goal is conversation that is pleasant and helpful, not hostile. Try these suggestions for improving your talks with your parents:

- **Take time to get to know your parents.** Simple questions about their lives pave the way for more involved talk.
- **Be positive.** So often it is not what is said, but how it is said. A short, snippy response may set a negative tone and even end a conversation.
- **Look for easy approaches to tough topics.** Talk about a television show or a movie to ease you into touchy subjects. Parents are just as uncomfortable as you are about some topics.
- **Use humor.** When things start to get heavy, look for ways to lighten up.

Limits and Rules

Parents do not set limits and rules for fun. Enforcing rules is not always easy. It is needed for several reasons. Parents set limits and rules to direct family life. They want to be sure the family's values are carried out. Rules can also help children develop positive traits, such as caring and honesty. Parents also set rules in order to protect their family. Rules about crossing the street and curfews are set with safety in mind.

Limits and rules can be a source of conflict for families. As teens become more independent, they may feel that some rules are too strict. Teens may feel ready for more freedom. Calmly discussing the subject with parents is the best way to reach agreement. Parents loosen rules at a pace they are comfortable with. Teens who have earned parents' trust are often given more privileges.

✓ **Reading Check** **Identify** What quality is necessary in a good relationship with parents?

Follow the Rules
Parents often set rules and limits to protect their children. *Why are limits and rules sometimes a source of conflict between teens and their parents?*

Relate to Siblings

A **sibling** is your brother or your sister. Relationships with siblings tend to be the longest of all family ties. They last as long as the siblings' lives. They are also among the most complex. Sisters and brothers in a family usually have very distinct personalities. Psychologists have been **intrigued**, or interested, by this and have looked for explanations.

Heredity and Environment

The family provides the two major factors that affect personality. These are heredity and environment. **Heredity** (hə-'re-də-tē) involves the genetic traits received from parents at birth. Environment is the surroundings that shape growth. It includes both people and experiences. Combining heredity and environment make siblings similar and different. Social scientists have studied identical twins that were raised apart. These studies have shown how heredity affects people. The twins were raised in different home environments. Still, they showed striking likenesses. These were linked to their common heritage. From studies like these, most researchers have concluded that heredity plays a large role in shaping personality.

The question of environment is also very interesting. Experience contributes a great deal to personality. Environment does have an effect. The process is more complex than you may think. Each child experiences the family environment subjectively. **Subjective** means relying on one's personal feelings and opinions. The facts of family life are filtered by the child's personality and perceptions. Thus, similar experiences in the family can lead to very different results in siblings.

Birth Order

Some psychologists believe that birth order shapes a person's personality. **Birth order** is the order in which each child is born. It affects the family environment for each child. As a first child, for instance, Erin was born to **novice**, or new, parents. They gave her their full attention. When her sister was born, the couple had more confidence in their skills and roles as parents. They had less time to spend on a baby. When Rich was born, he came into a family of four. He had to find a place in the ongoing relationships the four had with each other. In a sense, the three children were each born into a different family environment. Their personalities and ideas about relationships were bound to be different as well.

◀◀ *Build Sibling Relationships*
Building a relationship with one sibling may be different from building a relationship with another sibling. *What effect do you think age has in building sibling relationships?*

Sibling rivalry is competition between brothers and sisters. They compete for love, recognition, and to be treated fairly by parents. Some look for signs of favoritism. Feeling mistreated leads to complaints, fights, and even low self-esteem. If sibling rivalry is a problem for you, ask these questions:

- Do you keep track of the privileges that come your way as well as the unfair treatment? It is human nature to notice a sibling's special moment and forget yours.
- Could parents have reasons that are not clear to you? Often they do.

- Are you exactly like your siblings? Differences can account for different treatment.
- Do your siblings feel that you are favored? If so, then who is right?

Problem-Solving Joel is jealous of his sister. Suze is good at many sports. Their parents go to her games and are proud of her. Joel is a musician. Their parents attend his concerts, but he feels that they do not seem as excited about his solos as they do when Suze scores points. What can you say to Joel to help him overcome his sibling rivalry?

First-Born Children

Parents tend to expect a great deal of their first-born child. Oldest children tend to grow up responsible, independent, and ambitious. They help teach or take care of younger siblings. Many first-born children become leaders and achievers.

Middle Children

Second or middle children are less involved with parents than the older sibling was. They are often cheerful and practical. They thrive on social activities and friendships. Middle children also tend to be peacemakers and strive to please others.

Youngest Children

Youngest children must learn early in life to get along with others. The experience can make them popular, fun loving, and generous. Sometimes, the youngest child is spoiled by parents and siblings. This can lead to being self-centered. Growing up in the shadow of older siblings can be a challenge. The youngest child often has to work hard to find his or her own identity.

Only Children

Children without siblings usually get a lot of attention from their parents. They are often watched more closely than children in larger families. Lacking siblings, they may relate better to adults than to other children. They may try harder to please their parents. Only children tend to be fast learners, good students, and high achievers. They tend to lead busy, productive lives.

It is interesting to look at the possible effects of birth order. Still, not every person fits the profiles. Each person is an individual. Some fit the overall patterns, some do not.

Manage Sibling Relationships

Studies have shown that siblings do share one trait. They constantly compare how they are treated in the family. Their view of the treatment, however, is not always accurate. Other studies have found that parents, in general, treat their children in much the same way at specific ages. They have little control, however, over how their children perceive what they do.

Feelings of being at odds with siblings are normal. Managing those feelings can make family life smoother. To get along better with siblings, try the following ideas.

- **Work on settling disagreements with siblings yourself.** Parents will not always know who is right and who is wrong. Asking them to support one of their children against another is unfair. Any decision they make may be held against them.

- **Talk about your feelings.** As a child, your parents had to help you recognize your feelings. Now you must communicate your feelings to your siblings.

- **Look for your own strengths instead of comparing yourself to siblings.** Siblings are as different from you as friends are, so why compare?

- **Avoid serious conflict with siblings.** They will be important people in your life for many years to come. It makes sense to take good care of these relationships.

The stress of daily life with siblings may make relationships hard to manage. It is worth making the effort. Your bonds with your siblings will last a lifetime. How you get along with your family affects how everyone gets along. Be an example for others to follow. Begin now with a personal commitment to family strength.

Section 8.2 After You Read

Review Key Concepts

1. **Explain** why a family system is compared to a web.
2. **Describe** why good relationships with parents are important in the teen years.
3. **Identify** what siblings are.

Practice Academic Skills

English Language Arts

4. Make a list of four reasons parents set limits and rules. Then write a paragraph that explains why your parents set limits and rules.

5. Write a letter to your parents that explains why parents often see issues differently from their children.

NCTE 12 Use language to accomplish individual purposes.

NCTE 4 Use written language to communicate effectively.

Check Your Answers Check your answers at this book's Online Learning Center through **glencoe.com**.

CHAPTER SUMMARY

Section 8.1
Qualities of Strong Families

Families have to learn skills and qualities to become strong. They learn to communicate effectively. They affirm, or give positive input, to each other to show their support. They show respect for each other. Family unity happens when a family works together as a team. Family members are committed to each other. They share trust, values, and beliefs. Strong morals are a part of family life. Members act responsibly. Teamwork helps them overcome problems. Strong families spend time together. They establish and enjoy traditions as a family.

Section 8.2
Strengthen Family Relationships

Every family has a family system. This is how the personalities and roles of family members act together. What affects one person affects all of them. When teens build strong ties with parents, they will make a base for years to come. Empathy will help teens understand parents' concerns and perspectives. Parents and teens need to talk. Limits and rules are set to direct family life. They also keep members safe. Siblings are brothers and sisters. Sibling relationships tend to be the longest lasting of any in life. Heredity, environment, and birth order affect sibling relationships.

Content and Academic Vocabulary Review

1. Use each of these content and academic vocabulary words in a sentence.

Content Vocabulary
◇ affirmation (p. 140) ◇ sibling (p. 149)
◇ commitment (p. 141) ◇ heredity (p. 150)
◇ tradition (p. 143) ◇ subjective (p. 150)
◇ family system (p. 146) ◇ birth order (p. 150)
◇ nurture (p. 146)

Academic Vocabulary
■ stable (p. 139)
■ tact (p. 140)
■ intrigued (p. 149)
■ novice (p. 150)

Review Key Concepts

2. Identify the qualities and skills needed to build a strong family.
3. Explain the importance of spending time together in the family.
4. Describe a family system.
5. Suggest ways that teens can improve relationships with parents or guardians.
6. Identify ways that teens can build stronger ties with siblings.

Critical Thinking

7. Evaluate How do video and computer games or television affect family strength?
8. Analyze Why is giving affirmation difficult for people in some families?
9. Explain Why do you think many parents are reluctant to share personal concerns with their children?

Real-World Skills

Interpersonal Skills

10. Show Understanding Todd's mother has been upset. Todd asks her what is wrong. His mother says, "I'm sorry. It is nothing to worry about." Todd's grandmother has been sick. He thinks this is causing his mother's moods. What should Todd do?

Communication Skills

11. Practice Affirmations Set a goal to give ten affirmations a day to family members for a week. Each day, make a record of the affirmations you gave. At the end of the week, write a paragraph about what happened. Were affirmations easier to give with practice? How did you feel when you affirmed others? Did you get more affirmations when you gave more?

Decision-Making Skills

12. Family Traditions Bethany's family has family fun night on Sundays. Bethany feels she has outgrown this tradition. Her parents and siblings still enjoy it. She knows they would be hurt if she did not join in. What should Bethany do?

Critical Thinking Skills

13. Identify Values Follow your teacher's instructions to form into groups. List five topics on which parents set rules. Half of the group will write rules for these topics as if they were the parents. The other half will write rules that teens think are reasonable. Discuss your results. Compare your rules. Compare and contrast the values that are shown in each list.

14. Family Network Follow your teacher's instructions to form into groups. Each person needs a ball of yarn to make a large loop several yards in length. Members should now put their loops around their waists, connecting the group members. The loops represent the family system. Move around the classroom. What conclusions can you draw from this activity? How do these connections compare with those in a real family?

15. Investigate Look for resources in your community that strengthen families. This can include student organizations such as FCCLA. Are there classes to improve communication or volunteer activities for the whole family? Compile your findings in a brochure.

16. Make a Scrapbook Photo albums and scrapbooks can become a family tradition. With another family member, make a family scrapbook. Put photos and captions together in a positive, creative way.

17. Activities Go to this book's Online Learning Center at **glencoe.com** to find **Web Links** for **Family Activities**. Choose an activity that would promote quality family time for your family.

Additional Activities For additional activities, go to this book's Online Learning Center at **glencoe.com**.

Academic Skills

Mathematics

18. Calculate Costs Anna has asked to borrow money from her mother to prepare materials for her first job. She wants to give her mother a breakdown of the costs. Stationery will cost $23.45, envelopes will cost $18.63, stamps will cost $7.80, and a new pen will cost $3.99. What will the total expenditures be?

Math Concept **Adding Decimals** To add decimals, simply list the numbers vertically. Add normally from right to left, carrying when necessary. Be sure to bring the decimal point down into the answer.

Starting Hint: List the numbers ($23.45, $18.63, $7.80, and $3.99) in a vertical line with the decimal points lined up. Then add, starting with the hundredths place. Be sure to place the decimal point correctly in the answer, and label the answer.

 For math help, go to the Math Appendix at the back of the book.

> **NCTM Number and Operations** Compute fluently and make reasonable estimates.

English Language Arts

19. Write a Paper Think about the different sibling relationships described in this chapter. If you could choose, would you be an only child, a child with one sibling, or a child with several siblings? Write a short paper explaining your choice. Explain the advantages and disadvantages of your decision.

> **NCTE 4** Use written language to communicate effectively.

Social Studies

20. Research Alfred Adler was one of the first psychologists to suggest that birth order affects personality. Conduct research to find more information on birth order, including only children. Write a one-page report that describes your findings. Do you think birth order has affected your personality? If you are an only child, has that affected your personality? Why or why not?

> **NCSS IV.d** Apply concepts, methods, and theories about the study of human growth and development.

STANDARDIZED TEST PRACTICE

MULTIPLE CHOICE
Read the following paragraph. Then read and answer the question that follows.

21. How can you build strong family relationships? Here are some suggestions: Take time to get to know your parents, try to have a positive attitude, look for easy approaches to difficult topics, and use humor when appropriate.

Based on the paragraph above, which of the following statements is true?

a. Humor can always defuse a negative situation.

b. All topics should be treated seriously.

c. Always look for the best, most complicated approach to solving family issues.

d. Getting to know your parents can help build strong family relationships.

Test-Taking Tip With multiple choice questions that rely on information given, read the paragraph very carefully to make sure you understand what it is about. Read the answer choices. Then read the paragraph again before choosing the answer.

CHAPTER 9

Working with Others

● **Section 9.1**

Working Relationships

● **Section 9.2**

Teamwork and Leadership

▶▶ *Explore the Photo*
Working together in school and in the community prepares you for the future. *In what ways can a working relationship at school affect your relationships in a future career?*

Chapter Objectives

After completing this chapter, you will be able to:

- **Identify** elements of good working relationships.
- **Explain** the importance of relationships on the job.
- **Describe** the benefits of good working relationships at school and in the community.
- **Suggest** qualities and skills that improve teamwork.
- **Summarize** the qualities needed for leadership.

Writing Activity Personal Letter

Dedication You are dedicated when you devote yourself to or commit yourself to something you value. You can show dedication when you:

- Rehearse every night with the drama club for an upcoming musical.
- Become president of a group that supports a good cause.
- Volunteer to work at an animal shelter.
- Go to a grandmother's birthday party instead of out with friends.

Think about a cause or an event to which you are dedicated. Write a letter to one of your friends that promotes the cause and shows why it is worthy of your dedication.

Writing Tips To write an effective letter, follow these steps:

1. Give information about the cause and why it is important.
2. Tell others how they can participate in the cause.
3. Express your thoughts and feelings clearly.

Working Relationships

Reading Guide

Before You Read

Prior Knowledge Write down what you already know and what you want to find out about each key concept in this section.

Read to Learn

Key Concepts

- **Identify** elements of good working relationships.
- **Explain** the importance of relationships on the job.
- **Describe** the benefits of good working relationships at school and in the community.

Main Idea

Good working relationships are needed on the job, at school, and in the community.

Content Vocabulary

◇ working relationship
◇ cooperation
◇ reciprocation
◇ etiquette
◇ authority

 **Graphic Organizer** Go to this book's Online Learning Center at **glencoe.com** to print out this graphic organizer.

Academic Vocabulary

You will find these words in your reading and on your tests. Use the glossary to look up their definitions if necessary.

■ initiative   ■ foresight

Graphic Organizer

As you read, look for skills and attitudes that help build good working relationships. Use a concept web like the one shown to help organize your information.

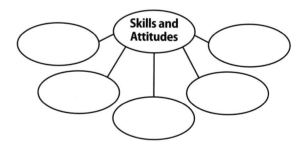

Skills and Attitudes

Academic Standards • • • • • • • • • • • • • • •

English Language Arts

NCTE 7 Conduct research and gather, evaluate, and synthesize data to communicate discoveries.

NCTE 12 Use language to accomplish individual purposes.

Mathematics

NCTM Problem Solving Apply and adapt a variety of appropriate strategies to solve problems.

NCTE *National Council of Teachers of English*
NCTM *National Council of Teachers of Mathematics*

NSES *National Science Education Standards*
NCSS *National Council of the Social Studies*

Elements of Good Working Relationships

A **working relationship** is one that exists to accomplish a task or goal. For teens, the two most common working relationships are those at school and on the job. You may also work with people in your neighborhood or other community groups.

Who influences your working relationships the most? You do. Your actions affect how others act. You can take the **initiative**, or the first step, to improve a relationship. Some people let pride or insecurity get in the way of taking action. They wait for others to make the first move. A strong, confident person is willing to reach out—and enjoys the results.

Skills and Attitudes

As you grow older, you will probably have more working relationships. Certain skills and attitudes will help you in all of them. A good working relationship blends personal warmth with respect and kindness.

A Friendly Attitude

A friendly attitude toward others creates a good impression. It helps others feel good. People feel noticed when you smile, look them in the eye, and use their name. You show that you like people, even if you do not know them well. Friendly people are a pleasure to work with.

Of course, no one can be friendly and upbeat all the time. Nearly everyone has times when they are down. Constant complaining and bad moods, however, bring the people around you down as well.

Vocabulary

You can find definitions in the glossary at the back of this book.

As You Read

Connect Think of some ways your actions can affect how others act.

◀) *Building Work Relationships* The actions you display in your work now can set the stage for your work in the future. *What actions would you consider important in a good working relationship?*

Sometimes you can pull yourself out of a bad mood if you try. If you have a problem that needs attention, talk with someone who can help. Working relations improve when people solve serious personal problems.

Respect

Have you ever given a speech in class and noticed that some of your classmates were talking or reading a book? How did you feel? When someone is talking, a respectful person listens. If a person has a problem, they show concern and offer to help. A respectful person takes other people and their opinions seriously.

Cooperation

The ability to work with others towards a common goal is called **cooperation**. Cooperation allows people to accomplish what they need. Owen, for example, works weekends at a hospital. One of his teachers requested his help with a school fund-raiser. Owen asked his manager for that weekend off. He offered to make up the time on other days. This showed cooperation. His manager agreed to the plan.

Reciprocation

Good working relationships are based on giving and receiving in return. This is called **reciprocation** (ri-,si-prə-'kā-shən). People tend to get back what they give. If you approach people in a friendly way, they tend to be open to you. If you show that you respect others, they are more apt to regard you highly. If you show a willingness to cooperate, others are more likely to meet you halfway.

Etiquette

Good manners, or **etiquette**, are the rules of appropriate behavior. These will help you deal personally and professionally with others. Being courteous and showing kindness can make your life run smoothly.

Dwayne, for example, keeps his relationship with his dentist smooth by remembering his appointment date and arriving on time. At work he holds the door open for others to enter. He also greets people as they arrive. Something as simple as good table manners can affect how people see you at work and in the community.

Good manners can often be forgotten at home because family members spend so much time together. Words such as "please" and "thank you" should be a regular part of a family's vocabulary. They say "excuse me" when they get in someone else's way. Family members who have etiquette also let others know where they will be when they are away from home. They take messages for each other.

Financial Literacy

Breaking Even

Your team leader at work has asked you to help the company solve a problem. The company you work for is going to make 2,000 roasting pans. Each roasting pan will sell for $16. It costs the company $10 to manufacture each pan. The company needs to make enough money to pay for the cost of manufacturing the pans. How many pans will the company need to sell to break even?

Math Concept **Writing and Solving Equations** The unknown quantity in this problem is the number of pans which, when sold at $16 each, equals the cost of manufacturing all of the pans. Write an equation that can be used to solve this problem.

Starting Hint: First, find the total cost to manufacture the pans (2,000 × $10). Then find how many pans will need to be sold at $16 to equal the total cost of manufacturing the pans.

 For math help, go to the Math Appendix at the back of the book.

NCTM Problem Solving Apply and adapt a variety of appropriate strategies to solve problems.

These are just a few examples of common courtesies. Etiquette rules can be found to go with all sorts of situations, both formal and informal. Books and the good examples set by others can help you learn what you should do. When in doubt, remember that good manners are based on treating people as you want to be treated.

Understand Authority

In most working relationships, someone has **authority**. This is the right to give orders, make decisions, and enforce rules. Some people with authority earn it. It is a result of the qualities, skills, or knowledge they have. A position may give the person who holds it authority. Examples of this include teachers, managers at work, and police officers. Anyone may hold a position of authority at some time. Have you ever taken care of young children? Then you had authority.

Get Along with Authority

To work well with others, you have to learn to accept and get along with those in authority. This may be difficult for some people. Learning to get along with people in authority is easier to do if you remember that:

- **Exercising authority is often part of a job.** The person in authority is simply doing what is expected of them.
- **Authority is used to keep order, promote safety, and make sure jobs get done.** The purpose of authority is to make life easier and more efficient, not more difficult.
- **People in authority have strengths and weaknesses, just like everyone else.** It is not fair to expect a person in authority to never make mistakes.
- **Being in authority can be difficult.** Managing the actions of others can be a challenge.
- **Authority is a responsibility.** People who are in charge are often held accountable for the actions of those under their authority.

Respond to Authority

Authority can have different effects on everyone. These are often linked to personality. For example, when faced with authority, some people work hard to please. They do what the person in charge wants. These people accept authority easily.

In contrast, some people rebel against authority. They tend to do the opposite of what is asked of them. They may create problems when they question those in charge.

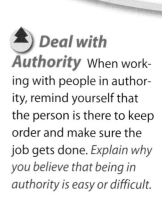

Deal with Authority When working with people in authority, remind yourself that the person is there to keep order and make sure the job gets done. *Explain why you believe that being in authority is easy or difficult.*

Each of these approaches can be a problem if they are carried to an extreme. Pleasing others by following directions and doing your work, of course, is usually wise. A cooperative and positive attitude is easy to get along with. It is also within reason, however, to question authority. It can be done in an acceptable way. The result can lead to change and knowledge that benefit everyone.

Control Your Urge to Rebel

During adolescence, some teens feel like rebelling against authority. As teens form their own ideas, they may question what others expect of them. This may be part of seeking independence. In trying to find their own ways, they reject the ways of others.

In the long run, everyone must live and cope with authority. Too much rebellion will eventually hurt the rebel. A teen can learn to be an individual while still getting along with those who have authority.

✓ **Reading Check** **Explain** What is a working relationship?

Relationships on the Job

On the job, good relationship skills are as important as good work skills. Most people will not be hired if they cannot get along with others. As a worker, you have two basic relationships. The first one is with your manager. The other is with your fellow employees.

Understand Your Manager

A manager or supervisor has two responsibilities. The first is to get work done. The second is to take care of workers' needs. These responsibilities often conflict with each other. For example, Gretchen needed to take some time off for a personal matter. She knew it was possible that her project would be held up if she took the time off.

▶ Common Goals
When coworkers work together to get a job done, everyone benefits. *What kinds of experiences have you had working with others to get a job done?*

She also knew her manager would be held accountable for missing the deadline. Gretchen took off only the time she needed. She worked hard to finish her work by the deadline.

Most managers care about their employees' personal lives. However, the job is still critical to them. If work does not get done, businesses cannot survive. People can lose their jobs. Managers count on employees to show up, do the work as scheduled, and keep absences to a minimum. They appreciate and reward those who make their job as a supervisor less stressful.

Get Along with Coworkers

Have you ever been with people who obviously did not want to be around each other? This may have been friends who had a fight or a sibling in conflict with a parent. If so, you can appreciate the value of working with people who get along. Good relationships make a job more satisfying. Unpleasant tasks are easier to handle. One of the most important traits of a worker is being able to get along with others. **Figure 9.1** outlines some tips to build good relationships at work.

Coworkers should be willing to help each other finish a task. If this happens, the job can be more enjoyable for everyone. For example, Eduardo worked at a small advertising firm. Everyone at the firm got along well. Workers pitched in to help each other. One night Eduardo stayed late to finish a Web page he was designing. Two coworkers brought take-out meals and urged him to take a dinner break. Refreshed by their kindness and company, Eduardo returned to his work re-energized.

Figure 9.1   Get Along with Coworkers

Apply these principles to get along with your coworkers better. *Why do coworkers who apply these principles build an effective work team?*

How to Get Along with Your Coworkers

- Do your share of the work.
- Be willing to help your coworkers get the job done.
- Give credit to your coworkers when they do well.
- Humbly accept credit from others.
- Recognize each other's good qualities.
- Do not gossip about your coworkers.
- Respect your coworkers even when they are not close friends.

As with all relationships, getting along with coworkers takes effort. People who are liked by their fellow employees do their part and help others willingly. They lighten the work environment with a positive attitude. They look for strengths in people and make light of weaknesses. They avoid gossip. You may not like all the people you work with. You can, however, get along with them if you try.

✓ **Reading Check** **Identify** What are the two types of relationships workers usually have at their jobs?

School and Community Relationships

Working relationships also occur in school and in the community. When these relationships work well, life goes more smoothly. Teens benefit when they have good relationships with others in these settings.

Make the Most of School

Teens spend many hours in school. During this time, they relate to other students as well as teachers, administrators, and support staff. Similar to how relationship skills are needed for the workplace, they are also needed in school. For example, a teen with a positive attitude may be able to motivate an entire classroom. Teens need to cooperate during group assignments in order to reach the common goal of completing the project. When teens show respect in the classroom, it can lead to encouragement in their peers. When people know they are respected, they feel more confident to share their opinions.

▶▶ *School Rules*
Doing well in school can depend on following the rules. *In what ways can following rules help you do better in school?*

Following the Rules

Can you imagine the result if schools did not have rules and procedures to follow? Doing well in school often hinges on following rules. Therefore, those who cooperate do better in school than those who rebel. Schools have rules and procedures so learning can take place. This prepares students for the future. Consider these questions when thinking about your school's rules: What happens when you break the rules? What happens when you follow them? Which behavior benefits you more in the long run? It is your choice how you want to act.

If you have the **foresight**, or are able to look forward, to see how today affects tomorrow, you will want to get along well at school. Make the most of your school relationships. They can have long-term effects on your life.

Everyday Encounters in Your Community

Every day, you relate to others you do not know well. It could be the receptionist at a medical clinic or a post office clerk. Cooperating with these people is a good idea. You need their help today, and you may need it again in the future. Your manners may decide whether you and the other person finish your business in a positive or negative way. You may never see that person again—but that is no reason to be rude. A considerate response is a cost-free way to improve the quality of someone's life.

Section 9.1 — After You Read

Review Key Concepts

1. **Define** a good working relationship and identify its five elements.
2. **Identify** the two main responsibilities of a work supervisor.
3. **Explain** why doing well in school often depends on following rules.

Practice Academic Skills

English Language Arts

4. Think about the different types of people you work with on a daily basis, such as classmates, coworkers, and friends. Consider how your relationship skills now will benefit you in your career. Write a paragraph explaining why being able to work with diverse people is a valuable skill.

> **NCTE 12** Use language to accomplish individual purposes.

5. Conduct research on etiquette in the workplace. How do your findings relate to the discussion on etiquette in this section? Give an oral report to your classmates on your findings.

> **NCTE 7** Conduct research and gather, evaluate, and synthesize data to communicate discoveries.

Check Your Answers Check your answers at this book's Online Learning Center through **glencoe.com**.

Teamwork and Leadership

Reading Guide

Before You Read

Look It up If you hear or read a word while reading this section that you do not know, look it up in the glossary at the back of this book or in a dictionary. Before long, this practice will become a habit.

Read to Learn
Key Concepts
- **Suggest** qualities and skills that improve teamwork.
- **Summarize** the qualities needed for leadership.

Main Idea

The most effective groups are those that function as teams. Group members cooperate to achieve a common purpose. Leaders are those who guide or influence others.

Content Vocabulary
◇ teamwork
◇ leader
◇ motivate
◇ participatory leadership
◇ directive leadership
◇ free-rein leadership
◇ diplomacy

Academic Vocabulary

You will find these words in your reading and on your tests. Use the glossary to look up their definitions if necessary.
- hallmark
- competent

Graphic Organizer

As you read, look for three styles of leadership. Identify when each style is most effective. Use a chart like the one shown to help organize your information.

Leadership Style	Most Appropriate When

 Graphic Organizer Go to this book's Online Learning Center at **glencoe.com** to print out this graphic organizer.

Academic Standards •
 English Language Arts

NCTE 4 Use written language to communicate effectively.

NCTE 12 Use language to accomplish individual purposes.

NCTE *National Council of Teachers of English*
NCTM *National Council of Teachers of Mathematics*

NSES *National Science Education Standards*
NCSS *National Council of the Social Studies*

Teamwork

The most effective groups are those that function as teams. Cooperating to achieve a common purpose is called **teamwork**. A choral group, a marching band, and a football squad all need teamwork to perform well. Teamwork is just as necessary in the family and on the job. People who work together are usually the most successful.

Sooner or later most people join with others in some kind of group. One type of group is an informal gathering of people with a common interest. This may be a neighborhood book club. Another type is a formal group with a set purpose, such as a city council. The common interests of the members in the group help them work toward the group's goals. Some groups will not achieve their goals unless they become a team. What marks a group as a team? A team:

- Is a small group of people who regularly interact.
- Has a common goal.
- Shows loyalty, enthusiasm, and a cooperative attitude.
- Relies on contributions from all team members.
- Coordinates its activities.

Qualities of Effective Teams

Teamwork is based on cooperation. It meets people's need for companionship and positive interaction. Teamwork means that people help each other and share information. Teams also work together for their mutual benefit. The team uses the strengths of its members. It helps them work on their limitations. Team members can accomplish more by cooperating than each could alone.

Teamwork requires an open flow of information. Sports teams need to communicate on a play before they run it. In the same way, team members in a work setting must know what is happening. They need to know what is expected of them and what resources they have to do their jobs. Teamwork in the family helps it fulfill its functions and meet its goals.

Effective teams are built on give-and-take. Each person is involved in setting goals and making decisions. Everyone is included in team activities. New members are welcomed. Team members pitch in, even when it means making sacrifices.

Vocabulary

You can find definitions in the glossary at the back of this book.

As You Read

Connect How do you practice teamwork at home?

▶▶ **Work as a Team**

When you work together with other people on your team, you establish common goals. *How would your team be affected if you did not have goals?*

Team members trust, support, and rely on each other. They appreciate each person's efforts and ideas. This mutual support helps them cooperate to achieve their goals. Together they build team spirit.

Teamwork Skills

Certain skills help people become valuable team members. Cooperation is probably the most important. Teams work with and for one another. Team players help strengthen each other.

Effective communication skills allow messages to flow freely among group members. Workers must know how to speak and listen. This will help the team complete their goal or task.

Teams have a hard time functioning if they cannot settle conflicts. Disagreements are a fact of life when people work together. Team members must use conflict resolution skills to solve problems. They will then be able to make progress.

Unselfishness is the **hallmark**, or distinguishing trait, of the best team members. They are committed to the team's goals and do their best to help achieve them. Getting credit for what they do is less important than seeing the team succeed.

✓ **Reading Check** **Define** What is teamwork?

INDEPENDENT Living

HOW TO Be an Effective Team Member

What do your classes, family, and part-time job all have in common? They all require you to be a good team player. Follow these guidelines to be an effective team member:

1. **Be results-oriented.** Focus on making progress. Do not worry about taking credit or placing blame. This will help you put aside personality conflicts and your own pride.
2. **Appreciate diversity.** Respect each team member's cultural background and personal qualities. Find ways to use everyone's differences to make the team stronger.
3. **Keep an eye on the big picture.** Ask, "how does my work affect your work?" Be aware of how your job affects the job of other people on your team. This can help you be responsible for a job well done.
4. **Understand human nature.** Be aware of the times other people need praise, support, and even gentle criticism. Tell people how you feel in a way that inspires them to give their best.

Take Action Choose a situation in which you can act as a team member. This can include helping a younger sibling prepare for school or working on a small group project for school. How do you think using the teamwork strategies described above help you in everyday situations?

Leadership

A **leader** is a person who guides or influences others. Effective leaders create results. They attain goals more quickly and at a higher level of quality than ineffective leaders. Most leaders who emerge from within a team have been highly involved with the group. They are major contributors who are seen as leaders by the others. Sometimes leaders are appointed. In that case, they then have to earn the respect of those already on the team.

Leadership Roles Both strong leaders and effective team players possess useful skills that help them in their positions. *Explain whether you believe that some people are born leaders.*

Leaders go by many names. Captain, president, teacher, parent, manager, and chair are a few of their names. They are needed in the family, the workplace, and the community. Whatever their title, leaders set the tone and direction for the group they lead.

Leadership can be practiced at many different levels. For example, it is shown by the president of a country. The student body president and the principal are leaders in your school. Parents are leaders in the family. In a group of friends, one may take a leadership role. The leader gives direction to the group's activities.

Leadership Skills

A leader may show any number of useful traits. Three general skills, however, are useful to all leaders. These skills include technical skills, working well with others, and thinking skills.

The first type of skill good leaders possess is technical skill. A technical skill is knowledge about how to do specific tasks and the ability to do them. Knowing how to use a computer is an example of a technical skill. Leaders must keep their technical skills fresh. They may need to adapt to changes that occur.

Secondly, leaders must be able to work effectively with people. They know how to make people want to do things, which means they are able to **motivate** others. They inspire others with their energy and enthusiasm. They must also be able to communicate and resolve conflicts. The ability to work with people and help solve their problems makes a good leader.

Dealing with ideas is part of leadership. Thinking skills help the leader direct the activities of the group. Leaders need to:

* Think critically and creatively.
* Make and carry out plans.
* Create and adjust to change.

Leadership skills are not easy to learn. If you want to be a leader, you must practice them. As you learn them, you will develop into a leader.

The work of a group, especially a formal one, often begins in meetings. To use meeting time well, many groups use rules of order, or parliamentary procedure. Parliamentary procedure is a method of running a meeting so that things go smoothly. It requires all points of view to be heard.

Bylaws are another set of rules that can help a group run an effective meeting. A set of bylaws is written and accepted by the group as the authority on how the group functions.

Problem-Solving The environmental group that Regan started a few years ago has grown from a handful of concerned citizens to several dozen. Meetings are disorganized as members try to plan activities and voice opinions. How can Regan help her club run its business more efficiently?

Leadership Styles

The way in which leaders use their skills is called leadership style. Outgoing, enthusiastic people may lead in one way. Those who are quietly **competent**, or qualified, are apt to lead in another. There are three general leadership styles. These are participatory, directive, and free-rein.

With **participatory leadership**, the leader and group members work together to make plans and decisions about what they will do. Under this type of leadership, group members tend to show interest in their work. They are most apt to become a team. Because they have input, they are enthusiastic about the group. They work with or without the leader's supervision. This type of leadership is most effective when group members are self-disciplined and responsible.

In **directive leadership**, the leader sets the group's goals. The leader plans and controls all of its activities. Directive leadership is most useful when people must be told what to do. It is also helpful when jobs must be done in a hurry, such as in emergencies. If used in other settings, however, members may be less motivated. This is due to their lack of input.

The **free-rein leadership** style allows group members to plan and complete their work on their own. The leader only partakes when asked direct questions. Free-rein leadership may be the best style to use when group members are trying to learn certain skills. It is also useful when creative thinking is needed. A team of self-motivated people may enjoy this type of leadership.

Leadership Tasks

Leaders of groups have two major tasks. The first is to accomplish the work of the group. The second is to promote teamwork. These two equally important tasks sometimes compliment each other and sometimes conflict with one another. It takes a talented leader to do both well.

Accomplish the Work

To get a team to accomplish its work, the leader motivates members to reach their goal. A leader must also coordinate schedules, solve problems, and manage resources. For example, Stuart was chairman of the committee that builds sets for the school's spring play. He created a plan so his team would finish the work by the deadline. Stuart called to remind people when they were needed to come set up. He made sure supplies had arrived and were available. When work sessions started to turn too social, Stuart would urge people to stick to the task at hand.

Promote Teamwork

The second task of a leader takes social skills. The leader needs to increase the team spirit and personal worth that people feel. This makes people want to put forth the effort it takes to reach team goals. Members who do not get along or feel good about the team can have a negative effect on everyone. They are also apt to leave the group.

A leader needs to make others feel important and essential to the effort. Praise for good work is one way to do this. Appreciation and enthusiasm motivate others to do their best.

Good leaders use **diplomacy** to develop teamwork. This is the ability to handle situations without upsetting the people involved. One way to be diplomatic is to speak in a polite manner. A good leader is not rude or aggressive. Diplomatic leaders use words in ways that do not offend others.

How would you react if a leader said, "We only have one more day to get this job done. What can I do to help you?" Would your reaction be different if you heard, "Why is that job not done yet?" Use qualifiers when speaking to show diplomacy. For example, start statements with phrases like "I think" and "It seems to me." This helps a leader avoid sounding too judgmental.

 **Skill Required**
A strong leader must have good technical skills, people skills, and thinking and planning skills. *Why does a good leader also need to be a good team player?*

Followers

No leader can exist without followers. The right combination of leaders and followers is what makes a team effective. A team must have more followers than leaders in order to work well.

Help the Group Succeed

A group's success depends as much, or more, on followers as it does on leaders. Without good followers, leaders accomplish little or nothing. Leading a group is time consuming. When followers are willing workers, a leader has more time to manage. The group can be more productive. It is more likely to develop into a team.

Many people prefer to be followers. They may lack the leader's time or commitment to the goal. They may want to contribute in a certain way. Whatever their involvement, however, all members must help out in order for the group to succeed.

Do Your Share

There are those who join a group only for what they can get out of it. They have fun but contribute little. These people are quickly recognized by the rest of the group. They are often resented by the others. If you join a group, plan to do your share. Each person works less when all work together.

Some people are quick to criticize the leader. Many of these people, however, would never accept the leadership role. Many leaders are volunteers. It can be hard to find people to assume a leader's duties without pay. How many people would stay in that role if they heard only criticism for their efforts? When you see people freely giving many hours to a group, show your appreciation. If you want change, volunteer your time and make the changes you want to happen.

Section 9.2   After You Read

Review Key Concepts

1. **Describe** at least four characteristics that show a group is a team.
2. **Explain** what a leader is.

Practice Academic Skills

English Language Arts

3. Most teams have leaders. Do you think a group with a weak leader can be effective? Write a paragraph that answers the question and explains the reasons for your answer.

4. Imagine you have been asked to interview a person who is running for student body president of your school. Write five questions to ask the person that would help you find out about the person's leadership skills.

NCTE 12 Use language to accomplish individual purposes.

NCTE 4 Use written language to communicate effectively.

Check Your Answers Check your answers at this book's Online Learning Center through glencoe.com.

CHAPTER SUMMARY

Section 9.1
Working Relationships

Working relationships are those that exist to accomplish a task or goal. A friendly attitude, respect for others, and good manners help make these work. When someone has authority, they have the right to give orders, make decisions, and enforce rules. People have to learn to handle authority to get ahead in life. On the job, working relationships exist between a worker and manager and among coworkers. Good working relations help people get the most out of school and community contacts.

Section 9.2
Teamwork and Leadership

Teamwork is needed in many working relationships. It means cooperating to achieve a common purpose. Effective teams communicate. They are able to solve their problems and resolve conflict. Leaders are those who guide or influence others. They must be able to get the job done. Different leadership styles are effective in different settings. Leaders need to handle situations without upsetting the people involved. Followers are also important in the success of any group.

Content and Academic Vocabulary Review

1. Use each of these content and academic vocabulary words in a sentence.

Content Vocabulary
◇ working relationship (p. 159)
◇ cooperation (p. 160)
◇ reciprocation (p. 160)
◇ etiquette (p. 160)
◇ authority (p. 161)
◇ teamwork (p. 167)
◇ leader (p. 169)
◇ motivate (p. 169)
◇ participatory leadership (p. 170)

◇ directive leadership (p. 170)
◇ free-rein leadership (p. 170)
◇ diplomacy (p. 171)

Academic Vocabulary
■ initiative (p. 159)
■ foresight (p. 165)
■ hallmark (p. 168)
■ competent (p. 170)

Review Key Concepts

2. Identify elements of good working relationships.
3. Explain the importance of relationships on the job.
4. Describe the benefits of good working relationships at school and in the community.
5. Suggest qualities and skills that improve teamwork.
6. Summarize the qualities needed for leadership.

Critical Thinking

7. Identify Alternatives Why are some people difficult to work with? What can be done to get along with these people?
8. Predict Which leadership style would be most effective with a group of five-year-old children? Explain.
9. Recognize Assumptions How much of a role do you think popularity plays in leadership?

Real-World Skills

Accountability Skills

10. Understand Responsibility Doug works at a restaurant and is scheduled for a pay raise. He is sometimes rude to the customers. His manager said he would not increase Doug's wages until customers stopped complaining. Write a paragraph explaining what Doug should do.

Self-Evaluation Skills

11. Assess Your Skills Think of a leadership position you would like to hold. Identify at least three leadership qualities you would need in this position. Write a plan of specific ways to strengthen the qualities you have identified.

Leadership Skills

12. Solve Problems Lara is leading a school committee that is planning the spring dance. Committee members do not agree on anything. Each has ideas and will not accept other ideas. Meetings have ended with yelling. Write a letter to Lara offering your advice.

Problem-Solving Skills

13. Misuse of Authority People with authority sometimes misuse it. If you were in a situation where you felt like someone was abusing their authority, what would you do? Write a paragraph explaining what actions you would take.

14. Build Awareness Spend the next day being more aware of others. Introduce yourself to those you do not know. Smile and say hello to those you meet. Ask questions to learn more about the people around you. Write a report about the reactions you got. What skill were you practicing? Was this an easy or difficult task for you? Why?

15. Community Groups Research your community to learn about groups in your area. You may find groups that focus on books, business, health, charity, travel, or sports. Select a group that interests you. What are its goals? When and where does it meet? What are the costs to belong? Create a table and fill in the information you collect.

16. Technology Many working relationships in the community have been replaced by technology. For example, automatic teller machines have replaced bank tellers. Make a list of examples where technology has replaced human contact. What are the advantages and disadvantages of these situations? Explain your answers in a paragraph.

17. Flag Etiquette Go to this book's Online Learning Center at glencoe.com to find **Web Links** for **Flag Etiquette Rules**. Make a list of at least five of these rules.

Additional Activities For additional activities, go to this book's Online Learning Center through glencoe.com.

Academic Skills

Mathematics

18. Teamwork Jan works at a landscaping company. She and her team are designing a garden for a public library. They must determine how much fencing they need to enclose the garden. The garden is in the shape of a right triangle. The sides of the triangle measure 6 yards, 8 yards, and 10 yards. How much fencing is needed to enclose the garden?

Math Concept **Finding Perimeter** The perimeter of an object or space is found by adding the length of all of the sides of the object or space. This is also known as the sum of all sides.

Starting Hint: Make an addition problem that includes the length of the three sides of the triangle, or garden (6 + 8 + 10).

 For math help, go to the Math Appendix at the back of the book.

> **NCTM Measurement** Apply appropriate techniques, tools, and formulas to determine measurements.

English Language Arts

19. Speaking Think of the importance of getting along with coworkers. Prepare a two-minute speech about getting along with others on the job. Include specific examples of how this could be done. Give your speech to your classmates.

> **NCTE 12** Use language to accomplish individual purposes.

Social Studies

20. Research Team-Building Training You are part of a team that is developing a team-building program to occur once a month at your company. Your job is to research the ways companies here and in one other country build strong teams. Conduct Research to find information about how teams are used in business. Summarize your findings in a one-page report.

> **NCSS I.a** Analyze and explain the ways groups, societies, and cultures address human needs and concerns.

STANDARDIZED TEST PRACTICE

MATH WORD PROBLEMS
Read the word problem. Then read all of the possible answers. If necessary, use a separate piece of paper to complete any math equations you may need. Choose the correct answer.

Test-Taking Tip Solve a word problem in two steps. First, translate the words into an equation of numbers and variables. Then solve each equation in order to get the correct answer.

21. You have written your landlord a letter telling her the date when you are going to move out of your apartment. Your landlord responds by telling you that she is deducting 32% of your security deposit for carpet cleaning and minor repairs. Your check will amount to $578. What was the original amount of your security deposit?
a. $800
b. $610
c. $850
d. $393

Find a Role Model

In this unit you have learned to use communication skills to keep your relationships healthy. You have also learned about the many different roles you lead in your life. In this project, you will find a role model in your community. You will use what you learned to write and perform a short script. The script will dramatize a situation in which your role model displayed a relationship quality that you admire.

My Journal

If you completed the journal entry from page 82, refer to it to see if your thoughts have changed after reading the unit.

Project Assignment

- Choose a person in your community who you think is a good role model.
- Identify and list three to six good relationship qualities this role model has. Think of at least one example for each quality.
- Choose one trait to explore further. Expand the example to represent a way your role model demonstrates this trait.
- Arrange to meet and interview your role model. Show the example. Bring a pen and paper to write down feedback.
- With a classmate, act out a one-minute script that you have written.

Academic Skills You Will Use

English Language Arts

NCTE 5 Use different writing process elements to communicate effectively.

NCTE 9 Develop an understanding of diversity in language use across cultures.

STEP 1 Choose a Role Model

Your role model can be anyone, as long as it is a person in your community who would be willing to be interviewed by you. If you already have a role model in your community, you may use him or her for this project. Some examples of possible role models may include the following:

- Parent or guardian
- Teacher
- Counselor
- Neighbor
- Manager
- Business owner

STEP 2 Make a List of Good Relationship Qualities

A person who displays good relationship qualities demonstrates mutuality, trust, self-disclosure, rapport, empathy, and shared interests. Make a list of three to six of these qualities that your role model has. Under each quality, write down one or two examples of a time when your role model showed this quality.

Writing Skills

- Organize your thoughts.
- Use examples that illustrate your points.
- Write in complete sentences.
- Write concisely (briefly but completely).

STEP 3 Connect to Your Community

Choose the relationship quality and the example you like best. Expand the example to clearly represent how your role model shows this trait. Arrange to speak to your role model, and show the example to him or her. Ask for feedback about how you have portrayed the situation. Ask how he or she felt during that situation, and why he or she communicated in a certain way. Take notes during your discussion.

Interpersonal Skills
- Listen attentively.
- Demonstrate understanding of your role model's situation.
- Ask for feedback.
- Be aware of nonverbal communication.
- Ask additional questions in order to gain a better understanding.

STEP 4 Plan and Present Your Script

Use the Unit Thematic Project Checklist on the right to plan and create your script and make your presentation.

STEP 5 Evaluate Your Presentation

Your project will be evaluated based on:
- Appropriateness of your example.
- Completeness of your script.
- Quality of presentation.

Evaluation Rubric Go to this book's Online Learning Center at **glencoe.com** for a rubric you can use to evaluate your final project.

Unit Thematic Project Checklist

Script	✓ From the example you shared with your role model, write a one-minute script with at least two characters that illustrates a relationship skill of your role model.
	✓ Be sure your script has a beginning, middle, and end.
	✓ Your script should use only dialogue and stage direction.
Presentation	✓ Make a presentation to your class to share your script and discuss what you learned.
	✓ Invite the students in your class to ask you any questions they may have. Answer three questions.
	✓ When students ask you questions, demonstrate in your answers that you respect their perspectives.
	✓ Turn in the notes from your research and your script to your teacher.
	✓ Act out a one to two-page story.
Academic Skills	✓ Write in the voices of your characters.
	✓ Speak clearly and concisely.
	✓ Be aware of your audience.
	✓ Use creativity in stage directions.

Unit 3

Decision-Making Skills

Unit

Thematic Project Preview
Manage Your Time

After completing this unit, you will learn about the skills you need to make decisions. In your unit thematic project, you can make a schedule that helps you balance work, school, and family life.

My Journal

Find a Balance Write a journal entry about one of the topics below. This will help you prepare for the unit project at the end of the unit.

- Describe how you handled a day when you were overscheduled.
- Explain how an adult you know leads a balanced life and makes time for their work and family.
- Identify what an ideal day of school, work, and family time would be like.

Explore the Photo
Poor time management can cause problems in life and in the family. *How do your family members manage their time to find a balance in their life?*

CHAPTER 10

Solve Problems in Your Life

Section 10.1

Decision Making

Section 10.2

Manage and Take Action

▶▶ Explore the Photo

Throughout your life, you will have to make decisions in order to solve problems. *What decision have you made in the last week that has helped you solve a problem?*

Chapter Objectives

After completing this chapter, you will be able to:

- **Identify** the steps in the decision-making process.
- **Determine** what makes a sound decision.
- **Describe** management skills useful in the decision-making process.
- **Explain** how ethics impact your actions.

Writing Activity

Coherent Paragraphs

Fairness If you want to be treated fairly, the decisions you make and actions you take should be fair to others. You can show fairness when you:

- Talk to a friend about a problem rather than ignoring the person or starting an argument.
- Help two classmates see both sides of an issue when they have a quarrel.
- Let a sibling tell his side of the story before drawing any conclusions about why he did not show up after work as planned.
- Walk to the end of the line instead of cutting in front of others.

Write two coherent paragraphs about yourself and how fairness affects your life.

Writing Tips To write coherent paragraphs, follow these steps:

1. Use transition words and phrases.
2. Use repeated words, parallel structures, or synonyms to link sentences and paragraphs.
3. Use pronouns to avoid unnecessary repetition.

Decision Making

Reading Guide

Before You Read

Check for Understanding If you have questions as you are reading, that means you are checking your understanding of the material. To get the most out of the text, try to answer those questions.

Read to Learn
Key Concepts
- **Identify** the steps in the decision-making process.
- **Determine** what makes a sound decision.

Main Idea
The decision-making process is a way to approach choices and problems. It has six steps that lead to sound decision making.

Content Vocabulary
◇ decision-making process
◇ decision
◇ problem
◇ option
◇ resource
◇ consequence
◇ risk
◇ prioritize
◇ procrastination
◇ denial

Academic Vocabulary
You will find these words in your reading and on your tests. Use the glossary to look up their definitions if necessary.
- strategy
- merit

Graphic Organizer
As you read, list the steps of the decision-making process. Use a chart like the one shown to help organize your information.

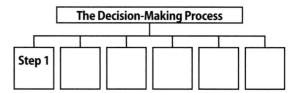

The Decision-Making Process					
Step 1					

 Graphic Organizer Go to this book's Online Learning Center at **glencoe.com** to print out this graphic organizer.

Academic Standards •

 **English Language Arts**

NCTE 4 Use written language to communicate effectively.

NCTE 6 Apply knowledge of language structure and conventions to discuss texts.

 **Mathematics**

NCTM Problem Solving Solve problems that arise in mathematics and in other contexts.

NCTE *National Council of Teachers of English*
NCTM *National Council of Teachers of Mathematics*

NSES *National Science Education Standards*
NCSS *National Council of the Social Studies*

The Decision-Making Process

To make decisions and solve problems, you need a **strategy**. A strategy is a process to help people make choices and solve problems. The **decision-making process** is a series of steps to identify and evaluate possibilities and make a good choice. It can also be called the problem-solving process. The steps may be labeled in a different way. Both processes, however, are basically the same. They are a way to deal with choices and problems.

Some of the differences in what the process is called involve how people see the situation. For example, a **decision** is a choice that is made. A **problem** is a dilemma that must be solved or worked out. Making decisions may seem easier than solving problems. A choice, however, is a problem. Problems may mean making many choices.

Vocabulary

You can find definitions in the glossary at the back of this book.

Identify the Problem

The first step in making a choice is to identify what needs to be decided. Great or small, problems and decisions need your attention. A simple choice or problem may be easy to put into words. You may need to choose an entrée at lunch in the school cafeteria. A problem may be that you cannot find your warm gloves to wear to shovel snow. Every day people face these small issues. They take them in stride and work them out. There is no need for a formal process.

As problems and decisions become more complicated, they have a greater impact on your life. They also become harder to handle. When ignored or unrecognized, they can threaten your health and well-being. The impact can last a long time. It is important to have a way to deal with these issues.

Sometimes choices and problems can seem overwhelming. No problem, however, is too big to handle. You can break a big problem down into parts. Then you can tackle one part at a time. If you discover several reasons for a problem, you can deal with each one as a separate problem. Start at the beginning and patiently work through the issues.

As You Read
Connect What are some of the small decisions you make every day?

Symptom or Problem?

When you have a fever, it is a symptom of a problem. The real problem is the sickness and its cause. That problem is what needs to be treated. People may not be able to see the real problems they face if they cannot look past the symptoms.

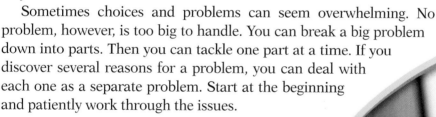

Everyday Problems
You solve problems every day, from the simple to the more difficult. *What are some easy decisions you have had to make recently and what are some difficult problems you have solved?*

For example, a parent and teen may argue over curfew rules. Is this a symptom or a problem? The real problem could be about independence and arguing over curfew may be a symptom.

Symptoms are useful because they offer clues that help point out serious problems. If you are confused, concerned, or upset, you need to figure out why. When these feelings last, a problem may need to be faced. In a feuding family, for example, the symptom is that they argue too much. The problem is the reason or reasons why they argue so often.

Be persistent in trying to identify real problems. If you solve problems, the symptoms will go away. If you only treat symptoms, the problems are still there and the symptoms will return.

List Your Options

Once you have a clear idea of the problem you want to tackle, what do you think you should do next? Look for ideas about what you can do. A possible course of action to choose from is called an **option**. The more options you can identify, the better prepared you are to make a choice or solve a problem.

Write down all the ideas that occur to you, even the bad or silly ones. Good solutions are not always apparent at first. Even a poor idea can trigger thoughts about better ones.

Remember that two heads are often better than one. Someone else may think of an option that you did not. As you look for options, you can involve friends you trust, family members, or experts. Ask yourself whose help would be valuable. Then turn to those people.

▶▶ *Identify Options*

Once you have identified a problem, you can develop a list of options. *What are some ways to identify all your options?*

Evaluate Your Options

Once you have a complete list of options, examine each one. For example, ask yourself if there will be different financial costs for each? How does each option match your values and goals? Think about these questions as you look at the **merit**, or positive quality, of each option:

- What are this option's strengths as a solution?
- What are its weaknesses?
- Is the choice realistic for you and your family at this time?
- Would this option meet the needs and wants of you and your family?
- Will you be happy later if you choose this option?

When all options seem about equal, try writing down the advantages and disadvantages of each one. Write them in two separate columns to clarify the option's merits.

Another way to evaluate options is to assign each advantage and disadvantage a number value from zero to five. Zero can indicate items that are not that important to you. Five can represent items that are the most important to you.

Whichever way you choose to look at your options, think about what an ideal outcome to the problem would be. Set a goal to be reached when the problem is solved. Achieving exactly what you want may not happen, but you need to know how you are working towards your goal.

Gather Information

As you evaluate options, you may need information about them. That means using resources. A **resource** is something you can use to reach goals and solve problems. If you have learned to recognize and locate resources, you will know where to turn.

Reliable Resources Finding the right information takes time. You may need to locate books and magazines, search the Internet, or talk to others. The more important the problem is, the more relevant good information becomes.

As you use resources, look at information carefully. This will help you judge how useful information is. You can also ask yourself these questions:

- Where did the information come from?
- What are the credentials of the source?
- Does the source have a special interest in this subject? Is the information biased?
- Is the information current?
- Does the information seem logical?
- Is the information supported by reputable research?

Financial Literacy

Health Care Costs

Drew has a health problem. He is concerned about how much money he will need to spend on doctor's appointments and medicines. He has a health insurance plan with a deductible of $750. The cost Drew paid for a doctor's appointment was $120. The prescription he was given costs him $90 each time he gets it filled. How many times will he need to get his prescription filled to reach his deductible?

Math Concept **The Deductible** The deductible in an insurance policy is the portion of any claim that is not covered by the insurance provider. It is usually a fixed amount that must be paid by the insured before the full benefits of a policy can apply. Adding each out-of-pocket expense the insured makes will indicate how close he or she is to reaching the deductible.

Starting Hint: Begin with $750 and subtract the cost of the doctor's appointment ($120). Divide that answer by the cost for each prescription ($90).

 For math help, go to the Math Appendix at the back of the book.

NCTM Problem Solving Solve problems that arise in mathematics and in other contexts.

Consider the Consequences

Any option you choose will have consequences. A **consequence** ('kän(t)-sə-ˌkwen(t)s) is the result of an action. Some are good. Some are not. It is important to look at consequences before a decision is made. You can prevent serious consequences from happening. As you analyze options, think about their effects on you. Also consider other people. How will your family and friends be affected by each option on your list? What will the impact on society be? These are important questions to ask. The answers will help guide what you do.

Sometimes consequences are not clear. You may not know for sure what will happen. For example, when someone starts a new business, there is no guarantee that it will be a success. There is most likely a great deal of risk involved in the decision. **Risk** is the possibility of loss or injury. People must weigh risks as they solve problems.

Some people are more willing to take risks than others. Some risks are more worth taking than others. Many great successes have come from risk taking. Many failures and tragedies have also come from taking risks. Are you willing to take risks? If you do not know exactly what will happen, think carefully about what can happen after you make your choice.

Choose the Best Option

Once you have carefully looked at your options, you are ready to choose one. Sometimes the right choice becomes clear as you review your options. If the decision is difficult, you may need to eliminate options until you have only the best one left.

When choosing a solution, let your values be your guide. Does the option you are considering support what you value? Fewer regrets are likely when you base your decision on what you believe.

Carry Out Your Solution

After you have decided what to do, put your decision into action. Sometimes this is the easiest step in the decision-making process. The hard part may have been deciding what to do. Prioritize the tasks to be done. To **prioritize** means to order things from first to last or from most important to least important. **Figure 10.1** shows different factors you can use to help you prioritize.

Changing Your Mind

Have you ever heard of a bride or groom whose mind changed at the altar? Changing your mind is not easy, but it may be the wise thing to do. New evidence and more thought may suggest a different path of action.

It is hard to admit that you made the wrong choice. There may be difficulties to overcome. It is far better to face them now than to live with the long-term effects of a bad decision. Knowing that it is all right to change your mind can give you the courage to do so. It could lead to a better long-term solution to your problem.

Figure 10.1   **Prioritizing**

When deciding what to do first when making a decision or solving a problem, take these factors into account: logic, importance and feasibility, and time. *How do you prioritize school assignments and activities?*

Logic Sometimes it is only logical to complete one task before going on to the next one. For example, a housepainter paints the ceiling of a room first, because any paint splatters that get on the walls will be covered when the walls are painted.

Time Sometimes it is best to finish short tasks before beginning more time-consuming tasks. For example, it might be easiest to answer several e-mails before returning a call to someone who needs extensive advice.

Importance and Feasibility If two tasks are equally important, start with the one that you know you can complete. Ask an adult for guidance if you are unsure about the importance of a task.

Evaluate the Results

A good decision maker does not stop after the decision has been made. Step back to look at your level of success. When you evaluate, you study the results of your actions. Were they effective? Did your decision solve the problem? If it did not, why? What can you do better the next time? Here are other questions to ask as you evaluate your decision:

- Did you accurately identify the problem? If not, how did that affect what happened?
- Was your goal realistic? Did it lead you to a solution?
- Did you identify enough resources? What else should you have used?
- Did you miss any options that might have been better?
- Did you make a good decision?
- Did you skip any steps in the process? Did this affect the solution to your problem?
- Did you solve your problem and reach your goal? What did you like and dislike about how your problem was solved?
- What could you have done to improve your decision making?

If you evaluate your decision, you can see what works for you as a problem solver. By evaluating, you can improve your decision-making skills. This may also help you make future decisions.

Following a decision-making process may feel awkward at first as you work through basic steps. Think of it as learning a new dance or how to play a new game. Once you know the steps, it is easier. You can even add variations to make the process fit different situations.

✓ **Reading Check** **Define** What is the decision-making process?

▶▶ *Family Decisions*
Families work together to make choices. *What choices has your family made recently?*

Make Sound Decisions

The decision-making process will help you make good decisions. It is important to think about how your decision may impact your life. With these pointers, you can make sound decisions and guard against mistakes:

- **Learn to recognize important decisions.** A decision that could affect you needs to be taken seriously. For example, when a choice is simple, you may be able to think quickly about what needs to be done. Then you can take action. In important situations, do not be afraid to take your time and say, "I will have to think about it."

- **Avoid impulsive reactions.** Impulsive, or sudden, decisions are ones that are made too quickly. Emotions rather than thought usually guide them. Allow yourself time to make large and important decisions.

- **Base decisions on your values.** Ignoring your values can lead to regrets. Ask yourself if your choices match what you believe in. The choices you make that are based on your core values are the ones that you will be the most proud of.

- **Make decisions when you are clear-headed.** In some cases, postponing a decision may be a better choice. For example, you may need to get some rest first. If you are upset, wait until you calm down.

- **Make your own decisions.** If you let others make your decisions, you will be living by their ideas and values, not your own. In the end, you will have to live with the results. Such decision making can be dangerous, especially if the person who controls the decision is unreliable.

- **Base your decisions on research and facts.** Take the time to do your research. Consider your options, risks, and consequences. When you are armed with knowledge, it is much easier to make sound decisions.

Attitudes Toward Decision Making

Your attitude toward a problem can sometimes harm you more than the problem itself. Why is that? People react differently when facing choices or problems. Some reactions can prevent you from finding a solution.

Procrastination

Have you or someone you know ever said, "I do not know what to do, so I will just wait." **Procrastination** (prō-ˌkras-tə-ˈnā-shən) means putting something off. People who procrastinate plan to take care of things, but they never do. They may feel uncomfortable or lack confidence, even with a minor issue.

This approach to a serious decision can be very costly. The longer you wait, the longer the problem goes unresolved. The effects of procrastination can cause increasing harm.

Life Skills CHECKLIST

Management Skills

Beat the Procrastination Trap Even with a goal in mind, procrastination can still be a trap. You will overcome procrastination if you:

- ✓ Write down when and where you will start working on your goal.
- ✓ Identify the tools and information you need.
- ✓ Start with the short, easy tasks.
- ✓ Do your least favorite jobs before the easier ones.
- ✓ Find support through others who have the same problem.
- ✓ Promise yourself a reward once your goal is reached.

One of the reasons some people procrastinate is because they may be trying to avoid failure. When people procrastinate, however, their chances of failing often increase. This is due, in part, to the fact that these individuals delay actions or decisions. Putting things off usually increases stress and decreases options. The result may be poor decisions and unsolved problems. Another result is the failure to handle the situation.

Denial

Some people do not want to face the fact that a problem exists. This is called **denial**. Denial makes a person struggle on without ever acknowledging the choice that needs to be made.

For example, Estefan noticed that his grandmother was having trouble walking. She often had to hold on to furniture to get around the house. Estefan tried to talk to her about her physical problems. She told him she was not having any problems. She was in denial about her health. She did not acknowledge the problem until the day she fell and injured her leg.

People often spend their time dealing with simple problems that have little importance but let the big problems go. Ignoring an overwhelming problem may seem easier. People may think the problem will go away if they ignore it. A tough problem can be hard to face. It will not be solved, however, until it is recognized and dealt with.

Denial can even be subconscious. A person might put an overwhelming problem aside without realizing it. You might see the person's problem, but he or she genuinely thinks it does not exist. This can be very serious. The person in denial cannot seek a solution to a problem that supposedly is not there.

Confronting a problem may mean handling unpleasant emotions and situations. A serious look at what can happen often gives people the strength to do what needs to be done.

A Positive Approach

When you have knowledge and skills, your confidence grows, even when confronted by problems. People need to see problems for what they are: something that you can solve. With this view, you can take positive steps to decrease trouble and pain in your life. Learning to make choices and solve problems can make your life easier and better.

Take Responsibility for Decisions

You are responsible for the decisions you make. You may be wondering though, "Why should I be?" It may seem like it would be easier to let someone else take the blame when things go wrong. It may also seem better to have an excuse if you make a mistake. Here are some reasons to be responsible for your decisions:

- Making mistakes is common. By denying your mistakes, you give the impression that you believe you are above making them, yet no one really is. Mistakes happen to everyone at some point.
- People do not respect you when you make excuses. They see excuses as a sign of weakness. People may also question your honesty when you try to come up with excuses.
- Others do not want to be blamed for your mistakes any more than you want to be blamed for theirs. Blaming others is a quick way to lose friends.
- Logically, if you take credit for what goes right, you have to take responsibility for what goes wrong. It would not be fair to accept praise for what you did right when you are not responsible for things that went wrong.
- You can learn from your mistakes. Denying them may cause you to make similar mistakes again.

Owning your decision means saying, "This is what I decided. I am responsible for the results." When decisions turn out well, taking credit is a pleasure. If choices do not turn out well, you show strength when you admit that you made a mistake. You can try to set it right if possible. People admire that.

Section 10.1   After You Read

Review Key Concepts

1. **Describe** why it is important to have and evaluate your options in the decision-making process.
2. **Explain** the effect procrastination and denial have on making sound decisions.

Practice Academic Skills

English Language Arts

3. Some people are too proud to admit when they are wrong. Write a paragraph explaining how this attitude could cause harm when solving problems.

4. Think of the steps in the decision-making process discussed in this section. Create an outline of these steps. Under each step, write a tip that will lead to a sound decision.

NCTE 4 Use written language to communicate effectively.

NCTE 6 Apply knowledge of language structure and conventions to discuss texts.

Check Your Answers Check your answers at this book's Online Learning Center through **glencoe.com**.

Manage and Take Action

Reading Guide

Before You Read

Be Organized A messy environment can be distracting. To lessen distractions, organize an area where you can read this section comfortably.

Read to Learn
Key Concepts
- **Describe** management skills useful in the decision-making process.
- **Explain** how ethics impact your actions.

Main Idea
Management skills are useful when making decisions and solving problems. Ethical actions are based on personal standards and ethical decision-making.

Content Vocabulary
◇ long-term goal
◇ short-term goal
◇ support system
◇ resourceful
◇ standard

Academic Vocabulary
You will find these words in your reading and on your tests. Use the glossary to look up their definitions if necessary.
- channel
- accountability

Graphic Organizer
As you read, look for different types of resources that can be used in management. Give an example of each. Use a chart like the one shown to help organize your information.

Types of Resources	Examples
1._____	_____
2._____	_____
3._____	_____

 Graphic Organizer Go to this book's Online Learning Center at **glencoe.com** to print out this graphic organizer.

Academic Standards •

 English Language Arts

NCTE 4 Use written language to communicate effectively.

NCTE 12 Use language to accomplish individual purposes.

NCTE *National Council of Teachers of English*
NCTM *National Council of Teachers of Mathematics*

NSES *National Science Education Standards*
NCSS *National Council of the Social Studies*

Management Skills

What is the difference between a person who makes decisions with ease and someone who does not? Often it is the skills they have. With certain skills at your command, you can approach decisions and problems with greater confidence.

Management is a useful skill in many of the steps of decision making. Management is using what you have to get what you want. People use management when they set goals and take carefully planned steps to reach them. Management skills are a basic part of getting along in life.

Management goes hand-in-hand with the decision-making process. If you identify your problem and want to solve it, that is your goal. The steps in the process are those you take to reach your goal. You use resources to gather information and to evaluate your options. When you have made a choice or solve the problem, you have reached the goal.

Set Goals

Goal setting is a valuable skill. If you learn to set goals, you can use them in several ways. First, goals help you accomplish tasks. Second, goals **channel**, or focus, the direction of your life. They reflect your values. You might set goals about education or the family you wish to have. Having such goals encourages you to take early steps toward reaching them. Third, goals can help you solve problems. A goal guides your efforts toward a solution.

Goals are influenced by many factors. The family is a major influence, as are friends. The media and community may affect goals. Needs and wants often create goals. These factors combine with personality to create the goals that a person works toward.

Families and groups set and work toward goals, which are related to their functions. The goals grow out of the purposes and values of the group. Group members cooperate to achieve the goals.

As You Read

Connect What are some decisions to which you might apply management skills?

Vocabulary

You can find definitions in the glossary at the back of this book.

Reach Your Goal Management skills can help you set and reach your goals. *To reach the goal of becoming class president, what management skills would you need?*

Part of being a group member is being committed to the group's goals. To be effective, goal setting should follow certain guidelines.

- **Make goals specific.** Do not just say that you will do better. State exactly what you want to achieve.
- **Establish a time frame for reaching goals.** Decide when you should reach a goal. A goal that takes months or years to achieve is a **long-term goal**. For example, career plans and saving for a cross-country trip are long-term. A **short-term goal** requires only a short period to achieve the goal. When you make a list of things to do on a Saturday, you are setting short-term goals. Sometimes short-term goals help you reach those that are long-term.
- **Show accountability, or a willingness to accept responsibility.** If possible, involve someone in your goals. Report what your plans are, so you will have more reason to follow through. When you know someone is holding you accountable, your motivation often increases.
- **Write goals down.** Write your goals down so that you will have a reminder that can help you stay focused.

INDEPENDENT Living

HOW TO   Set Goals

When you were a child, you probably had exciting ideas about what you could do when you grew up. Now that you are older, you can set realistic goals. These goals can be exciting to achieve. Follow these guidelines to learn how to set goals:

1. **Be specific.** Give yourself a very clear idea of your goal. That way, you can follow your progress easily and keep yourself on track. Achieving exactly what you set out to do gives you a great sense of satisfaction and confidence.
2. **Look at the big picture.** Think about how your goal may affect the other areas of your life. Will you still have time for everything you did before? Deciding in advance what is important can help you if conflicts arise later.
3. **Be realistic.** It is good to push yourself to reach an ambitious goal. You should, however, still be realistic about your abilities.
4. **Plan for potential problems.** Try to imagine potential problems. Plan positive, creative ways to deal with them. Being prepared for a problem will keep you from being caught off guard if your plan hits a snag.
5. **Stay active with your goal.** Action, not wishful thinking, is the key to success. Do something every day to work toward your goal.

Take Action Choose a goal for yourself that you think is possible, but challenging. Mentally work through this goal using the steps listed here. On reflection, does the goal seem more realistic or unrealistic? What would you have to change, if anything, to reach your goal? Can you make these changes? If so, would the effort be worthwhile? Why or why not?

Goal setting is important in several of the steps of the decision-making process. To be goal oriented, identify the problem to be solved or the choice to be made. Consider your options based on your goal. If an option does not lead to the goal, it will not solve the problem. You should select the best choice based on your goal. Finally, whether the solution turns out good or bad will depend on the goals you have for solving the problem.

Identify Resources

You do not have to solve problems or make choices alone. In fact, some problems require many different kinds of help. You need to learn to identify your resources. Good managers know how to find and use resources. Resources are also used to help families fulfill their functions and meet their needs.

Resources are often sorted into three types. These include human, material, and community resources. As you read about these types of resources, think about where you can find them in your own life. That way you will become skillful at identifying them. You will also be better equipped to find them when you need them.

Human Resources

Human resources are what people can offer you. They include skills and talents. Time and energy are human resources that are important in solving problems. You have personal resources that you can use to help yourself and others. From others, you can gain information, expertise, and sometimes a willing hand.

Families are an important human resource to their members. Friends and coworkers also are resources. Who helps you when you have a problem? The Krause family, for example, used human resources to help meet their goal of building a basement. Mr. Krause's brother is a carpenter. He put up panelling and built cabinets for them. The rest of the family helped paint and lay tile. Human resources made their goal come true.

Build a Support System People need support when problems arise. A **support system** is a group of resources that provide help. People and families need support systems. A support system is there when human resources are needed. Support works in two directions. When you help others, they will be willing to help you. Individuals and families need to build a support system before problems occur.

Use Your Resources To reach her goal of becoming first chair in the orchestra, this violinist used human, material, and community resources. *Can you identify the resources she might have used?*

Good managers often avoid problems by managing well. One of their skills is using time effectively. You can use this skill by doing the following:

- **List and prioritize.** To prioritize means to rank things according to importance. Numbering each item in order of importance can help you do this.
- **Schedule your week.** Get a daily planner and divide each day into one-hour blocks. Fill them in with activities you know you will have. Do not forget to leave time for things you enjoy.
- **Multitask.** When convenient, do two things at the same time, such as thinking about your homework while cooking dinner.

- **Organize your space.** Keep related items together. Paper, pens, and textbooks can be in a box near where you study. You save time when supplies are ready to use.

Problem-Solving

Lily was worried about the week ahead. She had to study for three tests. Her tennis team was scheduled to play. Her father's birthday was on Wednesday. She and her brother needed to make some plans. Then her boss at the restaurant asked if she could put in some extra hours. What would you suggest Lily do to make the next week manageable?

To help your family build a support system, try these ideas:
- Talk with your family about who would help you in a crisis. If you have few options, explore new possibilities.
- Develop a list of family resources and hang it for all to see.
- Check the telephone book or library for lists of community resources.
- Get to know your neighbors.
- Offer to help a neighbor, friend, or family member. You may say, "I am pretty good at raking leaves. May I help?"
- Ask for support. You may say, "I am looking for a job. Do you know anyone who needs a babysitter?"

Material Resources

Physical items are material resources. If you are planning a trip, for example, a car can be used for travel. Technology provides many material resources, such as phones and computers. Money is also a material resource. If you were taking a class, you could use money to buy books.

People who have few financial resources can still solve problems and reach goals. Creativity and the use of other resources can make up for a lack of money.

Community Resources

Every community has resources and services to help people. There are also many state and national agencies for people to seek management help. There are many ways to find resources in your area. Your phone book, school, library, and the Internet are all examples of where to start looking.

Communities provide services as well. Government programs offer everything from food stamps to health care. For example, Mrs. Cornwell's father lived with her family. No one was home to be with him during the day. The community's senior center turned out to be a great resource. Companionship and recreation were added bonuses.

Be Resourceful

Resourceful people recognize and make good use of resources. They know how to find them and how to make substitutions. This quality is valuable when you are solving problems. Solutions often depend on locating whatever and whoever can help you. People who are resourceful do not give up when something seems like an obstacle. They learn to stop, think, and ask questions. Resourceful people dig for answers and approaches.

Think Critically and Creatively

Thinking helps you use the decision-making process. Use your brain rather than your emotions to seek a solution to your problem or to make a choice. Logical thinking means using reasoning to reach a conclusion. It involves looking at the ideas and facts about a problem. The decision-making process itself is an example of logical thinking. When you use it, you collect evidence and information and identify facts. You think your way through the problem.

◀ *Make Good Use of Resources* Simple resources are always available to help you solve a problem. *How is this woman being resourceful?*

Another type of thinking is critical thinking. Critical thinking involves analyzing and evaluating. People who think critically look at a problem from all sides. They do not just take a person's word for it. This type of thinking is needed when evaluating options. Creative thinking means coming up with new ideas. Good creative thinking is original. It is useful when listing options in the decision-making process.

Make Plans

After a decision has been made, you may need a plan to carry out the decision. Planning is a way of getting organized. It also helps you see the whole picture before you start to act.

The ability to make a plan is part of good management. A plan is the road map between you and your goal. It requires resources and the ability to think. Ask yourself the questions in **Figure 10.2** to help you make a plan to carry out your decisions.

Balance Your Time

An action plan for solving problems is often easier when major tasks are broken down into smaller tasks. You can then schedule each smaller task with a different time. This may help you balance your time between each task in order to complete the larger one.

When you know the answers to the questions below, write them down. By writing the steps of your plan, you will be less likely to leave out something important. You will also be able to check your progress as you work through your plan.

✓ **Reading Check** **Explain** What is management?

Figure 10.2 **Make a Plan**

A good management plan will help you make the best decisions. *In what way is a good plan like a road map?*

STEP	1	What steps need to be taken?
STEP	2	In what order should the steps be taken?
STEP	3	What resources will be used in each step?
STEP	4	Who will take each step?
STEP	5	How long will each step take?
STEP	6	When should each step be carried out?

Take Ethical Action

Ethics are the moral rules of society. They are the principles that help people decide what is right or wrong. They guide people's actions. Ethical thinking takes you beyond yourself. It asks you to consider what happens to others as well as to you. When people act ethically, they look out for each other in positive ways.

How do you know when your actions are ethical? Generally, ethical actions:

- Show respect for others.
- Benefit others.
- Do no harm and take no unfair advantage.
- Are fair and honest.
- Comply with the law.

Personal Standards

These simple moral principles set a high standard. A **standard** is a basis for comparison. Personal standards are based on the values and moral codes of each person and of society. They guide people's decisions and actions. When people hold high personal standards, families and society benefit.

Personal standards also have a direct effect on your relationships. You should treat others ethically. If you do, they are likely to respond positively. Ethics are the basis for strong relationships in your life.

Ethics are important in the workplace. A successful business puts its customers first. It treats them fairly and honestly. In turn, it expects workers to behave ethically too.

Many groups have codes of conduct. These are ethical principles that the group says it will follow. The code of conduct reflects the group's goals and values. Group members may be asked to pledge that they will follow these rules.

Ethical Decisions

Many decisions you make and problems you solve involve ethics and personal standards. Would you make fun of a coworker's appearance? That is an ethical decision. What you do reflects on you. If you make fun of a coworker, others see that you do not have respect for that person. How will that affect what they think of you?

 **Take Responsibility**
We all need help sometimes.
How is this man demonstrating respect for others?

Many ethical questions are complicated. Deciding what to do is not always easy. Some ethical issues cause opposing points of view. You can be tolerant and respect the other's viewpoint. You can also show your own personal standards at the same time.

Ethics can guide you as you make decisions and solve problems. Think about these questions:

- What will happen to you and others over time?
- Would you be willing to change places with those most affected by what you plan to do?
- Would this be the right approach in a similar situation?
- Would there be good results if everyone chose this action?
- Will this solution help the overall well-being of yourself and others?

Your Values Affect Your Ethical Decisions

The stronger your value system is, the more comfortable you will be in dealing with ethical situations. You can look at the questions above with greater confidence. In making choices, the solutions you reach are likely to be better for you. They will benefit others and society as well.

A sound value system guides decisions and actions. Values provide meaning and satisfaction. If a person's life if carried out according to their value system, it is usually rewarding and fulfilling.

As you grow older, you will have more chances to make your own decisions and solve your own problems. You can set goals and find resources. You will learn to make ethical decisions and put management skills into action.

Now is the time to ask yourself what you want for the future. You have choices. You can let circumstances and problems take charge of your life. You can think, decide, plan, and act. What will you choose?

Section 10.2   After You Read

Review Key Concepts

1. **Identify** three benefits of setting goals.
2. **Describe** the role of personal standards in taking ethical action.

Practice Academic Skills

English Language Arts

3. Write a paragraph to explain how you can use resources—human, material, and community—to accomplish a short-term goal. Identify the goal, the resources you would use, and how you would use the resources to accomplish your goal. Accomplish one short-term goal.

> **NCTE 12** Use language to accomplish individual purposes.

4. Money is a material resource. Is it a useful resource or an essential resource? Write a paragraph that explains your answer to the question.

> **NCTE 4** Use written language to communicate effectively.

Check Your Answers Check your answers at this book's Online Learning Center through **glencoe.com**.

CHAPTER SUMMARY

Section 10.1
Decision Making

Decision making and problem solving are more effective when a logical process is used. The decision-making process has six steps. These include identifying the problem, listing and evaluating your options, choosing the best option, carrying out the option, and then evaluating the decision or solution. People who make sound decisions do not procrastinate or deny their problems. They are responsible for their own decisions.

Section 10.2
Manage and Take Action

Management skills are used to make decisions and solve problems. Management is using what you have to get what you want. It means setting goals and using resources to reach the goals. Resources can be human, material, or community based. Being resourceful means knowing how to find and use resources. Ethics are the basis for personal standards of behavior. Ethical decisions take into account the effects on others as well as on the decision maker.

Content and Academic Vocabulary Review

1. Use each of these content and academic vocabulary words in a sentence.

Content Vocabulary

◇ decision-making process (p. 183)
◇ decision (p. 183)
◇ problem (p. 183)
◇ option (p. 184)
◇ resource (p. 185)
◇ consequence (p. 186)
◇ risk (p. 186)

◇ prioritize (p. 186)
◇ procrastination (p. 189)
◇ denial (p. 190)
◇ long-term goal (p. 194)
◇ short-term goal (p. 194)
◇ support system (p. 195)
◇ resourceful (p. 197)
◇ standard (p. 199)

Academic Vocabulary

■ strategy (p. 183)
■ merit (p. 185)
■ channel (p. 193)
■ accountability (p. 194)

Review Key Concepts

2. **Identify** the steps in the decision-making process.
3. **Determine** what makes a sound decision.
4. **Describe** management skills useful in the decision-making process.
5. **Explain** how ethics impact your actions.

Critical Thinking

6. **Predict** Do you think that human or material resources are more important in solving problems? Explain your answer.
7. **Evaluate** Why do you think some people are successful even though they had few resources as they grew up?
8. **Analyze** Of the following, who should be the most concerned about making ethical decisions: parents, politicians, doctors, writers, teachers, your friends, or you? Why?
9. **Assess** Is procrastination always negative? Could there be a good reason to procrastinate? When might it be better to delay making a decision or taking action?

Real-World Skills

Problem-Solving Skills

10. Make a Choice Jani's grandmother needs to renew her driver's license and has asked Jani to help her study for the exam. Jani's parents think her grandmother is a danger to herself and others when she drives. They would prefer that she fail the exam so they do not have to take her keys away. They have asked Jani not to help her. What should she do?

Self-Management Skills

11. Set Goals Make a list of your goals. Include goals for all parts of your life, such as personal goals, work goals, and community goals. Once you have listed your goals, mark each goal as short or long term.

Technology Skills

12. Create a Puzzle Make a list of terms and their definitions related to decision making and management. Use software to create a hidden word puzzle that includes the terms and the definitions. Write the directions to say: Identify the term being defined, then find and circle it in the puzzle. Print your puzzle and have classmates solve it

Management Skills

13. Planning Plan a party for a family member or a friend. Use the tips on page 198 to guide your planning. Write out the steps you will take, the resources you will use, and when you will do each step. If possible, carry out your plans.

14. Graphic Arts Design a chart or graph that shows the relationship among goals, resources, decision making, problem solving, and management.

15. Identifying Skills Write down the stages of the family life cycle (from Chapter 3). For each stage, list a management skill that would be useful in meeting the family's needs. Explain why the skill would be useful for that stage.

16. Identifying Resources List helpful resources for each of these goals: learning a foreign language; building a birdhouse; deciding on a career. Identify each resource as human, material, or community.

17. Evaluating Information Go to this book's Online Learning Center at **glencoe.com** to find **Web Links** for variations of the **Decision-Making Process** such as those found in FCCLA. Choose one of the links and evaluate the information using the questions found on page 185 of this chapter. Decide whether the Web site provides useful information based on facts and data. Would you recommend this Web site to others? Why or why not?

 Additional Activities For additional activities, go to this book's Online Learning Center through **glencoe.com**.

Academic Skills

Mathematics

18. Analyze Population Data Dan's family is moving to a new area. Dan decides to analyze the demographics, or population, of the new community. Through research, he finds that there are about 25,000 people over 50 years old in the area. If this group represents about 8% of the population, what is the total population?

Math Concept **Variables and Expressions**
A variable is a place holder for a changing value. Any letter, such as x, can be used as a variable. Expressions such as $x + 2$ and $4x$ are algebraic expressions because they represent sums or products of variables and numbers.

Starting Hint: Change the percent (8%) to a decimal (.08). Use the decimal to create an algebraic expression where x represents the total population ($.08x = 25,000$). Then solve for x by isolating x on one side of the equation.

 For math help, go to the Math Appendix at the back of the book.

> **NCTM Problem Solving** Solve problems that arise in mathematics and in other contexts.

English Language Arts

19. Design a Brochure Using a publishing software program, design a brochure about overcoming procrastination. Use the tips in the Life Skills Checklist. Research to find out more. If possible, print the brochure and make copies. You can make these available in the school counseling office.

> **NCTE 6** Apply knowledge of language structure and conventions to discuss texts.

Social Studies

20. Public Decision Making Research how laws are made. What kind of process does the group making the law go through? How does this compare with the decision-making process discussed in this chapter? If possible, attend a session of a local government body such as the city council. Write a report that evaluates how decision making is done when making laws. If you were able to attend a meeting, write a report on what you observed regarding decision making.

> **NCSS X.c** Locate, analyze, and apply information about selected public issues.

STANDARDIZED TEST PRACTICE

MULTIPLE CHOICE
Read the question. Then read each answer choice and choose the best answer to fill in the blank.

> **Test-Taking Tip** In a multiple choice test, read the questions carefully. Look for negative words such as not, never, except, unless and positive words such as always or sometimes, which can affect how you answer the question.

21. The problem-solving process does not include _____.
   a. identifying the problem
   b. waiting two weeks before making a final decision
   c. evaluating the outcome
   d. choosing the best option

Section 11.1

Technology and the Family

Section 11.2

Technology in the Community

▶▶ *Explore the Photo* The development of new technology has changed lives dramatically. *In what ways has technology affected your life?*

Chapter Objectives

After completing this chapter, you will be able to:

- **Describe** the effects of technology on family life.
- **Identify** benefits and costs of communication technology in the family.
- **Summarize** the effect of technology in the workplace.
- **Explain** technology issues that impact society as a whole.
- **Suggest** guidelines for dealing with technology in the future.

Writing Activity

Business Letter

Ethical Behavior Ethical behavior is based on an individual's morals and values. It means doing what is right. You can show ethical behavior when you:

- Purchase software, rather than copying it illegally.
- Respect the privacy of other people's computer files.
- Keep a friend's confidences.
- Do the right thing, even though no one may know it.

Write a business letter to a local library asking if they provide information on ethical behavior involving technology. Explain why the free flow of information on the Internet makes ethical behavior important in society today.

Writing Tips To write an effective business letter, follow these steps:
1. Be clear about the purpose of ethical behavior.
2. Be brief and considerate.
3. Arrange the details of your argument in an organized, logical way.
4. Proofread to correct errors in the conventions of grammar, usage, spelling, and punctuation.

Technology and the Family

Reading Guide

Before You Read

Adjust Reading Speed Improve your comprehension by adjusting reading speed to match the difficulty of the text. Reading slower may take longer, but you will understand and remember more.

Read to Learn
Key Concepts
- **Describe** the effects of technology on family life.
- **Identify** benefits and costs of communication technology in the family.

Main Idea
Technology affects families in many areas. There are benefits and drawbacks to technology that families can recognize and manage.

Content Vocabulary
◇ technology   ◇ futurist

Academic Vocabulary
You will find these words in your reading and on your tests. Use the glossary to look up their definitions if necessary.
■ leisure   ■ access

Graphic Organizer
As you read, write down the areas of family life that technology has affected. List one benefit and one challenge of technology in each area. Use a chart like the one shown to help organize your information.

Area of Family Life	Benefit of Technology	Technology Challenge

 Graphic Organizer Go to this book's Online Learning Center at **glencoe.com** to print out this graphic organizer.

Academic Standards · · · · · · · · · · · · · · · · · ·

 English Language Arts

NCTE 7 Conduct research and gather, evaluate, and synthesize data to communicate discoveries.

NCTE 12 Use language to accomplish individual purposes.

 Mathematics

NCTM Problem Solving Solve problems that arise in mathematics and in other contexts.

NCTE *National Council of Teachers of English*
NCTM *National Council of Teachers of Mathematics*

NSES *National Science Education Standards*
NCSS *National Council of the Social Studies*

Manage Technology

Technology is the use of science to do practical things. Through technology, new products and tools change the world daily. These changes affect families in a number of ways.

Technology is one of many resources that families have. It can make family life better. It can also conflict with the family's goals and values.

How families manage technology has a huge impact on how well these families function. Technology can help families by making everyday tasks easier. At every stage of family development, there are also challenges in the use of technology.

People have their own approaches to technology. These are based on their personalities, interests, and values. For example, everyone does not have to have the newest gadgets. Many people manage well with the technology they have. People make choices that will fulfill their needs. These choices can also help their families function well.

A person who studies and predicts what may happen in the years ahead is called a **futurist**. Over the years, futurists have tracked the enormous number of changes that have occurred in society. The rate of change has also been increasing.

People can benefit when they learn to manage technology. It can help families with special needs. For example, voice recognition programs let people with limited mobility type on their computers.

People learn to overcome the challenges of technology. To get along well with technology, you need to know what can happen. You have to manage technology, rather than simply use it.

◆ Vocabulary

You can find definitions in the glossary at the back of this book.

As You Read

Connect How does technology make your family life better, and how can it conflict with family life?

Family Entertainment

Technology has brought new forms of entertainment into the lives of family members. DVDs and DVRs let you watch what you want, when you want. Cable and satellite television networks and satellite radio increase viewing and listening choices. MP3 players play the music you choose.

Video and computer games are everywhere. Through the Internet, people can play games with people on the other side of the world. The special effects and plots of the games can make them addictive.

▶▶ **Get Along with Technology** Families have to learn to manage the technology that has entered their homes. *What effect can video games have on a family?*

Financial Literacy

Develop a Budget Spreadsheet

On her home computer, Ahra set up a spreadsheet to track her monthly finances. For each month, she enters data about what she earns (earnings) and what she spends (expenditures). On your computer or by hand, create a spreadsheet that will show this information. Also include a formula for determining total cash flow.

Math Concept **Determine Total Cash Flow** Spreadsheets are tables with rows and columns used to display information. Total cash flow is determined by adding earnings and subtracting expenditures from earnings.

Starting Hint: Enter data into the cells of the spreadsheet. Create an equation for total cash flow using earnings and expenditures. The equation for total cash flow is: Total Cash Flow = Earnings − Expenditures.

 For math help, go to the Math Appendix at the back of the book.

NCTM Problem Solving Solve problems that arise in mathematics and in other contexts.

Challenges of Entertainment

At first glance, the entertainment options seem positive. There are, however, some drawbacks to the vast number of choices as well. Think about the impact of entertainment on the family. The effect may be beneficial or challenging. It all depends on how families manage their entertainment. How would you respond to these questions?

- Do televisions, computers, and video games divide families when members are involved for hours at a time?
- Does outside entertainment, such as movie theaters or amusement parks, pull family members away from home more than is reasonable?
- Do people neglect the quiet pleasures of nature or reading because they want more thrilling entertainment?

Leisure time, or free time, is important to the family. How families find this time depends on their values and goals. One family may limit computer use. Another may promote the latest video games. A third may ensure they spend quality time together.

Family Health and Safety

Technology has had a great impact on the health and safety of family members. One of the major effects has been in how people prepare and eat food. Some foods are ready to eat in minutes. Microwave ovens prepare food in seconds. Dishwashers make cleanup easy.

Eating on the run, however, can mean families are not together. Family ties may weaken when members are not able to share meals. For example, mealtimes are a good way to catch up on what everyone in the family did that day. When families do not have the time to eat together, they may not be as aware of the events in their family members' lives.

Nutrition

Good nutrition requires sound decision making. Fast food, both at home and in restaurants, is readily available. Fast food is often high in calories, fat, and salt. Families need to choose a variety of healthful foods. This is true both at home and in restaurants. Look for foods that are low in calories, fat, and salt.

Many foods now contain synthetic ingredients. This means they are produced by chemical means. For example, artificial sweeteners reduce calories. Artificial fats help people lower their intake of fat. Technology has produced leaner meat and low-cholesterol eggs. There are many improvements in preserving, shipping, and handling food. This makes fresh fruits and vegetables accessible year-round in most parts of the country.

Exercise

Technology can lead to an inactive lifestyle. In other words, many people sit rather than exercise. Products such as riding lawn mowers and computers lead to this. DVDs and video games can keep people inside in front of television sets and computer monitors. People may watch sports on televisions rather than play sports. The convenience of technology products can also lead to challenges in keeping up with exercise and a healthy lifestyle.

Many people do less physical activity than they need in the course of a day. As a result of this knowledge, the interest in exercising has grown over the years. People know that they need physical activity in their lives. Technology has lead to many helpful options to meet this goal. Exercise equipment is available for use at home and in health clubs. People who walk for exercise may use a treadmill rather than walk outside.

Security and Protection

Technology provides new ways of assuring safety. Security systems are installed in homes, offices, and cars. Air bags and children's car seats make travel safer. In a car accident or fire, equipment and rescuers arrive quickly. People get the care they need as soon as possible, often as a result of technology.

Families can use these advances to protect their members. Technology can make filling this family function easier. It is not possible to protect against every bad thing that can happen. People can use common sense in choosing protection. They should protect against the things that are most likely to happen to them.

Family Finances

Technology affects how families deal with their money. Automatic teller machines (ATMs) provide cash at any time of the day. Families can pay bills online. Checks can be deposited directly into bank accounts. Debit cards pull money from an account without having to write a check.

Software programs help people manage their money. The software tracks income and expenses. It shows where money is spent. These records can help people plan and budget better.

At the same time, technology makes matters more complex. Instant **access**, or availability, to cash and credit, for example, can cause trouble. It can lead to debt and spending money without thinking. Debt is easy to create and hard to get out of. If families use technology to their advantage, they can actively manage their money.

Use Technology to Stay Healthy Technology can promote good health. *What are some ways you think technology can contribute to your good health?*

New technology is interesting, but do you need everything you see? You have to weigh the costs and benefits. Many products, especially electronics, become outdated quickly. They are often replaced by more advanced products. To get the most for your money, you need to look for quality and buy carefully.

Cell phone makers continue to add new features. Phones now let people call, text, e-mail, surf the Web, take pictures, listen to music, and watch videos. Some of the new features help people stay connected to family and friends. Others are not used enough to be worth the cost. The media and advertisements create pressure to buy. Careful decision making helps people get the most for their money.

Problem-Solving Britt thinks her cell phone is old and not as useful. She wants a phone that has Internet access. Her old one can only call and text. Her parents say her old phone is fine. If she wants a new one, she has to pay for it and pay the added costs of using it. What should Britt do?

Housing

There are many technological advances that affect the home. What people used to do by hand, such as compress garbage, they can now do in seconds with modern appliances.

Reduce Energy

Advances in technology help reduce energy use in the home. Heating and air conditioners are more efficient than they used to be. More natural products are being used in household goods. There are items made from recycled materials that can be purchased for the home.

Household Management

Technology can make household management more convenient. Some families now have what is called a smart home. In smart homes, computers control many devices. These devices can turn off and on automatically in these homes. This type of technology was created for the security and comfort of the people living there.

In smart homes for example, lights turn on when people enter a room. Sensors adjust room temperatures and open garage doors. Families need to be sure that new housing technology will help them. Sometimes, older methods of running a house are just as effective.

✓ **Reading Check** **Define** What is technology?

Family Communication

Family members are linked to each other and the world by modern communication. Writing letters has been replaced by telephones, e-mails, instant messages, and text messaging. Answering machines and voice mail mean that you do not miss a call. Cell phones let you talk almost anywhere. Communication technology helps families. They can keep in touch with each other easier than before.

Communication Challenges

Family communication has grown stronger due to technology. The tools that help families keep in touch, however, can also pull them apart. For example, text messaging may lessen the amount of time families spend talking face-to-face. Families have to learn how to manage communication tools.

Communication tools can cause other problems as well. Here are some examples:

- When a cell phone rings in a theater, class, or library, it disturbs others. Remember to be courteous to people around you when using a cell phone.
- People often have private conversations on a cell phone in public. Everyone around the person has to listen to his or her personal business. This may be uncomfortable for others.
- It is common for people, especially teens, to have an accident when using technology while driving. Studies show that reduced attention to driving, such as talking on a cell phone or changing a CD, may cause an accident.
- Computer chat rooms sometimes lead to troublesome, even dangerous, relationships. People need to be cautious about the friendships they build on the Internet.

These are only a few examples. Can you think of other problems connected to communication technology? How can these problems be managed?

Communication technology is like any other resource. How you use it will affect whether or not it improves the quality of your life. These choices can enrich your communication and relationships with others if you manage the technology well.

Section 11.1　After You Read

Review Key Concepts

1. **Describe** five areas in which technology affects families.
2. **Identify** three challenges that can be created by communication technology.

Practice Academic Skills

English Language Arts

3. Research a feature that would be found in a smart home. Write a report of your findings. Include benefits of the feature, its cost, and whether you think it would be useful to have.

4. Select a communication device that you would like to own. Write five questions to ask a salesperson about the device. The questions should help you learn about the new product and its features and drawbacks.

NCTE 7 Conduct research and gather, evaluate, and synthesize data to communicate discoveries.

NCTE 12 Use language to accomplish individual purposes.

Check Your Answers Check your answers at this book's Online Learning Center through glencoe.com.

Technology in the Community

Reading Guide

Before You Read

Prepare with a Partner Work with a partner to ask each other and answer questions about the topics that will be discussed in this section.

Read to Learn
Key Concepts
- **Summarize** the effect of technology in the workplace.
- **Explain** technology issues that impact society as a whole.
- **Suggest** guidelines for dealing with technology in the future.

Main Idea
Most jobs today require technology skills. Communities and society are concerned about technology issues.

Content Vocabulary
◇ telecommute
◇ entrepreneur
◇ information society
◇ identity theft
◇ intrusive

Academic Vocabulary
You will find these words in your reading and on your tests. Use the glossary to look up their definitions if necessary.
▪ economic   ▪ sufficient

Graphic Organizer
As you read, write down tips to prevent identity theft. Use a concept web like the one shown to help organize your information.

 Graphic Organizer Go to this book's Online Learning Center at **glencoe.com** to print out this graphic organizer.

Academic Standards • • • • • • • • • • • • • • • •

 English Language Arts
NCTE 4 Use written language to communicate effectively.

NCTE 12 Use language to accomplish individual purposes.

Science
NSES Content Standard E Develop understandings about science and technology.

NCTE *National Council of Teachers of English*
NCTM *National Council of Teachers of Mathematics*

NSES *National Science Education Standards*
NCSS *National Council of the Social Studies*

Technology in the Workplace

Technology has drastically changed the workplace. Computers, for example, perform every kind of function at great speed. Laptops are replacing desktop computers. This lets people work faster and more efficiently from many different locations.

Very few jobs exist that do not involve computers. Think of the many ways the computer is used. Factories have computerized assembly lines. Retail stores can get information on sales per hour and the amount of the average sales by using a computer.

Wireless networking means that people are no longer tied to desks or workstations. This allows people to work at a distance. More people are working at home today than ever before. Many of them **telecommute**. This means they use telephones, faxes, and computers to do the same work at home that would be done at the workplace.

Technology also allows people to become entrepreneurs. An **entrepreneur** is someone who organizes and runs a business. Many businesses have been started by people using computers at home. Computers can now do what used to require teams of people and special equipment.

Technology means that workers need to be flexible. They must continue to update their knowledge and skills. Being open to change is a required skill of workers at every level.

✓ **Reading Check** **Explain** What does it mean to telecommute?

Society and Technology

Many communities use technology to help people. Computerized traffic lights, for example, control the flow of cars. This helps reduce traffic jams and accidents. Communication about services and activities can be sent through electronic sources. In other words, a town may e-mail its monthly newsletter and trash bills, rather than sending paper copies through the mail.

Communities often grant their citizens access to their technology resources. For example, libraries may have audio books to rent. They may loan CDs, DVDs, and computer games. Most have computers and an Internet connection that the public can use. Many cities have wireless Internet networks available to their residents.

The use of technology raises questions for society as a whole. What are the costs? What are the benefits? Which innovations will strengthen society? Which will weaken it? Which new technology will make life easier?

As You Read
Connect How do you see technology and computer skills used in the workplace?

◇ **Vocabulary**
You can find definitions in the glossary at the back of this book.

Work from Home Telecommuting is popular because it allows workers to balance their jobs with their lives. *What kinds of technology allow telecommuting to be possible?*

The Information Society

We are living in an **information society** where the main **economic** activity is creating and distributing knowledge. Economic means relating to production and consumption of goods and services. This activity may be in the form of text, pictures, sound, or video. The computer is the main tool that is used to spread this information.

Through computers and the Internet, people have instant access to every kind of information. People can get data from around the world. At the same time, the volume of information that exists has increased. As a result, the focus today is not on trying to remember everything about a topic. Instead you need to know how to find and judge the information.

The free flow of information on the Internet helps people at home and at work. The challenge is to know what is fact and what is not. A good portion of Web content may be opinion. Web site addresses that end in .edu or .gov are sponsored by educational groups or governments. The information on them is apt to be factual and based on research.

Management of e-mail can also be a concern. Computer viruses are spread through e-mails. Some of these can make computers useless. Spam is also a concern. Spam is unsolicited e-mail. Many people get more spam e-mail than real e-mail. Spam can also be a source of viruses. A spam filter is a program that can screen out unwanted e-mails. You should not open e-mails unless you know the sender. Never reply to spam or click on links within a spam e-mail.

Age of Information Today we have instant access to all kinds of information and knowledge. *Where in your community can you instantly access information?*

Protect Personal Identity

Identity theft is a crime. An identity thief will use personal information to commit other crimes, such as spending your money or running up debts in your name. Follow these guidelines to protect your personal identity:

1. **Secure your mail.** Drop your bills in a public box. Try not to leave them in your house or apartment mailbox. If you go on vacation, ask a friend to pick up your mail. You can also ask the post office to hold your mail.
2. **Keep personal information private.** Only give your personal information to sources you trust. Do not give personal information to strangers.
3. **Choose creative passwords.** Letter and number combinations make the best passwords. Do not choose obvious words and numbers like birth dates or names.
4. **Secure wireless computer connections.** Make sure the connection on your wireless home computer is secure.

Take Action Read the privacy policy on a Web site you visit regularly. What information about users does the company gather? How does it use this information? How does it protect against identity theft? Do you think these measures are enough?

Identify Theft

As information spreads, people worry about privacy. They want to protect personal information. They do not want the numbers for their telephone, bank accounts, and credit cards to get in the wrong hands.

It is essential to guard against identity theft. **Identity theft** is using a person's personal information to steal money or credit. Never give personal data to strangers who call on the phone. Be careful about putting it on the Internet as well. If you order products on the phone, make the calls yourself and only to companies you trust. When you buy items on the computer, make sure to use secure Web sites. Tear up or shred personal papers before throwing them in the garbage. Avoid leaving mail in an unlocked mailbox.

Intrusiveness

Technology can be **intrusive** (in-'trü-siv, -ziv). That is, it enters your life without your invitation. For example, does spam fill your e-mail inbox? Many people are annoyed by these and other intrusions.

You do have some options. You can sign up for national and state Do Not Call lists. If you do this, marketers are prohibited from contacting you without your prior permission. If they do, they can be fined. You can look for an Internet provider who has **sufficient**, or adequate, spam controls. Simple solutions can sometimes ease the frustrations that people feel.

The Cost of Technology

The cost of technology can be high. This is both a public and a personal issue. Equipment can cost hundreds or thousands of dollars. There are many public and personal questions related to the costs of using new technology. A community has to make choices, just as people and families do.

What is spent on technology is not available to be spent on other items. Sometimes, choices go back to the issue of needs and wants. Most new technology is a want, not a need. Once basic needs are met, then wants can be indulged. This is true of both communities and families. For example, the benefits of a high-speed subway system are wasted if there is no money to pay workers to keep it clean and working.

Health Care Costs

One area of concern in society is how to pay for health care. Medical technology saves lives but it is costly. People want new and better treatments, but they worry about how to pay for these treatments. Families without health insurance may struggle if faced with the cost of paying for treatment of a serious illness. How the costs of new types of medical care will be covered is an ongoing debate in society.

Medical technology saves, lengthens, and enriches lives. Some examples of this technology include artificial limbs and transplants. Some technology also makes medical care easier than it used to be.

Technology often creates hard choices in the areas of health and medicine. Some questions, like these, create debate:

- If a person has a terminal disease, how should it be treated?
- How should the use of life support systems be handled?

People are wise to stay informed about medical care issues. When looking for work, find out what employers offer. The better job may be one that has a good health plan. Taking care of health helps many people avoid the costs of some medical care.

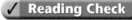

Advances in Science Advances in medical science and technology have saved millions of lives. *What technology do you think has contributed to people living longer?*

✓ **Reading Check**

Describe What is an information society?

Technology and the Future

As this chapter points out, technology has both rewards and costs. Technology, of course, is here to stay. You can be in control of the technology in your life. You do not have to let it control you. You and your family can manage technology if you keep the following in mind:

- **Have a sense of humor.** Devices fail and strange things happen. Laughing is better than getting upset.
- **Make time for activities that do not involve technology.** Your family can enjoy simple pleasures in life, too. These can include a day at the park or reading a book.
- **Use only what is important to you.** It can be helpful to narrow down what technology to use. You can do this by deciding what you need to use.
- **Stay informed.** Technology is fascinating. Knowing something about it can make you feel more comfortable and prepare you for the future.

Technology can improve life and help solve problems. Sometimes, however, technology may cause problems. When this happens, people need to step back and reflect. They can look at their resources and see if there is another way to manage them. They can plan what to do based on what is important to them. People find it helpful to know their goals and values. This can lead to easier decisions about how to manage technology. They will balance the costs and rewards of a device's new features. They will make decisions with care. In these ways, they will be able to manage technology successfully.

Life Skills CHECKLIST

Management Skills

Technology at Work You will manage technology at work effectively if you:

✓ Follow your company's policy on the personal use of technology.

✓ Ask questions when you do not know how to use equipment or software.

✓ Update your technology skills when you have the chance.

✓ Find someone to help you if you have technology problems.

Section 11.2 After You Read

Review Key Concepts

1. **Describe** why flexibility is a needed skill for workers today.
2. **Discuss** why finding and evaluating data is an important skill today.
3. **Explain** how a sense of humor can help manage technology.

Practice Academic Skills

English Language Arts

4. Think back to when you started school. Write a report identifying changes in educational technology since then. Do you think these changes have improved learning? Explain your answer.

5. If you could create a new technology, what would it be? What would it do? Write a paragraph describing your invention and its purpose.

NCTE 4 Use written language to communicate effectively.

NCTE 12 Use language to accomplish individual purposes.

Check Your Answers Check your answers at this book's Online Learning Center through **glencoe.com**.

CAREER SPOTLIGHT

Disabilities Accommodations Specialist

Ron Venable
Denton, Texas

For many students, getting an education can be difficult. It can be especially difficult for those with disabilities. That is where people like Ron Venable come in. Ron works with college students. He determines if their physical or mental condition qualifies as a disability under the Americans with Disabilities Act. If it does, he helps ensure their education meets their specific needs.

"All students are individuals," Venable states. "We must do everything possible to ensure we review their situation on a personalized basis. This will help us come to a solution for that individual."

After meeting with a student, Venable works with that student to create a plan. He looks into what can be done to overcome the limitations a student faces. He then acts as a liaison between the student body and the faculty. He manages a budget for special programs and tools, and works with teachers to help create accessible course content.

Venable says his job is always challenging and never boring. He explains, "What would you do if a dog who was supposedly on campus to help a person with a disability decided to attack another student? There is something new every day."

CAREER FACTS

Education and Training Master's degrees in vocational rehabilitation counseling are common, as are undergraduate programs in vocational rehabilitation.

Nature of the Work Disability accommodations specialists work with individuals with disabilities to help assess their needs, and with other agencies and groups to help connect with those individuals.

Aptitudes, Abilities, and Skills This career requires strong communication skills, great listening skills, and a strong sense of compassion and empathy.

Academic Skills Required English, biology, psychology, an understanding of political science

Student Organizations To prepare for this career, look for groups that allow you to help others, like a volunteer group that assists fellow students with disabilities around campus.

Career Outlook Jobs as disabilities accommodations specialists are expected to grow faster than the average over the next ten years.

Career Path This career often begins in a state vocational rehabilitation agency. There is one in every state in the United States.

Critical Thinking

Accommodations What kind of aid is there at your school for students with disabilities?

 Research Careers For more information on this and other careers, visit the Occupational Outlook Handbook Web site through the link on this book's Online Learning Center at **glencoe.com**.

CHAPTER SUMMARY

 ### Section 11.1
Technology and the Family

Technology affects all parts of family life. Families need to manage technology so that they can reach their goals. Values are important when making decisions about technology. Technology has changed entertainment choices. Some weaken and others strengthen the family. Technology has also changed the way people cook, eat, and exercise. It has brought about ways of promoting security and protection. The way a family handles their money can be both helped and hurt by technological advances in financing. Housing reflects changes in technology. Family relationships can be strengthened by wise use of communication technology.

 ### Section 11.2
Technology in the Community

The workplace has changed due to technology. Most jobs use computers. Workers must have technology skills and keep them up to date. Computers allow workers to telecommute and entrepreneurs to start new businesses. Communities use technology to provide services to citizens. Controlling the privacy of information and the cost of technology are two issues society faces. Personal information is widely available. This can lead to identity theft. Technology can also be intrusive. There are difficult decisions regarding health care and costs facing society. Individuals and communities need to make careful choices as they deal with more technology changes in the future.

Content and Academic Vocabulary Review

1. Use each of these content and academic vocabulary words in a sentence.

Content Vocabulary
- ◇ technology (p. 207)
- ◇ futurist (p. 207)
- ◇ telecommute (p. 213)
- ◇ entrepreneur (p. 213)
- ◇ information society (p. 214)
- ◇ identity theft (p. 215)
- ◇ intrusive (p. 215)

Academic Vocabulary
- ▪ leisure (p. 208)
- ▪ access (p. 209)
- ▪ economic (p. 214)
- ▪ sufficient (p. 215)

Review Key Concepts

2. Describe the effects of technology on family life.

3. Identify benefits and costs of communication technology in the family.

4. Summarize the effect of technology in the workplace.

5. Explain technology issues that impact society as a whole.

6. Suggest guidelines for dealing with technology in the future.

Critical Thinking

7. Analyze Think about how technology is used in four jobs or careers.

8. Evaluate Consider the danger involved in communicating with others on the Internet. Explain your answer.

9. Compare and Contrast How has technology affected the family? How has it affected society? What are the ties? The differences?

Real-World Skills

Problem-Solving Skills

10. Self-Management Larry's phone rings constantly with calls from coworkers, telephone solicitors, friends, and family. When it is not the cell phone, it is his e-mail. He feels as though he cannot escape. Write a paragraph explaining what he should do.

Management Skills

11. Organize E-mail Imagine that you have a job where you get e-mails from coworkers and customers. Your e-mail system lets you make folders for messages. Make a plan to organize your e-mail. Make a list of folders that would be useful, and write a paragraph explaining how you would prioritize the messages.

Critical Thinking Skills

12. Job Applicants Some employers search Web sites for the names of job applicants. They reject applicants who reveal certain personal details about themselves. Should employers be able to use the sites in this way? Write a letter to the school newspaper with your opinion.

Collaborative Skills

13. Decision Making Jonathan noticed that his mom was having trouble finding a place to store all of her kitchen appliances and gadgets. He began to think about all the things his family owned that they seldom or never used. Write an advice column explaining what you think Jonathan and his family should do.

14. Do Not Call Lists Follow your teacher's instructions to form into groups. Conduct research to find out how to get on Do Not Call lists. Write a summary of how people can get on these lists.

15. Public Access Find out where there are public computers in your community. Is there a cost to use them? Are there rules for their use? Are there wireless network connections? Who pays for the networks? Do you think your community has good public access to computers and networks? Why or why not? Write a paragraph to share your findings.

16. Interview Interview a parent about the television or movies his or her child watches. Are there restrictions on what is watched? How much time is spent watching? Is it educational? Take notes of your interview.

17. Millionaire Calculator Go to this book's Online Learning Center at **glencoe.com** to find **Web Links** for **A Millionaire Calculator**. Enter the necessary information into the calculator. The site will tell you how long it will take to have a million dollars. Print out the results.

Additional Activities For additional activities, go to this book's Online Learning Center through **glencoe.com**.

Academic Skills

Mathematics

18. Timing a Presentation Elena is going to give a speech at a luncheon. Her speech will be accompanied by a slideshow on her computer. The presentation time limit is 15 minutes. Elena figures that she will use 25 slides. How many seconds should she spend on each slide without going over the time limit?

Math Concept **Calculate Average Time** A minute has 60 seconds, an hour has 60 minutes, and a day has 24 hours. It is helpful to convert before you divide to calculate an average. To convert minutes to seconds, multiply by 60. Do the same to convert hours to minutes. To convert days to hours, multiply by 24.

Starting Hint: Convert the total number of minutes for the speech (15) to seconds by multiplying by 60. Divide your answer by the number of slides (25). Be sure to label your answer with the correct unit of time.

 For math help, go to the Math Appendix at the back of the book.

> **NCTM Number and Operations** Understand the meanings of operations and how they relate to one another.

English Language Arts

19. Research Conduct research to find out what futurists are predicting in the field of technology. What new devices do they expect to be invented in upcoming years? How will current technology evolve? Will there be any changes in costs of technology? Give an oral report to your classmates describing the most interesting prediction you found in your research.

> **NCTE 7** Conduct research and gather, evaluate, and synthesize data to communicate discoveries.

Social Studies

20. Survey Research how your local government uses technology to serve citizens. Does it use computers to provide service? Does it use video technology so that citizens can view public meetings? Does it use technology to monitor water quality or traffic flow? Write a short report of your findings. Make suggestions for other ways your local government can use technology to help its citizens.

> **NCSS VI.c** Analyze and explain ideas and mechanisms to meet needs and wants of citizens.

STANDARDIZED TEST PRACTICE

TRUE/FALSE
Read each statement. On a separate sheet of paper, write T if the statement is true, and write F if the statement is false.

> **Test-Taking Tip** Make sure you understand the full statement. All parts of a statement must be correct for the statement to be true. Statements that contain extreme words, such as all, none, never, or always, or that have unsupported opinions, are often false.

21. Decide if each statement is true or false.
  a. _____ Technology affects all aspects of daily life.
  b. _____ Privacy issues can be a negative consequence of technology.
  c. _____ All technology is beneficial.

CHAPTER 12

Balance Work and Family Life

Section 12.1

Work and Families

Section 12.2

Managing Busy Lives

 Explore the Photo
Families are leading busier lives than ever. *How does finding time for family and leisure make you a better person?*

Chapter Objectives

After completing this chapter, you will be able to:

- **Describe** two types of work that families do.
- **Summarize** how jobs and family life can affect each other.
- **Identify** ways that employers can support family life.
- **Explain** strategies that families can use to manage the work at home.
- **Suggest** ways families can use help from others to balance work and family life.

Writing Activity
Write a Dialogue

Courtesy Courtesy is using polite behavior and good manners. It is most difficult when you are frustrated, stressed, or in a hurry. You can show courtesy when you:
- Do an unpleasant household chore without complaint.
- Say please and thank you to family members.
- Greet others cheerfully when reporting for work.
- Carry a neighbor's groceries when she needs help.
- Behave politely to a difficult and demanding customer.

Some people believe that courtesy is a lost art in today's society. Write a dialogue between two people that shows courtesy.

Writing Tips To write an effective dialogue, follow these steps:
1. Let the people in your dialogue express themselves and their purpose through the words you write.
2. Use language that sounds real and appropriate to the people talking.
3. Use quotation marks appropriately.

Work and Families

Reading Guide

Before You Read

Helpful Memory Tools Successful readers use tricks to help them remember. For example, the acronym HOMES is a memory aid where each letter stands for one of the five Great Lakes. As you read the section, look for opportunities to make up your own memory aids.

Read to Learn
Key Concepts
- **Describe** two types of work that families do.
- **Summarize** how jobs and family life can affect each other.

Main Idea

Families do household and income-producing work. The work can be assigned so that there is balance in family members' lives. The quality of family life and job performance are related.

Content Vocabulary
◇ work ethic
◇ household work
◇ income-producing work

 Graphic Organizer Go to this book's Online Learning Center at **glencoe.com** to print out this graphic organizer.

Academic Vocabulary

You will find these words in your reading and on your tests. Use the glossary to look up their definitions if necessary.

■ satisfaction   ■ appropriate

Graphic Organizer

As you read, list the two types of work done by families in the left column under the heading Type of Work. Describe the work in the right column under Description. Use a chart like the one shown to help organize your information.

Type of Work	Description

Academic Standards . . . .

English Language Arts

NCTE 4 Use written language to communicate effectively.

NCTE 5 Use different writing process elements to communicate effectively.

Mathematics

NCTM Number and Operations Compute fluently and make reasonable estimates.

NCTE *National Council of Teachers of English*
NCTM *National Council of Teachers of Mathematics*

NSES *National Science Education Standards*
NCSS *National Council of the Social Studies*

The Value of Work

Work is a valuable part of life. It brings purpose and order to each day. Work not only provides something worthwhile to do, but it also brings income and other rewards. Good work allows you to feel proud of a job well done. You will feel **satisfaction**, or fulfillment, in the contributions you make.

People often talk about their work ethic. **Work ethic** is a set of values based on the moral virtues of hard work and diligence. It is an attitude that values honest work. It means you want to work hard to take care of yourself and your family. People with a good work ethic get things done.

Two basic kinds of work exist for families. One is the work that keeps the household going. The other is the work that produces income.

Household Work

Some work must be done simply for the well-being of people. The work a family does in the home to keep up with day-to-day living is **household work**. The management skills needed for household work are similar to those required to run a business. Both require using resources wisely. They involve dealing with people. Scheduling and cooperation are important in both places. Although people are seldom paid for household work, it is of value and should be appreciated.

Some jobs that keep a household going are easy to identify but others are not. Feeding the family is an obvious job. Meals must be planned, food purchased, recipes prepared, and cleanup done. Some people are not aware of what others do. If someone else cleans the refrigerator, you may not even notice. Still, someone in a family handles these and other tasks regularly.

Not all household chores are related to cooking and cleaning. Many families have repairs to make and errands to run. A car may need servicing. These jobs are also important in families.

Vocabulary

You can find definitions in the glossary at the back of this book.

As You Read

Connect What are some rewards that you think work provides?

◀◀ *A Job Well Done*
Taking pride in your work gives you a feeling of self-worth. *What qualities do you need to take pride in your job?*

When family members cooperate to get household work done, they enjoy many positive results that can include:

- **Less Stress** A person does not have to carry most of the workload when others are available to help.
- **Time for Other Activities** When family work is shared, it takes less time to do.
- **New Skills** The skills learned, such as planning and decision making, will be useful when teens are on their own.
- **A Strong Work Ethic** Family members discover a sense of accomplishment.

- **Positive Feelings** When people receive support, they are willing to support others.
- **Responsibility** A person who helps out is valued in the family. This gives that person a sense of purpose and commitment to the family.

Problem-Solving

Mrs. Kane cleaned the living room yesterday. Today it is a mess again. Everyone in her family left for the day without cleaning the living room. She had planned to sit and read a magazine before her friend Rosie came for a visit. What would you do if you were Mrs. Kane?

A Variety of Jobs

Household jobs differ in several ways. For instance, some are done more frequently than others. Mowing the lawn may be a once-a-week summer job, but unnecessary in winter. Other jobs may need to be done daily or monthly. Most household jobs can be categorized according to how often they need to be done.

Jobs also differ in the amount of time they take. Time management can be a factor in how well household work gets done. Small blocks of time can be used to do small chores. You could fold clothes during the ads of your favorite television show. You may be able to do two things at once. While you are talking on the phone, you can empty the dishwasher. If family members work together, they may be able to finish jobs faster than if they work alone.

Some jobs are simpler—even more fun—than others. People do not always agree on which jobs are better. While one person may love to cook, another may dislike it. What happens if everyone dislikes cooking?

Families have different feelings about work in the house. What they want and are able to get done depends on their attitudes and available time. The willingness of family members to share the work load is also a factor.

Income-Producing Work

Families also do **income-producing work**. This type of work provides money for needs and wants. The amount of time people devote to this work varies. Many people work full time. This option usually brings the most money and can include benefits. Some people prefer part-time work. This may allow flexibility if the worker has other duties to attend to. In some families, one person provides all the income. In many families today, however, more than one family member earns income.

Who Does the Work?

Who does the work in a family? Who should do the work? These questions can cause debate in almost any household.

Traditionally, the daily care of the home and family was the mother's job. The father's responsibility was to provide financially for the family and make decisions about how money was used. At home, he did some jobs, like mowing the lawn, and fixing things around the house.

Over the years, the way people have handled work has changed. Traditional ways of dividing work may not be **appropriate**, or suitable, today because life is different. Single-parent families have only one adult to do the work. In many families, both the mother and father hold jobs and share the household work. Children and teens also do useful work to help the family as a whole.

Each family deals with questions of roles and responsibilities in their own way. For example, women who are married, have children, and are employed work about as many hours at home as they spend on the job. Many husbands may share household work. However, their jobs tend to be assigned differently. Women still do about two-thirds of the everyday jobs at home. Men are more likely to be responsible for paying bills, doing car maintenance, yard work, and home repair. Their work is apt to be more flexible. Men often have more control over when they do household work and how much they do.

Men share child care more often than they perform household tasks. Men tend to play with and educate the children. Women are more likely to feed the children or take them to the doctor.

Younger families are less influenced by traditional roles. They are more likely to view work as something that a family must do together. As a result, they share household and income-producing work.

✓ **Reading Check** **Explain** What does work ethic mean?

Life Skills CHECKLIST

Communication Skills

Household Work Families need to communicate clearly about household work. A family will communicate well if they:

✓ Agree on the household tasks that need to be done.

✓ Understand family members' feelings and ideas about the household work.

✓ Listen to suggestions for improving the system of getting the work done.

✓ Remain aware of each family member's time commitments.

✓ Support each other when there are difficulties.

✓ Know what to do when problems arise.

◄◄ *Everyone Can Help* It is not just the mother's job to handle the daily home care. *Why should family members want to share in the work at home?*

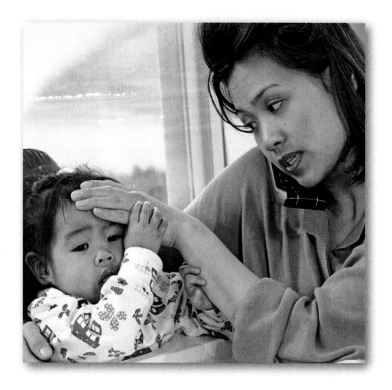

Jobs and Family Life

There is a definite interrelationship between job and family life. A job that produces a family's income is usually a big commitment of time and energy. House-hold work is too. Combining both can be like having two full-time jobs. Problems come when one person bears too much of the burden. Even when workloads are shared equally, managing life at home and on the job can still be a challenge.

Family Life Affects Jobs

Suppose you work a part-time job. You may notice that some of the employees have problems. What has happened to them at home may be affecting their job performance. Take a look at some examples of how family life affects jobs.

- **Home Pressures** Allyson is a single parent with two children. She often stays up late to get things done at home. She is tired and not very alert at work. She misses days at work when her children are sick.
- **Family Problems** Trevor and his wife recently divorced. Trevor's son stays with him every other week. Trevor's emotional state is fragile. He is often distracted at work.
- **Lack of Family Training** Pearce has a poor work ethic. He also does not take responsibility for his actions. Pearce is missing certain qualities that he should have learned while growing up.

Math in Action

Cost of Going Out to Eat

Dining out can be more convenient than making meals at home. It can also be more expensive. Compare the costs of dining out and eating at home. Use these steps:

1. List two meals you would typically eat when you go out.
2. Contact two restaurants and ask the cost of the meals you have listed.
3. List the ingredients for making the same food items at home.
4. Go to a grocery store and find prices for the ingredients you have listed.

Math Concept **Multi-Step Problems** When solving problems with more than one step, think through each step first.

Starting Hint: Calculate the average cost of dining out. Then total the cost of the ingredients for eating in. Subtract the smaller number from the larger number and determine which is more economical.

Building Academic Skills
Go to this book's Online Learning Center through glencoe.com to complete a worksheet for this activity.

NCTM Problem Solving Apply and adapt a variety of appropriate strategies to solve problems.

 Math For math help, go to the Math Appendix at the back of the book.

As you can see, each of these employees needs to improve their job performance. Their personal lives are affecting their jobs. Employers need workers whose personal lives are healthy and in order.

Jobs Affect Family Life

Just as jobs are affected by family life, family life is also affected by what happens on the job. Look at these examples to see how your job can affect your family life.

- **Job Loss** Pete lost his job, leaving his family with little income. He is trying to find another job but feels frustrated and worried. He is cross and short-tempered at home.
- **Relocation** Karen has been offered a job transfer. She and her family must decide if they want to move.
- **Work Challenges** Corbin is a medical technician. Although he likes the work, it is very challenging. His family often feels his emotional strain.
- **Difficult Work Schedules** As a doctor, Rebecca is called to duty at all hours of the day and night. Her family never knows for sure when she will be home.
- **Work Stress** Juan works with very tight deadlines at his job. He often carries his tension and frustrations home to his family.

Families are heavily influenced by what happens to individual family members at their jobs. For families to function well, they need cooperation from employers and help from all family members.

The need to balance work and family life is getting a lot of attention in society today. As a teen, you can help your family manage. The skills you learn now can help when you are the leader of your own family someday.

Section 12.1 After You Read

Review Key Concepts

1. **Explain** In what ways do household tasks differ from each other?
2. **Identify** situations at home that can affect job performance.

Practice Academic Skills

English Language Arts

3. Employers value workers who have a good work ethic. Write a paragraph that explains what a work ethic is and what employees can do to show their work ethic.

4. How families divide household work varies. The trend is toward more shared work. Write a report that describes what you believe is the ideal division of labor in a family. Include a chart, table, or other graphic to demonstrate your division. Explain the reasoning for your division.

> **NCTE 4** Use written language to communicate effectively.

> **NCTE 5** Use different writing process elements to communicate effectively.

Check Your Answers Check your answers at this book's Online Learning Center through glencoe.com.

Managing Busy Lives

Reading Guide

Before You Read

Use Notes When you come upon a section or term you are unfamiliar with, write the word or a question on the paper. After you finish the section, look up the terms or try to answer your questions based on what you have read.

Read to Learn

Key Concepts

- **Identify** ways that employers can support family life.
- **Explain** strategies that families can use to manage the work at home.
- **Suggest** ways families can use help from others to balance work and family life.

Main Idea

Managing the work at home depends on management skills and sharing the work. Families also use help from others to manage.

Content Vocabulary

◇ flextime
◇ leave of absence
◇ reimbursement

Academic Vocabulary

You will find these words in your reading and on your tests. Use the glossary to look up their definitions if necessary.

■ compress
■ grant

Graphic Organizer

As you read, look for the different types of child care that are available. Use a concept map like the one shown to help organize your information.

```
          Types of
         Child Care
    ┌─────────┼─────────┐
  [    ]    [    ]    [    ]
```

 Graphic Organizer Go to this book's Online Learning Center at **glencoe.com** to print out this graphic organizer.

Academic Standards • • • • • • • • • • • • • • • • •

 English Language Arts

NCTE 8 Use information resources to gather information and create and communicate knowledge.

NCTE 12 Use language to accomplish individual purposes.

 Mathematics

NCTM Number and Operations Compute fluently and make reasonable entries.

NCTE *National Council of Teachers of English*
NCTM *National Council of Teachers of Mathematics*

NSES *National Science Education Standards*
NCSS *National Council of the Social Studies*

Employer Support

Some employers believe that income-producing work is a person's first priority. That is not true for everyone. Many people believe that, while work is important, their families come first. They want a lifestyle that will balance their work and family lives.

For example, an employer saw this when one of her best workers left for another job. She offered him a large raise to stay. A raise, however, was not what the employee wanted. He wanted a job that only required 40 hours of work a week. He did not want to stay late or work on weekends. He wanted time with his family. In the end that was more important to him than a higher income.

As employers realize what people truly want and need, they are making changes. They are creating more flexible policies. These appeal to people who want to blend family and personal life smoothly with their careers.

As You Read

Connect Should people consider their families to be first priority over their income-producing work?

Work Schedules

Working an eight-hour shift for five days of the week does not work for some people. Demands on time include personal business and family duties. When rigid job schedules do not let people do what needs to be done, stress and anger are a common result.

Not Working

9 to 5 Some careers require people to work at different hours of the day or night. *How does working odd hours affect the family?*

What happens to children when workers are tied to a set schedule? Parents miss school events. Children may be home alone or unable to get to activities. Doctor visits are hard to schedule. Many people miss work because of sick children or other parent responsibilities.

Many working parents may prefer part-time work. One problem is that few part-time jobs provide benefits. Many families also need a full-time paycheck. Most employed parents work full time.

Although employers have business needs, most want workers to feel in control of their lives. With creative thinking, employers can provide flexible work schedules. These can ease the lives of their workers. The benefit is a happier, more productive workforce.

Flexible Hours

Some companies have flexible working hours. With **flextime**, workers construct their work schedules to suit their lives. This allows employees control over the time period that they work. Having a choice means that people with different needs do not have to live and work by the same schedules.

Flexibility has benefits. Giving workers some control over their lives makes them feel better about their jobs. They tend to be more productive and miss less work. Most employers find the effort is worth it.

Compressed Week

Long weekends are another option. An employee may **compress**, or squeeze together, their work week. This is called a compressed week. This may include working four 10-hour days. Another option can be three 12-hour days. The days can be long, but the schedules are right for some people.

Job Sharing

When two people divide the time and duties of one job, they are job sharing. They may each work four hours a day. They share the income and benefits that go along with the full-time job.

Workplace Policies

Many companies offer leaves of absence to workers. A **leave of absence** provides time off from work to use for some purpose. Employers may **grant**, or permit, leaves of absence when a child is born or adopted, or when a family member is ill. Companies over a certain size must offer these benefits. These leaves of absence are most often without pay. However, employees have the comfort of knowing they will not lose their jobs.

At one time many companies moved workers on a regular basis. If this caused family problems, the company did not do much to help. The companies may not have realized at the time that the move would affect the family. In the end, they saw that unhappy families meant problems on the job. Today many businesses limit transfers.

Personal and family problems can affect job performance. Some employers offer help for problems. A company may offer counseling for addictions or other personal problems. Concerned employers want to support and help their workers. They would rather help than let the problem continue or ask an employee to leave.

✓ **Reading Check** **Identify** What are some examples of work schedules that may be more accommodating to families?

◆ **Vocabulary**

You can find definitions in the glossary at the back of this book.

Financial Literacy

Determine the Best Buy

Dena and Miguel have decided that using paper towels instead of cloth towels saves them time. They try to find the best buy on paper towels. Paper towels come in regular and jumbo sizes. A regular roll costs $0.89 and contains 80 sheets, each 11 × 9 inches. A jumbo roll costs $1.37 and contains 146 sheets, each also 11 × 9 inches. What is the cost per sheet for the two sizes? Which roll is the best buy?

Math Concept **Dividing Decimals by Whole Numbers** When dividing a decimal by a whole number, place the decimal point in the quotient directly above the decimal point in the dividend. Then divide as you do with whole numbers.

Starting Hint: First, use long division to determine the price per sheet in both the regular and jumbo rolls. Divide the price of the roll (the dividend) by the number of sheets in each roll (the divisor). The answer will be the price per sheet (the quotient). Compare the two quotients to find the best buy.

 For math help, go to the Math Appendix at the back of the book.

NCTM Number and Operations Compute fluently and make reasonable estimates.

Management at Home

A balanced life depends on how the work is shared at home. Family members may have negative feelings that no one else is aware of. Finding out may be the first step to better family management. It may also be the first step to a happier family life.

There are many ways families can work together to manage the work at home. These are most needed when both parents work outside the home. This is mainly because both parents have to balance work and family life.

Family members benefit when they each do their assigned jobs cheerfully. They should try to cooperate and accept responsibility. This will build positive feelings among other family members. These feelings can lead to better relationships within the family.

Tools for Managing

There are some useful tools to help family life run more smoothly. Management tools may appear to be fairly simple. However, the tools work best when everyone understands their purpose. Everyone also needs to agree to use them.

INDEPENDENT Living

HOW TO Manage at Home

Balancing work and family life may be difficult when there are so many household tasks that need to be done. Family members can help by sharing the work load. Follow these guidelines to help manage the work at home:

1. **List work to be done.** List the time each task takes, how often it is done, and who now does it. A chart can help organize the data.
2. **Evaluate standards.** Can any task be done less often or more simply?
3. **Assign tasks to family members.** Talk about what each person wants to do. Think about ages, skills, and strengths. Some tasks can be handled by one person. Others can be done as teams.
4. **Set up a schedule.** Show when each task is to be done. Enter the final schedule on a calendar or in a chart or notebook where everyone can see it.
5. **Evaluate progress.** After some period of time, check what is happening. Is everyone being responsible? What changes are needed?

Take Action Using the steps above, write down a chore management schedule for your family. As you create it, think not only of the skills of the people in your family, but of their personalities. Is there someone who does not like to work at all? How would you address these issues to make your schedule work?

A Family Calendar

A family calendar can solve many problems. For example, Julia wanted to schedule a family outing when no one else had plans. However, she did not have a calendar with her family's plans. Tony had to pick up his younger brother after a field trip. His mother wrote the time on a calendar so Tony was able to remember what time he needed to be there.

To start a calendar, find one that is large enough to write on. Post it in a place where everyone will see it. All family members can enter their own schedules. When they do, the calendar becomes a useful information center. For example, a family can easily see who will be at home to help make dinner. **Figure 12.1** shows how a schedule and other management tools can help a busy family plan their meals. With a calendar, family members will have an easier time reaching each other and avoiding schedule conflicts.

Family Meetings

Families need regular communication. This helps them understand what the others are thinking. Important issues get overlooked when daily life always comes first. To solve this, many families set aside a regular time to meet and talk. They can discuss work, complaints, values, and goals.

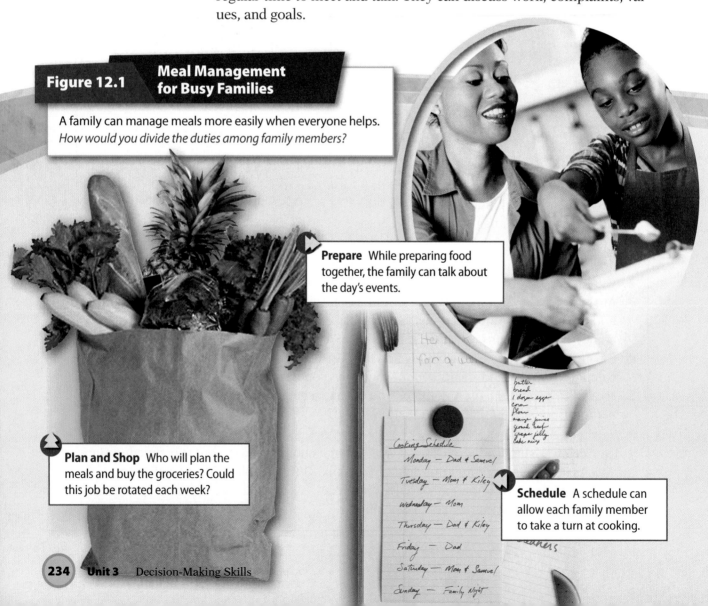

Figure 12.1 Meal Management for Busy Families

A family can manage meals more easily when everyone helps. *How would you divide the duties among family members?*

Prepare While preparing food together, the family can talk about the day's events.

Plan and Shop Who will plan the meals and buy the groceries? Could this job be rotated each week?

Schedule A schedule can allow each family member to take a turn at cooking.

Cooking Schedule
Monday — Dad & Samuel
Tuesday — Mom & Kiley
Wednesday — Mom
Thursday — Dad & Kiley
Friday — Dad
Saturday — Mom & Samuel
Sunday — Family Night

A Family Bulletin Board

A family bulletin board can be helpful for successful family management. This allows family members to communicate through writing. Leave notes for each other. Put them in a central location. The bulletin board can hold notes, lists, and messages.

Child Care

When employed parents cannot be home to take care of children, what happens? They want quality child care at a good price. That combination can be hard to find.

To find child care, parents can talk to family, neighbors, or physicians. Social service agencies often have lists of licensed child-care providers. These people have met local and state guidelines. There are three main types of child care available.

- **In-Home Care** This care is provided in the child's home. It is the most convenient and often the most expensive.
- **Family Child-Care Homes** The child goes to someone else's home for care. This may be a neighbor or relative's home. The cost varies greatly, as does the quality of the care.
- **Child-Care Centers** Children are cared for at a place that has organized activities for children. The government regulates child-care centers. Some have a sliding fee scale that matches the fee to a person's income.

Eat Together Sharing a meal with pleasant conversation builds family bonds.

Involve Everyone Each person can have a job, even small children. The habit of helping can be started young.

Clean Up If one person does most of the preparation, another could do the cleanup.

Adjusted Work Schedules

Some families arrange staggered work schedules so one parent is always home to care for children. Such plans save on child-care expenses and let each parent spend time with the children. A drawback is the limited time for two parents to spend with each other. It also cuts down the amount of time all family members are together.

After-School Supervision

Once children are in school, child-care issues do not end. Supervision after school is a concern. Transportation is another need. Many youngsters are unable to participate in activities because they do not have an adult to take them there.

Many parents who want after-school care cannot afford it or find it. Children who stay alone at home after school are sometimes called latch-key children. These children need to learn certain skills to keep themselves safe, such as calling an adult when they get home from school. They may be supervised by telephone from the parent's workplace.

⬆ *Workplace Care*
Some employers offer child care on-site for their employees. *Is the cost of providing child care a good investment for the employer?*

Employer Programs

An employee who is worried about children may have a difficult time working. Employers may assist workers by helping with child care. Some companies offer lists of approved child-care facilities. Companies may offer families a **reimbursement** (ˌrē-əm-ˈbərs-mənt). This means companies pay money back to the working parent. This helps the parent afford child care of their own choosing.

Some large companies have child care at the place of business. Parents and children can arrive and leave together. Parents may be able to spend their breaks and lunch periods with their children. These facilities may also have a sick bay, or sick area where children can be when they do not feel well. This helps prevent other children in the facility from getting sick. When companies have child care at the place of business, it can be quite costly. On the other hand, it cuts down on the time workers take off because their children are close by. It also keeps worker turnover low.

✓ Reading Check **Identify** What are the three main types of child care?

Help from Others

A support system can make life run more smoothly for a family. Common sources of support are extended family, neighbors, friends, and community services. It takes effort to build a solid support system.

Family, Friends, and Neighbors

Neighbors and friends are a good resource. Many families find ways to exchange with others in order to manage. For example, one family formed a car pool with neighbors so that their daughters could get to soccer games. Another family exchanged babysitting hours with friends. This way the parents could have some time away without the cost of a babysitter.

Community Services

Although not every family can afford it, some pay to get the support services they need. A family may hire someone to clean the house or do yard work. They may pay to have groceries delivered. Some families may hire a home health aide to stay with elderly family members who need company and care.

Help from others is a resource that many people do not use. They may not want to bother others. They may be too proud to ask for help. Efficient management means using all the available resources. Families can work with employers and others to improve the balance of work, personal, and family life.

Section 12.2   After You Read

Review Key Concepts

1. **Describe** the benefits of a job with flexible work hours.
2. **List** three tools that can help in family management.
3. **Identify** sources that can make up a support system for a family.

Practice Academic Skills

English Language Arts

4. Select one of the work schedules described in this section: flexible hours, compressed week, or job sharing. Research how the schedule works. What are the benefits and drawbacks for workers and employees? Would you like to work those hours? Write a paragraph to answer the questions and explain your answer.

5. Imagine that you are looking for child care for your two-year-old. A friend has suggested a woman who lives nearby. She cares for children in her home. What would be important to look for when you visit? Write a list of questions that would help you judge the situation.

> **NCTE 8** Use information resources to gather information and create and communicate knowledge.

> **NCTE 12** Use language to accomplish individual purposes.

Check Your Answers Check your answers at this book's Online Learning Center through glencoe.com.

CAREER SPOTLIGHT

Human Resources Manager

Christy Decker
Louisville, Kentucky

In any company, there is one role that touches all of the employees. That is the role of people in Human Resources. They are responsible for hiring new employees, managing existing employees, and facilitating training programs. They are also in charge of developing company policies and benefits packages and dealing with insurance-related issues like worker's compensation.

According to Christy Decker, an HR manager, she also has to serve as an unbiased third party when conflicts arise between the company and an employee.

Decker explains, "A human resources manager often acts as a mediator in employment disputes." She continues, "This requires one to have a strong sense of ethics."

An HR manager has to be able to have an honest, empathetic conversation with an employee when these situations arise. They have to make sure the outcomes are fair. Decker says she also needs to stay involved with the people she represents, in order to do the best job possible. "Spending time getting to know the employees is a key to success within the company."

CAREER FACTS

Education or Training A college degree is required, and an emphasis in business is preferred.

Nature of the Work Human resource professionals handle the hiring of new employees, deal with existing employees, and manage all of the aspects of the company/employee relationship – benefits, working conditions, training, and disputes.

Aptitudes, Abilities, and Skills Strong organizational and people skills are essential. HR professionals are often involved in budgeting decisions, so math skills are a plus.

Academic Skills Required English Language Arts skills are essential. The ability to speak a second language is a plus.

Student Organizations To prepare for this career, look for groups that foster leadership and honesty, such as an honor society.

Career Outlook Jobs as human resources and training specialists are expected to grow faster than the average over the next ten years.

Career Path Companies look for people with either a degree in human resources or a field that is closely tied to the company's business.

Critical Thinking

Working Parents What do you think a human resources manager could offer to help a working parent?

 Research Careers For more information on this and other careers, visit the Occupational Outlook Handbook Web site through the link on this book's Online Learning Center at **glencoe.com**.

Section 12.1
Work and Families

Work is valuable for the income and satisfaction it brings. A work ethic is a set of values based on the moral virtues of hard work and diligence. Families do household work and income-producing work. Who does each type of work can be a source of debate in families. Most families share both types of work. Men and women, however, tend to do different types of tasks. Careers and family life affect each other. Problems and issues in one area will impact the other area.

Section 12.2
Managing Busy Lives

It takes help and support to manage busy lives. Employers help when they offer options in work hours such as flexible hours, a compressed week, or job sharing. Some companies have policies to assist families. These may include leaves of absence or services to help with problems. Families can use tools for managing, such as a family calendar, meetings, and a bulletin board. Parents with children may need child care. Support from others can help balance work and family lives.

Content and Academic Vocabulary Review

1. Use each of these content and academic vocabulary words in a sentence.

Content Vocabulary
◇ work ethic (p. 225)
◇ household work (p. 225)
◇ income-producing work (p. 226)
◇ flextime (p. 232)
◇ leave of absence (p. 232)
◇ reimbursement (p. 236)

Academic Vocabulary
■ satisfaction (p. 225)
■ appropriate (p. 227)
■ compress (p. 232)
■ grant (p. 232)

Review Key Concepts

2. Describe two types of work that families do.
3. Summarize how jobs and family life can affect each other.
4. Identify ways that employers can support family life.
5. Explain strategies that families can use to manage the work at home.
6. Suggest ways families can use help from others to balance work and family life.

Critical Thinking

7. Evaluate If one person does all the work in a family, how will that affect others? How will it affect their relationships?
8. Analyze Suppose a family could afford to pay for services that can give support. Why would they choose to exchange services with other families instead of paying for services?
9. Recognize Alternatives Do you think home care standards need to be lowered for busy families (for example, they might only make beds on the weekends)? What could happen if the family does not agree on the level of cleanliness needed? Explain your answers.

Real-World Skills

Communication Skills

10. Problem Solving Tom's mother gives him a list of chores to do. He dislikes the list and usually does not finish it. When Tom asks his mother for the car and other privileges, she often says no. She says Tom is not responsible, which upsets Tom. Write a letter to Tom offering advice for his problem.

Management Skills

11. Team Shopping Some families use teamwork when grocery shopping. They enjoy the time together and shopping gets done more quickly. Make a plan for your family to try team shopping. Outline the steps that would be needed, such as who decides what to buy.

Technology Skills

12. Create a Spreadsheet Use a spreadsheet to create a chart of who does household chores in your family. List the chores in the left column. List the people in your family across the top row. Put an X in the appropriate cell to indicate who does which chores. What conclusions can you draw from your spreadsheet?

Problem-Solving Skills

13. Managing Employees Several of Isaiah's best workers are parents who have trouble managing the schedule that he sets. A few employees have grumbled about covering when one of the parents leaves for family issues. Write a paragraph about what you think he should do.

14. Create a List With a partner, brainstorm ways to help families manage and balance their work and family lives. Create a list of five to ten tips that families could use to manage time efficiently.

15. Interview Talk to someone who works in child care. Find out what happens when a child becomes sick at child care. Does the child-care provider care for sick children? Do parents have to pay when the child does not attend due to illness? Write a report of your findings.

16. Employee Benefits Contact a local employer in your community. Ask what benefits are offered to help workers balance work and family life. Do you think this would be a family-friendly place to work? Why or why not? Write a paragraph explaining your findings and opinions.

17. Child Care Standards Go to this book's Online Learning Center at glencoe.com for **Web Links** to **Child Care Standards**. Find out who sets these standards. What qualifications do child-care workers need? What are the rules about facilities? How might this information help you in choosing child care? Write a list of answers to these questions.

Additional Activities For additional activities, go to this book's Online Learning Center through glencoe.com.

Academic Skills

 Mathematics

18. Time for Household Jobs Follow your teacher's instructions to form into groups. With your group members, discuss the different chores you all do around the house. Then develop a list of common household jobs. Think about the jobs that you or other family members typically do in a week or month. Consider how long it takes to do each household job.

Math Concept **Calculate Average Times** As a class, compare each groups' ideas on how much time it takes to do each job. Find the average time for each job.

Starting Hint: List all of the times classmates give for a particular job. For example, washing dishes: 15 minutes, 10 minutes, 5 minutes, 7 minutes. Add the times (15 + 10 + 5 + 7) and divide by the number of times you added (4). Do this for each job on your list.

 For math help, go to the Math Appendix at the back of the book.

> **NCTM Number and Operations** Understand numbers, ways of representing numbers, relationships among numbers, and number systems.

 English Language Arts

19. Write a Survey Imagine you are an employer who wants to offer flexible hours. Right now, all your employees work from 8 A.M. to 5 P.M. with a one-hour lunch break. You want to know if your workers would enjoy a new program and what times people would prefer to work. Many of your employees bring their lunches to work. Would they like a shorter lunch break in order to arrive later or leave earlier? Write a survey for your workers that asks these questions.

> **NCTE 8** Use information resources to gather information and create and communicate knowledge.

Social Studies

20. Effects on Society Think about the effects of work ethic on culture or society. What effects would you expect if people had a strong versus a weak work ethic? Write a one-page essay that describes the relationship between work ethic and its effects on society.

> **NCSS I.c** Apply an understanding of culture as an integrated whole that explains the functions and interactions of language, traditions, beliefs and values, and behavior patterns.

STANDARDIZED TEST PRACTICE

ESSAY
Use a separate sheet of paper to write a one-page response to the following writing prompt.

Test-Taking Tip Before answering an essay question, think about what you want to say. Write down a few notes to help you organize your thoughts. Number your thoughts in the order you will write about them.

21. Suppose your brother is very active at school. He is involved in sports, school government, and many clubs. He also has a part-time job. Because you are not involved in so many activities, you end up doing more work around the home than he does. This is creating resentment and tension between you and your brother, and it is beginning to affect the rest of the family. Describe some possible solutions to this problem.

Unit 3 Thematic Project

Manage Your Time

In this unit you have learned tools for making good decisions. You have also learned that it can be a challenge to maintain a good balance among school, work, activities, and family life. In this project, you will interview a professional. You will use what you learn to create a schedule for yourself that balances school, work, family, and any other activities you are involved in.

My Journal

If you completed the journal entry from page 178, refer to it to see if your thoughts have changed after reading the unit.

Project Assignment

- List all of the activities you are involved in every day.
- Write a list of interview questions for a professional who creates schedules. Ask about managing scheduling conflicts.
- Identify and interview a professional in the community such as a retail or restaurant manager who regularly creates schedules.
- Use a computer program to create a seven-day schedule for yourself.
- Present your schedule to your classmates and explain how you came to the decisions that you did.

Academic Skills You Will Use

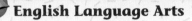

English Language Arts

NCTE 7 Conduct research and gather, evaluate, and synthesize data to communicate discoveries.

NCTE 8 Use information resources to gather information and create and communicate knowledge.

STEP 1 List Your Activities

The list below contains examples of activities you may be involved in on a daily or near-daily basis. Write down every activity that you need to schedule, even if it is not included below.

- School
- Work
- Family
- Volunteer work
- Religious activities
- Extracurricular activities such as sports, band, student government, and so on.

STEP 2 Write Your Interview Questions

Make a list of questions to ask a retail or restaurant manager about creating schedules. Make sure you ask how the manager handles employees' scheduling requests and scheduling conflicts. Also ask how the manager mainatins his or her own schedule, and ask for strategies for balancing work and family life.

Writing Skills

- Phrase open-ended questions to get the information you want.
- Consider your audience.
- Organize your questions in the order you want to ask them.
- Write concisely (briefly but completely).

STEP 3 Connect to Your Community

Identify and interview a manager of a retail store, restaurant, library, or any business in your community where employees work in shifts. Managers in these industries have to coordinate many different employees' needs when creating a schedule for the work week. Use the interview questions you wrote in Step 2.

Interview Skills

- During the interview, record responses and take notes.
- Use standard English to communicate.
- Listen attentively.
- When you transcribe your notes, write in complete sentences and use correct spelling and grammar.

STEP 4 Create and Present Your Schedule

Use the Unit Thematic Project Checklist on the right to plan and create your schedule and make your presentation.

STEP 5 Evaluate Your Presentation

Your project will be evaluated based on:

- Thoroughness of your interview and questions.
- Completeness of your schedule.
- Mechanics—presentation and neatness.

Evaluation Rubric Go to this book's Online Learning Center at glencoe.com for a rubric you can use to evaluate your final project.

Unit Thematic Project Checklist

Schedule	✓ Create a seven-day schedule that is a visual representation of your daily activities.
	✓ Color-code the items on your schedule. Write family activities in red, school activities in black, work activities in blue, extracurricular activities in green, and other activities in other colors.
	✓ Make room in your schedule for time to relax and for last-minute commitments.
Presentation	✓ Make a presentation to your class to share your schedule and discuss what you learned.
	✓ Invite the students in your class to ask you any questions they may have. Answer three questions.
	✓ When students ask you questions, demonstrate in your answers that you respect their perspectives.
	✓ Turn in the notes from your interview and your schedule to your teacher.
Academic Skills	✓ Set priorities.
	✓ Make decisions regarding conflicts.
	✓ Speak clearly and concisely.
	✓ Explain ideas clearly.

Unit 4

Support Family and Friends

Unit

Thematic Project Preview
Offer Helpful Advice

After completing this unit, you will learn skills to support your family and friends during times of change. In your unit thematic project, you can demonstrate your ability to research and give advice.

My Journal

When You Need Guidance Write a journal entry about one of the topics below. This will help you prepare for the unit project at the end of the unit.

- Describe a situation where you would ask for advice.
- Identify the skills that are important for a counselor or therapist.
- State the best advice you have ever received and why.

Explore the Photo
Family and friends are a great support group in difficult times. *How do you support your family and friends when they face problems?*

CHAPTER 13

The Challenge of Change

Section 13.1

Facing Change

Section 13.2

Stress Management

 Explore the Photo

When a family faces change, it can bring about many different feelings. *What are some ways you deal with change in your daily life?*

Chapter Objectives

After completing this chapter, you will be able to:

- **Explain** the process of change.
- **Describe** how families can adjust to various life changes.
- **Identify** causes and symptoms of stress.
- **Determine** how people can manage stress.

Writing Activity

A Descriptive Paragraph

Strength Becoming psychologically strong takes work, but it is worth the effort. This kind of strength lets you confront problems and changes in your life with less stress. To show strength, you can:
- Join a club to make friends at a new school.
- Ignore thoughtless comments about personal appearance.
- Help others by becoming a teen counselor.

Write a descriptive paragraph that explains what it means to be psychologically strong. Make sure to support your idea clearly with details.

Writing Tips To write a descriptive paragraph, follow these steps:
1. Decide what mood you want to create in the paragraph.
2. Write a strong topic sentence.
3. Orient the reader by presenting details in a logical order.
4. Select precise transition words.

Facing Change

Reading Guide

Before You Read

Preview Understanding causes and effects can help clarify connections. Ask yourself, "Why does this happen?" to help you recognize cause-and-effect relationships in this section.

Read to Learn
Key Concepts

- **Explain** the process of change.
- **Describe** how families can adjust to various life changes.

Main Idea

There is a process people go through as they adapt to change. Life changes can include moving, financial problems, unemployment, and natural disasters.

Content Vocabulary

◇ resilient
◇ sacrifice
◇ debt
◇ creditor
◇ bankruptcy
◇ unemployment
◇ identity

Academic Vocabulary

You will find these words in your reading and on your tests. Use the glossary to look up their definitions if necessary.

■ transition　　■ plan

Graphic Organizer

As you read, look for the steps in the process of change. Use a chart like the one shown to help organize your information.

Steps in the Process of Change
1._____
2._____
3._____
4._____

 Graphic Organizer Go to this book's Online Learning Center at **glencoe.com** to print out this graphic organizer.

Academic Standards • • • • • • • • • • • • • • •

 English Language Arts

NCTE 4 Use written language to communicate effectively.

NCTE 7 Conduct research and gather, evaluate, and synthesize data to communicate discoveries.

 Mathematics

NCTM Number and Operations Understand numbers, ways of representing numbers, relationships among numbers, and number systems.

NCTE *National Council of Teachers of English*
NCTM *National Council of Teachers of Mathematics*

NSES *National Science Education Standards*
NCSS *National Council of the Social Studies*

The Change Process

Change is a part of life. Some changes are expected. There may be others that catch you off guard. Change can bring gain or loss, joy or frustration. No matter what, you can count on change occurring in your life.

Change occurs at every level of society. For a family, a move to a new town or a divorce brings major change. Businesses also experience change. They may adopt new technology. They may be sold or closed. Each of these changes affects workers and their families. Changes occur in society when new laws are passed. There are also changes brought about by warfare or natural disasters. These affect the broader society as well as the people who live in it.

Change also occurs over the course of the family life cycle. Simply moving through the life cycle stages causes changes in the family. These changes need to be dealt with. Some of these changes are the addition of members to the family. Others are when family members leave. Changes in society today can affect parents and children in the future. Families must be ready to adapt at every stage of development.

Social scientists have studied change and how people react to it. They have found that there is a five-step process for how people deal with change.

1. **Denial** Often, the first reaction to change is to deny it is happening. People may feel numb. They want to continue as usual—as if nothing has changed.

2. **Resistance** The next step is to resist the change. People start thinking about the effect of the change on them personally. Anger and frustration are normal feelings in this stage.

As You Read

Connect What changes can you expect throughout life? What changes may catch you unaware?

Feelings About Change Moving often means leaving friends and family behind. *How do you think you would feel if you moved to a new city?*

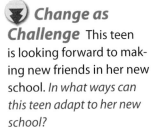
Vocabulary

You can find definitions in the glossary at the back of this book.

3. **Acceptance** Gradually people accept that the change will or has occurred. They regroup and start thinking about how to manage the change.

4. **Transition** When people **transition**, or pass from one stage to another, they begin to focus on the future. They figure out what they have to do to make the change work for them.

5. **Commitment** Finally, people are committed to the change. They become comfortable with the new way of doing things.

Reactions to Change

People react differently to change. Some people are very open to it. They enjoy it because they are ready for a change. Others are more cautious. Some people try out new ideas, but carefully. Others wait until most people have adopted the change. Traditional people tend to adopt a change only when it has become the new tradition.

Those who handle change well are resilient. **Resilient** (ri-'zil-yənt) means to be able to recover from or adjust easily to misfortune or change. People who are resilient are aware of what is going on in their world. They often anticipate change. They **plan**, or make a strategy, so they can take advantage of the changes they see coming. This lets them adapt to the changes more easily.

People who deal easily with change see it as a challenge. They want to learn new skills. They look at change as a barrier to see how they can overcome it. They seek out positive solutions to the problems brought by change. They show leadership in working through the change.

✓ **Reading Check** **Identify** What are normal feelings in the resistance step of the change process?

Change as Challenge This teen is looking forward to making new friends in her new school. *In what ways can this teen adapt to her new school?*

Life Changes

Coping with change is harder than most people expect. The best results occur when people plan how to react in order to manage the change. They identify their resources and figure out how to best use them. They rely on decision-making and problem-solving skills.

Moving

You live in the most mobile society ever. That does not make moving easy, however. A family is apt to feel sad about leaving their old home. They may be anxious about their new place. They also feel the strain of the work involved in moving.

Career changes can often lead to a move for the family. New jobs may pay more money or be a promotion. The impact of the change, however, is felt throughout the family. Before a move, families should discuss their plans openly and honestly. Visiting the area first helps everyone feel more comfortable.

Before a move, it can be beneficial to go to the local chamber of commerce. They may have useful information about the new location. You can learn whether the area has a swimming pool and where the library is located. You can find points of interest to visit or explore once you have moved. Many people also use the Internet to research a new location before they move.

Helping in the move gives a sense of control over the event. For example, children can pack toys and arrange items in a new room. A teen may take care of practical details, such as filling out a change-of-address card at the post office. Parents can arrange for the telephone and utility services to be set up.

Adjust to a Move

No matter how well you prepare, you cannot expect to feel at home right away. Making an effort is part of the process. Those who have a job are likely to adjust quickly. Others may need to look for ways to get involved. Community newcomer clubs are a good resource. Parents can make the effort to meet other parents in the neighborhood. This can help children make friends as they get to know others who live nearby.

Moving can be an exciting family challenge. It can draw a family closer. Members can rely on each other until they develop new routines. A new location offers new experiences that can help members grow as people.

Financial Problems

Many changes occur over the family life cycle due to financial, or money, problems. A family member may lose a job which can lead to a lower income. Some families may overspend the money they earn. Others may face financial problems as a result of medical issues. For example, some illnesses or injuries can lead to expensive medical bills.

Life Skills CHECKLIST

Leadership Skills

Welcome Others When someone moves to your school or neighborhood, you can help him or her get off to a good start when you:

✓ Introduce yourself to the newcomer as soon as possible.

✓ Take a housewarming gift or make some other friendly gesture.

✓ Offer to help in some way.

✓ Include him or her in an activity you have planned.

Financial Literacy

Calculate Housing Costs

Many families have financial problems. It is helpful to know how much of their income goes toward housing and household expenses. The average U.S. family spends about 16 percent of its income on housing. They spend about 12 percent on household expenses. If a family's monthly income is $3,125, how much does it spend on housing and household expenses?

Math Concept **The Distributive Property** The Distributive Property states that $a \times c + b \times c = (a + b) \times c$

Starting Hint: You can use this property to solve this problem. Multiply each percent (a and b) by the monthly income (c). Then add the products ($a \times c + b \times c$). Or you can add the percents and multiply their sum by the monthly income (($a + b) \times c$).

 For math help, go to the Math Appendix at the back of the book.

NCTM Number and Operations Understand numbers, ways of representing numbers, relationships among numbers, and number systems.

Some stages of the family life cycle tend to have more financial problems than others. For instance, if a family is thinking about having children, they need to be aware of the costs involved. Meeting a child's needs can be expensive. If a family decides to pay for a member to go to college, it can stretch a family's budget.

Financial problems can be upsetting for families. Some are quick to blame others. Money problems are most often due to an entire family's spending and saving habits. One person is rarely to blame.

People should take time to learn about their finances. It is best to do this before a financial problem occurs. There are many places to go for help. Taking action can help prevent more serious problems.

Deal with Financial Problems

Preparing for financial problems is one of the best ways to prevent them. Experts suggest saving up to three months of living expenses. The savings will act as a buffer in hard times.

Another way to deal with financial problems is to economize. This means finding ways to spend less money. This is also a way to help prevent problems. Some expenses are needed and unchanging. Others can be controlled or postponed. For example:

- Eat homemade meals. Meals made from scratch can be cheaper than restaurant meals. Watch the food ads to find the best buys.
- Put off buying new clothes. You might find well-cared-for items in shops that sell used clothing at low prices.
- Look for free or low-cost entertainment. Check out library books and videos, rather than buying them new. Attend a free concert in the park.

When money is tight, families may need to change their outlook on life. Solving money problems often means making a **sacrifice**, or giving something up. Family members may have to put aside their own wants. When everyone works together, getting through tough times is much easier.

Get Help

Financial problems can become too difficult for a family to solve alone. When this happens, a family needs outside help. Many communities have classes that offer guidance. Credit counselors are also a source of advice. They can be found in telephone or online directories under Consumer Credit Counseling Services. This and other nonprofit groups can help solve problems. They are usually at a lower cost to the family. There are also for-profit firms that offer help. They charge more for their services, which may cost more in the end.

Many families are in **debt**. A debt is something that is owed. A **creditor** is someone to whom a debt is owed. Most creditors will help people find ways to pay the debt. They may agree to smaller payments or accept property instead.

In extreme cases, **bankruptcy** ('baŋk-(ˌ)rəp(t)-sē) may be an option. This legal process declares a person unable to pay debts. Any assets the person has may be used to pay part of what is owed. Bankruptcy should be a last resort only. It gets people out of a huge debt. It also seriously hurts a person's access to funds in the future.

Some people have severe financial problems. They may not be able to afford a place to live. Homelessness is a growing problem. Homeless people often turn first to family and friends for help. Shelters have temporary housing until people can afford a place to live. Other organizations may provide job training and child care.

For families in serious financial trouble, states and local communities can offer public help. Departments have been set up to help with child care and food programs.

Unemployment

Unemployment means not having a job. Of all the reasons for financial problems, unemployment is one of the hardest on families. When people need a job and do not have one, life is not easy. Losing income is only part of the unemployment problem. Work is important to people for many reasons. Not having work can be mentally difficult for the person who lost a job.

Effects of Unemployment

Unemployment can damage a person's identity. Your **identity** is your view of yourself as a person. Losing a job can make people feel as though they have failed. They may begin to doubt themselves and grow anxious or depressed.

The longer unemployment lasts, the stronger its effects. The jobless person may feel guilty, irritable, and sensitive to criticism. Some people withdraw into themselves. Others turn to substances, such as alcohol, to dull their feelings. This often just makes them feel worse.

▶▶ **Search for Employment** Finding jobs you are qualified for can be stressfull. *What kinds of problems face the unemployed?*

Health Problems The stress of unemployment can cause health problems for the jobless person. Headaches, upset stomachs, and high blood pressure are a few common problems. If these become severe, they can strain an already tight financial situation.

Depression These physical and emotional effects can make finding a new job harder. A person who is depressed and filled with self-doubt is not apt to do well in a job interview. The person may even think that looking for a job is pointless.

Effects on the Family While the jobless person is suffering, the family is too. The effects of unemployment can cause changes in family life. Working together to solve the problems can bring family members closer at first. Conflict may arise as families make hard choices about the conditions they are living in. Long-term unemployment can cause a family breakdown.

Young children are often hit hardest by the loss of a parent's job. They tend to get sick more often than children of employed parents. They are less able to understand what is happening. They may have fewer friends and outside resources for support than older children.

Coping with Unemployment

Unemployment is a family problem. The family can be its own best resource for coping. Families can use other strategies as well.

Most workers are eligible for some type of unemployment insurance. It usually covers basic expenses. It also only lasts about one year. This is why it is important to have money saved. The insurance will not make up for a lack of savings.

The unemployed person needs to be persistent in looking for work. An employment agency or the state job service office has job listings. Job counseling may be helpful. Short-term work may help the family until a permanent position is found. Most people who lose their jobs do find new ones.

Older children can help. They can babysit, run errands, and help with cleaning or yard work. The feeling of being able to help out is a bigger benefit than any money they bring in.

Teens can work to increase the family income. It may make them feel proud that their money can benefit the entire family. Showing support and understanding, however, may be just as meaningful. A parent often feels bad about being unable to provide. Blame and complaints only deepen the hurt. Caring, love, and support are helpful.

🔺 *Pitch in to Help*
To help ease financial pressures in the family, children can help. *In what ways can children help out when an unemployed parent looks for a job?*

It is helpful to have open communication with family members during or before a time of unemployment. Family discussions can help form a plan when unemployment occurs. These discussions help the family feel secure by having a plan in place.

A family can use community resources as well. Medical clinics provide low-cost services. Food pantries are available when supplies run low. Families should find a support system. They can get advice from talking to those who know what unemployment is like. This can also help ease emotional problems.

Disasters

Many people have to face the changes caused by natural disasters, such as floods, fires, and hurricanes. The forces of nature cannot be controlled. As a result, it is wise to make a plan for dealing with disasters. The family's physical safety is the first concern in a natural disaster. To prepare, families can practice emergency responses at home.

Disasters in society, such as war, cannot be controlled either. They can cause drastic changes in family life. Families may have members who are gone from home for long periods of time. Families will need to prepare for this adjustment. Sometimes, a member of the family may pass away. Death is another change that families will have to face.

Planning for life after a disaster is important. For example, is the family's insurance enough to protect them in the most likely disasters? Does the family have a safe supply of food and water in case of emergency? Where would they stay if they had to leave their home? What financial assets do they have if their bank were unable to open? Learning the answers to questions like these helps families prepare. Preparation can ease the shock if a disaster occurs in your community.

Section 13.1 — After You Read

Review Key Concepts

1. **Describe** personal qualities of people who handle change well.
2. **Identify** personal skills useful in dealing with change.

Practice Academic Skills

English Language Arts

3. Moving is a big change for family members. Write a paragraph explaining whether you think moving is easier for young children or for teens.
4. A disaster causes communities and families to take action. Research a recent disaster. Find out what happened. What were the effects of the disaster on the community? On families? What changes did people face as they coped after the disaster? Write a report that explains the disaster and outlines the actions people took to deal with the disaster.

> **NCTE 4** Use written language to communicate effectively.

> **NCTE 7** Conduct research and gather, evaluate, and synthesize data to communicate discoveries.

Check Your Answers Check your answers at this book's Online Learning Center through **glencoe.com**.

Stress Management

Reading Guide

Before You Read

Pace Yourself Short blocks of concentrated reading repeated frequently are more effective than one long session. Focus on reading for 10 minutes. Take a short break. Then read for another 10 minutes.

Read to Learn
Key Concepts
- **Identify** causes and symptoms of stress.
- **Determine** how people can manage stress.

Main Idea
Stress is physical, mental, or emotional strain or tension. People can recognize, limit, and manage their stress.

Content Vocabulary
◇ stress
◇ stress management
◇ epinephrine

Academic Vocabulary
You will find these words in your reading and on your tests. Use the glossary to look up their definitions if necessary.
■ prone
■ optimistic

Graphic Organizer
As you read, look for signs of stress and ways to reduce stress. Use a chart like the one shown to help organize your information.

Signs of Stress	Ways to Reduce Stress
1. _____	1. _____
2. _____	2. _____
3. _____	3. _____
4. _____	4. _____
5. _____	5. _____

 Graphic Organizer Go to this book's Online Learning Center at **glencoe.com** to print out this graphic organizer.

Academic Standards . . . .

 English Language Arts

NCTE 7 Conduct research and gather, evaluate, and synthesize data to communicate discoveries.

NCTE 8 Use information resources to gather information and create and communicate knowledge.

NCTE *National Council of Teachers of English*
NCTM *National Council of Teachers of Mathematics*

NSES *National Science Education Standards*
NCSS *National Council of the Social Studies*

Understand Stress

What happens if you leave a tea kettle full of water on the range to warm? As the heat increases, the pressure inside the tea kettle rises. Left alone, the water boils over. People are like tea kettles. Pressure can build up inside until they boil over. The cause is not heat. It is **stress**—physical, mental, or emotional strain or tension.

When a tea kettle gets hot, you need to prevent it from boiling over. You can turn down the heat, let some steam escape, or remove the pot from the burner. Likewise, people must act to prevent stress from becoming a problem in their lives.

Many everyday situations cause stress. Being late, losing a textbook, and getting caught in traffic can be stressful. Tough working conditions and strained relationships with friends or family cause stress to build.

Troublesome events cause significant stress in people's lives. Even pleasing events can be stressful. Would accepting an award before an audience make you tense? What about playing in a championship game in your sport?

Symptoms of Stress

Everyone feels stress. That is normal. Not everyone feels stress in the same ways, however. When you take a test, for instance, the tension you feel is different from what other classmates feel.

What are some of the symptoms of stress? Stress can affect people physically. They may feel a pounding heart or be weak and dizzy. They may sleep too much or not be able to get enough sleep. Neck and back pain, sweating, and headaches are also common.

Stress can affect people mentally and emotionally as well. They can be irritable or depressed. They may be tense and afraid. They may tap fingers, pull hair, or grind teeth.

Vocabulary

You can find definitions in the glossary at the back of this book.

As You Read

Connect Why do you think stress is harmful to your well-being?

◀◀ *Everyday Stress*
Ordinary day-to-day events may cause stress if you allow them to upset you. *What methods do you use to handle everyday stress, such as studying for an exam?*

Stress can affect every part of a person's life. It can make people lose confidence in their abilities. It can hurt their relationships. It often reduces workers' effectiveness. Too much stress can cause both physical and mental diseases. The higher your stress level becomes, the more **prone**, or likely, you are to become ill.

✓ **Reading Check** **Define** What is stress?

Manage Stress

Do you long for a stress-free life? That might not be as good as it sounds. When properly handled, stress puts you in motion and keeps you going. The urge to create and accomplish something is positive stress. Some people need a little push. Those who say they work best under pressure are admitting that stress motivates them.

You do not need to be overwhelmed by stress. Learning to manage stress can control the negative impact it may have on your life. You can learn strategies to help you cope with the demands of life. This is called **stress management**. You may experience stress at home, school, work, or in the community. As a result, stress management can be used in all these places.

INDEPENDENT Living

HOW TO   Handle Stress

Being a teen is stressful. You have to juggle homework, family, friends, dating, and after-school activities. You may also be handling other stressful situations, such as parental divorce and peer pressure. Too much stress can take a toll on your emotional and physical health. Follow these guidelines to manage your stress:

1. **Exercise regularly.** It is a good idea to be physically active at least 60 minutes each day. Take a walk, swim some laps, or ride your bike.
2. **Eat for your health.** Eat regular meals instead of eating on the run or indulging in junk food. When you are in a hurry, reach for fruit, yogurt, and other healthy foods.
3. **Get plenty of sleep.** When you are well rested, you are better able to tackle what life throws at you. In addition, sleep gives your body a chance to recover from stress.
4. **Prioritize your activities.** Avoid overbooking yourself. Make sure that the things you choose to do are those that have the highest priority.
5. **Talk it out.** Talk about your problems with an adult or trusted friend. Sometimes letting out your fears or frustrations can reduce your stress level.

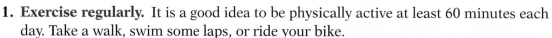

Take Action You may be putting pressure on yourself to be perfect. Of course, no one is perfect, but that can be hard to remember when your stress level is high. On a piece of paper, write down a promise to accept yourself at your best, not at a level of perfection you cannot achieve. Sign and date the promise, and keep it somewhere visible.

People who have busy schedules can be rushed and impatient. Family members work, keep appointments, and maintain the home. There is not much time to relax and relate. You can take steps to help reduce stress in your family.

- Lower expectations. Talk with others and set priorities for what must be done.
- Keep laughing. Post jokes, cartoons, and inspirational messages on the family bulletin board.
- Offer to help others when you can.
- Organize work teams to do tasks quickly.

Problem-Solving

The dinner hour is always stressful at the Gomez household. Everyone is hungry by the time Mrs. Gomez gets home from work. She does not like to start cooking the minute she walks in the door. By the time supper is ready, her two children are bickering and angry with each other. They often keep quarreling as they eat. By the time supper is over, Mrs. Gomez is angry at them. What would you suggest to reduce the stress in the Gomez household?

You will be able to deal with stress when you know what causes it for you. Certain signals show that you are under stress. These signals or often different for everyone. If you pay attention to physical and emotional signals, you can link them to the cause of stress. Then you can take action to deal with the problem.

It is important to learn to manage stress. If stress lasts a long time, it can lead to a range of medical problems. Stress symptoms are related to heart disease and high blood pressure. Emotional problems can result from extended stress as well. Learning to manage the stress in your life can empower you to feel in control of your emotions and reactions to difficult situations.

Limit Stress in Your Life

If you know that being late makes you tense and upset, what should you do? Eliminate what causes you to be late, right? The simple principle of cause and effect can be applied to cut down on the stress in your life. When you know what causes your stress, you can take action to reduce it.

Maintain Good Health

Teens that are not healthy often have a harder time coping with stress. They may even create stress for themselves. Low levels of energy and mental alertness can signal a fitness problem. Staying fit means having good habits. A person who maintains good health does the following:

- Eats a healthful diet, including breakfast.
- Gets at least eight hours of sleep each night.
- Exercises regularly and maintains a healthy weight.
- Stays away from drugs and tobacco products.
- Has regular medical checkups.

Manage Your Life Well

When you do not know what is going to happen to you, the feeling creates stress. Gaining a sense of control increases confidence and reduces stress. You can set goals and make plans to meet them. You can use the resources you have to reach your goals. As part of good management, you plan for the unexpected. When you are prepared, stress is easier to manage.

Managing time according to your priorities also puts you in charge. When time is going to be tight, make a plan. Make sure that the most important items are done first. Wasting time is a stress creator, just as time pressures can be. Satisfaction, instead of stress, comes when you feel good about how your time is spent.

Deal with Stress

No matter what you do, some stress will occur. Be sure to take time to relax, as shown in **Figure 13.1**.

Be sure that what is causing you stress is really stressful. Give each incident in life no more or less weight than it deserves. For instance, a stain on a new jacket may seem stressful. This is small in comparison, however, to studying for a final exam in one of your classes. Remember, too, that other people have survived worse.

Figure 13.1 Learn to Relax

When you feel stressed, try these activities to help you relax.
Which of the ideas shown would help you relieve stress?

Listen Soothing music can help you calm down.

Make Time Take time to enjoy a hobby.

Get Active Exercise to help relieve tension.

Use Your Support System

When you are faced with a stressful situation, what do you do? Do you confide in someone or keep your worries to yourself? Stress creates feelings you need to talk about. Sharing your problems and emotions with someone lightens the burden. Brain scans have shown that putting feelings into words reduces stress. Talking provides an immediate connection to another person.

A parent or older sibling may have been through something similar. It takes courage to ask for advice or help. The effort is worth it. People want to help, just as you would if someone confided in you.

People who have many strong relationships cope better with stress. They tend to have less stress. They are apt to have fewer stress symptoms as well.

Release Emotions

Did you know that crying may actually be a good way to deal with tension? Science has shown that emotional tears are chemically different from those caused by irritations like onions. Stress-related tears have more protein than other tears. They often contain high levels of minerals and hormones. Crying can bring relief by ridding the body of these chemicals. People who cry to relieve anxiety seem to have fewer stress-related diseases than those who do not cry.

The myth that tears are only for females is slowly breaking down. Both males and females cry at times. The stereotype that men do not cry is outdated now that men are more in tune with their emotions.

Meditate Imagine you are in a safe and beautiful place.

Reflect Think about the good things in your life.

Discuss Talk to someone about the situation.

Tears are not the only emotional outlet for stress. Some people have feelings so strong that they need to release them in some nondestructive way. Those who feel like lashing out can exercise instead. Many forms of exercise help release tension and soothe emotions.

Take Appropriate Action

When a stressful situation looms, take action. Research shows that taking charge lowers levels of **epinephrine** (ˌe-pə-ˈne-frən). This is the human hormone that causes the physical reactions to stress.

What actions you take depends on the situation. For everyday stress, you may be able to ease the symptoms right away. When you feel pressure, breathe deeply for a while.

You can take constructive action to deal with a stressful situation. You may be worried about a speech you have to give. Lower your stress by practicing the speech. If you are nervous about taking a driver's test, do something to relax before you go. If a serious problem is causing stress, use the decision-making process to take action.

Use Positive Self-Talk

All people talk to themselves and about themselves in their minds. This self-talk increases stress when it is negative. For example, Hiro was waiting his turn at bat in a softball game. He thought, "I will probably strike out again. I will never be any good at this game." Where do you think Hiro's stress level was as he stepped up to the plate?

Positive, but realistic, self-talk increases confidence. It eases the moment and often leads to success. Work to master the art of positive self-talk. It can lead you to think in a more **optimistic**, or hopeful, way. It will help to reduce the stress in your life.

Section 13.2   After You Read

Review Key Concepts

1. **Identify** some of the symptoms of stress.
2. **Describe** two ways to limit stress.

Practice Academic Skills

English Language Arts

3. Many people have favorite stress relievers, such as playing the guitar. With classmates, compile a list of these. Create a Stress Relief handout that can be given to other students or placed in the school newspaper.

4. Research information on the stress hormone epinephrine. What causes its release in the body? What are its effects? Write two paragraphs about your findings and share it with the class.

> **NCTE 8** Use information resources to gather information and create and communicate knowledge.

> **NCTE 7** Conduct research and gather, evaluate, and synthesize data to communicate discoveries.

Check Your Answers Check your answers at this book's Online Learning Center through **glencoe.com**.

CHAPTER SUMMARY

Section 13.1
Facing Change

Change is a constant in life for families, businesses, and society as a whole. It is a part of every stage of the family life cycle. Change is a five-step process. People react differently to change. Those who deal with it best are resilient. They see change as a challenge. There are many life changes. Moving can be a major change for a family. Financial problems and unemployment create many changes for families. Natural disasters, war, and terrorist acts also cause change for those whose lives are affected.

Section 13.2
Stress Management

Stress is physical, mental, or emotional strain or tension. It can cause physical, mental, or emotional symptoms. Stress management helps people cope with the demands of life. The first step is to recognize the symptoms of stress. Then people can take action to reduce the cause of the stress. In general, people who are in good health and who manage their lives well help limit the stress they feel. To deal with stress, people use their support systems. They release emotions and take action. They use positive self-talk.

Content and Academic Vocabulary Review

1. Use each of these content and academic vocabulary words in a sentence.

Content Vocabulary
◇ resilient (p. 250)
◇ sacrifice (p. 252)
◇ debt (p. 253)
◇ creditor (p. 253)
◇ bankruptcy (p. 253)
◇ unemployment (p. 253)
◇ identity (p. 253)
◇ stress (p. 257)
◇ stress management (p. 258)
◇ epinephrine (p. 262)

Academic Vocabulary
■ transition (p. 250)
■ plan (p. 250)
■ prone (p. 258)
■ optimistic (p. 262)

Review Key Concepts

2. Explain the process of change.
3. Describe how families can adjust to various life changes.
4. Identify causes and symptoms of stress.
5. Determine how people can manage stress.

Critical Thinking

6. Identify What are some pros and cons of having a personality that looks for change and challenge? List at least two pros and two cons.
7. Analyze An old proverb says, "It is better to bend than to break." Write a paragraph to explain how this relates to change and stress.
8. Describe Make a list of the sources of stress in your life. For each item on your list, describe one thing you could do to limit or reduce the stress that it causes.
9. Assess A friend says her goal in life is to eliminate stress. Is this a worthwhile goal? Why or why not? Write a letter to the friend to answer these questions.

Real-World Skills

Decision-Making Skills

10. Solve Problems Shannon's dad follows the same routine each day. Lately however, Shannon thinks he is not working and is looking for a job. How should Shannon handle this? How does ethics relate to her problem? Answer the questions in one or two paragraphs.

Stress-Reduction Skills

11. Deep Breathing Deep breathing can help you relax and reduce stress. One method is called the 4-7-8 method. Sit in a comfortable position. Inhale for a count of four. Hold for a count of seven. Exhale for a count of eight. Practice this for five minutes. How do you feel? Write a paragraph about how you can use this to manage stress.

Management Skills

12. Make Plans Drew's family is moving. He has worked hard to keep up his grades in order to get into college. Drew is worried that changing schools before graduation may hurt his chances. What can he do to ease his concerns? Write an advice column with suggestions for Drew.

Technology Skills

13. Create a Brochure Use a software program to create a brochure for young children on coping with change. As you write the brochure, think about the following: What changes are children most apt to experience? What information about change would be helpful to a child? How can you present the content so that a child could understand and use it?

14. Welcome New Students Find out what is done to help new students in your school feel welcome. Plan an activity that would contribute to this effort. Write a half-page report on what you can do personally to make friends with newcomers and help them feel at home.

15. Investigate Homelessness Find out if there is a homeless problem in your community. Create an information bulletin to answer these questions: What steps has local government taken to solve this problem? Are there shelters? Are there places where free meals are served? Who provides these services? What services do you think should be provided to homeless people? Explain your answer.

16. Roller-Coaster Analysis Write a paragraph in which you analyze the kinds of stress that could be produced by a roller-coaster ride.

17. Stress Tests Go to this book's Online Learning Center at **glencoe.com** to find **Web Links** for **Life Stress Tests**. Select one and take the test. Mark which events or symptoms apply, and write down your score. In a paragraph, evaluate whether you think the test is a valid one.

Additional Activities For additional activities, go to this book's Online Learning Center through **glencoe.com**.

Academic Skills

 ### Mathematics

18. Savings Plans It is important to have a healthy savings account. It can help prevent financial problems. Americans save less than 5% of their income. Other countries have a higher percentage of savings per capita, including Belgium (22%), Denmark (16.2%), and Japan (15.7%). Research the average per capita savings of at least five other countries. Display your findings in a bar graph.

Math Concept **Bar Graphs** Bar graphs can be designed so that the bars are horizontal or vertical. Each bar represents the quantity associated with a different category—in this case, the per capita savings of a country.

Starting Hint: Collect your data. Label one axis of the graph with the names of the countries. Label the other axis with the percentages of savings. Graph the data in the appropriate places.

 For math help, go to the Math Appendix at the back of the book.

> **NCTM Data Analysis and Probability** Formulate questions that can be addressed with data and collect, organize, and display relevant data to answer them.

 ### English Language Arts

19. Disaster Planning Follow your teacher's instructions to form into groups. Imagine that you are part of your school's disaster recovery team. Select a natural disaster. Work together to create a disaster plan. Identify preparations that should be made prior to the disaster. What procedures will protect people during the disaster? What supplies would be needed during and after the disaster? What might happen if the school building was being used as a community shelter? Present your plan to your classmates.

> **NCTE 11** Participate as members of literacy communities.

 ### Social Studies

20. Research Bankruptcy Laws Investigate the bankruptcy laws in your state. What is the process for declaring bankruptcy? What are the penalties? Find out whether the number of bankruptcies in your state is rising or falling. Why do you think this is so? Write a report of your findings.

> **NCSS X.i** Construct a policy statement to achieve one or more goals related to an issue of public concern.

 ## STANDARDIZED TEST PRACTICE

SHORT ANSWER

21. Answer each of the following questions in one to three sentences.

> **Test-Taking Tip** In a short answer question, write as neatly as possible. Double-check your grammar, spelling, and punctuation. Neatly written answers often get higher marks.

a. Explain how you can limit the stress in your life.

b. How can moving to a new home cause stress in one's life?

c. Natural disasters cannot be avoided, but there are precautions that can be taken to prepare in advance for a natural disaster. What can you do to prepare for a fire?

CHAPTER 14

Divorce and Remarriage

Section 14.1

When Marriages End

Section 14.2

Manage After Divorce

Explore the Photo
Ending a relationship can be a difficult decision. *What can couples do to prevent a relationship from ending in divorce?*

Chapter Objectives

After completing this chapter, you will be able to:

- **Explain** the changes that occur in a couple's relationship that can lead to divorce.
- **List** the three legal ways to end a marriage.
- **Identify** the major decisions that must be made during the divorce process.
- **Suggest** factors that help children cope with divorce.
- **Describe** adjustments a couple must make following divorce.
- **Summarize** the challenges that blended families face.

Writing Activity

Write an Explanation

Optimism You show optimism when you have a positive attitude and belief that things will work out well. You can show optimism when you:

- See a parent's remarriage as a chance to build a larger support system.
- Understand that the adjustment to having a new stepbrother or stepsister can work out well.
- Give others the benefit of the doubt.
- Believe in your abilities.

Write an explanation about why it is important to express optimism in your life. Include details so that others may see the importance of having optimism in their lives.

Writing Tips To explain something clearly, follow these steps:

1. Describe the major purposes of expressing optimism.
2. Arrange the details in an organized, logical way.
3. Make the explanation clear and legible for the audience.

When Marriages End

Reading Guide

Before You Read

Use Diagrams As you read, write down the main idea and any facts, explanations, or examples you find in the text. Draw arrows from the main idea to the information that directly supports it.

Read to Learn
Key Concepts
- **Explain** the changes that occur in a couple's relationship that can lead to divorce.
- **List** the three legal ways to end a marriage.
- **Identify** the major decisions that must be made during the divorce process.

Main Idea
Unstable couple relationships can lead to divorce. When this happens, there are many decisions to be made by the couple.

Content Vocabulary
◇ stability
◇ divorce
◇ invalidation
◇ betrayal
◇ annulment
◇ divorce mediation
◇ custody
◇ alimony

Academic Vocabulary
You will find these words in your reading and on your tests. Use the glossary to look up their definitions if necessary.
■ steadfast   ■ tolerant

Graphic Organizer
As you read, list and describe the stages couples go through as their marriages end. Use a chart like the one shown to help organize your information.

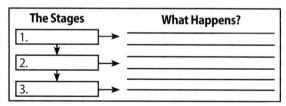

The Stages	What Happens?
1.	
2.	
3.	

 Graphic Organizer Go to this book's Online Learning Center at **glencoe.com** to print out this graphic organizer.

Academic Standards • • • • • • • • • • • • • • • • • •

 English Language Arts

NCTE 8 Use information resources to gather information and create and communicate knowledge.

NCTE 12 Use language to accomplish individual purposes.

 Mathematics

NCTM Problem Solving Solve problems that arise in mathematics and in other contexts.

NCTE *National Council of Teachers of English*
NCTM *National Council of Teachers of Mathematics*

NSES *National Science Education Standards*
NCSS *National Council of the Social Studies*

Stable and Unstable Relationships

In strong families, members have stable relationships with each other. **Stability** is the quality of being firm and steadfast. **Steadfast** means you are faithful to someone or something. Stable relationships tend to last over time.

Stable family relationships have certain qualities. These same qualities are also important with a married couple. A stable couple respects and trusts each other. They communicate and show unity. They share values and beliefs. They build strong morals. They spend time together and establish traditions.

An important trait of stable relationships is good communication. When a couple does not communicate, the relationship becomes less rewarding. Respect and trust may be reduced. A relationship that is not rewarding will not be stable. The costs begin to outweigh the rewards of the relationship. The couple may start to think that there are other choices.

Why Marriages End

Most relationships begin with love and high hopes. Some marriages, however, fail for a number of reasons. Sometimes partners grow apart. They no longer share the interests that once drew them together. Partners may not communicate well enough to maintain their ties. Problems may wear down a marriage. These can be financial, sexual, or role problems. Physical or mental abuse may cause a failed marriage as well.

Divorce is a legal action that ends a marriage. Ending a marriage leads to major changes for the whole family. Even the most cordial breakups cause pain and stress.

Not every troubled marriage is destined for divorce. Couples can seek counseling. These couples want help to solve the problems between them. They work to fix what is happening to prevent a divorce. Many couples have rebuilt strong marriages.

Vocabulary

You can find definitions in the glossary at the back of this book.

As You Read

Connect How can good communication help a relationship?

End of a Relationship Some relationships are unstable and may end in divorce. *What contributes to an unstable relationship?*

Society's View of Divorce

Society has grown more **tolerant**, or accepting, of divorce over the years. More flexible laws make it easier to get a divorce. Some people believe that divorce is too easy to obtain. They feel that couples have less reason to work at solving their problems. The effects of divorce are serious for everyone involved. Couples thinking about divorce need to consider the outcome for the family.

Breakups in Stages

Marriages seldom end without warning. Most breakups occur over the course of about two years. During this time, the relationship unravels through three basic stages:

- **Isolation** Partners withdraw from each other. They no longer share closeness. They may act like strangers. They talk politely about neutral subjects.
- **Invalidation** **Invalidation** ((ˌ)in-ˌva-lə-ˈdā-shən) means partners respond negatively to each other. They weaken their bond by making judgments. They blame each other. Negative feelings build up as a result.
- **Betrayal** **Betrayal** is the feeling that trust has been broken. The support each spouse expected from the other is no longer there.

The most important act in the breakup of a marriage is the choice to separate. Deciding to divorce can be harder than the divorce itself. Feelings are the most raw and painful at this time. How families handle the breakup at this point has a strong effect on all family members. This is especially true for children. Parents who stay positive about what is going on help children cope. Maturity on the part of parents gives everyone hope for the future.

✓ **Reading Check** **Define** What is divorce?

Real Life — Predictors of Divorce

Certain factors may predict whether a marriage will last or not. These include:

- **Age** The younger a couple is when they marry, the more likely they are to divorce. The risk for divorce also increases if the bride is pregnant.
- **Income** Unemployment and financial problems are closely linked to marriage failure. However, women who earn high incomes are more likely to divorce than women with low or no income.
- **Success of the Parents' Marriage** Those whose parents have divorced are more likely to end their own marriages.

- **Other Factors** People who are active in a religion are more likely to stay together. This is also true for couples who knew or dated each other for a long time. The more children a couple has, the less likely they are to divorce.

Problem-Solving Jake and Missy started dating at age fourteen. By age eighteen, they felt ready to marry. They planned to get jobs and live with Missy's stepmother until they could afford a place of their own. What do you think their chances are for a strong marriage?

The Legal Process

Sometimes one spouse simply leaves, or deserts, the other. Desertion may mark the end of their relationship, but their legal marriage remains. Marriages that cannot be saved may be ended legally. A marriage can be ended legally in one of three ways. These are:

- **Annulment** An **annulment** (ə-'nəl-mənt) states that a legal marriage never took place due to some prior condition. The marriage was not legal because it was not entered in good faith. A couple may get an annulment when their religious beliefs forbid divorce. This may let them continue in their faith.
- **Legal Separation** This lets couples live in separate homes. They cannot remarry. The partners make a legal agreement to live apart. Legal separation can be a halfway point between marriage and divorce. For some, however, it is permanent.
- **Divorce** This is the most common outcome of marital breakups. Divorce is governed by each state. Laws vary from state to state. Some states no longer use the term divorce. Instead they call the legal action the dissolution of marriage.

No-Fault Divorce Laws

Most divorces are granted under no-fault divorce laws. Partners simply claim that the marriage has broken down. Neither one is to blame. Time spent living apart may be all the proof needed that a breakdown has occurred. The legal process is simple. Still, a simple procedure does not solve the problems couples face. There are many challenges after people choose to divorce.

✓ Reading Check **Identify** What is an annulment?

Divorce Decisions

Ending a marriage means making many decisions. These are often difficult. Issues can include how to divide time with children. Personal items must be split. The final authority rests with the divorce judge. He or she legalizes the couple's decisions. When partners cannot agree, the judge decides for them.

Most couples need help in settling major divorce issues. This is especially true if children or complex financial affairs are involved. Some couples rely on **divorce mediation**. This is when the couple meets with a neutral third person. This person helps the couple work out a solution. Couples who go through successful mediation are usually happy with the results. Those who rely on a judge's decision tend to be less pleased.

▶▶ **Children and Divorce** Children and teens are hurt by divorce. *How can parents help children through the difficult process?*

Child Custody

When a couple has minor children, the divorce decree states how their care will be handled. **Custody** is the legal right to make decisions that affect children. It includes the duty to provide their physical care. These are the possible legal arrangements:

- **Sole Custody** One spouse keeps all legal rights and responsibilities of parenting. The other usually has the right to visit the child. Mothers often have sole custody. Many fathers today, however, seek and gain sole custody.
- **Joint Custody** Parents share equally in decisions about the children. Children live mostly with one parent or split their time in each parent's home.
- **Split Custody** Each parent has sole custody of one or more of the children. This arrangement can make the divorce harder on siblings who want to stay together.
- **Alternate Custody** Children live first with one parent for a long period of time, perhaps a year. Then the children live with the other parent for a period of time. Each parent has decision-making power during that time.
- **Third-Party Custody** Someone else, often a relative, is assigned as the children's legal guardian. The children may also be placed in a foster home.

Child Support

The custody arrangement defines how the child support will be handled. In single-parent custody, the parent who does not have custody usually pays support. This is often a set amount to be paid each month. Who pays the child support in joint custody varies.

Most children live with their mothers. Therefore, fathers tend to make most child support payments. A father is most apt to pay if he was involved with his children before the divorce. Having a good income also increases the chances that he will pay. Even so, child support tends to cover less than half the cost of raising a child.

Distance can lessen a parent's sense of duty to pay child support. This may be physical or emotional distance. Some refuse to pay because they cannot influence how the money is spent.

The problem of unpaid child support is a difficult one. The government has programs to locate parents who owe child support. It can deduct the money from their wages. Parents can be jailed or lose their driver's licenses. Offenders who are in jail or who lack transportation cannot earn wages. This kind of punishment, therefore, may not be the best solution. Many mothers feel it is not worth the effort to jail a father for lack of child support.

Financial Matters

Divorce means dividing property. This could be a home and furnishings. It may be cars, savings accounts, and investments. In most states, no-fault divorce calls for dividing property equally. This is mainly because a spouse who has been economically dependent on the other may suffer.

If spouses cannot reach a settlement that seems fair to both, the judge divides their property. Most judges look at what each has given to the marriage. They look at the length of the marriage and other factors. Women may have a right to part of their husband's Social Security or pension.

Alimony

Financial support of an ex-spouse is called **alimony** ('a-lə-ˌmō-nē). The spouse with more financial resources helps support the other. A spouse usually does not receive alimony for very long. Some people get spouse support until they find a job or remarry.

Section 14.1   After You Read

Review Key Concepts

1. **List** three reasons a marriage may fail.
2. **Describe** what is involved in a no-fault divorce.
3. **Explain** how child support is related to child custody.

Practice Academic Skills

English Language Arts

4. Research divorce mediation. What is the training to be a divorce mediator? What exactly does a mediator do? What kind of successes do mediators have in divorce cases? Write a report outlining your findings.

5. Create a chart that lists the five types of custody arrangements. Describe each type of arrangement. Identify the pros and cons of each for children and parents.

NCTE 8 Use information resources to gather information and create and communicate knowledge.

NCTE 12 Use language to accomplish individual purposes.

Check Your Answers Check your answers at this book's Online Learning Center through glencoe.com.

Manage After Divorce

Reading Guide

Before You Read

Look It up If you hear or read a word that you do not know, look it up in the glossary at the back of the book or in a dictionary. Before long, this practice will become a habit. You will be amazed at how many new words you learn.

Read to Learn

Key Concepts

- **Suggest** factors that help children cope with divorce.
- **Describe** adjustments a couple must make following divorce.
- **Summarize** the challenges that blended families face.

Main Idea

Children need stability as the divorce occurs. Divorce can create single-parent families. When divorced couples remarry, blended families face many challenges.

Content Vocabulary

◇ adjustment   ◇ favoritism

 Graphic Organizer Go to this book's Online Learning Center at **glencoe.com** to print out this graphic organizer.

Academic Vocabulary

You will find these words in your reading and on your tests. Use the glossary to look up their definitions if necessary.

◾ daunting   ◾ rigid

Graphic Organizer

As you read, look for at least four ways that families can provide stability for children during divorce. Use a chart like the one shown to help organize your information.

Ways to Provide Stability
1. _____
2. _____
3. _____
4. _____

Academic Standards • • • • • • • • • • • • • • • •

 English Language Arts

NCTE 11 Participate as members of literacy communities.

NCTE 12 Use language to accomplish individual purposes.

NCTE *National Council of Teachers of English*	**NSES** *National Science Education Standards*
NCTM *National Council of Teachers of Mathematics*	**NCSS** *National Council of the Social Studies*

Children and Divorce

Divorce creates major changes in the lives of children. Very young children may not understand the situation. Still, they can sense the anger and tension as a marriage ends. Studies have looked at how children cope with divorce. To cope well, children have to function on two levels. They must be able to manage daily life as well as live with the emotions caused by the divorce.

As You Read
Connect How does divorce affect a child's daily life?

How Children View Divorce

Young children often imagine that a divorce is somehow their fault. Parents need to make it clear that children do not cause a divorce. Children must be aware that they cannot prevent it. They also cannot make parents reunite.

Older children and teens know that the situation is complex. Some still hope their parents will get back together, even after a divorce. Sometimes divorce ends an abusive home life. Children's relief is often mixed with sorrow and guilt.

The Parents' Attitude Matters

Children tend to model their parents' attitude towards the divorce. Parents can stress that divorce is the best way for all of them to have a better life. When they do this, children tend to adopt this view. Parents can cooperate on matters affecting their children. When they do, the children may see themselves as now having two homes with a loving parent in each.

Support for Children Children tend to blame themselves when parents divorce. *How can families reassure and support children during this time?*

The Need for Stability

Children cope best with divorce when they have stability. This means there are few changes in the rest of their lives. It can mean living in the same home, going to the same school, and keeping the same friends. This gives reassurance that some things will stay the same. Stability helps balance the other changes caused by the divorce.

Keeping stable, loving relationships with both parents is important to a child. Children may feel they must choose between parents. This sense of torn loyalty is the most stressful part of the breakup for children. Children need to know that it is all right to love both parents after a divorce. This knowledge helps soften the effects of divorce.

Effects of Divorce

How divorce affects children is a controversial subject. Experts agree that the time around the parents' separation is the hardest on a child. The child grieves for what they feel is a death of the intact family. Feelings of guilt, rage, rejection, and helplessness are common. A child may need up to one year to sort out these feelings and adapt to the new life.

Studies of children of divorced parents have found that children can handle divorce. Emotional problems caused by the breakup tend to lessen with time. Having two loving, attentive parents helps. Some studies have also been done between children from divorced and nuclear families. They show no difference in school grades, intelligence, or self-esteem.

Divorce may have long-term effects for children. This may make them more careful in choosing a marriage partner. On the other hand, if their marriages break down, they are more apt to divorce.

A New Life Each person must adapt to life without the other after a divorce. *What are some changes they may face?*

✔ **Reading Check** **Explain** What are the two levels that a child of divorcing parents must function on?

Vocabulary

You can find definitions in the glossary at the back of this book.

The Divorced Couple

Families facing divorce must go through a period of **adjustment**. This means working to change routines and feelings to function in a new setting. A positive and determined attitude helps adjustment.

Both partners have to rebuild their lives following a divorce. Each must cope with loneliness, anger, depression, guilt, and feelings of failure. If a parent does not have custody, visits with children can help ease these feelings.

Some people have more financial, emotional, social, and community resources. These people tend to adjust more quickly. Even so, it takes from two to four years to get over the breakup of a marriage. The process is often hardest for those who withdraw from others.

Sometimes divorce affects careers. People going through a divorce may be less effective on the job. A move or promotion may mean one parent leaves children behind. A change of job may affect the ability of parents to support their children.

Dealing with the day-to-day care of children can also make adjusting harder. Parents with custody must often stretch their resources. They also need to hide their own anger and sorrow to help children deal with their feelings. The parent who does not have custody must work out new routines for seeing children.

Single Parenting

The move to a single-parent family following divorce is one of change and challenge. One parent must act as both mother and father for the child. The parent needs to earn the family's income and manage the household. These can be **daunting**, or discouraging, tasks even without the stress of divorce. Single parenting can cause strain and problems for both parent and child.

Money is often an ongoing problem in single-parent families. This is true especially when that parent is a woman. Household incomes for single mothers tend to drop after divorce. If child support payments are late or unpaid, problems can get worse.

Single parents who make good use of their support systems do best. They exchange help and services with family members and friends. They find community resources to help them.

Remarriage

Most divorced people marry again. Men remarry sooner than women do. The younger a person is, the greater the chance of remarriage. Most experts suggest waiting at least four years after a divorce to remarry. This is in order to heal the hurt caused by the breakup. People who remarry quickly to try to solve their problems rarely succeed. In most divorces, one partner remarries within two years.

INDEPENDENT Living

HOW TO Handle Divorce

It is important to remember that although the feelings divorced parents have for each other change, their love for their children stays the same. Follow these guidelines to manage stress when you or someone you know is going through a divorce:

1. **Do not blame yourself.** Whatever the reason your parents are divorcing, you did not cause the problem. It is important to remind yourself that it is not your fault.
2. **Do not choose sides.** You may feel pressure to choose one parent over the other. You do not have to choose sides in a divorce situation.
3. **Talk about it.** Discuss your feelings about the divorce with your parents and other trusted, supportive adults.
4. **Take care of yourself.** Eat nutritious foods, stay physically active, and get enough sleep. It is important to take care of yourself physically so that you can manage your stress.
5. **Join a support group.** Consider joining a support group for children of divorce. Doing so will help you realize that you are not alone.

Take Action Interview a trusted adult who is the child of divorced parents. Find out if he or she has any perspective on children of divorce. Ask if he or she has any advice for the children and teens of today whose parents get divorced.

▶▶ Starting Over
Most divorced people eventually remarry. *What challenges face couples who remarry?*

People who do wait often have happy second marriages. The two major issues in remarriage are money and children. If the partners can manage these issues well, the marriage is usually successful. The couple is older and wiser. This increases the chance for stability in remarriage. Partners are more apt to understand what they want and need in a spouse. They may be less **rigid**, or firm, about what they expect from each other.

Remarriages are the most successful when the couple has figured out what went wrong the first time. They understand that it was not all the former spouse's fault. Partners have learned from their past mistakes. Having a good working relationship with a former spouse is positive. The fewer issues there are with former spouses, the better the remarriage tends to be.

✓ Reading Check) **Define** What is adjustment?

Blended Families

More than half of all remarriages create blended families. A blended family is one where one or both spouses have been married before. The family includes children from previous marriages.

Blended families differ from nuclear ones. In a blended family, all members have lost a relationship from the past. The parent-child relationship is older than the couple relationship. In a nuclear family, the couple relationship is the first and older one.

Challenges of Blending

Life in any family has its challenges. The changes that occur as two families blend into one can present unique challenges that nuclear families may not face. These may include:

- **Favoritism** A parent may display **favoritism** to his or her own child over a stepchild. This means the parent favors one child over another. Some parents demand more of their own children.

- **Discipline** Children may have to adjust to new rules in the family. Parents may need to work out conflicting views on discipline.
- **Resources** Questions about dividing resources must be handled carefully. Sharing resources is basic to any family. However, some items might be kept for private use. All family members should be clear on which is which.
- **Values** Most members of a blended family do not share the same values. This is because they came from different families with different value systems. They must learn to understand each other's views and possibly form new values together.
- **Former Relationships** Parents and children of previous marriages may not support the new marriage. Blended family members must accept the needs of the other family.
- **Roles** Roles in blended families take time to define. Family members need to base behavior on the situation and people involved. They should look beyond the stereotypes.
- **Child-Spouse Competition** The new spouse may feel excluded at first. This may be because the parent-child relationship is older than the couple relationship. Jealousy and competition for attention are normal responses.

Blended families must work at maintaining relationships. First, the couple must be committed to each other and the marriage. Their children should not come between them. Adjusting to life in a blended family may take three to five years. Love takes time to grow. Those who make the effort are likely to be rewarded with a successfully blended family.

Life Skills CHECKLIST

Communication Skills

Getting Along in a Blended Family People who live happily in blended families have learned that communication skills are important. They use these skills to:

✓ Send I-messages to express ideas and feelings.

✓ Keep the lines of communication open among all family members.

✓ Show that they accept the new situation and will do their part to make it work.

✓ Express respect for the relationships in the new family, whether or not they are close ones.

✓ Show flexibility in managing space and time.

✓ Share a sense of humor.

Section 14.2 After You Read

Review Key Concepts

1. **Identify** the period of the divorce process that is most difficult for children.
2. **Explain** the role of resources in adjusting to divorce.
3. **Define** a blended family.

Practice Academic Skills

English Language Arts

4. Write down two negative terms, such as blame or favoritism, that come to mind regarding divorce and blended families. Then rephrase each to make it less judgmental. Use these positive references in your conversations with others.

NCTE 12 Use language to accomplish individual purposes.

5. Work in a group with other students to develop a list of rules for blended families. Include rules for parents and for children. Post your list of rules on the bulletin board.

NCTE 11 Participate as members of literacy communities.

Check Your Answers Check your answers at this book's Online Learning Center through **glencoe.com**.

CAREER SPOTLIGHT

Relationship Therapist, Clinical Psychologist

Judith Barnett
Chapel Hill, North Carolina

Couples that come to see Judith Barnett are often facing some of their toughest problems. These often include marital stress, unfaithfulness, lack of communication, and many other issues that arise over the course of a long-term relationship. Her job involves understanding what they are going through.

Barnett says, "Therapists need to be able to put their own self interest aside and fully engage in the world of the client." She explains that they need to be able to walk away from the client's problems when the session is done. They should not make the client's stresses their own.

Barnett has been working with couples for 20 years. Despite a solid background, she says real-world experience is the only way a therapist can develop his or her skills. She states, "The most relevant experience in this arena is hands-on experience, with supervision."

Despite the tough nature of the work, Barnett says she enjoys what she does. She especially likes helping people. "That's trite, but true," she says, "and it is also a great way to make a living."

CAREER FACTS

Education or Training Most states require a master's degree, 2 years of 3,000 hours of supervised clinical experience, and they have to pass the state-recognized exam.

Nature of the Work Marriage and family therapists apply principles, methods, and therapeutic techniques to individuals, families, couples, or organizations in order to resolve emotional conflicts.

Aptitudes, Abilities, and Skills Counselors must possess high physical and emotional energy to handle the array of problems that they address. They must have good communication and other interpersonal skills, and concern and empathy for others.

Academic Skills Required English Language Arts, Mathematics, Science, Social Studies

Student Organizations To prepare for this career, look for groups that foster communication skills, such as a debate team.

Career Outlook Employment of counselors is expected to grow faster than the average over the next ten years.

Career Path With additional preparation, education in family therapy may lead to supervisory positions, teachers, researchers, and clinicians in the discipline.

Critical Thinking

Get Advice Do you think a spouse should go to a relationship therapist alone? Why or why not?

 Research Careers For more information on this and other careers, visit the Occupational Outlook Handbook Web site through the link on this book's Online Learning Center at **glencoe.com**.

CHAPTER SUMMARY

Section 14.1
When Marriages End

When a marriage starts to come apart, it is often because of lack of communication or shared interests. A couple starts on a process that involves isolation, invalidation, and betrayal. This may take about two years. The couple can end the marriage by annulment, a legal separation, or divorce. There are many decisions to be made when a divorce happens. If there are children, custody and support issues must be settled. Property must be divided. Sometimes one spouse pays alimony or maintenance. The divorce judge has the final say in what is decided.

Section 14.2
Manage After Divorce

Children tend to see divorce in the same terms as their parents. If it is presented in a positive light, they see it that way too. Children need stability in their lives as they adjust to divorce. This means they cope better when there are few changes in the rest of their lives. There are few long-term effects of parental divorce. Two are a hesitation to marry and a tendency to divorce. Divorced couples may go through a two-to-four-year adjustment period. Being a single parent may make the adjustment more difficult. Many people remarry. A blended family has adjustments to make.

Content and Academic Vocabulary Review

1. Use each of these content and academic vocabulary words in a sentence.

Content Vocabulary

◇ stability (p. 269)
◇ divorce (p. 269)
◇ invalidation (p. 270)
◇ betrayal (p. 270)
◇ annulment (p. 271)
◇ divorce mediation (p. 271)
◇ custody (p. 272)
◇ alimony (p. 273)
◇ adjustment (p. 276)
◇ favoritism (p. 278)

Academic Vocabulary

■ steadfast (p. 269)
■ tolerant (p. 270)
■ daunting (p. 277)
■ rigid (p. 278)

Review Key Concepts

2. Explain the changes that occur in a couple's relationship that can lead to divorce.
3. List the three legal ways to end a marriage.
4. Identify the major decisions that must be made during the divorce process.
5. Suggest factors that help children cope with divorce.
6. Describe adjustments a couple must make following divorce.
7. Summarize the challenges that blended families face.

Critical Thinking

8. Compare What are some advantages and disadvantages when a couple stays together for the sake of their children?
9. Cause and Effect What benefits do family members gain when the parent who does not have custody pays child support as required?

Real-World Skills

Interpersonal Skills

10. Communication Will's parents are divorced. He enjoys one-on-one time with his father. His father is dating a woman with three children. The children are often there during Will's visits. Will misses his private time with his father. Write an advice column about what Will should do.

Management Skills

11. Planning Plan an activity for your family that will promote stability. It should encourage interaction among all family members. Write the steps you would need to take to make this activity happen.

Decision-Making Skills

12. Child Custody Choices Imagine that you are a judge in a divorce case. Two parents have asked for split custody of their two children. Neither parent wants to be alone. The children do not want to be separated. Write a paragraph that explains what you would decide.

Problem-Solving Skills

13. Make a Choice Bret has been divorced for three years and would like to get married to Sonja. His children do not like Sonja or her children. Write a letter to Bret sharing your advice for him.

14. Discuss Follow your teacher's instructions to form into groups. Discuss this issue: If divorces were more difficult to get, would society be stronger? Listen carefully as each person gives an opinion. Select one member of the group to summarize the discussion for the class.

15. Investigate CASA, court appointed special advocates, are trained volunteers who look after children in the court system. They work to be sure the judge's decision is in the best interest of the children involved. Is there a local branch of CASA in your community? Do they represent children in local divorce cases? If so, what is their role? Is this volunteer work that you would be interested in? Why or why not? Report your findings in an information brochure that can be shared with classmates.

16. Survey Ask 10 adults of various ages to explain if they think divorce is taken too casually today. Be sure to record their ages and answers. Compile your findings with those of your classmates. Are there differences by age groups? What conclusions can you draw from this survey?

17. Research Go to this book's Online Learning Center at **glencoe.com** to find **Web Links** for **The Fathers' Rights Movement**. What is the movement? How does it relate to divorce and child custody? Do you think the movement is valid? Explain. Write a brief report on your findings.

Additional Activities For additional activities, go to this book's Online Learning Center through **glencoe.com**.

Academic Skills

Mathematics

18. Calculate Child Support When marriages end in divorce, one or both parents are usually ordered to make child support payments. The judge has ordered a father to pay 20 percent of his after-tax income for child support. The father's take-home pay is $37,500 a year. How much child support should he pay each month?

Math Concept **Find Percentages**

A percent is a ratio that compares a number to 100. To multiply with percentages see the Starting Hint below.

Starting Hint: You can rewrite the percent (20%) as a fraction with a denominator of 100. Convert the fraction to a decimal. Multiply this decimal by the income ($37,500). Be sure to put the decimal point in the correct place in your answer. Remember this will give you the amount he must pay each year. The question asks how much he should pay each month. To find this number, you will need to divide your answer by 12.

 For math help, go to the Math Appendix at the back of the book.

> **NCTM Problem Solving** Apply and adapt a variety of appropriate strategies to solve problems.

English Language Arts

19. Persuasive Speaking Imagine that your aunt and uncle are in a custody battle over their fourteen-year-old child. Your cousin says to you, "I feel like I am being torn apart. Please talk to my parents for me." Plan what you might say to your aunt and uncle that will explain your cousin's feelings. Consider your relationship to and the emotional state of your aunt and uncle when you choose your words and tone. Write your answer in paragraph form.

> **NCTE 4** Use written language to communicate effectively.

Social Studies

20. State Laws Research divorce and child custody laws in your state. Find information on how long the waiting period is for divorce. Is mediation recommended? Are there requirements for alimony? Find out which is the preferred custody arrangement. What is the penalty if a parent does not pay child support? Write a report of your findings.

> **NCSS VI.a** Examine persistent issues involving the rights, roles, and status of the individual in relation to the general welfare.

STANDARDIZED TEST PRACTICE

MULTIPLE CHOICE
Choose the phrase that best completes the following statement.

> **Test-Taking Tip** In a multiple-choice test, the answers should be specific and precise. Read the question first, then read all the answer choices. Eliminate answers that you know are incorrect.

21. _____ is not a way to legally end a marriage.
a. Annulment
b. Legal separation
c. Divorce
d. Abandonment

CHAPTER 15

Relate to Older Adults

Section 15.1

Concerns of
Older Adults

Section 15.2

The Aging
Process

▶▶ *Explore the Photo*
Finding time to be with an older
adult can be rewarding to both of
you. *What are some activities you
may enjoy doing with an older family member?*

Chapter Objectives

After completing this chapter, you will be able to:

- **Describe** the types of concerns older adults have.
- **Explain** the effect ageism has on the image and lives of older adults.
- **Identify** the stages of aging.
- **Determine** the kinds of changes that occur as people age.

Writing Activity

Step-by-Step Guide

Caring Caring is concern for and interest in someone else. It gives a person attention and support. A caring person truly enjoys reaching out to others. You can show caring when you:

- Phone a grandparent frequently to see how he or she is doing.
- Listen with empathy when an older aunt or uncle talks about their health problems.
- Invite an elderly neighbor to a quiet family dinner.
- Take an older adult to a dental appointment when he or she has no transportation.

Think of a time when you or someone you know has been caring. Use this example to write a step-by-step guide for how someone can show that they care.

Writing Tips To write an effective step-by-step explanation, follow these steps:

1. Write the steps in chronological order.
2. Explain terms the reader may not know.
3. Use appropriate transition words.
4. Use precise verbs to make your explanation clear.

Concerns of Older Adults

Reading Guide

Before You Read

Be Organized A messy environment can be distracting. To lessen distractions, organize an area where you can read this section comfortably.

Read to Learn

Key Concepts

- **Describe** the types of concerns older adults have.
- **Explain** the effect ageism has on the image and lives of older adults.

Main Idea

Older adults have concerns such as decisions about finances and medical care. They need to live where they will be safe and cared for. Some societies tend to have a negative stereotype of older adults.

Content Vocabulary

◇ fixed income
◇ caregiver
◇ respite care
◇ chronic disease
◇ elder abuse
◇ ageism

Academic Vocabulary

You will find these words in your reading and on your tests. Use the glossary to look up their definitions if necessary.

- frugal
- frail

Graphic Organizer

As you read, identify six concerns of older adults. Use a chart like the one shown to help organize your information.

Concerns of Older Adults		

 Graphic Organizer Go to this book's Online Learning Center at **glencoe.com** to print out this graphic organizer.

Academic Standards •

 English Language Arts

NCTE 7 Conduct research and gather, evaluate, and synthesize data to communicate discoveries.

NCTE 9 Develop an understanding of diversity in language use across cultures.

 Mathematics

NCTM Number and Operations Understand the meanings of operations and how they relate to one another.

NCTE *National Council of Teachers of English*
NCTM *National Council of Teachers of Mathematics*

NSES *National Science Education Standards*
NCSS *National Council of the Social Studies*

Look at the Issues

In today's society, people do not grow old as fast as they used to. An older adult today may be a college student, athlete, or fast-food worker. Longer life spans have caused the older population in America to grow. The fastest growing age group is now over age 80. The numbers will grow even more quickly as another large group of people who were born between 1946 and 1964 reach retirement age. This group of people are commonly called baby boomers. This is a generation of people born during an increase in birth rates after World War II.

As a result, older people are apt to be part of your life. They may be coworkers, neighbors, family, and more. You can understand this age group better if you have an idea of what it means to grow older.

The needs of older adults differ from those of younger families. This may be because they are in a different stage of family development, the retirement stage. People in this stage face different management issues, such as not working anymore. They may also have fewer resources. This means they may need to be more resourceful.

In the long run, the concerns of older adults affect all generations. As you read about the issues facing older adults, think of their impact on younger people and families. This includes you and your classmates.

As You Read

Connect In what areas are older people a part of your life?

Financial Concerns

Many older adults live on a fixed income. A **fixed income** is a set amount that does not change. It is usually paid monthly. It may not cover the retired person's expenses. People without other financial resources often have a hard time making ends meet. There are older adults who live in poverty. Women, members of minority groups, and those over age 85 are most apt to be poor.

Fears about the future can add to the problem. Older adults cannot predict how long they will live. Some older adults are more **frugal**, or careful with how they spend their money, than necessary to save for later years. They may harm their health by skimping on food, heating, and other basic needs.

Vocabulary

You can find definitions in the glossary at the back of this book.

Longer Lives
People today are living longer than ever. *Why do you think this is happening?*

Financial issues of older adults are a concern in society. The two main government programs for older adults are Social Security and Medicare. Social Security pays a monthly amount to those over a certain age. Medicare helps with the cost of health care. Soon more baby boomers will retire and enroll in these programs. Funding will be a problem because there will be very few workers supporting each older adult.

Continue to Work

Many people continue to work after retiring. Some choose part-time or volunteer work. Some do jobs that are less demanding than those they held before. Many older adults enjoy the social aspects of the job. They like the company and the sense of purpose they feel at work. Most simply need or want the extra income.

The strains in the Social Security system may mean that more older people will need to work to make ends meet. Younger people will need to take a serious look at planning ahead for their older adult years. They will need to save and manage to have financial security in their older years and during retirement.

Medical Care

The aging process and illness take their toll on the body. Many older adults need a great deal of health care. This can be costly at a time that income is apt to be low. Programs like Medicare help pay expenses. Still, many older adults cannot afford the care they need. Health costs are a major issue for older adults.

Too much medication is another problem. The dosage of medicine a person needs can change with age. People with many health problems can have several doctors prescribing drugs. Some are harmful when mixed. Older adults may have trouble knowing how much of each medicine to take and when. These hazards make it vital that doctors be told about all drugs an older person is taking. Any side effects should be reported.

Living Arrangements

Like teens, older adults cherish their independence. The ability to care for themselves is basic to their sense of worth. Given a choice, most older adults want to stay in their own homes. Safety, however, is a concern as people age. Injuries are a major cause of death among people age sixty-five and older. Many of these occur in the home.

Some simple steps can make housing safer for older people. For example, furniture can be arranged to create clear, easy traffic patterns. Skid-resistant strips can be put on bathtubs and the backs of rugs.

Financial Literacy

Health Insurance

Your health insurance premium is currently $1,200 per year. If the cost of the premium increases 5 percent each year, what will your premium be in five years?

Math Concept Multiply by Percents
To multiply by percents, change the percent to a fraction with 100 in the denominator. Then change the fraction to a decimal. For example: $5\% = \frac{5}{100} = 0.05$.

Starting Hint: You will need to multiply the premium for each year by 5%. The starting premium is $1,200. You will multiply $1,200 by 5%. Then add your answer to $1,200 to get the premium for the second year. You will multiply the premium for the second year by 5% and add your answer to get the premium for the third year and so on for five years.

 For math help, go to the Math Appendix at the back of the book.

NCTM Number and Operations Understand the meanings of operations and how they relate to one another.

More adjustments may be needed to meet changes in health. At some point, older adults may be unable to live alone. Their choices in living arrangements depend on their resources, their families, and their needs. Options may include:

- **Shared Housing** Older adults may rent out rooms in their homes. Often the renter is younger and helps with household tasks.
- **Group Housing** In group housing, people live in the same building. They share meals and living space. They have their own rooms for privacy.
- **Living with Family** Older parents may move in with an adult child's family. The parent has to adapt to being dependent on the adult child. The adult child must adapt to being responsible for the parent. The adult child is considered part of the sandwich generation. This is a group of people who care for their aging parents while supporting their own children. All concerned lose some degree of freedom. They may gain stronger family ties.
- **Retirement Communities** These are housing units designed to meet the needs of older adults. Units are often arranged around a communal building. Residents can meet there for meals and social events. Many retirement communities provide maintenance services and transportation. Some offer several levels of care, including nursing care.

Caregivers

A **caregiver** is a person who provides direct care, usually for a child, older adult, or someone who is ill. Caring for an older adult can be stressful. Adjustments must be made. Some families sacrifice and make difficult decisions to care for older members. It is important for a family to know and use their resources during this time.

Some older adults need full-time care. Some families choose to have a family caregiver on call 24 hours a day. During this time, families may need to use stress management to handle the strains. Caregivers are often very busy. They should take good care of themselves. They need to stay healthy with good eating, sleep, and exercise habits. Caregivers often suffer from depression and chronic illnesses. They may try to do everything themselves. They need to remember to ask for help.

Many community groups offer respite care. **Respite care** is temporary care so that the main caregiver can have a break. Some groups offer home visits by respite care workers. Others provide care in a group setting.

Leisure Living
Most older adults have a variety of living options from which to choose. *What are some advantages and disadvantages to living in a retirement community?*

Selecting a nursing home for an older relative can be a challenge for many families. If your family ever has to face this duty, you can:

- Discuss possible choices with the older adult's physician.
- Ask people who have relatives in a certain home for their opinion.
- Choose a home that is near enough to visit.
- Meet with the staff to find out about costs and services.
- Inspect the rooms to see if they are clean and odor-free.
- Eat a meal at the home to determine if it is appealing and nutritious.

- Notice whether the residents appear clean, well cared for, and generally satisfied with the home.
- Observe if staff members are kind, capable, and respectful to the residents.
- View the home's recreational facilities and observe some activities.

Problem-Solving Geraldo's grandfather can no longer stay in his home alone, but his family has heard that the only nursing home close by is not good. What should the family do?

Nursing Homes

A nursing home may be the only option for a **frail**, or physically weak, person who needs skilled care. The older adult's family may not be able to provide the assistance required. The older adult may also require full-time care that the family may not be able to provide.

The percentage of older people living in nursing homes is small but rising. This increase is a result of several factors. One is the longer life span. Another is the number of older adults who have no one to care for them. Third is an increase in the number of older people who have chronic illnesses. A **chronic disease** is an illness or condition that occurs repeatedly or never goes away.

Nursing homes vary greatly. In some, residents may share a small room and bathroom. Eating and entertainment take place in common rooms. Others consist of small cottages or apartments. Some are for people needing a great deal of care. Others are for those who are more self-reliant. The cost of a nursing home varies depending on the location and the options included. Usually however, nursing homes can be expensive.

The decision to place a family member in a nursing home is not an easy one for most families. Older adults may not want to go. Adult children may feel guilty that they cannot care for the older adult at home. It is a decision that everyone in the family should discuss.

Safety

Older adults are often very concerned with personal safety. They may feel vulnerable to crime and violence. Some refuse to leave their homes. Others move to a different neighborhood where they feel more secure.

Crime

Loss due to crime may affect older adults more sharply than others. The theft of $100 may be much more serious to a person on a fixed income than to a working person. Physical injuries received during a crime can be life threatening. An older body does not usually heal quickly.

Elder Abuse and Neglect

A growing concern in society today is **elder abuse**. This is physical abuse of aging people. Often, the abuse is by adult children or caregivers. It has also occurred in some nursing homes. Sometimes caregivers just neglect the older adult. They may not feed or bathe them.

In some people, the stress of caring for an older adult is the trigger for violence. Those who take care of older relatives need a support system. All family members should share in the care, if possible. Community groups that work with older adults are another resource. Anyone who observes abuse or neglect must take action to end it.

✓ **Reading Check** **Identify** Why is a fixed income a concern for older adults?

Images of Aging

In some societies, people look forward to old age. It is seen as a time for reflection. In these societies, younger generations show their respect for older adults. In other societies, old age is feared and ignored. For example, look at the advertisements that sell certain items. What is the age of people who appear in these ads? Notice the products in stores that promise to hide the gray, reduce wrinkles, and cover age spots. Youth is seen as desirable. Aging often is not.

◀) *Mutual Benefits*
Teens can be a great help to older adults. *In what ways can you befriend an older person?*

Progress is being made against this attitude. Some people, however, are still biased against older adults. They feel that older people are not as alert, intelligent, and capable as younger people. This belief is called **ageism** ('ā-(,)ji-zəm). Like any prejudice, ageism unfairly views all people as alike. It does not see older adults as distinct people. It can prevent older adults from living their lives to the fullest. It also denies others the chance to benefit from the talents and wisdom of older adults.

Move Beyond Stereotypes

Understanding the aging process can help you see the concerns of older adults. You learn the facts that disprove the stereotypes. You see that older adults are not all alike, any more than teens are.

Spend Time with Older Adults

Spending time with older people also gives a truer picture than stereotypes. Teens have many chances to get involved in the lives of older adults. Perhaps you have older family members living with you or near you. Your local Agency on Aging can tell you what needs exist in your area. You can also ask about helping at a nursing home or hospital.

Resolve the Issues

As the older population increases, it is making its voice heard. Lawmakers and social agencies are working to resolve the concerns of older adults. The issues are complex, however.

As with any social situation, not all solutions lie in government. People need to care for each other. You can improve the situation of the older people around you. Perhaps someday someone will do the same for you.

Section 15.1   After You Read

Review Key Concepts

1. **Identify** two concerns older adults have with medical care.
2. **Describe** three ways you could get involved with older adults.

Practice Academic Skills

English Language Arts

3. Medication issues are becoming more important for older adults. Choose an issue, such as using too much medication or drug interactions. Research and write a report that explores the issue. What causes the problem? What could be done to solve it?

4. Research attitudes toward aging in another culture. Find out how older adults are treated in that culture. Write a report of your findings.

NCTE 7 Conduct research and gather, evaluate, and synthesize data to communicate discoveries.

NCTE 9 Develop an understanding of diversity in language use across cultures.

Check Your Answers Check your answers at this book's Online Learning Center through **glencoe.com**.

Section 15.2

The Aging Process

Reading Guide

Before You Read

Prepare with a Partner Read the titles of the heads in this section with a partner. Ask each other questions about the topics that will be discussed. As you read, answer the questions.

Read to Learn
Key Concepts
- **Identify** the stages of aging.
- **Determine** the kinds of changes that occur as people age.

Main Idea
People go through five stages as they age. The last third of life is sometimes called the third age. During the third age, older people go through many changes.

Content Vocabulary
◇ gerontology ◇ dementia
◇ disengagement ◇ Alzheimer's disease

Academic Vocabulary
You will find these words in your reading and on your tests. Use the glossary to look up their definitions if necessary.
■ reminisce
■ vibrant

Graphic Organizer
As you read, describe the physical, mental, emotional, and social changes that occur with aging. Use a concept web like the one shown to help organize your information.

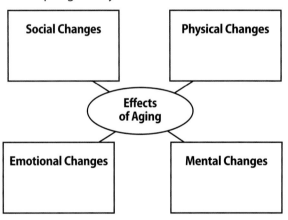

Graphic Organizer Go to this book's Online Learning Center at **glencoe.com** to print out this graphic organizer.

Academic Standards • • • • • • • •

English Language Arts
NCTE 7 Conduct research and gather, evaluate, and synthesize data to communicate discoveries.

NCTE 12 Use language to accomplish individual purposes.

NCTE *National Council of Teachers of English*
NCTM *National Council of Teachers of Mathematics*
NSES *National Science Education Standards*
NCSS *National Council of the Social Studies*

▶▶ Life Stories Older adults like to look back and assess their lives. *What are some activities older adults might pursue as they enter this stage?*

◀◇ Vocabulary
You can find definitions in the glossary at the back of this book.

As You Read
Connect How does breaking down aging into stages help those who study older adults?

The Stages of Aging

Aging is a natural life process. The study of the aging process is called **gerontology** (ˌjer-ən-ˈtä-lə-jē). It has helped people understand the rewards and problems of growing older. Social scientists have identified five general stages of life for older adults. These are:

- **The Honeymoon Stage** This stage starts when people retire. For a while, they may enjoy sleeping in, playing, and relaxing.

- **The Active Stage** At some point, older adults say, "What am I going to do with the rest of my life?" Some focus on their hobbies. They may turn a hobby into a business. Others may decide to do volunteer work. Whatever the choice, the person pursues new and old dreams.

- **The Slowing-Down Stage** Sooner or later, older adults slow down. They pause and reflect on life. They find new ways to enjoy old activities. Instead of driving across country, they may join bus tours. They may give up activities and find new ones they enjoy.

- **The Reminiscing Stage** In this stage, people **reminisce**, or look back, and assess their lives. They may enjoy visiting where they grew up. They think about old memories or write their life stories. They observe more and do less. Comfort and ease become important.

- **The Sunset Stage** People come to this stage ready to put things in order. They tie up loose ends. They may patch up poor relationships. This may be the stage where older adults enter a care facility.

As people move through these stages, activities change. Relationships also change. In the early stages, people are active. They stay involved. Gradually, there is some disengagement. **Disengagement** is withdrawal from others and from activity. Studies show that disengaged people are less happy. They are also less healthy and less satisfied in almost every area of life than those who remain involved.

✓ **Reading Check** **Define** What is gerontology?

The Third Age

One way of looking at life is to see it as three long stages. The first stage of life is spent developing as a person. The second stage is given to career and family concerns. The final years, or the third age, can be a time of creative learning and personal exploration. It is a time of life when people are free to do what they want. Work and family no longer define daily life. Men and women have the freedom to find new activities that they find meaningful, as shown in **Figure 15.1**.

Because the third age can last so long, no description fits everyone in the stage. People in their sixties and seventies are far from elderly. Some eighty-year-olds are more **vibrant**, or active and full of life, than those much younger. People handle aging differently. Many people in the third age do not show the effects of aging for a long time.

Physical Changes

The physical effects of aging are often the most visible changes. The body begins to change slowly. It seems to shrink as the tissues connecting the bones flatten and compress. Reactions and reflexes slow because the body replaces old cells with new ones slower than before. Many internal organs and systems work at a lower level.

Muscles may become weaker. Bones break more easily. The senses do not respond as they do in younger people. Some loss of hearing and vision is common. Sexual activity also slows down.

INDEPENDENT Living

HOW TO Reminisce with Older Adults

Reminiscing is more than recalling the good old days. Listening to stories lets you hear first-person accounts of history. Reflecting on the past also helps older adults see meaning in their lives. Follow these guidelines to initiate conversations with older adults:

1. **Ask about relationships.** Who was the adult's best friend and why?
2. **Ask about life choices.** What was the toughest decision the adult ever made? Did he or she make the right choice?
3. **Ask about the good times.** What was the happiest time of the adult's life and why?
4. **Ask about teen years.** What were their teen years like?
5. **Ask about the world.** What were some of the local, national, and world issues when the adult was young? How did they affect the adult's life?

Take Action Arrange to visit an older adult. Make a list of questions and topics to explore. Conduct the interview, allowing time for digression and storytelling. (You may get permission to record your interview so that you can preserve it.) Share your interview with the students in your class. Describe some of the facts and insights you have gained.

Some physical changes threaten good eating habits. A dulled sense of taste or smell can lead to less interest in food. Some people do not eat enough, and others may add flavor by using salt. This can lead to high blood pressure and heart disease. Tooth loss can interfere with eating enjoyment. Elderly people often have smaller amounts of saliva. This makes chewing and swallowing difficult. Physical problems may make shopping for and preparing healthy foods a challenge.

Dietary needs also change. Older people need to eat less food than before. They also, however, need greater amounts of some nutrients. For example, increasing calcium intake can help prevent broken bones.

Chronic diseases are a fact of life for many older adults. Examples include arthritis, high blood pressure, and heart conditions. These are more common as the body becomes less able to deal with the stresses of aging.

Maintain Physical Health

Some physical changes cannot be avoided. Older adults, however, can do a great deal to maintain their physical health. If properly done, exercise can be beneficial.

Good nutrition is also important. A poor diet can make many problems worse. Attitude, too, can have a major effect on physical ability. People need to know that aging is not a disease, and sickness is not a sure thing. Then they are more apt to work at keeping their health.

Figure 15.1   Improving with Age

The third age can be the best time in a person's life. *Why do you think older adults may think the third age is the best time in their lives?*

Continuing to Live Life People who are 65 years old can expect to live 18.4 more years.

Volunteering to Help Others About 60% of adults older than 55 volunteer in ways that help their families and communities.

Staying Connected Online More than 40% of adults age 66 or older use the Internet.

Mental Changes

Aging also affects thought processes. The mind often slows, just as the body does. Older adults sometimes have trouble with memory. Memory includes three functions:

- receiving data into the brain
- storing data in short-term memory
- storing data in long-term memory

To recall and use information requires all three functions. In younger people, this can be easy. In older adults, all three parts of memory still work, but data may not travel between them as well. This is why older adults may have trouble calling up information quickly.

Older adults may lack speed in their thought process, but their logic and understanding can often improve. Older adults who are students may work long and hard to learn new material. They are apt to learn it well.

Brain Disorders

Some mental changes involve brain disorders, such as dementia. **Dementia** (di-'men(t)-shə) is the progressive decline in cognitive function due to damage or disease in the brain. It can occur in any stage of adulthood, but is most common in elderly adults. It can affect a person's memory, attention, language, and problem solving. **Alzheimer's disease** ('älts-ˌhī-mərz) is one of the most common forms of dementia. It is a degenerative brain disease that causes memory loss, impaired thinking, and the inability to carry out daily activities.

Traveling to New Places Leisure travel is more common during the third age than in any other stage of life.

Contributing as Part of the Work Force About one quarter of older adults earn income from a job.

Owning a Home Eighty percent of families headed by an older adult own their homes.

Stay Mentally Healthy

The loss of mental abilities is not always an effect of aging. The greatest declines in thinking skills are often due to outside factors. These include depression, grief, poor health, poverty, and a lack of effort.

Older people need to use mental exercises to keep thinking skills sharp. Their activities should be active, not passive. They can learn new skills, join clubs, or become active in politics. Others may take part-time jobs, continue their education, or serve as volunteers.

Social Changes

Older adults may see differences in roles and relationships. As some roles become less important, new ones often develop. The greatest role change for older adults is the loss of the work role through retirement. This loss is most difficult for those whose sense of worth was tied to their careers.

Friendships often gain importance as people age. Older adults tend to have more friends than any other age group except teens and young adults. If grown children move away, friendships can become more needed and rewarding.

Older adults tend to keep the same types of social lives and interests as they did when they were younger. People who were less socially active continue in this pattern. For more outgoing older adults, community centers and clubs offer company.

Bridge Building

Building a bridge with older people can enrich your life. *How does becoming involved with older people benefit you?*

Grandparenting

One major role of many older adults is that of a grandparent. This role has become more important as people live longer. Grandparents can be involved in their family's lives for longer than they used to be. Involved grandparents can enrich a child's life. Older adults give children a sense of family roots. They can provide stability. This may be needed if divorce or other problems upset family life. Many grandparents find great pleasure in the grandparent role.

Emotional Changes

Some older people become depressed by thinking about the less-pleasant facts of aging. Some no longer see a purpose in their lives.

Others may feel that they are not needed. Unless older adults find new meaning in their lives, they risk falling into depression.

Preserve Emotional Health

Contacts with friends and family members are the best way to maintain emotional health. It can be helpful for younger people to talk to older adults. They can show respect for their wisdom and experience. Older people see that they still have something to offer. Older adults also need chances to talk about the past. Reminiscing helps them sort through their experiences and make sense of their lives. Older adults who adapt to new roles find satisfaction. This alone seems to slow down the aging process.

Older people can benefit from knowing you. Younger people can help older ones stay active, alert, and in touch with the community. Teens can provide practical services, such as running errands and mowing the lawn. Regular visits can also give older adults a sense of security. They know they can count on someone in case of illness or an accident.

Older people have much to offer. Years of experience give them a unique perspective on life. When older adults talk about the past, you can see how the world has changed and why. Listening to older adults recall challenges they have faced can provide insight into your life as well. It may give you new approaches to problems.

Section 15.2   After You Read

Review Key Concepts

1. **Explain** why the first stage of aging for retired adults is called the honeymoon stage.
2. **Describe** ways older adults can stay mentally healthy.

Practice Academic Skills

English Language Skills

3. Discuss with an older adult the five stages of aging. Before your discussion, write at least five questions to ask the older adult. Your questions should lead the adult to discuss his or her activities and feelings during each of the five stages.

> **NCTE 12** Use language to accomplish individual purposes.

4. Volunteering can help older adults stay mentally and physically active. Research the volunteer opportunities in your community. Create a brochure that includes the places people can volunteer and the contact information for these places. Ask permission to distribute the brochure at local senior centers.

> **NCTE 7** Conduct research and gather, evaluate, and synthesize data to communicate discoveries.

Check Your Answers Check your answers at this book's Online Learning Center through **glencoe.com**.

CAREER SPOTLIGHT

Activities Director

Derek Allen
Fern Creek, Kentucky

Families taking part in their community may not realize the level of planning and attention to detail that goes on behind the scenes. In most communities, several people work hard to make sure services, special events, and social activities are a fun experience for families.

Derek Allen coordinates events for sports teams and leagues, social gatherings, and dinners. Allen says he does not do it alone. Workers rely on members of the community to get the job done. He says he values honesty and integrity above all else.

"When I work with other people, I need them to be honest and to do their best, regardless of who may or may not be watching," he said. "Other people are crucial in the success of what I do. I must choose people to help who are dependable and trustworthy."

Allen believes that students should focus on working hard both in and out of the classroom. Everything students learn during their school years will benefit them in the "real world." He adds, "If you work hard and do your best at everything you are involved in, you will succeed."

CAREER FACTS

Education or Training A college degree in parks and recreation or leisure studies is usually required. A graduate degree or certification may be needed for some positions.

Nature of the Work Activities directors handle a wide variety of responsibilities. Many will plan, organize, and direct activities in local recreation areas, parks, community centers, religious organizations, and camps.

Aptitudes, Abilities, and Skills Strong interpersonal skills are important because most of the work in this career involves dealing with other people.

Academic Skills Required English Language Arts and Mathematics.

Student Organizations To prepare for this career, look for groups that work with people in the community, such as FCCLA.

Career Outlook Jobs as activities directors are expected to grow about as fast as the average over the next ten years.

Career Path Many activities directors work for local governments and personal care facilities. Activities directors may move into supervisory or administrative positions.

Critical Thinking

Improve Quality of Life Identify ways that older adults can benefit from planned activities.

 Research Careers For more information on this and other careers, visit the Occupational Outlook Handbook Web site through the link on this book's Online Learning Center at **glencoe.com**.

Section 15.1
Concerns of Older Adults

Older adults have a variety of concerns as they age. They may have financial and health concerns. They may also reach a point where they cannot live alone. They may share a house, live in a group home, move in with an adult child, or live in a retirement community. Nursing homes may be used for those who need skilled care. Older adults are concerned about safety from crime. Elder abuse and neglect can also be problems of aging. Older adults are individuals and should not be stereotyped. They are working to solve the problems they face.

Section 15.2
The Aging Process

Gerontology is the study of the aging process. There are five general stages of life for older adults. The final years of life are sometimes called the third age. During this time, people face many changes. Physical changes are the most obvious. These can be slowed by good health, nutrition, and exercise. There are also mental, social, and emotional changes. Older adults who stay involved can maintain their mental skills. The biggest social change is retirement. Many adults enjoy the role of grandparent. Preserving emotional health is vital for older adults.

Content and Academic Vocabulary Review

1. Use each of these content and academic vocabulary words in a sentence.

Content Vocabulary
◇ fixed income (p. 287)
◇ caregiver (p. 289)
◇ respite care (p. 289)
◇ chronic disease (p. 290)
◇ elder abuse (p. 291)
◇ ageism (p. 292)
◇ gerontology (p. 294)
◇ disengagement (p. 294)
◇ dementia (p. 297)
◇ Alzheimer's disease (p. 297)

Academic Vocabulary
■ frugal (p. 287)
■ frail (p. 290)
■ reminisce (p. 294)
■ vibrant (p. 295)

Review Key Concepts

2. Describe the types of concerns older adults have.
3. Explain the effect ageism has on the image and lives of older adults.
4. Identify the stages of aging.
5. Determine the kinds of changes that occur as people age.

Critical Thinking

6. Analyze Make a list of some of the stereotypes of older adults. What may have caused these stereotypes to be created?
7. Evaluate Society often has a negative view of aging. In what ways can this view affect older adults?
8. Explain If you owned a business, why would you want to hire an older adult?
9. Identify A family may have to make certain adjustments when a grandparent moves in with them. What are some of these adjustments?

Real-World Skills

Problem-Solving Skills

10. Identify the Problem Bailey is worried about her grandmother. The older woman stopped taking the newspaper and watching the news. She does not go out much any more. Write a paragraph about what Bailey should do.

Interpersonal Skills

11. Scams and Fraud Dishonest and fraudulent businesses often target older adults as their victims. Research at least one scam that has been used to steal from older adults. Make a list of suggestions to protect older adults from scams and fraud. Report your findings to the class.

Collaborative Skills

12. Group Project Follow your teacher's instructions to form into groups. Research the Social Security program. How is it funded? Will there be money to pay older adults when you retire? Present your findings to your class.

Management Skills

13. Evaluate Options Sheldon must find a nursing home for his father. One is close to his home. The cost is low, but it seems to lack enough staff. Sheldon likes another home, but it is farther away and more expensive. Explain in a short paper what Sheldon should do.

14. Nursing Home Tour Visit a nursing home. Use some of the actions from the Real Life feature on page 290 to evaluate the nursing home. Write a report of your conclusions. Was the home like you thought it would be? What stereotypes did you start with? Did your visit make you change your mind?

15. Analyze Advertising Identify a television program that appeals to your parent or guardian. Watch a program you enjoy and one your parent or guardian enjoys. List the ads during each program. Who is the target? How were the ads different? How were they similar? What conclusions can you draw?

16. Create a Flyer Find what programs and services are available to older adults in your community. Create a flyer that identifies the programs and the services. If possible, distribute your flyer at a senior center.

17. Research Careers Go to this book's Online Learning Center at **glencoe.com** to find **Web Links** for **Careers in Gerontology**. Select a career. What preparation is needed? What role does the career play in improving life for older adults?

Additional Activities For additional activities, go to this book's Online Learning Center through **glencoe.com**.

Academic Skills

 Mathematics

18. Graph Life Expectancy Insurance companies use life expectancy tables to determine insurance premiums. Use the following data to create a line graph. It should show life expectancy for males and females from age 65 to 85.

Life Expectancy		
Age	**Male**	**Female**
65	16.3	19.2
70	13.0	15.5
75	10.1	12.1
80	7.6	9.1
85	5.6	6.7

Math Concept **Line Graphs** A line graph shows how data changes over time. To create your line graph, put the ages along the *x*-axis. Put the life expectancy years on the *y*-axis, then plot the data.

Starting Hint: Since there will be two lines on the graph, use a blue line for male and a red line for female.

 For math help, go to the Math Appendix at the back of the book.

NCTM Data Analysis and Probability Formulate questions that can be addressed with data and collect, organize, and display relevant data to answer them.

 English Language Arts

19. Menu Planning Plan a day's menu for a senior citizens center. Choose foods that would be easy for an older adult to eat, are low in cost, are nutritious, and would be appealing. Take into account any special needs that the older adults may have in regards to food. Each morning, the center posts the following day's menus. Use a computer to design a one-page flyer. This flyer will be posted in the center. The flyer should include your menu and any information you think people should know about the food.

NCTE 12 Use language to accomplish individual purposes.

 Social Studies

20. Oral History Interview an older adult to create an oral history of the adult's life. Find out what inventions had the most impact on the person's life. What moments in history does the person remember most clearly? If possible, record your interview. Write your oral history, including the most important events your subject told you about.

NCSS IV.a Articulate personal connections to time, place, and social/cultural system.

STANDARDIZED TEST PRACTICE

OPEN-ENDED RESPONSE

21. Write one or two sentences to answer the following questions.

Test-Taking Tip Open-ended test questions are often looking for a specific response rather than an opinion. These may include definitions, comparisons, or examples.

a. Describe two ways the body changes as one ages.

b. What can an aging person do to help maintain his or her physical health?

c. Give two reasons why many people continue to work beyond retirement age.

CHAPTER 16

Coping with Crisis

● Section 16.1

Understand Crisis

● Section 16.2

The Crises People Face

▶▶ **Explore the Photo**

Resources for help are available when you are dealing with a crisis. *What resources can you use that would help you deal with a crisis?*

Chapter Objectives

After completing this chapter, you will be able to:

- **Determine** what makes a crisis different from an everyday problem.
- **Identify** resources that can be used to cope with a crisis.
- **Explain** the kinds of health issues that can lead to a crisis.
- **Summarize** the impact of harassment and abuse.
- **Describe** how people react to and adjust to death.
- **Suggest** ways that people can manage crises.

Writing Activity

Character Analysis

Courage When you have courage, you draw upon your mental and moral strengths to face danger, fear, or difficulty. Courage helps people get through their own crises in life. It also lets them step in when others need help. You can show courage when you:
- Develop your talents in spite of a disability.
- Cope with serious problems in constructive ways.
- Encourage a friend in a crisis to get help.
- Walk away from a situation where you feel peer pressure.

Analyze a person from a movie, book, or your personal life who has shown courage. Make sure to include details about the person.

Writing Tips To write a strong character analysis of a courageous person, follow these steps:
1. Describe his or her words and actions.
2. Analyze how his or her behavior shows courage.
3. Describe the reactions of others to the person.

Understand Crisis

Reading Guide

Before You Read

Preview A cause is an event or action that makes something happen. An effect is a result of a cause. To help yourself recognize cause-and-effect relationships in this section, ask, "Why does this happen?"

Read to Learn
Key Concepts
- **Determine** what makes a crisis different from an everyday problem.
- **Identify** resources that can be used to cope with a crisis.

Main Idea
A crisis is a situation so critical that it overwhelms usual coping methods. People react to crises in stages. There are a variety of resources that can be used to cope with crises.

Content Vocabulary
◇ crisis
◇ cope
◇ isolation
◇ adaptation

Academic Vocabulary
You will find these words in your reading and on your tests. Use the glossary to look up their definitions if necessary.
▪ overwhelm   ▪ ordeal

Graphic Organizer
As you read, find the three factors that determine if a problem is a crisis. Use a concept map like the one shown to help organize your information.

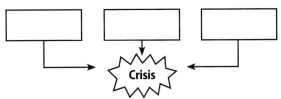

 Graphic Organizer Go to this book's Online Learning Center at **glencoe.com** to print out this graphic organizer.

Academic Standards · · · · · · · · · · · · · ·

 English Language Arts

NCTE 4 Use written language to communicate effectively.

NCTE 8 Use information resources to gather information and create and communicate knowledge.

Mathematics

NCTM Number and Operations Understand numbers, ways of representing numbers, relationships among numbers, and number systems.

NCTE *National Council of Teachers of English*
NCTM *National Council of Teachers of Mathematics*

NSES *National Science Education Standards*
NCSS *National Council of the Social Studies*

What Makes a Crisis?

A **crisis** ('krī-səs) is a situation that has reached a critical phase. People try to **cope** with the stress the crisis causes. This means they try to deal with and attempt to overcome problems and difficulties. The situation in a crisis is so critical that it can **overwhelm**, or overpower, usual coping methods and cause great emotional distress. For example, hostilities between two nations may grow into a military crisis. A major hurricane can create a crisis for victims and aid workers. Social problems, such as rising health care costs, may also cause crises. Some crises, such as a flood, hit quickly. Others, like the effects of alcoholism, build slowly.

Not every serious problem is a crisis. Crises stand out by their overwhelming nature. The things you do to cope well with other problems do not work in a crisis. A crisis is a threat to people. It can affect them physically, emotionally, and mentally.

There are three ways to measure if a problem is a crisis:

- **Hardship** Certain events can create hardship. The greater the hardship, the more apt it is to bring on a crisis. House fires, for example, cause loss of possessions and a place to live. Lives are disrupted in major ways.
- **Resources** Handling any problem well requires resources. If you do not have the needed resources, a problem may become a crisis.
- **Attitude** It is normal to be upset when trouble strikes. People do give in to feelings of shock and helplessness. This may mean a tough problem becomes unmanageable. If you can rebound and deal with the problem, it is less apt to overwhelm you.

Some people seem to have many crises in their lives. Crisis-prone families often do not have enough resources to solve their problems. A lack of self-confidence makes people anxious and fearful about life. They are more likely to define an event as a crisis.

▷ **Vocabulary**
You can find definitions in the glossary at the back of this book.

As You Read
Connect Why might the coping skills you use every day not work well in a crisis?

◀ *Facing a Crisis*
Crises take many forms. *What resources might be available to help deal with a natural disaster?*

Causes of Crises

What kinds of events are likely to cause a crisis? Outside events, such as an accident, job loss, or a natural disaster, can create one. Besides the hardship, the **ordeal**, or trial, can seem overwhelming because it is beyond your control.

Crises can also result from changes within the family. These can include the following:

- The loss of a family member through death or separation, such as by war or imprisonment.
- The unexpected addition of a family member. This can be adding aged grandparents or blended family members, such as in a remarriage. It also may include an unplanned pregnancy.
- The breakup of the family unit. This may be due to family members who are abusive or not supportive. It can also happen due to a divorce, health concerns, or legal problems.

Some crises result from a series of events. For example, imagine a family member needs to have emergency surgery. The family, however, lost its medical insurance due to a job loss. The strain of coping with both events is apt to cause a crisis for the family.

Families with members who have special needs are apt to be crisis prone. For example, a person may need around-the-clock care because of a disability. This often puts strain on the family's budget.

Figure 16.1   Where Can You Go for Help?

Every community has many resources to help during a crisis. These may include the phone book or community Web sites. *What resources are available in your community?*

Community Agencies Use a directory to locate agencies or groups that can help. Look for listings for the particular crisis you are facing.

Professional Help Call upon professiona for help. Most communities have clinics or health centers. These treat physical, menta and emotional conditions.

Support Groups Advice and support can be found in groups whose members have gone through similar crises.

It also affects them socially and emotionally. Any added problems may be enough to bring on a crisis. These families need a support system. The support system may include friends. Community human services resources, as shown in **Figure 16.1**, can also help the family.

Crises can strike in all stages of family development. There is no stage of family life that is immune to crises. Illnesses, accidents, and death can happen at any time. Changes in family membership can occur in several stages. Some events do tend to happen in specific stages. Children are apt to be added during the expanding years. The death of a spouse is most likely to occur during the retirement years.

Whatever your stage of life, it is wise to be prepared. You cannot ignore life's crises. They require action. By learning about crises that challenge people, you will be better able to respond when you need to.

Reacting to Crises

Typically people react to a crisis through a process of four stages. Time spent in each stage may vary, but the process is generally the same.

Stage 1: Impact

In this first stage, people experience shock and numbness. Whatever has happened hits them hard. Fear and helplessness are common emotions. The impact stage may last a few hours or several days. During it, a person may be too overwhelmed to even function. The first reaction a person normally has when diagnosed with a serious illness is an example of this stage.

Hotlines Hotlines are staffed by trained professionals or volunteers 24 hours a day. They can offer support and advice when needed.

Religious Organizations Most religious organizations are ready to help. They can provide spiritual support and guidance. In addition, they can offer practical help.

Shelters Many communities have shelters where victims of abuse can stay and be safe. A shelter can be located by calling a hospital emergency room, the police station, or a local abuse hotline.

Financial Literacy

Making Donations

Hector donates to a number of medical research charities. He does this because some of his friends and family members have had these diseases. He would like to give 25 percent more this year than he did last year. Last year he gave $100 for cancer research, $100 for HIV research, $75 for heart disease research, and $75 for muscular dystrophy research. How much will he donate in total this year?

Math Concept **Solving Problems Efficiently** There is usually more than one way to solve a problem. Often one way is quicker than another. It may save you time and involve fewer calculations and fewer chances to make a mistake.

Starting Hint: You can multiply each value donated by 125% (100% from last year + 25% more for this year) and add the four numbers together. This involves five separate calculations. On the other hand, you can add up the four values and then multiply the total by 125%. This makes only two calculations.

 For math help, go to the Math Appendix at the back of the book.

NCTM Number and Operations Understand numbers, ways of representing numbers, relationships among numbers, and number systems.

Stage 2: Withdrawal and Confusion

In this stage, people pull back from the crisis situation. Some people act emotionally cold and withdrawn. It looks as if they do not care about the things around them. They are in mental **isolation** (ī-sə-'lā-shən). This means they feel set apart from others and completely alone. Others maintain that no crisis exists. They busy themselves but do little. They get confused and have trouble focusing on what they are doing.

People sometimes use what are called defense mechanisms in this stage. These are emotions and thoughts that weaken the impact of the crisis. They may deny or hide what has happened. They may act childlike or claim there has been a mistake. They protect themselves until they can face what has happened.

Stage 3: Focus

People in this stage are ready to focus on reality. They admit that a crisis has occurred. They ask what action they must take to deal with it. Regaining some sense of control over their emotions lets them see the problems more clearly. They can begin to look at options and make plans to manage the crisis.

For example, Mrs. Dubin made a plan when she realized her son was an alcoholic. She compared treatment programs and costs. She contacted her insurance agent to see if any of the costs would be covered. She also found a support group through her religious leader to help her cope with what was ahead. This allowed her to feel as though she had control over the situation.

▶▶ **Focus on Reality**
Regaining a sense of reality helps people cope with a crisis. *Why do you think it is important to regain a sense of reality in a crisis?*

Stage 4: Adaptation

The final stage in responding to a crisis is dealing with it. The plans made in stage three are put into action. Through **adaptation** (ˌa-ˌdap-ˈtā-shən), people make changes. These should be practical and appropriate. After managing the crisis, life goes on, even though it may be different.

For instance, Seth's family adapted after a diving accident left him paralyzed. A ramp into the house was built for his wheelchair. The downstairs family room was turned into a bedroom so he could get to it with the wheelchair. Seth made arrangements to get to and from school. Adapting let Seth and his family move on with their lives.

✓ **Reading Check** **Define** What is a crisis?

Resources for a Crisis

During a crisis, people need the help of others. Recognizing that support is needed, and finding it, gives a sense of control. People should never be afraid to admit that they need help. Everyone needs help when a crisis occurs.

The family is the first source of help for most people. Friends are another option. When crisis strikes, most people are willing to help. Beyond family and friends, there are many other resources in local and national communities.

In your school, you can call upon teachers or counselors. They will provide support and help you decide what other kinds of resources are needed. The counseling office can help you locate these resources. Take advantage of all your resources when you must cope with a crisis.

Section 16.1 After You Read

Review Key Concepts

1. **Describe** at least six common causes of crises.
2. **Identify** the first source of help for most people when a crisis hits.

Practice Academic Skills
English Language Arts

3. A marriage, birth, or adoption is usually a happy event. Why might the addition of a family member cause a crisis? Write a paragraph to explain your answer.

4. Everyone has to learn to adapt as things change throughout life. But not everyone has to learn to adapt after a crisis. Research to learn about a person who had to adapt his or her lifestyle because of a crisis. The crisis might be a natural disaster, an injury, or a change in family. Write a report on your findings.

NCTE 4 Use written language to communicate effectively.

NCTE 8 Use information resources to gather information and create and communicate knowledge.

🖝 **Check Your Answers** Check your answers at this book's Online Learning Center through **glencoe.com**.

The Crises People Face

Reading Guide

Before You Read

Check for Understanding Ask questions as you are reading. This helps you check your understanding of the material. Try to answer those questions.

Read to Learn

Key Concepts

- **Explain** the kinds of health issues that can lead to a crisis.
- **Summarize** the impact of harassment and abuse.
- **Describe** how people react to and adjust to death.
- **Suggest** ways that people can manage crises.

Main Idea

People face a variety of crises. People can use management skills to get through crises.

Academic Vocabulary

You will find these words in your reading and on your tests. Use the glossary to look up their definitions if necessary.

- ■ degrade
- ■ belittle

Content Vocabulary

- ◇ addiction
- ◇ compulsion
- ◇ alcoholism
- ◇ harassment
- ◇ emotional abuse
- ◇ violence
- ◇ bereaved
- ◇ grief
- ◇ denial
- ◇ intervention

Graphic Organizer

As you read, list and summarize the types of emotional abuse. Use a chart like the one shown to help organize your information.

Types of Emotional Abuse	Summary
1.	
2.	

 Graphic Organizer Go to this book's Online Learning Center at **glencoe.com** to print out this graphic organizer.

Academic Standards • • • • • • • • • • • • • • • •

 English Language Arts

NCTE 2 Read literature to build an understanding of the human experience.

NCTE 12 Use language to accomplish individual purposes.

 Mathematics

NCTM Number and Operations Understand numbers and ways of representing numbers.

 Science

NSES Content Standard A Develop abilities necessary to do scientific inquiry.

NCTE *National Council of Teachers of English*
NCTM *National Council of Teachers of Mathematics*

NSES *National Science Education Standards*
NCSS *National Council of the Social Studies*

Health Issues

Health problems are an ongoing issue in life. Some cause minor problems. Sometimes illnesses, injuries, and disabilities, however, are more serious. When this is the case, the impact on families is much greater. The family will need to learn to cope with the resulting crisis.

When a family member encounters a major health problem, it can lead to many changes in the family's routines and schedules. People may feel tense and unsettled. The family will need to make adjustments. These differ in each setting. Communication and cooperation can help families deal with these problems.

Health Crises

Health crises can be major illnesses, such as cancer. Families can face a crisis when a baby is born too early or has a birth defect. Injuries, such as those from car accidents, may also cause crises.

Some families face a crisis because of mental illnesses, such as depression. This is often harder to assess than a physical disease or broken bones. Its effect can be just as harmful to the family. People who are mentally ill have trouble functioning on a daily basis. Their actions may often hurt or trouble others.

Many people think that while physical illness is not controllable, mental illness is. This is not so. Mental illness is just that—an illness. An ill person cannot snap out of it. A mental disorder can be a crisis for family and friends.

As You Read

Connect What kinds of health problems have impacted your family?

Helping the Family A doctor may need to explain an illness to a young child to lessen worry. *How can an older teen help during a family member's illness?*

Math in Action

Crime Data

Some families have their lives disrupted by crimes committed against them. Drugs or alcohol may play a part in these crimes.

1. Research some crimes, such as robbery, committed over the last year. List the number of crimes for each category.

2. Find out how many of the crimes were committed by people under the influence of drugs or alcohol.

3. Then find the percentages of the data found in step 2.

4. Present your data in a table.

Math Concept **Find Percents** Divide, and then move the decimal point two places to the right to find the percent.

Starting Hint: To find the percent, divide the number of people under the influence by the total number of crimes. For example, say there were 135 robberies and 40 of those were committed by people under the influence. Divide 40 by 135 to find the percent (40 ÷ 135 = 0.296 = 29.6%).

Building Academic Skills
Go to this book's Online Learning Center through **glencoe.com** to complete a worksheet for this activity.

NCTM Number and Operations Understand numbers, ways of representing numbers, relationships among numbers, and number systems.

 For math help, go to the Math Appendix at the back of the book.

Vocabulary

You can find definitions in the glossary at the back of this book.

Effects on the Family

Serious illness or disability may cause financial problems for the family. Income may be lost. Medical bills can add up. If a family has no medical insurance, they may not be able to pay the bills. Hospitals have staffs who offer advice about such problems. Some social service agencies and religious groups also provide counseling or help.

Medical Coverage Due to these situations, it is vital to think ahead. Every family needs medical insurance. Even when health is good, a person never knows what is in the future. Medical coverage should be purchased if it is not offered by an employer.

Emotional Effects Financial effects of a crisis are felt over time. The emotional impact of a family member's illness or disability, however, happens fast. Those who must take on added duties may feel the strain. Feelings of anger and resentment can surface. Young family members may not understand what is going on. All have worries about what will happen to them and their loved one.

Addictions

Another kind of health issue that can cause a crisis is addiction. You may joke while eating your favorite snack, "I am addicted to this." True addictions, of course, are more serious. An **addiction** (ə-'dik-shən) is a dependence on a particular substance or action. It is a mental or physical need to have a substance. It may also be a need to repeat a behavior in order to function.

A behavior addiction is called a **compulsion**. This can cause problems in families. Addictions to drugs, however, cause crises more often. Drugs are chemical substances, other than food, that change the way the body or mind functions. Alcohol and nicotine are examples of legal drugs that can be addicting. Few forces are as destructive to individuals and families as drugs.

Alcoholism

Alcohol takes control of people slowly. **Alcoholism** is an addiction to alcohol. Many people who drink a great deal do not believe they are alcoholics. They may deny their dependence on the substance and say they only use it casually. The people around them, however, most likely know the truth. These people may have witnessed the gradual change in behavior and personality of the alcoholic.

Sometimes there are no obvious differences between a user and an abuser. An alcoholic may not show signs of being addicted. However, alcohol abusers usually exhibit definite behaviors. They drink often, sometimes alone. They may drink in the morning or to face certain situations.

They may miss commitments, such as work or family outings. In its more serious stages, alcoholism leads to blackouts. These are periods when the person seems to be acting normally. Later, he or she has no memory of events. Some alcoholics display only some of these traits. It depends what stage of the disease they are in.

Families know when alcohol is a problem. For example, they may be embarrassed by the alcoholic's behavior. They worry at the damage done to the person's health. They can have feelings of blame and resentment. Some families may fear being hurt by the alcoholic's violence. Children can feel abandoned. Alcoholism is often a cause for family breakup and divorce.

Other Drugs

Many drugs cause serious problems. Both medicinal drugs and illegal drugs can be addictive. A person who abuses drugs may show several common signs of the addiction. He or she may miss school or work often and perform poorly when present. The person's behavior may not seem normal. It may be marked by mood swings. Aggression, attention seeking, and a poor focus are other signs. Physical symptoms may be seen. These can include an unhealthy look, slurred speech, and poor coordination.

People with drug addictions may neglect their duties. Employers and families can suffer. They may develop behavior problems. These will strain all their relationships. Violent behavior is often linked to drugs. Illegal drug use may result in criminal prosecution. The cost of drug or treatment programs can be expensive. The effects of drugs cause heavy burdens on a family.

✓ **Reading Check** **Identify** What is an addiction?

◀) *Harmless Fun*
Teens can have fun without harming themselves or others. *How do alcohol and drugs cause enjoyable occasions to become unpleasant or dangerous?*

In families where someone has an addiction, other family members can develop codependency. This means the person without the addiction becomes wrapped up in the addict's problems. He or she takes on the other person's responsibilities. This may help the addicted person hide the problem.

People who are codependent try hard to please others. They seek love and approval. An addicted person is usually not able to give what the codependent needs. Giving and receiving are out of balance in the relationship. Often, a codependent gets caught up in helping the addict. He or she may ignore what they need from the relationship.

Problem-Solving Sixteen-year-old Evan often comes home after school and finds his uncle sleeping. He hides any empty liquor bottles in the trash. He straightens up so that his parents will not come home to a mess. When his grandmother calls, he says that his uncle is not feeling well. What do you think is happening in this family?

Harassment and Abuse

There are many kinds of offensive behaviors. These can vary from annoying to life threatening. No matter what the poor behavior is, it damages people and relationships. At its worst, it brings on personal crises for the victim.

Harassment

Harassment refers to behaviors that are threatening or disturbing. They are actions that are not approved by society. The person doing the harassment wants power or control over the other person. There are several kinds of harassment:

- **Bullying** This is humiliating or abusive behavior by one person against another. It can include verbal comments, actions, or gestures. It can occur anywhere in any age group.
- **Racial Harassment** This abuse targets a person because of their race or ethnic group. The words or actions are designed to degrade the person, or lower his or her dignity.
- **Religious Harassment** This is verbal, mental, or physical abuse against a person because of his or her religious beliefs.
- **Sexual Harassment** This is unwanted words, gestures, or actions of a sexual nature. They make the victim feel uneasy.
- **Stalking** This is following someone so that a person's privacy is invaded. People who are being stalked often fear for their safety.

All types of harassment have negative outcomes. Some of the damage is mental. Some is emotional. They can occur at home, school, work, or in the community. Those doing it may think of harassment as fun. However, it is not fun for the victim and is never right.

Some harassment can be stopped by assertiveness. The other person may not realize that what is being said or done is offensive to you. A simple statement of your position may stop the behavior. In most cases, though, help is needed to stop harassment. Identifying a resource that can help is the place to start.

Emotional Abuse

Emotional abuse is the wrong or harmful treatment of someone's emotional health. It affects a person's sense of self-worth. Some types of this abuse are verbal attacks and withholding love. It causes invisible scars. They can last a lifetime.

There are five general types of emotional abuse. An abuser may:

- **Reject** Verbal comments **belittle**, or put down, the victim. The abuser pushes the victim away.
- **Terrorize** Threats of extreme or horrible punishments are made. The victim may be punished severely.
- **Ignore** The abuser is mentally unavailable to the victim.
- **Isolate** Normal contact with others is not allowed. A child may be kept at home. A spouse could be prevented from seeing family or friends.
- **Corrupt** The victim is taught to be antisocial or defiant. This may be in the areas of aggression or drug abuse.

Emotional abuse is extremely harmful when directed at a child. A child needs a loving relationship in order to develop normally. Abuse does not allow this to occur.

Physical Abuse

Some physical abuse takes the form of neglect. People neglect children when they fail to provide them with what they need. This can be adequate food, clothing, shelter, supervision, or medical care. Young children cannot be left to care for themselves under any circumstances. Older adults can be neglected in the same ways.

Violence occurs when physical force is used to harm someone or something. When this happens in the family, it is called domestic violence. Violent action can damage property. It can injure people. It can even kill. Reasons that people act violently are complex and often unclear.

Violent behavior is often learned. Those who grow up with it may see it as normal. They need to learn new ways to cope with stress and negative emotions. If they do not, violence may be passed to another generation.

Violence is a part of our culture. It can be found at home, school, work, and in the community. The media uses violence to entertain in movies and television shows. Some gangs create a culture of violence. No matter where it is found, violence damages people and relationships.

Keeping Others Safe No one ever deserves to be abused. *What actions can you take if you observe abusive treatment toward another person?*

Partner Abuse

Abuse between marriage partners occurs in some families. It may also happen in dating couples. Some abuse is emotional. Sometimes violence occurs. Abuse can break up a relationship. For some people, it becomes a way of life.

Some women are physically abusive toward men. Violence by men against women is more common. Men who batter women often hold rigid views of men's and women's roles. They believe this is how men always act. They tend to hold in their problems. Sooner or later, their rage explodes. Excessive drinking can add to partner abuse.

Abuse often occurs in cycles. First, the tension builds between partners. Then something triggers the abuse. Following the abuse, there is often a honeymoon stage. The abuser is sorry and apologizes. He or she may promise never to do it again. The partners enjoy a time of peace. Then, the tension starts again and the cycle repeats.

Why would a woman stay in an abusive relationship? She may not want to admit that abuse occurs. If she does not value herself, she may feel she deserves the abuse. A woman who was abused as a child is more apt to accept abuse from a partner.

Women who stay in abusive relationships make a tragic mistake. These relationships often get worse. Children get hurt, too. Many communities have shelters for abused women and children. Trained counselors can help a woman choose her next steps.

✓ **Reading Check** **List** What are the five general types of emotional abuse?

INDEPENDENT Living

HOW TO   Access Family Support Services

If your family were going through a crisis, where could you turn for help in the community? There are many community resources that provide help for families. Here are a few places to find support:

1. **Al-Anon** Supports families of people addicted to alcohol or other drugs.
2. **Alateen** A support group for teens living with someone addicted to alcohol or other drugs.
3. **Conflict Resolution Center** Offers support and training to help resolve conflicts.
4. **Family Services** Provides help for individuals, couples, and families.
5. **Teens in Transition** Offers help for teens coping with difficult life problems, such as divorce or death.

Take Action Follow your teacher's instructions to form into groups. Research support services in your community. Create a Community Family Support Directory with your group. Include the services, hours, and locations of each agency. Target the directory toward teens. Use clip art to make it visually appealing.

Death

Death is as natural as birth. It is the far end of the process of life. The circumstances of death may differ greatly. When a person has lived a long life, death is the next natural step. When death happens this way, people have the chance to put their lives in order. They can make their wills and pass on special heirlooms to the people they want to have them. Some older adults arrange their own funerals. All of these actions help ease the burden on others. With all loose ends tied up, these people may feel at peace when death finally comes.

Not everyone knows this kind of death, of course. Some people lose their lives suddenly. Dying in this way leaves little or no time to think about death, let alone prepare for it. Sometimes death comes early, but announced. Serious illness may force a person to come to terms with death without living a long life.

Grief

People who suffer the loss of a loved one are called **bereaved**. Losing a special person to death brings emotions and physical feelings that can be very painful. These feelings are known as **grief**. Because grief is so distressing, some people try to avoid grieving. Wanting to be strong, they push the pain deep inside. They tell themselves they do not hurt.

Experiencing grief is painful but necessary. When you lose a loved one, your mind and spirit suffer a great loss. You can hide outward signs of grief. The pain continues, however. Unless the reason for the suffering is addressed, greater problems will erupt later on. Unresolved grief may be linked to drug addiction, illness, and even death.

Symptoms of Grief

Most people are not prepared for the severe physical and emotional reactions they feel in grief. Grief can affect any area of the body or mind. People may not be able to eat or sleep. They may feel numb all over. Grieving people often are ill after the death of a loved one.

Emotionally, grief can be exhausting. Sadness and loss are some of the primary feelings. Anger and fear are also common. If the dying process took place over a long period of time, some people feel relief when death comes. They may then feel guilt for their relief. Mixed emotions like these are normal. People should not think it is wrong to feel them.

Life and Death
Death is the natural ending to life. *Why might someone prepare for death?*

Dealing with Grief

Many people, such as Elisabeth Kubler-Ross, have studied how people deal with grief. Kubler-Ross developed the five stages of grief that she believes people go through after experiencing the loss of a loved one. The stages are:

1. Denial and Isolation
2. Anger
3. Bargaining
4. Depression
5. Acceptance

Talk to at least two people who have experienced a loss in the past. Inquire, or ask, if they can recall the stages of grief they went through. Write a paragraph about your findings. (Be sensitive to people's feelings. Some of them may still have strong emotions over their loss.)

 Building Academic Skills
Go to this book's Online Learning Center through **glencoe.com** to complete a worksheet for this activity.

NSES Content Standard A Develop abilities necessary to do scientific inquiry, understandings about scientific inquiry.

The Process of Grieving

Grief is usually thought of in terms of death. However, any kind of loss, including the loss of a job, can cause grief. The grief process, also called grief work or mourning, includes three stages.

Stage One The first stage of grieving is shock and numbness, often coupled with denial. **Denial** (di-'nī(-ə)l) is refusing to believe the facts. A person in denial thinks and acts as if those facts do not exist. The bereaved may busy themselves with a flurry of activity. This helps them block out the painful truth that death has happened. They may want to bargain in this stage. For example, if the loved one really were not dead, the survivor would lead a reformed life.

Stage Two The reality of the situation sinks in during stage two. People feel an almost unbearable sense of loss. Anger, depression, and anxiety are common in this phase.

Stage Three The final step in the grief process is recovery. In recovery, people face and accept the loss as final. The bereaved person makes the adjustments needed to go on with life.

The time for grieving varies, but it is often a lengthy process. The age of the person who died and the cause of death can affect the time needed. The closeness of the relationship to the person also makes a difference. Grieving may last up to two years after the death of a parent and from four to six years after the death of a spouse. A parent may grieve for eight to ten years after the death of a child.

Grieving cannot be rushed. By working with the process instead of against it, however, a person can begin recovery sooner rather than later. Working through grief can help people learn to accept the loss. They need to take time to heal. Eventually, the pain fades and the good memories live on. They should get whatever help they need to make it through.

Suicide

Suicide has been called a permanent solution to a temporary problem. Suicide is one of the most common causes of death among teens. A suicidal person may believe that a problem is overwhelming. They think that there is no hope for future happiness. However, many people believe every problem can be solved in some way.

A person thinking about suicide sends out distress signals. Take them seriously. You should act if you notice these signs:

- Discouraged remarks, such as, "No one understands" or "There is no hope."
- Avoidance of and withdrawal from people and activities.

- Substance abuse and school problems.
- Creating artwork, poetry, or essays with themes of death.
- Purchase of a weapon, object, or substance that could be used harmfully.
- Giving away special possessions.
- Increasing depression and saying good-byes.
- Extreme anger, sorrow, or despair.
- Sudden happiness, which often indicates that a decision has been reached.
- Threats and suicide attempts.

Suicide is the one truly preventable kind of death. If you have suicidal thoughts, get help immediately. If you know a person who shows these signs, find someone who can help.

✓ Reading Check **Explain** Why do some people go into denial and deny their grief?

Crisis Management

In this chapter, you have read about some of the events that cause crises in people's lives. If the crisis happens in your family, you will need to face and manage it. If it happens to someone else, you may need to decide how to help. Some people avoid those in crisis if they can. Others want to help but do not know what actions to take.

Decision-Making Skills

Crisis management involves identifying the crisis. Then a plan to respond needs to be made. Finally, the crisis must be faced and resolved. Decision making and problem solving are important in crisis management. There are choices to be made and problems to solve. Management skills will help you plan and work your way through the crisis.

Communication

You need to be able to communicate with others during these times. Talking about what you are feeling helps reduce the power of negative emotions. Negotiation is often an important skill in a crisis. When you are stressed, you may need to relax and regroup. Conflict is apt to occur during a crisis. If you can help resolve the conflict, your family can move forward to deal with the crisis itself.

▼ **Check the Options** This teen thinks over his choices as he faces a crisis. *What options are available for families facing crises?*

▶▶ *Family Intervention* Family can step in and help out another family member when he or she is in a crisis. *Why are family members more likely to intervene in a crisis?*

Intervention

Intervention means taking direct action to cause change when someone else is in a crisis. A crisis may be beyond the ability of a person to handle. The person may be unable to think clearly. He or she may not be aware that the crisis requires outside aid. If this happens, the caring action of another person can bring help.

Harassment and emotional abuse often require intervention. People who are harassed or abused may not feel able to take action. In a work setting, a boss or human resource officer can help. They have steps to follow when an incident occurs. In school, those in authority need to know what is going on. If children are being abused at home, the appropriate agency needs to know. Those who abuse and harass others need to learn constructive ways of relating to people. They must face the damage they have done with their actions.

If you suspect someone is suicidal, do not be afraid to intervene. Say directly, "Are you thinking about suicide?" Ask what is wrong and listen rather than acting shocked or giving empty reassurances. Suggest options, people, and places that can help. Stay with the person, remove anything harmful, and seek help.

Someone with a mental illness may need professional help. Counselors can assist a person in controlling a minor problem before it becomes serious. Their advice and medication can make a huge difference. Ideally, a mentally ill person would make the decision to seek help for themselves. In extreme cases, however, family and friends may intervene to help the person get treatment.

Intervention is critical in drug addiction. No addict will seek help or stop using drugs until he or she is ready. A caring approach works best. People who are close to someone with this problem must take action. That may mean talking to a doctor to cut off access to prescription drugs. If illegal drugs are used, the police must be notified.

Intervening for a loved one sometimes requires courage and resourcefulness. It takes the kind of person who cares enough to try.

You have to be bold enough to risk interfering when the need is great. Friends and family members can begin the intervention process. With help, people can face and cope with life's crises.

Provide Help

Not all crises require intervention. Some just need the help of a friend or family member. Empathy is a good trait to have when someone you know is going through a crisis. Understanding what another person may be feeling helps you respond more positively. Helpful responses may take the form of:

- **A Touch or Hug** Physical closeness is comforting to many people, sometimes more so than words.
- **An Offer to Help** Offers of specific help are most useful.
- **Explanations** Children need the reassurance of simple, honest, positive explanations.
- **Knowledge** Learning about the crisis can give a sense of control. Knowing what to expect can lessen fear. Talk to others who are experts or who have faced the same crisis. You can share what you have learned.
- **Openness** Sharing feelings is beneficial. Encourage others to talk about what is happening and how they are feeling.
- **Be Direct** Help others by acknowledging the problem.

Many families face tough situations every day. It is important to stay positive. They can believe that help is available and go after it with determination. When that happens, a better life is ahead.

Life Skills CHECKLIST

Management Skills

Crisis You use your management skills to get through a crisis when you:

- ✓ Identify your goal for getting through the crisis.
- ✓ List the human resources you can call on, such as family and friends.
- ✓ Figure out what material resources you have that can help you in this crisis.
- ✓ Research the community resources that are available to you.
- ✓ Think logically, critically, and creatively about what you could do.
- ✓ Make a plan that will use your resources to reach your goal.

Section 16.2 — After You Read

Review Key Concepts

1. **Explain** why mental illness may cause more problems for a family than physical illness.
2. **Identify** five kinds of harassment.
3. **Describe** the stages in the process of grieving.
4. **Define** intervention.

Practice Academic Skills

English Language Arts

5. Recall a book or story you have read about a person or family in crisis. Write a half-page report about the book or story. In your report, briefly describe the crisis. Discuss the actions and interventions that occurred and how successful they were in resolving the crisis.

6. Create a poster that illustrates the management skills listed in the Life Skills Checklist above. With your teacher's permission, post your finished product on the classroom wall or in another area of the school.

NCTE 2 Read literature to build an understanding of the human experience.

NCTE 12 Use language to accomplish individual purposes.

Check Your Answers Check your answers at this book's Online Learning Center through glencoe.com.

CAREER SPOTLIGHT

Home Health Care Worker

Emily Chrysler
Richmond, Virginia

Sometimes, people suffer from diseases and afflictions that are incurable. In these instances, the best thing a medical professional can do is improve the quality of life, reduce suffering, and allow the patient to make the most of the time they have left. This is often called palliative care, or sometimes simply hospice care.

Emily Chrysler works as a liaison between health care providers and the families of patients. She coordinates care for the individual, while answering any concerns the patient may have. Her degree in nursing helps her understand the medical side of things. Her other degree in social work helps her connect with the patient.

Chrysler explains this career is not for everyone. It can be emotionally draining and at times disturbing. Those who are right for the job, however, find that they are making a difference in the lives of people who need comfort and understanding more than they ever have.

"Making a journey that seemed so frightening somehow approachable to patients and families—that's what I like most about my work."

CAREER FACTS

Education or Training Many care facilities require a mandatory state-approved training program to be completed. Knowledge of social skills and psychology are also helpful.

Nature of the Work Home health aides work with elderly or disabled persons to provide medical care that is more extensive than what family members or friends can give.

Aptitudes, Abilities, and Skills Hospice care providers need to have strong personal skills, patience, empathy, and tolerance, as they provide comfort to patients that are in pain or are nearing the end of their lives.

Academic Skills Required English Language Arts will help with communication skills. Knowledge of science, human anatomy, and medical terminology is also required.

Student Organizations To prepare for this career, look for volunteer groups that allow you to help out in a nursing home.

Career Outlook Excellent job opportunities are expected for this occupation, given the growing elderly population in the United States.

Career Path May begin with homemaker duties. Additional training, education, and licensing may help accelerate advancement.

Critical Thinking

Staying Balanced How can hospice workers keep an emotional distance from patients to remain effective?

 Research Careers For more information on this and other careers, visit the Occupational Outlook Handbook Web site through the link on this book's Online Learning Center at **glencoe.com**.

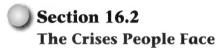

CHAPTER SUMMARY

Section 16.1
Understand Crisis

A crisis is a situation so critical that it overwhelms usual coping methods and causes great emotional distress. Three factors that can make a problem a crisis are hardship, resources, and attitude. People react to crises in a three-stage process. First they feel the impact of it. Then they withdraw and may act confused. Finally they are able to focus on the crisis. They adapt and resolve it. There are many resources available for those in crisis. People usually turn first to family and friends. School personnel and health care professionals can help. Community resources include hotlines, shelters, agencies, religious groups, and support groups.

Section 16.2
The Crises People Face

Some crises involve health issues. Disease, illness, and accidents have financial and emotional effects on families. Addictions are mental or physical needs to have a substance or to repeat a behavior in order to function. Harassment and abuse are behaviors that hurt others. Abuse can be emotional or physical. Death is another cause of crisis. People whose loved ones die may feel overwhelming grief. Suicide is a common cause of death for teens and can be prevented. Crisis management involves using skills to make decisions and solve problems. Interventions and helping others are ways to deal with crises.

Content and Academic Vocabulary Review

1. Use each of these content and academic vocabulary words in a sentence.

Content Vocabulary
- ◇ crisis (p. 307)
- ◇ cope (p. 307)
- ◇ isolation (p. 310)
- ◇ adaptation (p. 311)
- ◇ addiction (p. 314)
- ◇ compulsion (p. 314)
- ◇ alcoholism (p. 314)
- ◇ harassment (p. 316)
- ◇ emotional abuse (p. 317)
- ◇ violence (p. 317)
- ◇ bereaved (p. 319)
- ◇ grief (p. 319)
- ◇ denial (p. 320)
- ◇ intervention (p. 322)

Academic Vocabulary
- ■ overwhelm (p. 307)
- ■ ordeal (p. 308)
- ■ degrade (p. 316)
- ■ belittle (p. 317)

Review Key Concepts

2. Determine what makes a crisis different from an everyday problem.
3. Identify resources that can be used to cope with a crisis.
4. Explain the kinds of health issues that can lead to a crisis.
5. Summarize the impact of harassment and abuse.
6. Describe how people react to and adjust to death.
7. Suggest ways that people can manage crises.

Critical Thinking

8. Analyze Why do you think some people are reluctant to seek help in times of crisis?
9. Predict Why may intervention often be difficult to accomplish?

Real-World Skills

Problem-Solving Skills

10. Identifying Resources Bruce suffered an injury in a car crash. His doctors say he will need several months of intensive therapy to walk again. It could be up to a year before he recovers fully. Write a list of resources you would recommend to Bruce. How can these help?

Management Skills

11. Make a Plan Imagine that you have a friend who exhibits an addictive or destructive behavior. Make a plan to help your friend. Write out steps you could take to help your friend prevent the behavior in the future. What might be done to rehabilitate your friend?

Communication Skills

12. Music as Therapy Music can comfort a grieving person. Ask a religious leader or a funeral director about songs often used at services. Review the song lyrics. Create a play list of at least five songs you think would comfort someone who is grieving after the death of a loved one.

Interpersonal Skills

13. Make a Choice Colleen's cousin, Keith, has cancer. He read about a new treatment. His doctors warn that it is unproven. Keith is certain it will help. Colleen wants to support her cousin, but fears the doctors are right. Write a paragraph about what Colleen should do.

14. Brainstorm Follow your teacher's instructions to form into groups. Brainstorm to develop a list of strategies that can help prevent harassment and abuse. Discuss how the various ideas could be implemented.

15. Movie Review Recall a movie you have seen that portrays a crisis in a community. Write a review of the movie that describes the crisis. Evaluate how effectively the characters in the movie coped with the crisis.

16. Crisis Management Invite a school or community official to talk to your class about crisis management. What types of crises does their organization deal with? What is the plan for reacting to them? Who will carry out the plan in the event of a crisis? How much will it cost? Who will pay? Does the speaker think the plan will be effective? Why or why not?

17. Research Go to this book's Online Learning Center at **glencoe.com** to find **Web Links** for **Domestic Violence**. Choose a site to research domestic violence. How many cases of partner and child abuse are there? What types of abuse are reported? How do you know these statistics are valid? Write a report on your findings.

 Additional Activities For additional activities, go to this book's Online Learning Center through **glencoe.com**.

Academic Skills

 Mathematics

18. Calculate Medical Expenses Mr. and Mrs. Palos are calculating their family's yearly medical expenses. Their medical plan requires the Palos family to pay the first $200 in medical bills. This rule applies to each family member every year. This past year, Mrs. Palos' medical bills added up to $450. Mr. Palos had medical bills for $150. Their son had bills for $650. How much money did the Palos family have to pay in medical bills this past year?

Math Concept **Add Money** It helps to add money in a vertical column. When doing this, be sure to keep the decimal points in each dollar amount aligned.

Starting Hint: Remember that for any amount over $200, the Palos family only pays $200. For amounts under $200, the Palos must pay the entire cost.

 For math help, go to the Math Appendix at the back of the book.

> **NCTM Number and Operations** Understand numbers, ways of representing numbers, relationships among numbers, and number systems.

 English Language Arts

19. Crisis Guide Conduct research in your community to find out what resources are available to those who face crisis situations. Take notes of your findings. Follow your teacher's instructions to form into groups. Combine your findings with those of your group to create a community resource guide. The guide should tell citizens where they can go for help.

> **NCTE 7** Conduct research and gather, evaluate, and synthesize data to communicate discoveries.

 Social Studies

20. Research Conduct research to find funeral customs in another country or another culture. Choose one country or culture. Consider how the customs you researched differ from those you may practice. Are any customs similar? Describe the funeral customs and explain their purpose. Write your findings in a one-page report.

> **NCSS I.a** Analyze and explain the ways groups, societies, and cultures address human needs and concerns.

STANDARDIZED TEST PRACTICE

TRUE/FALSE
Read the following paragraph. Determine whether the paragraph is true or false.

Test-Taking Tip For true/false questions, look for clue words that usually make a statement false. Some of these words are always, all, only, none, and very. Words such as usually and generally are often used with true statements.

21. Experiencing grief at the death of a loved one is difficult, painful, and unnecessary. People tend to work through their grief in stages. These include shock, numbness, and denial. Then the reality sets in, and gives way to recovery.
a. True
b. False

Offer Helpful Advice

In this unit you have learned that change can be very challenging, even when it is good. You have also learned skills to handle changes, both large and small. In this project, you will discuss a problem with an adult who is trained to deal with crisis or change. You will use what you learn to create your own advice column.

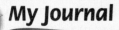

My Journal

If you completed the journal entry from page 244, refer to it to see if your thoughts have changed after reading the unit.

Project Assignment

- Choose a question about change or crisis that you feel is interesting or relates to your life.
- Research information to help answer the question, and list your resources.
- Identify and have a discussion with a professional in the community who is trained to deal with crisis or change.
- Use the information from your research to participate in the discussion. Take notes during the discussion. Type the notes.
- Use what you learned in the discussion and your research to create an advice column for the topic you chose.

Academic Skills You Will Use

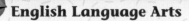

English Language Arts

NCTE 6 Apply knowledge of language structure and conventions to discuss texts.

NCTE 8 Use information resources to gather information and create and communicate knowledge.

STEP 1 **Choose a Question that Interests You**

Choose one of the questions below about a change or crisis people may face. You can also think of your own question to answer in your project.

- How can I reduce my stress level when I feel overwhelmed?
- How has or will my parents' divorce change my life?
- How can I help my grandmother who is in poor health feel more comfortable?
- What can I do to adjust after moving to a new location?

STEP 2 **Research the Situation**

Conduct research about the situation you chose in Step 1. Look for some of the effects of the change or situation. Then find healthy ways of coping with it. Take notes on your findings.

Research Skills

- Identify appropriate resources.
- Synthesize information.
- Organize your data.
- Take notes.

STEP 3 Connect to Your Community

Conduct a discussion with a member of the community who gives advice as part of his or her job, such as a spiritual leader or school counselor. Be prepared to participate in the conversation by using information you learned in your research.

Listening Skills

- Take notes during the discussion.
- Ask questions so there is a give and take of ideas and information.
- Listen attentively.
- Participate in the discussion.

STEP 4 Create and Present Your Advice Column

Use the Unit Thematic Project Checklist on the right to plan and create your advice column and make your presentation.

STEP 5 Evaluate Your Presentation

Your project will be evaluated based on:

- Depth and detail of discussion.
- Quality and composition of advice.
- Mechanics—format and neatness.

Evaluation Rubric Go to this book's Online Learning Center at **glencoe.com** for a rubric you can use to evaluate your final project.

Unit Thematic Project Checklist

Advice Column	✔ Create an advice column that answers a question and gives suggestions about how to solve a problem.
	✔ Format your advice column similar to advice columns you might see in a newspaper.
	✔ Write a clear, concise answer to the question that can be easily understood. You should offer concrete advice and different options for courses of action, when appropriate.
Presentation	✔ Make a presentation to your class to share your advice column and discuss what you learned.
	✔ Invite the students in your class to ask you any questions they may have. Answer three questions.
	✔ When students ask you questions, demonstrate in your answers that you respect their perspectives.
	✔ Turn in the notes from your research and discussion, and your advice column to your teacher.
Academic Skills	✔ Synthesize data from different resources into a concise document.
	✔ Be sensitive to the needs of different audiences.
	✔ Speak clearly and concisely.
	✔ Generate ideas and questions.
	✔ Communicate effectively.
	✔ Thoughtfully express your ideas.

Unit 5

Personal Development

Unit

Thematic Project Preview
Discover Citizenship

After completing this unit, you will learn that your behavior in the community reflects your personal development. In your unit thematic project, you can illustrate the way your citizenship skills help you understand yourself better.

My Journal

Help Your Community Write a journal entry about one of the topics below. This will help you prepare for the unit project at the end of the unit.

- Describe a type of volunteer work that appeals to you.
- Describe your ideal community.
- Explain why you think community leadership is important.
- Imagine you are in charge of a community fundraiser. Describe your first steps in planning it.

Explore the Photo
The values you have are often reflected in how others describe you. *What is the first thing you would like people to say when they describe you?*

A Closer Look at You

Section 17.1
Your Personality

Section 17.2
Develop a Positive Attitude

▶▶ Explore the Photo
Your personality develops as you learn and grow. *What traits do you have that help you keep a positive outlook?*

Chapter Objectives

After completing this chapter, you will be able to:

- **Describe** two factors that affect personality development.
- **Identify** the three main elements that make up personality.
- **Explain** how a positive attitude has a positive effect on a person's life.
- **Summarize** the relationship between self-esteem and attitude.
- **Determine** ways to build a positive attitude.

Writing Activity

How-To Paper

Generosity People show generosity by giving their time, talents, and other resources without expecting something back. You can show generosity by:
- Volunteering regularly at the local hospital.
- Donating wearable clothing to the homeless.
- Helping to register voters.
- Including an elderly neighbor on a trip to the grocery store.

Write a how-to paper explaining the resources a person needs in order to show generosity.

Writing Tips To write an effective how-to paper, follow these steps:
1. List all the materials and resources you will need.
2. List, in order, the steps you would take to show generosity.
3. Include an introduction and a conclusion.
4. Use transitional words and phrases.

Your Personality

Reading Guide

Before You Read

Adjust Reading Speed Improve your comprehension by adjusting your reading speed to match the difficulty of the text. Slow down and, if needed, reread each paragraph. This will help you understand and remember more.

Read to Learn
Key Concepts
- **Describe** two factors that affect personality development.
- **Identify** the three main elements that make up personality.

Main Idea
Personality develops from heredity and environment. There are three elements of personality. These are emotional traits, social traits, and intellectual traits.

Content Vocabulary
◇ introvert   ◇ extrovert

 Graphic Organizer Go to this book's Online Learning Center at **glencoe.com** to print out this graphic organizer.

Academic Vocabulary
You will find these words in your reading and on your tests. Use the glossary to look up their definitions if necessary.
- unique   - bias

Graphic Organizer
As you read, look for the three main elements that make up personality. Use a concept web like the one shown to help organize your information.

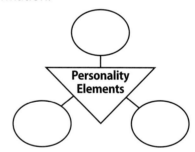

Personality Elements

Academic Standards •

 English Language Arts

NCTE 4 Use written language to communicate effectively.

NCTE 8 Use information resources to gather information and create and communicate knowledge.

 Mathematics

NCTM Geometry Analyze characteristics of two- and three-dimensional geometric shapes and develop mathematical arguments about geometric relationships.

NCTE *National Council of Teachers of English*
NCTM *National Council of Teachers of Mathematics*

NSES *National Science Education Standards*
NCSS *National Council of the Social Studies*

Personality Development

Have you ever thought about what makes all the people you know so different? For that matter, what makes you different from all the people you know? Personality is the answer. It is each individual's **unique**, or distinct, blend of qualities and behaviors.

Heredity and Environment

The process that creates personality is complex. It is shaped by both heredity and environment. No one can say for sure which contributes more. Instead, the two work hand in hand. Your environment molds the raw material you inherited. At the same time, your inherited traits have an impact on the environment around you.

Both heredity and environment affect personality. You cannot really blame either one for the problems you have. That is because people have the ability to make changes. It is much better to ask, "What can I do to change this?" than to say, "I was born this way."

Self-Improvement

How you deal with your personality affects where you go from here. It is possible to accept yourself and try to improve at the same time. Self-improvement keeps you learning and growing over the years. Take a closer look at your personality. This can help you understand how you got where you are. Then you can plan what you want for your future.

✓ **Reading Check** **Identify** What is personality?

Elements of Personality

Personality does not stay the same. It is always reacting to internal and external influences. There are many elements of each person's personality. Personality grows and changes as a person does. Be aware of this fact. You can work to shape the personality you want to have. Many different traits combine to make up your personality. Each trait falls into one of three categories. They are emotional, social, and intellectual.

▶ *Heredity* You may notice striking similarities at times when you are with your family. *What effect does heredity have on your personality?*

◆ **Vocabulary**
You can find definitions in the glossary at the back of this book.

📖 **As You Read**
Connect Do you believe your parents are responsible for your personality?

Emotional Traits

People experience eight basic emotions. These are fear, surprise, sadness, disgust, anger, anticipation, joy, and acceptance. How strongly you experience each one, and how often they occur, is part of your personality.

Emotions are elements of personality that are easily seen. Sometimes, however, they can be misinterpreted. Tyler, for example, was timid. He did not like meeting new people. His new classmates interpreted his actions as arrogant. After they got to know him better, they realized how wrong they were.

Control Your Emotions

You cannot control how you feel. What you can control is your response to your emotions. How you react is largely up to you. Emotions such as anger and frustration are often the hardest to control. These are negative emotions. Unfortunately, they can also do the most damage if you let them take over.

When emotional control is a challenge for you, taking the steps described in the Independent Living feature on this page can help. You gain more control over your personality. You can turn negative emotions into a chance to grow and improve. Sorrow for another person's loss may encourage you to give support.

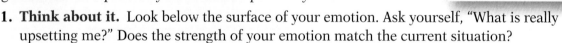

INDEPENDENT *Living*

HOW TO Control Your Emotions Positively

It is important to express emotions in healthy ways. Follow these guidelines to respond to your emotions positively:

1. **Think about it.** Look below the surface of your emotion. Ask yourself, "What is really upsetting me?" Does the strength of your emotion match the current situation?
2. **Consider the future.** Consider whether the situation you are in will matter tomorrow, next week, or next year.
3. **Wait to act.** Do not act on a strong feeling until you have considered the possible results of your actions.
4. **Take positive steps.** Relieve upsetting feelings by doing physical activities or by talking to a family member or trusted friend.
5. **Seek help.** If a negative feeling does not go away, seek help from a trusted adult or a health care professional.

Take Action Write down three situations that may cause negative emotions. (For instance, an argument with a friend, doing poorly on a test, and a relative who is ill.) For each situation, write down two or three ways you can respond positively to these emotions.

Not every negative emotional response can be overcome. Some things will always be sources of irritation or anxiety. For these, you can use the stress management skills you have learned.

Social Traits

Social traits affect how you relate to others. All people show certain social personality traits. For example, they may be polite or rude, accepting or judgmental. Most people behave somewhere between the extremes. It is natural to express different traits in different settings. For instance, you may judge people you do not know more harshly than you judge your friends.

Introverts and Extroverts

Everyone relates to other people in his or her own way. In most people, however, personality tends to lean toward two types. An **introvert** is a person focused inward, or on himself or herself. Introverts tend to prefer activities that let them focus on their own interests. Their opposites are extroverts. An **extrovert** is focused outward, or on others. Extroverts do not like being alone. They may enjoy playing team sports, performing, or taking part in discussions. They are open with their feelings and opinions. While they may also enjoy quieter activities, they choose first to be with others.

Most mental health experts agree that a balance of these two traits is best. Full social development means being able to enjoy time spent with others and time spent in quiet reflection.

Chapter 17 A Closer Look at You **337**

Math in Action

What Shape Fits You?

People have many different types of personalities. Follow these steps to complete this activity.

1. Choose a geometric shape (square, circle, triangle, and so on) that represents your personality.

2. Draw the shape on a piece of paper. Base the size of the figure on how you view your personality.

3. Write a paragraph that explains why you chose the shape and size you did.

Math Concept **Geometric Shapes** Geometric shapes can be circles or many-sided polygons. They can be two-dimensional triangles or squares, or three-dimensional pyramids or cubes.

Starting Hint: First, decide which shape you will use. Draw it to fit your personality. Then write your paragraph.

Building Academic Skills Go to this book's Online Learning Center through **glencoe.com** to complete a worksheet for this activity.

NCTM Geometry Analyze characteristics of two- and three-dimensional geometric shapes and develop mathematical arguments about geometric relationships.

Math For math help, go to the Math Appendix at the back of the book.

◄◄ *Your Inner Life*
Some people want time alone to pursue favorite interests. *In what ways do introverts achieve a balance in their lives?*

Personal qualities affect how relationships are built. People who are introverted may build relationships more slowly and carefully. Their ties to others may be strong and deep. The time spent alone may mean less time to relate to others. On the other hand, extroverted people often enjoy many relationships. They may not take time to develop strong or deep ties. They enjoy others without feeling the need to examine each relationship they form.

Intellectual Traits

Intellectual traits deal with the mind and mental abilities. These skills include logical processes, such as making conclusions and predicting outcomes. Critical thinking skills are also part of this trait. This includes evaluating arguments and seeing **bias**, or an attitude that favors one point of view.

The intellect is also the source of the imagination. This is expressed through the creative process. Writing a poem or finding a better way to finish a task are examples of creativity. Your intellectual traits are in continuous use. They come into play when you read a book, decide what to eat for lunch, or understand a friend's joke.

Any one of us can work at developing our mental abilities. School is a perfect opportunity. Read the everyday situations in the list below. In what way can these events lead to developing mental abilities?

- An older shopper in the checkout line comments to you on how prices have risen.
- Your car needs an oil change.
- You spot an unusual rock while walking to school.
- You see a painting that you admire in a friend's home.
- You hear a song by an unfamiliar band when riding the subway.

Section 17.1   After You Read

Review Key Concepts

1. **Describe** how personality is shown in daily life.
2. **Identify** the eight basic emotions people feel.

Practice Academic Skills

English Language Skills

3. The main part of the word personality is person. Research the origins of the term personality. Find the definition that reflects what you have read in this chapter. List five synonyms or related terms.

4. What environmental factors can be used to help an extreme introvert or extrovert come to a more balanced level between the two types of personalities? For example, what factors could help an extreme introvert feel more comfortable about giving a class presentation? Develop a strategy of using environmental factors to find a balance.

> **NCTE 8** Use information resources to gather information and create and communicate knowledge.

> **NCTE 4** Use written language to communicate effectively.

 Check Your Answers Check your answers at this book's Online Learning Center through **glencoe.com**.

Develop a Positive Attitude

Reading Guide

Before You Read

Helpful Memory Tools Successful readers use tricks to help them remember. Some students may try to create a song using the information. As you read, look for opportunities to make up memory aids.

Read to Learn
Key Concepts

- **Explain** how a positive attitude has a positive effect on a person's life.
- **Summarize** the relationship between self-esteem and attitude.
- **Determine** ways to build a positive attitude.

Main Idea

A positive attitude helps in many areas of life. It is important in self-esteem. There are ways to improve self-esteem and build a positive attitude.

Content Vocabulary

◇ attitude
◇ optimist
◇ pessimist
◇ serotonin
◇ self-esteem

Academic Vocabulary

You will find these words in your reading and on your tests. Use the glossary to look up their definitions if necessary.

■ recognize   ■ asset

Graphic Organizer

As you read, look for actions you can take to develop a positive attitude. Use a chart like the one shown to help organize your information.

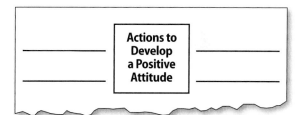

Actions to Develop a Positive Attitude

 Graphic Organizer Go to this book's Online Learning Center at **glencoe.com** to print out this graphic organizer.

Academic Standards . . . .

 English Language Arts

NCTE 3 Apply strategies to interpret texts.

NCTE 4 Use written language to communicate effectively.

 Mathematics

NCTM Number and Operations Understand the meanings of operations and how they relate to one another.

NCTE *National Council of Teachers of English*
NCTM *National Council of Teachers of Mathematics*

NSES *National Science Education Standards*
NCSS *National Council of the Social Studies*

What Is Attitude?

◆ **Vocabulary**

You can find definitions in the glossary at the back of this book.

Attitude is a person's state of mind or feeling. It is a basic outlook on life. Attitude is linked to heredity. An attitude can be described as positive or negative. The automatic response you have to most situations and people tells you whether you have a positive or negative attitude overall. A positive view puts the focus on strengths and what can be done. An **optimist** is someone with a positive point of view. A **pessimist** is someone with a negative point of view.

Serotonin (ˌsir-ə-ˈtō-nən) is a brain chemical. It affects mood and attitude. People who have high levels of serotonin tend to be more optimistic. Those with low levels may be more easily discouraged. Brain chemistry, however, only tells part of the story. Your environment plays a major role in shaping your attitude. This is also where you learn values and behavior. Your outlook is shaped by personal experiences at home, in school, and with friends. Your role models also affect your attitudes.

The Impact of Attitude

As You Read

Connect Why do you think a positive attitude is so important to your future?

A positive attitude serves a person best. Being an optimist is worthwhile for several reasons:

- A positive attitude helps build relationships. Do you enjoy being around someone who always complains and expects the worst? Most people prefer upbeat, eager, and optimistic company.

- Positive thinking aids problem solving. You see more options when you focus on solutions. Optimism gives you the spirit to tackle problems instead of being overwhelmed.

- Thinking positively can help you reach goals. When you believe you can succeed, you make the effort to meet challenges. If you expect failure, any problem may be a reason to quit trying.

- Positive thinking is better for your physical health. Studies have shown that optimistic people get sick only half as often as those with a more pessimistic attitude.

◀) *A Positive Attitude* People enjoy being around others who have positive attitudes. *Do the people you enjoy being with most have positive or negative attitudes?*

If a person has a negative attitude most of the time, others will eventually lose respect for that person. Relationships tend to fade away. On the other hand, sometimes people are too intent on being positive. They do not **recognize**, or acknowledge, when something is truly wrong. This attitude can get them in trouble, as well.

Change Your Attitude

Many things happen in life that can discourage people. As a result, it is sometimes a real challenge to think positively. A person needs to make a conscious effort to change how he or she views the situation. Some people look for ways to improve their overall outlook. This is not always easy. A person's attitude, fortunately, is like most personality traits. It can be improved. It may take one step at a time to adjust your attitude, but it can be done.

Your Reactions Affect Your Attitude

Your outlook on life shows in the way you view people, topics, issues, and even yourself. For example, think of a topic you feel strongly about. You will have three basic reactions. These combine to make up your attitude about the topic:

- **Mental** You have beliefs about the topic that come to mind.
- **Emotional** You sense feelings related to the topic.
- **Behavioral** You behave in certain ways because of how you think and feel.

If you want to change an attitude, you need to tackle each of these basic reactions. Take little steps to make changes. Begin with the mental aspect. That is often the easiest to change. You can gather new knowledge and use logical thinking. This can help you broaden your view of the topic.

Changing your behavior takes willpower. If you learn something new, however, you may be able to change your behavior. For example, if you learn something while changing your mental reaction, it may affect your behavior reaction. Feelings, or emotional reactions, usually resist change more than the other two reactions.

Interestingly, behavior is often the most vital of the three parts in changing an attitude. The reason for this is because when you act a certain way, your thoughts and feelings tend to follow. Understanding your attitude is important. It may help you build strong relationships and lead to a healthier life.

✓ Reading Check **Define** What is attitude?

Financial Literacy

Personal Finances

Knowing the state of your personal finances can often relieve some anxiety. This can affect your attitude. To figure out your personal finances, start by making a list of items that relate to your finances. This includes savings, monthly income (job earnings, allowance), and monthly expenses (money you spend).

Math Concept **Calculate Income and Expenses** Use a spreadsheet or another document. Categorize your expenses over a set period of time, such as a day, a week, or a month.

Starting Hint: You will need to create at least two columns of numbers. One will list your income. The other will list your expenses. Total both columns to see whether your income or expenses are greater.

 For math help, go to the Math Appendix at the back of the book.

NCTM Number and Operations Understand the meanings of operations and how they relate to one another.

Most people will feel moments of sadness at some point in their lives. Depression, on the other hand, is a long-lasting feeling of helplessness or hopelessness. It is not normal.

Depression often has no apparent cause. However, researchers believe an imbalance of chemicals in the brain may be one cause. This can make a person more prone to depression. Certain personality traits, such as a lack of self-confidence, may also make a person more prone to depression. A tendency toward depression appears to be inherited in some cases. Stress and crisis can also be triggers.

There is help for depression. Physical and mental fitness help. Sharing feelings of sadness can keep them from growing worse. Depression can require the advice and care of trained medical and human services professionals. Depression is not cause for shame or embarrassment. It shows that something is not right and needs attention.

Problem-Solving

Michelle walked self-consciously down the hall of her high school on a Friday afternoon. She thought about the weekend ahead and imagined that she would just sleep most of the weekend. Maybe she would not even come back on Monday. She wondered if anyone would notice if she was not there. What do you think is causing Michelle to feel this way? What would you say to her?

Self-Esteem and Attitude

Having a positive outlook on life is not easy if you do not feel good about you. **Self-esteem** is the way you feel about yourself. Self-esteem can also be called self-concept or self-worth. Positive self-esteem leads to self-confidence. When people have self-confidence, they are more likely to cope well with their failures.

People with low self-esteem often believe that they cannot do anything on their own. New settings make them anxious. They credit successes to luck. They think failures prove how inadequate they are. Those with low self-esteem are often defensive. They are sensitive to the words and actions of others. They may also be hurt or easily offended.

Positive Self-Esteem and Relationships

Self-esteem is closely tied to relationships. Positive relationships build self-esteem. When people relate well, they feel good about the relationship and themselves. In much the same way, positive self-esteem helps build good relationships. Those who feel good about themselves have confidence. They are apt to reach out to others. This helps build rapport and trust. People with high self-esteem are likely to disclose information about themselves. This also promotes good relationships.

Family Affects Self-Esteem

The family has a major impact on the self-esteem of its members. This is important when a family member has special needs. Family members teach each other skills and attitudes. When family members are accepted for who they are, all can grow and thrive.

Improve Self-Esteem

If you could bottle and sell the formula for self-esteem, you might become wealthy. Since there is no such formula, however, those who need a boost will have to make a personal effort. A sense of self-esteem builds from meeting four emotional needs:

- **Identity** Accepting yourself, including your flaws, makes you feel comfortable with who you are.
- **Belonging** This is your connection to people. You can find one small way today to strengthen a tie to another person. This may be a family member, friend, classmate, or group. Every day you can find one more way to belong.
- **Security** In this sense, security is psychological safety. To feel secure, find someone who accepts you, is reliable, and is worthy of trust. Then support each other.
- **Purpose** Knowing what you want to be or achieve gives meaning to what you do every day. To gain purpose, set a few short- and long-term goals.

When these four needs are met, self-esteem flows naturally. Success comes more easily. Many of these four needs are first met in the family. In addition, interpersonal skills help build self-esteem in family members. For example, listening sends the message that the other person is worthwhile. I-messages can build and increase another's self-esteem. They get the message across without blame. Hugs and other physical actions are supportive. Being able to resolve conflict helps prevent destructive messages and hurt feelings.

✓ **Reading Check** **Explain** Why is behavior often the critical factor in changing an attitude?

◀◀) **Express Confidence** Confidence will come naturally when your needs are met. *How does self-confidence lead to future successes?*

Build a Positive Attitude

On some days, it may be more challenging than on others to think positively. For those days, you may need ideas for adding joy to your life.

Thinking Skills

Evaluate Your Self-Esteem
Your self-esteem and attitude can improve if you:

✓ Avoid comparing yourself to others.

✓ Realize that your value as a person does not depend on money, social position, or friends.

✓ Accept your weaknesses as well as your strengths, and your failures as well as your successes.

✓ Set goals for yourself and follow through on them.

✓ Accept responsibility for your choices and actions.

✓ Believe you are in control of your own life.

- **Take positive action.** Just taking the first steps toward solving a problem can make you feel better.
- **Talk positively.** Dare to be an optimist. If things do not work out, remind yourself that such events often teach you the most. Say, "What can I do better tomorrow?"
- **Accept yourself.** You have weaknesses as well as strengths. Forgive yourself for mistakes and learn from them. Set reasonable goals and reward yourself for reaching them. Learn to measure progress in terms of where you are versus where you were.
- **Stay open to learning.** Learning new skills and knowledge increases your self-esteem.
- **Reach out to others.** Develop good relationships with a variety of people. Make positive thinkers your role models. Remember that it is qualities you want to imitate, not people.
- **Assert yourself.** You have a right to speak up and act on your beliefs. Preserve a positive atmosphere by saying what you think and feel in ways that are not offensive.
- **Accept and respect others as they are.** Treat people with respect to show that you think of them as worthwhile individuals.

A positive attitude can be a real **asset**, or resource, in life. Other people will welcome you. When you know that someone else feels good about you, you feel the same way about yourself.

Section 17.2 After You Read

Review Key Concepts

1. **Describe** the effect of serotonin on attitude.
2. **List** the emotional needs that must be met to improve self-esteem.
3. **Identify** ways that you can work to accept yourself.

Practice Academic Skills

English Language Arts

4. People who focus on what they have rather than what they do not have tend to be satisfied with their lives. People who focus on what they do not have tend to want more and are never satisfied. Think of people you know or know about. Do they focus on what they have or on what they do not have? Do they appear to be satisfied? Write an advice column explaining how this would affect a person's attitude.

   NCTE 3 Apply strategies to interpret texts.

5. List three ways you can build a positive attitude. Look at the list above to help you form your own examples.

   NCTE 4 Use written language to communicate effectively.

Check Your Answers Check your answers at this book's Online Learning Center through **glencoe.com**.

CHAPTER SUMMARY

⦾ Section 17.1
Your Personality

Personality is a result of heredity and environment. It is not fixed. It is influenced by internal and external factors. The three elements of personality are emotional, social, and intellectual traits. People feel a range of emotions. What counts is how they react to them and control them. Social traits affect how people interact with others. People tend to be introverts or extroverts. These affect how relationships are built. Intellectual traits include how a person thinks and learns.

⦾ Section 17.2
Develop a Positive Attitude

Attitude is a person's basic outlook on life. It affects all aspects of life. People tend to be optimists or pessimists. A positive attitude makes a good impression. It helps people in different areas of life. Emotional, social, and behavioral factors affect attitude change. Self-esteem is the way you feel about yourself. Those with a good attitude often have high self-esteem. Improving self-esteem is based on meeting four emotional needs. There are ways to help build a positive attitude.

Content and Academic Vocabulary Review

1. Use each of these content and academic vocabulary words in a sentence.

Content Vocabulary
◇ introvert (p. 337)
◇ extrovert (p. 337)
◇ attitude (p. 340)
◇ optimist (p. 340)
◇ pessimist (p. 340)
◇ serotonin (p. 340)
◇ self-esteem (p. 342)

Academic Vocabulary
■ unique (p. 335)
■ bias (p. 338)
■ recognize (p. 341)
■ asset (p. 344)

Review Key Concepts

2. Describe two factors that affect personality development.
3. Identify the three main elements that make up personality.
4. Explain how a positive attitude has a positive effect on a person's life.
5. Summarize the relationship between self-esteem and attitude.
6. Determine ways to build a positive attitude.

Critical Thinking

7. Analyze What is the result when both positive and negative emotions are controlled? Explain your answer.
8. Draw Conclusions How could having an inflated sense of self-esteem be a problem?
9. Evaluate Why might a person with few apparent successes in life have a positive attitude?

Real-World Skills

Self-Management Skills

10. Make Choices Jeremy prefers to be alone or with one or two close friends. He feels tense in crowds or among strangers. He knows, however, that success in life depends on working well with others. Write an entry for Jeremy's personal journal outlining things he can do to become more at ease with people.

Collaborative Skills

11. Personal Traits Follow your teacher's instructions to form into groups. Create a list of a variety of personal traits. These can be emotional, social, or intellectual. Together, analyze your list. Are the traits inherited or acquired? Would heredity or environment have the greatest effect on the trait?

Critical Thinking Skills

12. Career Analysis List your personality traits. Analyze these traits in terms of careers that may suit your personality. Choose three possible careers and find out more about them. Would the personality traits you have identified be a good match for the careers you chose? Write a paragraph to summarize your thoughts.

Problem-Solving Skills

13. Make a Plan Ashley needs to be around people. If she is not with friends, she is talking on the phone or text messaging with them. When she is alone, she feels moody and unsettled. Her mother says that Ashley needs to learn to entertain herself. What could Ashley do? Write a list of suggestions for Ashley.

14. Gratitude List For a week, make a list of at least five things that you are grateful for each day. At the end of the week, look over your lists. How many days were your friends included in the lists? Your family? Were you most apt to be grateful for people or for things? Why do you think this was so? Write a paragraph to explain your answers.

15. Comment Log For three days, keep a log of the negative things you hear people say about themselves. What faults do people seem to criticize most in themselves? How can you encourage positive attitudes?

16. Positive Images Talk to a teacher or a coach who uses positive images to teach others to imagine positive outcomes. How do students or players carry out these images? Write a report on what you learned.

17. Research Go to this book's Online Learning Center at **glencoe.com** to find **Web Links** for **Serotonin**. Locate information about how the study of serotonin has affected ideas about personality and the treatment of mental and emotional illness.

Additional Activities For additional activities, go to this book's Online Learning Center through **glencoe.com**.

Academic Skills

Mathematics

18. Calculate Living Expenses Worrying about finances causes many people to have negative attitudes. Dania was concerned about the cost of rent. She learned that most Americans spend approximately 30% of their yearly income on housing expenses. Dania earns $27,000 per year. What can she expect to spend on housing in one year?

Math Concept **Multiply Decimals by Whole Numbers** A percent is a ratio that compares a number to 100. To multiply with percentages, follow the steps below.

Starting Hint: You can rewrite the percent (30%) as a fraction with a denominator of 100. Convert the fraction to a decimal. Multiply this decimal by the number ($27,000). Remember to put the decimal point in the correct place in your answer.

Math For math help, go to the Math Appendix at the back of the book.

> **NCTM Number and Operations** Understand numbers, ways of representing numbers, relationships among numbers, and number systems.

English Language Arts

19. Analysis Recall an article or book you have read about a well-known person. Think of clues in the article or book about the person's personality. What is his or her attitude toward life and self-esteem? Compare your findings to those of classmates. What qualities seem to link to success and happiness? Which qualities seem to have a negative effect? Write a paragraph about your findings.

> **NCTE 2** Read literature to build an understanding of the human experience.

Social Studies

20. Factors in Development Write an essay on the ways that society affects personality development and self-esteem. What role does family, religion, ethnic group, nationality, or gender play in development? What effect does the media have? What do you think is most important? Explain your conclusion.

> **NCSS IV.c** Describe the ways family, religion, gender, ethnicity, nationality, socioeconomic status, and other group and cultural influences contribute to the development of a sense of self.

STANDARDIZED TEST PRACTICE

MULTIPLE CHOICE
Read the question. Then read each answer choice. Choose the best answer.

> **Test-Taking Tip** In a multiple-choice test, pay attention to key words in the question and each answer choice. In this question, the key words are positive attitude. Which answer choice refers specifically to positive attitude?

21. Which of the following helps to build a positive attitude?
a. trying to change others
b. letting people take advantage of you
c. talking positively
d. not learning any more when you realize that you know enough

Development Lasts a Lifetime

▶▶ Explore the Photo
You will go through major changes as you grow older. *What are some major developmental changes you think you have experienced?*

Chapter Objectives

After completing this chapter, you will be able to:

- **Identify** the major areas of human development.
- **Explain** how development is interrelated.
- **Describe** life-span development.
- **Summarize** the life tasks of adolescence.
- **Explain** how life structures relate to adult development.

Writing Activity

Cause and Effect

Honesty A person who is honest is truthful. Honesty is more than simply not lying. It means being true to your feelings and beliefs. You can show honesty when you:

- Tell a sales clerk that he or she gave you too much change back after you paid cash for a purchase.
- Give a coworker credit for a good job rather than accepting unearned praise.
- Tell details of weekend plans to parents, knowing that they might not approve.

Write a paragraph about the results of a time when you were honest with someone, or when someone was honest with you.

Writing Tips To write an effective cause-and-effect paragraph, follow these steps:

1. Focus on how the cause, wanting to be honest, created a positive effect.
2. Write a clear thesis statement. Make sure your paragraph takes a position on the effects of honesty.
3. Include an introduction and a conclusion in your paragraph.
4. Use appropriate transitional words, such as therefore and because between the cause and the effect.

Your Development

Reading Guide

Before You Read

Use Notes If you come upon something you are unfamiliar with, write a question on a piece of paper. After you have finished the section, try to answer your questions based on what you have read.

Read to Learn
Key Concepts
- **Identify** the major areas of human development.
- **Explain** how development is interrelated.

Main Idea
Development is the process of growth and change over the course of life. People develop physically, mentally, emotionally, socially, and morally. All development is interrelated.

Content Vocabulary
◇ hormone
◇ body image
◇ auditory learning
◇ visual learning
◇ kinesthetic learning
◇ temperament
◇ interrelate

Academic Vocabulary
You will find these words in your reading and on your tests. Use the glossary to look up their definitions if necessary.
- ■ perspective
- ■ evaluate

Graphic Organizer
As you read, look for the five areas of development. Use a concept web like the one shown to help organize your information.

Graphic Organizer Go to this book's Online Learning Center at **glencoe.com** to print out this graphic organizer.

Academic Standards •

English Language Arts

NCTE 4 Use written language to communicate effectively.

NCTE 5 Use different writing process elements to communicate effectively.

 Science

NSES Content Standard F Develop understanding of personal and community health.

NCTE *National Council of Teachers of English*
NCTM *National Council of Teachers of Mathematics*

NSES *National Science Education Standards*
NCSS *National Council of the Social Studies*

Areas of Development

The process of growth and change is called development. This includes all areas of life, such as physical, mental, emotional, social, and moral development. It has already taken you a long way from childhood. It will take you further still in the years to come. In some ways, you may stay the same. In other areas, changes may make you look back and ask, "Was that really me?" Will these changes bring you closer to the person you want to be? That remains largely up to you.

As you know, heredity has shaped part of what you are today. The environment also affects development. These are some of the environmental influences you encounter every day.

- Technology influences the information you have at your fingertips, the way you handle work and free time, and your health.
- Economic conditions may affect the opportunities you have.
- Social factors make an impact as well. For example, laws protect you from discrimination. Changing gender roles allow you to have a wider range of choices than people of earlier eras had.
- Life events, or the experiences that people have, can have strong effects on development. For example, injury or a health problem causes change.
- Support from others gives you a foundation for living. It adds incentive to do well in life.

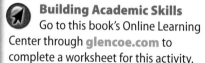

◀◀ **Your Changing Environment** Both heredity and environment affect your development. *How do environmental influences affect you as you develop?*

As You Read

Connect Do you think heredity or the environment has had more effect on your development?

Vocabulary

You can find definitions in the glossary at the back of this book.

All of these have an influence. The area most affected depends on your personality. It also depends on your needs. How you grow has an effect on your relationships as well. People who develop in the same ways see their relationship grow stronger. The relationship weakens when their development takes them in different directions.

Your Physical Self

Your physical self is made up of your body's outward appearance and internal functions. Your basic body type was inherited from your birth family, as were your physical traits. During the teen years, the physical self undergoes rapid change. It changes more than in any other age except infancy. This process generally begins and ends a few years earlier in females than in males. A **hormone** is a chemical substance. It regulates activity in the cells of the body. Changes in the production of hormones allow teens to develop adult traits.

Body Image

Physical change in the teen years is normal and healthy. It can still be disturbing. A teen who develops more quickly or slowly than peers may feel out of place. This new awareness of the body can cause trouble with **body image**. This is the way you see your physical self. When people have a poor body image, it affects how they relate to others. They may withdraw. They may have a harder time getting along.

Problems with body image start when people try to live up to some ideal. This is often a celebrity or model seen in the media. The pressure to live up to unrealistic images can cause teens to overlook their good points. They magnify what they believe is negative. The features that people dislike in themselves are usually not noticed by others. A winning personality tends to outweigh any flaws. As people get to know each other better, in fact, physical traits seem to disappear.

Physical Changes Physical changes can be dramatic during the teen years. *Do you think the physical changes teens experience have a positive or negative effect on their self-image?*

Telling yourself that looks are only skin deep is one thing. Believing it may be harder. What can you do?

- Act outgoing and upbeat. Attract people with a smile and a positive attitude.
- Focus on your good qualities (everyone has them).
- Stand tall and carry yourself with confidence.
- Follow the principles of good health and exercise.
- Be realistic about what you can be and work toward that.

- Learn to like what you see in the mirror.
- Use positive self-talk. Treat yourself to a compliment.

Problem-Solving Mark is a handsome guy. He works out at the gym every other day. You have told Mark how great he looks, but he does not believe you. He thinks maybe a few more hours in the gym will make a difference. What do you think is going on with Mark? What can you do or say to help?

Your Mental Self

The mental, or intellectual, self is the thinking self. You develop mentally as you learn. You begin to use knowledge, logic, and reason more effectively. Understanding ideas and the relationships among them shows mental growth, too.

Some people believe that mental abilities are shown only through school work. In fact, intelligence shows in many other ways as well, such as musical talent, creative skills, and problem-solving abilities. People also do not have the same strengths to the same degree.

During the teen years, you develop a more adult way of thinking. You come to see that actions have consequences. Sometimes these outcomes are positive. They can also, however, be negative. Your thinking will mature. As a result, you will be able to choose the behavior that brings rewards and fulfillment.

Predicting outcomes improves planning. When you understand the possible outcomes of actions, you may be able to solve them before they occur. Your plans are more likely to succeed.

Learning Styles

People learn through their senses. Learning by listening is called **auditory learning**. Learning by seeing is **visual learning**. Learning by doing is **kinesthetic learning**. You learn in all of these ways, but one may be more effective for you than the rest. Your preferred way of learning, or learning style, helps facts and concepts stick.

Auditory learners do best with the spoken word. They learn most from discussions and taped material. Visual learners understand written material best. They do well with computers, charts, and videos. Kinesthetic learners learn best with some type of physical action. It may be writing, speaking, or performing skits.

Learning is reinforced if you use more than one style. When you take notes in class, for instance, you are both listening and doing. Knowing how you learn best can help you develop your learning skills.

INDEPENDENT Living

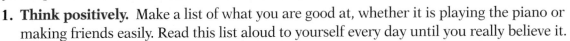

HOW TO Develop Self-Confidence

A strong sense of self-confidence will help you in every area of your life. It will help you master new skills and feel better about yourself when a situation does not go the way you expected. Follow these guidelines to develop self-confidence:

1. **Think positively.** Make a list of what you are good at, whether it is playing the piano or making friends easily. Read this list aloud to yourself every day until you really believe it.

2. **Do not go it alone.** When you feel overloaded by school, family, and outside activities, call a friend or parent to talk about it. Asking for support is a sign of strength, not weakness. Allow others to help you when they offer. It can help eliminate stress.

3. **Push yourself.** Challenge yourself to tackle new skills or situations. Instead of imagining all the ways something could go wrong, imagine yourself succeeding.

4. **Find people to cheer you on.** Build a support network of people who really believe in you. These people can be friends, parents, teachers, or counselors. When you are feeling down, they will be able to see your situation more clearly than you can.

5. **Keep trying.** You may not reach all your goals the first time. But by staying realistic about your ambitions, you can be proud of all your improvements along the way.

Take Action Create a personal to-do journal. On each page, write one of the above tips. Write two ways that you can use each tip in your daily life. Draw an empty box next to each example and add a check mark as you accomplish each one.

Your Emotional Self

Emotions are often pleasant. They are sometimes painful though. They provide information you can use to understand yourself and others. Emotions can vary in strength. Anger may be felt as mild irritation or red-hot rage. The basic emotions combine to make other ones. For example, disappointment is a blend of sadness and surprise.

As a young child, you were focused on yourself. You expressed emotions freely. Part of growing up is to understand and manage your emotions. You begin to see that emotional control and tact are vital to getting along with others. You learn to use communication skills in ways that promote development in yourself and others.

Handling Emotions

The teen years can be a stumbling block to handling emotions. During this time you start to feel new emotions. Hormonal changes in your body may also bring on mood swings. Feelings themselves are not right or wrong. What is right or wrong is how you deal with your emotions. The ability to cope effectively with emotions is one sign of growing up. It is the mark of being an adult.

People who are in control of their thoughts, feelings, and behaviors have good mental health. They feel good about themselves. They have strong relationships with others. The problems they face are kept in **perspective**, or within view. They have learned to cope with stress and problems.

Your Social Self

Your social self is the side of you that relates to other people. Each person has an inborn style of reacting to the world and relating to others. This is called **temperament**. A person's temperament is shown very early in life.

Infants reveal temperament in how active and persistent they are. They show it in how well they adapt to new people and events. How intensely they respond to their environment is another way temperament is revealed.

Basic temperament is inherited. Its effect tends to last throughout life. It affects the way people react to events and to others. Having a certain type of temperament, however, does not lock you into certain behavior. You can learn effective ways to deal with people. For example, an excitable person can begin to control reactions. A cautious person can work at trusting others. Someone with an easygoing nature can learn assertiveness.

Your Moral Self

You are also developing morally. When you were very young, you had no concept of right or wrong. Your actions were driven mostly by self-interest. Gradually, you learned that some behavior is not acceptable. You found that what you do has an effect on others. This is a powerful concept when making choices about behavior.

Your moral values are first learned within the family. Often, religious teaching influences moral codes. You develop your ability to **evaluate**, or determine, issues according to these values.

Moral development is vital, not only to individuals but to society as well. Society is weakened when people do not consider others. The bonds that tie people together fray when people act only in self-interest. When each person follows morally sound principles, people can be strong together as well as apart.

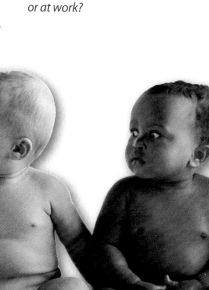

▼ **Different Temperaments**
Temperament is developed at a very early age. *How do you go about dealing with the different temperaments of people you meet at school or at work?*

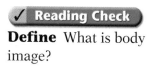
✓ **Reading Check**
Define What is body image?

Development Is Interrelated

All the areas of development are interrelated. To **interrelate** means to link in a mutual relationship. What affects one area can affect them all. For example, Ron grew 4 inches over the summer. He was self-conscious about his new height. This made him shy around others. He withdrew because he was embarrassed by his awkwardness. A physical change caused other changes in his social and emotional development.

Development is also affected by other interrelationships. Gender, ethnic group, and culture act to affect all areas of development. For example, imagine there is a stereotype that females are not good at science. This attitude may prevent some women from learning as much as they could.

Development also depends on how well a person's needs are met. When needs are met, the person can focus on other issues. Then development can occur. In the same way, a setback in development can cause needs to not be met.

Relationships can also impact development. When relationships are strong, people feel good. They are confident about their lives. They are ready to try new activities or learn new things. When there is a problem with development, relationships may suffer.

Your development as a person has just begun. What is ahead for you? The path from now through your adulthood will be filled with change and opportunity. How you develop in one area will affect the others. Right now you are setting the stage for adulthood. You can make decisions and plans that will give direction and purpose to your life.

Communication Skills

Show Confidence Healthy social and emotional development leads to self-confidence. You will communicate confidence if you:

✓ Stand up straight and look people in the eye when talking to them.

✓ Go out of your way to do something nice for someone.

✓ Focus on other people not yourself.

✓ Learn a new skill.

✓ Make a plan for improving yourself and carry it out.

Section 18.1   After You Read

Review Key Concepts

1. **List** the three main learning styles.
2. **Explain** what interrelated means.

Practice Academic Skills

English Language Arts

3. Think about how a person's moral development impacts the world at large. Write a case study about a specific example. Think about a news story you have heard or read. Describe what happened. Then describe the impact the action had on the people involved and society.

NCTE 4 Use written language to communicate effectively.

4. Why do you think some people have trouble with their body image? What can a person do to become more comfortable with his or her body image? Explain your thoughts in a two-paragraph response.

NCTE 5 Use different writing process elements to communicate effectively.

Check Your Answers Check your answers at this book's Online Learning Center through **glencoe.com**.

Life-Span Development

Reading Guide

Before You Read

Pace Yourself Short blocks of concentrated reading repeated frequently are more effective than one long session. Focus on reading for 10 minutes. Take a short break. Then read for another 10 minutes.

Read to Learn
Key Concepts
- **Describe** life-span development.
- **Summarize** the life tasks of adolescence.
- **Explain** how life structures relate to adult development.

Main Idea
Development continues throughout the life span. Adolescents have life tasks to complete. Adult development is based on moving through various life structures.

Content Vocabulary
◇ life-span development
◇ life task
◇ adolescence

Academic Vocabulary
You will find these words in your reading and on your tests. Use the glossary to look up their definitions if necessary.
■ aspect   ■ facet

Graphic Organizer
As you read, think of three examples for each part of a life structure. Use a graphic organizer like the one shown to help organize your information.

Roles	→	
Relationships	→	
Physical World	→	

 Graphic Organizer Go to this book's Online Learning Center at **glencoe.com** to print out this graphic organizer.

Academic Standards . . . .

 English Language Arts

NCTE 2 Read literature to build an understanding of the human experience.

NCTE 4 Use written language to communicate effectively.

 Mathematics

NCTM Data Analysis and Probability Formulate questions that can be addressed with data and collect, organize, and display relevant data to answer them.

NCTE *National Council of Teachers of English*
NCTM *National Council of Teachers of Mathematics*

NSES *National Science Education Standards*
NCSS *National Council of the Social Studies*

Development Throughout Life

As You Read

Connect Why do you think growing up is a lifelong process?

Vocabulary

You can find definitions in the glossary at the back of this book.

Do you remember, as a child, wanting to be grown up? Actually, you may never reach that point. Growing up is a lifelong process. Development in adulthood may be less apparent than in younger years. It can still have a major impact on life.

Have you ever had a good look at a tree that has been cut down? The tree's life story, year by year, shows in the cross section of rings in the trunk. The rings are not always evenly shaped or equally spaced. You see warps, scars, and discolored places. Each event the tree experienced has been imprinted in its very core. These events affected the tree's growth and health and left a lasting mark.

In the same way, each of your experiences leaves a lasting impression on you. You cannot erase the scars from the past, any more than the tree can. You, can, however, move beyond them.

Life-span development is the growth and change that occurs throughout a person's life. Every **aspect**, or angle, of life—physical, mental, emotional, and moral—involves ongoing growth and development.

Figure 18.1 Pioneers in Development

These social scientists were pioneers in the study of human development. Their work changed the way people looked at the life span. They were the first to study how people develop over their entire lives. *What is the common theme among these theories?*

Social Scientists and Their Theories

Social Scientist	Theory	Main Idea
Abraham Maslow	1943 Hierarchy of Needs	People can only develop to their fullest if their needs are met. Physical and safety needs must be met before higher needs such as love, esteem, creativity, and morality can be addressed.
Erik Erikson	1950 8 Stages of Development	There are eight stages of development: Infancy, Early Childhood, Preschool, School Age, Adolescence, Young Adulthood, Middle Adulthood, and Maturity. Each stage has a conflict to solve.
Robert Havighurst	1953 Developmental Tasks	Developmental tasks arise at certain times in life. If they are completed successfully, the person is able to move to the next stage of life. For example, a developmental task for an infant is to learn to walk.
Daniel Levinson	1978 Adult Development	Each person has a life structure, which is the underlying pattern of life at any one time. These patterns change about once a decade as people grow and develop throughout their adult lives.

Every day people get another chance to work toward becoming who they want to be. People never really finish developing. They are more like works in progress.

Life-span development is only a guide to future growth. It is not a blueprint. Although all people follow similar patterns, development is as unique as each person's circumstances and personality. You will meet life's challenges and tasks in your own time as your life unfolds.

Stages of Life

Social scientists study people and how they develop. They often sort what they observe into stages. The way these stages are divided and labeled can vary. **Figure 18.1** lists four of the more famous social scientists. They were pioneers in the study of life-span development.

Like development itself, the stages of life are interrelated. Each stage has its own potential, traits, needs, and problems. Each stage builds on the ones before it. Managing each stage successfully provides a solid base for the next. Within you are elements of the child you once were. These elements influence the teen you are now and the adult you are becoming.

The idea of life as a series of stages is useful for looking at and measuring growth. On the other hand, it may suggest a precision that does not really exist. The stages of personal development are like the stages of family development. They do not arrive and depart on a schedule. You may enter a stage ahead of another person, yet remain there longer.

Life Tasks

A **life task** is a challenge to be met at each stage of growth. It can be the skills, habits, knowledge, or attitudes you need to cope with the events in that stage. Completing a life task brings feelings of competence and success. You feel ready to meet the tasks of the next stage. In contrast, failure at a task leads to feelings of inadequacy. It makes success at future tasks more doubtful.

✓ **Reading Check** **Explain** How are the stages of life interrelated?

Adolescent Life Tasks

Adolescence (ˌa-də-ˈle-sᵊn(t)s) is the time of life between childhood and adulthood. This is where you are now. People move through the teen years at their own pace. No one route through the teen years works for everyone.

For most teens, adolescence is an exciting and satisfying age. It is a time of rapid growth and development. Teens work to build good relationships and form strong ties with family and friends. Most teens accept their parents' religious, political, and social views. They find ways to work toward independence without the conflict that some expect of these years.

The teen years are portrayed as a constant clash with parents, siblings, teachers, friends, and employers. Some teens do find adolescence to be an uphill battle. Rapid change and development can bring problems in relationships. Still, over two thirds of all teens are happy with their relationships with parents. To make the teen years a happy time, you need to work through the three main life tasks of adolescence.

▶▶ **Discover Your Identity** As a teen, you will search to discover your identity and decide on your future goals. *In what ways can you begin the search for your own identity?*

Build Your Identity

Before you can figure out what you want from life, you must know who you are as a person. A secure sense of self gives you the confidence to deal with the demands made of you. You can plan for the future and move toward adult responsibilities.

As a teen, you start to ask, "What are my values and my goals? What do I want for the future?" With growth and experience, you form a solid understanding of yourself. In other words, you find your identity. Building a sense of identity is the main life task of adolescence.

The search for identity involves every **facet**, or part, of life. During these years, teens keep working, searching, learning, and growing. They discover their unique goals, talents, and styles. They gradually begin to see who they are and where they fit in society.

Another part of forming an identity is known as integrating personality. This means putting together the parts of your personality to create a unique identity. You discover what you want to pursue as an adult. Your emotions stabilize and form a pattern to help you deal with life. You mold your roles and talents into a unified whole. Your attitudes and values also fit into your identity.

Financial Literacy

Compare Salaries

At the Frontier Company, an administrative assistant makes $35,000 a year, an office manager makes $40,000 a year, and the president makes $50,000 a year. Draw a bar graph of the three salaries.

Math Concept **Represent Data in a Graph** A bar graph represents data using shaded bars to show each value. The graph's axes should always be labeled, and the graph should have a title.

Starting Hint: Create a legend to show what each bar color represents.

Math For math help, go to the Math Appendix at the back of the book.

NCTM Data Analysis and Probability Formulate questions that can be addressed with data and collect, organize, and display relevant data to answer them.

Become Independent

A second task of adolescence is becoming independent. At some point, most people separate themselves from their parents. They leave home, marking the end of childhood and adolescence. They earn their own money and control their own lives. The young person is seen as a separate, self-sufficient adult. To live independently, you must have problem-solving, decision-making, and management skills. Learning these skills prepares teens to depend less on parents.

Plan for Employment

Another task of adolescence is planning for your life's work. Much of adult life is spent earning a living, often in more than one job. People who choose and prepare for careers tend to be happier than those who do not. To choose the right career, you need to know your talents and interests. Jobs that offer greater challenge, satisfaction, and income require preparation. The teen years are the time to start.

Some fields you choose may require a college education. You need certain courses in high school to be admitted. The better your grades, the better chance you have of getting into the school of your choice. Other fields offer on-the-job training. Technical training from a community college or trade school is required for other jobs.

✓ **Reading Check** **Identify** What is the most important life task of adolescence?

Adult Development

As teens move toward adulthood, the life tasks of adolescence should be finished. Young people should have a sense of who they are and who they want to be. They are ready to be independent and move on with life. Many years and more life tasks lie ahead.

Establish Life Structures

As you enter adulthood, you will begin to establish a structure for your life. A life structure is based on three components:

- **Roles** You will select the roles you want, such as parent, spouse, and worker.
- **Relationships** You will build relationships with family members, friends, coworkers, and others. Your stage of development affects these relationships.
- **Physical World** You will choose the physical world in which you live. This includes your home, your neighborhood, and your community.

There are many choices to make as you build your first life structure. What do you want to do or be in life? How will your life structure differ from what it is now? Your ability to make sound decisions will help you adopt a life structure that suits you.

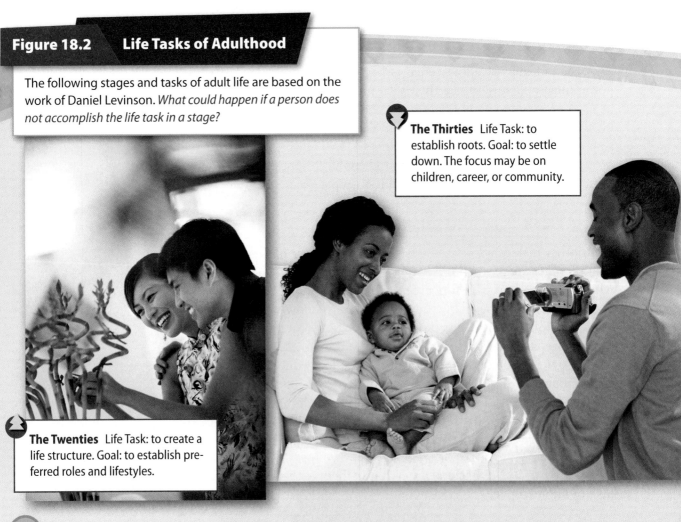

Figure 18.2   Life Tasks of Adulthood

The following stages and tasks of adult life are based on the work of Daniel Levinson. *What could happen if a person does not accomplish the life task in a stage?*

The Thirties Life Task: to establish roots. Goal: to settle down. The focus may be on children, career, or community.

The Twenties Life Task: to create a life structure. Goal: to establish preferred roles and lifestyles.

Changes in Life Structures

In adult life, there are times of stability and times of change. During stable periods, the life structure stays the same. In times of change, the life structure shifts.

Shifts in Life Tasks

These shifts tend to occur about every ten years. Each decade of life seems to be defined by a basic life task. **Figure 18.2** shows what these life tasks are according to Daniel Levinson. Many experts who study adult development have found a similar pattern applies to most people. However, other social scientists apply the tasks of The Sixties to the sixties and the decades that come after that. Of course, exceptions always exist. Each adult handles life tasks and structures in an individual way.

What causes the life structure to change? Both external and internal influences can impact life structures. Externally, a new job or a health problem can cause change. Internally, feelings of dissatisfaction or interest can lead a person to make changes. Changes can be major or minor. Will you take on a new role or leave an old one behind? Will you build a new relationship or end an old one? Will you move near or far? Adult development is based on these kinds of issues.

Change gives adults opportunities for growth. Through change, they move on to the next life task. By handling each task as it comes, adults prepare themselves for the next stage of life.

The Fifties Life Task: to find stability and peace. Goal: to have freedom from child-rearing, more contact with friends, a happy marriage, and few money problems.

The Forties Life Task: to reevaluate life. Goal: to see whether it is time to seize new opportunities and develop new interests.

The Sixties (and Beyond) Life Task: to come to terms with life's end. Goal: to retire and come to terms with how life has been.

A Lifetime to Develop

As a teen, it may seem impossible to imagine what you will feel and what you will think as a forty-, fifty-, or sixty-year-old. It may seem far away. It is important to consider this, though. It may help you consider if you should do things differently now.

No Regrets

Too often, adults look back with regrets. Some are sorry they ignored certain rules. Some wonder why they started a bad health habit. Some wish they had tried harder to make a relationship work. Some regret that they did not plan for a career they would enjoy.

Any older adult will tell you how quickly life passes by. It is a mistake to think you will not care how your life is going when you are older. You will want to live an enjoyable life as a mature adult just as much as you want to live an enjoyable life as a teenager. In fact, you may wish it even more as you grow older.

You will never be able to go back and change the past. Right now, however, you are creating your future. This is an opportunity for you. You can get ready for a lifetime of growth, development, and change. You can make decisions and plans to give your life direction and purpose. You can aim for a good life throughout all your years. You need to start right now.

Section 18.2 — After You Read

Review Key Concepts

1. **Explain** what a life task is and why it is important to complete life tasks at each stage of life.
2. **Summarize** why choosing and preparing for a career is important.
3. **Identify** the three parts of a life structure.

Practice Academic Skills

English Language Arts

4. Divorce is a major change in an adult's life. Describe the impact divorce would have on an adult's life structure. What are the emotional and physical changes that would take place in the life of an adult who becomes divorced?

    NCTE 4 Use written language to communicate effectively.

5. Recall a biography that you have watched or read about a person whose life interests you. Think about the adult development and life structures in that biography. How did these change over the course of the person's life? How did these relate to the periods of stability and change the person experienced? Summarize your analysis in an oral report to the class.

    NCTE 2 Read literature to build an understanding of the human experience.

Check Your Answers Check your answers at this book's Online Learning Center through **glencoe.com**.

CHAPTER SUMMARY

 ### Section 18.1
Your Development

Development is the process of growth and change. It occurs in several areas. Physical development is dramatic in the teen years. Body image can be an issue if teens look to unrealistic role models. Teens can show mental growth in school. They also find it in other talents. They develop an effective learning style. This can be auditory, visual, or kinesthetic. Teens build relationships as they develop socially. They learn acceptable behaviors, called moral growth. This also means they consider the effects of actions upon others. They learn that all development is interrelated.

 ### Section 18.2
Life-Span Development

Growth and change occur throughout a person's life. This is called life-span development. Social scientists look at life as a series of stages. Each stage has life tasks to do in order to pass to the next stage. The life tasks of adolescence include building an identity, becoming independent, and planning for employment. Adult development is based on life structures. These are the roles, relationships, and physical location that shape each person's life. Life tasks help people move to the next stage of adult development and the life structure for that stage.

Content and Academic Vocabulary Review

1. Use each of these content and academic vocabulary words in a sentence.

Content Vocabulary
◇ hormone (p. 352)
◇ body image (p. 352)
◇ auditory learning (p. 353)
◇ visual learning (p. 353)
◇ kinesthetic learning (p. 353)
◇ temperament (p. 355)
◇ interrelate (p. 356)
◇ life-span development (p. 358)
◇ life task (p. 360)
◇ adolescence (p. 360)

Academic Vocabulary
■ perspective (p. 355)
■ evaluate (p. 355)
■ aspect (p. 358)
■ facet (p. 361)

Review Key Concepts

2. **Identify** the five major areas of human development.
3. **Explain** how development is interrelated.
4. **Describe** life-span development.
5. **Summarize** the life tasks of adolescence.
6. **Explain** how life structures relate to adult development.

Critical Thinking

7. **Predict** Which life task of adulthood do you think will be most difficult? Explain.
8. **Analyze** Look at your own development over the last three years. How have you changed in those three years? In what areas of development have you changed most? Least? Can you see a pattern in your progress? What do you think the future may hold for you?
9. **Explain** Think about the stages of family development (starting as a couple, parenting, the middle years, retirement). How do they fit with the stages of adult development shown in Figure 18.2? Explain your answer.

Real-World Skills

Problem-Solving Skills

10. Plan for the Future Darrin's father wants to return to school for his college degree. Darrin plans to go to college when he graduates. He wonders if his family will be able to help him pay for college. He does not want to sound negative about his father's plans. Write a letter to Darrin offering your advice.

Interpersonal Skills

11. Look at Role Models Choose three people whom you admire, such as a friend, parent, teacher, coach, or famous figure. Describe each of the people you chose. What is he or she like? What makes you admire him or her? How has he or she influenced you or others? Write your answers in a one-page report.

Information Skills

12. Research Research the changes that occur in muscles, bones, and hormones during the teen years. Describe the changes and tell why they happen. What factors affect the time when the changes occur? What factors affect the rate at which the changes occur? Write a report of your findings.

Communication Skills

13. Self-Direction Morgan is trying to be more outgoing. She has made many new friends. Her long-time best friend says Morgan no longer has time for her and has outgrown their friendship. Morgan still cares, but she likes what she is becoming, too. Write a paragraph about what Morgan can say to her friend.

14. Learning Styles Survey ten students on what learning style is best for them. Use auditory, visual, and kinesthetic learning as the choices. Figure out what percent of the students surveyed named each style. Make a pie chart of the results. Write your conclusions in a paragraph.

15. Interview Talk with an adult about the various life structures he or she has experienced. Looking back, which part of his or her life structures changed the most often? Why? Were the changes because of external or internal factors? Write a report about what you learn.

16. Community Resources Make a chart of the community resources for people in their 20s, 30s, 40s, 50s, 60s, and 70s+. Under each heading, list resources and services available in your community.

17. Research Go to this book's Online Learning Center at **glencoe.com** to find **Web Links** for **Learning Style Tests**. Choose one and take a test to figure out which learning style you are. List three ways that knowing this can help you in your school activities.

Additional Activities For additional activities, go to this book's Online Learning Center through **glencoe.com**.

Academic Skills

 Mathematics

18. Calculate Average Work Time At his job at a local restaurant, Bill and two others spend a total of four hours working together. As a group, they prepare food for the salad bar so it is always full. What is the average number of minutes Bill spends to keep the salad bar filled?

Math Concept **Use Variables and Operations** Translating words into algebraic expressions requires knowledge of the meaning of the verbal descriptions. In algebra, a variable is a symbol used to represent a number. Arithmetic functions include addition, subtraction, multiplication, and division.

Starting Hint: If x = the average number of hours each worker spends to keep the salad bar filled, then the algebraic expression for the problem is $3x = (4 \times 60)$. Solve for x.

 Math For math help, go to the Math Appendix at the back of the book.

NCTM Algebra Represent and analyze mathematical situations and structures using algebraic symbols.

 English Language Arts

19. Write Questions One of the life tasks of adolescence is planning for employment. Choose a job that you think you would like. If you were to interview a person in this job, what questions would you ask about the job? What do you want to find out? Write ten questions that you could ask in an interview.

NCTE 12 Use language to accomplish individual purposes.

Social Studies

20. Investigate Research and write a report on ideas of beauty in other cultures or different times in history. Explain why certain physical features are or were thought to be attractive. Compare them with the ideas of beauty that you see today. Your report should point out any similarities or differences between the ideas about beauty in the other cultures and times, and the beauty you see today.

NCSS I.b Predict how data and experiences may be interpreted by people from diverse cultural perspectives and frames of reference.

STANDARDIZED TEST PRACTICE

TIMED WRITING
Read the writing prompt and respond in a one-page essay.

Test-Taking Tip When writing an essay test response, it is important to take a few moments to plan. Read the question several times and underline key words or phrases. Key words or phrases tell you what you have to do. For example, "explain how you made your choice" is a key phrase in this writing prompt.

21. High school students are faced with many choices upon graduation. Some choose to go to college. Others choose technical schools or apprenticeships. Write an essay explaining what you will do after high school and how it will affect your finances. Be sure to explain how you made your choice, the events or people who influenced your choice, and the impact your choice will have on your finances. Support your explanations with details and examples.

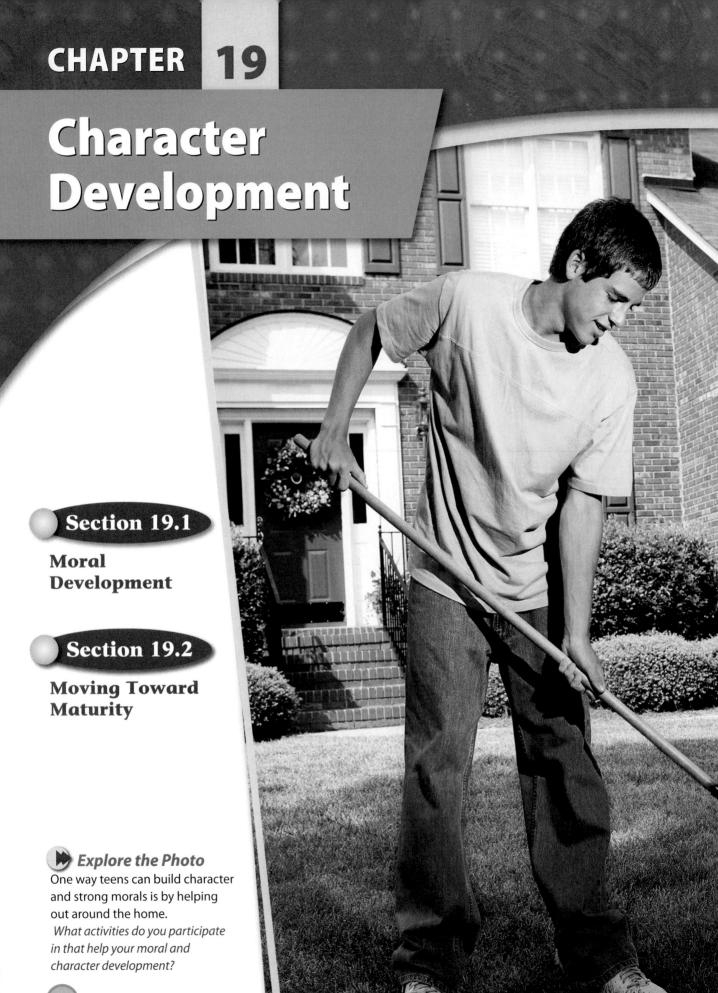

CHAPTER 19

Character Development

Section 19.1

Moral Development

Section 19.2

Moving Toward Maturity

▶▶ *Explore the Photo*
One way teens can build character and strong morals is by helping out around the home. *What activities do you participate in that help your moral and character development?*

Chapter Objectives

After completing this chapter, you will be able to:

- **Summarize** how morality develops in people.
- **Describe** moral reasoning.
- **Explain** what a code of ethics is.
- **Identify** qualities that show maturity.
- **Determine** what is needed to build a philosophy of life.

Writing Activity

Persuasive Paragraph

Tolerance When you recognize and respect the beliefs or practices of others, you are displaying tolerance. You can be tolerant if you:
- Do not confuse what is right with what is popular.
- Have the same expectations of yourself as of others.
- Look for ways to help others mature.
- Listen before forming an opinion.
- Accept that there are some unchangeable things about every person.

Write a persuasive paragraph about why tolerance is an important quality. Include specific details that support your opinion.

Writing Tips To write a persuasive paragraph, follow these steps:
1. State your position clearly.
2. Make sure each sentence in the paragraph includes details to support the main idea.
3. Use facts to back up your position.

Moral Development

Reading Guide

Before You Read

Use Diagrams As you are reading through this section, write down the main idea. Draw arrows to the information that directly supports it. Then draw arrows from these examples to any information that supports them.

Read to Learn
Key Concepts
- **Summarize** how morality develops in people.
- **Describe** moral reasoning.
- **Explain** what a code of ethics is.

Main Idea
Moral development occurs in stages and levels over time. Moral reasoning is using logic and critical thinking to solve moral problems. A code of ethics is a set of rules or principles that guide actions and decisions.

Content Vocabulary
◇ morality
◇ character
◇ conscience
◇ pre-conventional level
◇ conventional level
◇ post-conventional level
◇ moral reasoning
◇ code of ethics

Academic Vocabulary
You will find these words in your reading and on your tests. Use the glossary to look up their definitions if necessary.
■ thrive   ■ understand

Graphic Organizer
As you read, list and describe the three levels of moral development identified by Lawrence Kohlberg. Use a chart like the one shown to help organize your information.

Level of Moral Development	Characteristics

 Graphic Organizer Go to this book's Online Learning Center at **glencoe.com** to print out this graphic organizer.

Academic Standards • • • • • • • • • • • • • • • •

 English Language Arts

NCTE 4 Use written language to communicate effectively.

NCTE 6 Apply knowledge of language structure and conventions to discuss texts.

 Mathematics

NCTM Problem Solving Solve problems that arise in mathematics and in other contexts.

NCTE *National Council of Teachers of English*
NCTM *National Council of Teachers of Mathematics*

NSES *National Science Education Standards*
NCSS *National Council of the Social Studies*

The Development of Morality

Suppose you return the extra dollar you got in change. When you do this, you are practicing morality. **Morality** is a system of conduct based on what is right and wrong. It is the basis of order and good-will in the world. The broad themes of morality are justice and caring. Most people try to behave morally. Knowing which actions are right—and acting upon them—can be a challenge at times.

High standards of morality are important to individuals and to a community. The morality of each member contributes to the moral strength of the group. When each person learns and practices moral principles, order and goodwill can **thrive**, or prosper. How you treat others affects their treatment of you. You gain self-respect when you follow a moral course. This will also lead to the respect and coopera-tion from other people. People with **character** are morally strong, with the ability to think, judge, and act with maturity.

Rules for behavior can seem like a burden at times. Ask yourself: what would the world be like without them? How do you react when you are treated unfairly? Everyone wants to be treated well.

People are not born knowing right from wrong. They learn as they grow. Families teach children their earliest lessons in morality. Later influences are friends, religious leaders, and teachers. Moral-ity thrives or dies by example. People can choose to set good moral examples for others.

A child's conscience begins to form at about age six. A **conscience** ('kän(t)-shǝn(t)s) is an inner sense of what is right and wrong in a person's own behavior or motives. In healthy moral growth, the conscience grows with a person's experience and ability to **understand**, or know, the meaning of concepts. The con-science of an eight-year-old is far different from that of an eighteen-year-old.

Levels of Moral Development

Psychologist Lawrence Kohlberg did some of the basic research on moral development. He found that as the moral self develops, it moves through three general levels. Each level has two stages, totaling six stages.

Vocabulary

You can find definitions in the glossary at the back of this book.

As You Read

Connect Who has influenced you the most in teaching you right from wrong?

▶ *Set a Good Example* By choosing to set good moral exam-ples for others, you are developing your own good character. *How does setting a good example help you develop morality?*

Pre-Conventional Level

The **pre-conventional level** is the first level of moral development. This is the level where moral thinking focuses on the outcome of behavior. Acts are good or bad according to their results. A parent or other authority figure usually sets the rules for children.

Stage One In the first stage of this level, children obey rules to avoid negative outcomes. They have learned that some things are right or wrong, but they do not know why. They only know what will happen if they disobey.

Stage Two At the second stage, children obey to earn rewards or to have favors returned. Again, children do not question why something is right and wrong. They know what behavior others desire.

Conventional Level

The next level of moral development is the **conventional level**. At this level, the rules, expectations, and judgment of the group become the standard for behavior. The group may be family, classmates, or a unit of government. This level includes stages three and four. Most people have reached this level by age thirteen.

Stage Three In stage three, people obey to avoid disapproval or dislike from others. Good behavior is whatever pleases other people. Those who go along to win the approval of their friends are at this stage.

Stage Four Obeying rules because they represent authority is the theme of stage four. People accept and respect that laws are to be upheld. They understand that rules are needed for an orderly society.

Post-Conventional Level

The last level is reached around age sixteen. In this level moral beliefs are based on moral principles. This is the **post-conventional level** of moral behavior. People begin to evaluate customs, rules, and laws in terms of their personal standards.

Stage Five In stage five, people may decide that not all laws are good ones. They may work within the system to change laws they find unfair. In this stage, personal agreements between people gain moral importance. Decisions are based on the individual's idea of what is fair and fitting.

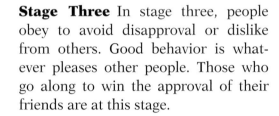

▼ *Respect Authority* At the conventional level, people have learned to respect authority. *How will learning respect for authority help you in the future?*

Stage Six Morality in stage six is based on universal principles. These include the fact that life is sacred. It may also be based on the equality of all people. People in this stage adopt these principles as their own and act on them. At the highest degree of this level are those who devote their lives to others, such as Mother Teresa and Dr. Martin Luther King, Jr.

Like other parts of personality, moral growth is not the same for everyone. Some adults show less-advanced moral thinking than do some teens. Also, moral behavior is not always consistent. Some people who have reached the higher stages may act improperly at times. True moral growth is shown by a person's attitudes and actions as a whole.

✓ **Reading Check** **Define** What is morality?

Moral Reasoning

Even if everyone reached the same level of moral development at the same time, they still would not agree on every matter of right and wrong. People are raised differently. They learn different principles and values. Some values that you hold might not be the same as someone else's. You may both be certain of your beliefs. Can you both be right?

Some situations are moral dilemmas. No option is entirely satisfactory. For example, many people believe in honesty as a moral value. However, if you dislike a friend's new outfit, should you say so? Is it dishonest for a person to steal food if he or she is starving?

Difficult questions such as these will always exist. You will face your share throughout life. **Moral reasoning** is dealing with moral issues by using logic and critical thinking. As with any decision, the goal is to understand the issue as clearly as possible and then make an informed choice.

First, ask questions to get the facts you need. Talk to those who can help you. Then, as you reflect on your options, consider if and how anyone may be hurt. Look for actions that do no harm, balancing the needs of others with your own well-being. Next, turn to the principles and values that you know are right. Positive values are the guiding force in moral behavior. Without them, many arguments can sound right, yet lead to a wrong choice.

Finally, think for yourself. It may be comforting to go along with the crowd, even if the crowd is only one other person. It may not be the right direction for you, however. Strong moral convictions can help you act with confidence.

✓ **Reading Check** **Explain** What is a moral dilemma?

Financial Literacy

Calculate Bonuses

John's boss is pleased with his skills and work ethic. She admires John's ability to work with others. She is going to give John a 20% bonus at the end of the year. This is in addition to his $500 holiday bonus. John's salary is $34,000. What will his total earnings for the year be with the two bonuses?

Math Concept **Multi-Step Problems**
When solving problems with more than one step, think through the steps before you start.

Starting Hint: To set up this problem, first write an equation for the amount of the end-of-the-year bonus:

$34,000 \times 0.20 = x$.

Then write an expression for his total earnings: $34,000 + x + $500

 For math help, go to the Math Appendix at the back of the book.

NCTM Problem Solving Solve problems that arise in mathematics and in other contexts.

A Code of Ethics

One of your greatest allies when you make moral decisions is your code of ethics. A **code of ethics** is a clear set of rules or principles that guide actions and decisions. It is the real-life application of a person's values. It takes into consideration your welfare as well as the welfare of others. When you value honesty, for instance, part of your code of ethics says, "It is wrong to lie."

Your code of ethics has an impact on your relationships with others. When you treat others fairly and with honesty, relationships grow. Problems can arise when people's codes of conduct clash. On some differences, tolerance may be enough to keep the relationship. For example, you may not agree with the other person, but the difference may be small. It is more a result of values than a matter of principle. Sometimes differences are more basic and a choice must be made. At some point, you may need to break off the relationship.

Organizations also need codes of conduct and ethical standards. These shape the goals of the group. They guide how people are treated. When people join groups or businesses with professional standards, they are required to follow them. This makes the group stronger. It creates the basis for good business relationships.

A code of ethics is not created overnight. Rather, it takes shape as you confront the issues and problems of daily life. You build a code of ethics as you think and make decisions about what is right and what is wrong. A strong code of ethics is a mark of true moral development.

Section 19.1 After You Read

Review Key Concepts

1. **Identify** the two broad themes of moral development.
2. **Describe** the goal of moral reasoning.
3. **Explain** how a code of ethics can affect relationships.

Practice Academic Skills

English Language Arts

4. There are three levels of moral development: pre-conventional, conventional, and post-conventional. What do the prefixes pre- and post- mean? Why would these terms be used to describe the levels of moral development?

5. A double standard is an ethical or moral code that applies more strictly to one group than to another. For example, school policy states that students who are late to class must go to detention after school. However, many teachers allow seniors to come to class late without having to spend time in detention. This is a double standard based on class status. Write a paragraph that explains how a double standard relates to morality.

> **NCTE 6** Apply knowledge of language structure and conventions to discuss texts.

> **NCTE 4** Use written language to communicate effectively.

Check Your Answers Check your answers at this book's Online Learning Center through **glencoe.com**.

Moving Toward Maturity

Reading Guide

Before You Read

Two-Column Notes Two-column notes are a useful way to study and organize what you have read. Divide a piece of paper into two columns. In the left column, write down main ideas. In the right column, list supporting details.

Read to Learn

Key Concepts
- **Identify** qualities that show maturity.
- **Determine** what is needed to build a philosophy of life.

Main Idea

The development of maturity continues throughout life. There are qualities that show a readiness for adult life. A philosophy of life is the sum of a person's beliefs, attitudes, and values.

Content Vocabulary

◇ mature
◇ maturity
◇ conform
◇ self-discipline
◇ egocentrism
◇ prejudice
◇ philosophy of life

 Graphic Organizer Go to this book's Online Learning Center at **glencoe.com** to print out this graphic organizer.

Academic Vocabulary

You will find these words in your reading and on your tests. Use the glossary to look up their definitions if necessary.
- individuality
- remember

Graphic Organizer

As you read, look for qualities that describe a mature person. Use a concept map like the one shown to help organize your information.

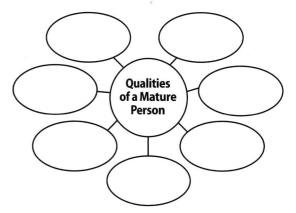

Academic Standards • • • • • • • • • • • • • • • •

English Language Arts

NCTE 4 Use written language to communicate effectively.

NCTE 12 Use language to accomplish individual purposes.

NCTE *National Council of Teachers of English*
NCTM *National Council of Teachers of Mathematics*

NSES *National Science Education Standards*
NCSS *National Council of the Social Studies*

Qualities of Maturity

Vocabulary

You can find definitions in the glossary at the back of this book.

When a person is **mature** (mə-'tûr), it means they have completed natural growth and development. No one wants to be labeled immature. The word brings up images of selfishness and helplessness. Instead, people want to be known as mature. How do they earn that label? **Maturity** is the state of being mature. In one sense, maturity is never entirely achieved. This is because personal development never stops. It continues over a lifetime.

People advance toward maturity in all developmental areas. These include physical, mental, emotional, social, and moral areas. Development in each area is not at the same pace. It is not to the same degree either. Maturity commonly means grown-up or adult. It means having the qualities and traits needed for adult life. Some of these qualities are described in this section.

Independence

As You Read

Connect What are some of the qualities of maturity you can demonstrate in your everyday life?

As people grow, they move from dependence on others to independence. Mature people have established their identities. They earn their own living and typically live apart from their parents. More important, they solve their own problems and make their own decisions.

When you are an independent person, problem solving can become more complicated. As you get older, more of your decisions have a long lasting impact. For example, Alise wanted to work in a certain women's clothing store but applied at several other places too. When a gift shop offered her a job, Alise hesitated. Should she take the sure offer of the gift shop, or take a chance by waiting for the job in the clothing store? Alise did not want to make a mistake that would affect her for a long time to come.

Rewards of Maturity Learning to drive responsibly is an important passage in a teen's life. *How do you plan to demonstrate maturity when driving?*

INDEPENDENT *Living*

HOW TO   Show Character with Others

You can build a foundation for healthy relationships by displaying traits of good character. Follow these guidelines to develop character with others:

1. **Be trustworthy.** You show trustworthiness when you are honest, reliable, and loyal. Trustworthy people do not cheat, steal, or deceive. They have the courage to do what is right.

2. **Be respectful.** You show respect by using good manners, being considerate of others, and being tolerant of differences. You are respectful when you deal with anger and disagreements in a peaceful way and treat other people and property with care.

3. **Be responsible.** You show that you are responsible when you do what is expected of you and are accountable for your choices. Being responsible also means that you use self-control, think before you act, and always try your best.

4. **Be fair.** You show fairness when you play by the rules and share. It means you do not blame or take advantage of others. A fair person listens to others and is open-minded.

5. **Be caring.** You show that you are caring when you are kind and compassionate. Caring means putting in time and energy to help others.

Take Action On a piece of paper, think of examples of each of the above traits. You can use an experience from your past or you can imagine a new situation. When you are finished, trade papers with a friend or classmate. Discuss why the actions chosen in your examples show good character.

You rarely can know exactly what will come from a particular choice or solution to a problem. The problem-solving process helps mature people make thoughtful decisions. You can evaluate solutions before you carry them out. A good solution or decision for you is one that:

- Fills your needs and wants, not someone else's.
- Causes no physical or emotional harm to you or anyone else.
- Is based on fact, rather than on hope, wishes, or fantasy.
- Has acceptable short- and long-term results.

Handle Conformity

As you become more independent, you learn to think for yourself. You make decisions about when to follow your own ideas and when to conform. To **conform** is to follow the customs, rules, or standards of a group. Some conformity is needed for life and society to run smoothly. At other times **individuality**, or something that distinguishes a person, is acceptable and even preferable. Knowing what action to take in any given situation takes good judgment. At Kellen's office, for example, men are required to wear ties. Kellen does not think wearing a tie affects his ability to do the job. He follows the rule because he values his job more than making an issue about the dress code.

Character develops when you recognize and live by positive values. Some people will tell you what they value, but their actions speak louder than their words. Do you have a clear set of guidelines or principles for your life? Use these steps to help you identify what is most important to you:

- Look at how you spent money in the last month. Purchases are one reflection of what you think is important.
- Keep a log of how you spend your time over a week. How do activities, and the time you spend on them, reflect your values?
- Think about your favorite leisure activities. What values are seen in these pastimes?
- Survey your possessions. Are the things you have a reflection of what is important to you?

- Consider your relationships. What do the people you spend time with say about your moral judgment?

Problem-Solving

Jessie manages a small business. Marcus, her newest employee, is a hardworking, cheerful young man. However, because he is a single parent, taking care of his young daughter keeps him from working certain hours or joining coworkers in some after-work activities. Some employees complain that Marcus is hard to get along with. They say he does not do his share of the work. Jessie sees no proof of this. She suspects they are acting out of prejudice. However, the business owner says to fire Marcus because he is bad for morale. What should Jessie do?

Self-Discipline

Self-discipline is the ability to direct your own behavior in a responsible way. Developing self-discipline is a strong sign of growth toward personal maturity. You show this trait when you resist negative temptations. You also show it when you stick to a difficult job until it is done.

Self-discipline is needed to work toward long-term goals. It may not be easy to give up today's pleasures for something you expect will happen in the future. Self-discipline today can bring rewards later.

Responsibility

The word responsible is often linked to maturity. When you are responsible, you are dependable. People know you will do as you say and complete the tasks assigned to you. Responsible people think about what their actions may cause. If something goes wrong, they accept their mistakes gracefully and follow up appropriately. They look out for other people as well as themselves.

Good Work Habits

Good work habits show at home, at school, on the job, and in your relationships. Taking care of your responsibilities is easier if you have formed good work habits. You can develop a system of good work habits with these ideas:

- **Decide what you want to accomplish.** You are more apt to be motivated if you set meaningful goals.
- **Make time to get things done.** Instead of saying, "I just do not have time," find the time.

- **Make deals to motivate yourself.** If you have several jobs, save your favorite for last. Promise yourself some kind of treat after finishing an unpleasant task.
- **Make lists.** Write down your plan for doing the work. Include the steps you need to take and the rewards you have set out for yourself after you complete the steps.
- **Tackle each task as if it were the most important.** Give a job your full attention and best effort, no matter how important it is.

Respect for Others

One mark of maturity is the willingness to appreciate others and respect their needs and feelings. You cannot do this if you are egocentric. **Egocentrism** is seeing life only from your own point of view. Children are naturally egocentric. Their reaction to a situation is: "How does this affect me? What will I gain or lose?"

As they grow, children start to see that they are not the center of the world. They learn to see what concerns other people and how they feel. As teens become more sensitive to others, they develop empathy. They move past egocentrism and toward social maturity.

Reject Prejudice

Respect for others means one does not put up with unfair judgments. An unfair or biased opinion is called **prejudice** ('pre-jə-dəs). Prejudice is often aimed at certain religious, political, racial, or ethnic groups. It is based on stereotypes. It is not based on knowledge and facts. Stereotypes thrive when people make assumptions about an entire group. To stop stereotypes, people need to get to know others as individuals.

Prejudice is a problem for society. Because of prejudicial attitudes, people are ignored, challenged, injured, and denied fair treatment. As you become aware of prejudice, you may uncover biases of your own. Confronting and working through these feelings is also part of social maturity. To help stop prejudice from spreading, you can:
- Point out the qualities that make people individuals.
- Speak out against name calling.
- Avoid conversations that put people down.
- Get involved with efforts to fight prejudice.

▶▶ **Respect** Including others in activities shows that you are mature and fair-minded. *What else does it say about you when you include others in your activities?*

▶▶ Learn from Mistakes Everyone makes mistakes, but we can learn from them. *How can you recognize a mistake and what can it teach you?*

Competence

People use many mental, emotional, and social skills in dealing with everyday life. Mature people have learned to use their skills competently, or effectively. With maturity, people recognize their own level of competence. They know when they have the ability to try something that could lead to success. They do not let pride and pressure lead them into situations they cannot handle. Mature people also know how to deal with success. They do not become overly confident, nor do they live in dread of failure.

Grow Through Mistakes

Even the most competent person makes mistakes. Using errors as a means of improvement is a mark of maturity. How can failure work for you? It can:

- **Educate.** You gain new information by discovering what does not work.
- **Push you in new directions.** You may work to improve skills or learn new ones.
- **Make you more realistic.** Failure can teach you what you can and cannot achieve. It can help you set a series of attainable goals to reach your final goal.
- **Give you freedom.** Having survived one failure, you feel freer to risk another. You know you can bounce back.
- **Bring others closer to you.** Supporting a friend through disappointment deepens the relationship and makes it more satisfying. It is harder to care about someone who rarely needs comforting.

Remember, or recall, that there is a world of difference between failing and being a failure. In this competitive world, everyone fails at something. Failures and mistakes are nothing to be ashamed of. They only mean that what you did was not effective. What counts is how you react. If you can accept what happened and learn from it, you can use any setback as a means to growth.

Keep Learning

Competent people need knowledge and skills. Mature people value knowledge and know where to find it. They can apply their knowledge to problem solving, decision making, and resource management.

Practical knowledge also is needed. For example, mature, independent people are able to choose nutritious foods. They have knowledge of other information that is useful for everyday living.

✓ **Reading Check** **Define** What is maturity?

A Philosophy of Life

You begin to develop a **philosophy of life** as you become a mature person. This is the sum of your beliefs, attitudes, values, and priorities. This philosophy affects the goals you work toward. It affects the personal traits you work toward and the way you treat others.

You may already have a philosophy of life without realizing it. Try listing your values and ask yourself which are most important. Write down your goals. Are they consistent with your values?

Think about the principles you follow. What things would you do? What would you avoid at all costs? When you can answer questions such as these, you are well on your way to understanding and developing your philosophy of life. You can then work to live by it.

One of the highest compliments you can give a person is, "You have real character." People with character act with maturity. Their code of ethics enables them to face life's challenges with confidence. Their personal philosophy of life guides them. Because of this, they are admired.

Life Skills CHECKLIST

Management Skills

Are You Mature? This checklist contains measures of maturity. You are mature if you:

✓ Accept responsibility for your mistakes.
✓ Accept what cannot be changed.
✓ Work to change what you believe needs changing.
✓ Control strong emotions if they are inappropriate.
✓ Remain open to other points of view.
✓ Can do a job well without praise from others.
✓ Keep your promises.
✓ Think for yourself.
✓ Are willing to put the needs of others first.

Section 19.2 After You Read

Review Key Concepts

1. **Explain** why some people never reach maturity.
2. **Define** philosophy of life.

Practice Academic Skills
English Language Arts

3. Select one of the qualities of maturity discussed in this section, such as independence, self-discipline, responsibility, good work habits, respect for others, or competence. In a short paragraph, describe three ways you can improve this quality in your life.

   NCTE 12 Use language to accomplish individual purposes.

4. Think of some people you know who have finished high school in the last year or two. Think about their maturity level. Do you think that most people, as they leave their teens, are mature enough to handle adult life? Explain your answer in a five-minute oral report to your class.

   NCTE 4 Use written language to communicate effectively.

Check Your Answers Check your answers at this book's Online Learning Center through glencoe.com.

CAREER SPOTLIGHT

Family and Consumer Sciences Teacher

Kendra Naef
Kimberly, Wisconsin

Kendra Naef's job as a Family and Consumer Sciences teacher involves working with high school students on a daily basis. She teaches students life skills such as money management, child development, nutrition, and food preparation. In addition to working with students in the classroom, Naef works with colleagues, administrators, parents, and members of the community.

Teaching is not a career for everyone. It can be exhausting and time-consuming. Those who are right for the job find that they do make a

difference in the lives of their students and their communities. FACS teachers know that they serve an important role in improving the lives of their students and their communities.

"I love the variety in my work," Naef says. "I enjoy daily interactions with students and leading them through the process of acquiring new knowledge and skills. I also thrive on providing students with real-world opportunities to make a difference in the lives of individuals, families, or their community."

CAREER FACTS

Education or Training Career requires a college degree with courses in communications, English, chemistry, or other sciences. Teaching jobs require state certification.

Nature of the Work Family and Consumer Science teachers teach subjects that can include child development, money management, grooming, consumer awareness, nutrition, menu planning, and food preparation.

Aptitudes, Abilities, and Skills Excellent communication skills are needed. Teachers must also have effective questioning skills to prompt student learning as well as to reflect on and refine teaching practices.

Academic Skills Required English Language Arts, Mathematics, Science, and Social Studies

Student Organizations To prepare for this career, look for student organizations involved in human services, such as FCCLA.

Career Outlook Jobs as teachers are expected to grow faster than average over the next ten years.

Career Path Careers may begin with teaching. Advanced degrees can lead to writing books and articles. Others may serve as advisers.

Critical Thinking

Help Others Why would someone considering this career need a strong desire to help and serve others?

 Research Careers For more information on this and other careers, visit the Occupational Outlook Handbook Web site through the link on this book's Online Learning Center at **glencoe.com**.

CHAPTER SUMMARY

Section 19.1
Moral Development

Morality is a system of conduct based on what is right and wrong. People learn morality first in the family. As they grow, they pass through three levels of moral development: pre-conventional, conventional, and post-conventional. Moral reasoning is dealing with moral issues by using logic and critical thinking. It leads to a code of ethics which is a clear set of principles that guide actions and decisions.

Section 19.2
Moving Toward Maturity

Maturity is full growth or development. It means having the qualities and traits needed for adult life, such as independence, self-discipline, and responsibility. It also means a person has a good work ethic. Respect for others and competence are also part of maturity. As you mature, you develop a philosophy of life. This is the sum of your beliefs and attitudes, as well as your values and priorities.

Content and Academic Vocabulary Review

1. Use each of these content and academic vocabulary words in a sentence.

Content Vocabulary

◇ morality (p. 371)
◇ character (p. 371)
◇ conscience (p. 371)
◇ pre-conventional level (p. 372)
◇ conventional level (p. 372)
◇ post-conventional level (p. 372)
◇ moral reasoning (p. 373)

◇ code of ethics (p. 374)
◇ mature (p. 376)
◇ maturity (p. 376)
◇ conform (p. 377)
◇ self-discipline (p. 378)
◇ egocentrism (p. 379)
◇ prejudice (p. 379)

◇ philosophy of life (p. 381)

Academic Vocabulary

■ thrive (p. 371)
■ understand (p. 371)
■ individuality (p. 377)
■ remember (p. 380)

Review Key Concepts

2. Summarize how morality develops in people.
3. Describe moral reasoning.
4. Explain what a code of ethics is.
5. Identify qualities that show maturity.
6. Determine what is needed to build a philosophy of life.

Critical Thinking

7. Analyze Do you believe an egocentric person can respect others? Explain your answer.
8. Evaluate Schools and government agencies are public institutions. Should they play a role in shaping a society's values? Explain your answer.
9. Recognize Bias Two reports on the Internet described a riot. One report said the leader of the riot was hysterical and stopped a company's deliveries. The second report said the deliveries were stopped because the company unfairly fired an employee. Did both reports state the facts in an ethical and responsible way? Explain your answer.

Real-World Skills

Interpersonal Skills

10. Problem Solving James showed his sister the new camera he signed out from work to take pictures of his son's birthday party. His sister asked to use it to take photos for an art show she had entered. Write a paragraph about what James should do. Relate your answer to one of the stages of moral development.

Planning Skills

11. Work Ethic You have agreed to call area businesses. You are to ask them to donate items to the animal shelter, which is planning a fund-raising event. Write out a plan you can use to accomplish the job. The suggestions about good work habits on page 378 and 379 will help you make your plan.

Collaborative Skills

12. Code of Ethics Follow your teacher's instructions to form into groups. Develop a code of ethics for students in your school. What beliefs, values, and actions do you think are important for students? When you have completed your code, ask for your teacher's permission to post it in the classroom.

Self-Management Skills

13. Personal Standards Kent's French class reads French literature. Kent knows that some students cheat and use English translations. As a result, the others perform better in class. Kent's teacher said he needs to improve to keep his grade. Write a paragraph describing Kent's options and what the outcomes may be.

14. Identify Values Make a list of your values and an example of how you rely on your values in everyday life. Are these values the basis of your moral development and philosophy of life? If not, how can you change your life to more closely reflect your values?

15. Observe Watch adults interact with children or teens. Observe three examples of the adult teaching habits that promote maturity. What concepts were taught? Write a summary of the three examples.

16. Ethics at Work Follow your teacher's instructions to form into groups. Discuss how ethics and morality apply to the workplace. What shows ethical actions on the part of employers? Workers? Develop a list of ethical practices in the workplace.

17. Ethics Go to this book's Online Learning Center at **glencoe.com** to find **Web Links** for **Workplace Code of Ethics**. Read one of the company's codes. What behaviors are required or encouraged by the code? Does the code of ethics seem fair? Describe any changes you would make.

Additional Activities For additional activities, go to this book's Online Learning Center through **glencoe.com**.

Academic Skills

Mathematics

18. Calculate Fair Pay Your boss wants to present a report to a group that makes sure employees in your industry receive fair pay. He has asked you to calculate summary statistics of salaries. These statistics would include the range and the mean. The salaries are: $48,000, $41,000, $29,000, $48,000, and $32,000. Provide the statistics for your boss.

Math Concept **Summary Statistics** Summary statistics provide important information about a data set. They do this without listing the entire data set. The range is simply the highest number in a data set minus the lowest number in the set. The mean is the average of all the numbers in the data set.

Starting Hint: Calculate the range by subtracting the lowest number from the highest number. Calculate the mean by adding all of the salaries together. Then divide by the total number of salaries (5).

 For math help, go to the Math Appendix at the back of the book.

NCTM Problem Solving Build new mathematical knowledge through problem solving.

English Language Arts

19. Literature Recall a coming of age story you have read or heard. Choose one in which characters undergo an experience that helps them mature. In your own words, summarize the plot in a paragraph. Explain how the events and character's response to them aided that person's progress toward adulthood. Think about how the topics in this chapter relate to character's change.

NCTE 2 Read literature to build an understanding of the human experience.

Social Studies

20. Civil Rights Movement The civil rights movement in the United States grew out of racial prejudice and inequality. Research one of the leaders of the movement. What led that person to join it? What role did the person play? How did the person evaluate their experiences? Give a short oral report to your class summarizing your findings.

NCSS II.f Apply ideas of historical inquiry to analyze historical and contemporary developments, and to inform and evaluate actions concerning public policy issues.

STANDARDIZED TEST PRACTICE

ESSAY
Read the following prompt and then write a one-page essay in response to the prompt.

Test-Taking Tip Read, reread, and think about the essay question first. Then write a short outline with your main points. Make sure your outline addresses all the questions in the essay topic. Include your own original ideas, but support every major statement with specific facts and examples.

21. Businesses have an ethical responsibility to their employees. Describe the type of ethics you would look for in an employer. Explain why this is important to you.

CHAPTER 20

Support Your Community

Section 20.1
Citizenship

Section 20.2
Service to Others

 Explore the Photo
Citizens have responsibilities as well as rights. *In what ways can citizens participate in their community?*

Chapter Objectives

After completing this chapter, you will be able to:

- **Explain** the rights and responsibilities of citizens.
- **Suggest** ways that people can work to create the community they want.
- **Describe** the benefits of volunteer work.
- **Identify** opportunities for volunteering.

Writing Activity

Advertisement

Compassion People who feel compassion have a deep awareness of and sympathy for another person's needs. You can show compassion when you:

- Stop to help.
- Listen when others want to talk.
- Offer your resources to help those in need.
- Look for lasting solutions.
- Comfort others without regard to race, gender, faith, age, or nationality.

Write an advertisement to encourage compassion. Think of a situation when a volunteer showed compassion toward something or someone in the community. Include this in your ad to help encourage others to show compassion and volunteer.

Writing Tips To write an effective advertisement, follow these steps:

1. Select your audience.
2. Check that your ad draws interest and causes action.
3. Appeal to people's feelings, but be truthful.

Citizenship

Reading Guide

Before You Read

Think of an Example Look over the Key Concepts for this section. Think of an example of when you could use one of the concepts from the Key Concepts. Think of how this concept is important to your life.

Read to Learn
Key Concepts
- **Explain** the rights and responsibilities of citizens.
- **Suggest** ways that people can work to create the community they want.

Main Idea

Citizens have rights and responsibilities. Citizens who care about their communities work to respect property, control crime, care for the environment, and promote understanding.

Content Vocabulary

◇ citizenship
◇ ecology
◇ pollutant

 Graphic Organizer Go to this book's Online Learning Center at **glencoe.com** to print out this graphic organizer.

Academic Vocabulary

You will find these words in your reading and on your tests. Use the glossary to look up their definitions if necessary.
- ■ disastrous
- ■ produce

Graphic Organizer

As you read, look for the rights of citizenship. Use a chart like the one shown to help organize your information.

A Citizen's Rights		

Academic Standards •

 English Language Arts

NCTE 8 Use information resources to gather information and create and communicate knowledge.

NCTE 12 Use language to accomplish individual purposes.

NCTE *National Council of Teachers of English*
NCTM *National Council of Teachers of Mathematics*

NSES *National Science Education Standards*
NCSS *National Council of the Social Studies*

What Is Citizenship?

Citizenship is membership in a community that guarantees certain rights. It also comes with certain responsibilities. Citizenship usually refers to a person's position in a nation or other large community. A community can be a neighborhood, a workplace, or a school. It can also be a state. It survives and improves only if each person works to make it a better place for everyone. The role of citizen was given to you at birth. How you fill that role is up to you.

◆ Vocabulary
You can find definitions in the glossary at the back of this book.

Citizens' Rights

Being a citizen provides you with certain rights. In the United States, these are listed in the Bill of Rights. These are the first ten amendments to the U.S. Constitution. They provide the right to:
- Vote for government representatives.
- Express your opinion freely and publicly.
- Receive an education.
- Travel freely within the country.
- Receive a fair and speedy trial.
- Enjoy equal protection under the law, regardless of gender, race, or ethnic group.

▼ Good Citizens
Voting in all elections is one of the responsibilities of good citizens. *What are some other ways to participate in your government?*

Citizens' Responsibilities

The advantages of being a citizen are balanced by its responsibilities. When you assume the responsibilities of a citizen, you are assuring rights for yourself and for others. The most important duty of citizenship may be participation. This can be in community events. It may be in government. Those who are involved in their communities are often more satisfied with them. They are more apt to know how to work for solutions when problems arise.

When you think of citizen participation, you may think first of voting. Electing government officials is important. Accepting or rejecting laws are vital duties and rights. Your vote influences the quality of life for the community. This includes what your family pays in taxes and the availability of parks, museums, and other community resources. Government affects daily life. Your vote affects government.

Citizens also support the government by financial means. Taxes are the main source of income for governments. There are different kinds of taxes. These include sales, income, property, and gasoline taxes. There are also charge fees for licenses and services.

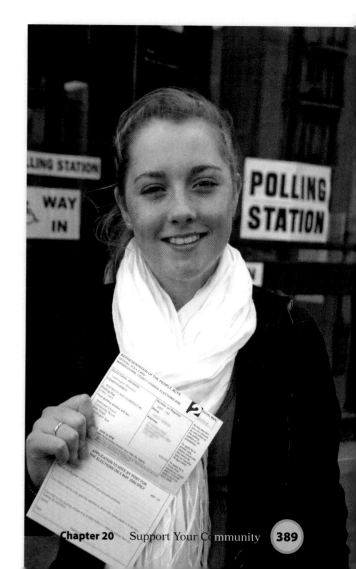

INDEPENDENT Living

A good citizen must get involved in his or her community. Follow these guidelines to practice citizenship:

1. **Do your share.** Offer to pitch in and help. Look for ways that you can lend a hand to family members, neighbors, teachers, and friends.
2. **Show respect for others.** Treat others as you would like to be treated. For example, wait your turn instead of trying to get to the front of the line. Speak respectfully to adults—including parents, grandparents, teachers, and police officers. Remember to show respect for everyone, not just people you know well or really like.
3. **Help other students.** Make new students feel comfortable and introduce them to other people. If someone holds different values than yours, be open and accepting. When you disagree with someone, give that person a fair chance to explain his or her opinion.
4. **Take care of shared property.** Treat shared property, such as library books, school books, or park equipment, as you would treat your own possessions. Then the next person will be able to use and enjoy them too.

Take Action Find community groups in your area. Attend a board meeting or read a record of the events. Then, write to one of your community leaders with a suggestion for a community project, such as a fund-raiser for the library.

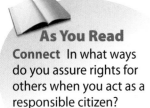

As You Read

Connect In what ways do you assure rights for others when you act as a responsible citizen?

Stay Informed

Citizens need information in order to vote wisely. They must know what issues affect their communities. One way to stay informed is through education. Schools teach skills that are needed to make good choices. Student government is a way to learn about making fair, workable laws for a community.

Most communities provide information to help citizens make wise choices. The media covers many issues. Most units of government have Web sites. Political leaders hold press conferences. Agencies hold public hearings on matters that they plan to act on. These hearings give citizens a chance to ask questions and voice concerns. Libraries and the Internet can help citizens learn more about issues.

Provide Leadership

Sometimes keeping informed and voting do not bring the results you want. Then you have the duty to get more involved. It takes a variety of skills to help communities reach their goals. Communities need leaders who can listen to all sides of the issues and make wise choices. Leaders must be able to manage and communicate well. There are often opposing points of view of societal issues.

Every community has elected positions where citizens can serve. Some of these positions are paid. They also have citizen boards and advisory groups where people can provide leadership. Most of these jobs are not paid positions. Anyone can learn what is happening in the community. You can attend board meetings or read accounts of the proceedings. You can write or talk to leaders. They are influenced by citizens.

✓ Reading Check **Identify** What is citizenship?

The Community You Create

People want to live in strong, happy communities. They want to be able to walk the streets safely. They want a clean and healthful environment. They want friends, not enemies. When people work to build up a community, they are less tolerant of those who tear it down. A feeling of pride and satisfaction comes from practicing good citizenship. It comes from contributing to the solutions instead of the problems.

A strong community helps build strong families. It provides a safe place to raise children. It has agencies that offer services to those in need. The laws and policies of the government affect people and families. It is due to the efforts of citizens and their leaders when these strengthen the family. The best communities help people and families meet their needs.

Respect Property

Respecting public property is a duty of citizenship. Just as your belongings are important to you, so do other people value theirs. You do not want your own possessions harmed. Neither does anyone else. Good citizens understand this. They work to ensure everyone's right to enjoy their own property. They take care of their possessions so they are positive assets in the community.

Real Life   Safety at Home

Discouraging crime starts at home. For safety at home, follow these suggestions:

- Keep entrances well lit at night.
- Lock doors and windows, especially when no one is home.
- Never hide a key under a mat or where it can be easily found.
- Do not allow shrubs to grow tall around entryways and windows.
- Never give out personal information to strangers.
- Keep expensive items in a safe place where they cannot tempt a thief.

Problem-Solving Vanessa overheard her brother Reggie on the phone. She heard him say, "Yes, that is our address. My parents will get home about six." When she asked who he was talking to, he said, "I don't know. Someone wanted to know if he had our address right and to talk to Mom or Dad." What should Vanessa say?

Clean up Your World Good citizens are aware of their responsibility to keep the environment clean. *In what ways do you think the efforts you make can help the environment?*

Control Crime

Good citizens understand that laws protect the rights of everyone in the community. Not breaking the law is the first step to controlling crime. You can help keep your neighborhood safe. Get to know your neighbors and their habits. Stay alert for unusual activities.

You may want to organize a neighborhood watch. This is where neighbors promise to look out for possible crimes. They help each other in emergencies. When crime occurs, your response can help keep it from happening again. Report illegal activity when you see it. Cooperate with police officers. Contact elected officials to tell them you support their efforts to catch and prosecute lawbreakers.

The key to controlling crime is involvement. Crime happens when people become afraid to get involved. Crime hurts everyone through:

- Higher taxes to hire more police.
- Higher prices to pay for stolen goods.
- Higher insurance costs to protect property.
- Less trust and more suspicion among citizens.

Good citizens do what they can to prevent these damaging outcomes. People need help when crime occurs. Hoping that someone else will do it can be **disastrous**, or cause great damage. A good citizen responds to an urgent need.

Care for the Environment

The quality of a community's environment depends on the people who live there. Those who act responsibly care for the environment. They care about its **ecology**. Ecology is the relationship of living things and their environment. People who care about the environment want to live in harmony with the environment. Their concerns may be for their local area or for the world as a whole.

To preserve the environment, you must begin by maintaining what exists. You can make a difference. Buy products with little packaging. Choose recycled products. Select items that you can reuse over ones that you throw away. Reuse disposable items as long as possible.

Responsible people help protect the environment. They conserve energy. Producing energy creates pollutants. A **pollutant** is an impurity in the environment. Turn off lights when they are not in use. Walk instead of driving. These are ways to save energy. Recycling helps too. It takes less energy to produce, or make, items from recycled material.

Environmental concerns such as global warming are worldwide. What happens in one place eventually affects others. It will take work to keep the world's benefits for future generations.

Promote Understanding

Business and education have grown increasingly international. You have more chances to contact a wider variety of people today than ever before. Your school, workplace, and community are becoming more diverse. They are made up of a number of different racial, ethnic, and social groups. Respect and understanding grow as you talk to people about their beliefs and customs.

Diversity may create different points of view in your community. As a citizen, it is your duty to make sure that everyone is heard. Government policies can respect the rights of all. Laws and policies should uphold the beliefs and traditions of all citizens.

In today's world, it is important to learn all you can about other cultures. Diversity is everywhere. The more you know, the more you can appreciate the differences among people. Make an effort to learn and to appreciate the diversity in your life.

Life Skills CHECKLIST

Communication Skills

Respect Property You demonstrate respect for the property of others when you:

✓ Ask permission before borrowing from others.

✓ Return other's property that you have borrowed.

✓ Save chewing gum and candy bar wrappers until you find a trash can.

✓ Organize a group to clean up the graffiti that was painted on a wall in your neighborhood.

✓ Lead your younger sibling away from the flowers he or she wants to pick from the neighbor's lawn.

✓ Avoid walking through the neighbor's yard even when you are late.

Section 20.1   After You Read

Review Key Concepts

1. **Identify** where the rights of United States citizens are listed.
2. **Explain** why it is important to respect both public and personal property.

Practice Academic Skills

English Language Arts

3. Our rights as citizens are listed in the Bill of Rights and other amendments. Did you know that these rights were not included in the original Constitution? Write a report that explains how the Constitution came to be amended by the Bill of Rights. Be sure to use proper grammar and sentence structure in your report. At the end of the report, list the sources of the information you used.

> **NCTE 8** Use information resources to gather information and create and communicate knowledge.

4. Do research to learn more about saving energy. Write a list of at least ten tips for saving energy. Select one tip that you can use. Write a paragraph that explains how you would carry out the tip and what its effect may be. Be sure to include specific examples of what you can do to carry out the tip.

> **NCTE 12** Use language to accomplish individual purposes.

Check Your Answers Check your answers at this book's Online Learning Center through glencoe.com.

Service to Others

Reading Guide

Before You Read

Buddy up for Success One advantage to sharing your notes with a buddy is that you can fill in gaps in each other's information. You can also compare notes before you start quizzing each other.

Read to Learn

Key Concepts

- **Describe** the benefits of volunteer work.
- **Identify** opportunities for volunteering.

Main Idea

Every community needs volunteers. Volunteers gain practical benefits as well as emotional rewards. Certain qualities are needed to volunteer successfully. There are many opportunities to volunteer.

Content Vocabulary

◇ volunteer   ◇ altruism

Academic Vocabulary

You will find these words in your reading and on your tests. Use the glossary to look up their definitions if necessary.

▪ generosity   ▪ obligation

Graphic Organizer

As you read, look for the benefits of being a volunteer. Use a list like the one shown to help organize your information.

Benefits of Volunteering
• _____   • _____
• _____   • _____
• _____

 Graphic Organizer Go to this book's Online Learning Center at **glencoe.com** to print out this graphic organizer.

Academic Standards ● ● ● ● ● ● ● ● ● ● ● ●

 English Language Arts

NCTE 6 Apply knowledge of language structure and conventions to discuss texts.

NCTE 7 Conduct research and gather, evaluate, and synthesize data to communicate discoveries.

 Mathematics

NCTM Number and Operations Understand numbers, ways of representing numbers, relationships among numbers, and number systems.

NCTE *National Council of Teachers of English*
NCTM *National Council of Teachers of Mathematics*

NSES *National Science Education Standards*
NCSS *National Council of the Social Studies*

Wanted: Volunteers

A **volunteer** is a person who gives unpaid help to others in the form of time, service, or skills. Has a volunteer ever helped you? They have if you have used a library or played on a sports team. If you have enjoyed events sponsored by youth programs, you have benefited from the giving of volunteers. Although not always obvious, volunteers are working in many parts of your community. Being a volunteer is one way to fulfill your responsibilities as a citizen.

Service to others is a part of a well-rounded life. Service involves **generosity**, or the act of giving, and unselfish kindness. It will give meaning to your life and help others as well. It strengthens you, your family, and your community. In contrast, when people act only in self-interest, society is weakened. Society is strong when people are willing to serve others.

The demand for volunteers always exceeds the supply. The mission of social service agencies is to help others. They work to serve and protect those who cannot help themselves. Often, they have too few funds for the many jobs that need to be accomplished. Meanwhile, the need for their services is growing. When economic times are tight, programs are cut because salaries cannot be paid. The answer? Find someone who will work without pay. Find a volunteer.

People Who Help

As more family members enter the workforce, fewer believe they have time for volunteer work. Retired people have filled some of the need. Many older adults find that volunteer work gives purpose and meaning to their lives. Longer life spans and better health let retired people give back to their communities through volunteer work.

Teens are an excellent volunteer resource. They have high levels of energy and spirit. They may have time to spare. Many want to do something useful with their time. The world of volunteering offers them plenty of opportunities for personal satisfaction.

Why Volunteer?

Every community has needs that are not met. There are many jobs left undone. Filling these needs through volunteer work is one of the best ways for citizens, and especially teens, to show commitment to their community. Some examples of volunteer work are shown in **Figure 20.1**. Most people know how important volunteers are to the groups they help. Fewer people realize how giving time and talent enriches the life of the volunteer.

Vocabulary

You can find definitions in the glossary at the back of this book.

As You Read

Connect How can volunteer work help you choose a career?

Financial Literacy

Calculate Donations

Many companies donate to charities. Some give back to the communities in which they operate their businesses. One company had $20 million in profits at the end of the year. It decided to give 15% of the money to projects to clean up the environment in their town. How much will the company donate?

Math Concept **Multiply Decimals by Whole Numbers** A percent is a ratio that compares a number to 100. To multiply with percentages see the starting hint.

Starting Hint: You can rewrite the percentage of money the company wants to give (15%) as a fraction. Make 15 the numerator with a denominator of 100. Convert the fraction to a decimal. Multiply this decimal by the amount of money the company made in profits ($20,000,000). Remember to put the decimal point in the correct place in your answer.

Math For math help, go to the Math Appendix at the back of the book.

NCTM Number and Operations Understand numbers, ways of representing numbers, relationships among numbers, and number systems.

Practical Benefits

Doing volunteer work allows you to practice current skills and learn new ones. You will enjoy the work more and do a better job if you choose a field where you feel confident. You may also expand your skills and knowledge into related areas. This can be a plus when going after future goals.

Career Exploration Imagine you are an artist who offered to help design an ad campaign for a charity's fund-raising drive. When you did this, you learned how to use a graphics program on the group's computer. Later, you used this skill as you worked toward your goal of becoming an architect. People who are undecided about their careers can learn what they may enjoy and be able to do by volunteering.

References When you volunteer, you meet many different people. This can be a bonus in a career hunt. New acquaintances can provide help. They can offer information about job openings and career choices. Often volunteers can list people they work with as references. These can be valuable additions on school, scholarship, and job applications.

Relationships Volunteering can help strengthen personal relationship skills. You can improve your leadership skills and ability to work with others. Volunteering can also help you learn to follow directions and communicate clearly.

Figure 20.1   Catch the Volunteering Spirit

The spirit of volunteerism is alive and well. Teens are pitching in to make a difference. *What volunteer opportunities are in your community?*

Care Animal shelters often have limited funds, so volunteers who care are needed.

Recycle Recycling helps reduce the amount of trash.

Beautify Parks and roadsides are improved when people work to beautify the area.

Another benefit of volunteering is that donating resources now can save other resources in the future. For example, Randall learned that many convicted criminals return to prison. This is partly due to the fact that they lack the reading and writing skills needed to get jobs. He became a tutor for a literacy program at a state prison. His work helped the inmates. It also, however, may have helped reduce the amount of tax money spent on returning the people to prison.

Emotional Rewards

Any volunteer work is a valuable experience. Learning new skills provides a feeling of personal growth and satisfaction. Working with others who share your concerns is a good way to make friends. As a volunteer, you may also come in contact with people you would not otherwise meet. These may be hungry or homeless people, or people who are simply lonely. These encounters can leave you with greater empathy and compassion for others.

Perhaps the greatest benefit to volunteers is the feeling of improving life for someone else. Volunteers often get to see the effects of their work. For example, Gil volunteers at his community's day camp for children from poor, urban neighborhoods. As he explained, "I see those kids eating a good lunch and playing. They are learning new things the way kids are supposed to. I know that I have made a positive difference in this world."

Read Wherever there are groups of children, volunteers are needed to read, teach, or play with them.

Help Volunteers in retirement homes provide help for older adults.

Support Many people need support from others just to get through the day.

The Qualities You Need

Volunteer work is much like a paying job, except that you do not receive a salary. When you volunteer, you make a commitment. Others count on you to be present and on time. They need your honest effort. To volunteer is to be entrusted with an important job. Letting down the organizers hurts them, your reputation, and the people you were going to serve.

Good work skills come in handy when you volunteer. Depending on your situation, you may need leadership skills or be able to work in a group. You may be needed for your technical skills and knowledge. You could be asked about the rules of a sport, how to use a computer, or the words of a nursery rhyme. As you volunteer, you are developing and refining your talents.

One trait shared by volunteers is altruism. **Altruism** ('al-trü-ˌi-zəm) is an unselfish concern for the welfare of others. Altruistic people are moved to help when they see a need. Altruism is a universally admired quality. Many well-known people display it.

✓ **Reading Check** **Define** What is a volunteer?

Be a Volunteer

There are many opportunities for volunteering. Anywhere that people need help, volunteers are welcome. Here are some examples of the places and organizations that need volunteers:

- Children's sports leagues may need volunteers to help referee a game, coach the children, or manage finances.
- Religious organizations depend on volunteers to organize many religious events.
- Music and theatre groups may need volunteers in the form of actors, musicians, clean up crews, stage managers, or people to help plan and organize the event.
- Libraries need the extra help of volunteers to keep materials looking new, shelves stocked, and customers informed.

◀) **Helping Others**
Caring for others requires special qualities. *What qualities do you have that would make you a good volunteer?*

Volunteer in Your Area

Many national charities may have local branches in your area. These branches often have openings for local volunteers. Some examples of national charities include the following:

- The American Red Cross offers a broad range of services to people, such as blood donation drives.
- Big Brothers/Big Sisters pairs up children from single-parent homes with adults who act as friends and role models.
- Habitat for Humanity helps low-income families find housing.
- The Salvation Army provides numerous services for the homeless, elderly, and others in need of aid.

To offer your services as a volunteer, first consider your interests. Think about your abilities. Figure how much time you are able to give. Then learn about the different groups in your area. Libraries often carry information that tells about these groups. Most groups have Web sites. To call a group directly, look in the telephone directory under social service organizations.

Local newspapers often have a listing of volunteer needs. Some larger communities have volunteer coordination services. They can tell you what groups exist and what kinds of help are wanted. While looking into your choices, persuade a friend to join you. You, your friend, and the organization will all reap the rewards.

Is volunteering a huge **obligation**, or something you have to do? Certainly you should take your duties to a group seriously. If you have the time, make a regular commitment of hours and energy. However, once you start to think like a volunteer, you can find little ways to serve in everyday life. Volunteering comes in many sizes. You can find choices that fit your life. All you need to do is say, "Yes, I would be glad to help."

Section 20.2 After You Read

Review Key Concepts

1. **Explain** why teens are often volunteers.
2. **Describe** how to find volunteer work that interests you.

Practice Academic Skills

English Language Arts

3. Check a dictionary for the origin of the word volunteer. What is its base word? In what language was it originally used? What is the date associated with the early use of the word? Why do you think this is important?

4. Find out more about one of the large national charities. What is its mission? What specific services does it provide? How is it funded? Does it rely on paid staff or volunteers? Write a paragraph to summarize your findings.

Check Your Answers Check your answers at this book's Online Learning Center through glencoe.com.

> **NCTE 6** Apply knowledge of language structure and conventions to discuss texts.

> **NCTE 7** Conduct research and gather, evaluate, and synthesize data to communicate discoveries.

CAREER SPOTLIGHT

Volunteer Coordinator

Erin Chernisky
Fairfax, Virginia

Erin Chernisky recruits volunteers for branches of her library system. She matches their skills and interests with the needs of the various branches. She also makes sure the volunteers receive proper training, and she makes sure they get recognition for a job well done.

Chernisky states, "I like that I get to work with different people throughout the community." She continues, "It is a great feeling to be part of a job that is constantly a win-win situation for both the volunteers and the library branches."

Volunteer coordinators need to have a creative eye for problem solving. The issues and needs that arise are often coming up for the first time. Figuring out how best to handle them involves out-of-the-box thinking. They also need to be extremely good with people of all types.

"Spending time volunteering in an agency that you think you might like to work for," according to Chernisky, "is a great way to get training for a career."

CAREER FACTS

Education or Training A degree is required. The degree can involve speaking and writing skills. Knowledge of government and the social studies is also helpful.

Nature of the Work Volunteer coordinators manage a network of people willing to devote their time and energy to a certain cause. They work to match volunteers with specific needs based on skills and availability.

Aptitudes, Abilities, and Skills Volunteer coordinators need to have strong communication skills. They also have to have strong organizational skills. They must be patient, persistent, and creative in their approach to solving problems.

Academic Skills Required Depending on what field the career is in, background in that field may be required. English Language Arts skills are needed.

Student Organizations To prepare for this career, look for groups that allow you to lead service programs and people who work on those programs, such as the Key Club.

Career Outlook Jobs as volunteer coordinators are expected to grow faster than average over the next ten years due to the growth of business.

Career Path Many volunteer coordinators work for hospitals, social service and government agencies, and nonprofit associations. With additional preparations, they may move into supervisory or administrative positions.

Critical Thinking

Recruitment Why would a library spend the money to have a full-time volunteer coordinator on staff?

 Research Careers For more information on this and other careers, visit the Occupational Outlook Handbook Web site through the link on this book's Online Learning Center at **glencoe.com**.

CHAPTER SUMMARY

Section 20.1
Citizenship

Citizenship is membership in a community. It guarantees certain rights. It comes with certain responsibilities. The rights of U.S. citizens are listed in the Constitution and its amendments. Participation is an important responsibility of citizens. Good citizens vote and stay informed. They participate by getting involved. Citizens also participate by providing leadership. People build the communities they want. They do this through their actions. Strong communities help families meet their needs. Citizens build strong communities when they respect property and control crime. They also do this when they care for the environment and promote understanding.

Section 20.2
Service to Others

Volunteers are people who give unpaid help to others in the form of time, service, or skills. Service to others is part of a well-rounded life. The demand for volunteers always exceeds the supply. Volunteer work is one way for citizens to show commitment to their community and care for others. One of the benefits to volunteers is improving life for others. Volunteers may practice skills and learn new ones. They meet a variety of people and may make new friends. Volunteers need to honor their commitment. They need good work skills. Every community has many opportunities to volunteer. Many national organizations also have opportunities for volunteers.

Content and Academic Vocabulary Review

1. Use each of these content and academic vocabulary words in a sentence.

Content Vocabulary
◇ citizenship (p. 389)
◇ ecology (p. 392)
◇ pollutant (p. 393)
◇ volunteer (p. 395)
◇ altruism (p. 398)

Academic Vocabulary
■ disastrous (p. 392)
■ produce (p. 393)
■ generosity (p. 395)
■ obligation (p. 399)

Review Key Concepts

2. Explain the rights and responsibilities of citizens.
3. Suggest ways that people can work to create the community they want.
4. Describe the benefits of volunteer work.
5. Identify opportunities for volunteering.

Critical Thinking

6. Cause and Effect How does failing to assume a responsibility result in losing a right? Give an example.
7. Analyze Why do people sometimes not want to volunteer? How might they be persuaded to participate? How might their attitude affect their experience?
8. Predict When people destroy public property, who is it that pays?
9. Compare In what ways is a successful community like a successful family?

Real-World Skills

Management Skills

10. Make a Plan Tammy has noticed trash piling up in a vacant lot in her neighborhood. Motorists sometimes toss fast-food wrappers and cups from car windows. Bags of garbage appear overnight. Write a plan that describes what Tammy can do.

Communication Skills

11. Interview Talk to a member of a local volunteer group. Learn about its function. Find out about its opportunities for teens. Share this information with the class. Put together a class list of volunteer opportunities.

Research Skills

12. Corporate Volunteer Programs Some businesses encourage their workers to do volunteer work. Find out about some of these volunteer programs. What are the benefits of these programs? What do employees do? Write a short report on your findings.

Problem-Solving Skills

13. Take Action Deke read in the paper that only 11 percent of local voters turned out to elect school board members. He thinks this is disgraceful and more people should be involved. Write a paragraph describing what Deke can do.

14. Recycling The U.S. Environmental Protection Agency reports that in 2005 each person in the country created 4.5 pounds of waste each day. For one day, keep a list of what you put in the trash and what you recycle. List and describe at least two actions you could take that would help you reduce waste on a long-term basis.

15. Citizen Responsibilities Find out what the procedures in your state are to register to vote. What documents are required? When can registration be done? Create a flyer that lists the steps to take to register to vote in your state.

16. Trash and the Environment Find out where the garbage produced by your community is taken. Is it put in a landfill? When will the landfill be full? Are there alternative methods of disposal available or in planning? Write a brief news article to present the information you collect.

17. Cost of Crime Go to this book's Online Learning Center at **glencoe.com** to find **Web Links** for **The Cost of Crime**. What are the various costs of crime? What kinds of costs are associated with the criminal justice system? What is the cost of loss of life and work? What kinds of costs are associated with crime prevention? Present your information in a chart.

Additional Activities For additional activities, go to this book's Online Learning Center through **glencoe.com**.

Academic Skills

Mathematics

18. Calculate Time Sam will participate in a running event to help raise money for new trees to be planted in town. Yesterday, he went to the track near his house and ran one mile. The track is exactly one quarter of a mile in length. His split times for each lap were as follows (in minutes and seconds): 2:05, 1:53, 2:03, and 1:49. How long did it take Sam to run one mile?

Math Concept **Adding up Time** When you add time, remember that there are 60 seconds in a minute and 60 minutes in an hour. Carry a number when the ten seconds place or the ten minutes place reaches six.

Starting Hint: Add the times, remembering to carry a one to the minutes place when the ten seconds place reaches six.

 For math help, go to the Math Appendix at the back of the book.

> **NCTM Number and Operations** Understand numbers, ways of representing numbers, relationships among numbers, and number systems.

English Language Arts

19. Citizen Input Write a letter to a government representative. This can be someone in your local community or at the national level. Identify a problem that you believe this person can help solve. Describe the problem. Give examples of the problem and what the effects of the problem are. Explain what you would like to see done as a solution to this problem.

> **NCTE 12** Use language to accomplish individual purposes.

Social Studies

20. Voting Records Contact the local election office to find out how many registered voters live in your precinct, or district. How many of them voted in the last election? What percentage of registered voters actually voted? Do you think this is an acceptable percentage? Why or why not? Write a paragraph to explain the information you find.

> **NCSS X.c** Locate, access, analyze, organize, synthesize, evaluate, and apply information about selected public issues.

STANDARDIZED TEST PRACTICE

MULTIPLE CHOICE
Read the following question, and then choose the appropriate answer.

21. Which of the following is not a characteristic of a good citizen?

> **Test-Taking Tip** Look for negative words such as *not* and *no* in multiple-choice questions. These words can be easily missed but can change the entire meaning of a sentence.

a. They stay informed and participate in the community.
b. They work to protect the local world and the environment.
c. They care for their own property and the property of others.
d. They spend all of their free time on favorite pastimes and have no time left to volunteer.

Thematic Project

Discover Citizenship

In this unit you have learned about the importance of self-awareness in developing a positive attitude and good self-esteem. You have also learned that demonstrating citizenship is a key factor in your personal development. In this project, you will volunteer in your community. You will use what you learn to create a collage that illustrates the way your experience affected you.

My Journal

If you completed the journal entry from page 330, refer to it to see if your thoughts have changed after reading the unit.

Project Assignment

- Choose a volunteer opportunity.
- Write a paragraph describing how you think you may feel about volunteering.
- Volunteer at the establishment that you chose.
- Bring a pencil and paper to take notes about your experience. You may also want to bring a camera to take photos for your collage.
- Use your notes, photos, or other materials to create a collage that expresses your feelings about your day.
- Present the collage to your class. Explain why you chose certain pictures to represent your experience.

Academic Skills You Will Use

English Language Arts

NCTE 5 Use different writing process elements to communicate effectively.

NCTE 9 Develop an understanding of diversity in language use across cultures.

STEP 1 Choose an Opportunity that Interests You

The ideas below are examples of volunteer opportunities in your community. Choose one of the opportunities for your volunteer experience. If you think of an opportunity not on this list, check with your teacher before choosing that opportunity.

- Homeless shelter
- Literacy program
- Humane society
- Community clean-up
- Hospital visits
- Local government
- Food bank
- Elder care

STEP 2 Write a Paragraph

Write a paragraph that describes your feelings about your upcoming volunteer experience. Think about the eight basic emotions from Chapter 17: fear, surprise, sadness, disgust, anger, anticipation, joy, and acceptance.

Writing Skills

- Use complete sentences.
- Use correct paragraph structure.
- Clearly express your feelings.
- Use correct spelling and grammar.
- Write concisely (briefly but completely).

STEP 3 Connect to Your Community

Volunteer at the establishment you chose in Step 1. Bring a notebook and pencil to write down observations and feelings about your experience. Be sure to pay attention to the differences and similarities between what you thought you might feel, as expressed in your paragraph, and how you actually feel while doing your volunteer work. Make notes of anything that surprises you, and any interesting people you meet. You may also want to bring a camera to take photos during your experience.

Leadership Skills
- Take initiative.
- Manage your time.
- Listen to instructions.
- Ask questions whenever necessary.
- Ask for feedback.

STEP 4 Create and Present Your Collage

Use the Unit Thematic Project Checklist on the right to plan and create your collage and make your presentation.

STEP 5 Evaluate Your Presentation

Your project will be evaluated based on:
- Content of your paragraph.
- Completeness, organization, and creativity of your collage.
- Mechanics—presentation and neatness.

Evaluation Rubric Go to this book's Online Learning Center at glencoe.com for a rubric you can use to evaluate your final project.

Unit Thematic Project Checklist

Collage	✓ Use photos, pictures from magazines and newspapers, or drawings to create a collage that illustrates your feelings after you have volunteered. ✓ Organize your collage to tell a story of your experience. ✓ Use the eight basic emotions from Chapter 17 to guide your visual choices.
Presentation	✓ Make a presentation to your class to share your collage and discuss what you learned. ✓ Invite the students in your class to ask you any questions they may have. Answer three questions. ✓ When students ask you questions, demonstrate in your answers that you respect their perspectives. ✓ Turn in your paragraph, notes, and your collage to your teacher.
Academic Skills	✓ Communicate effectively. ✓ Speak clearly and concisely. ✓ Be sensitive to the needs of different audiences. ✓ Use effective organizational strategies when creating your collage.

Unit 6

Move Toward Independence

Unit

Thematic Project Preview
Learn for Life

After completing this unit, you will learn that becoming an independent adult means being responsible for many areas of your life. In your unit thematic project, you will show the importance of continuing your education throughout your life.

My Journal

Career Choices Write a journal entry about one of the topics below. This will help you prepare for the unit project at the end of the unit.

- Imagine yourself ten years from now and describe your life.
- Explain which is more important to you in a job: a high salary or a light workload.
- List ten aspects of a job that would be important to you.

Explore the Photo
Having independence in aspects of your life, such as your health and thinking about your career options, can start now. *In what ways do you feel you are independent?*

CHAPTER 21

On Your Own

● **Section 21.1**

Move Away from Home

● **Section 21.2**

Manage on Your Own

▶▶ *Explore the Photo* You may soon be living on your own. *What are you looking forward to and what are you unsure of as you move toward independence?*

Chapter Objectives

After completing this chapter, you will be able to:

- **Describe** the rewards and challenges of independence.
- **Identify** housing options when living on your own.
- **Determine** the kinds of decisions that must be made when living independently.
- **Explain** why the purchase, storage, and preparation of food are important skills.
- **Suggest** guidelines for the purchase and care of clothing.
- **Summarize** factors that influence why people may choose life as a single.

Writing Activity

Personal Narrative

Self-Reliance Self-reliance is when you meet responsibilities with minimal help from others. You can be self-reliant when you:

- Buy clothes with money from a part-time job.
- Follow safety rules when the car breaks down on the highway.
- Use a personal checking account responsibly.
- Go to bed early to be alert in the morning.
- Arrange for transportation to school and activities.

You can be self-reliant now. Self-reliance is also useful when you live on your own. Write a personal narrative about how the self-reliance you have now will help you when you are on your own.

Writing Tips To write a personal narrative, follow these steps:

1. Test your ideas by talking them through or by freewriting.
2. Ask yourself questions to fill out details of the narrative.
3. Construct a time line or other graphic organizer for your narrative.

Move Away from Home

Reading Guide

Before You Read

How Can You Improve? Before starting the section, think about the last exam you took on material you had to read. Make a list of ways to improve your reading strategies in order to succeed on your next exam.

Read to Learn

Key Concepts
- **Describe** the rewards and challenges of independence.
- **Identify** housing options when living on your own.

Main Idea

When people live on their own, they are responsible for their own lives. Many young adults live in apartments, either alone or with others. Some live on their own and then move back home.

Content Vocabulary

◇ security deposit   ◇ landlord
◇ lease   ◇ tenant

 Graphic Organizer Go to this book's Online Learning Center at glencoe.com to print out this graphic organizer.

Academic Vocabulary

You will find these words in your reading and on your tests. Use the glossary to look up their definitions if necessary.

■ venture   ■ décor

Graphic Organizer

As you read, think of seven questions you could consider when looking for an apartment that will best meet your needs. Use a figure like the one shown to help organize your information.

What to Look for in an Apartment
1.
2.
3.
4.
5.
6.
7.

Academic Standards . . . .

📖 English Language Arts

NCTE 3 Apply strategies to interpret texts.

NCTE 4 Use written language to communicate effectively.

Mathematics

NCTM Number and Operations Understand numbers, ways of representing numbers, relationships among numbers, and number systems.

NCTE *National Council of Teachers of English*
NCTM *National Council of Teachers of Mathematics*

NSES *National Science Education Standards*
NCSS *National Council of the Social Studies*

Choose Independence

Does the phrase "on your own" fill you with excitement, anxiety, or some of both? Mixed emotions are a normal response to the thought of leaving home. Living on your own is a milestone in growth toward maturity. You assume responsibility for managing your life. You are the one preparing meals, handling finances, taking care of personal safety, and much more. You will have many adjustments to make as you take on the duties of living on your own.

When you are on your own, you will make choices and explore new options that let you learn more about yourself. You continue to shape your identity as you discover it. This practical and emotional independence offers great rewards and risks. It also brings satisfaction and frustration. It is all waiting for you.

If you are like many young adults, you may delay the move awhile. Living on your own can be costly. Some people see the advantages of staying at home for a few years after completing their education. They work and save money until they can better afford the style of living that they want. People today are waiting longer to marry. Those who would have left home to start their own families are now staying at their parents' home. Some young adults still want the support and closeness of their families. **Figure 21.1** shows the percentage of young adults who are living at home.

The best time to move out on your own depends on you and your plans after high school. Will you join the working world? Do you plan to attend college or get other training? Perhaps you will join the military. The option you choose will affect your decision. There is no set time for moving out that is right for everyone. You must support yourself financially and take on the responsibilities of adult living. You will need to make the adjustment from child to adult. When you are ready, you will be eager to make the move.

✓ **Reading Check** **Explain** What are the advantages of living at home as a young adult?

As You Read

Connect What does the phrase "on your own" mean to you?

| Figure 21.1 | Young Adults at Home |

Many young adults live with their parents rather than on their own. *What are some reasons you think young people might choose to live at home?*

Age of Young Adult	Percent of Males Living at Home	Percent of Females Living at Home
18–24 Years	53	46
25–34 Years	13.5	8.1

Select Housing

Your first big challenge after deciding to leave one home is to find a new one. Across the life span, people and families must find housing that meets their needs. They need to be able to take care of the physical needs of family members. Families want to feel safe at home. They have emotional and social needs that housing can help fill. Family members with special needs will have specific housing needs. For example, someone in a wheelchair cannot use stairs, and doorways may need to be widened to fit the wheelchair. These needs must be taken into account when making choices about housing.

Decision making plays a large role. At any age, using the decision-making process will help people make wise choices when selecting housing. Options can vary from the rental of single rooms to the purchase of large homes.

Families need to decide what they can afford. Experts suggest that 30 to 35 percent of take-home income can be spent on housing. This includes rent, utilities, maintenance, and furnishings. There are government housing programs that can help families that have trouble paying for housing.

As a teen, your choices are somewhat easier than those of a family. Your housing options may depend on what you do. If you attend a college or university for example, some may require students to live on campus for the first year or two. Those entering the military often live in barracks. Young adults in other settings have other options.

Apartment Living

Apartment living is the choice for many young adults. An apartment can offer privacy and freedom from housing maintenance. Finding an apartment can be an interesting **venture**, or risk. Newspapers and the Internet have listings of apartments for rent. You can also check rental agencies and real estate companies for additional properties.

Rent an Apartment

What do you look for when choosing an apartment? First you need to know whether you can afford the place. In addition, most rental agreements require a **security deposit**. This is a one-time payment often equal to one month's rent. The deposit is returned to you when you move out if you have not damaged the apartment. Otherwise, the cost of any needed repairs is deducted from the amount. Sometimes the initial payment includes the first and last months' rent in addition to the security deposit. The rent may include utilities. If not, ask what the average cost of utilities is for the apartment.

▲ A Place of Your Own When looking for your first place to live, you have many decisions to think about. *What would be your main needs in finding a place of your own?*

◆ Vocabulary

You can find definitions in the glossary at the back of this book.

Find out what the terms are for the lease. A **lease** is a written agreement between the landlord and the tenant. The **landlord** is the property owner. The **tenant** is the renter. The lease states the rights and responsibilities of each person. It is important to get these conditions in writing.

Inspect the apartment before signing the lease. Does it look and smell clean? Is everything in good repair? Find out what, if any, furnishings are provided. Many apartments are equipped with larger appliances, such as a refrigerator and a range.

Check the safety of the apartment. What are the locks on the doors and windows like? Is any additional security provided? How safe is the neighborhood in general? Consider whether the location will be convenient for you. Is it near places you go frequently? If not, you may need to add transportation costs to your expenses.

You may have other concerns as well. For example, if you have pets, you will need to check if they are allowed. What parking and laundry facilities are available? You may want to make a checklist of the features you consider most important in an apartment.

You may have trouble finding the ideal apartment. This is especially true if your income is limited. Still, making an effort to find the best apartment available is time well spent.

Furnish Your Apartment

Have you ever thought about all the furnishings in your home that you use? There are larger pieces such as a couch, bed, and television. You also need smaller items such as towels, sheets, and kitchen supplies. One of the challenges of life on your own is outfitting your apartment to suit your needs and tastes. This is often done on a tight budget.

Most first-time apartment dwellers gather items from a number of sources. Friends and family members may offer linens, tables, lamps, or kitchen supplies they do not need or use anymore. Otherwise, check out thrift or discount stores, garage sales, online auctions, or classified ads.

Furnishing your apartment will most likely take time. You will need to think about how your furnishings can meet your needs. You can use the elements and principles of good design in your **décor**, or style and layout of your furnishings. The way you furnish your first home can show your creativity and resourcefulness.

In addition to furnishing your apartment, you need to keep your place clean and maintained. A regular schedule of cleaning and maintenance will help you keep things in good order. This will work to your advantage when you move out of the apartment and want a refund on your security deposit.

Financial Literacy

The Cost of Renting an Apartment

Toni is trying to decide whether she would rather live in the downtown area of the city or in a suburb. She is comparing rent costs to help make her decision. She found a one-bedroom apartment downtown that rents for $600. She found a one-bedroom apartment in the suburbs that rents for 75% of the cost of the downtown apartment. What is the rent of the apartment in the suburbs?

Math Concept **Multiplying by Percents** To determine the cost of the apartment in the suburbs, multiply the cost of the apartment in the downtown area by 75%.

Starting Hint: To multiply by a percent, you must change the percent to a decimal. To do this, move the decimal point two places to the left. In this problem, 75% becomes .75, which you will multiply by $600.

 For math help, go to the Math Appendix at the back of the book.

NCTM Number and Operations Understand numbers, ways of representing numbers, relationships among numbers, and number systems.

INDEPENDENT Living

HOW TO   Furnish Your Living Space

The way you decorate your home is a reflection of who you are. Follow these guidelines to furnish your living space:

1. **Consider the residents.** Think about the needs of the people who live in the home. Are there little children who may damage breakable objects? Does anyone have a physical disability that needs to be accounted for?
2. **Consider the house itself.** Think about the space you are working with. If it is small, limit the amount of items you buy. If it is a large, open space, you may need screens or room dividers. If it has no overhead light, you will need floor and table lamps.
3. **Invest wisely.** Furniture is usually accumulated gradually since it is expensive. Set priorities for what is most important to buy first. To stretch your budget, you can buy pieces that serve more than one need. For instance, you can put a sofa bed in the living room for overnight guests, or use your kitchen table as a place to pay bills.
4. **Reflect your personality.** There are endless possibilities for home accessories. No matter what you choose, these personal touches give a room personality and tell your guests something about you. It does not matter whether the objects are sophisticated or simple, elegant or rustic. What matters is that they mean a lot to you.
5. **Take care of your possessions.** It is important to take good care of your furniture and accessories. Do not let that hard work go to waste by neglecting your possessions.

Take Action Create a How to Decorate book for yourself. Research information on interior design. Write down five to ten rules of thumb for decorating, based on what you have learned. Cut out pictures from interior design magazines, or print pictures from the Internet of room designs you like. Paste them in your book, for future reference.

Live with Others

Renting an apartment is one option for independent living. Renting a room in a private home is another. This option can be helpful to both parties, especially when the homeowner is an older person. You might get lower rent in exchange for helping with housework.

Young adults often cut costs by living with a roommate. Sharing an apartment or a house with a roommate or two has benefits. It is usually less costly than living alone. Many people enjoy having a companion. As with any relationship, communication and cooperation make it work.

Before roommates begin sharing space, they should decide how to divide expenses. They need a plan to share household tasks. They can set up guidelines for behavior and privacy. A good attitude can prevent potential conflict. Sharing life with a roommate can be an opportunity for growth.

Move Back Home

Many young adults, after living on their own awhile, decide to move back to their parent's home. This may happen when a college student finishes school, or returns from the military. For some, it is difficult to meet all of their expenses when living on their own. Others may decide they need more guidance or better skills to handle independence. Some people move home to recover from the stress and pain of divorce. A lengthy illness or disabling injury can send people home for physical and financial healing. Moving back home works best if the young adult has a clear-cut need for help.

When young adults move back home, all family members will find that their roles and relationships have changed. Clear communication about duties is important. Everyone needs to know what is expected. All members should agree on who is responsible for which household expenses and chores.

It helps if the return is temporary. It also helps if it is a one-time event. Adjustments and compromise will be needed for both the young adults and the family members still at home.

A move back home is more apt to be successful if the adult child gets along well with his or her parents. It helps if the adult child pays rent or contributes to the household in some way. This can include household chores, such as yard work or cooking. Being cheerful and responsible can prevent many problems.

Very few people live permanently with their parents. Moving back home usually lasts until the young adults get their bearings, emotionally or financially. Then it is time to start out on their own again.

Section 21.1   After You Read

Review Key Concepts

1. **Describe** the emotional response people often have when moving away from home.
2. **Explain** what a lease is.

Practice Academic Skills

English Language Arts

3. List some of the pluses and minuses of living in a group setting. The setting can include a college dorm or military barracks. After you complete your list, write a paragraph to describe how you would feel about living in a group setting. Also explain why you would feel this way.

   NCTE 4 Use written language to communicate effectively.

4. Obtain an example of an apartment lease. Read and summarize the main points of the lease. What are the rights and responsibilities of the landlord? What are the rights and responsibilities of the tenant? Can the landlord or tenant break the lease? If so, under what circumstances?

   NCTE 3 Apply strategies to interpret texts.

   Check Your Answers Check your answers at this book's Online Learning Center through **glencoe.com**.

Manage on Your Own

Reading Guide

Before You Read

Get Your Rest The better rested you are when you study, the more likely you will be to remember the information later. Studying in the same state of mind as when you take a test helps ensure your best performance.

Read to Learn
Key Concepts
- **Determine** the kinds of decisions that must be made when living independently.
- **Explain** why the purchase, storage, and preparation of food are important skills.
- **Suggest** guidelines for the purchase and care of clothing.
- **Summarize** factors that influence why people may choose life as a single.

Main Idea
There are many decisions to make when living on your own. Management skills are used in the purchase and preparation of food, and in the care and purchase of clothing. Some people like the single lifestyle.

Content Vocabulary
◇ autonomy
◇ pathogen
◇ cross contamination

Academic Vocabulary
You will find these words in your reading and on your tests. Use the glossary to look up their definitions if necessary.
- create
- analyze

Graphic Organizer
As you read, look for ways to handle fresh meat safely. Use a figure like the one shown to help organize your information.

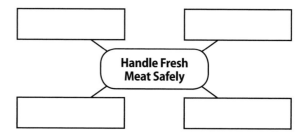

Handle Fresh Meat Safely

 Graphic Organizer Go to this book's Online Learning Center at **glencoe.com** to print out this graphic organizer.

Academic Standards · · · · · · · · · · · · · · · · ·
 English Language Arts

NCTE 4 Use written language to communicate effectively.

NCTE 12 Use language to accomplish individual purposes.

NCTE *National Council of Teachers of English*
NCTM *National Council of Teachers of Mathematics*

NSES *National Science Education Standards*
NCSS *National Council of the Social Studies*

Make Important Decisions

Every day, independent adults plan for and manage all parts of their lives. They have many choices to make. Such choices are part of **autonomy**. This is the ability to direct your life independently. For singles, autonomy can be rewarding. When you live on your own, you can choose your own lifestyle. These choices will depend on where you live, the amount of money you earn, and your values and beliefs. For the first time, you will be able to decide exactly how you want to live.

There are many choices to make as you begin to manage on your own. One of the most important choices is how you will manage your money. Single adults are usually their own source of income. They are also their own money managers. They need to make sure their bills are paid accurately and on time. They decide whether remaining money is saved or spent. They rely on their own values and priorities when making these choices. You will learn more about managing your money in Chapter 23.

You will need to make decisions about your personal safety when you are on your own as well. Teens often believe that they will be safe no matter where they live. They can be careless and act in ways that may put them in personal danger. Single adults learn that they need to take care of themselves as part of their autonomy.

Transportation is another issue that requires decision making when you are on your own. Many young adults who live at home have access to a car. They may use the family car or share rides with friends when they need transportation. When they move out, however, getting from one place to another can test their resourcefulness. A single person may have to buy a car, use public transportation, ride a bicycle, or walk. The decisions you make in this area will affect how you manage your time, money, and energy.

✓ Reading Check **Define** What is autonomy?

◆ Vocabulary

You can find definitions in the glossary at the back of this book.

As You Read

Connect What will be your highest and lowest priorities in managing your money?

▶ Manage Your Money One of the most important decisions you make when living on your own is how to manage your money. *What are some needs you will have to budget for?*

As a single adult living alone, you will need to be aware of your personal safety. These guidelines can help:

- Make sure your home's doors and windows have reliable locks.
- If you suspect someone has broken into your home, leave immediately. If you do not have a cell phone with you, call the police from a neighbor's phone.
- Know your neighbors. Recognizing those who live nearby will help you identify strangers. It will also give you someone to turn to if you need help.
- Be familiar with your surroundings. Notice anyone or anything that seems unusual or out of place.

- If you are out after dark, walk and park your car in well-lit areas. Lock your car when you leave it and have your keys ready in your hands when you return.
- If you think you are being followed, go to a well-lit place where there are people. Report the incident to the police.
- Tell the police if you often receive odd or disturbing phone calls or many wrong numbers.

Problem-Solving Toby sees lots of strangers in his neighborhood. This makes him uncomfortable. But because he just moved in, he is not sure whether the strangers are really his neighbors. What should Toby do?

Food Management

Good health starts with healthful eating. When you live on your own, you will be responsible for what you eat. You will have to shop for and store food, and prepare your own meals as well. Each of these areas requires management skills. You will need to plan how you want to manage each of these areas before you begin.

Purchasing Food

The amount of money spent on food varies from family to family and person to person. People select food because of likes and dislikes. Choices may be made based on nutrition and health. Food allergies may affect what they buy. Some religions have rules about diet. The amount of food needed may vary as well, depending on the number of people in the household. Individuals and families, regardless of the reason for their choices, need to consider the funds available when they shop for food. Up to a point, the more money a person has, the more they are able to spend on food.

Figure out how much money you are able to spend on food. How many meals do you need to cover with the cash you have? With that in mind, plan some menus. If you have some idea of what food costs, you will be better able to match your menus to the amount of money you have to spend.

Next, make a list of foods used in your menus. This will help you get what you need and control your spending as you shop. It is easy to overspend at the grocery store. Food is attractively displayed and arranged to encourage you to buy. It is tempting to buy your favorite things without regard for cost. A list can help you use self-discipline at the grocery store so you buy just what you need.

As you shop, look for quality products. Fruits and vegetables should be clean and free of spots and blemishes. Meat and deli products should be refrigerated and look fresh. Check sell-by dates to be sure of freshness. Look at labels to see how nutritious foods are. Focus on fruits and vegetables and whole grain products for healthful eating.

Food Safety

Food safety is often overlooked. How food is stored, handled, and prepared can mean the difference between health and illness. There are many illnesses that can be caused by food that has not been stored or cooked properly. One key to good health is to be sure to wash surfaces and hands often while you are handling food.

When you are shopping and storing food, be sure to keep fresh meat separate from other groceries. Uncooked meat is a source of a disease-causing organism called a **pathogen**. Avoid **cross contamination**, which means moving pathogens from one food to another. Be sure to wash your hands and equipment with hot, soapy water after touching any raw meat. Do not touch other food or reuse the equipment until you have washed. Any food that has touched raw meat should be cooked or thrown away.

Food Preparation

Frequently purchasing take-out or prepared foods is too costly for most people. Snacks and eating out are also not healthful or budget-friendly options. Young adults need food preparation skills. You can start simply, with a few easy, healthful dishes. If you enjoy cooking, you may want to learn more complex recipes. Learning to cook well helps save time and energy in food preparation. Processed foods also help save time and energy. They are often less healthful than foods made with fresh ingredients, so these foods should be chosen carefully.

Cooking can be a way to express yourself. Eating should be a pleasure for your taste buds, as well as your other senses. You can use design elements and principles to make your food attractive. Food presentation is one way to show your creativity.

✓ Reading Check **Identify** What are two benefits of using a list when shopping for food?

►► *Gourmet Chef*
Cooking can be an enjoyable experience where you can be creative. *How would you go about preparing your favorite home-cooked foods?*

Clothing Management

Clothing is an important part of everyday living. It protects the body from the elements. It is also a means of personal expression. Clothing is a way to communicate nonverbally. What does your clothing say about you?

Across the life span, clothing needs differ. Children's clothing needs to be sturdy and durable. Teens are often interested in trendy, fashionable clothing. Adults may select more classic designs. Older adults may want comfort and ease of dressing. When people purchase clothing, it should suit the needs of the one who will be wearing it.

Clothing affects a person's comfort in many ways. Clothing should be physically comfortable. It should not restrict movements or be too tight. Clothing can give psychological comfort. You feel good when you know you look good. Social comfort comes when your clothing lets you fit in with others in a group. Managing your clothing needs means choosing garments that will help you become comfortable in all settings.

Learning basic sewing skills can be rewarding. **Figure 21.2** shows some of the skills that can help you **create**, or design, clothing. These skills will also help you alter or repair clothing. When you can sew, you have a chance to make exactly what you want. This also allows you to show your creativity and flair.

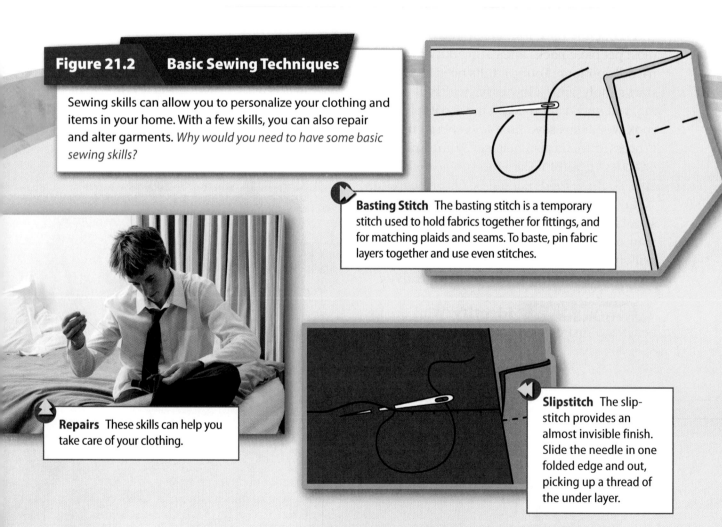

Figure 21.2   Basic Sewing Techniques

Sewing skills can allow you to personalize your clothing and items in your home. With a few skills, you can also repair and alter garments. *Why would you need to have some basic sewing skills?*

Basting Stitch The basting stitch is a temporary stitch used to hold fabrics together for fittings, and for matching plaids and seams. To baste, pin fabric layers together and use even stitches.

Repairs These skills can help you take care of your clothing.

Slipstitch The slipstitch provides an almost invisible finish. Slide the needle in one folded edge and out, picking up a thread of the under layer.

Purchase Clothing

You do not have to spend a lot of money on clothing to dress well. Select garments that are well designed. Consider the elements and principles of design when you shop. Look for quality fabrics that will not fray or tear easily. A well-made garment is sewn with even stitching, enough width in seams and hems, and smooth zippers or buttonholes.

Before you shop for clothing, **analyze**, or examine closely, the clothing you already have. Figure out what other garments you will need. Set a realistic, but flexible, amount of money to spend.

Clothing Care

Take care of clothing so it lasts. Garments that last longer are replaced less often. In the long run, taking care of your clothing saves you money. Promptly treat stains. Do small repairs before they turn into major problems. Clean garments according to the care instructions. Store them properly.

Before laundering, zip zippers and hook hooks. Turn clothing inside out to prevent rubbing and wear on the outside of the garments. Use the right water temperature for the color and type of clothing. Do not over-dry clothing. Fold or hang garments as soon as they come out of the dryer.

✓ **Reading Check** **Explain** How do clothing needs differ across a person's life span?

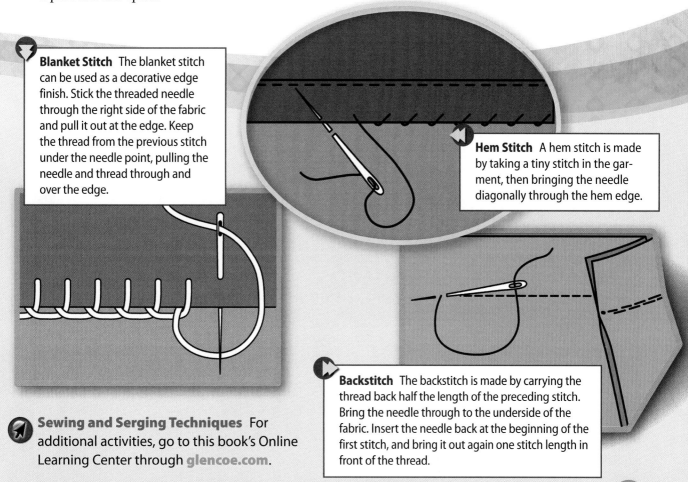

Blanket Stitch The blanket stitch can be used as a decorative edge finish. Stick the threaded needle through the right side of the fabric and pull it out at the edge. Keep the thread from the previous stitch under the needle point, pulling the needle and thread through and over the edge.

Hem Stitch A hem stitch is made by taking a tiny stitch in the garment, then bringing the needle diagonally through the hem edge.

Backstitch The backstitch is made by carrying the thread back half the length of the preceding stitch. Bring the needle through to the underside of the fabric. Insert the needle back at the beginning of the first stitch, and bring it out again one stitch length in front of the thread.

Sewing and Serging Techniques For additional activities, go to this book's Online Learning Center through glencoe.com.

The Single Life

People are attracted to the single life because of the opportunities for personal growth. Without a spouse or children, singles are free to commit more fully to a career. They may pursue volunteer work, travel, or more education. There can be time for friends and family. Singles may engage in hobbies and attend social events. When it comes to creating a pleasing home environment, they can furnish the home and prepare the foods they enjoy. These are decisions on which couples and parents often must compromise.

Getting to know others is not always easy for singles. Some places for meeting people include volunteer groups, work, theatre and musical groups, sports activities, and religious-based groups. The kind of life you choose will be based on your values and your heritage. Your experiences with family members and others will also influence the way you live.

Some people enjoy the freedom and independence of the single life. They are in control of their time and money. They may not want the responsibilities of a family. Still, those who remain single throughout their lives are only a small part of the population. Most people look forward to marriage and family life some day. They want the closeness and support families provide.

Finding a way of life in which you feel comfortable and confident is the challenge and opportunity of living on your own. It means successfully managing all areas of your life. The more you know now, the better you can use your time to prepare.

Section 21.2   After You Read

Review Key Concepts

1. **Identify** three areas of life that an autonomous person must handle alone.
2. **Explain** how to select fresh, nutritious products when shopping for food.
3. **Describe** three steps to take before shopping for clothing.
4. **List** places where singles can meet others.

Practice Academic Skills

English Language Arts

5. Many people believe that young adults today expect too much too soon. Compared to previous generations, they want more in terms of finances, housing, clothing, and transportation. Do you agree? If so, is this trend necessarily negative? Explain your answers.

6. Write two paragraphs to explain your plans for living on your own. The first paragraph should tell where you expect to live after high school and why. The second should describe what skills you will need to live successfully in that setting and how you could develop those skills.

> **NCTE 4** Use written language to communicate effectively.

> **NCTE 12** Use language to accomplish individual purposes.

Check Your Answers Check your answers at this book's Online Learning Center through **glencoe.com**.

CHAPTER SUMMARY

Section 21.1
Move Away from Home

Teens often approach living on their own with mixed emotions. If they are attending college or going into the military, they may live in dormitories or barracks. Many young adults rent apartments. Finding a good apartment means knowing what you want. It also means knowing what you can afford. You must evaluate each one you look at carefully. There will probably be a lease and a security deposit. Furnishing an apartment is a way to show creativity and resourcefulness. Roommates need to communicate and cooperate to successfully share a home. Many young adults move home after living on their own.

Section 21.2
Manage on Your Own

There are many important decisions to make when living on your own. These choices are part of being autonomous. They include decisions about money, safety, and transportation. Food management is a part of daily life. It involves planning, purchasing, storing, and preparing food. Food safety is important to prevent illness. Clothing is a means of expressing yourself. Clothing management involves purchasing and caring for clothing. Some people enjoy the benefits of living as a single. These include making their own choices about money and time. They enjoy the chance for personal growth.

Content and Academic Vocabulary Review

1. Use each of these content and academic vocabulary words in a sentence.

Content Vocabulary
◇ security deposit (p. 412)
◇ lease (p. 413)
◇ landlord (p. 413)
◇ tenant (p. 413)
◇ autonomy (p. 417)
◇ pathogen (p. 419)
◇ cross-contamination (p. 419)

Academic Vocabulary
■ venture (p. 412)
■ décor (p. 413)
■ create (p. 420)
■ analyze (p. 421)

Review Key Concepts

2. **Describe** the rewards and challenges of independence.
3. **Identify** housing options when living on your own.
4. **Determine** the kinds of decisions that must be made when living independently.
5. **Explain** why the purchase, storage, and preparation of food are important skills.
6. **Suggest** guidelines for the purchase and care of clothing.
7. **Summarize** factors that influence why people may choose life as a single.

Critical Thinking

8. **Recognize Stereotypes** Some people think that those who choose to stay single are selfish and trying to avoid responsibility. Do you agree? Explain your answer.
9. **Analyze** Moving back home works best if the adult child has a clear-cut need for help. Why do you think this is so?

Real-World Skills

Critical Thinking Skills

10. Analyze Look at ads in magazines and newspapers that show some aspect of single living. What products seem aimed at single people? How are their lives depicted? Make notes of your findings. Describe for your class the image of life as a single that you found.

Problem-Solving Skills

11. Build Relationships Roman, age 22, lives with his parents. He works full-time, pays rent, and does chores. Roman's parents worry because he does not have a lot of friends. They think he will make more friends if he finds his own place. Write a letter offering Roman advice about what to do.

Self-Management Skills

12. Rate Your Skills Make a list of responsibilities involved in living on your own. Using a scale of one (lowest) to ten (highest), rate yourself on how well you think you would handle each one. Write a short paragraph explaining whether you feel ready for independence.

Decision-Making Skills

13. Personal Safety Candy works and goes to school part-time. She cannot afford a car. Public transportation is not convenient, so Candy rides a bike. When the weather turned cold, a neighbor she does not know well offered her a ride. Write a list of things Candy should do before accepting a ride from the neighbor.

14. Evaluate Your Wardrobe Try on all of your clothes. Put your clothing into three piles. The first pile is clothes you like that fit well. The second pile is clothes that fit but need cleaning or mending. Take care of these garments. The third pile is clothes that do not fit, are outdated, or worn out. Discard or donate these items. Write a report of your wardrobe evaluation. What surprised you most about this activity?

15. Investigate Find out what kinds of government programs for housing are available in your state. What are the requirements for each program? Write about your findings in a one-page report.

16. Cookbook Have each person in your class locate an easy recipe that would be appealing to a young adult. Create an On Your Own Cookbook of the recipes. If possible, prepare some of the recipes.

17. Housing Needs People with special needs often have problems finding housing that meets their needs. Go to this book's Online Learning Center at **glencoe.com** to find **Web Links** for **Housing Features**. Find features that meet these needs. Write a summary of your findings.

Additional Activities For additional activities, go to this book's Online Learning Center through **glencoe.com**.

Academic Skills

Mathematics

18. Compare Housing Costs Raji is currently paying $675 a month to lease a one-bedroom apartment. The cost of all utilities is included in the rent. He is thinking about renting a house with his friend, Jon. The monthly rent for the house is $900, not including utilities. Utilities will total an extra $300 a month. Raji and Jon have agreed to split all costs evenly. Calculate how much the move would save or cost Raji each month.

 Solve Multi-Step Problems with Money Solving word problems sometimes requires several mathematical steps. Read the situation described carefully in order to figure out what the steps should be.

Starting Hint: First, find how much Raji will pay each month sharing the house with Jon [($900 + $300) ÷ 2]. Then subtract this from Raji's current cost of rent to find the difference between the two costs.

 For math help, go to the Math Appendix at the back of the book.

> **NCTM Problem Solving** Solve problems that arise in mathematics and in other contexts.

English Language Arts

19. Create a Brochure Do research to learn more about food safety. Create a brochure that explains why food safety is important to teens. Give specific guidelines for handling food safely and checking the sell-by date on products. Include information on keeping kitchen surfaces clean and throwing away items that have been in the refrigerator too long.

> **NCTE 8** Use information resources to gather information and create and communicate knowledge.

Social Studies

20. Investigate Find out what your local and state laws are for renters' rights and responsibilities. What are tenants' options if they have a disagreement with their landlord? What are the landlord's rights if a tenant does not keep the lease agreement? Present your findings in a table similar to the following:

	Rights	**Responsibilities**
Tenant		
Landlord		

> **NCSS X.b** Identify, analyze, interpret, and evaluate sources and examples of citizens' rights and responsibilities.

STANDARDIZED TEST PRACTICE

TRUE/FALSE
Read the following statement and determine whether it is true or false.

> **Test-Taking Tip** When taking a test, if you have time at the end, check your answers. Did you answer each part of every question? Did you answer the questions asked? Do your answers look reasonable?

21. The single life is most rewarding if you develop a way of life that fits you and your values.
a. True
b. False

CHAPTER 22

Health and Wellness

Section 22.1

Learn About Wellness

Section 22.2

Positive Health Habits

 Explore the Photo

Your personal choices for health and wellness can prevent illness and protect your health. *What good choices have you made to ensure your wellness?*

Chapter Objectives

After completing this chapter, you will be able to:

- **Describe** the role of personal choice in wellness.
- **Identify** actions you can take to promote wellness.
- **Summarize** positive habits that contribute to good health.
- **Suggest** personal and community resources for health and wellness.

Writing Activity

Purpose and Audience

Self-Respect Self-respect means valuing yourself as a person. You care enough about yourself to do and be your best. It also means avoiding what could hurt you. You can show self-respect when you:

- Exercise daily to take good physical care of your body.
- Take a walk to release anger and stress constructively.
- Join a school club to help overcome shyness.
- Make the decision not to use harmful drugs.
- Practice a skill daily to develop a talent.

Write a one-page paper that will show your knowledge of self-respect. When writing this paper, keep in mind your purpose and audience.

Writing Tips To write for a specific purpose and audience, follow these steps:

1. Determine if your purpose is to inform, persuade, entertain, or describe.
2. Consider what style of writing is suitable for your audience.
3. Think about the background of your audience and how familiar they will be with your topic.

Learn About Wellness

Reading Guide

Before You Read

Use Color As you read this section, try using different colored pens to take notes. This can help you learn new material and study for tests. You could use red for vocabulary words, blue for explanations, and green for examples.

Read to Learn
Key Concepts
- **Describe** the role of personal choice in wellness.
- **Identify** actions you can take to promote wellness.

Main Idea
Over the years, wellness has improved due to medical advances and care. Personal choices about wellness affect health and disease. There are many ways to work toward personal wellness.

Content Vocabulary
◇ wellness
◇ preventive medicine
◇ antibiotic
◇ laparoscope
◇ obesity
◇ cardiovascular disease

Academic Vocabulary
You will find these words in your reading and on your tests. Use the glossary to look up their definitions if necessary.
▪ organize   ▪ contagious

Graphic Organizer
As you read, look for four diseases that are linked to lifestyle choices. Use a chart like the one shown to help organize your information.

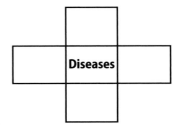

 Graphic Organizer Go to this book's Online Learning Center at **glencoe.com** to print out this graphic organizer.

Academic Standards . . . .

🌐 English Language Arts

NCTE 2 Read literature to build an understanding of the human experience.

NCTE 4 Use written language to communicate effectively.

NCTE *National Council of Teachers of English*
NCTM *National Council of Teachers of Mathematics*

NSES *National Science Education Standards*
NCSS *National Council of the Social Studies*

What Is Wellness?

Wellness is a positive state of physical and mental health. It is more than just the lack of disease or sickness. It is an optimal state of health. A pledge to wellness means you have made a choice to live in a way that promotes good health. You can prevent many health problems by choosing wellness.

Your behavior changes when you have the right attitude toward health. For example, you can take charge of having good health habits. You can find ways that health experts suggest to stay healthy. Then you can make these actions part of your routine. This is part of **preventive medicine**, which is behavior that serves to deter or avoid disease or an adverse condition.

Wellness pays. When you are healthy, you not only look and feel good, you feel good about yourself. You also save money. Health care is costly. A serious illness can create thousands of dollars in bills. Many illnesses can be prevented when people make good choices related to their health. No one else can make these choices for you.

Improvements in Health

Overall, people today are healthier across the life span than they have ever been. There are several reasons for this. Vaccines have helped reduce the rate of many illnesses, such as measles, that were common in the past. An **antibiotic** is a special medicine that destroys disease-causing bacteria. It is the main treatment for many diseases and infections.

New ways of doing surgery have improved health. Many surgeries can be done using a **laparoscope**. This is a tiny telescope that lets the surgeon see inside the body. Only small incisions need to be made to do the surgery. It is also usually less painful and has a faster healing time. Organ transplants and joint replacements have improved the quality of life for many people as well.

Improvements in medical care affect everyone from premature babies to older adults. Better health means longer lives. This is mainly because of better health care.

The overall standard of living today has also had an impact on people's health. With better housing and sanitation, people enjoy healthier lives. In general, this standard of living allows people to have more money to spend on health care.

Vocabulary
You can find definitions in the glossary at the back of this book.

As You Read
Connect How does wellness save money?

▶▶ *Take Charge* You can take charge of your wellness by choosing healthful habits. *What are some ways you can take charge of your health?*

Personal Choices About Health

The overall level of health may be better than what it used to be, but not everyone enjoys good health. Serious illnesses today include heart disease, cancer, and stroke. Another major health problem is obesity. **Obesity** means being more than 30 percent over the ideal body weight. It is linked to heart disease and diabetes.

A **cardiovascular** (ˌkär-dē-ō-ˈvas-kyə-lər) **disease** is a heart-related disease. Examples can include strokes and high blood pressure. They are the leading cause of death in the United States. Smoking and poor eating habits are linked to heart diseases. Stress and lack of exercise also are factors. Cancer is the second leading cause of death in the United States. Many kinds of cancer are linked to smoking.

Personal choices can affect many of these diseases. Sometimes they are called lifestyle diseases. For instance, eating habits can cause obesity. Lack of exercise and a poor diet can lead to heart disease. Smoking has been linked to lung cancer as well as heart disease. Lifestyle choices can have a direct impact on your health.

You cannot control everything that affects your health. Some health conditions, such as heart disease and diabetes, run in families. Due to heredity, the chances of getting the disease go up. Certain diseases are more common in one gender than the other.

That does not mean, however, that good health habits are not needed. People may have a family history of a certain illness. For them, good health practices may be even more vital to reduce the risk of developing the disease. If you can, find out about your family's health history. This will give you helpful data about possible health problems.

Another factor is money. People who have lower incomes tend to have more health problems. They may not eat as well, or they may lack needed health care. In this case, people must use resources carefully to stay in good health.

▶▶ **Choose Exercise**
Exercise is one personal choice you can make to prevent getting many lifestyle diseases. *What lifestyle diseases might exercise prevent?*

A support group is a gathering of people who share a common condition or interest. A support group can help people:

- Make connections so they feel less alone.
- Give and receive emotional support.
- Find new coping skills.
- Be motivated to stick to a treatment or a health plan.

Many support groups focus on health and wellness issues. Some groups deal with specific diseases such as diabetes. Others focus on weight loss or exercise. When you find a support group, attend a few meetings to see how you like it. If you are uncomfortable or the group is not useful, try another one.

Problem-Solving

Monique knows she needs to lose weight. She has tried several diets without much success. The local hospital is starting a weight-loss support group led by a nurse. Monique is considering joining it. She does not know if the group will help her. She also knows she will be embarrassed in front of others to admit she cannot lose weight on her own. What should Monique do?

The Role of Mental Health

To be well, your mental health is as important as your physical health. Stress, crises, and other mental strains affect the body. They can cause both physical and mental illnesses. Physical illness from stress may include nausea or even a stroke. About half of those who seek treatment have physical illnesses directly related to stress.

To deal with mental health issues, look at how you manage your life. Review what you have learned about setting priorities and time management. Look at how you **organize**, or plan and arrange, your time and activities. Both relaxation and exercise help relieve stress. When tension and nervous energy are controlled, you improve your physical health as well.

When you have support from others, it helps keep emotions and stress under control. Family and friends can help when you have problems. Joining a support group is a way to find understanding and help from others.

✓ **Reading Check** **Describe** What is wellness? How does wellness affect both physical health and mental health?

Work Toward Wellness

Wellness is not just a personal issue. A person's health affects their entire family. Health care costs impact the money a family has for other expenses. For example, if a person has costly medical bills, their family may not be able to afford family activities. Family events may also be limited when a member has a disabling illness.

Health and wellness also affect a community. Healthy people are needed to work and volunteer. There are many costs to society when people are ill or disabled. There may be direct costs when government programs pay for health care. A person who is unable to work is not paying taxes. This is an indirect cost to society.

Wellness Tips

The personal decisions you make about health can have a ripple effect in your family and society. Your decisions can affect relationships. They may also affect work. When people work to be healthy and fit, they benefit others as well as themselves. The following ideas can help as you aim for wellness:

- **Practice cleanliness.** Washing your hands several times a day with soap can prevent many **contagious** illnesses. These are illnesses that are spread by direct contact.
- **Get regular dental and medical checkups.** Health problems are more easily managed when discovered early.
- **Gain knowledge.** You can locate Web sites, books, television programs, and magazines that will keep you up-to-date on new developments in health.
- **Be wary of false information.** You will hear about many treatments and programs that may be inaccurate. Find out the facts.
- **Surround yourself with people who will support you.** School clubs and religious groups are good places to start.
- **Choose your own path to wellness.** If people close to you have poor habits, you do not have to follow them.

When it comes to wellness, you are in charge of following good health habits. Nothing comes with guarantees. You have a better chance for good health when you practice wellness.

Section 22.1 After You Read

Review Key Concepts

1. **Identify** some of the improvements in health care that help people enjoy good health today. Include at least one type of medicine, one surgical technique, and one other improvement in your answer.
2. **Explain** why regular dental and medical checkups are important for people at all age levels.

Practice Academic Skills

English Language Arts

3. Write a paragraph describing the role of wellness in your life. What habits do you have that promote wellness? Which of those habits promote physical wellness? Which habits promote mental wellness? What could you do better to improve wellness?

    NCTE 4 Use written language to communicate effectively.

4. Recall an article in a magazine or on a Web site you have read about a lifestyle disease. Summarize the article. Compare the information in the article to what you have learned about lifestyle diseases. What are the qualifications of the article's author? Do you think the information in the article is trustworthy? Explain.

    NCTE 2 Read literature to build an understanding of the human experience.

Check Your Answers Check your answers at this book's Online Learning Center through glencoe.com.

Positive Health Habits

Reading Guide

Before You Read

Study with a Buddy It can be difficult to review your own notes and quiz yourself on what you have just read. According to research, studying with a partner for just twelve minutes can help you study better.

Read to Learn
Key Concepts
- **Summarize** positive habits that contribute to good health.
- **Suggest** personal and community resources for health and wellness.

Main Idea

It takes planning and management to work toward wellness. It is important to eat right, exercise, get enough sleep, and reject harmful drugs. There are personal and community resources for health and fitness.

Content Vocabulary

◇ anorexia nervosa
◇ bulimia
◇ compulsive eating
◇ immunity
◇ endurance

◇ aerobic exercise
◇ strength
◇ flexibility
◇ sleep deprivation

Academic Vocabulary

You will find these words in your reading and on your tests. Use the glossary to look up their definitions if necessary.

☐ diet   ☐ induce

Graphic Organizer

As you read, look for nutrition guidelines that will help you eat right. Use a figure like the one shown to help organize your information.

Follow MyPyramid Guidelines

To Do for Good Nutrition

Graphic Organizer Go to this book's Online Learning Center at **glencoe.com** to print out this graphic organizer.

Academic Standards . . . .

English Language Arts

NCTE 4 Use written language to communicate effectively.

NCTE 12 Use language to accomplish individual purposes.

Mathematics

NCTM Number and Operations Understand numbers, ways of representing numbers, relationships among numbers, and number systems.

NCTE *National Council of Teachers of English*
NCTM *National Council of Teachers of Mathematics*

NSES *National Science Education Standards*
NCSS *National Council of the Social Studies*

Plan for Good Health

As You Read

Connect Why do you think healthy habits take effort on your part?

Healthy habits do not happen by accident. It takes planning and management to make them happen. Most healthy habits take effort. They need to be scheduled into a busy life. Effective time management is needed. You will need to plan when to exercise, get enough sleep, and make nutritious meals and snacks. Value your health enough to make the effort to build positive health habits.

You may need to improve in several areas as you work toward good health. You will be more successful if you work on your goal in small steps. You may want to focus first on healthful eating. When you have made improvements in that area, you can make a plan to increase your activity or exercise. With each success, you will be ready to make more improvements.

Families need to focus on health and wellness. In some families, there is not enough money for good health care. In such families, it becomes more important to work on good health. If someone in the family is disabled, those who care for that person need to stay well. Family members who stay healthy and fit are better able to cope with their life problems.

Vocabulary

You can find definitions in the glossary at the back of this book.

Eat Right

A good **diet**, or food and drink that you consume, while you are young helps you grow and develop normally. Throughout your life, good nutrition will remain vital to wellness. Eating right can help fight heart disease, weight problems, diabetes, and some types of cancer.

The eating patterns of family members have a major impact on health across the life span. Children who learn healthful eating patterns and habits are apt to continue them as adults. Eat three balanced meals a day. Breakfast is the most important meal of the day. It provides fuel for your morning activities. Each meal should contain healthful foods from each of the food groups. Choose healthful snacks when eating between meals. As you plan menus for yourself and your family, make sure your choices meet the nutritional needs of family members. When you eat out, make healthful choices from the menu.

A poorly nourished body has a lower resistance to illnesses. It takes longer to heal when injured. A poor diet can lead to tooth decay. Do you know anyone who has a hard time focusing or is irritable? The reason may be because of a poor diet.

Plan for Healthful Family Meals This family has planned ahead to cook a healthful meal. *What are some ways you can plan to be healthy?*

How do your current eating habits rate? Here are some basic nutrition guidelines to help you stay healthy:

- Follow the MyPyramid shown in **Figure 22.1**. You need the recommended number of food servings each day.
- Learn about serving size. Follow the guidelines.
- Study good nutrition. Find out your nutrient and calorie needs.
- Read the labels on food packages. Learn what the nutritional information means.
- Eat regular meals instead of grabbing sugary or salty snacks.
- Avoid sugary foods and soft drinks.
- Limit sodium and fats by eating fewer fried foods and fatty meats. Most fast food is high in both fat and salt. It should be eaten in moderation.

Maintain a Healthy Weight

Weight management is an important part of health and wellness. Excess weight is a common cause of many diseases. High blood pressure, arthritis, heart disease, and diabetes are more apt to strike those who are overweight. Being underweight may not be healthy either. It can weaken the body and make fighting off illness harder.

For the best health, your weight should fall within the range shown for your gender and height in current, standard weight tables. Consult your physician before developing a plan to gain or lose weight.

Figure 22.1 MyPyramid

Choose a variety of foods each day, including the recommended number of servings from each group. *Where do your favorite foods fit in the pyramid?*

| Grains Make half your grains whole. | | Vegetables Vary your veggies. | | Fruits Focus on fruits. | Oils | Milk Get your calcium-rich foods. | Meat & Beans Go lean with protein. |

Know the limits on fats, sugars, and salt.

Food Groups	Female 14–17 years	Male 14 years	Male 15 years	Male 16–17 years
Grains	6 ounces	8 ounces	9 ounces	10 ounces
Vegetables	2.5 cups	3 cups	3.5 cups	3.5 cups
Fruits	2 cups	2 cups	2 cups	2.5 cups
Milk	3 cups	3 cups	3 cups	3 cups
Meat & Beans	5.5 ounces	6.5 ounces	6.5 ounces	7 ounces

Eating Disorders

Eating disorders are mental problems related to food and eating. They result in abnormal eating behaviors. Often these disorders are about issues of power and control. Stress and crisis may also be involved. The teen years are a time of high risk for eating disorders. In most cases, professional help is needed to overcome these problems.

Anorexia nervosa (ˌa-nə-ˈrek-sē-ə (ˌ)nər-ˈvō-sə) is a disorder that shows itself in a fear of being overweight. It affects more females than males. The person refuses to eat enough to maintain a healthy body weight. He or she over-controls the body. This mental illness can cause death. Patients must often be hospitalized for treatment.

Bulimia (bü-ˈlē-mē-ə) is an eating disorder that involves binge eating. A person who has bulimia eats huge amounts of food in a short period of time. Then the person will **induce**, or cause, themselves to vomit. It can lead to an unhealthy body weight. It causes damage to the teeth and esophagus from vomiting.

Compulsive eating is a disorder in which people are unable to resist food. They cannot stop eating. It is a lack of control over eating habits. The cause is often emotional distress. Compulsive eating plays a major role in obesity.

INDEPENDENT *Living*

HOW TO Choose Nutritious Restaurant Meals

Calories add up when you dine out regularly. But you can make healthful selections almost anywhere. The menu and your choices, not the restaurant type, determine the nutrition in your meal. Follow these guidelines to make nutritious food choices when dining out:

1. **Get information.** For wise choices, learn about the type of food the restaurant serves. In addition, you should be familiar with menu terms such as appetizer, entrée, and side dish. This will help you understand the portion size of the meal.

2. **Include nutrition and variety in your order.** Fast-food meals are often limited in whole grains, vegetables, and fruits. For more nutrition, order sandwiches on whole wheat bread, choose salad or a vegetable side dish, and have fruit for dessert.

3. **Order on the light side.** Pay attention to the way foods are prepared. Stay healthy by avoiding fried foods and limiting heavy cheeses and sugary desserts.

4. **Keep portions small.** Restaurant portions are often large. To lower calories, ask for a half-portion or split an order with a friend. You may also choose to order an appetizer and side dish for your meal, instead of an entrée.

Take Action Look at menus from local restaurants. Choose a wide variety of types, such as gourmet and fast food, and determine which are the healthiest menu choices for each restaurant. Using these various menus, make healthy choices for every meal of the day. Include breakfast, lunch, dinner, and a snack.

Exercise

Exercise helps keep your heart strong. It keeps your muscles toned, your lungs working well, and your blood circulating smoothly. Nutrients and oxygen can move more easily to all parts of your body. If you exercise regularly, you are likely to feel better. You will have more energy. Your immunity increases. **Immunity** is a condition of being able to resist a particular disease. Without exercise, your muscles, including your heart, weaken. Your breathing becomes shallower.

Types of Exercise

The length of time you are able to work or exercise is called your **endurance**. You build endurance through **aerobic** (ˌer-'ō-bik) **exercise**. This is strenuous activity that raises the heart rate. It increases the amount of oxygen taken into the lungs. Walking, swimming, jogging, and cycling are great ways to build endurance. Experts suggest at least thirty minutes of aerobic exercise three to four times a week.

Your ability to apply force is known as **strength**. Strength training is also called weight training. It builds strong muscles and bones. It also helps prevent the loss of muscle that occurs with age. Machines are available to strengthen all the major muscle groups. You may find them in schools and health clubs. Weights and stretchy bands are also used and can be bought at lower costs.

With **flexibility**, you are able to move your muscles to a great extent, sometimes to their fullest extent. Stretching exercises promote flexibility. They help keep muscles long and limber. Stretching helps muscles relax. Short, tight muscles cause stiffness and pain. When you stretch, gradually increase the stretch without straining the muscles. Hold for 10 to 15 seconds. Bouncing while you stretch tends to cause small tears in your muscles.

You do not need to work on all three areas every time you exercise. Alternating exercises allows muscles to rest. It may prevent you from becoming bored. Always warm up first. This prevents injury. Before beginning any exercise program, you should see your doctor. Adding more exercise to everyday activities, however, is generally safe and helpful.

Plan to Add Exercise

Where in your daily schedule can you include exercise? It may be easier than you think. The following exercise ideas can be added safely to your normal everyday activities:
- Use the stairs instead of an elevator or escalator.
- Walk instead of driving short distances.

Financial Literacy

Food Costs

You want to get the best value for your money on your food budget. Research the nutritional value and cost of several different foods to fill in the chart below. Then, evaluate the nutritional value and the cost of the foods you researched. Share your findings with your classmates.

	Snacks	Fast Food	Dining Out	Home-Cooking
Food Item				
Calories				
Total Fat				
Sodium				
Total Carbs				
Sugar				
Protein				
Cost				

Math Concept **Evaluating Data** To evaluate the data, look at the numbers. Do they have good nutritional value at a reasonable cost? For example, if you list a food item that is high in calories, total fat, sodium, and sugar, the nutritional value would not be good. However, the cost might be acceptable.

Starting Hint: Determine what levels of the items listed are acceptable. Then determine acceptable costs.

 Math For math help, go to the Math Appendix at the back of the book.

NCTM Number and Operations Understand numbers, ways of representing numbers, relationships among numbers, and number systems.

- Park your car in the far corner of a parking lot rather than close to the door.
- Stand while talking on the telephone. You can also try marching in place.
- Walk in place or ride a stationary bike while watching TV.
- Get up to change the TV channel instead of using the remote.

You will be more apt to maintain a fitness program if you have a plan. Make time in your schedule every day for exercise. Be sure to include all three types of exercise in your overall plan.

Get Enough Sleep

With the right amount of sleep, you should wake up feeling restored and alert for the day. Most teens need close to nine hours of sleep each night. Heredity and health influence the amount of sleep you need. People who do not get enough sleep are more likely than others to develop mental health problems. Lack of sleep can affect memory, learning, and logical reasoning.

The study of sleep disorders is gaining attention today. Depression, stress, and tension may cause sleep problems. **Sleep deprivation** (‚de-prə-'vā-shən) means not getting enough sleep. People with this problem often do not realize why they are so tired. They cannot concentrate. They are depressed. Researchers have found that chemical factors can affect how much sleep people actually get. A growing number of sleep clinics now treat sleep problems.

Refuse Harmful Drugs

Staying away from and refusing harmful drugs is your right as well as your responsibility. Your wellness depends on the choices you make about harmful drugs. Drugs affect the mind and behavior by changing feelings, mood, and perceptions. They can lead to addiction. They have destructive effects on the lives of those who take them and of the people around a drug user.

Depending on the drugs used, long-term damage can include permanent injury to the liver, heart, kidney, lungs, and brain. Depression, severe mood changes, and mental illness are common. Harmful drugs can cause permanent damage. They may prevent you from ever being healthy again.

◀) **Sleep for Health** It is important to your health to get enough sleep each night. *Why do you think so many people have difficulty getting the proper amount of sleep?*

Tobacco

Tobacco use is a leading cause of illness. Smoking is the most common preventable cause of death in the United States. Smoking is linked to many cancers, as well as heart disease, stroke, and other serious diseases. Cancer of the lip and mouth has been linked to pipe smoking and the use of smokeless tobacco. Cigar smoking is also dangerous.

The drug in tobacco is nicotine. It is very addictive. It is not easy to stop smoking once a person has started. Many people need help and support to stop. Nicotine patches and smoking cessation materials help many people. Smokers are more apt to quit if they use all of their available resources.

Alcohol

Alcohol causes serious problems. Brain damage, heart disease, liver damage, and cancer have been linked to alcohol use. Ulcers and gastritis also result from its use. Alcohol use is also linked to poor mental health for both drinkers and their families.

About half of all fatal car accidents in America are linked to drivers using alcohol. This is because alcohol can slow reflexes and cause poor judgment. People, regardless of their age, should never consume too much alcohol. **Figure 22.2** shows the long-term effects alcohol can have on a person who drinks too much.

✓ **Reading Check** **Identify** What are the three types of exercises?

Figure 22.2 Long-Term Effects of Alcohol

Alcohol has a negative effect on many of the body organs, and excessive long-term alcohol use can cause death. *What are some interpersonal skills people can use to resist peer pressure to drink alcohol?*

The Brain	The Cardiovascular System	The Digestive System	The Pancreas
Addiction Physical dependence can lead to the inability to control the frequency and amount of drinking. **Loss of brain functions** Loss of verbal skills, visual and spatial skills, and memory. **Brain damage** Excessive use of alcohol can lead to brain damage and to a reduction of brain size. The learning ability and memory of adolescents who drink even small amounts can be impaired.	**Heart damage** The heart muscles become weakened and the heart becomes enlarged, reducing its ability to pump blood. This damage can lead to heart failure. Reduced blood flow can also damage other body systems. **High blood pressure** Damages the heart and can cause heart attack and stroke.	**Irritation of digestive lining** Can lead to stomach ulcers and cancer of the stomach and esophagus. **Fatty liver** Fats build up in the liver and cannot be broken down, leading to cell death. **Alcoholic hepatitis** Inflammation or infection of the liver. **Cirrhosis of the liver** Liver tissue is replaced with useless scar tissue. Cirrhosis can lead to liver failure and death.	**Swelling of the pancreas lining** The passageway from the pancreas to the small intestine can become blocked, and chemicals needed for digestion cannot pass to the small intestine. The chemicals begin to destroy the pancreas itself, causing pain and vomiting. A severe case of pancreatic swelling can lead to death.

Resources

Wellness cannot be taken for granted. To preserve wellness, what can you do? You have your own strengths to turn to, and you can also look for help around you. There are personal and community resources to explore for opportunities to improve your wellness.

Personal Resources

Poor health is often preceded by excuses. Have you ever said, "I do not have time to exercise"? You can try these ideas to overcome excuses. First, be a leader. If others around you are making poor health choices, you can be the one to suggest something new. Look for ways to exercise that are fun. A dance class or talking with a friend while you take brisk walks may not seem like exercise at all.

Use Your Resources There are a variety of resources available in your area to help with your wellness plans. *What types of wellness resources can you find in your area?*

Use your management skills for your health. Set goals, look for your resources, and make a written plan. Involve a friend or relative who also wants to make health improvements. You can work together. When you are committed to making wellness a priority in your life, excuses will not get in the way.

Health Insurance

Health insurance gives you financial protection from health care costs. It is very risky to think you will not need insurance. Teens are typically covered by a parent's policy, but this does not last when you are on your own. If you do not have insurance where you work in the future, you will want to get good advice about buying insurance.

Like everyone else, young people can have illnesses and medical emergencies. For example, when Justin fell and broke his leg, there was one bill for the emergency room. Another was for the person who took X-rays of the leg, and another was for the X-rays themselves. There was a bill for the doctor who set the leg. There was even one for the crutches he used. Justin spent most of his savings on his part of the medical bill. Can you imagine the total without insurance?

Community Resources

Managing your health is not out of reach. You can take advantage of community resources, too. These are some that are available:

- **Health Care Services** Doctors, nurses, hospitals, and clinics help when you are ill. Some clinics offer free or low-cost services. These range from medical care to treatment of mental illness. It is a good idea to have a family doctor who knows your history.

- **Government Health Programs** Most counties have public health departments. They can provide various services. There are two major federal health programs. Medicare is for older adults. Medicaid is a program to help low-income people with medical bills. Other federal programs cover research on diseases. There are services for mother and child health. Other programs prevent and control the spread of disease.
- **Recreational Facilities** Public parks, tennis courts, and pools provide places to exercise. Belonging to a health club is another way to enjoy exercise.
- **Nonprofit Service Organizations** These groups are devoted to raising awareness about health issues. They include the American Red Cross and the American Heart Association.
- **The Library and Internet** In the public library, you will find books and magazines. There also may be health-related programs. A librarian can show you how to use the resources. The Internet has many health-related Web sites. Be sure that the site offers information you can trust.

Maintaining wellness does not have to be difficult. Making healthy choices, such as carefully deciding what to eat and how to exercise, can make it easier. By combining personal and community resources, good health habits can gradually become a way of life for you. They have for many others.

Section 22.2 After You Read

Review Key Concepts

1. **Describe** three ways you can add exercise into your daily routine. Think about what you do throughout the day. Then think about how you can add exercise into three different parts of your day.

2. **Identify** two skills that can be used to work toward good health. Explain how these skills can help you plan for good health.

Practice Academic Skills

English Language Arts

3. Write a paragraph explaining the impact self-discipline has on a person's health. Be sure to focus your answer on the positive effects self-discipline can have on a person's health.

4. Imagine that you have just joined a health club. You want to attend a step aerobics class in the morning before work. You will have to adjust your work schedule to do this. You have talked with your manager and she said she would let you adjust your schedule on the days you take the class. Write an e-mail telling your manager what days you will be attending class, how much time your schedule will be delayed, when this time will be made up, and any other needed information.

> **NCTE 4** Use written language to communicate effectively.

> **NCTE 12** Use language to accomplish individual purposes.

Check Your Answers Check your answers at this book's Online Learning Center through glencoe.com.

CAREER SPOTLIGHT

Wellness Specialist

Adam Thompson, Ph. D., ATC, LAT
Marion, Indiana

Dr. Adam Thompson works with student athletes to prevent injuries. He diagnoses and cares for the inevitable injuries that can happen. He also does long-term work with athletes that need rehabilitation and reconditioning after serious incidents.

As the director of the athletic training department, Thompson is responsible for the administrative details. He also works with the school to develop new training and education programs.

Interpersonal skills are essential in his work. He deals with a wide variety of patient groups. It is important that he be friendly and flexible with all of them. Thompson enjoys working with an energetic and ambitious group of people. "They can be invigorating and a positive influence to the health care providers servicing them."

According to Thompson, the most important thing to strive for is "balance. Every aspect of your life must be appreciated to avoid stress and negative situations."

CAREER FACTS

Education or Training Most professions in this field require courses or a degree in science and anatomy, health care, nursing, or sports medicine.

Nature of the Work Wellness specialists work with a variety of groups, training them in healthy practices and habits ranging from diet and exercise to lifestyle choices.

Aptitudes, Abilities, and Skills This career requires not only a disciplined mind and body, but also strong interpersonal skills. Wellness specialists work with a wide variety of people, and being able to communicate with them is essential.

Academic Skills Required Science and an understanding of how the human body works

Student Organizations To prepare for this career, look for groups that allow you to work with student athletes, such as your school's sports training facility.

Career Outlook Opportunities are expected to be good for fitness workers because of rapid growth in the fitness industry.

Career Path Many fitness and wellness specialists begin by teaching classes in gyms or fitness centers. However, higher-profile positions within companies usually require medicine- or wellness-specific degrees and training.

Critical Thinking

Different Settings Identify how this career in a hospital may differ from the duties described in this feature.

 Research Careers For more information on this and other careers, visit the Occupational Outlook Handbook Web site through the link on this book's Online Learning Center at **glencoe.com**.

CHAPTER SUMMARY

Section 22.1
Learn About Wellness

Wellness is a positive state of physical and mental health. There have been many advances in wellness over the years. Vaccines and antibiotics have helped. Surgery can be done with a laparoscope. Organ transplants and joint replacement are possible. Some diseases can be related to lifestyle choices. These include cardiovascular diseases, cancer, obesity, and diabetes. People can make choices that could decrease some of the risk of getting these diseases. Mental stress and illness can contribute to physical diseases. There are many ways to work toward wellness.

Section 22.2
Positive Health Habits

Positive health habits take planning and management. Healthful eating is based on MyPyramid. It is important to maintain a desirable weight. Eating disorders are mental problems. A good exercise plan includes exercises for endurance, strength, and flexibility. Most people need eight hours of sleep a night. Good health means rejecting harmful drugs. Personal and community resources can be used in working toward health and wellness. Personal leadership and management skills help in developing a more healthful lifestyle.

Content and Academic Vocabulary Review

1. Use each of these content and academic vocabulary words in a sentence.

Content Vocabulary
- ◇ wellness (p. 429)
- ◇ preventive medicine (p. 429)
- ◇ antibiotic (p. 429)
- ◇ laparoscope (p. 429)
- ◇ obesity (p. 430)
- ◇ cardiovascular disease (p. 430)
- ◇ anorexia nervosa (p. 436)

- ◇ bulimia (p. 436)
- ◇ compulsive eating (p. 436)
- ◇ immunity (p. 437)
- ◇ endurance (p. 437)
- ◇ aerobic exercise (p. 437)
- ◇ strength (p. 437)
- ◇ flexibility (p. 437)

- ◇ sleep deprivation (p. 438)

Academic Vocabulary
- ■ organize (p. 431)
- ■ contagious (p. 432)
- ■ diet (p. 434)
- ■ induce (p. 436)

Review Key Concepts

2. **Describe** the role of personal choice in wellness.
3. **Identify** actions you can take to promote wellness.
4. **Summarize** positive habits that contribute to good health.
5. **Suggest** personal and community resources for health and wellness.

Critical Thinking

6. **Predict** Some people do not live with their biological families and may not know them. What impact might this have on their approach to wellness?
7. **Evaluate** Why do some people ignore the harm that can result from dangerous drugs?
8. **Analyze** Does learning more about diseases help people? Do you think it might make them overly sensitive to their health? Explain your answer.
9. **Compare** What are the outcomes of the three types of eating disorders?

Real-World Skills

Self-Management Skills

10. Problem Solving Melissa decided to train her body to need less sleep so she would have more time. Gradually, she has decreased the time she sleeps each night. She now has afternoon slumps and often feels groggy. Write an advice column for the local newspaper of what you think Melissa should do.

Critical Thinking Skills

11. Evaluate Keep track of everything you eat for a day. Create a food diary to record what you eat. Use the MyPyramid guidelines on page 435 to evaluate your diet. At the end of your diary, make suggestions for how you could improve your diet on another day.

Collaborative Skills

12. Teach Others Follow your teacher's instructions to form a team with your classmates. Plan a lesson on one of the following topics: nutrition, exercise, sleep problems, drug use, or mental health. Narrow the topic to a more specific subtopic and find additional information. Present your lesson to the class.

Problem-Solving Skills

13. Decision Making Kevin is on the wrestling team. He often forces himself to vomit secretly before weighing in to meet weight requirements. He wants to be in a higher weight class, but his coach wants Kevin at the lower weight. Write a letter to Kevin about what he should do.

14. Demonstrate Follow your teacher's instructions to form into groups. Look at various exercises. Select one to improve strength and one to improve flexibility. Find out how to properly do the exercises you have chosen. Demonstrate your exercises to the class.

15. A Healthy Workplace Suppose you own a business. How would you promote employee wellness? Brainstorm with a partner to develop a list of ideas. Are the ideas something employees would really do? Would the ideas take time away from the employees' work?

16. Assessment Make a list of resources available in your community that help promote wellness. Do you think wellness is a priority? Write a paragraph to explain your answer.

17. Nutritious Choices Go to this book's Online Learning Center through **glencoe.com** to find **Web Links** for **Restaurant Nutritional Information**. Select a restaurant from the list. Study the nutritional information for the menu choices. Choose healthful foods for a meal that is low in fat and sodium. Write out a menu for a healthful breakfast, lunch, or dinner.

Additional Activities For additional activities, go to this book's Online Learning Center through **glencoe.com**.

Academic Skills

Mathematics

18. Calculate Workout Time Anna started an exercise program to help her maintain a healthy weight. The amount of time she spent exercising is shown in the table. How much time did Anna spend exercising this week?

Day	Time
Sunday	$\frac{1}{2}$ hour
Monday	$\frac{1}{3}$ hour
Tuesday	$\frac{1}{4}$ hour
Wednesday	$\frac{2}{3}$ hour
Thursday	$\frac{3}{4}$ hour
Friday	$\frac{1}{2}$ hour
Saturday	$\frac{1}{2}$ hour

Math Concept **Adding Fractions** To add fractions, all of the fractions must have the same denominator.

Starting Hint: Find the lowest common denominator (12) and change all fractions so they have that denominator. After you add, be sure to reduce your answer.

 For math help, go to the Math Appendix at the back of the book.

> **NCTM Number and Operations** Understand numbers, ways of representing numbers, relationships among numbers, and number systems.

English Language Arts

19. Creative Writing Write a humorous essay. Title it "An Unhealthy Day in the Life of . . ." In it, describe what happens to a person with an irresponsible attitude toward health. Include the types of foods the person eats throughout the day. Also include the amount of exercise he or she gets during the day.

> **NCTE 5** Use different writing process elements to communicate effectively.

Social Studies

20. Investigate People in other parts of the world have different diets than people in the United States. Some also tend to have fewer lifestyle diseases. For example, people who live in Mediterranean countries have less heart disease. Select a country that has a different diet than you are used to. Find out how diet appears to affect health in that country. Compare the outcomes to those in the United States. Write a report of your findings.

> **NCSS I.a** Analyze and explain the ways groups, societies, and cultures address human needs and concerns.

STANDARDIZED TEST PRACTICE

TIMED WRITING
Read the writing prompt. Set a stop watch for 30 minutes and write a one-page essay using details and examples to illustrate your points.

> **Test-Taking Tip** Plan out your essay before you begin writing. Jot down the main points or details you want to focus on in the margins. Refer to these points frequently as you write.

21. Tim considers himself to be in perfect health. He rarely gets sick, he eats right, and he is not overweight. His blood cholesterol and blood pressure are within the acceptable range. He insists there is no need for him to participate in any type of exercise program. Do you agree with Tim? Explain your answer.

CHAPTER 23

Manage Your Money

○ **Section 23.1**

Use Your Money Wisely

○ **Section 23.2**

Make a Financial Plan

▶▶ *Explore the Photo*
When you shop, it is important to know how to manage your money. *What are some ways you have managed your expenses?*

Chapter Objectives

After completing this chapter, you will be able to:

- **Compare** present-oriented spenders and future-oriented spenders.
- **Explain** how to use a checking account to handle money.
- **Describe** three types of credit.
- **Identify** ways to protect your future through insurance, saving, and investing.
- **List** the steps in making a financial plan.
- **Determine** the factors to be considered in making a family financial plan.

Writing Activity

Write a First Draft

Resourcefulness If you are resourceful, you use what you have to get what you need and want. You use resources creatively and substitute one resource for another when necessary. You can show resourcefulness when you:

- Find a way to earn extra money to pay for music lessons.
- Make a gift instead of buying one.
- Offer to tutor a friend in exchange for help with painting a room.
- Ask your history teacher to recommend sources for researching a paper.
- Plan tomorrow's dinner menu while waiting in line at the store.

Think about what it takes to be resourceful. Write a first draft of a one-page paper that describes a person who is resourceful.

Writing Tips To effectively write a first draft, follow these steps:

1. Arrange your ideas in an order that makes sense.
2. Organize your draft into paragraphs.
3. Make sure that each paragraph is organized around one main idea.

Use Your Money Wisely

Reading Guide

Before You Read

Guilt-Free Rest If you feel guilty about resting, you create more stress. Your reading skills are more effective if you are relaxed and ready to learn.

Read to Learn
Key Concepts
- **Compare** present-oriented spenders and future-oriented spenders.
- **Explain** how to use a checking account to handle money.
- **Describe** three types of credit.
- **Identify** ways to protect your future through insurance, saving, and investing.

Main Idea
People differ in how they spend money. Manage your money wisely with a checking account, savings account, or credit.

Academic Vocabulary
You will find these words in your reading and on your tests. Use the glossary to look up their definitions if necessary.
- assess
- compare

Content Vocabulary
- check
- electronic funds transfer
- debit card
- credit
- interest
- loan
- down payment
- insurance
- premium
- deductible
- investment
- asset
- share
- stock
- mutual fund

Graphic Organizer
Use a chart like the one shown to write three credit options and two tips for using each wisely.

Credit Options	Tips for Using
	1. 2.

 Graphic Organizer Go to this book's Online Learning Center at **glencoe.com** to print out this graphic organizer.

Academic Standards · · · · · · · · · · · · · ·

 English Language Arts

NCTE 4 Use written language to communicate effectively.

NCTE 8 Use information resources to gather information and create and communicate knowledge.

 Mathematics

NCTM Number and Operations Understand the meanings of operations and how they relate to one another.

NCTE *National Council of Teachers of English*
NCTM *National Council of Teachers of Mathematics*

NSES *National Science Education Standards*
NCSS *National Council of the Social Studies*

Spending Styles

Managing daily life is easier when you can pay for what you need. Most people would also like to indulge their wants. Doing this takes money. Some people put more value on money than others do. What people truly need to be happy has provoked many debates.

Often, attitudes toward money spring from emotional needs rather than practical ones. One teen may build up low self-esteem by buying designer clothes or the latest sound system for a car. Another person may save every penny to feel more secure. To feed a desire for power, a person may pay for objects that buy the loyalty of family and friends. Another may buy gifts to show that they love a person.

How a person spends money says a lot about the person's values and goals. There are two basic spending styles that people have:

- **Present Oriented** With this approach, people tend to buy what they want sooner rather than later. They do less financial planning and saving. They are also less likely to consider how their spending habits affect the family. On the other hand, they may enjoy life more because they worry less. These spenders can easily go into debt. They may be devastated if they have an emergency.
- **Future Oriented** People who focus on the future think more about saving. They rarely lose sight of their goals. They make purchases with care to reach those goals. These spenders are prepared when something unforeseen happens. The future-oriented style can be taken to the extreme. A person might not enjoy money or want to spend it at all. This frugality could annoy others. The person could take advantage of those who are willing to pay.

Very few people are purely one style or the other. Most people are a mixture, with one style being more dominant. Whatever style fits you will need to be blended with good management to avoid money problems. Most teens are responsible for only part of their expenses. Adults usually take care of housing, food, medical care, and maybe some clothing and leisure costs. As you become more independent, you will take on more financial responsibility. When you are on your own, you will need management skills to handle your own money.

As You Read

Connect Does money buy happiness? Why or why not?

> ✓ **Reading Check**

Explain What does present-oriented spending mean?

▶▶ *Your Spending Style* Some people are present-oriented spenders and others are future-oriented spenders. *What is your spending style and why?*

Checking Accounts

At some point, you will discover that keeping enough cash on hand to pay all your bills is not safe or convenient. With a checking account, however, your money is safe. It is also ready to use when you need it.

Vocabulary

You can find definitions in the glossary at the back of this book.

With a checking account, you deposit money in a financial institution. You can use a bank or savings and loan association. Many people use a credit union. The institution holds your money safe until you are ready to use it. You can withdraw it in person. It also can be taken out electronically or by writing checks. A **check** is a written document that transfers money from a bank account to a person or business.

Although convenient, checking accounts can be abused. Sometimes people write checks for more money than they have in an account. They have insufficient funds. When this happens, the check is said to bounce. The check is returned unpaid to the person who wrote it. The check writer will still have to pay for the purchase. Businesses charge a fee for bad checks to cover the cost of collecting their money. The financial institution may **assess**, or charge, a fee as well.

INDEPENDENT Living

HOW TO Save and Invest

People today are living longer, healthier lives than they did in the past. In order to make the most of a long and healthy life, it is important to save and invest your money. The choices you make now can impact your lifestyle many years into the future. Follow these guidelines to save and invest your money:

1. **Savings Accounts** Most people begin saving their money by opening a savings account at a bank, a savings and loan association, or a credit union. Before you choose a bank, find out what fees you will have to pay. Some accounts charge a maintenance fee or a fee for some deposits and withdrawals.
2. **Investments** Investments are financial products you can purchase to make your money grow. A low-risk investment choice will pay a steady amount of interest over a long period of time. Low-risk options include savings bonds, money market accounts, and certificates of deposit.
3. **Pension Plans** A pension plan is a retirement plan funded, at least in part, by an employer or union. Your company may pay you a fixed amount at retirement, which is called a defined-benefit plan. Or, as in a profit-sharing plan, your employer contributes a set amount to the plan each year.

Take Action Imagine you have $100 to invest. Choose a local bank and find out the interest rates for their savings accounts. Calculate the interest on your $100 in ten years if you were to put it in the savings account. Next, choose a stock to invest in. Using the newspaper, find out the interest rates for that stock. Assuming the interest rate does not change, calculate the profits for your $100 invested in that stock over ten years.

There are several ways that money can be moved by electronic means. An **electronic funds transfer** (EFT) moves money from one account to another by electronic means. Your paycheck may be deposited in your bank account this way. You can also move money from a checking account to a savings account this way.

ATMs

Most financial institutions have automatic teller machines (ATMs). These are very convenient. They allow you to access your account when the business is not open. Some ATMs are available 24 hours a day. You can withdraw cash from your account and make deposits. To do this, you need an ATM card. You will also need a personal identification number (PIN), assigned by the institution. Some financial institutions charge a fee to use an ATM.

Money you withdraw from an ATM is taken immediately from your account. You should keep accurate records of ATM transactions. This way you will know how much money is in your account at all times.

Debit Cards

Another way to pay for purchases with checking account funds is with a debit card. A **debit card** is a plastic card used to buy goods and services without cash. The money is deducted electronically from your checking account when you use the card.

You need to keep good records of what money has been taken out of your account with the debit card. Overdrawing the account can easily happen if you are using a debit card and writing checks. Debit cards need to be kept safe.

Online Banking

Most banks offer some type of online banking. You are able to see your account with a computer and Internet access. You can look at your transactions and balance. You may be able to initiate transactions online, such as bill paying. There are banks that have no physical locations but only offer online services.

Online banking is convenient. It is available any time, day or night. Transactions are processed quickly. It may take some time to get your accounts set up and to learn how to use the institution's Web site. You will need a user name and password. Security is very important for online banking. Look for the security lock or key icon on your screen when you are banking online.

ATM Transactions When you use an automatic teller machine (ATM), you can quickly take money out of your account. *Why is it important to keep good records when using an ATM?*

✓ **Reading Check** **Define** What is a check?

Credit

Credit means borrowing or using someone else's money and paying it back later. You can buy larger purchases, such as houses and cars, this way. You can also buy many other kinds of goods and services today and delay payment for them.

Credit is rented money. Any time you rent something, a fee is involved. **Interest** is what you pay to use someone else's money. After adding interest, the cost of what you buy goes up. There is a relationship between time and money. The longer you borrow a certain amount of money, the more you pay in interest.

Companies keep track of whether or not people use their credit responsibly. Those who use it well and pay promptly earn good credit ratings. Credit ratings go down when people make late payments or carry too much debt. Whether you can get more credit and how much interest you will pay is related to your credit rating. A credit report outlines the credit a person has and how well it is being managed. Lenders look at your credit report before they decide whether to lend you money. You are entitled to one free credit report each year. This helps you know what your credit rating is.

Credit is regulated by many laws. There are laws that set limits on interest rates. Other laws require that certain information be given to a person who applies for credit. Laws govern credit reports and how they can be used. You should learn all you can about credit laws so that you can use your credit wisely.

Use Credit Cards Appropriately Credit cards are convenient, but they need to be used appropriately. *What are some benefits and drawbacks to using credit cards?*

Types of Credit

Many people may be willing to loan you money. Lenders only make money when they loan it to consumers. The more they loan and the longer the time the money is loaned, the more lenders earn. There are several types of credit.

Credit Cards

Credit cards are much like debit cards. With a debit card, however, you are spending your own money. With a credit card, you are borrowing the money from the credit card company. Most credit cards have a limit. That is the most credit that you can have with the card. You must agree to the credit card agreement that sets out your rights and responsibilities. It identifies the interest rate and payment schedule. Be sure to read the agreement carefully.

Some credit card accounts start charging interest immediately after you make a purchase. Others do not charge interest if you pay the full amount due each month. The amount of interest charged varies among cards. Rates are often very high. Many have annual and late-payment fees, in addition to the interest.

Be sure to write down the number of your credit card and the telephone number of the company. Keep these numbers in a safe place. If your credit card is lost or stolen, call the company immediately. They will take steps to prevent anyone else from using your card.

Loans

A **loan** is an agreement to borrow money and to pay back more than the borrowed amount. Banks and credit unions are sources of lower-cost loans. More expensive sources of cash include small loan companies, cash advances on credit cards or paychecks, and pawnbrokers.

Federal laws control the information supplied when you borrow money. This helps you **compare**, or find relations between, costs and terms on different loans. Read and analyze the loan contract. Before signing, find out what the consequences will be if you do not meet the terms of the agreement.

Installment Buying

Larger items, such as cars, furniture, and appliances, may be bought with an installment plan. This kind of credit is offered through the business that sells the product. It is often more costly than loans from other sources. Check the terms carefully before signing the papers.

With installment buying, you pay a **down payment**, an amount you pay in cash. You then sign a contract to pay the remaining amount in monthly installments. How much the monthly payments are can be misleading. You need to look at the interest rate as well as other possible costs. High-interest rates are often linked to low monthly payments. A clear understanding of the contract helps you make better decisions.

Use Credit Carefully

Buying on credit is an easy way to get what you want, but debt problems are extremely common. These problems have serious outcomes, such as stress or loss of property. You can also ruin your credit record, and you may not be able to get other credit you may want or need.

Stop and think before you use credit. If you cannot pay cash for what you want to purchase, is it worth it to use credit? Will you be able to make the required payments? Learning to manage money well is the best way to protect your credit record.

✓ Reading Check **Describe** What is credit?

Financial Literacy

Installment Plans

Michelle bought new bedroom furniture on an installment plan. The price of the furniture was $1,500. She paid 10 percent down and must pay the remainder in 16 monthly installments of $100 each. How much total interest will she pay?

Math Concept **Multi-Step Problems** To solve this problem, calculate how much Michelle paid as a down payment by multiplying $1,500 by 10%. Then calculate how much her total payments cost. Add these two numbers. Then subtract the cost of the furniture ($1,500) from your answer to find the interest paid.

Starting Hint: To multiply by a percent, change the percent to a decimal (10% = .10).

 For math help, go to the Math Appendix at the back of the book.

NCTM Number and Operations Understand the meanings of operations and how they relate to one another.

Protect Your Future

Managing your money is not just about what you spend today. It is also about protecting your future. Ways to protect your future are through insurance, savings, and investments.

Insurance

One way to protect your future is to buy insurance. **Insurance** is a promise of payment in the case of loss. For this, you make a periodic payment called a **premium**. Insurance protects you against the financial impact of an unexpected event or problem.

Types of Insurance

Insurance can be complicated. Most policies have a **deductible**. This is the amount you pay when a loss occurs. The insurance company then pays the rest of the bill. You can reduce insurance costs by choosing a higher deductible. Learn exactly what the policy that you are buying covers. The most common types of insurance are:

- **Health Insurance** This protects people against large medical bills. **Figure 23.1** describes the three basic types of health insurance.
- **Life Insurance** This protects a family against the loss of income if a family member dies. A wage earner may buy life insurance to protect against the loss of income. Term insurance buys a death benefit only. Cash value insurance has a savings portion as well.
- **Auto Insurance** This protects car owners against damage done to others. It also protects against damage others do to them. It is required in most states. Collision insurance covers losses to your car from a collision. Comprehensive coverage takes care of most non-collision damage to the car. Auto insurance also covers bodily injury and property damage.
- **Homeowners Insurance** This protects owners if their home and possessions are damaged or destroyed. Renter's insurance covers the value of possessions when the insured rents a home or apartment.

Savings

Regardless of your spending style, saving should be one of your goals. Saving money for the future is not easy. You might have to give up some things, but the benefits outweigh this drawback. Saving is usually easier for future-oriented spenders. Present-oriented spenders may need more self-discipline to get in the habit of saving.

Money that you put in a savings account earns interest. As the account balance grows, you build a fund for emergencies. It can also be for some special goal, such as a new computer. Sometimes people face an unexpected major expense, such as car repairs. When these expenses occur, people realize the usefulness of savings. Experts suggest that you keep three to six times your monthly salary in an emergency fund.

With a savings account, you loan money to a bank, savings and loan association, or credit union. Most of them allow you unlimited access. You can usually deposit and withdraw money as you like. Some institutions will offer higher interest rates but place restrictions on how often you can withdraw money from the account. Interest rates on regular savings accounts are often low.

Certificates of deposit (CDs) offer higher rates of interest. Government savings bonds also do this. These types of plans, however, do not allow you access to your money for a certain period of time without a penalty. Be sure to research which options are best for you when you begin saving.

Figure 23.1 Types of Health Insurance

There are three main types of health insurance plans for individuals and families. *Which type of insurance would be best if you traveled a lot on business or pleasure?*

Type of Plan	Plan Description	Fee Structure
Fee-for-Service	Insured can go to almost any doctor or hospital and be covered for most procedures.	The insured pays for the doctor visit or procedure. The insurance company pays back part of the money spent after proper paperwork is filed.
Preferred Provider Option (PPO)	Insured can go to any doctor or hospital on an approved list and be covered for a wide variety of services.	Insurance money goes to provider. Insured has a co-pay in addition to premiums.
Health Maintenance Organization (HMO)	Insured is assigned or chooses an HMO primary care doctor. Care is limited to that approved by the HMO.	HMOs are prepaid health plans. Insured pays a monthly premium to the HMO and may pay a small co-pay.

Investments

An **investment** is the purchase of an asset to make money. The difference between saving and investing is the difference between lending and owning. When you save, the money is still yours. You earn interest by loaning it to others. With investing, you might buy real estate or part of a company. You own an **asset**, which is something of value. You expect the asset you bought will increase in value.

Most large companies are publicly owned. This means their shares are available for the public to invest in. A **share** shows an ownership position in a company. The shares are called **stock**. Shares are bought and sold through a stock market. When you invest your money in the stock market, you are buying shares of a company. Your shares will increase and decrease in value over time. People try to select companies to invest in that they think will do well, and gain value in the long term.

Many small investors start with mutual funds rather than stocks. A **mutual fund** is an investment company. These companies raise money and then pool it to invest it in stocks, bonds, or other investments. Investors in a mutual fund own a part of the assets of the mutual fund.

Many young people think investing is something they will do later. They think there will be time when they are older. Once you have some savings, however, you can begin investing for long-term financial security. Successful investing requires study. There are many decisions to make. These will affect your financial future.

Section 23.1 After You Read

Review Key Concepts

1. **Explain** the problems that a future-oriented spending approach might bring.
2. **Identify** what is needed to do online banking.
3. **Define** a down payment.
4. **Describe** the difference between saving and investing.

Practice Academic Skills

English Language Arts

5. Decide if you are a present-oriented spender or a future-oriented spender. Write a paragraph describing your approach to spending. Include what is good about your type of spending. Describe the problems you may have and changes you should make.

   NCTE 4 Use written language to communicate effectively.

6. Obtain an agreement for making a purchase on an installment plan. Read the agreement. Summarize in one paragraph the main points that the buyer should know.

   NCTE 8 Use information resources to gather information and create and communicate knowledge.

Check Your Answers Check your answers at this book's Online Learning Center through **glencoe.com**.

Make a Financial Plan

Reading Guide

Before You Read

Think of an Example Think of an example of how or when you could use one of the Key Concepts in this section. This can help motivate your learning by showing you why the skill is important.

Read to Learn

Key Concepts
- **List** the steps in making a financial plan.
- **Determine** the factors to be considered in making a family financial plan.

Main Idea

Creating a financial plan is important in managing money. Family financial plans are more complex because there are more people's needs and wants to consider.

Content Vocabulary
◇ financial plan
◇ fixed expense
◇ flexible expense

 Graphic Organizer Go to this book's Online Learning Center at **glencoe.com** to print out this graphic organizer.

Academic Vocabulary

You will find these words in your reading and on your tests. Use the glossary to look up their definitions if necessary.
- determine
- category

Graphic Organizer

As you read, list what you need to know to make a good financial plan. Use a graphic organizer like the one shown to help organize your information.

estimate income	**What I Need to Know**	

Academic Standards • • • • • • • • • • • • • • • • • •

 English Language Arts

NCTE 4 Use written language to communicate effectively.

NCTE 12 Use language to accomplish individual purposes.

NCTE *National Council of Teachers of English*
NCTM *National Council of Teachers of Mathematics*

NSES *National Science Education Standards*
NCSS *National Council of the Social Studies*

A Financial Plan

Vocabulary

You can find definitions in the glossary at the back of this book.

Having enough money to buy all you would like is seldom possible. A **financial plan** guides spending and saving. Also known as a budget, it can make managing money go more smoothly. With a financial plan, you can make your money lead to an enjoyable life.

Five basic steps can lead you to a financial plan. Each step takes effort and honesty in order to work. As you look at where your money goes and how to spend it, keep your values and priorities in mind. You will need to look at both short- and long-term goals. What do you want to do with your money? What expenses are necessary and which are luxuries?

Estimate Income

The first step in creating a financial plan is to estimate income. Think about the effect that the economic system might have on your personal income. If you lose your job, will you be able to find another at the same pay? Estimating conservatively is wise.

As You Read

Connect Why is it important to estimate income based on the pay you take home rather than your hourly wages?

If you are working, base your income on the pay you take home. Do not base it on your hourly wage or salary. If your hours are irregular, estimate what your average pay is. Money for taxes, social security, and any benefits is deducted from a paycheck. Add any allowance and other regular income.

Record Expenses

Set a Financial Plan When you make a financial plan, look at your short- and long-term goals. *What are some of your long-term financial goals?*

Secondly, you need to **determine**, or settle on, exactly what your expenses are. You will need to keep records. Keeping accurate records will help you see where your money really goes. You may use a computer money management program to help track your expenses.

Analyze Spending

Third, analyze your spending habits. You will probably be surprised at how much money you spend. For example, consider how much money you spend each month on clothes, music, or snacks. Financial software or spreadsheets can help you make these judgments. Once you are aware of your spending habits, you can decide what to do about them. Some expenses may be important enough to include in your plan. A plan can also help you decide where you can easily cut back on spending.

As you look at your records, you will notice certain regular expenses. Each of these is called a **fixed expense**. They might include a car insurance payment or school activity fees. When you are still living at home, you probably do not have as many fixed expenses as you will when you live on your own.

Would you recognize a financial problem in the making? Problems require planning and management to get you back on track before things get out of hand. Some financial danger signals include:

- Paying only the minimum amount due on credit accounts.
- Paying regular monthly bills with loans or savings.
- Using credit to pay for items that are normally paid for with cash.
- Not knowing how much your total debt is and how much interest you are paying.

- Depending on irregular income, such as overtime or tax refunds, to pay bills.

Problem-Solving For the third week in a row, Eddie asked his brother to borrow a little cash just to get by. His brother was annoyed, asking where Eddie's paycheck had gone. He said he was not loaning Eddie any more money until Eddie paid back the money he had already borrowed. Eddie started thinking about who else might loan him some money. What would you suggest to Eddie?

Next, look at each **flexible expense**. These do not occur regularly. They may be extras, such as a gift. They could be needed, such as a textbook. Flexible expenses can be adjusted. For example, if you need a new pair of shoes but do not have the money, you may try to include them in your spending plan for next month.

Plan for Spending and Saving

The next step in making a financial plan is deciding how to spend your money. List and total your fixed expenses. Include savings as a fixed expense, even if the amount is small. Then subtract that total from your income.

The money that is left is what you have for flexible expenses. You will want to set up categories. These may include school supplies, clothing, transportation, and entertainment. Look at what you have been spending and what you would like to spend. Assign a financial limit for each category of flexible spending. Use your plan to guide and control your spending. Continue to keep track of expenses. Stay within the spending limits you have set.

Evaluate Your Plan

As the final step in managing the plan, you will need to make periodic checks to see how well it is working. Remember, what works for you might not be right for someone else. As you use the plan, make adjustments to fit your changing situation. If you save money in a spending category, or group, you can boost your savings. Then you may have money for something extra. A carefully considered plan can set the stage for good money management for life.

✓ Reading Check **Explain** Why is one of the steps in making a financial plan keeping track of what you spend?

Attaining Your Goals A financial plan can help a family reach its goal for buying a house. *What financial goals would you set up for your future family?*

The Family Financial Plan

The steps in personal financial planning can also be used to make a family financial plan. Like an individual, each family has an income and expenses. Some expenses are the same for all families. Others are based on a particular family's goals. These goals will affect the financial decisions of the family.

A family's financial plan is apt to be more complex than an individual's. In a family, there are more people whose needs and wants must be considered. The first step is meeting the basic family needs of shelter, food, and clothing. These can vary a great deal. The choices that are made depend on the amount of money available and the family's values. Then parents must consider the needs and wants of all family members. The many expenses connected to taking care of a family add up quickly. These expenses can include school supplies; transportation costs to school, jobs, and activities; and uniforms and equipment for sports or clubs.

Some families have special needs. These must be considered when making a financial plan. If a child has a physical disability, that must be considered. Health conditions that need treatment or special care will also affect planning. These families may need to be especially resourceful in planning and managing. The extra demands of those with special needs are not always easy to meet. The family may have to consider medical expenses, special transportation costs, or even in-home care costs for some people with illnesses or disabilities.

Make Financial Decisions

Usually younger family members do not have a clear picture of the family's finances. It may be easy to ignore insurance costs, medical bills, and the money for groceries. If a younger family member knows all the details, they will know if the family expenses are being met.

How a parent decides to distribute any extra income may not always be your choice. Discussion may make the decision clearer. Look at the long-range impact of choices made today. Remember that parents' decisions about spending are not easily made.

Plan for Family Development

The special qualities of each stage of family development will affect how a family spends money. When a couple forms a family, both partners may be working. As children join the family, the expenses of raising them are added to the financial plan. In addition, one parent may cut back on work to be at home.

Financial pressure is probably greatest when children are teens. Costs for education, transportation, and personal care can be high. These pressures often decrease as children go off on their own. Adults in their middle years are often at the peak of their earning power. During retirement, when income usually decreases, adjustments must again be made. Adults who have made a plan for retirement can feel secure at this time.

Specific family situations may require special money management plans. For example, if a teen plays the piano well, a family may want to save money for lessons. Money may be set aside for an annual trip to visit grandparents or a family vacation. Without a financial plan, a family may face disappointment. With a financial plan, families have a tool to help them reach their goals.

Section 23.2   After You Read

Review Key Concepts

1. **Explain** why it is important to identify values and short- and long-term goals before making a financial plan.
2. **Describe** the first priority in making a family budget.

Practice Academic Skills

English Language Arts

3. Identify a goal that you would like to achieve within the next year. What kind of financial resources will it take to reach that goal? Write a one-page report that explains how you will achieve the goal and the impact this goal will have on your financial plan.

> **NCTE 12** Use language to accomplish individual purposes.

4. Imagine you are attending college. You have just discovered that you need another costly book for your chemistry class. You do not have the money to pay for the book. Your grandmother has told you that she would be happy to help with your college expenses if necessary. Write a letter to your grandmother asking if she will loan you the money to get the book. Outline when and how you will pay back the loan.

> **NCTE 4** Use written language to communicate effectively.

Check Your Answers Check your answers at this book's Online Learning Center through glencoe.com.

CAREER SPOTLIGHT

Consumer Education Specialist

Sandra McKinnon
Franklin County, Missouri

Handling money wisely is one of the most important skills an adult can possess. People do not learn everything about finance from family and school. Specialists such as Sandra McKinnon help a wide variety of people learn enough to make smart decisions about their money.

McKinnon says her topics include saving and investing, budgeting, avoiding identity theft, comparison shopping, insurance, estate planning, and home ownership. "I address the needs of women, youth, the aged, social service agencies, employers, and offenders," she says.

It is a job that puts her in front of a lot of different people, and as a result, strong communication skills are a must. "You need to be able to form coalitions and facilitate groups, speak and present ideas clearly, have the ability to be self-directed but also work with the public and colleagues, and have a strong understanding of adult education principles and interactive teaching strategies."

She says the reward at the end of the day is that she gets the satisfaction of knowing she has helped adults learn real-world skills that will make their day-to-day lives better.

CAREER FACTS

Education or Training Bachelor's or Master's degrees in economics, sociology, business, accounting, and finance.

Nature of the Work Consumer education specialists work with individuals and groups, creating and implementing educational programs to help them master their finances.

Aptitudes, Abilities, and Skills Candidates for this career need to work well with a wide variety of people, must be good communicators, and should be sympathetic and caring. Often, the people coming for help may be in poor financial condition, and will need a kind voice in addition to the education.

Academic Skills Required Finance and accounting, language skills, public speaking

Student Organizations To prepare for this career, look for groups that involve peers teaching each other how to make, save, and spend money wisely, such as FCCLA.

Career Outlook Opportunities are expected to be good for this career, but it is a field that fluctuates with the economy.

Career Path Consumer education specialists often work for public agencies or universities. Charitable organizations also offer adult financial counseling as part of their services.

Critical Thinking

Money Management Do you have the math and money management skills for a job like this one?

 Research Careers For more information on this and other careers, visit the Occupational Outlook Handbook Web site through the link on this book's Online Learning Center at **glencoe.com**.

CHAPTER SUMMARY

Section 23.1
Use Your Money Wisely

People tend to be present oriented or future oriented in their approach to spending. A checking account is a way to hold money safely in a financial institution until you need it. Money can be transferred by writing a check. It can also be moved electronically through ATMs, debit cards, or online banking. Credit is paying interest to use someone else's money. Insurance helps protect against financial losses. Savings are needed for emergencies. Investments involve buying an asset, such as stock, a mutual fund, or real estate.

Section 23.2
Make a Financial Plan

One of the best tools for managing money is a financial plan. Goals, values, and priorities need to be considered when making a financial plan. Income should be estimated. A record of expenses is made. Then spending is analyzed. The plan is developed by setting amounts for the categories of spending. The plan should be evaluated to see how well it is working. Family financial plans are more complex because there are more people involved. The stage of development a family is in affects how it plans and manages money.

Content and Academic Vocabulary Review

1. Use each of these content and academic vocabulary words in a sentence.

Content Vocabulary
◇ check (p. 450)
◇ electronic funds transfer (p. 451)
◇ debit card (p. 451)
◇ credit (p. 452)
◇ interest (p. 452)
◇ loan (p. 453)
◇ down payment (p. 453)
◇ insurance (p. 454)
◇ premium (p. 454)

◇ deductible (p. 454)
◇ investment (p. 456)
◇ asset (p. 456)
◇ share (p. 456)
◇ stock (p. 456)
◇ mutual fund (p. 456)
◇ financial plan (p. 458)
◇ fixed expense (p. 458)
◇ flexible expense (p. 459)

Academic Vocabulary
■ assess (p. 450)
■ compare (p. 453)
■ determine (p. 458)
■ category (p. 459)

Review Key Concepts

2. Compare present-oriented spenders and future-oriented spenders.
3. Explain how to use a checking account to handle money.
4. Describe three types of credit.
5. Identify ways to protect your future through insurance, saving, and investing.
6. List the steps in making a financial plan.
7. Determine the factors to be considered in making a family financial plan.

Critical Thinking

8. Analyze Why do you think many people have trouble managing credit cards wisely?
9. Identify Certain skills you use in personal relationships can be used to prevent conflicts when dealing with family finances. What are some of these skills?

Real-World Skills

Decision-Making Skills

10. Solve a Problem Jeri tried to cash her paycheck at a bank. They would not cash it since she does not have an account there. It costs $5.00 at the supermarket to cash the check. Jeri does not want to spend $5.00 every time she gets a paycheck. Write a paragraph to explain what Jeri should do.

Management Skills

11. Plan a Budget Suppose you take home $1,865.00 a month. Set up a monthly budget. Include food, housing, savings, and utilities, transportation, insurance, clothing, entertainment, and miscellaneous items. Be sure that you balance the budget.

Technology Skills

12. Create a Spreadsheet Research three different credit cards. Compare their interest rates and how the interest is calculated. What fees does each card have? What other information would a user need to know about each card? Use a spreadsheet to organize the information you collected.

Problem-Solving Skills

13. Manage Credit Ted charged several items when he got his first credit card. When the bill came, he paid the minimum payment. The amount of interest charged on his second bill was too high to pay. Write a financial advice column that addresses Ted's problem.

14. Interest Rates Compare what the interest rate would be on a car loan at a local bank, credit union, finance company, and car dealership. Why would someone pay the higher rates when lower rates are available? Write a paragraph to explain your reasons.

15. Electronic Banking Research options for banking by electronic means. Who offers it? Are there charges for the service? What can be done electronically? Create a brochure that answers these questions.

16. Interview Talk to an older adult. Learn about his or her attitudes toward money. What events in the person's life affected how he or she manages money? Did attitudes change with age? Write a report comparing the older adult's attitudes with the attitudes of young adults you know.

17. Money Management Software Go to this book's Online Learning Center at glencoe.com to find suggested **Web Links** for **Money Management Software.** Choose one of the programs and learn more about it. Write a report describing the software, its cost, its features, and how this software could help you manage your money.

Additional Activities For additional activities, go to this book's Online Learning Center through glencoe.com.

Academic Skills

Mathematics

18. Calculate Interest Yasmin has saved $5,000 from her part-time job. She can open a checking account at First Bank at a two percent interest rate. Her other choice is a checking account at Second Bank at a four percent interest rate. How much more money will she make with the account at Second Bank?

 Math Concept **Subtracting Percentages** To subtract percentages, first convert them to decimals. You can do this by dividing the percent by 100. For example, 2% would be $2 \div 100 = .02$.

Starting Hint: Subtract the interest rate for the account at First Bank (2%) from the interest rate for the account at Second Bank (4%). Then multiply your answer by the total amount Yasmin has invested ($5,000).

Math For math help, go to the Math Appendix at the back of the book.

NCTM Problem Solving Solve problems that arise in mathematics and in other contexts.

English Language Arts

19. Create a Brochure Conduct research to learn more about how to manage credit. Use a word processing program to write a brochure that will help teens manage credit when they are on their own. Create an interesting design and layout. Plan a way to distribute the brochure to older teens.

NCTE 8 Use information resources to gather information and create and communicate knowledge.

Social Studies

20. Credit Laws Investigate the laws that control the use of credit in your state. What is the highest interest rate that can be legally charged? Are there any limits on the fees that can be assessed? What happens when people cannot or do not pay their bills? Write a report of your findings.

NCSS VI.c Analyze and explain ideas and mechanisms to meet needs and wants of citizens and establish order and security of a just society.

STANDARDIZED TEST PRACTICE

MULTIPLE CHOICE
Read the following sentence. Then read the question below the sentence. Read the answer choices and choose the best answer to fill in the blank.

Test-Taking Tip In a multiple-choice test, the answers should be specific and precise. Read the question first, then read all the answer choices. Eliminate answers that you know are incorrect.

21. With installment buying, you make a partial cash payment and sign a contract to pay the balance in monthly installments. In this sentence, the word balance means _____.
 a. an instrument for weighing
 b. physical equilibrium
 c. remaining amount
 d. mental steadiness

CHAPTER 24

Consumer Skills

Section 24.1

Be a Good Consumer

Section 24.2

Consumer Rights and Responsibilities

 **Explore the Photo**

A good consumer knows how to judge quality and compare prices. *What are some ways you make wise shopping decisions?*

Chapter Objectives

After completing this chapter, you will be able to:

- **Describe** the traits of skillful consumers.
- **Determine** ways to use advertising to be a skillful consumer.
- **List** the rights and responsibilities of consumers.
- **Explain** an effective procedure for making consumer complaints.
- **Identify** resources for consumers.

Writing Activity Compare and Contrast

Diligence When you do things fully, you do them diligently. Diligence is being determined to perform a task well. You can show diligence when you:

- Follow through in writing a letter of complaint and getting a refund for a defective product.
- Compare prices before making a major purchase.
- Double-check to be sure a school assignment has been done correctly.
- Take care of all home responsibilities, doing jobs promptly, completely, and well.

Write a report comparing and contrasting the ways you made a well-thought-out purchase and a purchase made with little thought. Describe your satisfaction with both purchases.

Writing Tips To write an effective compare and contrast report, follow these steps:

1. Choose two purchases to compare and contrast.
2. Organize your paper by comparing purchase processes and satisfaction levels.
3. Use appropriate transitions between comparisons and contrasts.

Be a Good Consumer

Reading Guide

Before You Read

How Can You Improve? Before starting the section, think about your last exam. What reading strategies helped you? Make a list of ways to improve your strategies in order to succeed on your next exam.

Read to Learn

Key Concepts
- **Describe** the traits of skillful consumers.
- **Determine** ways to use advertising to be a skillful consumer.

Main Idea

A skillful consumer is one who knows how to judge quality and price, comparison shop, and control impulse buying. The purpose of advertising is to get consumers to buy more.

Content Vocabulary

◇ consumer
◇ bargain
◇ comparison shopping
◇ warranty
◇ impulse buying

Academic Vocabulary

You will find these words in your reading and on your tests. Use the glossary to look up their definitions if necessary.

■ entice   ■ subtle

Graphic Organizer

As you read, look for tips for effective comparison shopping. Use a chart like the one shown to help organize your information.

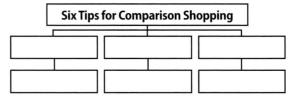

Six Tips for Comparison Shopping

 Graphic Organizer Go to this book's Online Learning Center at **glencoe.com** to print out this graphic organizer.

Academic Standards •

 English Language Arts

NCTE 3 Apply strategies to interpret texts.

NCTE 8 Use information resources to gather information and create and communicate knowledge.

 Mathematics

NCTM Number and Operations Compute fluently and make reasonable estimates.

NCTE *National Council of Teachers of English*
NCTM *National Council of Teachers of Mathematics*

NSES *National Science Education Standards*
NCSS *National Council of the Social Studies*

Traits of Skillful Consumers

One pleasure of earning money is buying what you need and want. Do you ever want more than your financial plan allows? Businesses **entice**, or attract, you in many ways. They use clever ads, tempting packaging, and determined salespeople. Whether you are in charge is your choice.

A **consumer** is a person who purchases goods and services. Making good decisions is the basis of being a good consumer. To be a skillful consumer, you must:

- Become familiar with products, prices, and standards of quality.
- Read and do research to learn what features to look for or avoid in products.
- Use self-discipline to resist society's message to buy more than you need.

You can learn the skills you need to be a smart consumer. First, you have to want to do so. When you are serious about making the most of your dollars, you will be inspired to discover how.

Judge Quality and Price

A cautious consumer wants to get top quality at a fair price. Do you look at how well something is made before you buy it? How do you know if the price is reasonable? These are decisions that consumers make.

What Is Quality?

Something that has quality is well made, works right, and will last. Well-made products can prevent frustration and save money. Experience teaches about quality. For example, Merle bought a new shampoo. After using it, his hair was oily and limp. Merle said, "I will never buy that brand again!" Sometimes learning by experience can be costly. Most people want to know ahead that a product or service is worth buying.

◆ Vocabulary

You can find definitions in the glossary at the back of this book.

As You Read

Connect How can you learn the skills needed to be a good consumer?

◀ Be a Good Consumer Different factors influence your decision to make a purchase. *What influences you the most when you purchase an item?*

If you saved a dollar a week by making careful purchases, in a year you would have $52 to save or spend. Saving more would give you even greater spending power. Here are some ideas for making that happen:

- Take advantage of sales and specials.
- Try private brands and lesser-known brands.
- Shop at discount stores.
- Shop at garage sales, thrift stores, and through the want ads when you can judge quality.
- Pay cash since credit may lead to debt.

- Use coupons unless quality house brands are cheaper.
- Check the unit price, a measure of the cost per unit of weight or volume, to compare prices on different-size packages.

Problem-Solving Max has a $.75 coupon for a brand-name toothpaste that costs $3.45 without the coupon. He usually buys the house brand. It is the same size as the brand-name toothpaste and costs $2.65. Which toothpaste costs less?

You can learn about quality by reading about the product. Consumer magazines may rate the product you want. There are also Web sites that report on products. These groups also rate the manufacturers that produce the products. Consumers Union is one such group. It tests products in laboratories. It then reports its findings in its magazine, *Consumer Reports*. Another group is Consumers Research. It publishes *Consumers Research* magazine. You can also find facts at public libraries. The Internet can offer you quality information if you choose reliable sites.

A Fair Price

No one wants to pay too much for an item. Deciding the best quality for the best price is not easy. Sometimes the lowest price is not the best buy. Four conditions make a purchase a true **bargain**, or a good buy:

- The product is one you need, want, and will use.
- The item's quality is suitable.
- The product sells at a price you are willing to pay.
- A reliable dealer sells the item.

Comparison Shopping

Comparison shopping means you look at the same item in several stores. Comparing quality and price before you buy helps you find good quality at the lowest price. If you use the Internet, there are sites set up to allow you to compare prices from various sources in one place.

You can compare prices on everything from small grocery items to major purchases. This includes cars, furniture, and large appliances. With large items, the amount saved can be substantial. On the other hand, regularly saving a little can add up. For example, when Dylan buys detergent, he checks the cost of different brands on the shelf. By comparing quantities and prices, he saves money with very little effort.

Tips for Comparing

When you do comparison shopping, following a few suggestions leads to satisfying results:

- **Know what you want.** Before you begin, write down the features you want. Look for these and avoid features you do not need. The more features, the more you are likely to pay.
- **Use the Internet.** If you know what you want, check the Web sites of several stores. You will learn who has the item and how much it costs at each. Going online first can save you time.
- **Compare similar items.** Read labels carefully so you can tell whether the products are comparable. For example, do not compare the prices of silk and cotton shirts.
- **Check any warranty.** The **warranty** is a written guarantee. Check if there is a warranty and what it covers. If it covers parts, check which parts. Labor for repairing the product may be covered. Also, check the length of time the warranty is in effect.
- **Compare credit terms.** If you are planning to purchase something with an installment plan, compare the plan on different brands.
- **Check the return policy.** Be sure to find out whether the store or company backs its products. Find out what the conditions are for returning a product before buying.

Control Impulse Buying

Impulse buying is the purchase of items without previous thought. You see something you like, so you buy it. Impulse buying is typical of present-oriented spenders. They often buy without thinking.

Retailers promote impulse buying in the store layout. Items they want you to grab are often close to the front of the store, so you see them as you enter. They are also placed near checkout aisles. People see them while waiting and are tempted to buy.

To control impulse buying, you must know what you truly need and can afford to pay. A shopping list will help you focus on what you intend to buy when you start out. For example, Adrienne decided ahead of time what she was going to get when she made her shopping list. While she was at the store, she stayed focused on her list. That way, she was looking for something specific rather than just looking. It also helps to take only enough money to cover what you have planned to buy. Impulse shoppers find it easy to spend extra money they are carrying.

✓ Reading Check **Explain** What makes a purchase a bargain?

Math in Action

Compare Prices

Comparing prices on different brands of the same item can help save you money. Go to a grocery store, drugstore, or discount store. Choose three items that you regularly use, such as toothpaste, chocolate cookies, or socks, to compare. Follow these steps:

1. Write down the price for a national brand of your products. Then write the price of a store brand for the same products. Make sure the size is the same for both items.

2. For each pair of products, subtract the lower number from the higher number.

3. Determine which brand is the best buy and how much you would save by buying that brand.

Math Concept **Subtracting Money**
You can subtract money just as you would subtract other numbers. Make sure the columns are aligned and regroup when necessary.

Starting Hint: Be sure to have the decimal points aligned before you begin subtracting.

Building Academic Skills
Go to this book's Online Learning Center through **glencoe.com** to complete a worksheet for this activity.

NCTM Number and Operations Compute fluently and make reasonable estimates.

 Math For math help, go to the Math Appendix at the back of the book.

Advertisements can help
you be a better shopper.
*In what ways do advertise-
ments help you as a
consumer?*

Analyze Advertising

Advertising can be very helpful to consumers. You keep up to date on new and existing products. It gives you price information and tells you when sales occur. You learn where to find products and services. Being a good shopper would be much harder without advertising.

A wise consumer, however, is also cautious about ads. The purpose of advertising is to get you to buy more goods and services. Businesses use it to create needs and wants that did not exist before.

Advertising is everywhere—on television and radio, in newspapers and magazines, and on buses, subways, and billboards. It is on clothing and everywhere on the Internet. If you are smart, you will use advertising and not allow it to use you.

Advertising Techniques

Companies advertise in two ways. It can be done directly and indirectly. Direct advertising tries to get you to buy a particular product by aiming directly at your values. One common approach focuses on glamour. Other values may include health, happiness, success, good looks, and love. Ads that are based on new technology may have special appeal to young people.

Indirect advertising is more **subtle**, or not obvious. For example, celebrities are often associated with products even though they are not selling them. The hero of a movie drinks a well-known soft drink. The star in a television series gets on an airplane from a major airline. This is called product placement. Companies pay to have their products featured in this way.

Another form of indirect advertising is the printing of product names on clothing. You may have a T-shirt with a brand name on it. You are advertising every time you wear it. What other examples of indirect advertising come to mind?

A Critical Eye

To use advertising successfully, you must watch out for deceptive ads. These suggestions can help you decide whether buying is wise:

- **Learn to separate fact from fiction.** Advertising is not always reliable. For example, an ad for cereal may claim to have the highest amount of vitamins of all cereals tested. This may refer to a test that included only two other brands.
- **Recognize "no-promise" promises.** Beware of certain words in ads, such as "can" and "often." Your cold medicine may promise to relieve symptoms for up to 12 hours. Does that mean one hour, 12 hours, or something in between?
- **Watch out for below-cost sales.** Sometimes a store will sell below cost to get you to come in to shop. They assume you will buy other items as well. If you have compared prices, you will be able to tell whether the price is truly low.
- **Be careful of percent-off ads.** If a store raises its prices, then advertises "30 percent off selected items," you may pay more on sale than you would otherwise.
- **Get the whole story.** Advertised prices sometimes do not include other fees or the cost of everything else you will need.

For example, when Mitzi saw a computer advertised at an incredibly low price, she went to check. The advertised price was for the computer only. When she added the price of the monitor, keyboard, printer, cables, and programs needed to make the computer run, the advertised price was not a bargain.

Section 24.1   After You Read

Review Key Concepts

1. **Describe** a quality product.
2. **Explain** the difference between direct and indirect advertising.

Practice Academic Skills

English Language Arts

3. Select an electronic product that you would like to own. Conduct research to find out the features and price of this item. Write a summary of your findings that could be used by others as a buying guide. Compile your summary with those of your classmates to create an Electronics Buying Guide. If possible, print your guide and make it available to other students.

> **NCTE 8** Use information resources to gather information and create and communicate knowledge.

4. Find an advertisement for a product with which you are familiar. Analyze the ad. What values is the ad appealing to? What age group is the ad directed at? Is there any misleading information in the ad? How do you know? Overall, how would you rate this ad? Explain your rating.

> **NCTE 3** Apply strategies to interpret texts.

Check Your Answers Check your answers at this book's Online Learning Center through **glencoe.com**.

Consumer Rights and Responsibilities

Reading Guide

Before You Read

Understanding Write down questions while reading. Many of them will be answered as you continue. If not, you will have a list ready for your teacher.

Read to Learn
Key Concepts
- **List** the rights and responsibilities of consumers.
- **Explain** an effective procedure for making consumer complaints.
- **Identify** resources for consumers.

Main Idea
Consumers have both rights and responsibilities. Consumer complaints are best resolved in person. There are government and business resources for consumers.

Content Vocabulary
◇ small claims court
◇ Better Business Bureau
◇ Consumer Action and Advisory Panel

Academic Vocabulary
You will find these words in your reading and on your tests. Use the glossary to look up their definitions if necessary.
■ explain   ■ deception

Graphic Organizer
As you read, think of a benefit of each of the seven rights of consumers. Use a figure like the one shown to help organize your information.

Consumer Right	Benefit of that Right
Be Informed	
Choice	
Safe Products	

 Graphic Organizer Go to this book's Online Learning Center at **glencoe.com** to print out this graphic organizer.

Academic Standards · · · · · · · · · · · · · · · ·

 English Language Arts

NCTE 8 Use information resources to gather information and create and communicate knowledge.

NCTE 12 Use language to accomplish individual purposes.

 Mathematics

NCTM Number and Operations Understand the meanings of operations and how they relate to one another.

NCTE *National Council of Teachers of English*
NCTM *National Council of Teachers of Mathematics*

NSES *National Science Education Standards*
NCSS *National Council of the Social Studies*

Rights and Responsibilities

Consumers have both rights and responsibilities in the marketplace. State and federal laws protect consumers' interests, or rights. At the same time, however, consumers also have duties. You must earn your rights as a consumer. You have to live up to your responsibilities.

Consumer Rights

As a consumer, you have seven major rights. These are the right to:

- **Information** Federal agencies make sure that companies provide you with accurate information about products. This includes both advertising and labeling.
- **Choose** Fair competition is encouraged. As a result, you can choose from any number of similar products. You may purchase any you want.
- **Safe Products** Some goods are dangerous. They may be banned by law. In other cases, labels warn you that the product can be dangerous. Exact directions are given for the safest use.
- **Be Heard** If you are not satisfied with a product or service, you should receive a full hearing and fair treatment. Also, the government considers consumers when making choices that affect the public. You must make your views about products and services known. You should inform your representatives and government agencies.
- **Have Problems Corrected** Businesses should replace a defective product or issue a refund.
- **Consumer Education** You should have the chance to learn consumer skills. These include comparison shopping, reading labels, and knowing how to identify quality products.
- **Service** You have a right to receive good service. This means being treated with respect and courtesy. It means being treated without discrimination.

Consumer Responsibilities

Consumers have responsibilities as well as rights. They must be careful, considerate shoppers. They must treat merchandise as carefully as if they owned it. Consumers have the responsibility to pay for all products. Shoplifting losses cut into a store's profits. The costs are passed along to shoppers when they pay higher prices.

Consumers have the responsibility to be informed. They should know what they are buying. They can read labels. Research will help them learn more about products and their features. They can learn and use consumer skills.

As You Read
Connect How have you exercised your rights as a consumer?

Consumer Rights You have the right to let companies know how you feel about their products. *How can you inform a business about its product if you have a problem?*

Financial Literacy

Paying Interest

For your birthday, you received $100. You could use the money to buy the $100 snowshoes you want. You go to the mountains four times each winter and rent snowshoes for $6 each time. On the other hand, you could use the money to pay off the $100 you owe on your credit card. This would help you avoid paying the 27% annual interest charge, which amounts to $2.25 per month. How much money would you save in one year if you bought the snowshoes? How much interest would you pay in a year if you did not pay what you owe on the credit card? Which is the better option?

Math Concept **Comparing Costs** Figure how much you would save by purchasing snowshoes by finding the cost to rent them four times a year (4 × $6). Then figure how much interest you will pay in a year if you do not pay off the credit card debt (12 × $2.25).

Starting Hint: Compare the cost of renting snowshoes to the cost of interest.

 For math help, go to the Math Appendix at the back of the book.

NCTM Number and Operations Understand the meanings of operations and how they relate to one another.

 **Vocabulary**

You can find definitions in the glossary at the back of this book.

The consumer is responsible for acting if a product or a service is not acceptable. This means saving sales records and receipts in case a product needs to be returned or exchanged. Consumers can speak out about products that are not up to standard.

Consumers are responsible for following instructions that are listed on products. You must understand and follow the directions. That way, you will avoid the dangers of not using them in the right way.

✓ **Reading Check** **Identify** How are consumers' rights protected?

Consumer Complaints

You must file a consumer complaint when you have a problem with goods or services. It is both a right and a responsibility. You have the right to be treated fairly and honestly. You also have the responsibility to save others from unfair treatment if you can.

Refunds and Replacements

Returning unsatisfactory merchandise for a refund or replacement is common. Handled correctly, these situations are resolved successfully. As with any consumer problem, first contact the business involved. You will have the best success if you go in person. Take your product and receipts. State your problem. **Explain** clearly, or make known, what you want done. Do this as often as needed until the issue is resolved. Remember: two points of view exist on an issue. Many stores must deal with irresponsible shoppers.

Returning an item is fine, as long as the reason is a good one. Stores that have to deal regularly with **deception**, or dishonesty, may seem strict with their policies. The reason for this is due to the actions of some consumers.

Sometimes writing a letter of complaint is the best approach when you have a problem. Information that comes with a product may tell you where to send such a letter. You could use the same address if you wanted to write a letter to compliment a company.

Billing Problems

Incorrect billings upset many consumers. People may be billed for items they did not buy. Their payments may have been credited to the wrong account. Human error and computers sometimes make these problems difficult to solve. Be sure, however, that the problem is corrected as soon as possible. Information that is not correct may go to credit reporting companies. Then you may have trouble getting credit later.

The best course of action for ensuring a billing error is corrected is to write a letter to the company. When you report a billing error in writing, the company is required by law to reply within 90 days of the date your letter was received. If you are right, the company is responsible for correcting the billing. Any interest charges will be removed from your account. If you are found to be wrong, you are expected to pay the bill within ten days.

✓ **Reading Check** **Explain** Why is making a consumer complaint both a right and a responsibility?

Resources for Consumers

As a consumer, you have many resources to help you. The government operates some of these resources. Businesses and industries run others.

Government Agencies

The federal government has consumer affairs offices. So do all state governments. They may have different names in each state. The attorney general of each state enforces laws that protect consumers. Many county and city governments also have agencies that are set up to deal with consumer problems. These agencies are most concerned with the serious problems of fraud in goods and services. They deal with unfair or deceptive selling methods. They are less apt to deal with inadequate goods and poor service.

INDEPENDENT Living

HOW TO | Get Financial Help

Even if you have excellent budgeting skills, you may need financial help at some point in your life. Unexpected events can cause major financial problems. For those who run into trouble, help is available. Follow these guidelines to get financial help:

1. **Read about it.** Visit a library for books that offer financial advice.
2. **Take a class.** Sign up for a money management class at a local community college.
3. **Visit the bank.** Ask your bank if it offers free financial advice to its customers.
4. **Use the Internet.** Research Web sites that offer information, useful statistics, and practical advice on money management.

Take Action Write down two economic changes that might cause you financial hardship. Write a paragraph explaining the steps you would take to get the help you need. Include two of the sources from the list above.

Some consumer disputes are resolved in **small claims court**. These courts handle cases that do not exceed a money limit set by each state. You can sue only for the actual cost of the time or services lost. Most consumers use small claims court only as a last resort because of the time, cost, and effort that are involved.

Lawyers are not required in small claims court. In some states, they are not allowed. The judge works to bring out the facts of the case and to understand the issues. The decision will either be announced right away or mailed.

Business Organizations

Honest businesses treat their customers in a fair way. They know satisfied customers are the reason they are in business. Many companies have set up their own groups to regulate themselves.

The **Better Business Bureau** (BBB) is an independent group. It is sponsored by businesses in a community. The BBB watches over advertising. It keeps files on local companies. The information on file may include how long a company has been in business, how often complaints have been made against the company, and how the company handles complaints. The BBB does not advise consumers. It only shares information with them. Citizens can make a complaint or get information by calling the BBB, or through its Web site.

A **Consumer Action and Advisory Panel** (CAP) is formed by a specific industry to help solve consumer problems. The appliance, automobile, furniture, and travel industries all have a CAP. If you have a problem with a business, a CAP may be able to help you.

Section 24.2   After You Read

Review Key Concepts

1. **Describe** what the government does to insure that products are safe.
2. **Explain** why it is important to get billing problems solved quickly.
3. **Identify** information that can be obtained from the Better Business Bureau (BBB).

Practice Academic Skills

English Language Arts

4. Find articles on the rights or responsibilities of consumers. Work with your classmates to create a poster. Title it "Rights and Responsibilities." Arrange the articles you collected on the poster.

5. Imagine you are angry at the service you received at a diner close to your school. Write a letter to the editor of your school newspaper. Outline what happened, how it was dealt with at the diner, and what you would like other students to do. Use reason and logic in writing your letter.

> **NCTE 8** Use information resources to gather information and create and communicate knowledge.

> **NCTE 12** Use language to accomplish individual purposes.

Check Your Answers Check your answers at this book's Online Learning Center through **glencoe.com**.

CHAPTER SUMMARY

Section 24.1
Be a Good Consumer

Skillful consumers have traits that help them make the most of their money. They know that a quality product is well made, works right, and will last. They can evaluate whether a price is fair. They comparison shop. Good consumers avoid impulse buying. Advertising can be direct or indirect. Direct advertising aims directly at your values. Indirect advertising is not as obvious. Consumers can use information from advertisements. They should use a critical eye to question and evaluate ad claims.

Section 24.2
Consumer Rights and Responsibilities

Consumers have rights that are set by federal and state laws. They also have responsibilities. Consumer complaints may be best done in person. The consumer should state the problem. He or she should explain the outcome wanted. Sometimes a letter is more effective. Billing problems should be settled quickly to prevent incorrect credit reports. Government agencies serve as resources for consumers. In addition, business groups are also resources.

Content and Academic Vocabulary Review

1. Use each of these content and academic vocabulary words in a sentence.

Content Vocabulary

◇ consumer (p. 469)
◇ bargain (p. 470)
◇ comparison shopping (p. 470)
◇ warranty (p. 471)
◇ impulse buying (p. 471)
◇ small claims court (p. 478)
◇ Better Business Bureau (p. 478)
◇ Consumer Action and Advisory Panel (p. 478)

Academic Vocabulary

■ entice (p. 469)
■ subtle (p. 472)
■ explain (p. 476)
■ deception (p. 476)

Review Key Concepts

2. Describe the traits of skillful consumers.
3. Determine ways to use advertising to be a skillful consumer.
4. List the rights and responsibilities of consumers.
5. Explain an effective procedure for making consumer complaints.
6. Identify resources for consumers.

Critical Thinking

7. Identify Evidence What should you look for *before* you buy something? What clues would tell that you are dealing with an honest business?
8. Explain Why do you think many people buy and wear clothes with advertising designs?
9. Evaluate Are consumers entitled to consumer rights? What if they do not live up to their responsibilities as consumers?

Real-World Skills

Consumer Skills

10. Problem Solving After a recent shopping trip, Olivia lined up her purchases for a look. Already she had second thoughts about several items. She wondered why she keeps buying things she does not need and seldom uses. Write a paragraph with your advice to Olivia.

Research Skills

11. Product Evaluation Find a product that is being compared in a consumer publication. Using the findings in the comparison, decide which brand of the product you would buy. Write a paragraph to explain your choice. Be sure to prioritize which features affected your decision.

Financial Literacy Skills

12. Billing Problems Cody's credit card bill showed a charge he had not made. He did not pay it, but did not write a letter explaining why. The next month, his bill contained a finance charge in addition to the original charge. Write a step-by-step list of actions Cody should take.

Interpersonal Skills

13. Group Work Follow your teacher's instructions to form into groups. Suppose you were going to market the class you are taking right now to younger students. With your group, create and present an advertising campaign that would sell the class.

14. Advertising Analysis Find five examples of advertisements. Identify the techniques used. What appeals are used in each? Which do you think is most effective? Least effective? Create a table for your findings. Share your advertisements and analysis with your classmates.

15. Investigate Find out about the consumer laws in your state. What protections do they offer? What are the penalties for breaking these laws? Write a summary of your findings.

16. Interview Talk to the manager of a retail store. Learn about examples of irresponsible consumers. How do their actions raise prices for other consumers? What can be done about this problem? Write a brief report of your interview.

17. Comparison Shopping Online Go to this book's Online Learning Center at **glencoe.com** to find **Web Links** for **Online Shopping Comparison Sites**. Find at least three DVD players to compare. Sort the listings. Would you want to purchase the DVD player from any of these stores? Why or why not? Present your findings in a report.

Additional Activities For additional activities, go to this book's Online Learning Center through **glencoe.com**.

Academic Skills

Mathematics

18. Calculate Unit Costs Jamie is at the local supermarket shopping for apple-sauce. He finds a 16-ounce jar of brand-name applesauce that costs $1.59. He decides to compare the price to other brands. He finds the supermarket house brand is a 14-ounce jar for $1.09. What is the cost per ounce of each jar? Which is the better buy?

Math Concept **Dividing Money** To divide money, make sure the decimal point in the quotient is directly above the decimal point of the dividend.

Starting Hint: Divide the cost of the brand-name applesauce ($1.59) by the number of ounces in the jar (16). Then do the same for the house-brand jar of applesauce. Compare your answers.

 For math help, go to the Math Appendix at the back of the book.

NCTM Number and Operations Understand numbers, ways of representing numbers, relationships among numbers, and number systems.

English Language Arts

19. Write a Letter Imagine that you have purchased a defective product. Write an effective letter of complaint to the company that sells the product, using the tips in this chapter. Be reasonable and logical with your argument. Do not attack the company. Also, clearly state what it is you want the company to do to make the situation right.

NCTE 4 Use written language to communicate effectively.

Social Studies

20. Evaluate Laws The government has laws in place that have increased the safety of consumers. Write a report on these laws and the effect they have had on the safety of consumers. Examples may include automobile safety and secondhand smoke. Include in your report some specific examples of changes manufacturers have made because of these laws.

NCSS X.b Identify, analyze, interpret, and evaluate sources and examples of citizen's rights and responsibilities.

STANDARDIZED TEST PRACTICE

ESSAY
Use a separate sheet of paper to write a half-page response to the following writing prompt.

Test-Taking Tip Budget your time. Make sure you have sufficient time to study so that you are well prepared for the test.

21. You have just purchased your very first car. It is used, but the salesperson says it is fully guaranteed. Two weeks after you have the car, the muffler falls off. When you return to the dealer, you are told that the parts are guaranteed but the labor is not. Write an essay expressing why you feel its policy is misleading.

CHAPTER 25

Think About Your Career

Section 25.1

Prepare for a Career

Section 25.2

Join the Work World

▶▶ *Explore the Photo* You should consider your interests when thinking about your career. *How can identifying your interests help you succeed in your career?*

Chapter Objectives

After completing this chapter, you will be able to:

- **Describe** the process of making a plan for a career.
- **Explain** why it is important to set career goals.
- **Identify** what it means to have a professional approach to the work world.
- **Evaluate** the advantages and disadvantages of being an entrepreneur.

Writing Activity

Editing

Perseverance The ability to keep working at a task, in spite of difficulties, is called perseverance. It means to reach for a goal with insistent effort. You can show perseverance when you:

- Fill out job application forms even when businesses say they are not hiring.
- Take summer school classes to raise your grades high enough to get into a training program.
- Run every morning before school to better your chance of making the track team.
- Speak cheerfully to a shy neighbor who rarely returns the greeting.

Write a paragraph that identifies a situation in your life where you showed perseverance. After you have written the paragraph, go back and edit it.

Writing Tips To effectively edit your paragraph, follow these steps:

1. Edit your sentences so they make sense.
2. Be objective when editing your own work.
3. Proofread closely to find errors.

Prepare for a Career

Reading Guide

Before You Read

Two-Column Notes Divide a piece of paper into two columns. In the left column, write down main ideas. In the right column, list supporting details.

Read to Learn
Key Concepts
- **Describe** the process of making a plan for a career.
- **Explain** why it is important to set career goals.

Main Idea
The time to plan for a career is now. Interests and abilities may lead to possible careers. Decisions about education and training need to be made. Goals can be set to outline a possible career path.

Content Vocabulary
◇ career
◇ aptitude
◇ career counselor
◇ career cluster
◇ apprentice
◇ career path

Academic Vocabulary
You will find these words in your reading and on your tests. Use the glossary to look up their definitions if necessary.
■ interpret ■ qualify

Graphic Organizer
As you read, look for the kinds of tests used in career counseling. Use a concept map like the one shown to help organize your information.

Career Counseling Tests

 Graphic Organizer Go to this book's Online Learning Center at **glencoe.com** to print out this graphic organizer.

Academic Standards • • • • • • • • • • • • • • • • • • •

 English Language Arts

NCTE 5 Use different writing process elements to communicate effectively.

NCTE 8 Use information resources to gather information and create and communicate knowledge.

 Mathematics

NCTM Number and Operations Understand the meanings of operations and how they relate to one another.

NCTE *National Council of Teachers of English*
NCTM *National Council of Teachers of Mathematics*

NSES *National Science Education Standards*
NCSS *National Council of the Social Studies*

How to Plan Your Future

Are you ready to enter the work world when you finish your schooling? It is time to plan and set goals now. Some people do not think about where they want to be in ten or fifteen years. They may find themselves drifting from one unrewarding job to the next.

A **career** is a series of related jobs or occupations done over a period of years. Personal satisfaction is one reason to plan for a career. Financial concerns are another. The well-being of you and your future family may depend on the choices you make now. A good job offers a family more than a way to pay the bills. It gives them chances to make choices in life. It supports their efforts to remain strong.

You may want to think whether your career choice fits with the view of the family life that you want. Are you looking at a career where flextime or job sharing would be possible? Would you like a career where you could telecommute? Are you willing to be away from your family if the job requires travel?

Throughout your life, your career choices will be tied to your family. If you change jobs or careers, your family will feel the impact. You will need to act wisely to think about your needs as well as those of other family members. If you meet your career goals, you can help your family meet its needs and goals.

Your community also has a stake in your career. When families are self-sufficient, they can help others, rather than need to be helped. Strong families help build strong communities.

Another factor to think about in planning for the future is technology. The world of technology is one of rapid change. In your career, you are apt to use devices and software that have not yet been invented. You need a solid grasp of the way technology affects jobs and job trends. You will need to be prepared to keep up to date. This will require continued training and education.

You need to develop a strategy to choose and prepare for your career. You will have many personal opportunities in the future. If you do not start now, time and events may make it harder to achieve your goals.

Evaluate Your Interests and Abilities

Have you ever noticed that when you are doing something you really enjoy, it does not seem like work? Think of how rewarding it would be to have a career that you like and are good at, too. What are your skills and interests? Can they be channeled into a worthwhile career? A number of resources can help you answer these questions.

Vocabulary
You can find definitions in the glossary at the back of this book.

As You Read
Connect Why is it important to plan and set career goals now?

Set Career Goals
Setting a career goal now will help you attain it later. *What goals do you have that will help you attain your dream career?*

Tests

Certain tests identify interests and abilities. They are matched to fields of employment. Some tests reveal broad, general skills. Others focus on specific, job-related talents. Commonly used tests include:

- **Intelligence Tests** These rate mental abilities, such as reasoning and problem solving.
- **Aptitude Tests** A natural talent and capacity for learning a certain skill is called **aptitude**. Aptitude tests can cover many areas, such as mechanical understanding or physical skills.
- **Activities Preference Tests or Interest Tests** This type of test helps you translate your likes and dislikes into specific work preferences. Test results show patterns of interest. You can then compare these patterns to career descriptions. This helps you see what you might enjoy doing.
- **Job Preference Tests** This test lists pairs of tasks. Then it asks you to choose between them. When the test is scored, you are given a list of jobs that should suit your interests.

Except for intelligence tests, these tests have no right or wrong answers. The tests are useful, but limited. They cannot tell you what job to pursue. They cannot guarantee happiness and success. The purpose of these tests is to point out careers that indicate a chance for success.

Career Counseling

Career counselors can help you identify your skills and interests. A **career counselor** helps people choose and succeed in their work. They can answer questions about the education or training needed for jobs. They will know about working conditions. They can give you incomes of specific careers. Guidance counselors at school often serve as career counselors. Counselors are also found in employment agencies and private firms.

Career counselors talk with you about your interests and talents. They look at your career and personal goals. They are trained to **interpret**, or explain, the tests. This will help you discover your work strengths. Based on your tests, a counselor might suggest looking at a specific career cluster. A **career cluster** is a group of occupations and broad industries that have something in common. **Figure 25.1** lists examples of careers found in the Human Services Career Cluster.

▲ The Right Fit
What you enjoy doing now can help you decide on your future career. *What interests do you have now that could become your chosen career?*

The following is a list of the 16 career clusters:
- Agriculture, Food, and Natural Resources
- Architecture and Construction
- Arts, Audio/Video Technology, and Communications
- Business, Management, and Administration
- Education and Training
- Finance
- Government and Public Administration
- Health Sciences
- Hospitality and Tourism
- Human Services
- Information Technology
- Law, Public Safety, Corrections, and Security
- Manufacturing
- Marketing, Sales, and Service
- Science, Technology, Engineering, and Mathematics
- Transportation, Distribution, and Logistics

Decisions About Education and Training

Good workers are needed and valued everywhere. Remember, though, that you need a long-distance view of work. The job you have or can get now may not support your family. You may outgrow a job and wish for something that interests you more. You may want something that pays more, too.

It is important to look at job trends when making choices about training. Your interests may point you in a specific direction. The ideal situation is when your interests match a career that is projected to grow.

Figure 25.1   Human Services Career Cluster

Jobs caring for the needs of people and families are found in the Human Services Career Cluster. *What personal qualities would be needed to work in this career cluster?*

Career Categories	Examples of Jobs
Early Childhood Development and Services	Childcare worker, parent educator, teacher aide
Counseling and Mental Health Services	Social worker, marriage counselor, psychologist
Family and Community Services	Domestic violence shelter administrator, religious counselor, adoption placement worker
Personal Care Services	Beautician, personal shopper, elder services specialist
Consumer Services	Credit counselor, consumer complaint investigator, consumer media specialist

Compare Hourly Wages

Tim is trying to decide which job offer to accept after graduating from school. The hourly wage at Company A is $10 and the hourly wage at Company B is $12. What percentage of Company B's hourly wage would Company A's hourly wage be? Round to the nearest whole percent.

Math Concept **Dividing Decimals** To divide decimals, move the decimal point in the divisor until it is no longer a decimal and move the decimal point in the dividend the same number of places.

Starting Hint: First, set up a division problem with the divisor and the dividend. Move the decimal point two places to the right in both numbers. Divide until you reach the thousandths place. Your answer will be a decimal that you can write as a percent.

Math For math help, go to the Math Appendix at the back of the book.

NCTM Number and Operations Understand the meanings of operations and how they relate to one another.

Another factor to look at is how the education or training can be used. Are you looking for general or specific training? Training that is too specific may be outdated quickly. Skills that will help you in many situations may be more useful in the long run. You may be able to use job skills in other settings as well. Some skills will transfer to home or community roles.

People often find that they need education or training past high school to **qualify**, or meet the requirements, for the jobs they would really like to have. The amount of education you receive depends on your interests and your work goals. Your financial situation is another factor. What your family expects of you and what you expect of yourself will affect your plans. You need to weigh all of these factors. Then you can make decisions about education that are right for you. You can obtain education or training in several ways.

Career or Technical Schools

If you know what job you want, you may choose a career or technical school. These schools provide specialized training for a specific career. It could be in culinary arts, dentistry, or electronics. Courses consist of both classroom study and hands-on experience. Programs are intense since students receive training only for one job.

Apprenticeships

For many occupations, you can receive on-the-job training. These can include plumbing, painting, and carpentry. As an **apprentice**, you receive training from a skilled worker in a trade. You gain experience and earn money at the same time. The career counselor in your school can help you find out more about programs in your area.

Colleges and Universities

Colleges and universities offer bachelor's degrees. Some also offer master's degrees. A bachelor's degree usually involves a four-year course of study. Many jobs require a college degree. Some jobs require an advanced degree, such as a master's degree or a doctorate. You will want to choose a college that has a quality program in the field you have chosen. The location, cost, and size of the college can also affect your choice.

Community colleges are two-year schools. They may offer classes that lead to a certificate. Examples might be computer repair or child-care worker. They also offer basic academic elective classes like writing and research skills to prepare students to transfer to a four-year college. One of the big advantages of community colleges is their cost.

Also, their credits are transferable, so they apply toward your degree requirements at another school you may want to attend. They often offer courses in the evening and on weekends. This helps those who are working while attending school.

Education and Training Costs

There are many alternatives for getting an education. Some cost more than others, but quality can be found at all prices. Tuition, fees, books, and living expenses are all parts of the price of an education. Some educations, like expert apprenticeships, cost years of hands-on work but no money. Many people attend inexpensive community colleges for two years and then transfer their credits to more expensive state colleges, where they receive bachelor's degrees.

The expense of education is an investment in your future. The more education you have, the more money you are likely to earn over the course of your lifetime. Education can help you get jobs and it can lead to promotions and higher pay.

✓ **Reading Check** **List** What are four kinds of tests that can help in choosing a career?

INDEPENDENT *Living*

HOW TO **Direct Your Career**

Some teens know their exact career path before they enter high school. For most teens, however, career plans are a little less clear-cut. Although you may not be ready to commit to a career yet, you want to be ready for whatever the future brings. Follow these guidelines to direct your career:

1. **Gain a variety of experiences.** When you try something new, you learn more about yourself. Experiences help you narrow down your skills and interests.
2. **Focus on goals.** Staying aware of your goals, values, and expectations can help you decide which career path to take.
3. **Develop transferable skills.** These are learned abilities that can be used in many job situations. For example, time management skills can help a cook create a work schedule for the kitchen staff.
4. **Look at general trends.** Always think about the economic power of trends in society. For instance, you know that many domestic and global trends have a growing effect on the local job market.

Take Action Ask an expert on careers, such as a school counselor or job recruiter, what skills are always in demand. Use this information to analyze the classes you are taking. Make a list of future classes that would help you gain necessary workplace skills.

Career Goals and Paths

Setting career goals helps you focus on what you need to do. You can identify resources and develop a plan to prepare for the kind of work you want. Because your work life will last a long time, you will need short-term goals that you will work for now. You will also want to set some long-term goals. These will help you focus on where you want to be in ten or twenty years.

In establishing career goals, your interests and skills can guide you. Changes in the job market, in your family situation, and in yourself might cause you to switch jobs and even careers. Workers today average six or seven job changes during their lifetime. Your goals, both long- and short-term, should help you stay flexible as well as focused.

Being flexible as you set career goals helps you see how one job can lead to another. This connection is called a **career path**. As you move along your career path, you gain skills and knowledge. You will have new roles and responsibilities. You will grow as a person. More challenging jobs will be ahead. As you look at a career path that interests you, think about what it involves. What kind of salary can you expect? Where will you need to live? What other factors are important? As the years unfold, you can adapt or change your goals to match your changing interests and circumstances.

At this point in your life, you may not be able to lay out a career path. What you do need are career plans and goals to give you focus over the next few years.

Section 25.1   After You Read

Review Key Concepts

1. **Explain** why the teen years are a good time to think seriously about a career.

2. **Describe** a career path.

Practice Academic Skills

English Language Arts

3. Should a person ever choose a career that does not match his or her interests and skills? Why or why not? Write a brief speech to answer these questions. The speech will be for younger students. As you write, keep in mind the age of your intended audience. Make sure the vocabulary you use is appropriate for the audience.

> **NCTE 5** Use different writing process elements to communicate effectively.

4. Gather information about the opportunities for education and training in your area. What colleges and universities are close? What career or technical schools? Are there apprentice programs available? What are the costs of each? Write a summary of your findings.

> **NCTE 8** Use information resources to gather information and create and communicate knowledge.

Check Your Answers Check your answers at this book's Online Learning Center through **glencoe.com**.

Join the Work World

Reading Guide

Before You Read

Get Your Rest The more well rested and alert you are when you sit down to study, the more likely you will be to remember the information later.

Read to Learn

Key Concepts

- **Identify** what it means to have a professional approach to the work world.
- **Evaluate** the advantages and disadvantages of being an entrepreneur.

Main Idea

Employers value workers who show professionalism. It can be shown when locating and applying for a job. It can be shown in interviews and when leaving a job. Some people become entrepreneurs rather than employees.

Content Vocabulary

◇ professionalism   ◇ reference
◇ résumé   ◇ interview
◇ application form ◇ notice

Academic Vocabulary

You will find these words in your reading and on your tests. Use the glossary to look up their definitions if necessary.

▪ hygiene   ▪ check

Graphic Organizer

As you read, identify sources for job leads. Use a chart like the one shown to help organize your information.

Resources for Job Possibilities
1.
2.
3.
4.

 Graphic Organizer Go to this book's Online Learning Center at **glencoe.com** to print out this graphic organizer.

Academic Standards •

 English Language Arts

NCTE 4 Use written language to communicate effectively.

NCTE 5 Use different writing process elements to communicate effectively.

 Science

NSES Content Standard 1 Develop an understanding of science unifying concepts and processes.

NCTE *National Council of Teachers of English*
NCTM *National Council of Teachers of Mathematics*

NSES *National Science Education Standards*
NCSS *National Council of the Social Studies*

A Professional Approach

Finding a job and succeeding at it are two different things. Having a good attitude toward your work is vital for success. How you think and feel about your job affects your job performance, as well as that of fellow employees.

The best workers have a spirit of **professionalism**. That is, they show a positive attitude. They have a sense of commitment. Employees with professionalism take pride in their work, whatever it may be. They carry out their duties cheerfully. They work to the best of their abilities. Their actions on the job reflect high moral standards. They use ethical behavior on the job. Self-discipline is an important trait of a professional worker. Others are responsibility and the ability to work without supervision.

Communication skills are a part of professionalism. Workers need to be able to speak. They must be able to listen. They need to write effectively. When there are multiple workplaces involved, communication techniques must be effective.

It is also important to dress professionally. You need to know if there is a dress code at work. There may be a uniform to wear. What you wear can affect how your manager looks at you and your work. Personal **hygiene**, or cleanliness, is also important.

You can start to develop a professional attitude now. You can be professional in your job as a student. You can use that attitude when you look for and apply for a job. When you do, you are building skills that can take you far in whatever career you choose.

Vocabulary
You can find definitions in the glossary at the back of this book.

As You Read
Connect What are some ways you can improve your communication skills?

▶▶ **A Positive Attitude** Your appearance and the way you conduct yourself show pride and commitment to your work. *In what ways can you show a positive attitude at school and at work?*

Write your résumé carefully. It will be a reflection of you and what you have to offer a company. Use the following tips to write an effective résumé:

- Use the library or Internet to learn more about writing a résumé.
- Highlight the education, training, and skills you have.
- Use a word processing program to prepare the résumé.
- Limit your résumé to one page.
- Proofread carefully so there are no errors in grammar or spelling.

Problem-Solving Dane wanted to apply for the job of editor of the school newspaper. One of the requirements was to turn in a résumé. Dane called his friend Scott to ask for help. Scott replied that it would be easy to create a résumé since Dane had done so much writing for both the school and some local newspapers. What other help could Scott give Dane? Write your answer as an interview between Scott and Dane. Scott will ask questions and Dane will give answers.

Locate Job Possibilities

The best-laid plans for a brilliant career will not do much good unless you can reach that early, all-important goal of getting a job. Job hunting is where the ideas in your head meet real life. Finding a job takes energy, spirit, and self-confidence. To track down and land a job can seem like an imposing task. It often requires using many resources to find possible jobs. The following are examples of where you can locate job possibilities.

- **Internet** Online you can find job banks, recruiters, and job listings from newspapers and associations. You can research employers and look at business and telephone listings. There are many mailing lists, newsgroups, and chat forums on finding a job. You can **check**, or inspect, jobs locally and in distant places.
- **Personal Contacts** One of the best ways to discover job openings is through others. Let family members, friends, and neighbors know you are looking for a job.
- **Placement Offices** School placement offices are good sources. Job openings are often posted. Community colleges usually have placement offices. Even if you do not attend the college, you can visit the office to see what is available.
- **Classified Ads** Newspapers and magazines run print ads for jobs. These are especially useful in smaller communities where jobs may not be posted online.
- **Employment Agencies** Employment agencies provide job listings, counseling, and testing. State-funded agencies offer these services for free. Private agencies charge a fee.
- **Businesses** A challenging tactic is to visit places of business in person. Ask if they are hiring. This approach takes courage. You are apt to be disappointed. However, your interest may impress a possible employer.

Apply for a Job

Suppose you find a job opening that sounds promising. Your next step is to submit a résumé. A **résumé** is a written account of your qualifications. It includes education, training, experience, skills, activities, and interests. If you do not have a lot of experience, it is best to organize your résumé around your skills and accomplishments.

You will probably be asked to fill out an **application form**. This form gives employers basic data about job candidates. They can quickly compare applicants to find the most promising ones. Read and follow all the instructions carefully. Answer every question, printing neatly in black or blue ink. If a question does not apply to you, write "not applicable" in the space given. Be sure to have your Social Security number and your employment record.

Most application forms ask for references. A **reference** is someone who will recommend your ability and character. Be sure to ask these people for permission before using their names.

A Successful Interview

Promising applicants are asked for an **interview**. This is a face-to-face meeting between an employer and a potential employee. It is normal to approach the interview with anxiety. First impressions in an interview are important. You want to project a professional image.

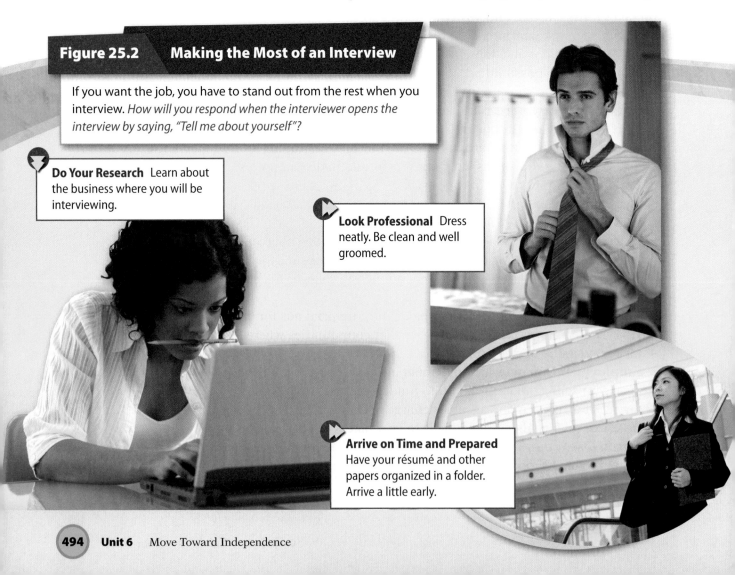

Figure 25.2 Making the Most of an Interview

If you want the job, you have to stand out from the rest when you interview. *How will you respond when the interviewer opens the interview by saying, "Tell me about yourself"?*

Do Your Research Learn about the business where you will be interviewing.

Look Professional Dress neatly. Be clean and well groomed.

Arrive on Time and Prepared Have your résumé and other papers organized in a folder. Arrive a little early.

What you say and how you act can make the difference between acceptance and rejection. You need to know what to expect and prepare for it carefully. Then you can calm your nerves and make the interview work in your favor.

Your goal is to convince the interviewer that you are the best person for the job. Plan ways to explain what you have to offer. Show self-confidence. Ask any questions you have about the job. Asking about wages and benefits is all right. Avoid giving the impression that they are your main concern. **Figure 25.2** will help you through the interview process.

Leave a Job

Sooner or later, most people leave a job. Again, you can leave in a professional manner. Whatever your reason for leaving, try to do so on a positive note. You never know when you may need the contacts you have made.

It is good workplace etiquette to give your employer **notice**. This is an official written statement that you are leaving. A letter of resignation is the most common type of notice. Depending on the job and the business, your employment may end at the time you resign. In other cases, you are expected to work a period of time after giving notice. This gives your employer time to hire a replacement.

✓ **Reading Check** **Describe** What is professionalism?

Have a Positive Attitude Smile and make eye contact. Be positive and show interest.

Speak for Success Talk about your strengths tactfully. Answer questions clearly and simply. Ask questions you have about the company and position.

After the Interview Express your thanks verbally. Send a note of appreciation.

Become an Entrepreneur

An entrepreneur is someone who organizes and runs a business. Entrepreneurs need to be highly motivated. They must be self-confident. They will have to work hard to develop the business. They must have the personal skills needed to run a business.

Successful entrepreneurs see a needed service and decide to provide it. They research the business and look at the risks and rewards. If they decide to take the challenge, they move forward with their businesses.

There are businesses that can be set up to serve families. Families are getting busier. They are more willing to pay others for tasks they usually do themselves. Many entrepreneurs run small businesses. They clean houses or plan parties. They offer child care or prepare meals. Many financial planners and tax preparers own their own businesses.

Entrepreneurs often work long hours, at least to start. There is no guarantee of success. The risk is great because the failure rate of new businesses is high. Entrepreneurs must be willing to sacrifice the security of a regular paycheck. They may need financial backing from others.

There is, however, deep personal satisfaction in working for yourself. There is also the potential for a good income. In the end, most entrepreneurs choose to start a business because they want to be in charge.

Section 25.2 After You Read

Review Key Concepts

1. **Identify** resources for finding information about available jobs.

2. **Describe** what an entrepreneur does.

Practice Academic Skills

English Language Arts

3. Imagine you have just completed a job interview. Write the interviewer a note of thanks for interviewing you. As you write, keep in mind the intended recipient, or audience, for your note. Write in a professional, respectful way that shows your appreciation.

> **NCTE 5** Use different writing process elements to communicate effectively.

4. Write a classified ad for an entrepreneur. Include the qualities needed to be successful in starting a business. Be sure to use language that will make the reader want to buy your product. Make the reader feel like this is the opportunity of a lifetime.

> **NCTE 4** Use written language to communicate effectively.

 Check Your Answers Check your answers at this book's Online Learning Center through **glencoe.com**.

CHAPTER SUMMARY

Section 25.1
Prepare for a Career

People need to start planning for their careers while still in high school. One of the first steps is to look at interests and skills. Various tests can help identify career fields that will match your interests. Some of the different tests are intelligence, aptitude, interest (activities preference) and job preference tests. Career counselors are good sources of information about careers. Education, training, and costs need to be considered. Long- and short-term goals help people stay focused yet flexible as they map out a career path.

Section 25.2
Join the Work World

The best workers show professionalism. This is a display of personal qualities and skills. Having high moral standards at work is also important. Job opportunities can be found on the Internet and through personal contacts. Placement offices, ads, employment agencies, and businesses are other resources. Application forms and résumés are usually asked for when applying for a job. An interview is a chance to make a good impression on an employer. Employees should give notice when leaving a job. Entrepreneurs start their own businesses.

Content and Academic Vocabulary Review

1. Use each of these content and academic vocabulary words in a sentence.

Content Vocabulary
- ◇ career (p. 485)
- ◇ aptitude (p. 486)
- ◇ career counselor (p. 486)
- ◇ career cluster (p. 486)
- ◇ apprentice (p. 488)
- ◇ career path (p. 490)
- ◇ professionalism (p. 492)
- ◇ résumé (p. 494)
- ◇ application form (p. 494)
- ◇ reference (p. 494)
- ◇ interview (p. 494)
- ◇ notice (p. 495)

Academic Vocabulary
- ■ interpret (p. 486)
- ■ qualify (p. 488)
- ■ hygiene (p. 492)
- ■ check (p. 493)

Review Key Concepts

2. Describe the process of making a plan for a career.

3. Explain why it is important to set career goals.

4. Identify what it means to have a professional approach to the work world.

5. Evaluate the advantages and disadvantages of being an entrepreneur.

Critical Thinking

6. Analyze During an interview, you should talk about your personal strengths. How can you do this without sounding like you are bragging?

7. Evaluate Testing can tell you if your present interests are ones you should base a career on. What are some other ways to find out if your interests are valid?

8. Predict You show professionalism at work. How does this assist your coworkers? How does it help your employers?

9. Recognize Values Which do you think is more important—doing work you love or having a career with a good income? Why?

Real-World Skills

Decision-Making Skills

10. Problem-Solving Anthony is a top student and a talented saxophone player. His dream is to earn a living as a jazz musician. He has been offered an academic scholarship, but wants to attend an arts school for music. Anthony's parents think he should accept the scholarship. Write a note with your advice for Anthony.

Technology Skills

11. Create a Presentation Create a list of tips that would be helpful in a job interview. Use software to prepare a presentation. Title it "Interviewing Tips." Be sure your presentation looks good so it catches the attention of your audience. Also, carefully check grammar and spelling.

Research Skills

12. Economics Conduct research on the requirements for three levels of employment in the same career. Examples may be preschool, high school, and college teacher. Compare the education needed with the salary for each position. Are the costs of the education a good investment? Show your findings in a table.

Communication Skills

13. Plan Answers Nicole's friend told her about some difficult questions that she was asked at a job interview. Nicole realizes that the questions would give her trouble, too. She has a job interview scheduled for next week. What could Nicole do? Write a list of suggestions.

14. Job Interviews Follow your teacher's instructions to form into pairs. Write down five questions that might be used at a job interview. Switch partners. The new partners will conduct a mock job interview in front of the class. The class will identify the best question and answer.

15. Job Application Obtain a job application from at least two different places of employment. Fill out the applications. Use the suggestions in the chapter to help you answer the application's questions.

16. Job Analysis Follow your teacher's instructions to form into groups. Develop a list of jobs that are commonly held by teens in your area. Discuss the skills and experiences teens could gain from these jobs. Write a summary of your group's discussion and share with the class.

17. Job Banks Go to this book's Online Learning Center through **glencoe.com** to find **Web Links** for **Job Banks**. Find one that lists openings where you live. Identify three listings that interest you and three that you are qualified for. Explain your answers in a paragraph.

Additional Activities For additional activities, go to this book's Online Learning Center through **glencoe.com**.

Academic Skills

Mathematics

18. Calculate Time You are becoming anxious to learn whether you have been accepted to attend the technical college where you sent your application. It has been about four and a half months since you filled out and sent in your application. You are literally counting the days until you receive word back from the college. About how many days has it been since you sent in the application?

Math Concept **Increments of Time** Weeks always have seven days. There are usually four weeks in a month. Months have varying numbers of days, from 28 to 31. Typically, however, 30 is used as an average to represent the number of days in a month.

Starting Hint: Set up an equation to figure out how many days, on average, are in 4.5 months, and solve: $4.5 \times 30 = x$

 For math help, go to the Math Appendix at the back of the book.

NCTM Number and Operations Understand numbers, ways of representing numbers, relationships among numbers, and number systems.

English Language Arts

19. Prepare a Résumé Imagine that you are applying for a job posting you found in the local newspaper. Prepare a personal résumé that you could use when applying for the job. Emphasize the skills you have that could be useful in the work setting. Include your work experience and activities. Also include any awards or recognitions you have earned. Use a word processing program to create and print your résumé.

NCTE 5 Use different writing process elements to communicate effectively.

Social Studies

20. Values and Money Some of the highest paid people in the world are athletes and entertainers. How do you think this reflects the values and beliefs of today's society? If these careers are highly paid, why would people choose to do anything else? Write your answer as a short article for an economics magazine.

NCSS VII.f Compare how values and beliefs influence economic decisions in different societies.

STANDARDIZED TEST PRACTICE

MULTIPLE CHOICE
Read the following paragraph. Then read the question. Read the answer choices and choose the best answer. Write your answer on a separate sheet of paper.

Test-Taking Tip When answering multiple-choice questions, read the question first, then read all the answer choices before choosing your answer. Eliminate answers you know are not correct.

21. Interviewing is an important part of the job-hunting process. There are many things you should do for a successful interview and some things you should not do. Which of the following should not be done during a job interview?
 a. Speaking clearly
 b. Making eye contact
 c. Being courteous
 d. Fidgeting in your chair

Learn for Life

In this unit you have learned living as an independent person comes with many responsibilities. You have also learned that the career you choose can help you feel satisfied with the quality of your life. In this project, you will interview a school admissions officer, or an adult who has chosen to continue his or her education. You will use what you learn to create a brochure about lifelong learning.

My Journal

If you completed the journal entry from page 406, refer to it to see if your thoughts have changed after reading the unit.

Project Assignment

- Choose a business and career that you might want to pursue.
- Research businesses, schools, and community programs that offer continuing adult education.
- Interview a school admissions officer or an adult who has decided to continue his or her education to advance his or her career.
- Arrange and take notes during the interview with the professional. Type your notes from the interview.
- Use the information you have learned to create a brochure that explains the benefits of lifelong learning.

Academic Skills You Will Use

English Language Arts

NCTE 5 Use different writing process elements to communicate effectively.

NCTE 6 Apply knowledge of language structure and conventions to discuss texts.

STEP 1 Choose a Business and Career that Interest You

Make a list of businesses that interest you. Then, add careers for each business. For instance, if you are interested in cars, you could be a designer, work on an assembly line, be a salesperson, or be a mechanic. Brainstorm types of lifelong learning that might help you achieve success in each of these careers. What sorts of classes should you take in order to stay current in your chosen industry?

STEP 2 Research Lifelong Learning

Research universities, colleges, trade schools, private businesses, and community programs in your area that offer adult education classes that relate to your chosen career. Look into specific courses or internships that are offered. Identify how these can be helpful for your chosen career.

Research Skills

- Gather information.
- Use a variety of research materials.
- Make phone calls if additional information is needed.
- Discriminate among sources.

STEP 3 Connect to Your Community

Interview an admissions officer at one of the educational institutions you researched, or an adult who has returned to school to help advance his or her career. Ask the person you interview why continuing education is important. List the benefits of lifelong learning. Take notes during your interview.

Communication Skills

- Ask questions that require more than a yes or no answer.
- Listen attentively and actively.
- Use positive body language.
- Communicate your questions clearly.

STEP 4 Create and Present Your Brochure

Use the Unit Thematic Project Checklist on the right to plan and create your brochure and make your presentation.

STEP 5 Evaluate Your Presentation

Your project will be evaluated based on:
- Design and content of your brochure.
- Quality of your presentation.
- Mechanics—presentation and neatness.

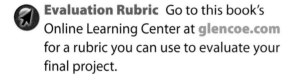 **Evaluation Rubric** Go to this book's Online Learning Center at **glencoe.com** for a rubric you can use to evaluate your final project.

Unit Thematic Project Checklist

Brochure	✓ Make a list of the main points and supporting details on the benefits of lifelong learning that were discussed in the interview. ✓ Use the main points to write headings and subheadings. Include information on how lifelong learning is becoming a major trend, and how this trend is creating more career opportunities. ✓ Write the supporting details under each heading and subheading. ✓ Add graphics to your brochure using computer software or personal drawings. ✓ Proofread your brochure to ensure everything is correct. ✓ Print the brochure and fold it into three panels.
Presentation	✓ Make a presentation to your class to share your brochure and discuss what you learned. ✓ Invite the students in your class to ask you any questions they may have. Answer three questions. ✓ When students ask you questions, demonstrate in your answers that you respect their perspectives. ✓ Turn in the notes from your interview and your brochure to your teacher.
Academic Skills	✓ Speak clearly and concisely. ✓ Organize information logically. ✓ Design effectively. ✓ Write clearly. ✓ Adapt and modify language to suit different purposes. ✓ Thoughtfully express your ideas.

Unit 7

Extend Your Relationships

Unit

Thematic Project Preview
Make Healthy Choices

After completing this unit, you will learn that the strength of your relationships can contribute to your personal happiness. In your unit thematic project, you can learn how to make healthy relationship choices for yourself.

My Journal

Find Your Lifestyle Write a journal entry about one of the topics below. This will help you prepare for the unit project at the end of the unit.

• Describe your personal life as you imagine it ten years from now.

• Identify five traits you have that you think are attractive to friends.

• State the reasons that a close friendship is important to you.

Explore the Photo
Relationships with people outside of your family, such as your friends, may be important to you. *How do you balance your relationships with your family and those with your friends?*

503

Relationship Decisions

 **Explore the Photo**
Friends share thoughts and feelings with each other. *Why is friendship important as you grow in your life?*

Chapter Objectives

After completing this chapter, you will be able to:

- **Determine** the importance of friends.
- **Suggest** ways of dealing with peer pressure.
- **Identify** the stages in learning to love.
- **Describe** how a relationship develops when two people become a couple.
- **Compare** infatuation and mature love.
- **Explain** how to cope with the end of a relationship.

Writing Activity Essay Question & Answer

Respect Respect is consideration for another person's feelings, beliefs, and rights. It means seeing another person's needs and wants as equal to your own. You can show respect when you:

- Abide by the curfew your friend has to obey when going out.
- Ask for a partner's suggestion about where to go for a date.
- Discuss calmly and reasonably in a dispute with a parent.
- Knock on closed doors before entering a room.
- Obey the law.

Write an essay question and answer about an action that shows respect. The question should be about recalling a time when respect was displayed. Answer the question in a detailed essay.

Writing Tips To write an effective essay question and answer, follow these steps:

1. Develop a question that is challenging but realistic.
2. Plan an answer that connects to the key words of the question.
3. Organize your answer with an introduction, a body, and a conclusion.

You and Your Friends

Reading Guide

Before You Read

Study with a Buddy Go over your notes with a study buddy and quiz each other on what you have just read. According to research, studying with a partner for just twelve minutes can help you study better.

Read to Learn
Key Concepts
- **Determine** the importance of friends.
- **Suggest** ways of dealing with peer pressure.

Main Idea
All kinds of friends are important in a person's life. Peer pressure can be positive or negative. Handling negative peer pressure takes courage and a strong sense of self.

Content Vocabulary
◇ reciprocity
◇ peer pressure

Academic Vocabulary
You will find these words in your reading and on your tests. Use the glossary to look up their definitions if necessary.
▣ mingle
▣ bolster

Graphic Organizer
As you read, look for three benefits of friendship. Use a chart like the one shown to help organize your information.

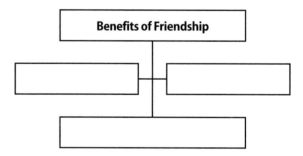

Benefits of Friendship

 Graphic Organizer Go to this book's Online Learning Center at **glencoe.com** to print out this graphic organizer.

Academic Standards •
 English Language Arts

NCTE 2 Read literature to build an understanding of the human experience.

NCTE 12 Use language to accomplish individual purposes.

NCTE *National Council of Teachers of English*
NCTM *National Council of Teachers of Mathematics*

NSES *National Science Education Standards*
NCSS *National Council of the Social Studies*

Friends in Your Life

Have you heard anyone describe a friendship by saying, "She is like a sister to me" or "We could be brothers"? These expressions show why it is important to develop and maintain friendships.

People gain three important benefits from friendships:

- **Emotional Support** Friends supply emotional needs such as comfort, caring, reassurance, acceptance, and understanding.
- **Models for Imitation** Friends teach useful social and physical skills. They learn from each other.
- **Opportunities to Practice Roles** Friends may try out different roles with each other. The teen years are a time for new experiences and growth. Friends provide an audience. They give you feedback as you work to create your identity.

Friendships are especially important to teens. They help bridge the gap to independence. Building relationships with others means relying on family a little less, while handling life on your own a little more. Friendship is real-life education. There are issues to be approached and problems to be solved.

As You Read

Connect When you think of your best friend, what quality first comes to mind?

All Kinds of Friends

When teens think of friends, they usually think first of people who are like themselves. It is most comfortable to be with others who share your interests and outlook. Good friends, however, can be found in people of all types.

Friends of Other Ages

Friendships with children can benefit you and children both. Many families today are very busy, especially when all the adults are employed. Children who care for themselves part of the day often need an older role model.

Younger children, always eager to grow older, look up to teens. They try to imitate teens. This is a chance to teach them in positive ways. When you listen to children and take them seriously, you enrich their lives. What can you gain from these friendships? First, you learn responsibility. When you are with children, you learn to respond to what they need. This knowledge may be useful if you decide to become a parent someday. Being with someone who admires you may inspire you to set a good example. Your sense of self-worth, as well as the child's, can also increase from the experience.

Just as a child can benefit from a teen's company, a teen can gain from friendship with adults. Older adults can help you put this time of your life in perspective. You can give companionship and a view of the younger generation.

Develop Your Friendships The support that friends give can help you learn and grow. *How do your friends help you in your everyday life?*

INDEPENDENT *Living*

Make New Friends

Making friends seems to come naturally to young children. But for many teens, especially those who are going to a new school, making friends can be awkward and stressful. Follow these guidelines to make new friends:

1. **Be positive.** Do you enjoy the company of people who always complain or feel sorry for themselves? Avoid behaviors and attitudes like these. They drive away potential friends. Remember to smile—people are more willing to begin a friendship with someone who appears positive.

2. **Strive for friendship, not popularity.** The desire for friendship leads some teens to take on what they think are the keys to popularity, such as wearing certain clothes. Actually, popular teens attract people through their personalities. You can do the same.

3. **Extend an invitation.** Instead of waiting to be asked, take the first step. You may be surprised to learn that the other person was hoping you would reach out. If someone turns you down, do not worry about it. Just try again later with another person.

4. **Lend a hand.** What could make a better impression than offering help? Ask first before helping, and make sure you know what you are doing. Give help in the spirit of service, not superiority.

5. **Keep expectations realistic.** Even best friends do not share every quality or interest. Do not let differences in taste discourage you from developing a friendship. Likewise, give people space. Do not overwhelm potential friends with constant demands on their time or energy. Give your friendship room and time to grow.

Take Action Choose one of the suggestions outlined above. Using creative thinking skills, list practical ways to help teens apply it. Compile your ideas with those of your classmates into an action plan for making friends.

Friends with a Difference

Friendships between males and females tend to be different from those of the same gender. Females typically like to share personal concerns and feelings with each other. Males tend to share interests and activities. A male-female friendship may combine both aspects. Such friendships often help you see issues from another point of view.

Getting to know people of all races, ethnic groups, and economic levels can help you grow as a person. Every contact with someone is a chance to learn. Spending time with those who are different from you can bring insights and knowledge that you would not otherwise gain. How can you benefit? You will understand all people better. You will be more aware of how people think and feel, and why. Broadening your outlook makes you a more interesting person.

We live in a world where so many diverse people **mingle**, or come together. It pays to be open to all of the people you meet. Being able to relate to people of many backgrounds will serve you well in school, on the job, and in the community. Society greatly benefits when people make an effort to reach out to one another in friendship. Fewer problems occur in communities where people understand and truly respect each other.

Vocabulary

You can find definitions in the glossary at the back of this book.

Promote Friendship

How many people do you know who can meet a stranger, chat for a while, and walk away with a new friend? Making friends is not always easy. Shyness, low self-esteem, and lack of experience make it hard for some people to talk to and be friendly and open with people they do not know.

If you feel unsure of yourself when making friends, think of two points. First, the other person may feel the same way. Second, you are worthy of being a friend. You have traits and abilities that others will enjoy. By working to become a better person, you become an even better candidate for friendship. Friendships grow more readily when people are pleasant to be around and easy to get along with. See **Figure 26.1** for some examples of qualities that lead to friendship.

Keep Your Friends

Often, building a friendship is easier than keeping it going. In fact, the oldest and strongest friendships require the most work. Long-time friends may begin to take each other for granted. Sometimes people can forget to always be thoughtful when they are secure in a long-term friendship.

Figure 26.1	**Learn the Qualities of Friendship**

There are several qualities that help you get along with others and can lead to friendship. *What qualities, besides those listed below, can you think of that may lead to friendship?*

Positive Attitude	A positive attitude goes a long way toward building friendships. People enjoy those who look on the bright side and have a sense of humor.
Accepting	No one wants to be criticized all the time. Someone who overlooks little faults is more fun to be with.
Caring and Courteous	People respond to those who show they care. A friendly smile and a kind word make a difference.
Cleanliness	People who are clean and neat are more pleasant to be around.

Real Life — How to Say No

When pressure to do the wrong thing makes you uncomfortable, remember these suggestions:

- Be assertive. You can be firm without offending others.
- Say no convincingly. Let the tone of your voice tell people that you mean it.
- Give reasons only if you want, but do not make excuses or apologize. You have the right to say no.
- Use facial expressions that show you are serious. Look steadily at the person and do not smile.
- Use forceful body language. Avoid using gestures that may indicate you are less than sure of yourself.

- Suggest another activity. This puts the pressure on those who are pressuring you.
- If the pressure is too much, leave.

Problem-Solving

Teri and her friend Jordan are the two finalists in a scholarship competition. The last stage of the selection process is a joint interview with the judges. Teri handles interviews well; it is easy for her to talk to people. She knows Jordan gets flustered and self-conscious. Jordan has told her that if he does not get the scholarship, he will not be able to go to college. He asked her to help him do well during the interview. What should Teri do?

Friendships are kept strong day by day through small, caring gestures. For friends to remain friends, each person must benefit from the relationship. An important trait of friendship is **reciprocity** (ˌre-sə-ˈprä-s(ə-)tē), or mutual exchange. Each friend gives to the relationship. Each friend also takes from it. Each person enjoys spending time together and sharing activities. Friends praise, appreciate, and listen to each other.

Friends do not always have to agree with each other. A solid friendship can survive differences of opinion. Honesty and respect should provide the foundation for the friendship. Then it can withstand differences. It can even build upon them.

✓ **Reading Check** **Identify** How do friends provide emotional support to each other?

Peer Pressure

Peer pressure is social pressure on somebody to adopt a type of behavior, dress, or attitude in order to be accepted as part of a group. Peer pressure often occurs among people in a similar age group or peer group. It is one of the most challenging situations teens face. When you want to join in an action or a belief because everybody else is, you are feeling peer pressure.

Peer pressure may be positive or negative. If someone encourages you to do something helpful, that pressure is positive. Pressure that keeps you from doing something wrong is also positive. The problems come with negative peer pressure. It pushes you to do something destructive. It may also tempt you away from what you know is right.

Sometimes the values and goals of the family are not the same as those of friends. It is hard to be caught in the middle. If this happens, consider what is truly important in your life. Recognizing possible consequences can help you avoid making a major mistake.

Teens are very sensitive to their peers' criticism and acceptance. Often they have not yet formed a strong personal identity. This uncertainty weakens their inner strength. As a result, they may not be able to resist when people push them. Thus, peer pressure convinces them to do what others are doing, even if they do not really want to do it.

In the disguise of friendship, peer pressure can be dangerous. People who use peer pressure often know that what they want others to do is not something they would do without pressure. True friends do not ask each other to do what either one feels is wrong or unwise.

Handle Negative Pressure

Learning to handle teen peer pressure is a major task. Walking away from peers who pressure you is not always easy, especially for the sake of a principle.

To stand up to negative pressures, you need a clear vision of what you believe. You also need courage and the willingness to let your convictions show. You need the confidence to take a stand and not let reactions bother you.

Submitting to negative pressure may seem easier than resisting it. To **bolster**, or boost up, your courage, think about this. The people who stand up for what is right for themselves and others are the ones who are most admired in the long run.

Section 26.1   After You Read

Review Key Concepts

1. **Explain** the benefits of making friends with different types of people.
2. **Define** peer pressure. Explain how it can be positive or negative.

Practice Academic Skills

English Language Arts

3. Friendship and loneliness are often the subjects of songs. Recall songs you have heard, or select a few examples from library resources. Listen to the lyrics carefully and try to understand and interpret what the author is saying. Then write a paragraph to explain what you think the author is saying in your own words. Share your interpretation with your classmates.

> **NCTE 2** Read literature to build an understanding of the human experience.

4. It is said that you can make more friends by showing interest in them than by trying to get them interested in you. Think about what makes you interested in another person. Then write a list of at least five things you can do to show interest in another person.

> **NCTE 12** Use language to accomplish individual purposes.

Check Your Answers Check your answers at this book's Online Learning Center through **glencoe.com**.

First Steps to Love

Reading Guide

Before You Read

Check for Understanding If you have questions as you are reading, that means you are thinking about how well you understand the material. To get the most out of the text, try to answer those questions.

Read to Learn

Key Concepts

- **Identify** the stages in learning to love.
- **Describe** how a relationship develops when two people become a couple.
- **Compare** infatuation and mature love.
- **Explain** how to cope with the end of a relationship.

Main Idea

People learn to love by going through stages. Attraction brings couples together. They may experience infatuation or mature love. It takes time to recover from the loss of a relationship.

Content Vocabulary

◇ mature love
◇ compatible
◇ dating
◇ infatuation

Academic Vocabulary

You will find these words in your reading and on your tests. Use the glossary to look up their definitions if necessary.

■ esteem   ■ abuse

Graphic Organizer

As you read, look for the stages of learning to love. Use a chart like the one shown to help organize your information.

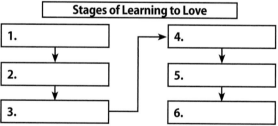

Stages of Learning to Love	
1.	4.
2.	5.
3.	6.

 Graphic Organizer Go to this book's Online Learning Center at **glencoe.com** to print out this graphic organizer.

Academic Standards •

 English Language Arts

NCTE 4 Use written language to communicate effectively.

NCTE 12 Use language to accomplish individual purposes.

 Mathematics

NCTM Number and Operations Compute fluently and make reasonable estimates.

NCTM Problem Solving Apply and adapt a variety of appropriate strategies to solve problems.

NCTE *National Council of Teachers of English*
NCTM *National Council of Teachers of Mathematics*

NSES *National Science Education Standards*
NCSS *National Council of the Social Studies*

Learn to Love

The idea of learning to love another person may seem strange. After all, the desire to love and to be loved is natural in nearly everyone. You learn to love through experience and observation. You learn about love by receiving love from others and seeing how love works in the relationships of others. Once you have received love, you can give it back and spread it to others. In this way, love multiplies.

As You Read

Connect How have you learned about love?

Learning to love is a lifelong process that goes through a series of stages. Each stage helps you build a stronger base for future love relationships. Each new stage builds on the previous ones. It is sometimes called the Ladder of Love. If love relationships at one stage are not satisfying, successfully going on to the rest of the stages is difficult. Here are the stages that people go through as they learn to love:

- **Stage 1: Self-Love** A person's first love is love of self. Even this is learned. Babies' basic needs are to be well-fed, diapered, kept comfortable and safe, and receive physical contact and attention. When these needs are met, children learn that they are worthy, lovable beings.

- **Stage 2: Love of Caregiver** As babies are cared for and loved, they gradually gain trust and love for their caregivers, typically the parents. If babies' needs are not fully met, they may never be able to give and receive love.

- **Stage 3: Love of Peers** As children interact with peers, they become attached to their playmates. They develop a strong relationship with one or two best friends of the same gender. The feelings they have are one form of love. Friends become very important at this stage.

- **Stage 4: Hero Worship** As children grow older, they develop a loving admiration for an older person. This may be a sibling or relative, a family friend, a coach or teacher, or even a celebrity. They imitate their chosen role model's talk, dress, and mannerisms. In this stage, children try out different qualities and traits.

Love Begins Early Children mimic the love they receive from their caregivers. *Since this child has been cared for with love, how do you think he will treat his puppy?*

- **Stage 5: Love of the Opposite Gender** During the preteens or early teens, children become interested in the other gender. At first, this interest is not specific. Later, the focus is on one person who catches their interest. These relationships are often short-lived and based on surface qualities. People at this stage focus on the thrill of being newly in love rather than the realities of a long-term loving relationship.

- **Stage 6: Mature Love** At the highest level of emotional development is **mature love**. It builds over time and lasts. This is the stage that most people find the hardest to recognize and attain. Not everyone is prepared for a mature love relationship at the same age. Some people never develop enough emotionally to be capable of lasting mature love.

In this six-stage process, most teens are likely to be in stage five. During this period, young people typically go through steps that take them from peer groups, to pairing, and on to love of the opposite gender. If they can maintain the loving relationship and be patient and caring, they may be able to achieve mature love.

✓ Reading Check

Explain Why are the stages in learning to love important?

Becoming a Couple

During the preteen and early teen years, most young people are involved in same-gender peer groups. During puberty, interest in the opposite gender builds. Groups expand to include both males and females. Within these groups, parties, dances, and spending time together take place.

Often these social groups continue throughout the teen years. The group gives protection in different ways. Being with the opposite gender can be less intimidating with other friends close by.

◀) *Mutual Attraction* Teens often become attracted to someone who is a very close friend. *What are some of the qualities that attract you to another person?*

Vocabulary

You can find definitions in the glossary at the back of this book.

Sexual pressures are more manageable in a group. As long as the group is reliable, peer pressure can be positive. Parents tend to feel more comfortable when teens associate in groups.

Eventually, people pair off as couples. Teens who spend time with a group may pair off informally within the group. At some point, however, couples pair off more exclusively. The couple begins to develop a personal bond. That relationship becomes more important and other friendships become less important.

Attraction

Couples are drawn to each other because of attraction. Your reasons for liking someone are as individual as you are. Many people are first attracted to someone for a physical reason. You might react to a person's smile, physique, or skills. These are good traits, but they alone do not make the person right for you.

When you spend time with someone special, it gives you a chance to find out what that person is really like. It is similar to finding the traits that make a good friend become more important. Traits that can lead to a positive dating experience include:

- **Compatibility** People who can exist together in harmony are **compatible**. They share interests. They have similar values and attitudes. They agree on many things.
- **Honesty** People in a good couple relationship are honest with themselves. They are also honest with each other. They can express their feelings to each other. They do not fear rejection.
- **Respect** Two people who respect each other honor and **esteem**, or highly regard, one another. They enjoy each other's personalities. Partners take a real interest in each other's activities and ideas.
- **Mutual Support** In any good relationship, the people involved must be caring. They need to be supportive. They help each other grow by giving encouragement.
- **Independence** Partners enjoy time and activities together. They also can enjoy time apart. Neither partner tries to limit the other's interests or relationships with family and friends.

It is natural to be attracted to people your friends find attractive. This can be limiting, however. What you like in a person will not be quite the same as what your friends like. Your personal tastes may be a better guide. What talents and traits do you admire? You may look for someone who makes you feel valued as a person. You are apt to be attracted to those who share some of your interests and values. What else may attract you to someone?

Math in Action

Dates and Dollars

Developing a budget for a date can help you spend your money wisely. To develop a date budget, follow these steps.

1. Decide how much money you will spend on the date.

2. Make a list of options for the date such as going to a movie, going bowling, eating pizza, and so on.

3. Write down the costs for the options listed in step 2.

4. Choose the options that will fit within your budget.

Math Concept **Multi-Step Problems** When solving problems with more than one step, think through the steps before you start making your plan for solving the problem.

Starting Hint: First decide how much you want to spend. Then decide the costs of your date options. Choose from your options and add the costs to find the options that fit within your budget. You may have to do some re-calculating to get the costs to fit within your budget.

Building Academic Skills Go to this book's Online Learning Center through **glencoe.com** to complete a worksheet for this activity.

NCTM Number and Operations Compute fluently and make reasonable estimates.

 For math help, go to the Math Appendix at the back of the book.

Financial Literacy

Dating Costs

Derrick spends 10 percent of his income on dates each year. But now he needs to save $1,000 a year to pay for technical school. The money for school will come out of his date money. If Derrick makes $20,000 per year, what percentage of his income can he continue to spend on dates?

Math Concept **Multiple-Step Problems**
To solve multiple-step problems, you first need to determine the exact information you need to find. Then determine the steps you must take to find that information.

Starting Hint: First, determine how much Derrick currently spends on dates each year. Subtract $1,000 from that amount and divide your answer by $20,000 to find the percentage of his income Derrick can continue to spend on dates.

For math help, go to the Math Appendix at the back of the book.

NCTM Problem Solving Apply and adapt a variety of appropriate strategies to solve problems.

Dating

Once attraction takes hold, two people may begin to go out together. Over the years, this shared social activity has commonly been called **dating**. A date can be something as simple as studying at the library or as involved as going to a school dance.

Dating customs and etiquette vary across cultures and age groups. In the past, the rules of dating were fairly rigid. In today's world, they are less so. Still, it is important to be polite and treat dating partners with courtesy. People should also behave in ways that support their personal values.

Teens gain poise and self-confidence through dating as they practice social skills. They discover what they might like in a mate and learn more about the opposite gender. Dating is also a way to just enjoy time with someone special.

Dating is difficult for many people. The less a couple knows about each other, the more awkward those first dates may be. Dating poses certain risks. You may be rejected. You may be shy or confused by what people expect. A date that does not turn out as you hoped is disappointing. It takes self-confidence to date. For most people, however, the chance to start a caring relationship outweighs the risks.

When should a couple dating begin? That is a common question for teens and parents. Family rules often dictate the age and conditions. Once a teen begins to date, new issues arise. Parents do not want dating to interfere with schoolwork and family duties. They also do not want teens to deal with sexual pressures too soon.

Some people do not date until they are older. Since people mature at different rates, some are ready before others. Differences in maturity rates are obvious during high school. Because females mature faster than males, more females than males may be interested in dating. This pattern tends to level off after high school.

Whatever the age, people need to be mature enough to handle the responsibilities of dating. They should behave in ways that support their values. Based on their values and goals, they can make personal rules or guidelines for behavior. They need to think through these choices ahead of time. This makes it easier to resist peer pressure.

Dating often causes concerns for teens. Some want to date but do not know anyone who interests them. Some feel odd because they are not interested in dating at all. Teens should understand that time takes care of most concerns. It is alright to concentrate on friends, activities, and school, rather than worrying about dating.

Date Abuse

While dating is fun, the smart teen is cautious. The possibility of **abuse**, or ill treatment, exists between dating partners. It should, however, have no place in any relationship.

Physical abuse includes shoving, slapping, punching, or worse. Abusive people see violence as a way to solve problems. When conflict occurs, one person may try to frighten the other with violence or the threat of it. Abusers often feel sorrow afterwards. They may promise never to do it again. However, if the abused partner does not take action, the cycle may start over.

Not all abuse is physical. Some is emotional. The person who cares less about the relationship controls it. Some people may misuse that power. The abuser may yell at or belittle the other. The victim feels intimidated and fearful. Emotional abuse can lead to lasting problems.

Ending a relationship is the only safe response when there is abuse. People who respect themselves leave such relationships. Leaving an abusive relationship lowers the risk of injury. It also prevents the abused person from becoming more involved in a destructive relationship.

✓ **Reading Check** **List** What are five traits that are important in attraction?

Infatuation and Love

Some kinds of love are wonderful while they last but do not sustain a couple for the long term. Mature love, in contrast, satisfies, nourishes, and lasts. It helps both partners grow stronger.

Telling one type of love from the others is not always easy, especially for those just starting to develop love relationships. Some feelings of love are fleeting. The question "Is this the real thing?" is answered only over time. There are clues, however, that can help you see whether loving feelings can lead to a lasting love relationship.

The Excitement of Infatuation

Infatuation (in-ˌfa-chə-'wā-shən) is an intense emotional involvement that begins with a sudden, strong attraction. It is often the first kind of love that most people experience. It is intense and emotional. It begins with a sudden attraction. It may be a person's physical appearance. It might be triggered by the person's self-confidence. It also may be that person's sense of humor. Infatuation is very real and powerful. The infatuated couple wants to spend all their time together. They share all their feelings. They are emotionally immersed in each other. They may feel overwhelmed by their own emotions.

*▼ **Infatuated** Infatuation is exciting, but it is very different from mature love. Do you think infatuation can last as long as mature love?*

Love that Lasts
Mature love involves feeling secure and comfortable with each other. *What are some other signs of mature love?*

While it lasts, infatuation is very enjoyable and satisfying. It is, however, self-centered. Partners focus more on how wonderful the relationship makes them feel and how it satisfies their own needs. They are less apt to focus on the feelings and needs of the other person during this time.

Infatuation is unrealistic. Infatuation leads people to not see important differences between them. Undesirable traits tend to be ignored. Infatuated people see only what they want to see.

Over time, the intense emotional high of the relationship dies down. When the attraction and emotions are not as new and strong, they no longer cloud judgment. Reality begins to set in. The partners may realize that the attraction was based only on surface traits. They see the lack of something more meaningful and lasting. They may recognize that the other person has traits or shortcomings they cannot accept or that they have very little in common.

Infatuation is natural. When young people are learning what a real loving relationship involves, it is useful. In some cases, infatuation is the beginning of a committed relationship. It can be a step on the way to true, mature love.

Recognize Mature Love

Mature love is what most people have in mind when they think of real love. It means mutual caring, sharing, respect, support, and commitment. Those who have reached a high level of emotional development are secure enough with themselves to commit to another person.

Mature love can begin with a sudden, strong attraction, but often it does not. Sometimes, in fact, the attraction builds slowly. Whether mature love begins slowly or quickly, it still has certain qualities that define it. These are what make it quite different from infatuation. See **Figure 26.2** to understand how to recognize mature love.

✓ **Reading Check**) **Define** What is infatuation?

When Relationships End

People enter a relationship with hope. No one can tell what the future will bring. Discovering that mature love will probably not develop may be the end of a relationship. That can mean pain and heartache. It is far better to end a relationship and move on. It is not wise to continue in a relationship that is not working for one or both partners.

Figure 26.2   Recognize Mature Love

There are a number of characteristics that define mature love. *How would you test a relationship to know if it is mature love or infatuation?*

Characteristics of Mature Love

Secure and Comfortable	Partners are confident about the love that each feels. They are trusting and faithful and do not need constant reassurances.
Shared Interests	The couple shares certain interests that will allow them to have good times together.
Similar Beliefs and Goals	Both people have similar goals in life and want to work toward them together. Important issues will not come between them.
Highly Focused on the Other Person	Each person holds the other's well-being in high regard, sometimes ahead of self. Neither one wants to lose personal identity in the relationship. Still, each cares deeply about the other's point of view, emotions, health, and happiness. The couple is willing to make sacrifices and compromises. Each wants to do things for the other to show caring and love.
Accepting but Realistic	Each partner sees the other as a real person. They know how each reacts to boredom, stress, and crisis. They do not ignore or overlook undesirable traits, but do accept small flaws.
Responsible	Partners take the relationship seriously. Each wants to contribute to the work needed to strengthen the relationship. Each wants to build a good life.
Respectful	Each has regard for the other as a person and would not say or do things that are hurtful on purpose. They are proud of each other's talents and skills.
Able to Put Attraction in Perspective	Physical attraction is important. It is not the main focus. Partners enjoy each other's company.
Lasting	The relationship stands the test of time. Few of the qualities described here are certain. It takes ample time to observe and analyze them.

If you are the one ending a relationship, be straightforward. Choose words that are not hurtful. You may wish to point out why you feel the two of you are not right for each other. Sometimes the other person may be emotional, lack understanding of the situation, or be unwilling to accept what is happening. Take a firm approach. Do not give false hopes when you know the relationship is over.

Recovery

Feelings of hurt, betrayal, and self-doubt are common when a relationship ends. You may feel you are to blame. You may vow to never get involved again. These are natural reactions that go away in time. Remember these ideas if you face such a situation:

- While exploring love, nearly everyone has relationships that end.
- Blaming yourself is not realistic. Most relationships end because they simply were not worth maintaining.
- A relationship that ends paves the way for finding a relationship that can develop into mature love.
- Learn from the relationship. Think about what you can do differently next time you are building a love relationship.

Regardless of why a relationship ends, you may go through a period of sadness. Recovery can be hastened in several ways. Some people write their thoughts in a journal. Talking to a close friend who is supportive often helps. You might pamper yourself a little.

You will start to feel stronger inside if you determine to move ahead with life. Remember that when people find real love, they are often thankful for what they have learned from past experiences. You will have a better idea of what you want and need in a partnership.

Section 26.2 After You Read

Review Key Concepts

1. **Describe** how people learn to love.
2. **Identify** benefits of the peer social groups that often precede dating.
3. **Explain** whether infatuation is the first step to mature love.
4. **Suggest** ways to kindly end a relationship that is not working for you.

Practice Academic Skills

English Language Arts

5. Some people do not seem to see the negative qualities of someone they are dating. What are the possible outcomes of this situation? Write a paragraph explaining them.

6. Imagine that you have met someone to whom you are attracted. Put together a text message you might send that person. It should show your interest.

> **NCTE 4** Use written language to communicate effectively.

> **NCTE 12** Use language to accomplish individual purposes.

Check Your Answers Check your answers at this book's Online Learning Center through **glencoe.com**.

CHAPTER SUMMARY

Section 26.1
You and Your Friends

Friends are an important part of life. They give emotional support. They are role models and provide a safe way to practice roles. Friendships across different ages and ethnic and cultural backgrounds can enrich life. Qualities that help promote friendship include a positive attitude. Others include being accepting, caring, and courteous. Friendships last when each person benefits from the relationship. Peer pressure is an attempt to influence someone in a similar age group. It can be positive or negative. Resisting negative peer pressure takes courage.

Section 26.2
First Steps to Love

People learn to love by receiving and observing it. There are stages in learning to love. A couple experiences attraction. They start spending time together either in a peer social group or through dating. Dating offers a chance to learn new skills and knowledge. It can be difficult for many people. A dating relationship should be ended if it involves physical or emotional abuse. Infatuation and mature love are different kinds of relationships with different characteristics. It is often necessary but never easy to end a relationship that is not working for one or both partners.

Content and Academic Vocabulary Review

1. Use each of these content and academic vocabulary words in a sentence.

Content Vocabulary
◇ reciprocity (p. 510)
◇ peer pressure (p. 510)
◇ mature love (p. 514)
◇ compatible (p. 515)
◇ dating (p. 516)
◇ infatuation (p. 517)

Academic Vocabulary
■ mingle (p. 509)
■ bolster (p. 511)
■ esteem (p. 515)
■ abuse (p. 517)

Review Key Concepts

2. Determine the importance of friends.
3. Suggest ways of dealing with peer pressure.
4. Identify the stages in learning to love.
5. Describe how a relationship develops when two people become a couple.
6. Compare infatuation and mature love.
7. Explain how to cope with the end of a relationship.

Critical Thinking

8. Analyze Which would you rather belong to: a small, close-knit group of friends or a large, loosely knit group? Why?
9. Evaluate Do you think love at first sight is possible? Explain why some people may disagree with you.

Real-World Skills

Problem-Solving Skills

10. Hero Worship Every time Tom steps outside his house, eight-year-old Marco from next door seems to show up. He follows Tom, chattering and peppering him with questions. Tom is getting annoyed. What should he do? Write a letter of advice to Tom.

Collaborative Skills

11. Fun for Less Follow your teacher's instructions to form into groups. Develop a list of free or low-cost activities suitable for a date. Which may be best for a new relationship? Which could be appropriate for a long-standing one? Share your list with your classmates.

Self-Management Skills

12. Deal with Peer Pressure Follow your teacher's instructions to work with a partner. Develop a skit that shows two teens in a situation where one is using positive pressure to encourage the other. Write a realistic dialogue between the two teens. Present your skit to the class.

Interpersonal Skills

13. Communication Chad now wants to cut back on expenses to save money for a car so he can take classes at a nearby college. He worries about how his girlfriend, Amy, will respond. How should Chad communicate his problem to Amy? Write your answer in a paragraph.

14. Brainstorm Follow your teacher's instructions to form into groups. Brainstorm qualities that you think friends should have. Write each quality on a separate slip of paper. Put the slips of paper in a bowl. Take turns drawing out a slip. Write down specific examples of how the qualities can be shown in a friendship. Share them with the class.

15. Personal Qualities Think of people whose company you enjoy. List the qualities they have that make them likable. Write a specific plan of action for developing or strengthening these qualities in yourself.

16. Analyze Select a television show or movie that you enjoy. Analyze the love relationships that are shown. Give examples and explain whether these relationships seem to be mature. Do you think they would last if the relationship existed in real life? Write your answers in a short essay.

17. Research Go to this book's Online Learning Center at **glencoe.com** to find **Web Links** for **Abuse in Teen Dating Relationships**. What are some of the signs of abuse? How widespread is it? How can a teen get out of an abusive relationship? What community resources are available to help? Create a brochure that provides this information.

Additional Activities For additional activities, go to this book's Online Learning Center through **glencoe.com**.

Academic Skills

Mathematics

18. Calculate an Entertainment Budget
John has budgeted to spend no more than five percent of his income on entertainment with his friends. He and his friends like to go to movies and concerts. Once or twice a year, they like to go to an amusement park. His annual income is $15,000. How much would he spend each year on entertainment?

Math Concept **Multiply Decimals by Whole Numbers** A percent is a ratio that compares a number to 100. Follow the steps in the starting hint below to multiply with percentages:

Starting Hint: You can rewrite the percent (5%) as a fraction with a denominator of 100. Convert the fraction to a decimal. Multiply this decimal by the number ($15,000). Remember to put the decimal point in the correct place in your answer.

 For math help, go to the Math Appendix at the back of the book.

NCTM Number and Operations Understand numbers, ways of representing numbers, relationships among numbers, and number systems.

English Language Arts

19. Book Summary Refer to the section of this book on relationships, or another book that you have read. Make a list of ten facts or suggestions that you think would be useful in your life. Items on your list should help you develop positive relationships. They should also help you better understand the relationships in your life. Share your list with your classmates.

NCTE 2 Read literature to build an understanding of the human experience.

Social Studies

20. Love in History Conduct research of the history of love in relationships. Has love always been a factor in picking a mate? What qualities were considered important in the past? Discuss the factors that were important for successful relationships in earlier eras. Write your discussion as a short essay.

NCSS II.e Investigate, interpret, and analyze multiple historical and contemporary viewpoints within and across cultures related to important events, recurring dilemmas, and persistent issues, while employing empathy, skepticism, and critical judgment.

STANDARDIZED TEST PRACTICE

OPEN-ENDED RESPONSE
Write one or two sentences to answer the following questions.

Test-Taking Tip Open-ended questions are often looking for a specific response rather than an opinion. These may include definitions, comparisons, or examples.

21. a. What three important things do people gain from friendships?
  b. List four attributes of people who are pleasant to be around and easy to get along with.
  c. What is peer pressure?

CHAPTER 27

Responsible Behavior

Section 27.1

Develop Your Identity

Section 27.2

Sexual Behavior

 Explore the Photo

Couples in a mature relationship are responsible when it comes to sexual behavior. *What do you think it means to be responsible in a relationship?*

Chapter Objectives

After completing this chapter, you will be able to:

- **Explain** how personal identity is affected by gender roles.
- **Describe** what sexual identity is.
- **Identify** some of the pressures and influences involved in sexual development.
- **Determine** the benefits of abstinence.
- **Suggest** possible consequences of sexual behaviors.
- **Describe** what it means to be sexually responsible.

Writing Activity

Step-by-Step Guide

Self-Discipline When you use self-control, you are being self-disciplined. You show self-discipline when you:
- End a date at a reasonable hour.
- Respect a partner's choice to refrain from sexual activity.
- Plan a study session with a date when others are home.
- Walk away from a disagreement without using physical violence or emotional and verbal abuse.

Write a step-by-step guide to self-discipline that teens can use when they feel themselves losing control.

Writing Tips To write an effective step-by-step guide, follow these steps:
1. Write the steps in chronological order.
2. Explain terms the reader may not know.
3. Use appropriate transition words such as: at first, in addition, also, and as a result.

Develop Your Identity

Reading Guide

Before You Read

Think of an Example Read the Key Concepts below. Think of an example of how one of the Key Concepts applies to your life.

Read to Learn
Key Concepts
- **Explain** how personal identity is affected by gender roles.
- **Describe** what sexual identity is.

Main Idea
Gender roles are part of your personal identity. They are the behavior and characteristics expected of a male or female. Sexual identity is the way people see themselves as males and females.

Content Vocabulary
◇ gender role   ◇ sexual identity

Academic Vocabulary
You will find these words in your reading and on your tests. Use the glossary to look up their definitions if necessary.
■ absorb   ■ contradict

Graphic Organizer
As you read, look for influences on sexual identity. Use a concept map like the one shown to help organize your information.

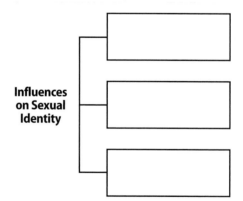

Influences on Sexual Identity

 Graphic Organizer Go to this book's Online Learning Center at **glencoe.com** to print out this graphic organizer.

Academic Standards • • • • • • • • • • • • • • • • • •
English Language Arts

NCTE 4 Use written language to communicate effectively.

NCTE 5 Use different writing process elements to communicate effectively.

NCTE *National Council of Teachers of English*
NCTM *National Council of Teachers of Mathematics*

NSES *National Science Education Standards*
NCSS *National Council of the Social Studies*

Personal Identity

Your personal identity is how you view yourself as a unique individual. Your identity is formed by your relationships, your likes and dislikes, and your experiences with other people. Your identity also depends on your age and circumstances. Your personal identity will continue to change throughout your life.

You develop your values, interests, beliefs, and goals through your experiences and choices. You may have some traits in common with friends or family members, but your personal identity is unique. It is what sets you apart from other people.

As You Read

Connect At this point in your life, what factors have helped form your personal identity?

Gender Roles

One way that society affects your personal identity is through gender roles. A **gender role** is the behavior and traits expected of a male or female. Your first ideas of what it means to be a male or female came from seeing how others define the genders. Whatever is thought to be acceptable for each gender is part of that gender role. Society as a whole has certain gender role expectations. Each individual person also has opinions about what a male or female should be like.

Vocabulary

You can find definitions in the glossary at the back of this book.

Heredity or Environment

Both heredity and environment are believed to have an effect on how people acquire gender traits. Many people agree that environmental influences affect gender roles. Some people believe that gender traits, like physical traits, are naturally present through heredity. For example, some people believe you learn to be sensitive from the people around you. Others believe you will be sensitive by nature, because your parent is sensitive.

Learn Gender Roles Gender roles are often learned by observing others. *How have you learned about gender roles in your family?*

Roles Have Changed

If you had to make one list of words that describes what females do and another list for males, what words would you put in each one? Would you put any words in both lists? The words in your lists may be very different from the words older generations would have listed. Your list may also differ from your friends' lists.

Remember that as society changes, so do roles. Stereotypes, the ideas about the qualities or behaviors of a certain group of people, also change. In traditional gender roles, many people viewed the man as the sole or primary wage earner in the family. In this stereotype, the woman was the homemaker and took care of the children and the family's daily care. Now it is much more common for men to be directly involved in the care of their children. Many families today rely on the woman's income.

While many gender roles have evolved, some people still have different expectations for male and female behavior. Some people are accepting of new gender roles, while others prefer traditional ones. Positive traits and behaviors are encouraged in everyone.

Family and friends often accept those people who do not conform to gender stereotypes. When a person is happy with his or her gender role, that person can have positive self-esteem and can build a satisfying and rewarding life.

✓ **Reading Check**) **Explain** What are some expectations of gender roles society has defined?

▶▶ *Female Roles Are Changing*
Gender roles defined by society are changing. *What roles for females may have been nearly impossible for your grandmother to consider?*

A Look at Sexual Identity

Sexual identity is the way people see themselves as males and females. There are many different influences on sexual identity, including family, peers, media, and society.

Sexual identity develops in childhood. Children **absorb**, or take in, information about gender from birth, most of it through observation. A child will watch how his or her parents, as well as older siblings and other adults, behave. Children learn feelings and responses that are thought to be appropriate for their gender. They earn approval for certain behaviors. They also earn disapproval for other behaviors. They draw conclusions from the way they are treated. The toys they are given and the games they play influence how they see themselves. Learning about the roles of men and women continues throughout school. Children become more aware of gender differences as they grow.

A child's gender affects how he or she is treated by others. For example, people may interact with an infant differently based on whether they are told the child is a girl or a boy. People who do not know an infant's gender may be unsure of how to relate to the child in many ways.

Often, people are not aware of the subtle ways their behaviors shape a child's outlook. Many people are not actively aware of the stereotypes they have. Stereotypes can harm people. For example, talent in scientific research and engineering has been typically viewed as a male trait. However, females do just as well in scientific research and engineering when given the same education and encouragement as males.

⬆ Sexual Identity
The toys children are given can influence their sexual identity. *Do you think it is reasonable to expect boys to want to play with cars and girls with dolls?*

Family and Other Adult Influences on Identity

Of all the influences on a person's gender identity, one of the strongest is the family. What it means to be female or male is first learned within the family setting. By the time they reach school age, children have a strong understanding of how they are expected to behave.

Children are also influenced by other adults. They observe and imitate what other adults of the same gender do. They build a sense of themselves as males and females from their contacts and experiences with a variety of different people.

Peer and Media Influences on Identity

Peers are an important influence on gender identity. Have you ever found yourself copying your friends' actions and attitudes? People of all ages want to be liked and have friends. Good friends often share an interest in similar activities. It is common for friends to adopt the actions and attitudes of each other.

Television and movies also influence sexual identity. Books, ads, and music videos all suggest ways men and women relate to each other. It is important to be aware that much of what people see in the media is not realistic. The actions of actors and characters in books, TV shows, and movies are often exaggerated. They are designed to be entertaining.

Your Identity

There are many different ideas about gender identity. Some even **contradict**, or say the opposite of, each other. No single gender identity standard fits everyone.

Throughout life, you will know people who appreciate you for the positive traits you have, rather than seeing you just as a stereotypical male or female. Appreciate and develop your relationships with these people. Develop all the special talents and qualities you have, whatever they may be.

It is important to remember that every person is unique and worthy of respect. If you respect yourself, you will be more likely to develop relationships with people who also respect you. This will help you to have confidence and peace of mind.

Section 27.1 After You Read

Review Key Concepts

1. **Explain** whether you think gender roles are more affected by heredity or environment.
2. **Describe** how your family members and other adults can influence your personal identity.

Practice Academic Skills
English Language Arts

3. Over the years there have been many changes in gender roles in our society. For example, many years ago, there were no female firefighters or police officers. What do you think causes changes in society's view of gender roles? Write your answer as an article for the opinion page of your local newspaper.

> **NCTE 4** Use written language to communicate effectively.

4. Make a list of the influences on your sexual identity. Then, write a paragraph comparing and contrasting how the influences on your list helped shape your view of yourself.

> **NCTE 5** Use different writing process elements to communicate effectively.

Check Your Answers Check your answers at this book's Online Learning Center through **glencoe.com**.

Section 27.2

Sexual Behavior

Reading Guide

Before You Read

Look It Up Look up the content vocabulary in a dictionary or in the glossary in the back of the book. This will help you to learn new words.

Read to Learn

Key Concepts

- **Identify** some of the pressures and influences involved in sexual development.
- **Determine** the benefits of abstinence.
- **Suggest** possible consequences of sexual behaviors.
- **Describe** what it means to be sexually responsible.

Main Idea

Teens experience many pressures toward sexual activity. Choosing abstinence helps avoid negative consequences of sexual activity.

Content Vocabulary

◇ sexuality
◇ abstinence
◇ sexually transmitted infection (STI)
◇ sterility
◇ rape
◇ date rape
◇ fidelity

Academic Vocabulary

You will find these words in your reading and on your tests. Use the glossary to look up their definitions if necessary.

■ prevalent   ■ refuse

Graphic Organizer

As you read, use a graphic organizer like th eone below to write the possible consequences of teen pregnancy.

Consequences of Teen Pregnancy
1.
2.
3.

 Graphic Organizer Go to this book's Online Learning Center at **glencoe.com** to print out this graphic organizer.

Academic Standards · · · · · · · · · · · · · · · · ·

English Language Arts

NCTE 4 Use written language to communicate effectively.

NCTE 12 Use language to accomplish individual purposes.

Mathematics

NCTM Number and Operations Understand the meanings of operations and how they relate to one another.

NCTE *National Council of Teachers of English*
NCTM *National Council of Teachers of Mathematics*

NSES *National Science Education Standards*
NCSS *National Council of the Social Studies*

Physical Attraction
During the teen years, curiosity about sexuality usually increases. *What can you do to deal with these feelings responsibly?*

**Vocabulary**
You can find definitions in the glossary at the back of this book.

Sexual Development

The teen years bring on many physical changes. These changes are the start of adult sexual development. Sexual traits develop. Teens become physically able to reproduce. Interest in the opposite gender increases. Sexual interest is common. The decisions you make about sexual behavior will have a great impact on your life. Choosing to make responsible decisions about sexual behavior is part of becoming mature.

Sexuality is your beliefs and values about sexual behavior. Sexuality is a basic part of your development. It affects your behavior. It affects your present relationships. It also has an effect on your future relationships.

Children learn values about sexuality from family. They also learn from society and religious beliefs. Families and religions may teach values that are different from those seen in society. In society today, talk and images of sexuality are **prevalent**, or generally accepted, in the media, such as on television, on the Internet, and in magazines. It is important for you to be able to determine if that information is useful or accurate.

Sexual Pressures

As You Read

Connect What are some other pressures that you experience in your life?

Pressure to become sexually active is intense for many teens. The reasons for this are complex. Messages about sexual behavior can be confusing. If you are confident about your values and goals, you will be more likely to make responsible decisions and effectively deal with sexual pressure. You need to know how to react to strong sexual feelings when they occur. Finding an outlet, such as exercise, may be a good way to constructively react to sexual feelings.

Sexual activity is not the same as intimacy. Intimacy is a closeness between two people. You can develop intimacy and express affection by holding hands, hugging, kissing, and by sharing thoughts, feelings, and dreams.

A lasting and loving relationship is not based on sexual activity. Sexual activity does not make you an adult. It cannot save a poor relationship either. Physical and emotional changes can often create a desire to act on sexual feelings. Even teens who reject the outside pressures to become sexually active have to be strong about resisting their sexual feelings. Sexual feelings are natural, and they can be powerful. Your best defense is to plan ahead and avoid situations where you may be tempted to engage in sexual activity.

Media Influences

Sexual messages are everywhere in society today. Sexual images are in the media. They are more explicit than ever. This may make some teens feel that sexual activity is acceptable. Behavior that is seen as acceptable is more likely to be imitated or copied. The many negative consequences of sexual behavior are not shown in these sexual images. Remember that these actions are not real.

Peer Influences

Your peers can also have a strong influence on your decisions about sexual behavior. Some speak and act as though sexual activity is okay, and that everybody is doing it. This is not true. This sort of talk is often exaggerated or comes from people who take dangerous risks. These people may seem exciting or glamorous. Do not follow their bad example. Teens who think for themselves do not give in to pressure from others. These teens, however, are often less vocal. You may have to pay close attention to receive their positive messages.

✓ **Reading Check**) **Explain** What is sexuality?

Abstinence

Choosing abstinence ('ab-stə-nən(t)s) from sexual activity allows you to take responsibility for your well-being. **Abstinence** is a deliberate decision to avoid high-risk behaviors, including sexual activity and the use of tobacco, alcohol, and other drugs. You show your values and beliefs if you choose abstinence. Abstinence, however, is not always easy. Use the tips in the Independent Living feature on the next page to stay firm in your decision.

◀◀ *Find an Outlet*
One way to effectively deal with sexual pressures it to find an outlet, such as exercise. *What are some other examples of healthy outlets?*

INDEPENDENT Living

HOW TO **Make a Responsible Decision**

Abstinence requires planning and self-control. Abstinence from sexual activity will help you achieve your goals for your future. Follow these guidelines to make a responsible decision:

1. **Set limits for expressing affection.** Think about your priorities and set limits for your behavior before you are in a situation where sexual feelings may build.
2. **Communicate with your partner.** Share your feelings with your partner. A sign of a mature and responsible relationship is being able to communicate openly.
3. **Talk to a trusted adult.** Sharing your thoughts with a parent or other trusted adult can be a safe way for you to manage your feelings.
4. **Seek low-pressure dating situations.** Choose safe dating locations and activities such as group dating or attending parties only where an adult is present.
5. **Date someone who respects and shares your values.** A dating partner who respects you and has similar values will understand your commitment to abstinence.

Take Action On a piece of paper, make a list of your goals and priorities. These can be for school, work, and dating. Next to each one, list an example of a risk or a distraction that can keep you from being responsible. In a third column, list an action you can take to avoid making a choice with negative consequences.

When you have a close relationship with someone, you can talk about your feelings before you get in an intimate situation. Make sure your partner understands your point of view and limits clearly. Find out what your partner is thinking, too. Respect your partner's wishes about sexual behavior. If you push someone into unwanted activity, it is a sign of selfishness and immaturity. Building a loving relationship takes time. Partners need to get to know each other. They need to share experiences, thoughts, and feelings.

You can say no to and **refuse**, or deny, any situation that does not feel right to you. Refusing to participate in something you believe is wrong is your responsibility to yourself. It is easier, however, to choose dating locations and activities that avoid the pressure for sexual activity, such as a group date or a party with adults present. Nearly any situation is more manageable when you plan for it.

There are nonsexual ways of showing love that can be satisfying. Affection can be shown when you hold hands, hug, or kiss. Also, love and affection can be shown in nonphysical ways. Talking and sharing dreams and interests can create a sense of intimacy and closeness. Small sacrifices can express caring more than sexual behavior does. Respect your partner's needs and goals, as well as your own. Choose ways of expressing feelings that feel right to you both.

✓ **Reading Check** **Explain** Give examples for nonsexual ways of showing love.

The Consequences of Sexual Behavior

Saying yes to sexual pressures as a teen has serious consequences. Those who engage in sexual activity too soon may have major problems. Some of these are emotional, such as trust issues, difficulty committing in future relationships, and a loss of self-esteem. These problems may also include physical consequences, such as sexually transmitted infections, HIV and AIDS, and pregnancy.

Sexually Transmitted Infections

A **sexually transmitted infection (STI)** is an illness that is spread through sexual contact. It is also called a sexually transmitted disease (STD). STIs are an epidemic in the United States. The Centers for Disease Control and Prevention (CDC) estimates there are 19 million new infections each year. About half of these occur in people ages 15 to 24. Some of the most common STIs are described in **Figure 27.1**.

Sometimes STIs are passed because a person is unaware that he or she is infected. Some people with STIs knowingly engage in sexual activity and do not tell the people they are sexually active with. These people are selfish and irresponsible.

Figure 27.1 Sexually Transmitted Infections

Five common STIs are described in the table. The CDC estimates that only about half of all cases of STIs are reported. *Why do you think only half of the cases are reported?*

Name of Infection	Symptoms	Treatment / Cure	Number of Infections
Chlamydia (klə-'mi-dē-ə)	Painful urination, nausea, low fever. May have no symptoms.	Antibiotics. Can be cured.	929,462 infected a year
Genital HPV (human papillomavirus) (ˌpa-pə-'lō-mə-ˌvī-rəs)	Most have no symptoms. May have genital warts or precancerous changes in genital tissue.	Treatment for warts or precancerous changes in tissue. No cure.	6.2 million infected a year
Genital Herpes ('je-nə-t°l 'hər-(ˌ)pez)	Open sores on the sex organs.	Antiviral medication can shorten and prevent outbreaks. No cure.	45 million currently infected
Gonorrhea (ˌgä-nə-'rē-ə)	Genital burning, itching, and discharge.	Antibiotics. Can be cured.	339,593 infected a year
Syphilis ('si-f(ə-)ləs)	Sores on the sex organs, fevers, rashes, hair loss.	Antibiotics. Can be cured.	8,724 infected a year

Females may develop a painful general infection in the pelvic area. This is known as pelvic inflammatory disease (PID). PID can damage the reproductive organs. PID can lead to sterility (stə-'ri-lə-tē). **Sterility** is the inability to have children. Some STIs can harm the fetus during pregnancy.

Some STIs can be cured. Others last a lifetime. A few can be fatal. All STIs are preventable. Avoiding sexual activity is the best prevention.

STIs cause hardships for everyone involved. People who are infected need medical care, which may be costly. Family members are likely to be disappointed in or worried about the person who is infected. The emotional consequences of having a sexually transmitted infection or disease can include depression, embarrassment, guilt, or shame.

HIV and AIDS

Acquired immunodeficiency syndrome (AIDS) is one type of STI. It is caused by a virus called the human immunodeficiency virus (HIV). The virus invades and kills the cells of the immune system. The body is then unable to defend itself from many diseases. HIV can live in the body many years before developing into AIDS. See **Figure 27.2** for the number of reported AIDS cases in males and females ages 13 to 19.

| Figure 27.2 | AIDS Cases Among Teens 13 to 19 Years Old |

AIDS has become an epidemic, even among teens. *What do you think might cause the number of AIDS cases to decrease in the coming years?*

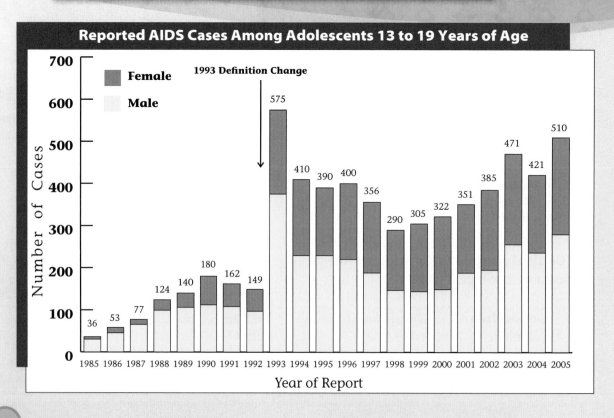

Reported AIDS Cases Among Adolescents 13 to 19 Years of Age

The CDC estimates that about one million people in the United States are living with HIV or AIDS. About 40,000 new cases occur each year. HIV has been spreading rapidly among teens. There is a time lag between initial infection with HIV and the onset of AIDS. Therefore, an infected teen may not show signs of AIDS until he or she is 20 years old or older. Meanwhile, the infected individual can pass on the disease to others.

HIV is spread through intimate sexual contact. The virus can also spread among drug users who share needles. An infected female can pass the virus to her baby if she becomes pregnant.

AIDS has no known cure. At one time, having AIDS was a death sentence. Current medical treatment uses a combination of drugs to delay HIV from developing into AIDS. These powerful drugs do slow the progress of the disease. They are expensive and can have serious, negative side effects. Saying no to all high-risk behaviors is the best way to protect yourself from getting AIDS.

Get Help

Those who suspect they have an STI should get medical help immediately. Most treatment is kept private. Patients are sometimes required to give the names of their partners. This is so they can also be tested if necessary. The consequences of avoiding treatment can be disastrous. There are STI support groups that provide care and help. These groups help people get accurate STI information. They are a forum to share experiences, fears, and feelings with others.

Teen Pregnancy

Many teens get pregnant each year in the United States. Many teens want to have a child to have someone love them. However, a child cannot give unconditional love until he or she is older. Parents must give, rather than receive, love. While parenting can be rewarding, it is also very demanding. Some teens may think that being a parent will prove they are adults. Even some mature adults find the challenges of parenthood difficult.

When teens become parents, the following results may occur:

- Many teen parents, both male and female, do not finish high school or go on for further education. This decreases their chances to get jobs that will support them and their children well. Many teen mothers fall into poverty and stay there.
- Many teen mothers do not get medical care during pregnancy. Teens are more likely to have complications in childbirth than are older women. Babies born to teens younger than 16 are more likely to die in the first year of life than those born to older women.

Financial Literacy

Cost of Having a Baby

Jan and Mike have been married for two years. They plan to have their first baby three years from now. They want to save $10,000 before they have the baby. How much money do they need to save each month to have the $10,000 saved in three years?

Math Concept **Dividing Decimals** To divide money, make sure the decimal point in the quotient is directly above the decimal point of the dividend.

Starting Hint: Before you divide, decide how many months are in three years. After you divide, round your answer to the nearest dollar.

 For math help, go to the Math Appendix at the back of the book.

NCTM Number and Operations Understand the meanings of operations and how they relate to one another.

Real Life | Avoid Date Rape

Personal responsibility plays a large role in avoiding date rape. You can:

- Avoid risky situations. Be careful about where you go, especially with people you do not know well.
- Set limits for yourself. Know beforehand what behavior for you and your partner is acceptable and unacceptable.
- Communicate. Make sure your partner understands and accepts your limits. Speak up when you feel he or she is pressuring you to do something that goes against your values.

- Recognize disrespectful behavior. Learn to identify signs that your partner is not taking your standards seriously.
- Be assertive. If a situation makes you uncomfortable, say so. Say it with verbal and nonverbal language. If it continues, get away or call for help.

Problem-Solving Fiona was looking forward to her date with Kyle. But she had heard some frightening things about him. As her friend, what would you say to Fiona? Write her a letter of advice.

- Teens are rarely prepared for the many duties of parenting. Children born to teens are more likely to be abused, abandoned, or need some type of foster care.
- Children of teen parents are often slow to develop. They tend to get lower grades in school and have more behavior problems.
- Many teen families are dysfunctional. Families that do not meet basic needs tend to produce people who cannot cope in society or make a contribution. A weak family weakens society.

There are ways to avoid teen pregnancy. Contraceptives can prevent pregnancy but they do not always work. Abstinence from sexual activity is the only guaranteed way to avoid getting pregnant. The reality of teen pregnancy and parenting is that negative outcomes far outnumber the happy endings.

Date Rape

Rape is forced sexual intercourse. It is an act of violence. Rape may occur between strangers or people who know each other. Rape that takes place in a dating situation is called **date rape**.

Date rape occurs more frequently than most people realize, and it often is not reported. Teens in particular often do not report date rape. They may mistakenly believe it was their fault or that it was not rape if they were on a date. Many think accusing someone of rape will cause them public shame and embarrassment. Sometimes they feel that no one will believe them.

Rape should never be tolerated. In a threatening situation, teens must be assertive. You could leave the situation or call for help. Any rape, in any situation, must be reported. States have different reporting requirements. Call the police to find out exactly what to do. Reporting the rape will raise awareness of the problem. It may also prevent the rapist from repeating the act.

Every person who experiences sexual violation reacts in a different way. Rape affects victims physically, emotionally, and socially. It may take help from professionals to heal. They can help victims work through the shock and trauma. Most communities have support groups that can help rape victims.

✓ **Reading Check** **Describe** What is an STI?

Take Responsibility

What does it mean to be sexually responsible? It means knowing the facts about sexuality. It means thinking about the outcome of your decisions and actions on yourself and others. It means knowing your values and living by them.

Most people want sexual activity to be special. They want strong feelings of desire to go along with a strong bond to one beloved person. Many people are willing to wait. They want a sexual relationship based on fidelity. **Fidelity** is faithfulness. Saving sexual activity for the committed framework of marriage provides a way to show your responsibility. It also shows respect for yourself and others.

Remember that you and your partner or date both deserve to be treated with consideration and respect. You should be able to communicate your thoughts and feelings honestly with one another. Talk with a trusted adult, such as a parent or guardian, to help you manage your feelings and make informed choices.

Life Skills CHECKLIST

Communication Skills

Refusal Strategies You can refuse any situation that feels wrong to you by using these tips:

✓ Say no in a firm voice.

✓ Explain why by saying you feel the activity goes against your values or beliefs.

✓ Offer safe, healthful alternatives to the situation.

✓ Stand your ground. Make it clear that you will not back down.

✓ Leave. If the other person continues to pressure you, simply walk away.

Section 27.2 After You Read

Review Key Concepts

1. **Describe** ways to cope with sexual pressures from peers and society.
2. **Identify** some methods for developing intimacy without sexual activity.
3. **List** and describe five common STIs.
4. **Explain** why people want a sexual relationship based on fidelity.

Practice Academic Skills

English Language Arts

5. Interview a woman who has had a child. Ask her questions about the impact of the pregnancy on her life. What does she feel she gained or lost by having a child? Ask how she thinks her life might have been different if she had had the child while in her teens. Write a report of the interview.

   NCTE 4 Use written language to communicate effectively.

6. You have just learned that a teenage cousin of yours is pregnant. You are certain that her parents are giving her a hard time. Write an e-mail that shows your support and offers your help if she needs it.

   NCTE 12 Use language to accomplish individual purposes.

🧭 **Check Your Answers** Check your answers at this book's Online Learning Center through **glencoe.com**.

CAREER SPOTLIGHT

Public Health Educator

Laura Linnan, ScD, CHES
Chapel Hill, North Carolina

Dr. Laura Linnan, like many health education professionals at the university level, divides her time between teaching and research. She researches the prevention and control of cancer. She also says she gets great pleasure out of teaching. She enjoys the contribution she can make to health care through the classroom.

Linnan says, "I teach graduate students. I place a high value on the professional preparation of the next leaders in health care." She continues, "My interests are in making a positive impact on the health of the public, especially those who are suffering the most."

Linnan explains that the lessons students can learn in a classroom setting are essential for health educators. For example, communication skills are beneficial for teaching a wide range of students. She also states that there are some basic life lessons that are just as important. These lessons can help people stay healthy for life.

"Pay attention to your own health," she recommends. Linnan offers several ways to do this. "Stay active, eat healthfully, and realize that health includes mental, emotional, physical, and spiritual health."

CAREER FACTS

Education or Training Most careers require undergraduate degrees in health and medicine, education, English, and language.

Nature of the Work Health educators work with various groups of people and communities to encourage and promote healthy behaviors.

Aptitudes, Abilities, and Skills Creative thinking, strong communication skills, public speaking, the ability to connect with a diverse group of people.

Academic Skills Required English, oral and written communication, science, health, public speaking, foreign language skills

Student Organizations To prepare for this career, look for groups that help you gain knowledge of health and nutrition, such as FCCLA.

Career Outlook Jobs as health educators are expected to grow faster than average over the next ten years.

Career Path Health educators may work at the university level or directly with affected populations in community agencies. High-level university degrees may lead to university teaching positions and research opportunities within the health field.

Critical Thinking

Routes to a Career There are many routes to becoming a public health educator. Which would you take?

 Research Careers For more information on this and other careers, visit the Occupational Outlook Handbook Web site through the link on this book's Online Learning Center at **glencoe.com**.

CHAPTER SUMMARY

 ### Section 27.1
Develop Your Identity

Personal identity is affected by gender roles. These are the behavior and traits expected of a male or female. Societal gender roles have changed over the years. Sexual identity is the way people see themselves as males and females. It begins to develop during the teen years. Family is a major influence. Later, peers and the media affect sexual identity. Each person must develop his or her own personal identity. People can be appreciated as individuals.

 ### Section 27.2
Sexual Behavior

Sexual development begins during the teen years. There are external sexual pressures from peers and the media. Abstinence is refraining from sexual intercourse and is the only guaranteed way to avoid the negative consequences of sexual activity. Sexual activity can bring serious outcomes, including sexually transmitted infections. Teen pregnancy will have a long-term impact on the teen parents' lives. You can take responsibility for your decisions about sexual activity.

Content and Academic Vocabulary Review

1. Use each of these content and academic vocabulary words in a sentence.

Content Vocabulary
◇ gender role (p. 527)
◇ sexual identity (p. 529)
◇ sexuality (p. 532)
◇ abstinence (p. 533)
◇ sexually transmitted
  infection (STI) (p. 535)
◇ sterility (p. 536)
◇ rape (p. 538)
◇ date rape (p. 538)
◇ fidelity (p. 539)

Academic Vocabulary
■ absorb (p. 529)
■ contradict (p. 530)
■ prevalent (p. 532)
■ refuse (p. 534)

Review Key Concepts

2. Explain how personal identity is affected by gender roles.
3. Describe what sexual identity is.
4. Identify some of the pressures and influences involved in sexual development.
5. Determine the benefits of abstinence.
6. Suggest possible consequences of sexual behaviors.
7. Describe what it means to be sexually responsible.

Critical Thinking

8. Analyze Imagine that your best friend has a twin brother. They both want to attend an out-of-state college. Your friend's parents approve of her brother's plans. They want your friend to live at home and attend the community college. She believes this is because she is a girl. Your friend has asked for your advice. What do you tell her?
9. Evaluate If behavior reflects values, what values might abstinence illustrate? What might sexual activity illustrate?

Real-World Skills

Self-Management Skills

10. Problem Solving Javon likes to write poetry. He has kept this a secret because he is afraid his male friends will laugh at him. Now he wants to test his skills in a school writing contest. He is struggling with his decision because of his fear. What should he do? Write your answer in a paragraph.

Critical Thinking Skills

11. Assess Roles Television programs that portray family life often reflect the gender roles of the times. Watch or recall a show from the 1950s that deals with family life. Look for ways in which gender roles are portrayed. Compare these to today's gender roles. Write a comparison of the gender roles in the two shows.

Communication Skills

12. Practice Assertiveness Follow your teacher's instructions to form into groups. Create a list of lines that some teens might use to try to persuade a partner to have sex. Write at least one assertive no response to each line. Be sure to label the lines and responses clearly, and respond assertively.

Problem-Solving Skills

13. Take Action Zane and Sheena see contradictory attitudes toward sexual behavior in their school. Some students are sexually active. Others are committed to abstinence until marriage. Zane and Sheena would like to find a way to help others choose abstinence. How could they do this?

14. Evaluate View your favorite music video. Do you see sexual behavior shown in the video? Are the sexual messages positive? Are they negative? Write a magazine article to share your findings with the class.

15. STI Testing Find out what resources are available in your community for testing for STIs, including HIV/AIDS. How much does testing cost? Create a brochure to report your findings.

16. Community Resources Find out what kinds of special programs are available in your community for pregnant teens. Does the school district sponsor any of these programs? Is low-cost medical care available? Are there support groups? Create a brochure summarizing your findings.

17. Research Go to this book's Online Learning Center at **glencoe.com** to find **Web Links** for the **Centers for Disease Control and Prevention**. Select an STI and find out more about the infection. Write a report summarizing your findings.

Additional Activities For additional activities, go to this book's Online Learning Center through **glencoe.com**.

Academic Skills

Mathematics

18. Calculate Lost Wages Stan has recently been diagnosed with a sexually transmitted infection (STI). He has not been feeling well enough to go to work and he has already had several medical appointments for treatment of the infection. He does not get paid if he does not go to work. He earns $12.00 per hour at work and has missed 45 hours of work because of the medical appointments and sickness. How much money has Stan lost so far because of the STI?

 Math Concept **Multiply Decimals**
Multiplying with money is the same as multiplying with decimals. Be sure to put the decimal point in the correct place in your answer.

Starting Hint: Set up a problem that multiplies Stan's hourly wage ($12.00) by the number of hours he has missed work (45).

 For math help, go to the Math Appendix at the back of the book.

NCTM Number and Operations Compute fluently and make reasonable estimates.

English Language Arts

19. Create a Flyer Use a word processing or design program. Design and write a flyer that informs teens about the different types of STIs. Do research to find information about these infections and how they are spread. Include their consequences to health and life in your flyer. Compare your flyer with those of your classmates.

NCTE 8 Use information resources to gather information and create and communicate knowledge.

Social Studies

20. History Research and find information about a person who was influential in changing societal views of gender. Examples may include Margaret Sanger or Susan B. Anthony. Write a short biography of the person. Highlight his or her activities and the changes the person helped bring about. Does the person's life and influence continue to affect people today? Why or why not?

NCSS II.c Identify and describe significant historical periods and patterns of change within and across cultures.

STANDARDIZED TEST PRACTICE

TRUE/FALSE
Carefully read the following statements and determine whether they are true or false.

Test-Taking Tip When taking a true/false test, if you have time at the end, check your answers. Did you read the statement carefully? Was there any part of the statement that was false? If so, the entire statement is false.

21. a. Giving in to sexual pressures can have serious consequences.
b. AIDS can be spread only by sexual contact.
c. Self-discipline can help you walk away from an intense argument rather than saying or doing something hurtful.

CHAPTER 28

Readiness for Marriage

Section 28.1
Understand Attraction

Section 28.2
Choose the Right Partner

 Explore the Photo
Sharing interests and values indicates a readiness for marriage. *What other factors show that you may be ready for marriage?*

Chapter Objectives

After completing this chapter, you will be able to:

- **Describe** various theories of attraction.
- **Compare** theories of attraction with the development of real-life relationships.
- **Identify** signs of readiness for marriage.
- **Determine** the warning signs of potential danger in a relationship.
- **Explain** what makes a realistic attitude toward marriage.

Writing Activity / Personal Essay

Dependability Dependable people prove themselves worthy of trust by keeping their word and meeting responsibilities. You can show dependability when you:

- Show up for an assigned shift at a volunteer event.
- Start dinner on time so it is ready when the rest of the family gets home.
- Stay late at the library to finish part of a group presentation for class the next day.
- Turn in an article for the school newspaper before the deadline.
- Make an effort to be patient and sympathetic when friends need support.

Write a personal essay that explains why dependability is important to you in a marriage partner. Make sure your essay has an introduction, a body, and a conclusion.

Writing Tips To write a strong personal essay, follow these steps:

1. Include a thesis statement, or your position on the issue.
2. Use vivid details and examples.
3. Compose complete and logical sentences.

Understand Attraction

Reading Guide

Before You Read

Stay Engaged One way to stay engaged when reading is to turn each of the headings into a question, then read the section to find the answers.

Read to Learn

Key Concepts
- **Describe** various theories of attraction.
- **Compare** theories of attraction with the development of real-life relationships.

Main Idea

Theories of attraction attempt to explain why people choose the mates they do. The theories are useful but not always realistic.

Content Vocabulary

◇ homogamy
◇ complementary needs
◇ propinquity

 Graphic Organizer Go to this book's Online Learning Center at **glencoe.com** to print out this graphic organizer.

Academic Vocabulary

You will find these words in your reading and on your tests. Use the glossary to look up their definitions if necessary.

■ exchange
■ criterion

Graphic Organizer

As you read, list and describe each filter from the filter theory of attraction. Use a chart like the one shown to help organize your information.

The Filter Theory of Attraction	
Filter	**Description**

Academic Standards • • • • • • • • • • • • • • •

 English Language Arts

NCTE 3 Apply strategies to interpret texts.

NCTE 5 Use different writing process elements to communicate effectively.

 Mathematics

NCTM Number and Operations Compute fluently and make reasonable estimates.

 Science

NSES Content Standard A Develop abilities necessary to do scientific inquiry, understandings about scientific inquiry.

NCTE *National Council of Teachers of English*
NCTM *National Council of Teachers of Mathematics*

NSES *National Science Education Standards*
NCSS *National Council of the Social Studies*

Theories of Attraction

How does a friendship develop into a long-term relationship? How does it develop into a solid marriage? Studies on human behavior have taken a detailed look at the way we select our mates. This research has resulted in several theories. No one theory explains all relationships. Each one gives insight into what causes people to choose their partners the way they do.

Homogamy

Many studies have found that people choose mates that are like themselves. This is the basis of the homogamy (hō-'mä-gə-mē) theory. **Homogamy** means sameness. People look for three levels of homogamy. These levels are found in outer qualities, inner qualities, and ideas about roles.

Outer Qualities

First, people are attracted to those who share their outer qualities. This makes sense. Likenesses create comfort and ease in a new relationship. Race, age, religion, education, and family background are some common traits that many couples share. You may know couples who have striking differences. In these basic traits, however, most couples are alike.

Gimel's experience shows the impact of shared outer traits. Gimel worked on the assembly line of an auto plant. His parents were immigrants who worked in the same plant. He lived in an extended family with strong ties to relatives in their native country. One night, Gimel met Mara, an attractive college student. Mara described her studies as an art major and her summer of touring art museums in Europe. She complained that she was having trouble getting along with her father's third wife. Do you think Gimel and Mara are likely to be attracted to each other?

Inner Qualities

Couples who share outer qualities look for homogamy in their inner qualities, which include goals, interests, and values. People who like and want the same things in life are more apt to have positive feelings for one another. Similar values makes acceptance of the other person easier. For example, two people who have received the same kind of education are likely to get along well. People with the same religion usually hold many of the same ideas on morals.

As You Read

Connect What attracts you to another person?

Vocabulary

You can find definitions in the glossary at the back of this book.

Theory of Homogamy Studies show that attraction is based on similarities. *Do you believe partners should be alike in all aspects?*

Roles

As couples become more serious about each other, their need to agree on roles becomes more important. What are the duties of each partner in a marriage? What should each person be like as a parent? The more alike the answers are, the more apt the relationship is to progress.

Roles became an issue for Charles and Pamela. Pamela dreamed of having several children soon. She wanted to stay home while the children were young. Charles wanted his wife to have a career. He hoped to travel and enjoy the benefits of two incomes. Any children could perhaps come much later. The couple ended their relationship after a long talk. They knew they would never see eye to eye on some very critical issues.

⬇ Understand Roles It is important to agree on roles in a relationship. *How can you avoid role conflict in a relationship?*

Complementary Needs

The expression opposites attract may be a comment on a pattern of attraction. This theory is called **complementary needs**. It says that people select others who complete, or complement, their personality needs. Each partner's strengths balance the other's. For example, an outgoing person may be attracted to someone who is quiet. Strong people may choose those who will support them.

At first glance, the theories of homogamy and complementary needs seem to contradict each other. In real life, they tend to work together. People are drawn first to those like themselves. From among this group, they seek someone who can help them meet their needs. People choose partners who affirm and support their sense of self.

Social Exchange

In some cultures, families arrange marriages between young people. These are based on what each family can offer the other. Some researchers believe that people select their mates on the same idea. They ask themselves what they want in a mate. They may look at material resources, personal qualities, and skills. Then they look at what they can offer in return. This theory is called the social exchange theory. It is related to the costs and rewards of the relationship.

You tend to choose someone who brings you the best practical and emotional rewards at a fair cost to yourself. People select and build those relationships that give the most value. For example, Judy is a professional musician. She spends much of her time traveling and rehearsing. Her husband manages her career and schedules her tours. She got both a husband and a manager when she married.

The idea of **exchange**, or giving or taking one thing in return for another, may seem somewhat calculating, but it is seen in many strong relationships. You and your friends probably practice some kind of social exchange. Still, your friendships are more than a list of favors given and received.

Propinquity

Propinquity (prə-ˈpiŋ-kwə-tē) is nearness in time or place. People are more apt to meet and get to know and stay with others who are physically close by. It is much harder to build a relationship when the couple is apart. The propinquity theory is linked to the social exchange theory. Relationships are more convenient when people live close to each other. They bring rewards without the costs that long-distance relationships bring. These costs include time and money for communication and travel. There are also emotional costs in being lonely.

Ideal Mate

Have you ever thought that a devoted, loving couple were made for each other? The ideal mate theory takes that saying to heart. With this theory, people have a mental image of an ideal mate. This is based on appearance, character, or other traits. They measure those they meet against this ideal. They are most attracted to those who come closest to their ideal.

Some people have a very clear image of their ideal. They can envision everything about that person. Often, the image of an ideal mate is based on parents. A person may idealize the parent of the opposite gender. Of course, a person may also be looking for someone who is the exact opposite of the parent.

Right Time

This theory says that people pick a mate when the time is right. This may be after graduating from high school or college, or when returning from time served in the military. For some people, the right time is when they are established in a career. The person may have met many suitable mates over the years. None were right until the time was right as well.

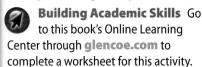

Science in Action

Magnetic Personalities

Social scientists study the way people interact with other people in groups and in society. Some people are said to have magnetic personalities. This means other people like to be around them. People are drawn to them much like items made of iron are drawn to a magnet. To determine whether someone has a magnetic personality, consider the following questions:

1. Does the person like to be around other people?
2. Do other people like to be around the person?

Survey ten people to find whether they believe they have a magnetic personality. Share your findings with your classmates.

Building Academic Skills Go to this book's Online Learning Center through **glencoe.com** to complete a worksheet for this activity.

NSES Content Standard A Develop abilities necessary to do scientific inquiry, understandings about scientific inquiry.

Filter Theory

The filter theory puts some of the other theories of mate selection together. It explains how a couple moves toward marriage. It says that a person chooses another according to a specific **criterion**, or standard. There may be several criteria. Each choice narrows the field. Then the final selection of a mate is made. The filters are:

- **Propinquity Filter** People meet and get to know others.
- **Attraction Filter** Different traits attract different people. This filter is similar to the social exchange theory. That theory says that people look for qualities that will be rewarding. It also involves the ideal mate theory. This says that people look for traits similar to those of their ideal mate.
- **Homogamy Filter** People look for those who are similar in age, education, religion, race, attitudes, and values.
- **Complementary Needs Filter** The couple fills each other's needs. This gives balance to the relationship.

Shared Interests

A shared interest can bring two people together. *Do you think a person should adopt an interest in order to please the other?*

- **Readiness Filter** When people are ready, they decide to marry. This is the right time theory. Males tend to take longer to get past this filter than females.

The filter theory suggests that when a couple goes through all the filters, they are ready to marry. This theory is the most complex. It also may come closest to describing how couples actually move toward marriage.

✓ **Reading Check** **Explain** What is homogamy and how is it linked to attraction?

Theories and Reality

The theories of attraction do not neatly describe every situation. They simply offer ideas to consider. Knowing why you find a potential mate attractive can help you see the value of the relationship more clearly. What has brought you together? What is keeping you together? Is your current attraction enough to build a strong relationship for the future?

Often, people find themselves in serious relationships without ever having considered what traits they value in a potential mate. They may be in the relationship because of poorly made decisions or pressures from peers or family. Some couples have no plans for their future as a couple.

Dating provides a chance to get to know people you find attractive. Most dating relationships do not progress to marriage. They will, however, help you learn what qualities you want and need in a spouse. They may also help you learn about yourself.

Certain qualities make a successful dating relationship. The couple has fun together. They enjoy going out with others to have a good time. The qualities that make dating a success may not be ones that make a good spouse. An ideal date does not necessarily make an ideal mate. At some point, however, dating is apt to lead to mate selection.

Marriage partners need to respect each other and have fun together. They also need many other skills and traits to make the marriage work. The qualities that attract partners may not be the qualities needed for a long-term marriage. As you think about the qualities you seek, you may start to ask what qualities you can bring to a marriage. It is important to take a long, hard look at what it takes to be ready for a life together.

Financial Literacy

Travel Costs

Jeff and Sarah began dating before she left for college. While she was away, Jeff visited her once a month for four years. It cost him an average of $248.50 for a round-trip ticket each time he visited. How much did Jeff spend on travel to visit Sarah?

Math Concept **Multiply Money** Money can be multiplied like regular decimals. Be sure to put the decimal point in the correct place in your answer.

Starting Hint: First, determine how many tickets Jeff bought (4×12). Then multiply your answer by the average cost of the tickets ($248.50).

 For math help, go to the Math Appendix at the back of the book.

NCTM Number and Operations Compute fluently and make reasonable estimates.

Section 28.1 After You Read

Review Key Concepts

1. **Describe** how the theories of propinquity and social exchange are linked.
2. **Explain** why a good dating partner may not be a good prospect for a long-term relationship.

Practice Academic Skills
English Language Arts

3. Conduct research for the roots of the word propinquity. You may want to look it up in a dictionary. Why do you think this word was chosen as the name of the theory? How does the theory relate to roots of the word? Write your answer in a short paragraph.

   NCTE 3 Apply strategies to interpret texts.

4. Do you think people are generally aware of the forces of attraction that are at work inside them? How could an increasing awareness of yourself and the knowledge of attraction be helpful? Write a paragraph explaining your answer.

   NCTE 5 Use different writing process elements to communicate effectively.

Check Your Answers Check your answers at this book's Online Learning Center through **glencoe.com**.

Choose the Right Partner

Reading Guide

Before You Read

Take Time to Rest The brain has a hard time absorbing new data when it is stressed. Your reading skills will be much more effective if you are relaxed.

Read to Learn
Key Concepts
- **Identify** signs of readiness for marriage.
- **Determine** the warning signs of potential danger in a relationship.
- **Explain** what makes a realistic attitude toward marriage.

Main Idea
There are a number of signs that a person is ready for marriage. There are also warning signs that could signal problems for a relationship. A realistic attitude toward marriage is needed.

Content Vocabulary
◇ readiness   ◇ institution of marriage
◇ jealousy

Academic Vocabulary
You will find these words in your reading and on your tests. Use the glossary to look up their definitions if necessary.
■ potential   ■ resolution

Graphic Organizer
As you read, look for factors that show readiness for marriage. Use a concept web like the one shown to help organize your information.

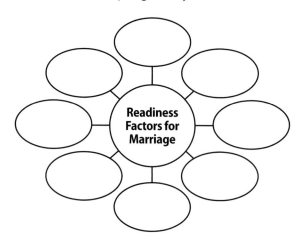

 Graphic Organizer Go to this book's Online Learning Center at **glencoe.com** to print out this graphic organizer.

Academic Standards • • • • • • • • • • • • • • •
English Language Arts
NCTE 4 Use written language to communicate effectively.

NCTE 8 Use information resources to gather information and create and communicate knowledge.

NCTE *National Council of Teachers of English*
NCTM *National Council of Teachers of Mathematics*

NSES *National Science Education Standards*
NCSS *National Council of the Social Studies*

Signs of Readiness

When two people are deeply in love, it is too late to ask, "Are you ready for this?" They are not likely to make an objective decision. **Readiness** is those traits and conditions that show whether a person is prepared for marriage. Questions about readiness need to be asked and answered early. Some should be asked even before a relationship is in sight.

The idea of readiness is simple. The more readiness factors partners have or acquire, the more tools they have for creating a long and rewarding marriage. No list of factors guarantees success in marriage or in life. You can, however, give yourself a much better chance by thinking ahead.

Age

Up to a point, the older two people are at the time of their wedding, the more apt the marriage is to be stable. Added years bring more life experiences. Age often leads to greater maturity and to better jobs and incomes. All of these tend to help make stronger marriages.

This effect levels off at about age 27 for men and 25 for women. A 32-year-old woman, then, is no more apt to have a good marriage than a woman of 29.

Independence

People who cannot stand on their own are not able to support someone else. Look at your own level of independence in readiness for marriage. Ask questions like those below. If your answers are yes, chances are you are well on your way to independence:

- Do I have the practical knowledge I need to survive on my own?
- Do I make good decisions?
- Can I make decisions without turning to family for help?
- Am I comfortable with the idea of living apart from the family that raised me?
- Can I support myself financially?

Remember to ask the same questions about a **potential**, or possible, partner. A good marriage takes two independent people. Otherwise, one person may rely too much on the partner. Both may depend too much on their families.

Bonds with parents and other family members should remain strong. However, a marriage is meant to form a new family. Partners who are not ready to shift their first loyalty to each other are not ready for marriage.

Vocabulary
You can find definitions in the glossary at the back of this book.

As You Read
Connect What other factors does age bring to a marriage?

Ready for a Marriage When two people are ready to commit to marriage, they will have prepared for the decision in a number of ways. *What are some ways couples need to prepare before marriage?*

Parental Approval

Parental approval should not be a main reason for choosing a mate. However, parental input can be very helpful. Parents genuinely want their children to be happy. They may have good reasons for disapproval of a partner. They may be bothered by the person's traits or think the timing is not right.

In most cases, couples are wise to postpone marriage if parents object, even if their worries seem unfounded. Over time the troublesome situation may be resolved. A sign of mature love is that it will wait.

Sometimes parents come to support their child's choice of partner. Some couples decide not to marry because they see their parents' reasons for concern. Marriage is a partnership for life. Spending a little extra time to make the decision is a worthwhile choice. Marrying against parents' wishes puts stress on all the relationships involved.

Importance of Parental Approval
It is important for parents to approve of a couple's upcoming marriage. *What steps can a couple take if parents do not approve?*

Know Each Other

In one study, researchers found that partners who had known each other for at least five years before marrying were the happiest. Five years, however, is not a magic number. The point is to know your partner well before making a lifetime pledge. This is essential to the success of a marriage.

Some couples marry after a very short time together. Couples in this situation simply do not have the chance to learn about each other and talk over important issues. The same may be true of couples who are apart prior to marriage. You will have a better understanding whether your relationship will last if you have experience facing life's ups and downs together.

To discover each other's views on important topics, partners need to have open communication. Do they agree on having children? How can they keep parents, stepparents, and other relatives happy? Where will they live? How will they make decisions about money? What kind of lifestyle will they build together?

Many couples use prepared checklists designed to help work through these kinds of issues. Counselors and clergy members have them. You can find them in resource books and magazines. Going over such checklists together, a couple may find questions that had not occurred to them. An example might be how and where they will celebrate holidays. They need to talk over the many issues they will face as a couple. This can bring greater understanding and confidence to the relationship.

A Sense of Responsibility

Think of all the duties the adults in your family have. They must meet the family's physical needs for food, clothing, and shelter. Emotional needs may be harder to meet. For a marriage to succeed, partners must be willing and able to take on these responsibilities.

Supporting a family takes financial resources. Before getting married, partners should be earning enough money to pay their expenses. They may have to delay marriage to finish their educations and get established in jobs. Low income often adds to problems. In fact, fights about money are the most often named cause of divorce. Financial preparation and planning help prevent added stress.

Spouses have other important duties to one another. They must be willing to share the work of the household. Emotionally, they must be ready to support each other.

Friends and Siblings

If you have friends, you have a better chance of contributing to a strong marriage. This is because the same skills are needed for both.

Siblings also can influence a person's readiness for marriage. Learning to get along with brothers and sisters is good training as a husband or wife. Close relations with siblings contribute to a happy childhood.

✓ **Reading Check** **Describe** What does marriage readiness mean?

INDEPENDENT Living

HOW TO Cook for Someone Special

Getting a meal on the table takes both preplanning and multitasking. Follow these guidelines to make sure each dish is ready at the right time:

1. **List the steps in each recipe and the time needed to complete each one.** Estimate times generously, especially when trying new skills or recipes.
2. **List any added time needed for cooking.** List it next to the task times.
3. **Figure out the starting time.** Subtract the total time from the time at which the meal should be ready. Again, add a few minutes.
4. **Make a schedule.** Put the tasks in order based on starting time, working backward from the time the meal should be ready. Fill gaps with tasks that have flexible starting times and others that can be completed at the same time.
5. **Carry out the plan.** Check off tasks as you complete them so that nothing is forgotten. Note any problems to help improve the results next time.

Take Action Plan and prepare a three-course meal of simple recipes, using the steps listed here. Was preparing the meal easier or harder when you put yourself on a schedule? How can the habit of scheduling help you make larger, more complicated meals?

Warning Signs

Some conditions can encourage couples to move ahead with their relationship, such as knowledge of each other's values. Other factors should make them put on the brakes. These factors are called warning signs. These signs warn of problems that are apt to keep a relationship from being healthy or strong.

Abuse

Abuse has no place in a loving relationship. Abuse, you will remember, may be physical or emotional. It shows a partner's inability to handle problems in a mature way. If abuse occurs, the couple should stop seeing each other. If they want to try to save the relationship, they need outside help. Without professional help, abusive relationships rarely improve and often get worse.

Substance Abuse

If a partner abuses alcohol or other drugs, it can lead to a troubled relationship. These people often have emotional problems in addition to substance abuse. Emotional problems make it hard for both partners to stay in a committed relationship. Substance abuse also decreases self-control. This makes the abuser more prone to acts of cruelty, such as physical violence.

Few people knowingly marry someone with a substance abuse problem. Partners often hide an addiction. This is especially true early in a relationship. Getting out of such a relationship can be difficult. A partner may feel that he or she is abandoning the other person just when he or she needs support the most. Abusers must solve their problems themselves, however. A partner can be supportive. It needs to be clear that a long-term relationship is possible only when the abuser has control over the problem.

Real Life | Differences

Too many differences can threaten a relationship. Before two people think seriously about commitment, they might ask each other:

- Will age make a difference? A large age difference presents a problem when two people cannot relate to each other's experiences.
- Will cultural differences be a problem? A couple may need to look at how their backgrounds have affected their attitudes, values, and what they expect.
- What role does religion play in their lives? If one person feels more strongly than the

other, the couple may have trouble bridging the difference.

Problem-Solving

Alex and Cynthia are in college together. They have been dating seriously for several months. Alex wants Cynthia to meet his family. He invites her to dinner. He has described his family's pride in their Latino heritage. Cynthia is not familiar with this culture. She wants to show respect. What can Cynthia do to show her interest in the family?

Jealousy

Jealousy is watchfulness in guarding a relationship with a loved one. Jealous people see their actions as signs of love. Their behavior is a desire to possess and control another person. They show a complete lack of trust in their partners.

Most jealous partners are not secure about themselves or their relationships. The victims of a jealous partner are often isolated and lonely. They have been cut off from their friends and families. Extreme jealousy is emotional abuse.

To some degree, jealousy is normal early in a relationship. This is when neither partner is sure of how the other feels. With committed couples, however, feelings of jealousy should be rare.

Arguments

True love may not always run smoothly. If couples spend much of their time arguing, however, they should seriously rethink their relationship. One or both of them may need to develop the qualities that make the relationship work, such as communication, compromise, and respect. The couple may not be as compatible as they thought.

Argument is different from discussion. Discussion is honest, thoughtful, respectful, and sticks to the subject. It leads to compromise and the **resolution**, or solution, of problems. Argument is emotional, poorly reasoned, and can be hurtful. It may even lead to physical abuse by some. Argument does not solve a problem. It becomes one.

 **Reading Check** **Explain** Why is substance abuse a warning sign for a relationship?

Be Realistic Partners need to look at each other, with all their negatives and positives, in a realistic light. *How is it possible to realistically look at the person you are most attracted to?*

A Realistic Attitude

Love alone is not enough to solve the problems that married life brings. You must have a strong belief in the **institution of marriage**, or marriage as a way of living. You must believe marriage is worth preserving in society. People who believe this have added encouragement to do what it takes to make marriage and family life work.

It takes many skills to make a successful marriage. Does having all of the qualities and conditions described here make someone ready for marriage? The answer is, not entirely. People can be prepared for marriage in many ways. Yet they may still have an unrealistic attitude toward married life. They may expect too much from themselves, their partners, or the relationship. They may not realize that choosing the right partner is only the first step toward a successful, long-term bond.

The following points can help you think realistically about marriage and potential marriage partners:

- **Love is more than sexual attraction.** Ideally, a strong, physical attraction would go along with a strong, loving marriage. When the sensual aspect becomes the focus, couples may fail to deal with other areas that are important to married life. Unresolved differences and problems can drive couples apart.

- **Marriage is not a cure-all.** Some people see marriage as a means to social status, financial security, or to have children. They may want marriage to get them out of a bad home environment. Some people feel pressure from family to marry. Marriages made in response to a problem are not typically strong.

- **What you see is what you get.** Planning to change a partner's habits after marriage is a mistake. If a person cannot or will not change before marriage, why should he or she change afterwards? It is wiser to marry someone whose traits you already find appealing.

- **Do not expect a perfect partner.** You cannot be one, and you are not going to find one.

Choosing whether to marry—and whom to marry—are among the most important decisions you will ever make. Your choice of a spouse will influence most of the other decisions you make throughout life. It will impact the kind of lifestyle you create. You need realistic ideas about married life and a real understanding of your future spouse. These will give you an advantage in making a happy marriage.

Section 28.2 After You Read

Review Key Concepts

1. **Summarize** why independence is a sign of readiness for marriage.
2. **Describe** the relationship between jealousy and emotional abuse.
3. **Explain** why it is important for a couple to have a belief in the institution of marriage, rather than just thinking love is enough.

Practice Academic Skills

English Language Arts

4. You know someone who is waiting for a partner who fits every point of readiness discussed in this chapter. How would you advise him or her to continue in their search for a relationship? Write an advice column directed to this person.

   NCTE 4 Use written language to communicate effectively.

5. Research the effect of alcoholism or drug abuse on family life. Write a report that summarizes your findings. Do you agree that these should be warning signs for a couple looking to marry? Why or why not?

   NCTE 8 Use information resources to gather information and create and communicate knowledge.

Check Your Answers Check your answers at this book's Online Learning Center through **glencoe.com**.

CHAPTER SUMMARY

 Section 28.1
Understand Attraction

Several theories explain why people are attracted to each other. The most common theory is homogamy. This says that people are attracted to those who are most like themselves. Others fall under the complementary needs and social exchange theories. Propinquity, ideal mate, and the right time are more theories. Filter theory combines other theories into one. It says that the theories act in a series of steps until a mate is selected. The theories are useful. However, they do not explain everything. They do not tell us how a relationship develops and a partner is chosen.

 Section 28.2
Choose the Right Partner

There are many signs that show that people are ready for marriage. These include being older and being independent. Relationships are stronger when parents approve. They are better when the couple knows each other well. Partners should have a sense of responsibility. People with many friends and those who get along with siblings are apt to have good relationship skills. Warning signs in a relationship include physical, emotional, and substance abuse. Jealousy or constant arguments are other signs. It is important to have a realistic attitude about marriage.

Content and Academic Vocabulary Review

1. Use each of these content and academic vocabulary words in a sentence.

Content Vocabulary
◇ homogamy (p. 547)
◇ complementary needs (p. 548)
◇ propinquity (p. 549)
◇ readiness (p. 553)
◇ jealousy (p. 557)
◇ institution of marriage (p. 557)

Academic Vocabulary
■ exchange (p. 549)
■ criterion (p. 550)
■ potential (p. 553)
■ resolution (p. 557)

Review Key Concepts

2. Describe various theories of attraction.
3. Compare theories of attraction with the development of real-life relationships.
4. Identify signs of readiness for marriage.
5. Determine the warning signs of potential danger in a relationship.
6. Explain what makes a realistic attitude toward marriage.

Critical Thinking

7. Analyze Behavior You may have known couples who seem to have very little in common. Yet they have successful relationships. How would you explain this?
8. Recognize Contradictions The text says that independence from parents is important for a strong marriage. So is approval from parents. These statements seem to disagree with each other. How do you explain this?
9. Compare Imagine you are allowed to base your selection of a partner on only one theory of attraction. Which would you use? Why?

Real-World Skills

Decision-Making Skills

10. Problem Solving Chelsea and John plan to marry after they graduate from college. They have little money, but both have been offered jobs with good pay. Chelsea's parents want to loan them money to help them pay expenses. Write a paragraph to explain what you think Chelsea and John should do.

Collaborative Skills

11. Ideal Mate Write down five traits that you find desirable in a partner. Combine your list with those of classmates. List the five most popular traits for male and female students. Would these lists represent an ideal mate? Should you expect to find all these traits in one person? Explain your answers in a short essay.

Communication Skills

12. Interview Talk to married couples from different generations—your own, your parents', and your grandparents', if possible. Ask: How did you meet? What traits did you look for in a spouse? What did you expect marriage to be like? Compare and summarize their answers in a short report.

Interpersonal Skills

13. Make a Decision Maria and Juan are planning their wedding, although Juan's father opposes the marriage. Juan told Maria that his father will not attend the ceremony. Maria knows that Juan and his father have grown very close since his mother died. What should she do? Write Maria a letter with your advice.

14. Checklist Follow your teacher's instructions to form into groups. Locate a marriage readiness checklist available in your community. Work with your group to design a brochure that encourages couples to obtain this checklist before marriage.

15. A Mobile Society Today's society is very mobile. Do you think this trend toward movement and travel affects mate selection? Explain. What theories of attraction might be involved? Write a newspaper article to express your answers.

16. Family History Imagine that you have two alcoholics in your family who are in recovery. You are dating someone special. You think it may develop into more. Should you disclose this family history? When should you mention it? Write your answer as an entry in your journal.

17 Marriage Readiness Test Go to this book's Online Learning Center at **glencoe.com** to find **Web Links** for **Marriage Readiness Tests**. Choose one test and write a one-page paper on how the test is useful for couples.

Additional Activities For additional activities, go to this book's Online Learning Center through **glencoe.com**.

Academic Skills

Mathematics

18. Saving Money Rosa and Jim plan to drive across the country to visit relatives. They each earn $100 a week and estimate that they will need $1,000 to make the trip. If they make the trip seven months from now, how much do they need to save each month to have the $1,000 in time for the trip? How much will they have left to spend each month?

Math Concept **Multiple-Step Problems**
Decide what you need to know and when you need to know it. In this problem, you must answer the first question before you can answer the second question.

Starting Hint: First, decide how much Rosa and Jim will need to save each month ($1,000 ÷ 7). Then calculate how much they make each month ($100 × 2 × 4 weeks). Then subtract the amount they need for the vacation to find what they have left to spend each month.

 For math help, go to the Math Appendix at the back of the book.

> **NCTM Problem Solving** Solve problems that arise in mathematics and in other contexts.

English Language Arts

19. Create a Poster Design and create a poster on the theme "Are You Ready for Marriage?" In your poster, be sure to include accurate information. The information can include the qualities needed to be ready for marriage. You might also include information about relationships with parents and siblings. Display your poster in the classroom.

> **NCTE 5** Use different writing process elements to communicate effectively.

🌐 Social Studies

20. Compare Read or recall a novel you have read that is set in the 17th or 18th century. As you read, look for how mates were selected in those eras. What theories of attraction can you find in the book? Write an essay comparing mate selection in that era to mate selection today. Give examples from the novel of the theories of attraction you found.

> **NCSS I.a** Analyze and explain the ways groups, societies, and cultures address human needs and concerns.

STANDARDIZED TEST PRACTICE

MULTIPLE CHOICE
Read the paragraph. Then read the question below the paragraph. Read the answer choices and choose the best answer to fill in the blank. Write your answer on a separate sheet of paper.

> **Test-Taking Tip** You can improve your score on multiple-choice items by covering the options while you read the question and trying to answer the question. Then select the option that most closely matches your answer.

21. Bill is a successful executive with a utilities company and can provide his family with a very comfortable living. He wants a wife who will be a stay-at-home mom and teach their children at home. This is an example of _____.

a. homogamy

b. propinquity

c. social exchange

d. jealousy

Make Healthy Choices

In this unit you have learned that you will enjoy strong relationships with people outside of the family throughout your life. You have also learned that to be a good friend or partner, you must be a healthy and self-aware individual. In this project, you will interview an adult in a healthy relationship. You will use what you learn to write an essay that describes how a good relationship can meet important needs.

My Journal

If you completed the journal entry from page 502, refer to it to see if your thoughts have changed after reading the unit.

Project Assignment

- Think about how your interests relate to a style of living. Choose a lifestyle that interests you.
- Consider places where you may meet people with similar interests.
- Identify and interview a trusted adult who is in a healthy relationship.
- Arrange to have an interview with the trusted adult. Take notes, then type a summary of your interview.
- Use what you learned to write an essay. The essay will describe how your interview subject's relationship meets his or her needs and interests.

Academic Skills You Will Use

English Language Arts

NCTE 5 Use different writing process elements to communicate effectively.

NCTE 9 Develop an understanding of diversity in language use across cultures.

STEP 1 Choose a Lifestyle that Interests You

Some people are active, some enjoy reading, and others are spiritual. These are all examples of different types of lifestyles. No one lifestyle is better than another. The topics below are examples of different lifestyles people enjoy. Choose one of the lifestyles that you think suits your personality.

- Active
- Travel-focused
- Academic
- Spiritual
- Urban
- Family-centered

STEP 2 Consider Places to Meet People

Think of activities or locations that match your lifestyle choice. These are places where you can meet people with interests similar to you own. These activities may include sports events, community service, museum tours, or adult education classes. When you meet people that share your lifestyle interests, you have already started building a foundation for a relationship.

Thinking Skills

- Identify your interests.
- Consider your own perspective.
- Set priorities.
- Organize your thoughts.

STEP 3 Connect to Your Community

Interview a trusted adult who is part of a healthy friendship or marriage. Ask the adult how his or her lifestyle matches the friend's or spouse's. Ask the adult how his or her needs are fulfilled by this relationship. Also ask how he or she fulfills the needs of the other person.

Interview Skills

- During the interview, record responses and take notes.
- Ask additional questions if necessary.
- Listen attentively.

STEP 4 Write and Present Your Essay

Use the Unit Thematic Project Checklist on the right to plan and create your essay and make your presentation.

STEP 5 Evaluate Your Presentation

Your project will be evaluated based on:
- Depth of interview and questions.
- Content and structure of your essay.
- Quality of presentation.

Evaluation Rubric Go to this book's Online Learning Center at **glencoe.com** for a rubric you can use to evaluate your final project.

Unit Thematic Project Checklist

Essay	✓ Write a one-page essay about an adult in a healthy relationship.
	✓ The essay should have an introductory paragraph, a body, and a conclusion.
	✓ The essay should describe the way the adult met the other person, how the adult's needs are met by the relationship, how the adult meets the needs of the other person, the similarities and differences the two adults share, and how those affect the relationship.
Presentation	✓ Make a presentation to your class to share your essay and discuss what you learned.
	✓ Invite the students in your class to ask you any questions they may have. Answer three questions.
	✓ When students ask you questions, demonstrate in your answers that you respect their perspectives.
	✓ Turn in the notes from your interview and your essay to your teacher.
Academic Skills	✓ Present ideas effectively.
	✓ Write creatively.
	✓ Speak clearly and concisely.
	✓ Draw conclusions based on information gathered.
	✓ Organize and distill information.
	✓ Thoughtfully express your ideas.

Unit 8

Forming Your Own Family

Unit

Thematic Project Preview
Build Successful Relationships

After completing this unit, you will learn that using teamwork skills can help people in relationships make big decisions. In your unit thematic project, you can show how these skills build successful relationships.

My Journal

Decision Making Write a journal entry about one of the topics below. This will help you prepare for the unit project at the end of the unit.

- Identify the big decisions people in relationships have to make.
- Describe how people can use teamwork skills to make decisions together.
- State how you would use teamwork skills to make a difficult decision.

Explore the Photo
Forming a family can be exciting and fun when you take the proper steps to prepare. *What are some ways you can think of to help form a happy family?*

CHAPTER 29

Choosing Marriage

Section 29.1

The Engagement

Section 29.2

Making Wedding Plans

▶▶ **Explore the Photo**

Finding the right person to marry is just as important as being the right person. *What can a person do to be the right person?*

Chapter Objectives

After completing this chapter, you will be able to:

- **Describe** the purposes of an engagement period.
- **Determine** when breaking an engagement is a wise choice.
- **Explain** the societal significance of weddings.
- **Identify** contracts and customs connected to weddings.
- **Suggest** ways to plan a successful wedding.

Writing Activity Descriptive Paragraph

Commitment People show commitment when they are true to their word and their values. You can show commitment to:

- A strong family.
- An education.
- Friends.
- A job.
- The environment.

Write a descriptive paragraph about one thing to which you are committed. Include specific actions you can do to strengthen your commitment.

Writing Tips To write a descriptive paragraph, follow these steps:

1. Decide what mood you want to create in the paragraph.
2. Write a strong topic sentence.
3. Orient the reader by presenting details in a logical order.
4. Select precise transition words.

The Engagement

Reading Guide

Before You Read

Predict Before starting this section, browse the content by reading headings, bold terms, and photo captions. Do they help you predict the information in the section?

Read to Learn
Key Concepts
- **Describe** the purposes of an engagement period.
- **Determine** when breaking an engagement is a wise choice.

Main Idea
Spend the engagement period learning more about your partner. It may help lessen problems in your marriage.

Content Vocabulary
◇ engagement   ◇ premarital counseling

Academic Vocabulary
You will find these words in your reading and on your tests. Use the glossary to look up their definitions if necessary.
■ affect   ■ trait

Graphic Organizer
As you read, name four general purposes of the engagement period. Use a web like the one shown to help organize your information.

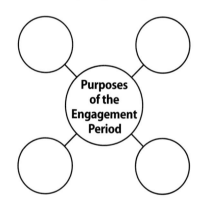

 Graphic Organizer Go to this book's Online Learning Center at **glencoe.com** to print out this graphic organizer.

Academic Standards • • • • • • • • • • • • • • • • • •

 English Language Arts

NCTE 4 Use written language to communicate effectively.

NCTE 12 Use language to accomplish individual purposes.

 Science

NSES Content Standard A Develop abilities necessary to do scientific inquiry, understandings about scientific inquiry.

NCTE *National Council of Teachers of English*
NCTM *National Council of Teachers of Mathematics*

NSES *National Science Education Standards*
NCSS *National Council of the Social Studies*

Purposes of Engagement

Before marriage, most people go through an **engagement**. An engagement is a promise or intention to marry. At this stage, couples may be ready for the commitment and responsibilities of marriage. The engagement period is a time to prepare for the wedding.

During this time, couples may buy a wedding dress and change their names on their bank accounts. These tasks may be necessary, but the wedding day is not the only thing couples prepare for during their engagement. More importantly, the engagement period is a time to prepare for marriage. It lets couples address issues that may **affect**, or influence, the success of their marriage. This is a time of transition that leads to the joining of two lives into one future.

Learn About Each Other

Couples should use their engagement time to make sure they really know each other. It is good to know and be comfortable with aspects of the other's life such as their family goals, spending patterns, cleanliness habits, and food preferences. If they do this, there tend to be fewer surprises that can lead to problems during marriage. Some experts say the engagement should last six to twelve months. This allows enough time for this discovery process.

Identify Differences

During an engagement, a couple can identify and deal with differences. They can then decide if the difference will enhance or weaken their relationship. What effect do you think the following differences may have on a marriage?

- Tia likes fast food. Scott is a vegetarian.
- Martha wants to have two children once she and Glen have secure jobs. Glen wants to have four children, beginning right away.
- Tanya wants to live in a small town and Barry likes the city.
- Marcus does not like to be around a large group of people and Tabitha loves to go to big parties.

Only the couple can determine if their differences will threaten the success of their marriage. Relationships are successful when each partner knows his or her values and expectations.

▷ **Vocabulary**
You can find definitions in the glossary at the back of this book.

As You Read
Connect Do you know any married couples? How long was their engagement period?

Look Closely
Spend time together to learn about your differences. *What are some differences couples may have?*

Practical matters that a couple will need to address before marriage include:

- Where will you live? Will you rent or buy? Will you live with other family members?
- How will you manage money? What are your spending and saving priorities?
- Who will be responsible for shopping and bill paying?
- Do you want children? If so, when? How many?
- Will you both have outside careers?

- How will you handle issues involving your in-laws or other family members? Where will you spend holidays?

Problem-Solving Whenever Michelle and Walter talk about their plans for married life, Walter has few opinions. When Michelle asked him about this, Walter replied, "Why are you surprised? I am just trying to be agreeable." Michelle still feels uneasy. What do you think she should do?

It is often easier to solve problems caused by differences before marriage, rather than after. When people deal with issues together, it strengthens the relationship and sets a pattern for the future. Couples can use the problem-solving skills that they will need in married life.

Some couples think about living together before marriage. They may believe it is a good way to find out if they are truly compatible. Recent studies, however, have shown that couples who try this are not as happy with their marriage as those who do not. They are also more likely to divorce.

Develop Teamwork

When couples are engaged, they start to think "we" rather than "I" when setting goals, making plans, and solving problems. A couple does not need to be exactly alike to make a good team. In fact, their different strengths and qualities can combine into an effective working relationship.

Use Teamwork Skills

Trust One way to use teamwork skills is to have trust in your partner. Engaged couples have to trust each other in order to talk about serious issues. They must confide in each other for a deeper understanding to develop.

Communication Another way a couple can use teamwork skills is by practicing good communication skills. Couples have a lot to discuss. They should talk about issues like housework, parenting, earning and managing money, and religion before they get married.

Compromise Finally, compromise is essential to teamwork. As a couple plans for the future, they must be thinking about what is best for both of them. A willingness to compromise is a sign that both partners are committed to making the marriage work.

Building Bonds
A stepparent can start building bonds with step-children well before the marriage. *What can help build those bonds?*

Establish New Relationships

During the engagement period, families and friends gain a new relationship with the couple. The new partner is often included in family events. This lets family and friends get to know the new person. It is also a good time for the new person to meet and become more comfortable around his or her future spouse's family.

When Children Are Involved

A large number of engagements today are between partners who have been married before and may have children from that previous marriage. These situations can be more complex. They involve more family members than first marriages. The couple's children, former spouses, grandparents, and other extended family are still connected by the children. In this situation, emotions and stress levels can run high.

In these cases, the engagement period can be a good time to address personal concerns. Children need patience and reassurance to cope with the stress of adjusting. For example, when Eugene and Jolene told his six-year-old son Trace that they were getting married, Trace seemed sad. The couple used the engagement period to help Trace see what their relationship would be like. It also helped Trace get used to the idea of them becoming a family.

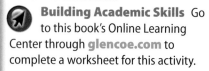

Seek Advice

Some people get **premarital counseling** before their marriage. Premarital counseling is when couples get advice from trained professionals before marriage. Good premarital counseling helps couples focus on their reasons for marrying. It lets them address questions about their relationship. Couples may be asked:

- How or why did you fall in love? Was it quick and unexplainable, or did it occur slowly for reasons you both understand?
- What, right now, is your partner's most endearing **trait**, or distinguishing quality? Is it long-lasting? If so, will it still seem as appealing in the future?
- Do you and your partner reveal your weaknesses, fears, and mistakes to each other? Are you both accepting of each other?

Counseling usually helps show potential trouble spots. It helps when a couple knows how they disagree on certain topics. It lets them handle their problems better and often resolve them before marriage.

There are other resources in the community that can help engaged couples. Religious organizations, social service agencies, and other educational groups may have classes or information on marriage issues.

The engagement period is an important step before marriage. It lets couples gain a deeper understanding of themselves and their relationship. This insight can help build an enduring marriage.

✓ **Reading Check** **Summarize** How can seeking advice from a premarital counselor be beneficial for engaged couples?

Get Help

Many couples seek professional advice before marriage. *Where can you find a premarital counselor in your community?*

Broken Engagements

When a couple gets engaged, a marriage usually follows. However, about one-third of all engagements are broken before marriage. Many of these are broken with good reason.

As their engagement proceeds, some couples find that they are not ready to make the needed sacrifices and compromises for marriage. Some couples have conflicting traits and values that may be too difficult to overcome.

As people grow and have different experiences, it may cause strain on a relationship. Annessa and Lamar got engaged just before Annessa enlisted in the navy. Six months later Annessa came home. She had changed so much that she seemed like a stranger to Lamar. He, too, had made new friends and found new interests. When couples like Annessa and Lamar no longer have much in common, they may rethink their engagement. The lack of parental approval ends some engagements as well.

Breaking an engagement can be a painful experience. Both partners may grieve for the loss of an important relationship. They may feel a sense of failure. Explaining the situation to family and friends can be awkward. Breaking the ties is easier if the couple can act with dignity and treat each other with respect.

Even though a broken engagement is hard, it is not as difficult as a troubled marriage or a divorce. Marriage is meant to be a lifetime commitment. It should only happen when both partners know they can live happily with the decision.

Section 29.1 After You Read

Review Key Concepts

1. **Name** four ways the engagement period prepares you for marriage.
2. **Explain** at least two reasons why a couple would consider breaking their engagement.

Practice Academic Skills

English Language Arts

3. Imagine that you are engaged. List and define five characteristics or qualities that you would want in your marriage partner. Give an example of how he or she could demonstrate each of those qualities in your marriage.

> **NCTE 4** Use written language to communicate effectively.

4. If you are engaged, you and your partner may get marriage advice from a premarital counselor. Brainstorm some ways you and your partner may differ. Then write down two questions you might ask a premarital counselor before you got married.

> **NCTE 12** Use language to accomplish individual purposes.

Check Your Answers Check your answers at this book's Online Learning Center through glencoe.com.

Making Wedding Plans

Reading Guide

Before You Read

Prior Knowledge Look over the Key Concepts at the beginning of the section. Write down what you already know and what you want to find out about each concept.

Read to Learn
Key Concepts
- **Explain** the societal significance of weddings.
- **Identify** contracts and customs connected to weddings.
- **Suggest** ways to plan a successful wedding.

Main Idea
Planning a wedding includes meeting all the legal requirements and adding any unique elements or customs.

Content Vocabulary
◇ contract   ◇ prenuptial agreement
◇ custom

 Graphic Organizer Go to this book's Online Learning Center at **glencoe.com** to print out this graphic organizer.

Academic Vocabulary
You will find these words in your reading and on your tests. Use the glossary to look up their definitions if necessary.
- valid
- require

Graphic Organizer
As you read, list three purposes of a prenuptial agreement. Use a chart like the one shown to help organize your information.

Purposes of a Prenuptial Agreement
1.
2.
3.

Academic Standards • • • • • • • • • • • • •

 English Language Arts

NCTE 4 Use written language to communicate effectively.

NCTE 12 Use language to accomplish individual purposes.

 Mathematics

NCTM Number and Operations Understand the meanings of operations and how they relate to one another.

NCTE *National Council of Teachers of English*
NCTM *National Council of Teachers of Mathematics*

NSES *National Science Education Standards*
NCSS *National Council of the Social Studies*

A Ceremony with Significance

Few occasions in people's lives are treasured the way weddings are. For centuries, cultures around the world have created and carried out different rituals for weddings. These rituals stress both the joy and the seriousness of the event.

Even though all weddings are different, they all have important purposes. They mark the personal and often spiritual union of a woman and a man. They are also a formal, legal display of commitment and the start of a new family. Weddings are also important because society wants to promote stable relationships. Marriage provides the structure for having and raising children. Within the framework of the family, children are cared for. They are also taken into the culture. In this way, society continues.

✓ Reading Check **Explain** What does marriage mean for society?

Contracts and Customs

When a couple marries, they enter into at least one **contract** with each other. A contract is a binding agreement between two or more people. Marriage is a contract overseen by the state and made official with a marriage license. A couple can also make other contracts before marriage.

Couples may also include marriage customs in their weddings. A **custom** is a common practice among many people that has been handed down from the past. The customs used in weddings can be regional, ethnic, or family traditions. Some marriage customs are influenced by regional and cultural groups. Customs give a sense of continuity with past generations.

 **Vocabulary**

You can find definitions in the glossary at the back of this book.

 **As You Read**

Connect What customs would you want to include in your wedding?

◀◀ Getting a License
All states in the United States require a license to marry. *Where can you get a marriage license in your community? What is the cost?*

Financial Literacy

Housing Costs

Jean and Alex want to buy a home before their wedding. They looked at two houses on the market for $346,113 and $272,895. Use front-end estimation to make a quick estimate of the difference in housing costs.

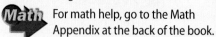 **Math Concept** **Front-End Estimation**
To make a quick estimate of the sum or difference between two numbers, you can use front-end estimation. Just add or subtract the digits of the two highest place values, and replace the other place values with zeroes. This will give you an estimate of the solution to a problem.

Starting Hint: Front-end estimate both numbers in the problem ($346,113 to $350,000 and $272,895 to $270,000). Now subtract using the new numbers.

Math For math help, go to the Math Appendix at the back of the book.

NCTM Number and Operations Understand the meanings of operations and how they relate to one another.

Marriage Laws

Society has a stake in marriage so the government creates laws to try and make sure successful marriages take place. Sometimes marriage laws have rules about minimum age, mental soundness, and certain diseases. In some states, marriage may be illegal among people with close blood ties, like cousins.

In the United States, marriage is controlled by each state. Couples have to meet the requirements of the state where the ceremony will be held. Once this is completed, their marriage will be **valid**, or legal.

Some states **require**, or demand as necessary, that a blood test be done before getting a marriage license. Blood tests check for many types of sexually transmitted and other communicable diseases. The purpose of the blood test is to make sure couples know about possible conditions. It is not meant to prevent marriage.

Each state has a time frame for getting a license. Some states may require partners to get a license at least three days, but not more than 30 days, before the wedding. A marriage ceremony must be performed by an authorized person and be witnessed. Once the witnesses and the person who marries the couple sign the license, the marriage contract becomes legal. The couple is now bound by the marital laws of that state.

Prenuptial Agreements

Some couples have special concerns and make additional agreements before the wedding. This is called a **prenuptial agreement** (prē-'nəp-shəl). Partners can make agreements on any topic they need to. To some people, starting a relationship by thinking about it ending shows a lack of commitment. Other people feel more secure with the protection of the agreement. Prenuptial agreements seem to deal with three main issues: protecting property, establishing ownership, and defining roles.

- **Protecting Property** A prenuptial agreement to protect property is often used when the couple is not marrying for the first time. The couple may want to make sure money or possessions from another marriage stay with the family of that marriage.
- **Establishing Ownership** Some prenuptial agreements decide how property will be divided if the marriage ends. These contracts are mostly used when the couple has a lot of assets.
- **Defining Roles** Finally, a prenuptial agreement can define a partner's rights and responsibilities in the marriage. It may state who will take time off from work to raise the children or who will manage the money. This type of agreement is less likely to be a legal contract.

Ceremonies

The bride and groom can add personal touches to their wedding, but they have to keep some conditions in mind. The ceremony must meet legal requirements. Couples can have a civil or religious wedding ceremony. Wedding vows are usually exchanged in both types of ceremonies. The vows declare the couple's promise of commitment to each other. Most religious faiths ask that a certain form be followed as well. The wedding and other festivities must also fit within a family's budget.

Civil Ceremonies

In a civil ceremony, a judge, justice of the peace, or other appropriate official marries the couple. When couples choose a civil ceremony, they are often able to personalize it to suit their tastes. Couples can have their civil ceremony take place almost anywhere. Some get married in a home, a courthouse, on a beach, or even on horseback. This type of wedding is usually not as formal as a religious ceremony.

Religious Ceremonies

Most faiths value family life. As a result, marriage is also an important religious ceremony. Many people choose to be married in a religious ceremony. These ceremonies are usually held in a house of worship. A religious official, such as a minister, rabbi, or priest, marries the couple. The readings, music, and vows all reflect the couple's beliefs. Religious services may be less flexible than civil ceremonies. However, couples may be allowed to include their own statements and music they find meaningful.

Wedding Receptions

Weddings are often followed by some type of reception. Here, the bride and groom are received by family and friends, and their wedding is celebrated. Like the ceremony, receptions can be simple or very elaborate.

In addition to customizing their wedding ceremony, many couples also add personal touches to their reception. A couple may choose to include specific food, music, and decorations to represent their interests. The reception can take place in many different places, such as a home, restaurant, or banquet room. The location of the reception often depends on the couple's budget, where the wedding ceremony is being held, and how many people will be attending the reception.

▲ *Plan Carefully*
Some people plan to have part or all of a wedding ceremony outdoors. *Why would a backup plan be a good idea?*

Customs

Wedding customs vary depending on factors such as ethnic background, religion, and even geography. The couple may choose to have customs and rituals with widely accepted meanings. These have both symbolic and practical value.

- Many couples exchange rings. A ring is a traditional symbol of marriage and sometimes engagement. It is a circle that represents unity and timelessness. Gold is a popular metal chosen for wedding rings. It has great value, strength, and enduring quality.

- Many couples have engagement parties or wedding showers. Family members or close friends usually give these parties to the couple. It allows families and friends to celebrate the upcoming wedding together. People bring gifts that the couple can use in their new life together.

Couples can customize the wedding ceremony in many ways. They just have to be sure they stay within the limits of the law and their religion. Some choose a special location. Some express their commitment in a personal way by writing their own vows.

🔺 **Unique Customs**
There are many different wedding customs. *What are some customs that you want in your wedding?*

The Honeymoon

Many couples go on a honeymoon after their wedding. This is a time for the couple to relax and spend time together. Couples can also use this time to start adjusting to marriage. Some couples also have destination weddings. The closest friends and family usually accompany the bride and groom to an exotic location for the wedding and vacation afterwards.

Some couples may travel or take time off of work to celebrate their honeymoon. When couples choose how to spend their honeymoon, they may consider their responsibilities and budget. The length of time couples are on their honeymoon may be different for each couple. It depends on how much time the couple can afford to be away from their daily life.

✓ **Reading Check** **Analyze** Why are wedding customs an important part of weddings?

Planning a Successful Wedding

Most weddings need a great deal of planning to go smoothly. It can be time consuming and complicated to make all of the decisions about the arrangements. Couples must take the time to prepare, though, if they want a successful wedding.

Managing Expenses

Traditionally, the bride's family paid the costs of the ceremony and reception. The groom's family paid for the rehearsal dinner the evening before. Today, expenses may be split differently. The groom's family may contribute to the cost of the wedding. If a partner's parents are divorced, costs may be divided in nontraditional ways. With more couples waiting until they are older to marry, many can and want to pay part or all of the cost. Usually, parents who are not paying for the wedding are not involved in the planning. Out of courtesy, however, couples should ask and consider their ideas.

A wedding can strain the budget at any income level. Thoughtful couples keep plans and expectations realistic. They do not pressure parents to give them an expensive wedding.

INDEPENDENT Living

HOW TO   Plan a Celebration

From the everyday to the once-in-a-lifetime, some events call for celebrating. Any celebration, even an informal gathering, can benefit from preplanning. Follow these guidelines to make your next event a memorable one:

1. **Extend invitations.** Send written invitations for casual events at least two weeks in advance. Allow four weeks for a major event. Include the date, time, address, and reason for the event. Add RSVP, meaning, "response, if you please."
2. **Set the menu.** Foods should fit the occasion. An elaborate meal may be right for a holiday. A selection of snacks or pizza might be better for a get-together with some friends.
3. **Consider space needs.** Space can be a limitation and an asset if it is creatively used.
4. **Plan your time.** You need to be creative to fit tasks into your schedule. If you are going to prepare foods, look to healthful convenience foods for help.
5. **Choose decorations.** Decorations can add a festive touch. Look for things you can borrow or buy at little cost. Decorations can even help you create a theme to your event.

Take Action In groups of four or five, plan a simple celebration for a small group, such as a lunch for adult volunteers who help your class. Discuss and assign each of the tasks described here. Carry out your plans if possible.

Thinking of Others

Many couples want to please their families, especially those members who are helping to pay for the ceremony. However, a wedding is meant to express the couple's tastes and values. When planning a wedding, keep these tips in mind to avoid conflicts among family members.

- Thoughtfully word announcements and invitations to make sure everyone that needs to be included is.
- Carefully plan photograph and seating arrangements.
- Get the advice of a professional wedding planner. There may be several areas in which this professional can help you.
- Have good communication with both families.
- Keep those involved with the wedding informed, especially about any changes.
- Be sensitive to the feelings of others so that the event is meaningful for everyone.

If a couple prevents conflicts before they arise, it will be easier to focus on what is really important during their wedding day: the love they feel for each other and the commitment they are making before family and friends. Most people look back on their wedding day as a high point in their lives. If they have selected the right partner and used the time during their engagement wisely, their wedding can be the beginning of a long and happy life together.

Section 29.2   After You Read

Review Key Concepts

1. **Explain** in a brief paragraph why weddings are significant to society as well as to the couple getting married.
2. **Define** a marriage contract and a marriage custom. Name one example of each.
3. **Identify** ways a bride and groom can plan for a successful wedding day.

Practice Academic Skills

English Language Arts

4. There are many purchases a bride and groom may make before a wedding. It can be helpful to keep track of what you buy. How do you currently track your purchases? How can tracking your purchases help make your wedding day more enjoyable? Write your responses in a two-paragraph summary.

> **NCTE 4** Use written language to communicate effectively.

5. List the reasons you might have a civil or religious wedding ceremony. How are these two types of ceremonies similar and different? Do you think either type of experience can affect the future of your marriage? If so, how? Write your responses in a one-page essay.

> **NCTE 12** Use language to accomplish individual purposes.

 Check Your Answers Check your answers at this book's Online Learning Center through **glencoe.com**.

CHAPTER SUMMARY

Section 29.1
The Engagement

Couples can use the engagement period to prepare for marriage. If a couple learns more about each other, they are less likely to have problems in their marriage. An engaged couple needs to see themselves as a team. The engagement period gives the couple's family and friends time to accept and adjust to their upcoming marriage. Many couples seek counseling before marriage. This can help ensure they are making the right decision. Wedding plans can be called off during the engagement period if a person has serious doubts.

Section 29.2
Making Wedding Plans

Weddings are important to society as well as to individuals. Marriage is a legal contract with certain rights and restrictions. A couple may make other contracts such as prenuptial agreements to cover personal concerns. Engaged couples can choose between a civil or religious wedding ceremony. There are also many customs they can include in their wedding. These customs can be regional, ethnic, or family traditions. When a couple takes time to plan for the wedding, the celebration can be less stressful.

Content and Academic Vocabulary Review

1. Use each of these content and academic vocabulary words in a sentence.

   Content Vocabulary
   ◇ engagement (p. 569)
   ◇ premarital counseling (p. 572)
   ◇ contract (p. 575)
   ◇ custom (p. 575)
   ◇ prenuptial agreement (p. 576)

   Academic Vocabulary
   ■ affect (p. 569)
   ■ trait (p. 572)
   ■ valid (p. 576)
   ■ require (p. 576)

Review Key Concepts

2. **Describe** the purposes of an engagement period.
3. **Determine** when breaking an engagement is a wise choice.
4. **Explain** the societal significance of weddings.
5. **Identify** contracts and customs connected to weddings.
6. **Suggest** ways to plan a successful wedding.

Critical Thinking

7. **Predict** Do you think people treat each other differently before marriage than they do after? How can a person prepare for this?
8. **Analyze** The bride traditionally receives more attention than the groom in wedding preparations. Why do you think this is? What change, if any, would you make in this custom?
9. **Explain** Which do you think is better, a simple wedding or an elaborate one? Explain the reasons for your choice.

Real-World Skills

Problem-Solving Skills

10. Make Decisions Jalen and Lakisha have been engaged for six months. Jalen began to notice differences in their values, so he told Lakisha he was unsure if he wanted to get married. She said that difference can make relationships interesting. What can Jalen and Lakisha do to be sure they want to get married?

Interpersonal and Collaborative Skills

11. Work in Teams Follow your teacher's instructions for working in teams. Research and compile a list of tasks that need to be done before a wedding. Research the order in which each task should be completed. Create a timeline that can help a bride and groom schedule their tasks. Share your list and timeline with your class.

Technology Applications

12. Create a Spreadsheet Imagine you are planning a wedding. There are many things you have to buy. You want to record the type of purchase as well as how much each purchase costs. Use spreadsheet software to create a document that lists all your wedding purchases and their costs.

Financial Literacy Skills

13. Determine Your Financial Situation Knowing your financial situation can help you and your partner plan for the future. Start by making a list of your possible finances: savings, monthly income, monthly expenses, and debts. Use a notebook or other document to categorize your expenses over a set period of time, such as a week or a month.

14. Discuss an Issue Follow your teacher's instructions to form into groups. Discuss this statement: Marriage can survive on love alone, because loving partners put their relationship first. Have a discussion with all group members contributing to the discussion.

15. Interview Married Couples Interview a married couple about their experiences being in a marriage. Ask them questions about how they met, what traits they looked for in a spouse, and what they expected marriage to be like. Share your findings with your class in an oral report.

16. Research Most communities offer resources that help couples prepare for marriage. Research where engaged couples can get marriage advice in your community. Share any materials you found with your class.

17. Marriage Requirements Go to this book's Online Learning Center at **glencoe.com** to find **Web Links** for **Marriage Documents**. List where in your state you can find legal documents you will need to marry.

Additional Activities For additional activities, go to this book's Online Learning Center through **glencoe.com**.

Academic Skills

Mathematics

18. Calculate Average Reception Costs
Most couples have a reception after their wedding ceremony to celebrate the marriage. Reception costs often include the catering, band, linens, and renting a hall. Most Americans spend about 48% of their wedding budget on the reception. If you have a wedding budget of $20,000, how much money will you need to cover the cost of the reception?

Math Concept **Multiply Decimals by Whole Numbers** A percent is a ratio that compares a number to 100. To multiply with percentages:

Starting Hint: You can rewrite the percent (48%) as a fraction with a denominator of 100. Convert the fraction to a decimal. Multiply this decimal by the number ($20,000). Remember to put the decimal point in the correct place.

 For math help, go to the Math Appendix at the back of the book.

> **NCTM Number and Operations** Understand numbers, ways of representing numbers, relationships among numbers, and number systems.

English Language Arts

19. Write a Thank You Letter Imagine that you just got married. Your family helped you with a lot of the wedding preparations. You would like to send a letter thanking your family for making your wedding day special. Draft a letter to thank them. Include details stating what you really appreciated. Share your thank you letter with the class.

> **NCTE 5** Use different writing process elements to communicate effectively.

Social Studies

20. Research Values Research another culture's system of values. If possible, interview someone who grew up in that culture. Name and describe the values in that culture. Explain how those values affect weddings and marriage in that culture. Share your findings with the class in a five-minute oral report.

> **NCSS 1.c** Apply an understanding of culture as an integrated whole that explains the functions and interactions of traditions, beliefs and values, and behavior patterns..

STANDARDIZED TEST PRACTICE

MULTIPLE CHOICE
Read the following paragraph. Then read the question below the paragraph. Read the answer choices and choose the best answer to fill in the blank. Write your answer on a separate sheet of paper.

> **Test-Taking Tip** In a multiple choice test, read the question before you read the answer choices. Try to answer the question before you read the answer choices. This way, the answer choices will not throw you off.

21. Lena's parents had premarital counseling and they have been married for 30 years. As a result, Lena is biased towards seeing a premarital counselor before she marries. In this sentence, the word biased means _____.

a. running diagonally across the weave of a fabric

b. a distortion of a set of statistical data

c. voltage applied across an electronic device

d. having a preference

CHAPTER 30

Build a Strong Marriage

● **Section 30.1**

Qualities of a Strong Marriage

● **Section 30.2**

Skills and Resources for Marriage

▶ **Explore the Photo** It takes a strong commitment to make a marriage a success. *What can couples do to ensure a successful marriage?*

Chapter Objectives

After completing this chapter, you will be able to:

- **Identify** qualities that help make a marriage strong.
- **Explain** what the U-Shaped Satisfaction Curve means for married couples.
- **Summarize** skills that can strengthen a marriage.
- **Suggest** resources for married couples.

Writing Activity

Expository Essay

Supportiveness When you give support, you help hold a person up, keep someone moving forward, or help someone reach a goal. Married couples show support when they:

- Listen uncritically as the other describes a difficult day at work.
- Encourage each other to find satisfying work opportunities.
- Both follow a healthful diet when one wants to lose weight.
- Offer comfort and support when times are hard.

Write an expository essay about someone who has shown supportiveness to you.

Writing Tips To write an effective expository essay, follow these steps:

1. Use comparison and contrast to show how things are the same and different.
2. Remember that cause and effect shows how events are related.
3. Write in chronological order to present events in time order.

Qualities of a Strong Marriage

Reading Guide

Before You Read

Use Color As you read this section, try using different colored pens to take notes. This can help you learn new material and study for tests.

Read to Learn
Key Concepts
- **Identify** qualities that help make a marriage strong.
- **Explain** what the U-Shaped Satisfaction Curve means for married couples.

Main Idea
Certain qualities help make a marriage strong. These include realistic expectations, commitment, acceptance, flexibility, and thoughtfulness. Marital satisfaction follows a U-shaped curve during the marriage.

Content Vocabulary
◇ marriage commitment
◇ expectation
◇ U-shaped curve

Academic Vocabulary
You will find these words in your reading and on your tests. Use the glossary to look up their definitions if necessary.
- underlie
- pattern

Graphic Organizer
As you read, look for five traits of strong marriages. Use a web like the one shown to help organize your information.

Five Traits of Strong Marriages

Graphic Organizer Go to this book's Online Learning Center at **glencoe.com** to print out this graphic organizer.

Academic Standards · · · · · · · · · · · · · · · · · ·

 English Language Arts

NCTE 4 Use written language to communicate effectively.

NCTE 12 Use language to accomplish individual purposes.

 Mathematics

NCTM Number and Operations Understand the meanings of operations and how they relate to one another.

NCTE *National Council of Teachers of English*
NCTM *National Council of Teachers of Mathematics*

NSES *National Science Education Standards*
NCSS *National Council of the Social Studies*

What Makes a Marriage Strong?

Strong marriages are important. They benefit society as well as the couple. In general, people who are married are healthier than single people. They tend to be wealthier and happier as well. Couples in successful marriages are apt to have successful children. Marriage gives many protections under the law. Society is stronger when marriage and family life are strong and stable. These marriages are satisfying to those who live in them.

Each couple has its own idea of what makes a marriage rewarding. In a strong marriage, partners work with each other to get what each wants from the marriage. Their way of doing that might be very different from another couple's. Still, both couples may be equally happy.

One couple may find that quiet talk over a simple dinner brings real closeness. Another couple may feel closest while joking around. This couple laughs as they work in the kitchen making a meal together.

What is it that makes such different types of relationships rewarding? Certain traits **underlie**, or are behind, all strong, happy marriages. That is true whatever their outer differences. A few of the most vital traits are described in this section. All are needed, but none come without effort, even sacrifice. Problems can arise when any of these qualities are absent. Couples who are willing to work on these traits can look forward to a happy married life.

Commitment

When partners truly want the relationship to last, they act to make this happen. They work together to overcome problems. They take satisfaction in finding solutions. Such couples have a high level of marriage commitment. **Marriage commitment** is the desire to make a marriage work.

A strong commitment to marriage means that partners put each other first. They put each other before work, extended family members, and even their children. This firm commitment is one thing that helps hold a marriage together through stressful times and even through crises. It can help prevent some problems as well.

Sometimes a couple must make an intentional decision to give their relationship top priority. They schedule time together as a couple. This may be as simple as taking a walk together. Whatever they do, the partners make sure to take care of their relationship.

As You Read

Connect What is your idea of what makes a marriage rewarding?

<>**Vocabulary**

You can find definitions in the glossary at the back of this book.

▶ *Rewards in Marriage* Every couple has their own idea of what defines a happy marriage. *What are some of the rewards of a successful marriage?*

Expectations
Knowing what partners expect from each other can make a marriage more enjoyable. *What expectations does this couple seem to have?*

Realistic Expectations

One of the most important factors in what makes a happy marriage is based on what the couple's expectations are. If they have realistic expectations, these are apt to be met. An **expectation** is a belief about or a mental picture of the future. When a marriage is what a partner thought it would be, he or she is more likely to be happy.

Many people enter marriage with higher expectations than can be met. Each person has ideas about how his or her spouse is supposed to be and act. He or she knows what should be done as well as how it should be done. One partner may feel that the other should meet all of his or her needs. When his or her spouse, for whatever reason, does not meet these expectations, the relationship feels its first strain. Another source of potential conflict is when a person does not feel his or her needs are being met or even addressed. Both individuals are responsible for the relationship. If one expects the other to keep the bond strong, frustration lies ahead. It takes two partners working together to create a strong and happy marriage.

Sources of Unrealistic Expectations

One source of unrealistic expectations is the way couples are portrayed in the media. They appear to be happy. They solve problems easily. They communicate well about important issues. Most of these couples live with little conflict. Real couples do not always communicate well. They may struggle to solve problems and resolve conflict. Conversation tends to be on the topics of everyday life. Couples should try to find other real-life married couples, rather than those in the media. They can look towards these real-life couples as role models. This will help the young couple have a more realistic idea of what to expect in a marriage.

Some couples believe that getting married means that their problems will disappear. Every marriage has problems. Couples have to expect problems and be ready to work together to solve them.

Beth, for example, had a job that required long hours. Drew was upset because Beth was not home to fix dinner for him every night. Beth was frustrated because Drew did not take initiative to start dinner when she was late. Each had the unrealistic expectation that the other would know what was upsetting them, so the issue was never mentioned. Because they did not communicate, they became more and more unhappy about their marriage.

INDEPENDENT Living

HOW TO Express Your Commitment

Healthy relationships depend on good communication. Sharing your thoughts and feelings in a productive way strengthens bonds with family and friends. Follow these guidelines to express your commitment:

1. **Show that you care.** People in good relationships show that they care for each other through words and actions.
2. **Be supportive, especially during tough times.** Whether the difficulty is small or very serious, talking about it can help you feel better. Remember to be a good listener when it is time for someone else to talk.
3. **Demonstrate trust.** Members of a good relationship trust one another. You may earn your friends' trust by caring for them and being honest. Likewise, your closest friends have most likely earned your trust the same way.
4. **Act responsibly.** Think before you act. Avoid risky behaviors. Ask for permission. Be accountable. These are all actions that show respect for yourself and the people closest to you.

Take Action On a piece of paper, make a list of the most important people in your life. This list can be long or short. Next to each person's name, write a step you can take to further express your commitment to the relationship.

Couples who communicate and who know each other well before the wedding are more likely to have realistic expectations. They have a sense of what their life together will be like. They are less likely to be disappointed as the excitement of a new marriage wears off and life settles into a routine. Their satisfaction with each other strengthens the relationship.

Acceptance

Acceptance is part of dealing with any aspect of life. Partners in a strong marriage accept and value each other for who they are. They see that they both have strengths and weaknesses. Both have attractive and unattractive points. They are tolerant of the differences between them. Each resists the urge to show the other what he or she thinks is the right way to act or think or feel.

Another part of acceptance is empathy. When partners show empathy they identify with one another's feelings, and they feel good about the marriage. Partners are more content with their relationships. They are happy when they know their spouses understand their thoughts and feelings.

Financial Literacy

Calculate Living Expenses

Tyrell has been offered a promotion at work. However, he will have to move to Atlanta to take the position. He will get a raise. He and his wife, Shawna, want to know how much their monthly expenses will increase. Since the cost of living is higher in Atlanta, they will have to pay $800 a month for an apartment; now, they pay $650. Tyrell will have to spend $4 per day to ride the train to and from work, and they estimate that their food costs will increase by $50 a week. If Tyrell works five days a week for 52 weeks a year, how much extra will they spend in a year if they move to Atlanta?

Math Concept **Multiple-Step Problem** First, determine the information you need to know. In this case, you need to know how much more they will pay in rent, how much Tyrell will pay for riding the train, and how much more they will pay for food.

Starting Hint: Make one problem to find how much more rent they will pay for one year [($800 − $650) × 12]. Then make a problem to find how much Tyrell will pay to ride the train (5 × 52 × $4). Next, determine how much their food costs will increase ($50 × 52). Lastly, add the three answers together.

 Math For math help, go to the Math Appendix at the back of the book.

> **NCTM Number and Operations** Understand the meanings of operations and how they relate to one another.

Respect Differences

Married couples sometimes try to improve their partners. Some even enter the marriage with this idea, though this approach rarely works. People change only if they want to, not because someone else tells them they should change. Attempts to make a spouse change are often met with anger and disappointment. When one person tries to force change on another, it is not likely to happen. It is much more likely to occur when spouses respect their differences.

Part of acceptance is having a positive attitude. Couples who accept each other tend to have positive connections. Lack of acceptance can lead to negative thoughts and actions. If there is too much negativity, the relationship will suffer.

Advice and helpful criticism can have a place in a marriage. This is especially true if one person's behavior is damaging. Loving partners, however, use criticism only for issues that are serious. They know in these cases they risk hurting their partners. They use I-messages that express personal feelings. They avoid you-messages that may be viewed as an attack.

Flexibility

Flexibility regarding change is part of building a strong bond. You, your partner, and the marriage itself will change. Changes in jobs, values, and ways of living can threaten a couple's commitment. Those who accept change and learn to make the most of it have a better chance of keeping a strong relationship.

For example, when Della wanted to go back to school for a degree, Bart was concerned. They talked, and Della said she was bored at work and needed more of a challenge. The move would make her happier and allow her to earn more money. This would benefit their family. Bart supported her. His flexibility improved their relationship.

Thoughtfulness

Dating or engaged couples often work hard to please each other. They buy small gifts or do unexpected favors. These gestures of caring may gradually decrease after the couple marries. Such acts of thoughtfulness are needed to build and maintain a strong marriage.

Thoughtfulness, of course, is more than just giving things. It involves showing empathy and concern when your partner has a problem. It means making an extra effort to support your partner.

✓ **Reading Check**) **Describe** Why should couples have realistic expectations about marriage?

The U-Shaped Satisfaction Curve

Many newlywed couples believe that the excitement of their wedding will last forever. Very few marriages keep that level of happiness. This can leave some partners disappointed.

Many family scientists have studied happiness and satisfaction in marriage. They found a **pattern**, or a repeated set of actions. It is called the U-shaped curve. A **U-shaped curve** describes something that starts at a high level, drops as time goes on, and then rises again. The pattern visually forms the letter U.

During the first years of marriage, couples set their daily pattern of living. They enjoy activities and make decisions together. They adjust to each other's needs and habits. They tend to be very satisfied.

There may be some surprises during the early days of marriage. However, newlyweds are generally happy. Marital satisfaction begins to lessen with the birth of a couple's first child. Time and money are stretched. The parents often do fewer things together. However, the stress of parenting does not always cause a drop in overall satisfaction. The joys gained from raising children may more than offset the drop in happiness in the marriage.

Marital satisfaction tends to hit a low when children enter school. Another other low point comes when children are teens. When children start to leave home and resources become more plentiful, marital satisfaction begins to rise again. It continues to increase into middle age. By then it often equals or surpasses the satisfaction that is felt by newlyweds.

Understanding the pattern to marital happiness can help a couple cope better. They realize that the change in their relationship is normal. Their relationship skills will help them lessen the decline. They can look forward to the better times that lie ahead.

Life Skills CHECKLIST

Leadership Skills

Thoughtfulness You can take the lead in showing thoughtfulness when you:

- ✓ Plan little surprises for your spouse.
- ✓ Leave unexpected notes of praise.
- ✓ Develop a signal that says "I love you."
- ✓ Say "thank you" for small kindnesses.
- ✓ Remember birthdays and anniversaries.

Section 30.1   After You Read

Review Key Concepts

1. **Explain** the effects of a high level of marriage commitment.
2. **Identify** the two lowest points in a marriage according to the U-Shaped Satisfaction Curve.

Practice Academic Skills

English Language Arts

3. Is gift giving the best way to show thoughtfulness in a marriage? Write a paragraph that explains whether you think this is or is not the best way.

4. Partners who are committed have stronger marriages. Write a list of ways a partner could show commitment when he or she is married.

> **NCTE 4** Use written language to communicate effectively.

> **NCTE 12** Use language to accomplish individual purposes.

Check Your Answers Check your answers at this book's Online Learning Center through **glencoe.com**.

Skills and Resources for Marriage

Reading Guide

Before You Read

Buddy up for Success One advantage to sharing your notes with a buddy is that you can fill in gaps in each other's information.

Read to Learn
Key Concepts
- **Summarize** skills that can strengthen a marriage.
- **Suggest** resources for married couples.

Main Idea
Interpersonal skills are needed to build a strong marriage. These include resolving conflict, communicating, building intimacy, decision making, and management skills. Resources for couples include family, friends, marriage enrichment programs, and marriage counseling.

Content Vocabulary
◇ intimacy ◇ mutual
◇ estranged

Academic Vocabulary
You will find these words in your reading and on your tests. Use the glossary to look up their definitions if necessary.
■ recall ■ intensive

Graphic Organizer
As you read, look for five tips to help couples manage their money. Use a chart like the one shown to help organize your information.

Help Couples Manage Money
1.
2.
3.

 Graphic Organizer Go to this book's Online Learning Center at **glencoe.com** to print out this graphic organizer.

Academic Standards . . . .

 English Language Arts

NCTE 6 Apply knowledge of language structure and conventions to discuss texts.

NCTE 12 Use language to accomplish individual purposes.

 Mathematics

NCTM Number and Operations Compute fluently and make reasonable estimates.

NCTE *National Council of Teachers of English*
NCTM *National Council of Teachers of Mathematics*

NSES *National Science Education Standards*
NCSS *National Council of the Social Studies*

Skills for Marriage

Marriage offers warmth, security, and protection to individuals. It promotes stability in society. It is founded on a firm commitment that does not shift over time. Couples who choose to marry expect to be happy. Happiness, however, does not happen without work. It requires time and effort from the partners.

Couples need to set goals for the marriage and the relationship. This gives the partners something to work toward together. Common goals can help a couple stay united in times of hardship. How do they want to relate mentally and emotionally? What do they want from their life together? They may value security, teamwork, adventure, or peace of mind. When couples have a similar vision for their life, they can make it happen.

There are many adjustments that must be made when a couple marries. They have to deal with new relationships, such as those with in-laws. The routines of daily life have to be established. Couples adjust to their sexual life as married partners. Adjusting to married life does not have to cause problems. If it does, the couple needs to work together to resolve them.

In Units 2 and 3 of this book, you read about skills for strengthening relationships. These skills are also the basis of a strong marriage. Couples use their interpersonal skills to build the relationship from dating to marriage. The skills can also help the marriage last. The more a couple uses their skills, the more rewarding their life will be.

As You Read

Connect What goals do you think are important for couples to have?

Resolve Conflicts

One skill that is important in a strong marriage is knowing how to resolve conflicts in a positive way. Every couple has conflict, but not everyone deals with it well. Some people believe that truly happy couples never disagree. They see any conflict as a sign of a troubled marriage. As a result, they avoid disagreement of any kind.

◀) **Deal with Conflicts** Couples should take time to discuss issues and resolve conflicts in their marriages. *Why is it important to deal with conflicts as they happen?*

 **Vocabulary**

You can find definitions in the glossary at the back of this book.

At the opposite end of the spectrum are couples whose every disagreement turns into conflict. You will **recall**, or remember, that excessive arguing is a warning sign in a relationship. It can signal a lack of basic compatibility. It can also be a sign of deeper problems. A healthy relationship avoids both extremes. Couples deal with disputes as they arise. They decide whether a difference is worth pursuing. They try to be sensitive to each other. They use reason, compromise, and negotiation to come to a choice that pleases both.

Common problems in a marriage involve money, sex, work, child rearing, in-laws, and how time is spent. Compromise and negotiation may be needed to resolve these issues. Empathy and respect for each other may help set the stage for solving these problems.

Resolving conflict in marriage should be a balance of give-and-take. When one person does most of the giving in, the marriage is rarely happy. Giving only as much as you feel you get is not a loving approach. If partners do not handle conflict well, negativity is apt to creep into their relationship. This may cause it to weaken.

Communicate

The ability to communicate well, as shown in **Figure 30.1**, is vital in marriage. It makes every other skill possible. Partners need to feel free to say what they think. They must be willing to listen in return.

Figure 30.1   Communication Counts

Does anything guarantee a successful marriage? Good communication may top the list. *Do you think these communication suggestions become easier or more difficult the longer two people are married? Why?*

The people closest to you are often the ones who affect your self-worth the most. When both partners communicate openly with each other, it can lead to a strong and fulfilling marriage.

Express Appreciation and Love
People need to hear such expressions.

Choose Kind Words
Say, "Thanks for dinner" when the other person takes time to make a meal.

Be a Good Listener
Eliminating distractions helps the listening process.

They should be able to explain their worries without fear of judgment or ridicule. Using I-messages can help couples communicate without being hurtful to their partner. Communication allows partners to build each other up through praise and affirmation.

Ideally, communication in marriage occurs in an atmosphere of complete trust. Partners know that private discussions will be kept private. They know that information will not be used to hurt each other or anyone else. To do so would damage the relationship.

The demands of children, work, and household tasks challenge communication in marriage. Couples may need to set aside specific times to talk. It could be in the morning or at night. It needs to be a time when there are no distractions. Making this effort shows their commitment to keeping the marriage strong.

Share Intimacy

When you share intimacy, you talk about problems you would not share with anyone else. **Intimacy** is closeness that develops from a personal relationship. Intimacy can be built in many ways. You can listen to your favorite music together. You can go for long walks while holding hands. Intimacy is part of a healthy marriage.

Although intimacy may be expressed through sexual activity, many other ways are just as valuable. A warm and loving conversation that shares deep feelings shows intimacy. A touch, hug, or look that says you care is intimate. Daily intimacies such as these keep a relationship fresh, healthy, and vital.

Show Trust Private discussions are just between the two of you.

Make Time to Talk This will help you grow closer.

Hold Back on Judgments Criticism and ridicule are destructive.

The Need for Intimacy

Partners may not have the same need for intimacy. Someone who wants to share every personal feeling can overwhelm a more reserved spouse. This is not a fault in a marriage, but couples do need to talk about their needs. They must find a level of intimacy that satisfies them both. A person may need to give his or her partner some space at times, while his or her spouse can learn ways to express feelings. This is part of the give-and-take of marriage.

Family and household needs can interfere with time spent together. Parents' needs often take a back seat to those of children. While spending time together as a family is important, so is time alone with your spouse. Couples may find that sharing household chores is a way to spend time together while also getting work done.

Intimacy can be shown in many small ways within a marriage. Partners feel an emotional closeness. When sex is linked to intimacy in this way, sexual attraction can last the lifetime of the marriage. When sex is related to physical pleasure alone, a marriage may be less secure and satisfying.

Intimacy in a marriage can break down for many reasons. One person may lose trust or a sense of commitment to the marriage. Another person might let day-to-day life interfere with closeness. Sometimes people simply forget that others need to be shown or told that they are loved.

When partners stop making an effort to be close, whatever the reason, they begin to feel estranged. **Estranged** means alienated. Expressions of intimacy decrease when this happens. Sexual relations are strained and unsatisfying.

As you can see, what couples think and feel affects how they act. How they act affects their thoughts and feelings. Emotional support leads to intimacy, yet intimacy provides emotional support. A wise couple knows how this cycle works, and makes it work for their relationship.

Real Life | About Intimacy

Intimacy is closeness between two people that allows them to share their deepest thoughts and feelings. They trust each other and show that they really care. Intimacy helps a relationship last. Even in marriage, sex without intimacy is unrewarding and meaningless. Intimacy develops in marriage when a couple:

- Learns more about each other each day.
- Shares their most personal ideas and possessions.
- Strengthens their relationship.
- Affirms their love and respect for each other.

- Laughs together frequently.
- Actively listens to each other.

Problem-Solving

Jenny had not felt close to her husband Pete in a long time. He was often heading out the door to the health club when she got home from work. She would be asleep before he got home. They had not talked much lately. Jenny had thought by now they would have had a baby, but it had not happened. What should Jenny do?

Spend Time Together

To married people, time can be more valuable than money. You can build a strong relationship without spending much money on each other. To build and keep intimacy, you must spend time together. Sharing activities, whether work or play, expresses love and builds closeness.

Make Decisions Together

As partners in marriage, people have major choices to make together. They must decide where to live. They need to decide whether to have children, and more. By sharing decisions, couples work toward the same goals in their marriage. Comparing options lets them choose the ones that seem best for both of them. Decisions that are mutual are more apt to be carried out. **Mutual** means agreed to by both partners.

When they make decisions, a couple tries to reach the fairest outcome. This does not mean that both partners must feel satisfied with every choice equally. Some decisions are often better for one person than the other. However, each person should feel that the sacrifices made and the benefits received even out.

Common Values

A couple who shares common values has an advantage in making choices. Knowing that your spouse cares about the same things you do helps you find options that will be right for you both. Shared values are important if one partner is deciding a matter that also affects his or her spouse.

Manage the Family Finances

Conflicts over money are a leading cause of marital breakup. To manage this resource while avoiding arguments, a couple can:

- **Talk about money.** Before marriage, discuss spending habits and attitudes about money. Will two incomes be pooled? Will each partner have some money for personal use? After marriage, talk about how you manage your money. Is one partner spending too much? Can you afford to splurge on something or to make a major purchase?
- **Make a financial plan and stick to it.** Decide how much money is available for family expenses. How much will be kept for individual use? Make sure both partners feel the plan is fair. Include the value of unpaid work.
- **Establish priorities.** Distinguish between needs and wants. Compromise about what is essential and what is a luxury. Decide on financial goals as well.

Enrich Your Marriage Marriage enrichment classes are a good resource for married couples. *Would happily married couples benefit from such classes?*

- **Assign financial responsibility to the one who handles it better.** This could mean that one person makes all the financial decisions. It could mean division of money management duties. For example, one person might keep track of the budget, while the other pays the bills.
- **Always save some money.** Even a small amount of money set aside regularly adds up. More important, it gives a feeling of security. It allows the couple to work toward shared goals.

✓ Reading Check **Explain** Why is communication an important skill in marriage?

Resources for Married Couples

For building a strong marriage, a couple's first resource is themselves. To reach some goals, however, they need help from others. To manage their lives and maintain a rewarding relationship, couples can turn to a number of outside resources.

Family and Friends

Like everyone, married couples can benefit from the help of families. Parents can give advice based on their own years of experience. Siblings may pitch in with child care or household projects. Extended family members may be willing to provide financial help. These acts of support can benefit both the couple and their families.

At the same time, ties with family members and between the couple can be strained if partners routinely turn to family for help. Marriage means accepting the responsibility of building a life with a partner. This includes dealing with problems. A couple should work out problems on their own. When they do, they develop the teamwork needed for a strong marriage.

As newlyweds, couples focus on each other and on establishing their relationship. Friendships often seem less important. Most partners soon rediscover the value of good friends, however. A spouse may not be able to meet all of his or her mate's emotional needs. Friends are a good resource.

Marriage Enrichment

Many programs are available to couples who want to make their marriages stronger. Their purpose is not to fix broken marriages. Their goal is to make average or good marriages better. Many such programs are sponsored by colleges or mental health centers. Others may be offered by religious groups. There may be a series of sessions. Some are held over several weeks. They could be **intensive**, or concentrated, weekend retreats. Topics covered include improving communication, solving conflict, and building intimacy.

Marriage Counseling

As the rate of divorce shows, married relationships can run into trouble. A couple may lose their closeness. They may be worn down by a conflict that they cannot solve. Their frustration at not knowing how to improve the relationship can threaten their commitment. These couples may be able to save their marriage through counseling.

Marriage counseling works best when both partners want to improve their relationship. Both have to be willing to work at it. Finding a skilled counselor can take some effort. Local family service and health care agencies may be able to locate a qualified person. Sometimes these groups provide counseling at a low cost. Many religious leaders have training in counseling couples.

It is not easy to go to marriage counseling. Couples find it hard to share details of their personal life with someone they do not know. It is discouraging to talk about so many negative parts of the marriage. A skilled counselor can help couples gain a sense of progress on their toughest issues.

A counselor acts as a referee and advisor during sessions. This helps couples learn to solve their own problems. Most problems involve a breakdown of communication. This is often where counselors begin. Couples may also need help in overcoming anger, resentment, and guilt. As they learn the skills they need, they find solving problems becomes easier. A successful outcome means that a troubled marriage is once again satisfying.

Section 30.2 After You Read

Review Key Concepts

1. **Identify** some of the problems that married couples encounter and must resolve.
2. **Explain** when marriage counseling works best.

Practice Academic Skills

English Language Arts

3. Write a paragraph to explain the quotation, "It takes two to make a marriage a success and only one to make it a failure." Do you agree or disagree with the statement? Explain your answer.

4. Look at the skills discussed in this chapter. List the skills in their order of importance to you. Explain why you placed them in this order.

Check Your Answers Check your answers at this book's Online Learning Center through **glencoe.com**.

> **NCTE 6** Apply knowledge of language structure and conventions to discuss texts.

> **NCTE 12** Use language to accomplish individual purposes.

CAREER SPOTLIGHT

Financial Planner

Russell Bailyn
New York, New York

Managing finances is an important part of a marriage. A financial planner can help couples in this process.

The financial world is complex. There are markets open 24 hours a day, all around the world. Money is constantly changing hands.

Russell Bailyn spends his days gathering information about his clients. This includes everything from tax returns and paycheck stubs to investment statements and budgets. Bailyn then puts together a plan to help them reach financial goals, like paying for college or saving for retirement.

"My passion for work is contagious," he says. "When I speak about the state of the markets or a smart financial planning strategy, people tend to listen. They can sense my love for what I do. This gets me referrals."

For people interested in a career in finance, Bailyn recommends some basic reading. "Try reading *The Wall Street Journal,* and see if the content is exciting to you." He continues, "Once you get to high school or college, try to find somebody who works in the field of investments or financial planning. Ask them if you can come to work for a day and observe what goes on."

CAREER FACTS

Education or Training A college degree is usually required, with an emphasis in accounting, finance, economics, business, mathematics, or law.

Nature of the Work Financial planners work with individuals, families, and businesses to develop plans for how to use income to meet specific goals.

Aptitudes, Abilities, and Skills A financial planner should have an analytical mind, be a good listener, and be comfortable with basic mathematical tasks.

Academic Skills Required English Language Arts, Math, and accounting skills

Student Organizations To prepare for this career, look for positions that foster money management skills, such as the Treasurer of a school committee.

Career Outlook Employment of financial planners and advisors is expected to grow faster than the average over the next ten years.

Career Path Entry-level financial advisors may advance to higher positions such as portfolio manager or high-level financial manager for one or more corporate clients.

Critical Thinking

Financial Help Would you pay someone to help you plan how to spend your money? Why or why not?

 Research Careers For more information on this and other careers, visit the Occupational Outlook Handbook Web site through the link on this book's Online Learning Center at **glencoe.com**.

CHAPTER SUMMARY

 Section 30.1
Qualities of a Strong Marriage

Strong marriages share some common traits. The couple has realistic expectations about what the marriage will be like. Partners are committed to each other. They show acceptance, flexibility, and thoughtfulness. Marriages vary in satisfaction. The U-Shaped Satisfaction Curve notes that most couples are very happy in the beginning. Satisfaction starts to decrease with the birth of the first child. It tends to be lowest when children enter school, and when children are in their teens. Satisfaction increases when children leave home.

Section 30.2
Skills and Resources for Marriage

Good relationships are needed for a strong marriage. Couples need to be able to resolve conflict. Partners must communicate well. They need to build and share intimacy between them. It is important to spend time together to maintain intimacy. Partners who share the same values often find making decisions easier. Good money management can help couples keep the marriage strong. Resources for couples include family and friends. Others are marriage enrichment programs and marriage counseling.

Content and Academic Vocabulary Review

1. Use each of these content and academic vocabulary words in a sentence.

Content Vocabulary
◇ marriage commitment (p. 587)
◇ expectation (p. 588)
◇ U-shaped curve (p. 591)
◇ intimacy (p. 595)
◇ estranged (p. 596)
◇ mutual (p. 597)

Academic Vocabulary
■ underlie (p. 587)
■ pattern (p. 591)
■ recall (p. 594)
■ intensive (p. 599)

Review Key Concepts

2. **Identify** qualities that help make a marriage strong.
3. **Explain** what the U-Shaped Satisfaction Curve means for married couples.
4. **Summarize** skills that can strengthen a marriage.
5. **Suggest** resources for married couples.

Critical Thinking

6. **Compare and Contrast** Discuss the ways in which marriage enrichment and counseling are similar. In what ways do they differ?
7. **Analyze** Some problems that come between couples develop slowly. The couple may not recognize the problem for months or years. How can this be prevented?
8. **Evaluate** A partner in a troubled marriage refuses to attend counseling. Experts urge the other partner to seek help alone. What are some advantages to one partner attending counseling alone? What are some drawbacks?
9. **Draw Conclusions** Do you think each marriage partner should spend time on personal activities on his or her own? If so, how much time do you think is acceptable?

Real-World Skills

Critical Thinking Skills

10. Think Logically After the birth of the first child, satisfaction in marriage tends to lessen. If a couple decides to have children later in a marriage, would the outcome be different? If yes, in what ways? Express your answer in a brief essay.

Interpersonal Skills

11. Communication Anne told Gilbert that she feels taken for granted now that they are married. "You hardly compliment me anymore or say thanks for the special things I do for you." Gilbert replied, "No one can do those things forever." Write an advice column to Anne.

Management Skills

12. Low-Cost Activities Many couples face a boring routine. Develop a list of low-cost activities that a couple can use to enhance their married life. They should help the couple maintain a closeness in their relationship.

Problem-Solving Skills

13. Identify Options After their two children were born, Maria became a full-time homemaker, and Ben supported the family. Six years later, the couple has little time or energy. They are starting to feel that they have little in common. Write a paragraph about they should do.

14. Scheduling Conflicts Follow your teacher's instructions to form into groups. Each group member should think of five activities that a married person may do. Write these on small slips of paper. Put everyone's slips in a bag. Take turns pulling out two slips. Suggest ways partners might respond if the two activities conflicted in a couple's schedule.

15. Community Activities Find out what activities are available in your area. These can include recreational, cultural, volunteer, or other types of activities. List three activities that couples might enjoy. How could they help make a marriage stronger? Explain your answer in a short essay.

16. Marriage Enrichment Programs Find out about programs to strengthen marriages that are offered in your community. Who sponsors the programs? How much do they cost? What kinds of topics are covered in the program? Create a brochure with your findings.

17. Use a Search Engine Go to this book's Online Learning Center at **glencoe.com** to find **Web Links** for **Search Engines**. Choose one and type the phrase "commitment quotations." Read the various quotations. Copy five that you think apply to marriage commitment.

Additional Activities For additional activities, go to this book's Online Learning Center through **glencoe.com**.

Academic Skills

Mathematics

18. Calculate a Savings Plan Ana and Li have decided to purchase a new computer for their home office. They have agreed on the model of computer they would like to have. They have also agreed that the price for the computer fits their budget. Ana and Li will need to save $1,350 over the next six months to buy the computer they want. How much will they need to save each week to buy the computer in six months?

Math Concept **Divide by Whole Numbers** When dividing money, recall how you would divide decimals. Be sure to put the decimal in the correct place in the answer.

Starting Hint: You must first determine how many weeks Ana and Li have to save money (6 months × 4 weeks). Once you have determined this, divide $1,350 by your answer.

 For math help, go to the Math Appendix at the back of the book.

> **NCTM Number and Operations** Compute fluently and make reasonable estimates.

English Language Arts

19. Literature Choose a novel, short story, or play that features a marital relationship. The literature should be from a different time period. Is the marriage strong or weak? What actions or details does the author show to convey this? How might this description of marriage be representative of that time period? Share your ideas in a short report to the class.

> **NCTE 2** Read literature to build an understanding of the human experience.

Social Studies

20. Cultural Images Study stories of the marriages of some famous people. You can choose movie stars or well-known athletes. What do these stories tell you? Do you find these images favorable? Unfavorable? Base your answers only on the descriptions you find. What recommendations would you have about marriage? Write your answers in a short report.

> **NCSS Standard I.g** Construct reasoned judgments about specific cultural responses to persistent human issues.

STANDARDIZED TEST PRACTICE

ESSAY
Use a separate sheet of paper to write a half-page response to the following writing prompt.

> **Test-Taking Tip** In an essay test, read the prompt carefully to be sure you understand what you are supposed to write. After you have finished writing, reread your answer and the prompt to make sure you have answered correctly.

21. Phil and Alexandra have been married for 12 years, but lately they seem to be growing apart. They are both very involved with their careers and sometimes go for days without talking to each other. They do not seem to enjoy each other's company like they once did. They are both committed to making their marriage work, but they do not know what to do. Give some suggestions for things they can do to grow closer to one another.

CHAPTER 31

The Parenting Question

○ **Section 31.1**

Examine Parenting

○ **Section 31.2**

Prepare for Parenthood

 **Explore the Photo**
Parents will experience both joys and challenges as they raise their children. *Do you think that the rewards of parenthood are greater than the challenges?*

Chapter Objectives

After completing this chapter, you will be able to:

- **Identify** why choosing parenthood is such an important decision.
- **Describe** the rewards and challenges of parenting.
- **Explain** reasons for adoption.
- **Determine** factors that are involved in parenting readiness.
- **Suggest** ways to prepare yourself for parenthood.
- **Summarize** resources useful to parents.

Writing Activity

Persuasive Essay

Think Realistically Having a realistic outlook means seeing life as it is—not as you would like it to be or as you fear it might be. You can show a realistic attitude when you:

- Observe that babies are lovable but that caring for them is work.
- Practice patience now in order to be a better parent someday.
- Talk to a career counselor about the education you need for a desired career.
- Save money for unexpected expenses.

Write a persuasive essay where you try to persuade your audience of the benefits of thinking realistically.

Writing Tips To write a strong persuasive essay, follow these steps:

1. Create a graphic organizer to help you organize and visually show the plan for your argument.
2. Keep your audience in mind. Your audience will probably include your peers, classmates, and teacher.
3. Remember your purpose—to present an opinion, acknowledge alternative viewpoints, and provide reasons for your opinion.

Examine Parenting

Reading Guide

Before You Read

Pace Yourself Short blocks of concentrated reading are effective. Focus on reading for 10 minutes. Take a short break. Then read for 10 minutes.

Read to Learn
Key Concepts
- **Identify** why choosing parenthood is such an important decision.
- **Describe** the rewards and challenges of parenting.
- **Explain** reasons for adoption.

Main Idea
Choosing parenthood is an important decision. There are rewards and challenges. Some couples undergo medical treatment to have children. Some couples try adoption.

Content Vocabulary
◇ parenting
◇ genetic disease
◇ fertility
◇ infertility
◇ adoption

Academic Vocabulary
You will find these words in your reading and on your tests. Use the glossary to look up their definitions if necessary.
■ forethought   ■ biology

Graphic Organizer
As you read, identify pressures to have children and not to have children. Use a chart like the one shown to help organize your information.

Pressures	
To Have Children	**To Remain Childless**
1._____	1._____
2._____	2._____
3._____	3._____

 Graphic Organizer Go to this book's Online Learning Center at **glencoe.com** to print out this graphic organizer.

Academic Standards •

 English Language Arts

NCTE 5 Use different writing process elements to communicate effectively.

NCTE 8 Use information resources to gather information and create and communicate knowledge.

 Mathematics

NCTM Problem Solving Solve problems that arise in mathematics and in other contexts.

NCTE *National Council of Teachers of English*
NCTM *National Council of Teachers of Mathematics*

NSES *National Science Education Standards*
NCSS *National Council of the Social Studies*

Choosing Parenthood

For some people, parenthood just happens. They do not ask themselves whether having a child is the right thing to do. They do not prepare themselves for the responsibilities. The pregnancy rate among teens is proof that parenthood can be taken lightly. However, anyone of any age who has children without **forethought**, or planning ahead, risks the same difficult outcomes.

Having a child is not something you can walk away from—emotionally, legally, or morally. You can quit a job or end a friendship. Parenthood, however, cannot be undone. It has a lifelong impact on parents and children. People who are not prepared to love and care for a child properly may make mistakes. If things go wrong, the child may not have the best possible chance at having a loving family. This can affect a child for a lifetime.

There is a better way to look at parenthood. People need to view it as a choice. Then they can make thoughtful decisions about whether, when, and how to parent. **Parenting** is the process of caring for children and helping them grow and learn. Parenthood is **biology**, the science of life. Parenting involves love and caring for all of a child's needs.

Making a careful decision to have a child benefits you and your child. As with any goal, you are more likely to succeed when you have chosen the role. Children deserve to be born to parents who are ready for parenthood. When parents choose to raise children, children stand a better chance at becoming happy, productive people.

Being a parent is one of the most important roles a person has in life. It is also a role that few people are educated and trained for. People rarely learn about children and the skills needed for parenting.

Pressures to Have Children

In many ways, society promotes the idea of having children. A society cannot continue without future generations to maintain it. The government promotes having children by providing income tax deductions for children. Society promotes having children in other ways, too. For example, lower-cost meals for children at restaurants help support people who choose to have children.

Children, too, learn the expectation of parenthood as they grow up. Small children practice parenting by playing house. Adults tell children, "You will understand when you have kids of your own." Such comments imply that parenthood is normal and expected.

 **Vocabulary**
You can find definitions in the glossary at the back of this book.

As You Read
Connect How do you think viewing parenting as a choice can help you look at parenthood?

Parenthood Readiness When a couple chooses to have a child, they are usually better prepared to care for the child. *Why would some couples think they are ready when they really are not?*

Among married couples, pressure to become parents may be more personal. The couple's parents often look forward to grandchildren. They may often hint that they are eager to become grandparents.

Peer pressure can also be strong in urging a couple to start a family. Friends may have children and talk of the joys of being a parent. A couple that does not have children can feel like they are missing something or they might feel selfish.

People need to be aware of all the pressures to have children. They need to realize that children should be born because parents honestly want them. They should be willing to make a commitment to their children's upbringing. Children are a source of joy and fulfillment to many people. This is rarely true for those people who want children for the wrong reasons.

Pressures to Not Have Children

Most pressure to not have children comes from the couple themselves. About 10 percent of people of childbearing age choose not to have children. They make this choice for a number of reasons.

Some couples take a global view of the issue. They believe the world already has too many people competing for limited resources. They may worry about bringing a child into a world troubled by terrorism, war, or environmental problems. Those who have such concerns tend to have few, if any, children. Some people simply do not enjoy children. Some have values and goals that conflict with parenting. People who are focused on their careers may decide that children would interfere with their success.

Some people may feel they have a chance of passing on a disease that runs in the family to a child. A **genetic disease** is a disease that is passed from parent to child. Not every child may get the disease. These diseases include hemophilia, sickle cell anemia, and cystic fibrosis. Couples with a family history of such diseases can have genetic testing. Counseling is also available. They can learn their chances of passing a genetic disease to a child.

◀◀ *Pressure* There are different types of pressure a couple may feel to become parents. *How do you think relatives of the couple can be a type of pressure?*

Thoughtful Decision Making

In the past, almost all married couples were expected to have children. This was true unless the couple was physically unable to have children. Today, modern methods of planning births allow choices about if and when to have children. These choices carry with them the duty to choose wisely.

The best choices come when all the options and outcomes are thoughtfully weighed. You need to see the values, factors, and pressures that affect your choice about whether to have a child. Sorting through all the facts can help you make choices that are right for you.

Children bring about a major change in a couple's lifestyle. They use a lot of family resources. They require time, energy, and money. Children affect parents physically. They also affect them socially and emotionally. They can change a family's goals. They can change how parents work toward these goals. They affect a couple's financial and legal responsibilities.

Only you can decide whether you want to parent. Your decision, however, has a major impact on your future and that of your children. Making the right choice now helps ensure a happy, satisfying life for yourself and for any children you might have.

 **Parenthood Is a Choice** Some couples make a choice to delay parenthood or not to have children at all because of their careers. *Do you think it is selfish for couples to choose not to have children?*

✓ **Reading Check** **Explain** What are genetic diseases?

Rewards and Challenges of Parenting

Raising healthy, well-adjusted children takes certain skills. It also requires lots of time, energy, patience, and understanding. Parents must provide for all of a child's needs. They make sure a child is safe, loved, educated, and guided. Handling these duties well can challenge even the most devoted and loving parent.

For many parents, of course, having children makes all the challenges worthwhile. To some couples, a family is not complete without a child to share in their love and affection. One reward of parenthood is the joy children provide. Seeing the world through a child's eyes can be a learning experience.

Parenthood can also bring a sense of fulfillment. Parents can take pride in caring for the needs of their children and watching them grow into happy, responsible adults. Many parents consider this their greatest success in life.

Financial Responsibilities

One of the challenges of parenting is the financial cost and responsibility it brings. Raising a child is expensive. Estimates set the cost of raising a child at two and a half to three times the family's yearly income at the time the child is born.

Where does the money go? Food and clothing are two regular expenses that grow as the children do, and children grow rapidly. Costs for medical care, child care, education, toys, and recreation cannot be overlooked, either. There are supplies and equipment needed at every age. Having a child may mean that a family needs a larger home. This brings higher utility bills and rent or mortgage payments. To cover these costs, a couple may have to lower their standard of living. They may go out less, buy fewer and less expensive clothes, and find less costly ways to have fun. They may be able to use technology to help educate and entertain themselves and their children. Financial planning software may help them manage their money more skillfully.

Personal Costs

As high as the financial costs are, the personal costs of having children can be even greater. These include the time and energy it takes to provide all the care that babies and children need. It includes the personal sacrifices involved as well.

Women tend to take on more parenting duties than men do. They are more likely to give up or change their career goals. Sharing parenting roles helps spread the personal costs of raising children more evenly between fathers and mothers.

The combined drain on parents' time, energy, and finances often leads to feelings of lost freedom. Parents may notice they have less time and energy left for themselves and each other. Technology can help sometimes. Baby monitors let parents keep track of the child from a distance. Sending instant messages or texting can be a way to keep in touch when caring for children. Wayne texts Traci each day to let her know what time he will be home. This helps her plan their baby's schedule so she and Wayne can eat dinner together.

▼ **Chosen Children** Adoption is a serious choice for many couples, but the love for their children is no less than what biological parents feel. *What are some options for couples who cannot have children of their own?*

✓ **Reading Check**

Identify What are some of the personal costs of parenting?

Infertility and Adoption

Fertility is the ability to have children. **Infertility** is the inability to have children. It affects about one in five married couples. A couple is said to be infertile if the female does not become pregnant after a year without using birth control. This peaks in a person's twenties. Infertility is most common among couples in their thirties and forties. Some couples find other ways to become parents.

Infertility Choices

Some couples who have fertility problems still have choices about whether to have a child. About half of these couples can have children with medical help. Complete medical histories and a series of special tests are taken. These may reveal the exact reason the couple cannot have a child. Once the source of the problem is found, treatments can be started. Certain procedures are morally unacceptable to some couples, however.

New technology has made the treatment of infertility more likely to be successful. New drugs and surgeries make fertility treatments more apt to work. There are legal issues in choosing to use these tools. There are ethical decisions as well.

Some couples who choose medical treatment find it a test of their commitment to having a child. They are asked to share details of the most private part of their life together with medical personnel. Several years and thousands of dollars' worth of treatments may yield no birth, one birth, or multiple births. A couple must be willing to take such risks and live with the results.

Adoption

Adoption is the legal process of taking a child of other parents as one's own. The parents and child are bound in every legal way until the child reaches age 18. The birth parents give up all the rights and duties of parenthood.

People adopt for many reasons. Infertile couples may not have success with medical treatment. They may be opposed to its use. Some adoptive parents fear passing on serious diseases, some genetic, to their offspring.

Sometimes people who can safely have children of their own prefer to adopt. They may be concerned with overpopulation. They may want to help a child who might otherwise not have a home. Such couples often adopt children who are older or have health problems or disabilities. Some single people who strongly wish to parent also choose adoption.

Financial Literacy

Childcare Costs

Kim and Ethan both work full time and have two children, Gregory, who attends preschool, and Dominic, who stays with a sitter while his parents are at work. Kim and Ethan are trying to decide whether it would save them money for Kim to quit her job and stay home with the children. Preschool costs $34.50 per day and childcare costs $25 per day. They pay these costs for five days a week for 50 weeks out of the year. Kim makes $14,000 per year. Would it be better financially for Kim to quit her job and stay home with the children?

Math Concept **Comparing Costs**

To determine whether it would be better financially for Kim to stay home with the children, you must first calculate the total amount they pay for preschool and childcare and then compare that number to Kim's salary.

Starting Hint: First, find the cost for preschool ($34.50 × 5 × 50) and the cost for childcare ($25 × 5 × 50) and add these together. Compare the total to Kim's salary ($14,000).

 For math help, go to the Math Appendix at the back of the book.

NCTM Problem Solving Solve problems that arise in mathematics and in other contexts.

The issue of identity is a sensitive one in adoptions. Birth and adoptive parents may believe in privacy. They choose closed adoption. This is where identities are not revealed. Closing adoption records, however, can make it hard to get vital information. Both personal and medical information is important to have. Adopted children with few facts about their birth parents may be bothered later by questions. Birth parents worry whether the child is healthy and loved.

Open adoptions are becoming more popular. In open adoption the identities are known. Personal information may be found in files. The birth mother and adoptive parents may meet.

They may remain in contact over time. Open adoption can provide the child with a sense of identity. However, involving several parents in raising a child can cause problems. It also can be confusing.

Problem-Solving Will and Elizabeth adopted their son in a closed adoption due to the birth mother's wishes. Jared, now 10 years old, is asking questions about his birth parents and background. The couple feels threatened and worried about violating the birth mother's privacy. What should they do?

Adopt an Infant

Many couples adopt infants in order to enjoy raising a child almost from birth. The supply of infants available for adoption, however, cannot meet the demand. The wait for a healthy infant or toddler averages five years. It can often stretch as long as ten years.

Some couples who want to have a baby turn to international adoption. They give a home to an orphan or an abandoned child from another country. International adoptions can be very costly. They require patience and perseverance. There can be many risks with this type of adoption.

Adopt an Older Child

The demand is high for infants and toddlers. The wait to adopt an older child is often shorter. The adoptive parents, however, must be prepared for special challenges. An older child may have emotional scars. A child who has a disability may require added patience and other adjustments. For parents who see both the limitations and the possibilities, however, raising such a child can be a great joy. The rewards can be great when a neglected child learns to love and be loved.

The Public Adoption Process

About three-fourths of all adoptions take place through public, state-approved agencies. These agencies are concerned with serving the best interests of the child. They also want to serve the birth parents and the adoptive parents.

Placing a child for adoption is usually a difficult decision. It is also a loving one for the birth parents. These parents, often teens, realize that they cannot provide the kind of home a child needs. They want their child to have a better chance at a happy life than they can offer. Agencies that specialize in adoptions help with this decision.

They counsel birth parents to make sure they understand all their options. Medical records and other information about them and the child are collected for the adoptive parents.

Prospective parents are screened and counseled to be sure that they are ready and able to care for a child. Once parents are approved, the agency tries to match them with a suitable child. That child is given to the parents for a trial period. Both the parents and agency must be satisfied that the match is successful. If so, a court awards permanent custody.

The Private Adoption Process

Adoptions can also take place privately. Clergy, doctors, and lawyers arrange these adoptions. These often are done more quickly than with a public agency. The adopting couple often pays the medical, hospital, and legal fees. In some cases, they pay the birth mother's living expenses. A fee for the child itself is considered buying the child. It is illegal.

Private adoption carries certain risks. Without consent from both parents when a baby is adopted, the adoption is not final. Birth parents' rights are legally more important than adoptive parents' rights. The birth parents may change their minds. If they do, the adoptive parents can do nothing.

A person can become a parent naturally, with medical aid, or by adoption. Still, the basic truth of parenting is the same. Raising a child involves risks and rewards, sacrifice and satisfaction. Are the pleasures worth the challenges? For those who see the reality of parenting and who love children enough to choose it, the answer is a definite yes.

Section 31.1   After You Read

Review Key Concepts

1. **Explain** the difference between parenthood and parenting.
2. **Identify** some of the financial costs of raising a child.
3. **Describe** some of the reasons people turn to international adoption.

Practice Academic Skills

English Language Arts

4. List some items that describe the importance of making the decision to become a parent. Items might include being prepared to meet a child's emotional and physical needs, and being willing to give up some things to raise a child. Create a poster to illustrate these ideas.

5. Research an article about adopting an older child. You could also choose an article about adopting a child with disabilities. Look for the special challenges and rewards of this kind of adoption. Write a summary of the article to share with your class.

> **NCTE 5** Use different writing process elements to communicate effectively.

> **NCTE 8** Use information resources to gather information and create and communicate knowledge.

Check Your Answers Check your answers at this book's Online Learning Center through **glencoe.com**.

Prepare for Parenthood

Reading Guide

Before You Read

Two-Column Notes Divide a piece of paper into two columns. In the left column, write down main ideas. In the right column, list supporting details.

Read to Learn

Key Concepts

- **Determine** factors that are involved in parenting readiness.
- **Suggest** ways to prepare yourself for parenthood.
- **Summarize** resources useful to parents.

Main Idea

Parenthood readiness is the degree of preparation for parenting. People prepare for parenthood by learning about children. They also prepare by learning about reproduction. There are many resources for parents.

Content Vocabulary

◇ parenting readiness
◇ child development
◇ conception
◇ placenta
◇ prenatal
◇ birth defect
◇ trimester
◇ miscarriage
◇ labor
◇ postpartum

Academic Vocabulary

You will find these words in your reading and on your tests. Use the glossary to look up their definitions if necessary.

■ restriction   ■ relate

Graphic Organizer

As you read, look for the effects of parenthood on mothers, fathers, and infants. Use a chart like the one shown to help organize your information.

Effects on Mothers	Effects on Fathers	Effects on Infants

 Graphic Organizer Go to this book's Online Learning Center at **glencoe.com** to print out this graphic organizer.

Academic Standards • • • • • • • • • • • • • • • •

 English Language Arts

NCTE 7 Conduct research and gather, evaluate, and synthesize data to communicate discoveries.

NCTE 12 Use language to accomplish individual purposes.

NCTE *National Council of Teachers of English*
NCTM *National Council of Teachers of Mathematics*

NSES *National Science Education Standards*
NCSS *National Council of the Social Studies*

Look at Readiness

Studies in life-span development show that the time an event occurs in life has as much impact as the event itself. Losing your job, for example, is almost always a negative event. It is apt to have a big impact if you are a 40-year-old parent and spouse. It may be less of a problem if you are 16 and in high school.

Likewise, having a child is a life-changing event. Responsibilities will increase and some sacrifices may have to be made. These demands are best handled in a stage of life that makes it easy for you to meet them.

How can a couple decide whether they will be able to handle the changes that come with parenting? The couple needs to examine their **parenting readiness**. This is their level of preparation. The following traits are extremely helpful when thinking about parenthood. They can also prevent serious effects on the mother, father, and child. These effects can last a lifetime.

Here are traits that mature parents often have:

- **Emotional Maturity** Emotional maturity brings patience and confidence. It includes a sense of duty and other traits that good parents need. Because teens are still developing, these traits may not be in place yet. Teens are still learning to take care of themselves. They may not be ready to take total responsibility for another person.
- **Financial Readiness** Would-be parents need to look ahead to future expenses and income. No one wants to feel financial burdens and stress. Careful planning before children enter the picture can make a difference.
- **Realistic Goals and Expectations** Couples should think about what will happen to their goals. Children can cause their plans to change. Deciding when to have children is the best insurance against having to give up something important.
- **Age** In a sense, age is the best way to judge parenting readiness. Age affects the other factors. Older parents tend to be more emotionally and financially stable. They have had more time to reach their goals. The experience and wisdom they have gained are resources for dealing with parenting.

Effects on Mothers

Age affects a woman's readiness for motherhood. Physical maturity also plays a part. There is a greater risk among teens. They have more problems in pregnancy and delivery than adult women. They are twice as likely to suffer complications.

As You Read

Connect What sacrifices do you think you may have to make if you become a parent?

Vocabulary

You can find definitions in the glossary at the back of this book.

Handle Parenting Situations
Parents need to be ready to deal with all situations, including a crying baby. *Why might a baby cry?*

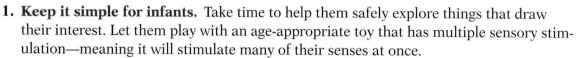

INDEPENDENT Living

HOW TO Entertain Children

Children like to be involved in activities. Yet if you ask, "What do you want to do?" a child may respond, "I don't know." Simple, low-cost activities can help you keep a child's hands—and mind—active. Follow these guidelines for how to entertain children:

1. **Keep it simple for infants.** Take time to help them safely explore things that draw their interest. Let them play with an age-appropriate toy that has multiple sensory stimulation—meaning it will stimulate many of their senses at once.

2. **Make mealtime fun.** Generations of parents have made train noises as a spoonful of strained peas pulls in to a child's mouth. You can make the train a honking car, an airplane, or rumbling truck.

3. **Make play out of work.** Encourage toddlers' can-do spirit and channel their energy by giving them jobs. They can help sort laundry or dust chair legs.

4. **Explore nature.** Most toddlers and preschoolers enjoy nature activities. Gather and crack acorns. Compare colors of autumn leaves. Watch ants at work. Feel different types of grasses and leaves.

5. **Play pretend with toddlers.** Pretend to be cats, dogs, or jungle animals. Toddlers are also great imitators. Teach them dance steps (but do not expect coordination).

Take Action In small groups, discuss ways to include a young child in daily activities. Choose one activity. Develop a simple lesson plan.

Early motherhood and education are often difficult to mix. Women who have a baby while in high school or college are less apt to graduate than those who wait. Strained by caring for a child and working, many women drop out of school. Without an education, it may be hard to get high-paying jobs. Therefore, young mothers tend to have low incomes.

The earlier a woman has a baby, the more apt she is to have other children soon after. The baby's and mother's health suffer for this. Supporting and caring for several children increases stress. Teen mothers have been found to have very high levels of stress compared to their peers who are not parents.

Finally, there is the frustration factor that affects many mothers. A younger mother may feel frustrated. She may have jumped directly from being taken care of by her own parents to taking care of someone else. If this is the case, she missed the period of growth and socializing that young single people enjoy. There are women who have already managed their own money and reached some of their goals. Those women may be more willing to accept the **restriction**, or limitation, that accompanies raising children.

Effects on Fathers

Physically, fathers can walk away from parenthood more easily than mothers, but the law holds them equally responsible. A father is legally bound to support his child until the child turns 18. This is regardless of the father's age or whether he is married to the child's mother. It does not matter if he ever sees his child. Fathers as young as 14 have been asked to pay child support.

As with mothers, young fathers may have to interrupt their education. They may drop out of school to meet their financial obligations. Some are able to resume their education later. They often do so under a double burden of work and study.

Like teen motherhood, teen fatherhood tends to lead to low-paying, unskilled jobs. These offer less security and chance for advancement. Earning money becomes a lifelong worry.

Teens who are also fathers often find that they do not quite fit into either the teen world or the adult world. Their duties isolate them from their more carefree peers. At the same time, they do not fully **relate**, or connect, to adults. They may feel lonely and confused about their roles.

Effects on Infants

Infants are also affected by a parent's lack of readiness. Babies born to teens face greater health hazards than those born to older mothers. They are likely to be premature, with low birth weight. Even full-term infants tend to be smaller and weaker. The younger a mother is, the more likely her baby is to die before celebrating a first birthday.

Many teens deny that they are pregnant. They tell no one. They try to hide the pregnancy from family and friends. They may delay going to the doctor for care. This can increase the chances of problems for the baby and themselves.

Sadly, infants born to young parents are at greater risk of abuse. Teen parents often do not understand infant development. They underestimate the baby's needs. They overestimate the baby's abilities. Some teens have unrealistic expectations. They expect an infant to love them very much. They do not expect an infant to cry much. When parents are not yet adults themselves, these disappointments and other strains of parenthood can lead to child abuse.

✓ **Reading Check** **Explain** Why is emotional maturity needed for parenting readiness?

A Day with Dad
More and more, fathers are realizing that their children need them. *How does a father benefit from a close relationship with his children?*

Prepare Yourself

Some parents may say that trying to learn about parenting by reading books is like trying to learn to swim on dry land. It is true that there is no substitute for experience. At the same time, however, you do not learn to swim by diving into the pool. First, you get used to the water temperature. Then you learn to float. Along the way, you decide whether swimming is for you.

Likewise, there are ways to prepare yourself for parenting before you have a child. Gain a truer picture of parenting now. This allows you to develop realistic expectations about what is involved. You will be better able to handle parenting problems. You will be able to appreciate the joy that raising a child should be if you decide to parent someday.

Learn About Children

People who have prepared themselves by learning about children assume the parental role most easily. Future parents need to know about **child development**. This is how children grow and change at each stage from birth through the teen years.

When parents understand what children can typically do at different ages, they can respond to them in the best way. Parents can be patient. They can also be realistic. They can feel more confident about providing what the child needs. Parenting produces less stress and greater satisfaction.

Gain Experience

One of the best and simplest ways to learn about children is to spend time with them. For people from large families, that is easy. The trend is toward smaller families, however. People may need to find other ways to be around children. Many teens babysit to earn money. The practice they get in caring for children may be more valuable than the pay.

Some people do volunteer work with children. Loy helped supervise a playground at a community center. He watched children play together. It taught him a lot about their physical, emotional, and social skills. Teaching a Sunday school class, coaching a sports team, and getting involved with a children's charity can also give insights about children.

Watch children and parents in public places. It can be interesting and informative. How do parents handle good behavior? How do they handle poor behavior? Observing parents in such situations can give you ideas about good parenting.

A Look at Reproduction

Learning about pregnancy and childbirth can help people prepare to be parents. The more a woman understands, the more comfortable she will be with the changes that are taking place in her body. The father can be a supportive partner.

The reproductive systems are among the most complex in the body. The purpose of these systems is to produce the male and female reproductive cells. The male cell is called the sperm and the female cells are called ova or eggs.

In the female, the ova are produced in the female sex glands called the ovaries. An ovary is one of two female sex glands. When the ova are released, they travel down the fallopian tubes. A fallopian tube is either of two tubes that carry the ova. The ova end up in the uterus, a hollow pouch inside the woman's lower abdomen. If they are not used for pregnancy, the ovum and other tissues move down the vagina, the passage from the uterus to the outside of the body. They are a part of the monthly flow of blood. This is called menstruation.

In males, the sperm are produced in the testicles. A testicle is one of two sex glands located inside the male's scrotum. The scrotum is the bag of skin that holds the testicles. The sperm is stored in fluid called semen in the prostate gland. Ejaculation is what happens when a male discharges semen from his body through his penis, the male sex organ.

A Healthy Pregnancy

Pregnancy begins with conception. **Conception** is the union of a sperm and egg. Each contains half the genetic material needed to create a new human being. During pregnancy, the cells divide, grow, and develop in the uterus. The developing child is called a fetus.

The **placenta** is the life-support system for a fetus during pregnancy. It connects the mother and baby. It does the work of the lungs, liver, and kidneys for the fetus. The umbilical cord connects the placenta to the baby. It brings nourishment from the mother's blood to the fetus. It carries wastes back to the placenta.

A woman who is healthy and physically fit before pregnancy will likely experience an easier **prenatal** period. This is the time from conception to birth. Her body will be able to nourish the baby. It will be able to cope with the stress of pregnancy and childbirth. Her baby will likely be healthier, too.

Good medical care during the prenatal period is vital to the health of mother and child. There are many problems that can occur with pregnancy. Good care cannot prevent all of them. It may help to find problems early so they can be treated.

In an ectopic pregnancy, the baby starts to grow in the fallopian tubes rather than the uterus. Ectopic pregnancies are dangerous for the mother. They do not end in a live birth. Toxemia is the presence of toxins, or poisons, in the mother's blood. It is linked to high blood pressure. The doctor will monitor blood pressure closely.

> **Learn Together**
> The more couples learn about their upcoming pregnancy, the more comfortable they will be with the changes that are occurring. *What are some ways couples can learn about pregnancy?*

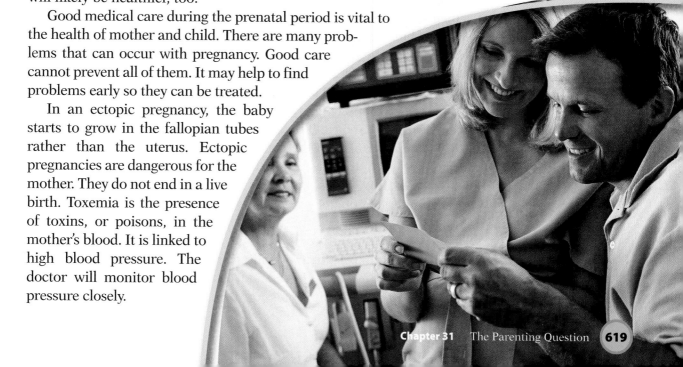

Tobacco, caffeine, and other drugs, including alcohol, are all potential dangers to a developing child. They can cause birth defects. A **birth defect** is a problem that happens while a baby is developing in the mother's body. Pregnant women should avoid substances that can be harmful to the child. Most birth defects happen during the first three months of pregnancy. A variety of tests are used to determine if a baby has a birth defect.

Pregnancy and Birth

A full-term pregnancy is 40 weeks. Infants born before the end of the 37th week are considered premature. Premature babies often have problems with breathing and eating. They may not yet be fully developed. Some babies are stillborn, which means they are not alive when they are born.

Pregnancy is broken into three time periods. Each one is called a **trimester**. Specific development in the fetus is seen in each period.

The first trimester is the most important. The baby's body structure and organ systems develop. A woman tends to feel the most discomfort at this time. She may have fatigue, nausea, and breast tenderness. Most miscarriages happen during this trimester. A **miscarriage** occurs when a fetus is born before it is able to live outside the mother's body. It can also be called a spontaneous abortion.

The second trimester tends to be easier on the mother. The fetus continues to develop. The first heartbeat is heard at around 12 weeks. The baby's first fluttering movements occur between 16 and 20 weeks.

The third trimester is the final stretch before birth. The baby's lungs develop and bones start to harden. The fetus packs on pounds. Movements become stronger. The mother may have symptoms such as shortness of breath, varicose veins, and sleeping problems. Most of these are due to the increase in the size of the uterus as the baby grows.

Labor is a series of contractions of the uterus. The contractions propel the baby out of the uterus. The baby goes into the vagina, then outside the mother's body. The placenta is pushed out of the body shortly after. Labor and delivery are hard work and uncomfortable. Many fathers are with the mother during this time. They may help the mother control the pain. She does this through relaxation and deep breathing. Decisions about pain medication are discussed by the mother and doctor prior to the birth.

Most new mothers have some postpartum symptoms. **Postpartum** is the period of time after the baby's birth. Between three and 14 days, many women have something called the baby blues. They may feel tense and anxious. They may feel sad and lack focus and energy. A few mothers develop postpartum depression after the birth of the baby.

Special Addition A new baby brings joy to the lives of his or her parents, along with a variety of issues to deal with. *What are some issues new parents must deal with during the first few weeks of a baby's life?*

Most couples find the first few weeks with a new baby a time of joy and fatigue. Babies eat often, so new parents do not get much sleep. At the same time, they are filled with love toward the tiny being that they made together.

✓ **Reading Check** **Define** What is a birth defect?

Resources for Parents

There are a great many resources that people can use to learn about parenthood. Courses on parenting and child development are a good place to start. You can find them at high schools or local colleges. Social and mental health agencies are other places to take classes. Religious groups and hospitals also offer them.

Many couples take childbirth classes during pregnancy. There, parents who are expecting learn what occurs during pregnancy and birth. They practice breathing and relaxation exercises. These will help ease the pain and stress of the birth process. Hospitals and clinics often offer these classes.

Many parents find their doctor is a good resource. Parenting books and magazines are others. Web sites of well-known parenting and child development groups may also be useful. The library or an Internet search will supply more references than you can read. You may choose to become a parent someday. These and many other resources can help you prepare for the job.

Section 31.2 After You Read

Review Key Concepts

1. **Explain** what is meant by parenting readiness.
2. **Describe** the importance of learning about reproduction and pregnancy.
3. **List** community groups that are likely to offer parenting courses.

Practice Academic Skills

English Language Arts

4. Anyone who is planning to marry and have children will benefit from knowing as much as possible about reproduction and pregnancy. Do research to learn more about some aspect of reproduction or pregnancy. Check your local library for information. You might also check with your doctor for any brochures or other information he or she might have available for patients. Write a report of your findings.

5. Research parenting classes that are offered in your community. First, make a list of the contact information for the classes, such as when and where they are offered. Then list the topics that are presented in these classes. Make an outline of the topics. Present your outline to the class.

NCTE 7 Conduct research and gather, evaluate, and synthesize data to communicate discoveries.

NCTE 12 Use language to accomplish individual purposes.

Check Your Answers Check your answers at this book's Online Learning Center through **glencoe.com**.

CAREER SPOTLIGHT

Preschool Teacher

Susan Goertzen
Leavenworth, Kansas

Preschool can be a scary time for children. It is often their first encounter with being away from home for a long period of time. It can also be an exciting experience. This is especially true when they get to spend the day with a preschool teacher who cares about them and creates a warm environment for them.

According to Susan Goertzen, you have to possess a real desire to be with children in order to thrive as a preschool teacher. "Having a love for children is the best advice I can give to prepare for this job," she says.

Goertzen spends her days doing more than just babysitting a group of children. She also gives the students skills to help them mature. Preschool is a place where key social and learning skills are formed. Her job involves creating activities that nurture those skills, and fostering a real love of learning.

Goertzen states, "I love watching the growth in the children over the year." She continues, "The look of excitement as they experience new things is so exciting."

CAREER FACTS

Education or Training Preschool teaching often involves on-the-job training, but degrees in education, child development, and child psychology are all useful.

Nature of the Work Preschool teachers work with young children, teaching them social and learning skills that they will need as they progress into the first grade.

Aptitudes, Abilities, and Skills This career requires patience, and a genuine love for children. Creativity is also important, as preschool teachers spend a great deal of time developing activities to keep the children interested and excited.

Academic Skills Required Develop strong skills across the board in all of the basics—English, math, communications, and science.

Student Organizations To prepare for this career, look for student organizations that foster involvement with and understanding of children, such as FCCLA.

Career Outlook Opportunities for this career will range from good to excellent.

Career Path Community childcare centers and Parents Day Out programs can be inroads to this career; a more conventional path involves getting a license from the State Board of Education and applying at a public or private school.

Critical Thinking

Enjoy Children Why do you think it is important to love children in order to do this career?

 Research Careers For more information on this and other careers, visit the Occupational Outlook Handbook Web site through the link on this book's Online Learning Center at **glencoe.com**.

CHAPTER SUMMARY

Section 31.1
Examine Parenting

The decision to choose parenting has a life-long impact on parents and children. There are pressures to have children and not to have children. There are many rewards of parenting, like love, affection, and joy given and received. Parents feel pride and satisfaction in helping a child grow and develop. Parenting also brings financial and personal costs. Some couples are infertile and may undergo treatments to have a child. People choose adoption for many reasons.

Section 31.2
Prepare for Parenthood

Parents need emotional maturity and financial readiness to prepare for parenthood. They should have realistic goals and expectations and be old enough to handle this new role. Parenthood affects the lives of the whole family. Experience with children helps people understand what skills are needed to raise a child. Learning about reproduction and pregnancy helps partners become comfortable with what is happening. There are a number of resources for parents.

Content and Academic Vocabulary Review

1. Use each of these content and academic vocabulary words in a sentence.

Content Vocabulary
- ◇ parenting (p. 607)
- ◇ genetic disease (p. 608)
- ◇ fertility (p. 611)
- ◇ infertility (p. 611)
- ◇ adoption (p. 611)
- ◇ parenting readiness (p. 615)
- ◇ child development (p. 618)
- ◇ conception (p. 619)
- ◇ placenta (p. 619)
- ◇ prenatal (p. 619)
- ◇ birth defect (p. 620)
- ◇ trimester (p. 620)
- ◇ miscarriage (p. 620)
- ◇ labor (p. 620)
- ◇ postpartum (p. 620)

Academic Vocabulary
- ■ forethought (p. 607)
- ■ biology (p. 607)
- ■ restriction (p. 616)
- ■ relate (p. 617)

Review Key Concepts

2. Identify why choosing parenthood is such an important decision.
3. Describe the rewards and challenges of parenting.
4. Explain reasons for adoption.
5. Determine factors that are involved in parenting readiness.
6. Suggest ways to prepare yourself for parenthood.
7. Summarize resources useful to parents.

Critical Thinking

8. Analyze Are parents who go through a lengthy adoption process or expensive medical treatments to have a child apt to be better parents? Why or why not?
9. Evaluate Having a child tends to strengthen a solid marriage. However, it weakens an already troubled one. Why do you think this is so?

Real-World Skills

Problem Solving Skills

10. Decision Making Tom and Kim's lawyer has an infant for them to adopt. However, the birth mother wants an open adoption. The couple is uneasy at having that much contact with the mother. They worry about her involvement in the future. In a paragraph, explain what Tom and Kim should do.

Self-Management Skills

11. Goals and Children Write down three short-term and three long-term goals that you have for yourself. Include the time by which you hope to reach them. Write a short essay describing how having a child now would affect whether you would reach those goals.

Technology Skills

12. Spreadsheet Use spreadsheet software to estimate and calculate costs, such as food and clothing, during a baby's first year. List these in the spreadsheet. Then find the costs for these items. Use the spreadsheet to help you calculate what the cost of these would be for a year. Total the year's costs.

Management Skills

13. Make a Plan At seventeen, Charlie left school to work full-time to help support his child. He is feeling alone. Make a plan that will help Charlie solve his problem. Write out all of Charlie's options. Then write a short summary explaining which options you think will work best.

14. Brainstorm Follow your teacher's instructions to form into groups. Develop a list of what actions and activities a woman can take to have a healthy pregnancy. Divide your list into two parts—what a woman can do before she becomes pregnant and what she can do while she is pregnant. Share your list with your classmates.

15. Community Opportunities Survey your community. Create a list of opportunities to work with young children. Arrange to take part in one that seems interesting to you. What did you learn about your readiness to be a parent? Write a one-page report about your experience.

16. Interview Talk to three people of various ages. Ask them about their feelings about children and parenting. Ask if their opinion has changed in the last five or ten years. If so, how? What happened to affect his or her thinking? Write a paper to summarize your findings.

17. Research Go to this book's Online Learning Center at **glencoe.com** to find **Web Links** for **Genetic Diseases**. Select a genetic disease. What progress has been made against the disease? What is the outlook for the near future? Write a summary of your findings.

Additional Activities For additional activities, go to this book's Online Learning Center through **glencoe.com**.

Academic Skills

Mathematics

18. Calculate the Cost of Giving Birth to a Child Talk to someone you know who has children and do research to find the average cost of giving birth. Present your data in a table.

Math Concept **Present Data in a Table** Create a three-column table in which to present your data. The first column should list different costs such as medical visits, hospital costs, and so on. In the second column, list the costs you get from talking with someone with a child. In the third column, list the costs you find during your research. Add the items in the second column and the items in the third column and compare the answers.

Starting Hint: Give your table a title, and label each column so that anyone who looks at your data will know what it represents.

 For math help, go to the Math Appendix at the back of the book.

> **NCTM Data Analysis and Probability** Formulate questions that can be addressed with data and collect, organize, and display relevant data to answer them.

English Language Arts

19. Research Gather information about the different types of medical procedures used to help infertile couples. What is involved? What is the success rate? What are the costs involved? Are there negative consequences to receiving these treatments? If so, what are they? Report your findings to the class.

> **NCTE 8** Use information resources to gather information and create and communicate knowledge.

Social Studies

20. International Adoptions Investigate adoptions from other countries. What is the current status of these adoptions? What countries allow them? What rules govern them? What are some of the advantages of these adoptions? What are some risks? How does the culture of the various countries affect their view of international adoption? Write your findings in a report.

> **NCSS IV.e** Examine the interaction of ethnic, national, or cultural influences in specific situations or events.

STANDARDIZED TEST PRACTICE

TRUE/FALSE
Carefully read each question. Pay attention to any key words.

21. Decide if the following statements are true or false.

Test-Taking Tip In a true/false test, be sure to budget your time. Go through the test items. Answer those you know first. As time allows, reread the items you are not sure about and try to answer them. Often, your first impulse is the correct one.

a. Family members often put pressure on a young couple to have children.

b. Learning about children before becoming a parent does not help when you have your own children.

c. There is no test to help people determine whether they are ready to be parents.

CHAPTER 32

Skillful Parenting

Section 32.1

Promote Children's Development

Section 32.2

Guide Children's Behavior

▶▶ *Explore the Photo*
Parents have the responsibility to help their children develop good behavior. *How do parents who spend time playing with their children teach them acceptable behavior?*

Chapter Objectives

After completing this chapter, you will be able to:

- **Explain** why parenting is most effective when it is a partnership.
- **Identify** specific ways to promote well-rounded development in children.
- **Describe** three basic parenting styles.
- **List** parenting skills needed to successfully discipline a child.
- **Suggest** four principles that help parents teach good behavior.

Writing Activity

Dialogue

Patience Patience is the ability to tolerate things that do not go as you want them to. Patient people are willing to move slowly toward goals. You can show patience when you:

- Make encouraging remarks to younger siblings.
- Read a younger sibling a favorite story over and over.
- Pass the time with conversation while waiting in a busy restaurant.
- Explain a math problem in careful detail to a classmate who needs help understanding.

Write a dialogue between a parent and child that illustrates how a parent can show patience.

Writing Tips To write an effective dialogue, follow these steps:

1. Let the parent and child speak for themselves.
2. Use dialogue for a purpose.
3. Use language that sounds real and age appropriate to the people talking.
4. Use quotation marks appropriately.

Promote Children's Development

Reading Guide

Before You Read

Be Organized A messy environment can be distracting. To lessen distractions, organize an area where you can read this section comfortably.

Read to Learn
Key Concepts
- **Explain** why parenting is most effective when it is a partnership.
- **Identify** specific ways to promote well-rounded development in children.

Main Idea
Parenting is best for adults and children when it is a partnership. Parents need to promote the areas of child development.

Content Vocabulary
◇ motor skill ◇ latch-key child
◇ monitor

 Graphic Organizer Go to this book's Online Learning Center at **glencoe.com** to print out this graphic organizer.

Academic Vocabulary
You will find these words in your reading and on your tests. Use the glossary to look up their definitions if necessary.
■ stimulation ■ quirk

Graphic Organizer
As you read, look for what children need to develop. Use a concept map like the one shown to help organize your information.

Developmental Area		Needs
1. Physical	→	
2. Social	→	
3. Intellectual	→	
4. Emotional	→	
5. Moral	→	

Academic Standards • • • • • • • • • • • • •

English Language Arts
NCTE 4 Use written language to communicate effectively.

NCTE 9 Develop an understanding of diversity in language use across cultures.

Mathematics
NCTM Problem Solving Solve problems that arise in mathematics and in other contexts.

NCTE *National Council of Teachers of English*
NCTM *National Council of Teachers of Mathematics*

NSES *National Science Education Standards*
NCSS *National Council of the Social Studies*

Parenthood as Partnership

Deciding to have a child is only your first parenting decision. It opens the gate to countless others. By becoming a parent, you agree to think for at least two people—yourself and your child. Children are born with minds of their own and the will to use them. However, making choices that keep them safe and healthy is the parent's job.

Have you ever thought of everything a parent is to a child? A parent is a provider, protector, teacher, nurse, chef, chauffeur, and more. Mothers have traditionally had the main role in raising children. Today, fathers are more involved in child rearing than they have been in the past. Parents work to be sure that all of the needs of their children are met.

With both mother and father present, parenting duties can be shared. The benefits go beyond having help with the cooking or laundry. Children have needs not easily met by one parent alone. Mothers and fathers are both important. Each parent responds differently. Each offers special strengths that complement the other. They also bring different personal interests, skills, and traits.

Whether parents live together or apart, they can provide support for their children. A stable relationship between parents is good for children. Children benefit when both parents are involved in their lives. It helps in all areas of child development.

Parents need to support their children financially. Children who live with single parents are more likely to have needs that are not met than those who live with both parents. Parents who do not live with their children can help by making regular child support payments.

Other family types may provide ways to share parenting. Extended families may have one or more grandparents. They often want to help care for children. Children in blended families may have stepparents who assist in their care. Foster parents serve in the role of parents while foster children live with them. Whoever fills the parent role is responsible for promoting the development of the children in their care.

✓ **Reading Check** **List** What are some of the roles that parents fulfill for their children?

Well-Rounded Development

The first three years of life are among the most important in the development of a child. A newborn's brain contains about 100 billion brain cells. These are not yet connected to each other. During the first three years of life, the brain forms connections between these cells. The more connections that are made, the better the brain functions.

As You Read

Connect What needs does a father fill in sharing parenting duties?

Parents Work Together Both parents can provide help in raising their children because they offer different things to the children. *What are the benefits of having both parents raise their children?*

Scientists have studied babies' lives. They looked at whether the babies seemed happy, heard lots of music or speech, and received hugs. What they found was that experience itself changed the physical development of the brain. The connections in the brain increased with more experiences. These are the connections that promote thought, emotions, and movement.

In order to promote brain development, children need to be exposed to a variety of experiences. Young children's brains are open to learning and enrichment. Infants prefer human contact to other kinds of stimulation. They respond to faces and voices. They need to be touched, held, comforted, rocked, and sung to. Talking and listening to children are the best ways to make the most of their critical brain-building years.

Toddlers need the **stimulation**, or excitement, of the outside world. They respond to sights, sounds, tastes, textures, movement, and touch. Toddlers enjoy nature, colors, music, and outdoor play. Indoors they can work simple puzzles, build block towers, and look at sturdy books. Trips to the grocery store, library, and parks build the brain in a variety of ways. Children need two loving, involved parents. They help them develop to their fullest in all areas, which is to become well-rounded. This includes physically, socially, mentally, emotionally, and morally.

Vocabulary

You can find definitions in the glossary at the back of this book.

Financial Literacy

Baby Food Costs

Ron and Stacy have been paying an average of $0.23 per ounce for name-brand baby food for their son Tyler. They usually purchase 200 ounces of baby food at a time. They have found that they can make their own baby food. It contains the same nutritional value for about $0.08 per ounce. How much will they save on 200 ounces of baby food by making their own?

Math Concept **Multiple-Step Problems** Solving some word problems requires more than one step. Read carefully so you can represent the problem in mathematical terms.

Starting Hint: First, calculate how much is spent on 200 ounces of brand-name baby food (200 × $0.23). Then calculate how much is spent on homemade baby food (200 × $0.08). Then subtract the smaller number from the larger numbe r.

Math For math help, go to the Math Appendix at the back of the book.

NCTM Problem Solving Solve problems that arise in mathematics and in other contexts.

Physical Development

A pregnant woman cares for herself physically in order to have a healthy baby. This concern for good health continues as a child grows. Parents see that children are properly fed and clothed. They encourage play as well as rest. Parents protect children from harm. Through physical care, children first become aware of their parents' love for them.

Nutrition

Parents have the responsibility to serve healthful, balanced meals. Children need nourishing foods to help them build strong, healthy bodies. To provide children with a good diet, you must know about their nutritional needs and eating habits. For example, small children have small stomachs. They frequently cannot eat enough at one meal to last them until the next. Therefore, parents must be ready with wholesome snacks, such as fresh or dried fruit, milk, or small pieces of cheese. Some children are picky eaters. It is important for parents to have a positive attitude toward all foods so that children have an open mind about trying different kinds of food, too.

Also, foods must be prepared so children can eat them safely and willingly. Pieces of food should be cut into small enough pieces that a child will not choke.

Some children develop irrational behaviors about eating, such as refusing to eat certain foods or foods that touched other foods on the plate. Skilled parents know how to satisfy a **quirk**, or an oddity, such as this without helping a child to develop a habit of being a picky eater. If parents take a healthy attitude toward eating, children are much more likely to also develop healthy eating habits.

Clothing

Protection from the weather is not a parent's only concern. Clothing must be durable and safe for an active child. Garments should be designed so that they allow freedom of movement. However, large or baggy clothes can interfere with play. They can catch on play equipment or cause a child to trip and fall.

When children have suitable clothing they are more able to learn to dress themselves. Parents look for clothes with elastic waistbands, snap closures, and hook-and-loop fasteners. These and other features help children dress themselves. Doing this task promotes competence and independence. The pride that children feel aids their emotional development.

Exercise

Exercise is important to children's physical and mental health. Physical activity lets children release pent-up energy. With exercise, children develop strong bones, muscles, and motor skills. A **motor skill** is the ability that depends on the use and control of muscles. This includes those in the arms, legs, hands, and feet. Picking a flower, throwing a ball, and riding a scooter are all activities that require motor skills.

Rest

A child's active, growing body needs plenty of rest to rebuild energy supplies. Tired children often do not learn well. They are more prone to illness and irritability. Parents need to make sure that children have regular opportunities to rest and nap through the day. They can teach good sleep habits by enforcing scheduled bedtimes. They can use calming techniques to help children get to sleep—and get back to sleep—on their own.

Medical Care

Concerned parents make sure children receive good medical care. This begins before birth and goes throughout childhood. Dental care begins as soon as a child has teeth. Regular physical and dental checkups help ensure that children are growing as they should. If parents make regular medical care a priority, problems can be detected early, improving the chances for a good outcome.

 Exercise Is Play Parents can show children that exercise can be fun. *How can a child benefit from regularly choosing to exercise?*

Parents also seek prompt medical help when a child is ill or injured. Infants and children need a series of vaccinations to protect them from diseases such as polio, measles, and mumps. Health insurance is a priority for parents. When needed, public health clinics offer medical services to families who cannot afford to pay for them.

A Safe Environment

Childproofing a home is one way that parents create a safe environment for children. No home can be made safe enough for an unsupervised child, however. Children are impulsive. They do not know what hazards their actions may bring. Covering unused electrical outlets with plastic plugs, putting locks on cabinets, using gates to close access to open stairways, and keeping dangerous household items out of reach are some of the precautions parents can take.

Children need monitoring. To **monitor** is to keep close watch over. Young children need constant watching. Three-year-olds are eager to test their physical skills. They can easily climb from a chair onto a counter and just as easily fall and get hurt.

Children need less watching over as they build their thinking skills. Parents prepare them to look out for their own safety. A skillful parent teaches a child to avoid dangerous substances and situations. Parents and children can practice ways to respond to emergencies.

Monitoring should not end entirely until children reach maturity. Even in the teen years, parents need to know where their children are. They need to know what they are doing. Teens who are monitored have lower rates of drug and alcohol abuse. They are also less likely to run away or break the law.

Self-Care

Parents help children gradually take over some of their own physical care. When children are old enough, parents show them how to do things such as brushing and flossing their teeth and gums. They teach children to wash their hands before eating. A well-cared-for child acquires healthy habits and a sense of independence.

Monitors for Safety Parents need to carefully monitor their children. *Why is it critical to be most concerned with the safety of very young children?*

Crying is the way babies communicate. A young baby who is crying needs your attention. Check first for any physical problem. Is it time for a feeding? Is the baby too hot or too cold? Does the baby need a diaper change? Perhaps the baby needs to burp.

You could try holding the baby close and rocking. You might walk around as you cuddle the baby. Talking softly and singing to the baby may help. The baby may be hungry or thirsty. Simply changing a baby's position can sometimes bring relief. You could use a toy to distract the baby.

A pacifier may comfort the infant. Older babies may need a special blanket or stuffed toy that they are used to having with them.

Problem-Solving

Trent was watching his sister's baby, Nona. When Nona woke up from her nap, she was screaming loudly. Trent changed her diaper and wrapped her in a warm blanket. He warmed a bottle but Nona refused to take it. The screaming started to bother Trent. What should he do?

A **latch-key child** is a child who is home alone after school. These children need to develop basic skills in caring for themselves. Safety is a main concern. Latch-key children learn to be self-reliant and independent. However, they are often lonely, bored, or afraid. Parents usually monitor latch-key children from work by phone, e-mail, or instant messages.

Social Development

Social development begins at birth, as infants are held, fed, and soothed by a calm voice. When babies are treated with care and concern, babies begin to develop socially. Babies thrive on the love and attention they receive from parents and others.

Show Affection

Showing babies affection does not spoil them. By two or three months of age, they show how much they enjoy attention. They coo, gurgle, and smile in return. Games of peek-a-boo and pat-a-cake also help social growth. Good social development can occur when there is positive contact between parents and child. Talking to children promotes social development. Children come to enjoy people and learn to laugh and have fun. Communication is an important skill for building relationships at any age.

As children grow, parents' expectations and attitudes remain a chief influence on social growth. A parent's smile or praise encourages children to repeat good behaviors. A frown or scolding discourages other actions. In this way, children learn how to act. This prepares them to get along with others.

All the positive exchanges that take place in the family are good for social development. Children learn relationship skills by observing the people around them. They learn by interacting with parents, other family members, and other adults. They will use these relationship skills throughout their lives. This aids them in building strong relationships.

Intellectual Development

There has been much research on how children learn, but many questions remain. Babies come into the world knowing nothing. Parents have a big responsibility to spur and guide learning so babies can reach their greatest potential.

Learning Experiences

Learning experiences fuel mental growth. By knowing how children learn, parents can provide activities to suit their child at each age. **Figure 32.1** outlines some of the ways small children learn.

Senses and Actions Young children learn through their senses and actions. They discover how things work with hands-on exploration and play. Thus, parents promote learning by exposing children to the sensory experiences the world offers. Sensory experiences include bright colors, a range of sounds, and intriguing smells and textures. Both active and quiet play help children learn.

Outings Children draw upon experiences to form ideas about the world. Outings to museums, zoos, parks, band concerts, and fairs are fun, and they can also help children learn about the world. They give children a greater understanding of the people, jobs, and events that make up their world.

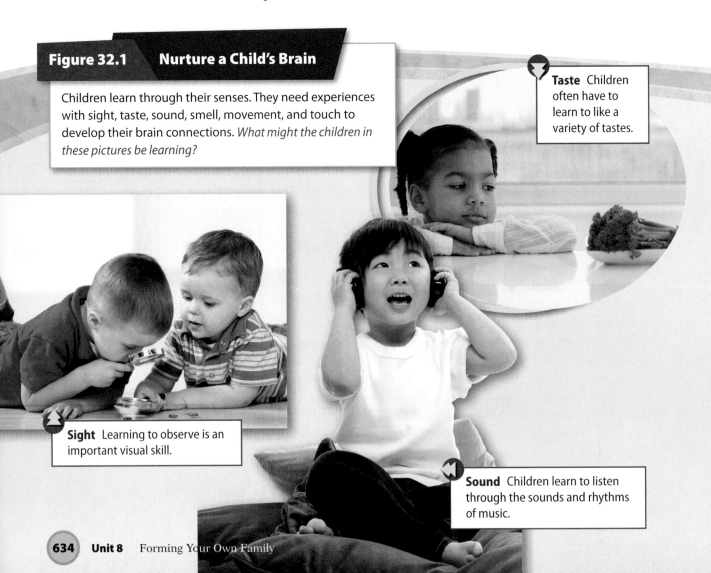

| Figure 32.1 | Nurture a Child's Brain |

Children learn through their senses. They need experiences with sight, taste, sound, smell, movement, and touch to develop their brain connections. *What might the children in these pictures be learning?*

Taste Children often have to learn to like a variety of tastes.

Sight Learning to observe is an important visual skill.

Sound Children learn to listen through the sounds and rhythms of music.

Logical Thinking At around age seven, children begin to think logically. This means that they are able to sort objects into broad categories. They still learn best through direct experience, however. Handling and sorting objects such as trading cards and shells strengthens children's ability to compare and contrast.

Abstract Thinking At age 11 or 12, most children begin to think in an abstract way. Thinking abstractly means that they use their imagination to predict what may happen in the future. They begin to see causes for events and experiences that have happened in the past. This allows children to solve some problems with thought alone.

Parents can teach by tailoring lessons to their child's gradually developing thinking skills. For example, Bree knew that warning about burns would not keep her two-year-old son, Kurt, from touching a hot oven. Instead, she taught him about temperature while washing his hands. As they held their hands under the running water, Bree noted, "This water is cold. Now it is getting warm. Now it is getting hot. Ouch!" When Kurt learned that hot was unpleasant, he stayed away from the hot stove. He also learned what ouch means and avoided all things labeled ouch, such as kitchen knives.

Language Development

Using language opens up new worlds for children. Throughout life, verbal skills are vital for sharing ideas. All types of growth and development are enhanced when a child can communicate with words.

Movement Children love physical activities such as dance, running, and climbing. They learn control of their bodies as they move.

Smell The world is full of smells that children can discover.

Touch Children learn about their world through touch.

Parents nurture language development from the day a child is born. Jorge's parents talked to him all the time when he was a baby. They named everyday items: crib, chair, banana, and blocks. Jorge loved their silly songs and rhymes that made language fun. All the while Jorge was learning the rules of language. As he developed speech skills, Jorge became an avid talker. He knew and could use several thousand words. If he did not always use them properly, his parents did not correct him. They simply modeled proper usage until Jorge caught on.

It is important that parents listen to children when children are talking to them. Children know when an adult is not listening. Full attention when listening gives children the message that they are important to you. It helps them develop their language skills.

When talking to children about their behavior, use I-messages. This can help you to avoid negative communications like blame and anger. Express your feelings about the child's actions but do not attack the child's character. Get down to the child's level so you can talk eye to eye.

Emotional Development

An important part of emotional development is the bond between parents and children. Parents need to appreciate the special qualities of each child. Children thrive when they are loved and nurtured. They need a loving, caring relationship with both parents.

A growing child experiences a growing range of emotions. These can be both positive and negative. Part of guiding emotional growth is helping children identify these feelings. Helping them express them acceptably is also important.

Children must learn how to handle negative emotions. Beginning around age two, parents set rules about negative actions. A parent may tell a five-year-old, "I know you are angry because you cannot go to the park, but screaming is not allowed. You can punch a pillow or run in the yard. I like to run when I am angry."

Accepting negative emotions is one way to help children feel emotionally secure. Children see that they are loved unconditionally. Unconditional love means being loved despite any problems. It is essential to healthy emotional development. Children who doubt their parents' love will grow up doubting themselves. They may fear losing that love by not living up to certain expectations. This can greatly undermine a child's sense of self-esteem and confidence.

Emotional Support Children will feel secure when parents teach them how to deal with their emotions. *Why is it important for parents to teach children how to deal with their emotions?*

Parents help build a child's self-concept by giving love, attention, and encouragement. They should offer the child many chances to succeed. They should encourage the child to pursue different activities based on the child's talents and interests. Parents should recognize and praise a child's achievements. Sincere praise builds self-esteem. It encourages children to take on new tasks and challenges.

Sometimes children have trouble learning a skill. Parents need to model persistence by not letting children give up. Leigh's six-year-old son Jacob struggled with handwriting. She told him, "I know this is not easy for you. Some things are hard to learn, but just because something is hard is no reason to give up. I know you can do this." Leigh praised every improvement she noticed. With Leigh's support, Jacob learned to handwrite and he also learned that overcoming difficulty is part of life.

Helping children learn mental skills needed for independence also promotes feelings of competence. Parents can strengthen decision-making skills by giving children some choices. They could choose what to wear or what activities to try. Some parents give children small allowances and allow the children to handle their own money. This teaches them to weigh options and manage resources. It is also provides a great opportunity to teach the importance of saving, consumer skills, and financial literacy skills. Parents must be sure that everyone can live with the outcome if the child makes a bad choice. This, too, is part of independence.

Encourage Good Behavior Parents set examples for their children by showing them how to be kind and caring. *How can parents model what is right and wrong?*

Moral Development

Through moral development, parents work to build character in their children. Infants and young children do not know right and wrong. They look to parents to tell them whether actions are good or bad. As children learn to relate to others, moral development takes on a strong social element. Parents can encourage children to act with kindness and caring and to have empathy toward other people. They can model other positive social behaviors like volunteering and community service. Children see the benefits of this behavior. Then they are more likely to accept kindness and caring as values worth having.

Parents need to guide moral growth by fitting their standards to a child's abilities. They might expect truthfulness from a six-year-old who has begun to develop a conscience. At the same time, they know that young children this age are very fanciful. Sometimes they do not fully understand the difference between fact and fiction. A child may need help in separating fantasy from reality, and may not always deserve punishment for lying.

Children with Special Needs

Some children face added challenges in development. They may have physical impairments. They may have emotional problems. They may also have learning disabilities. They must work harder to master physical or mental skills. Children with special needs have the same basic needs as other children. They require extra help to reach their fullest potential.

Parents of children with special needs require the same skills as other parents. However, parenting a child with special needs may demand more time, energy, and patience. Parents may have to work closely with doctors, therapists, and educators to plan and carry out specific goals for the child. A child with special needs may not be independent as soon as other children.

Families with members who have special needs are more likely to face financial challenges. There may be costs for equipment and supplies. Money for counseling or training may be required. Parents may need the help of a financial professional to achieve their financial goals.

Time is another resource that may take special management. Children with special needs may require more care. Caregivers may need help from others to manage. If the family cannot afford to hire help from professional caregiving agencies, family members will need to help. Raising a child with special needs can take extra effort. Frequently, however, even though the demands on parents' time are great, so are the rewards.

Section 32.1 After You Read

Review Key Concepts

1. **Explain** why child support payments are important when children live with a single parent.
2. **Identify** the kind of skills that are developed through exercise and other physical activities.

Practice Academic Skills

English Language Arts

3. Investigate what children call their mothers in other countries around the world. Make a list of the country name and the term children call their mothers. How are these terms similar or different? What are mothers called in your region of the country? Summarize your answers in a coherent paragraph.

> **NCTE 9** Develop an understanding of diversity in language use across cultures.

4. Look at a catalog of children's clothing. Select an outfit for a three- to five-year-old child that would allow the child to self-dress. Be sure to include a top, pants or skirt, shoes, and socks. Write a paragraph explaining what features led to your selection of those items of clothing.

> **NCTE 4** Use written language to communicate effectively.

Check Your Answers Check your answers at this book's Online Learning Center through **glencoe.com**.

Guide Children's Behavior

Reading Guide

Before You Read

Use Diagrams Write down the title of the section. This is the main idea. Start at the section title and draw arrows to the headers or subtitles that directly support the main idea.

Read to Learn

Key Concepts

- **Describe** three basic parenting styles.
- **List** parenting skills needed to successfully discipline a child.
- **Suggest** four principles that help parents teach good behavior.

Main Idea

There are three main parenting styles. Parents discipline a child when they encourage good behavior, set and enforce limits, and deal with misbehavior. Parents need to take action to develop good behavior in their children.

Content Vocabulary

◇ authoritarian style
◇ authoritative style
◇ permissive style
◇ discipline
◇ positive reinforcement
◇ time-out

Academic Vocabulary

You will find these words in your reading and on your tests. Use the glossary to look up their definitions if necessary.

■ chagrin　　　■ privilege

Graphic Organizer

As you read, look for three skills parents need to successfully discipline children. Use a concept map like the one shown to help organize your information.

Skills for Successful Discipline

Graphic Organizer Go to this book's Online Learning Center at **glencoe.com** to print out this graphic organizer.

Academic Standards ● ● ● ● ● ● ● ● ● ● ● ● ● ● ● ● ●

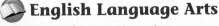

English Language Arts

NCTE 3 Apply strategies to interpret texts.

NCTE 12 Use language to accomplish individual purposes.

NCTE *National Council of Teachers of English*
NCTM *National Council of Teachers of Mathematics*

NSES *National Science Education Standards*
NCSS *National Council of the Social Studies*

Parenting Styles

As You Read

Connect What parenting styles are used in your household?

Vocabulary

You can find definitions in the glossary at the back of this book.

A parenting style is a pattern of relating to children. It reflects a person's idea of what the parent-child relationship should be. Parenting style is shaped by personality. It is also shaped by childhood experiences. It reflects a person's basic attitude toward children and beliefs on how children should be raised. Society also influences parenting styles. There are three basic styles of parenting:

- The **authoritarian style** is a parenting style in which parents expect children to trust and obey without question. Rules and goals are clearly and firmly stated. There is often little discussion. Failure to follow the rules is dealt with swiftly and firmly.
- The **authoritative style** is a parenting style in which parents consider a child's desires, abilities, and ideas. The authoritative style has much more flexibility than in the authoritarian style. Children are given a certain amount of freedom. They are allowed to make some decisions within set limits. When parents make rules or choices, they often give children reasons for the rules and choices that they make.

INDEPENDENT Living

HOW TO Be a Positive Example

You can have a positive influence on the development of children. When you set a good example it benefits them and you. Setting a positive example is good practice for when you start your own family as an adult. Follow these guidelines to set a positive example:

1. **Be consistent.** As often as possible, make your words match your actions and your actions match your values. When a person says one thing and does another, children can become confused and lose confidence in the person.
2. **Give reasons for your actions.** Examples are the most effective when a child connects your behavior to your values. Enforcing a bedtime may seem unfair to a child. You may need to explain that sleep is important to a child's physical and mental development.
3. **Admit your mistakes.** Children do not trust people who claim to never make mistakes. Let children know that you sometimes fall short, just like they do. This shows them that they do not have to be perfect to do well.
4. **Point to other role models.** Tell children why you admire your role models. Perhaps a parent taught you the importance of honesty and work ethic.
5. **Respect their limitations.** Expect no more than children are capable of. To a five-year-old, that may mean parting with one toy. As the child grows socially and emotionally, so will the ability to share.

Take Action For the next three weeks, make an effort to set a good example in situations where children are present. Write an essay to describe the effect on your actions. How did your actions affect your feelings about yourself?

- The **permissive style** is a parenting style in which parents use minimal authority. They provide limited structure. Children are allowed to set many of their own goals, rules, and limits. They may act within broad guidelines. They must be willing to accept the outcomes of their choices.

Skillful parenting often involves using all of the parenting styles. What works in one setting may not work in another. Any one style or combination of styles may be used. It is important that parents provide love, attention, security, and support no matter what parenting style they use.

There have been changes in the style of parenting over the years. Traditionally, parents have tended to be authoritarian. This has slowly changed and families have moved to the authoritative style. This style tends to have the best outcomes for children. Children raised in an authoritative style have good social skills. They show lower levels of problem behavior. This tends to make them good citizens in their schools and communities.

▲ **Parenting Style** The way a parent guides a child's behavior shows his or her parenting style. *In what ways can this parent display the three parenting styles while they make cookies?*

✓ **Reading Check** **Describe** How does a parent develop a parenting style?

Discipline

Discipline is the process of helping children learn to behave in acceptable ways. It helps children live up to what the family and society expect. It builds character. Discipline helps children learn to control their own behavior. This is called self-discipline.

Many people confuse discipline with punishment. In fact, punishment is only a small part of discipline. It should be used only when necessary. Discipline is more accurately called guidance.

In one study, parents said that of all their parenting skills, they had the least belief in their ability to discipline their children. It is not easy to shape a child's behavior. Learning some basic guidelines is a first step. The way a parent approaches discipline is closely linked to parenting style.

Effective guidance is a balance of three parenting skills. Parents need to encourage good behavior. They need to set and enforce limits. They need to deal with misbehavior.

Encourage Good Behavior

One of the best ways to encourage good behavior is to set a good example. Much of a child's learning comes from watching others. Children are great imitators. They adopt many of the beliefs and behavior patterns they see around them.

Parents should remember that children watch closely. For example, Chen did not go to school one morning, telling his father it was a teacher in-service day. When his father learned the truth, he grounded Chen for the weekend. He then called the school secretary and explained that Chen was home with a fever. What example did Chen's father set for his son?

Positive reinforcement is something that acts to encourage a specific behavior. Praising positive behavior is one way to help a child want to do it again. The following are examples of using guidelines or praise as positive reinforcement:

- **Be specific.** Saying, "You did a good job picking up the toys," is more helpful than just saying, "You are a good boy." Children who understand the specific action that was good are more likely to repeat it even without praise.
- **Be sincere and positive.** Give praise only when it is earned. Children know when praise is not deserved.
- **Give praise as soon as possible.** Children need to hear praise right away to associate the praise with the action or behavior.

▼ Rules and Limits Parents have valid reasons to set and enforce limits. *What do you think are this parent's reasons?*

Set and Enforce Limits

Parents set limits to tell children what is acceptable, appropriate, and safe. Limits may be physical, such as permitting a child to play only in the yard. There may be rules for behavior, such as throwing a baseball outside only. Useful limits are simple and clearly stated. They are reasonable and suitable for the child's age. They address situations that the child will face in daily life. Rules are most effective when they stress what children should do rather than what they should not do.

As children grow older, they often need fewer limits. They may earn this freedom by being responsible. Children who follow the rules are more likely to be rewarded with more freedom. Parents should revise rules and limits as necessary, based on the actions of their children. Needless or unfair rules can create feelings of resentment and anger in children.

Misbehavior

All problems are not prevented by promoting good behavior and setting limits. Everyone behaves poorly at times. Responses should be based on the misbehavior and the child.

Sometimes children will behave badly. They may want attention. Do not dwell on harmless misbehavior. A warning may be enough to remind a child about appropriate behavior.

In some cases, you can let children experience the consequences of their behaviors. A consequence is something that follows from an action. Deron dawdled while getting ready for school. He was not completely dressed when the school bus came. Deron rode to school still wearing his pajama top, with his shirt in his backpack. His **chagrin**, or embarrassment, was the consequence of his actions.

A young child may be given a time-out. During a **time-out**, the child is removed from the presence of others or from the activity for a short time. This gives children a chance to regain self-control.

Taking away a **privilege**, or a right, can also be an effective discipline technique. This works best when the privilege removed is related to the misbehavior. Older children can better make the connection between the action and outcome. Suppose a child left a bike out overnight after repeated reminders to bring it in. The privilege of riding the bike might be denied for a while to teach the value of following the rules.

Punishment should match the offense. A parent may need to cool off to avoid overreacting. When her son was late arriving home, Penny grounded him for a month. Within a few days, she realized that the punishment was too severe and reduced it. She will think before she speaks in the future so that her son will take her seriously.

Using more than one method often works best. The Kipps were trying to teach two-year-old Shawna to share. They pointed out how they shared things and talked about how good it felt. When Shawna grabbed toys from her playmates, they gave her a short time-out. They praised her when they noticed Shawna sharing with others.

Experts vary in their opinions on spanking. Some feel strongly that spanking does not help children learn good behavior. It teaches that hitting is acceptable. Others believe that using an open hand to strike a child's bottom without causing physical injury is sometimes okay. Getting the attention of a child who is out of control is an example. Most experts agree that spanking should not be done too hard or too often. Parents should never use spanking to vent their anger.

Deal with Misconduct When parents discipline with loving support, children can thrive. *How can parents deal with misbehavior in constructive ways?*

✓ **Reading Check** **Explain** What is the purpose of limits?

Take Action

Advice on guidance may seem overwhelming, but doing nothing is a poor option. Parents may not discipline perfectly. Still, a confident and loving approach is needed. These basics can help parents teach good behavior:

- **Start early.** Good habits are easier to instill when children are very young. If poor behavior is ignored in a young child, it may become harder to change when the child is older.
- **Be consistent.** Parents need to decide what is and is not appropriate. Then they should respond in a similar way each time the action occurs. Children should know whether an action will bring positive or negative outcomes.
- **Present a united front.** Parents need to agree on rules, limits, and techniques. If they do not, approaches may be confusing or not consistent. Children are more likely to misbehave when they know that parents disagree on basic points of discipline.
- **Follow through.** Warnings mean nothing unless misbehavior is met with action. For instance, telling a child not to pick the flowers is pointless if there is no consequence for disobeying.

Family life is much more enjoyable when behavior is under control. You may someday choose to have children. You will do a better job of parenting if you prepare now with guidance techniques.

Section 32.2   After You Read

Review Key Concepts

1. **Compare and Contrast** how decision making is handled in the three basic parenting styles.
2. **Identify** what positive reinforcement is.
3. **Describe** why good habits are easier to instill when children are young.

Practice Academic Skills
English Language Arts

4. Suppose a parent tells a child, "Come in before it gets late," or "You can stay out for a little while longer." Is this limit effectively stated? Why or why not? What may the child not understand? Is a specific time given? How would you restate the limit?

> **NCTE 12** Use language to accomplish individual purposes.

5. Locate a magazine or newspaper article about child guidance. Write a summary and a personal analysis of the article. In your summary, list the main points of the article and some supporting details or examples. In your analysis, state whether you agree or disagree with the article and explain why.

> **NCTE 3** Apply strategies to interpret texts.

Check Your Answers Check your answers at this book's Online Learning Center through **glencoe.com**.

CHAPTER SUMMARY

Section 32.1
Promote Children's Development

Parenting works best when it is a partnership between parents. Children need healthy, balanced meals, suitable clothing, exercise, and rest. Medical care helps keep them healthy. The environment should be safe for them. Children can learn self-care. Children need to develop socially. Intellectual development requires many learning experiences. Good language skills are also needed. Children also develop emotionally and morally. Children with special needs require more time and attention from parents.

Section 32.2
Guide Children's Behavior

The three basic styles of parenting are authoritarian, authoritative, and permissive. Discipline is guiding children to good behavior. It is different from punishment. Parents promote good behavior by setting good examples and giving positive support. Children need to know what behavior is safe, appropriate, and acceptable. Children may need to experience the result of poor choices. Time-outs are another way to deal with bad behavior. So is taking away privileges. Parents should start guiding children when they are young and be consistent in their actions.

Content and Academic Vocabulary Review

1. Use each of these content and academic vocabulary words in a sentence.

Content Vocabulary
- ◇ motor skill (p. 631)
- ◇ monitor (p. 632)
- ◇ latch-key child (p. 633)
- ◇ authoritarian style (p. 640)
- ◇ authoritative style (p. 640)
- ◇ permissive style (p. 641)
- ◇ discipline (p. 641)
- ◇ positive reinforcement (p. 642)
- ◇ time-out (p. 643)

Academic Vocabulary
- ■ stimulation (p. 630)
- ■ quirk (p. 631)
- ■ chagrin (p. 643)
- ■ privilege (p. 643)

Review Key Concepts

2. Explain why parenting is most effective when it is a partnership.

3. Identify specific ways to promote well-rounded development in children.

4. Describe three basic parenting styles.

5. List parenting skills needed to successfully discipline a child.

6. Suggest four principles that help parents teach good behavior.

Critical Thinking

7. Predict Children need self-esteem. They also must learn that the world does not revolve around only them. How can parents instill a balance between these perspectives?

8. Evaluate The members of a family agree to eat dinner together every night. Do you think this will help promote the development of the child or children in the family? In what ways?

9. Analyze Some parents threaten consequences that they cannot or will not carry out. Name two examples of this situation. What problems may result from this?

Real-World Skills

Interpersonal Skills

10. Make a Plan Lourdes is concerned about her four-year-old son, Elias. He is shy and clings to her when he is around other children. Lourdes knows that Elias will need to be comfortable with his peers when he starts school. Write a letter to Lourdes about what she should do.

Management Skills

11. Safety Check Suppose that you are the parent of a child just learning to walk. Develop a safety checklist for each room in the house. You could include the kitchen, bathroom, bedrooms, and the general living area. If possible, use your checklists to evaluate a real home. Share your evaluation with classmates.

Technology Skills

12. Healthy Snacks Imagine that you are teaching a class on parenting. You want to give your students a brochure about healthy snacks for small children. Identify some healthy snacks. Use a software program to create a brochure with this information and present it to your class.

Communication Skills

13. Problem Solving Stan thinks his wife, Belinda, is too strict with their children. Stan tolerates some behaviors that Belinda disapproves. He rarely hands out a serious punishment. Belinda feels Stan is weakening her authority. What should Stan and Belinda do? Create a bulleted list of suggestions.

14. Analysis Watch one hour of children's television programming. What do the shows teach, intentionally or otherwise? Would you want your child to watch these shows? Why or why not? Write an analysis of each program and answer each of the questions in your analysis.

15. Positive Reinforcement Volunteer to take care of a child for a few hours. Respond to the child's behavior in positive ways. Afterward, evaluate your approach and the child's reaction. How could you improve your technique? Write your evaluation in a half-page report.

16. Evaluation Read an article in a parenting magazine. What problem or situation does it describe? What advice does it recommend? Is the advice consistent with what you have read in this chapter? Present your information in one or more paragraphs.

17. Investigate Go to this book's Online Learning Center at **glencoe.com** to find **Web Links** for **Children with Special Needs**. Research one special need. How can children with this condition be helped to reach their potential? Share your findings in a short presentation.

Additional Activities For additional activities, go to this book's Online Learning Center through **glencoe.com**.

Academic Skills

Mathematics

18. Calculate Allowance Carlos and Maria give their 12-year-old son, Ben, $5.00 in allowance each week. To earn his allowance, Ben must do chores around the house and be courteous to his parents. However, each time Ben does not do a chore or talks back to his parents, $0.25 is deducted from his allowance. This week, Ben finished his chores, but he was disciplined six times. How much allowance will he receive?

 Math Concept **Problem Solving** Solving word problems sometimes requires several mathematical steps. Read the situation described carefully in order to figure out what the steps should be.

Starting Hint: First, you will need to know how much money will be deducted from Ben's allowance ($0.25 × 6). Then you will subtract this answer from the total allowance possible ($5.00).

Math For math help, go to the Math Appendix at the back of the book.

> **NCTM Problem Solving** Apply and adapt a variety of appropriate strategies to solve problems.

English Language Arts

19. Investigate There is ongoing scientific research being done on brain development. Conduct your own research to learn more about the current brain research. Study the development of the brain in children from ages 0 to 3 years. Use various forms of media to do your research. Summarize your findings in a one-page report.

> **NCTE 8** Use information resources to gather information and create and communicate knowledge.

Social Studies

20. Economics and Development Financial resources help parents meet needs in various areas of development. Research ways that these resources help. Write an article with examples. How might money help children develop physically, socially, intellectually, emotionally, and morally? Does money always help? Are there other resources available?

> **NCSS VII.h** Apply economic concepts and reasoning when evaluating historical and contemporary social developments and issues.

STANDARDIZED TEST PRACTICE

MULTIPLE CHOICE
Read the question. Read the answer choices and choose the best answer.

> **Test-Taking Tip** In a multiple-choice test, be sure to read all answers, paying attention to words like *correct* and *best*. If you are asked to choose the *best* answer, there may be more than one *correct* answer from which to choose.

21. Explaining and modeling principles of right and wrong can encourage a child's _____ development.
   a. intellectual
   b. emotional
   c. social
   d. moral

Build Successful Relationships

In this unit you have learned that to be successful in relationships, marriage, and parenting, teamwork skills are needed. You have also learned that teamwork takes trust, communication, and compromise. In this project, you will interview a professional. You will use what you learn to create a visual representation that shows two people using teamwork skills to build a successful relationship.

My Journal

If you completed the journal entry from page 564, refer to it to see if your thoughts have changed after reading the unit.

Project Assignment

- Choose a topic that you feel is a large decision to make when forming a family.
- Write a list of interview questions. Ask how trust, communication, and compromise help people make big decisions together.
- Identify and interview a professional in the community who helps build successful relationships.
- Arrange, take notes at, and type the interview with your candidate.
- Use what you learned in the interview to create a visual representation. It should show two people using teamwork skills to solve the topic you chose.

Academic Skills You Will Use

English Language Arts

NCTE 4 Use written language to communicate effectively.

NCTE 12 Use language to accomplish individual purposes.

STEP 1 Choose a Topic that Interests You

The topics below are examples of decisions two people make when forming a family. Choose one of the topics to talk about in your interview.

- Should we marry?
- Where should we live?
- Who will do the household chores?
- Should we have children?
- How will we parent?
- What religion should we practice?
- Who will manage the expenses?

STEP 2 Write Your Interview Questions

Make a list of interview questions. Ask how teamwork skills (trust, communication, and compromise) can be used to make a good decision about your topic. Also ask how they would walk a couple through the decision you chose.

Writing Skills

- Use complete sentences.
- Use correct spelling and grammar.
- Consider your audience.
- Organize your questions in the order you want to ask them.
- Write concisely (briefly but completely).

STEP 3 Connect to Your Community

Interview a member of the community who builds successful relationships as part of his or her job. Some examples are a religious leader, marriage counselor, school counselor, or social worker. Use the interview questions you wrote in Step 2.

Interview Skills
- During the interview, record responses and take notes.
- Use standard English to communicate.
- Listen attentively.
- When you transcribe your notes, write in complete sentences and use correct spelling and grammar.

STEP 4 Create and Present Your Visual

Use the Unit Thematic Project Checklist on the right to plan and create your visual and make your presentation.

STEP 5 Evaluate Your Presentation

Your project will be evaluated based on:
- Depth of interview and questions.
- Content of your visual presentation.
- Mechanics—presentation and neatness.

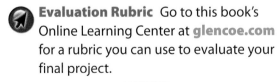 **Evaluation Rubric** Go to this book's Online Learning Center at **glencoe.com** for a rubric you can use to evaluate your final project.

Unit Thematic Project Checklist

Visual	✓ Make a poster, video, slide show, or other visual that illustrates how teamwork skills can be used to build successful relationships. ✓ In your visual, show how two people can communicate about and come up with a solution to a topic that you feel is a large decision to make when forming a family. ✓ Use the main points of trust, communication, and compromise as titles to each stage in your visual.
Presentation	✓ Make a presentation to your class to share your visual and discuss what you learned. ✓ Invite the students in your class to ask you any questions they may have. Answer three questions. ✓ When students ask you questions, demonstrate in your answers that you respect their perspectives. ✓ Turn in the notes from your interview and your visual to your teacher.
Academic Skills	✓ Communicate effectively. ✓ Organize your visual and your presentation so the audience can follow along easily. ✓ Speak clearly and concisely. ✓ Be sensitive to the needs of different audiences. ✓ Adapt and modify language to suit different purposes. ✓ Thoughtfully express your ideas.

Number and Operations

▶ *Understand numbers, ways of representing numbers, relationships among numbers, and number systems*

Fraction, Decimal, and Percent

A percent is a ratio that compares a number to 100. To write a percent as a fraction, drop the percent sign, and use the number as the numerator in a fraction with a denominator of 100. Simplify, if possible. For example, $76\% = \frac{76}{100}$, or $\frac{19}{25}$. To write a fraction as a percent, convert it to an equivalent fraction with a denominator of 100. For example, $\frac{3}{4} = \frac{75}{100}$, or 75%. A fraction can be expressed as a percent by first converting the fraction to a decimal (divide the numerator by the denominator) and then converting the decimal to a percent by moving the decimal point two places to the right.

Comparing Numbers on a Number Line

In order to compare and understand the relationship between real numbers in various forms, it is helpful to use a number line. The zero point on a number line is called the origin; the points to the left of the origin are negative, and those to the right are positive. The number line below shows how numbers in fraction, decimal, percent, and integer form can be compared.

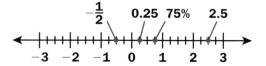

Percents Greater Than 100 and Less Than 1

Percents greater than 100% represent values greater than 1. For example, if the weight of an object is 250% of another, it is 2.5, or $2\frac{1}{2}$, times the weight.

Percents less than 1 represent values less than $\frac{1}{100}$. In other words, 0.1% is one tenth of one percent, which can also be represented in decimal form as 0.001, or in fraction form as $\frac{1}{1,000}$. Similarly, 0.01% is one hundredth of one percent or 0.0001 or $\frac{1}{10,000}$.

Ratio, Rate, and Proportion

A ratio is a comparison of two numbers using division. If a basketball player makes 8 out of 10 free throws, the ratio is written as 8 to 10, 8:10, or $\frac{8}{10}$. Ratios are usually written in simplest form. In simplest form, the ratio "8 out of 10" is 4 to 5, 4:5, or $\frac{4}{5}$. A rate is a ratio of two measurements having different kinds of units—cups per gallon, or miles per hour, for example. When a rate is simplified so that it has a denominator of 1, it is called a unit rate. An example of a unit rate is 9 miles per hour. A proportion is an equation stating that two ratios are equal. $\frac{3}{18} = \frac{13}{78}$ is an example of a proportion. The cross products of a proportion are also equal. $\frac{3}{18} = \frac{13}{78}$ and $3 \times 78 = 18 \times 13$.

Representing Large and Small Numbers

In order to represent large and small numbers, it is important to understand the number system. Our number system is based on 10, and the value of each place is 10 times the value of the place to its right.

MATH APPENDIX

The value of a digit is the product of a digit and its place value. For instance, in the number 6,400, the 6 has a value of six thousands and the 4 has a value of four hundreds. A place value chart can help you read numbers. In the chart, each group of three digits is called a period. Commas separate the periods: the ones period, the thousands period, the millions period, and so on. Values to the right of the ones period are decimals. By understanding place value you can write very large numbers like 5 billion and more, and very small numbers that are less than 1, like one-tenth.

Scientific Notation

When dealing with very large numbers like 1,500,000, or very small numbers like 0.000015, it is helpful to keep track of their value by writing the numbers in scientific notation. Powers of 10 with positive exponents are used with a decimal between 1 and 10 to express large numbers. The exponent represents the number of places the decimal point is moved to the right. So, 528,000 is written in scientific notation as 5.28×10^5. Powers of 10 with negative exponents are used with a decimal between 1 and 10 to express small numbers. The exponent represents the number of places the decimal point is moved to the left. The number 0.00047 is expressed as 4.7×10^{-4}.

Factor, Multiple, and Prime Factorization

Two or more numbers that are multiplied to form a product are called factors. Divisibility rules can be used to determine whether 2, 3, 4, 5, 6, 8, 9, or 10 are factors of a given number. Multiples are the products of a given number and various integers.

For example, 8 is a multiple of 4 because $4 \times 2 = 8$. A prime number is a whole number that has exactly two factors: 1 and itself. A composite number is a whole number that has more than two factors. Zero and 1 are neither prime nor composite. A composite number can be expressed as the product of its prime factors. The prime factorization of 40 is $2 \times 2 \times 2 \times 5$, or $2^3 \times 5$. The numbers 2 and 5 are prime numbers.

Integers

A negative number is a number less than zero. Negative numbers like −8, positive numbers like +6, and zero are members of the set of integers. Integers can be represented as points on a number line. A set of integers can be written {…, −3, −2, −1, 0, 1, 2, 3, …} where … means "continues indefinitely."

Real, Rational, and Irrational Numbers

The real number system is made up of the sets of rational and irrational numbers. Rational numbers are numbers that can be written in the form a/b where a and b are integers and $b \neq 0$. Examples are 0.45, $\frac{1}{2}$, and $\sqrt{36}$. Irrational numbers are non-repeating, non-terminating decimals. Examples are $\sqrt{71}$, π, and 0.020020002….

Complex and Imaginary Numbers

A complex number is a mathematical expression with a real number element and an imaginary number element. Imaginary numbers are multiples of i, the "imaginary" square root of −1. Complex numbers are represented by $a + bi$, where a and b are real numbers and i represents the imaginary element. When a quadratic equation does not have a real number solution, the solution can be represented by a complex number. Like real numbers, complex numbers can be added, subtracted, multiplied, and divided.

Vectors and Matrices

A matrix is a set of numbers or elements arranged in rows and columns to form a rectangle. The number of rows is represented by m and the number of columns is represented by n. To describe the number of rows and columns in a matrix, list the number of rows first using the format $m \times n$. Matrix A below is a 3×3 matrix because it has 3 rows and 3 columns. To name an element of a matrix, the letter i is used to denote the row and j is used to denote the column, and the element is labeled in the form $a_{i,j}$. In matrix A below, $a_{3,2}$ is 4.

$$\text{Matrix A} = \begin{pmatrix} 1 & 3 & 5 \\ 0 & 6 & 8 \\ 3 & 4 & 5 \end{pmatrix}$$

A vector is a matrix with only one column or row of elements. A transposed column vector, or a column vector turned on its side, is a row vector. In the example below, row vector b' is the transpose of column vector b.

$$b = \begin{pmatrix} 1 \\ 2 \\ 3 \\ 4 \end{pmatrix}$$

$$b' = (1 \quad 2 \quad 3 \quad 4)$$

▶ Understand meanings of operations and how they relate to one another

Properties of Addition and Multiplication

Properties are statements that are true for any numbers. For example, $3 + 8$ is the same as $8 + 3$ because each expression equals 11. This illustrates the Commutative Property of Addition. Likewise, $3 \times 8 = 8 \times 3$ illustrates the Commutative Property of Multiplication.

When evaluating expressions, it is often helpful to group or associate the numbers. The Associative Property says that the way in which numbers are grouped when added or multiplied does not change the sum or product. The following properties are also true:

- **Additive Identity Property:** When 0 is added to any number, the sum is the number.

- **Multiplicative Identity Property:** When any number is multiplied by 1, the product is the number.

- **Multiplicative Property of Zero:** When any number is multiplied by 0, the product is 0.

Rational Numbers

A number that can be written as a fraction is called a rational number. Terminating and repeating decimals are rational numbers because both can be written as fractions.

Decimals that are neither terminating nor repeating are called irrational numbers because they cannot be written as fractions. Terminating decimals can be converted to fractions by placing the number (without the decimal point) in the numerator. Count the number of places to the right of the decimal point, and in the denominator, place a 1 followed by a number of zeros equal to the number of places that you counted. The fraction can then be reduced to its simplest form.

Writing a Fraction as a Decimal

Any fraction $\frac{a}{b}$, where $b \neq 0$, can be written as a decimal by dividing the numerator by the denominator. So, $\frac{a}{b} = a \div b$. If the division ends, or terminates, when the remainder is zero, the decimal is a terminating decimal. Not all fractions can be written as terminating decimals. Some have a repeating decimal. A bar indicates that the decimal repeats forever. For example, the fraction $\frac{4}{9}$ can be converted to a repeating decimal, $0.\overline{4}$

Adding and Subtracting Like Fractions

Fractions with the same denominator are called like fractions. To add like fractions, add the numerators and write the sum over the denominator. To add mixed numbers with like fractions, add the whole numbers and fractions separately, adding the numerators of the fractions, then simplifying if necessary. The rule for subtracting fractions with like denominators is similar to the rule

for adding. The numerators can be subtracted and the difference written over the denominator. Mixed numbers are written as improper fractions before subtracting. These same rules apply to adding or subtracting like algebraic fractions. An algebraic fraction is a fraction that contains one or more variables in the numerator or denominator.

Adding and Subtracting Unlike Fractions

Fractions with different denominators are called unlike fractions. The least common multiple of the denominators is used to rename the fractions with a common denominator. After a common denominator is found, the numerators can then be added or subtracted. To add mixed numbers with unlike fractions, rename the mixed numbers as improper fractions. Then find a common denominator, add the numerators, and simplify the answer.

Multiplying Rational Numbers

To multiply fractions, multiply the numerators and multiply the denominators. If the numerators and denominators have common factors, they can be simplified before multiplication. If the fractions have different signs, then the product will be negative. Mixed numbers can be multiplied in the same manner, after first renaming them as improper fractions. Algebraic fractions may be multiplied using the same method described above.

MATH APPENDIX

Dividing Rational Numbers
To divide a number by a rational number (a fraction, for example), multiply the first number by the multiplicative inverse of the second. Two numbers whose product is 1 are called multiplicative inverses, or reciprocals. $\frac{7}{4} \times \frac{4}{7} = 1$. When dividing by a mixed number, first rename it as an improper fraction, and then multiply by its multiplicative inverse. This process of multiplying by a number's reciprocal can also be used when dividing algebraic fractions.

Adding Integers
To add integers with the same sign, add their absolute values. The sum takes the same sign as the addends. An addend is a number that is added to another number (the augend). The equation $-5 + (-2) = -7$ is an example of adding two integers with the same sign. To add integers with different signs, subtract their absolute values. The sum takes the same sign as the addend with the greater absolute value.

Subtracting Integers
The rules for adding integers are extended to the subtraction of integers. To subtract an integer, add its additive inverse. For example, to find the difference $2 - 5$, add the additive inverse of 5 to 2: $2 + (-5) = -3$. The rule for subtracting integers can be used to solve real-world problems and to evaluate algebraic expressions.

Additive Inverse Property
Two numbers with the same absolute value but different signs are called opposites. For example, −4 and 4 are opposites. An integer and its opposite are also called additive inverses. The Additive Inverse Property says that the sum of any number and its additive inverse is zero. The Commutative, Associative, and Identity Properties also apply to integers. These properties help when adding more than two integers.

Absolute Value
In mathematics, when two integers on a number line are on opposite sides of zero, and they are the same distance from zero, they have the same absolute value. The symbol for absolute value is two vertical bars on either side of the number. For example, $|-5| = 5$.

Multiplying Integers
Since multiplication is repeated addition, $3(-7)$ means that −7 is used as an addend 3 times. By the Commutative Property of Multiplication, $3(-7) = -7(3)$. The product of two integers with different signs is always negative. The product of two integers with the same sign is always positive.

Dividing Integers
The quotient of two integers can be found by dividing the numbers using their absolute values. The quotient of two integers with the same sign is positive, and the quotient of two integers with a different sign is negative. $-12 \div (-4) = 3$ and $12 \div (-4) = -3$. The division of integers is used in statistics to find the average, or mean, of a set of data. When finding the mean of a set of numbers, find the sum of the numbers, and then divide by the number in the set.

MATH APPENDIX

Adding and Multiplying Vectors and Matrices

In order to add two matrices together, they must have the same number of rows and columns. In matrix addition, the corresponding elements are added to each other. In other words $(a + b)_{ij} = a_{ij} + b_{ij}$. For example,

$$\begin{pmatrix} 1 & 2 \\ 2 & 1 \end{pmatrix} + \begin{pmatrix} 3 & 6 \\ 0 & 1 \end{pmatrix} = \begin{pmatrix} 1+3 & 2+6 \\ 2+0 & 1+1 \end{pmatrix} = \begin{pmatrix} 4 & 8 \\ 2 & 2 \end{pmatrix}$$

Matrix multiplication requires that the number of elements in each row in the first matrix is equal to the number of elements in each column in the second. The elements of the first row of the first matrix are multiplied by the corresponding elements of the first column of the second matrix and then added together to get the first element of the product matrix. To get the second element, the elements in the first row of the first matrix are multiplied by the corresponding elements in the second column of the second matrix then added, and so on, until every row of the first matrix is multiplied by every column of the second. See the example below.

$$\begin{pmatrix} 1 & 2 \\ 3 & 4 \end{pmatrix} \times \begin{pmatrix} 3 & 6 \\ 0 & 1 \end{pmatrix} = \begin{pmatrix} (1\times3)+(2\times0) & (1\times6)+(2\times1) \\ (3\times3)+(4\times0) & (3\times6)+(4\times1) \end{pmatrix} = \begin{pmatrix} 3 & 8 \\ 9 & 22 \end{pmatrix}$$

Vector addition and multiplication are performed in the same way, but there is only one column and one row.

Permutations and Combinations

Permutations and combinations are used to determine the number of possible outcomes in different situations. An arrangement, listing, or pattern in which order is important is called a permutation. The symbol P(6, 3) represents the number of permutations of 6 things taken 3 at a time. For P(6, 3), there are $6 \times 5 \times 4$ or 120 possible outcomes. An arrangement or listing where order is not important is called a combination. The symbol C(10, 5) represents the number of combinations of 10 things taken 5 at a time. For C(10, 5), there are $(10 \times 9 \times 8 \times 7 \times 6) \div (5 \times 4 \times 3 \times 2 \times 1)$ or 252 possible outcomes.

Powers and Exponents

An expression such as $3 \times 3 \times 3 \times 3$ can be written as a power. A power has two parts, a base and an exponent. $3 \times 3 \times 3 \times 3 = 3^4$. The base is the number that is multiplied (3). The exponent tells how many times the base is used as a factor (4 times). Numbers and variables can be written using exponents. For example, $8 \times 8 \times 8 \times m \times m \times m \times m \times m$ can be expressed $8^3 m^5$. Exponents also can be used with place value to express numbers in expanded form. Using this method, 1,462 can be written as $(1 \times 10^3) + (4 \times 10^2) + (6 \times 10^1) + (2 \times 10^0)$.

Squares and Square Roots

The square root of a number is one of two equal factors of a number. Every positive number has both a positive and a negative square root. For example, since $8 \times 8 = 64$, 8 is a square root of 64. Since $(-8) \times (-8) = 64$, −8 is also a square root of 64. The notation $\sqrt{}$ indicates the positive square root, $-\sqrt{}$ indicates the negative square root, and $\pm\sqrt{}$ indicates both square roots. For example, $\sqrt{81} = 9$, $-\sqrt{49} = -7$, and $\pm\sqrt{4} = \pm2$. The square root of a negative number is an imaginary number because any two factors of a negative number must have different signs, and are therefore not equivalent.

MATH APPENDIX

Logarithm

A logarithm is the inverse of exponentiation. The logarithm of a number x in base b is equal to the number n. Therefore, $b^n = x$ and $\log_b x = n$. For example, $\log_4(64) = 3$ because $4^3 = 64$. The most commonly used bases for logarithms are 10, the common logarithm; 2, the binary logarithm; and the constant e, the natural logarithm (also called $ln(x)$ instead of $\log_e(x)$). Below is a list of some of the rules of logarithms that are important to understand if you are going to use them.

$$\log_b(xy) = \log_b(x) + \log_b(y)$$
$$\log_b(x/y) = \log_b(x) - \log_b(y)$$
$$\log_b(1/x) = -\log_b(x)$$
$$\log_b(x)y = y\log_b(x)$$

▶ Compute fluently and make reasonable estimates

Estimation by Rounding

When rounding numbers, look at the digit to the right of the place to which you are rounding. If the digit is 5 or greater, round up. If it is less than 5, round down. For example, to round 65,137 to the nearest hundred, look at the number in the tens place. Since 3 is less than 5, round down to 65,100. To round the same number to the nearest ten thousandth, look at the number in the thousandths place. Since it is 5, round up to 70,000.

Finding Equivalent Ratios

Equivalent ratios have the same meaning. Just like finding equivalent fractions, to find an equivalent ratio, multiply or divide both sides by the same number. For example, you can multiply 7 by both sides of the ratio 6:8 to get 42:56. Instead, you can also divide both sides of the same ratio by 2 to get 3:4. Find the simplest form of a ratio by dividing to find equivalent ratios until you can't go any further without going into decimals. So, 160:240 in simplest form is 2:3. To write a ratio in the form *1:n*, divide both sides by the left-hand number. In other words, to change 8:20 to *1:n*, divide both sides by 8 to get 1:2.5.

Front-End Estimation

Front-end estimation can be used to quickly estimate sums and differences before adding or subtracting. To use this technique, add or subtract just the digits of the two highest place values, and replace the other place values with zero. This will give you an estimation of the solution of a problem. For example, 93,471 − 22,825 can be changed to 93,000 − 22,000 or 71,000. This estimate can be compared to your final answer to judge its correctness.

Judging Reasonableness

When solving an equation, it is important to check your work by considering how reasonable your answer is. For example, consider the equation $9\frac{3}{4} \times 4\frac{1}{3}$. Since $9\frac{3}{4}$ is between 9 and 10 and $4\frac{1}{3}$ is between 4 and 5, only values that are between 9×4 or 36 and 10×5 or 50 will be reasonable. You can also use front-end estimation, or you can round and estimate a reasonable answer. In the equation 73×25, you can round and solve to estimate a reasonable answer to be near 70×30 or 2,100.

Algebra

▶ *Understand patterns, relations, and functions*

Relation

A relation is a generalization comparing sets of ordered pairs for an equation or inequality such as $x = y + 1$ or $x > y$. The first element in each pair, the x values, forms the domain. The second element in each pair, the y values, forms the range.

Function

A function is a special relation in which each member of the domain is paired with exactly one member in the range. Functions may be represented using ordered pairs, tables, or graphs. One way to determine whether a relation is a function is to use the vertical line test. Using an object to represent a vertical line, move the object from left to right across the graph. If, for each value of x in the domain, the object passes through no more than one point on the graph, then the graph represents a function.

Linear and Nonlinear Functions

Linear functions have graphs that are straight lines. These graphs represent constant rates of change. In other words, the slope between any two pairs of points on the graph is the same. Nonlinear functions do not have constant rates of change. The slope changes along these graphs. Therefore, the graphs of nonlinear functions are *not* straight lines. Graphs of curves represent nonlinear functions. The equation for a linear function can be written in the form $y = mx + b$, where m represents the constant rate of change, or the slope. Therefore, you can determine whether a function is linear by looking at the equation. For example, the equation $y = \frac{3}{x}$ is nonlinear because x is in the denominator and the equation cannot be written in the form $y = mx + b$. A nonlinear function does not increase or decrease at a constant rate. You can check this by using a table and finding the increase or decrease in y for each regular increase in x. For example, if for each increase in x by 2, y does not increase or decrease the same amount each time, the function is nonlinear.

Linear Equations in Two Variables

In a linear equation with two variables, such as $y = x - 3$, the variables appear in separate terms and neither variable contains an exponent other than 1. The graphs of all linear equations are straight lines. All points on a line are solutions of the equation that is graphed.

Quadratic and Cubic Functions

A quadratic function is a polynomial equation of the second degree, generally expressed as $ax^2 + bx + c = 0$, where a, b, and c are real numbers and a is not equal to zero. Similarly, a cubic function is a polynomial equation of the third degree, usually expressed as $ax^3 + bx^2 + cx + d = 0$. Quadratic functions can be graphed using an equation or a table of values. For example, to graph $y = 3x^2 + 1$, substitute the values −1, −0.5, 0, 0.5, and 1 for x to yield the point coordinates (−1, 4), (−0.5, 1.75), (0, 1), (0.5, 1.75), and (1, 4). Plot these points on a coordinate grid and connect the points in the form of a parabola. Cubic functions also can be graphed by making a table of values. The points of a cubic function form a curve. There is one point at which the curve changes from opening upward to opening downward, or vice versa, called the point of inflection.

Slope

Slope is the ratio of the rise, or vertical change, to the run, or horizontal change of a line: slope = rise/run. Slope (m) is the same for any two points on a straight line and can be found by using the coordinates of any two points on the line:

$$m = \frac{y_2 - y_1}{x_2 - x_1}, \text{ where } x_2 \neq x_1$$

Asymptotes

An asymptote is a straight line that a curve approaches but never actually meets or crosses. Theoretically, the asymptote meets the curve at infinity. For example, in the function $f(x) = \frac{1}{x}$, two asymptotes are being approached: the line $y = 0$ and $x = 0$. See the graph of the function below.

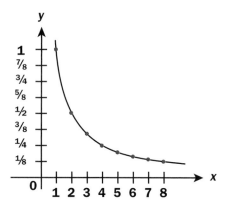

Represent and analyze mathematical situations and structures using algebraic symbols

Variables and Expressions

Algebra is a language of symbols. A variable is a placeholder for a changing value. Any letter, such as x, can be used as a variable. Expressions such as $x + 2$ and $4x$ are algebraic expressions because they represent sums and/or products of variables and numbers. Usually, mathematicians avoid the use of i and e for variables because they have other mathematical meanings ($i = \sqrt{-1}$ and e is used with natural logarithms). To evaluate an algebraic expression, replace the variable or variables with known values, and then solve using order of operations. Translate verbal phrases into algebraic expressions by first defining a variable: Choose a variable and a quantity for the variable to represent. In this way, algebraic expressions can be used to represent real-world situations.

Constant and Coefficient

A constant is a fixed value unlike a variable, which can change. Constants are usually represented by numbers, but they can also be represented by symbols. For example, π is a symbolic representation of the value 3.1415…. A coefficient is a constant by which a variable or other object is multiplied. For example, in the expression $7x^2 + 5x + 9$, the coefficient of x^2 is 7 and the coefficient of x is 5. The number 9 is a constant and not a coefficient.

Monomial and Polynomial

A monomial is a number, a variable, or a product of numbers and/or variables such as 3×4. An algebraic expression that contains one or more monomials is called a polynomial. In a polynomial, there are no terms with variables in the denominator and no terms with variables under a radical sign. Polynomials can be classified by the number of terms contained in the expression. Therefore, a polynomial with two terms is called a binomial ($z^2 - 1$), and a polynomial with three terms is called a trinomial ($2y^3 + 4y^2 - y$). Polynomials also can be classified by their degrees. The degree of a monomial is the sum of the exponents of its variables. The degree of a nonzero constant such as 6 or 10 is 0. The constant 0 has no degree. For example, the monomial $4b^5c^2$ had a degree of 7. The degree of a polynomial is the same as that of the term with the greatest degree. For example, the polynomial $3x^4 - 2y^3 + 4y^2 - y$ has a degree of 4.

Equation

An equation is a mathematical sentence that states that two expressions are equal. The two expressions in an equation are always separated by an equal sign. When solving for a variable in an equation, you must perform the same operations on both sides of the equation in order for the mathematical sentence to remain true.

Solving Equations with Variables

To solve equations with variables on both sides, use the Addition or Subtraction Property of Equality to write an equivalent equation with the variables on the same side. For example, to solve $5x - 8 = 3x$, subtract $3x$ from each side to get $2x - 8 = 0$. Then add 8 to each side to get $2x = 8$. Finally, divide each side by 2 to find that $x = 4$.

Solving Equations with Grouping Symbols

Equations often contain grouping symbols such as parentheses or brackets. The first step in solving these equations is to use the Distributive Property to remove the grouping symbols. For example $5(x + 2) = 25$ can be changed to $5x + 10 = 25$, and then solved to find that $x = 3$.

Some equations have no solution. That is, there is no value of the variable that results in a true sentence. For such an equation, the solution set is called the null or empty set, and is represented by the symbol $\varnothing$ or {}. Other equations may have every number as the solution. An equation that is true for every value of the variable is called the identity.

Inequality

A mathematical sentence that contains the symbols < (less than), > (greater than), ≤ (less than or equal to), or ≥ (greater than or equal to) is called an inequality. For example, the statement that it is legal to drive 55 miles per hour or slower on a stretch of the highway can be shown by the sentence $s \le 55$. Inequalities with variables are called open sentences. When a variable is replaced with a number, the inequality may be true or false.

Solving Inequalities

Solving an inequality means finding values for the variable that make the inequality true. Just as with equations, when you add or subtract the same number from each side of an inequality, the inequality remains true. For example, if you add 5 to each side of the inequality $3x < 6$, the resulting inequality $3x + 5 < 11$ is also true. Adding or subtracting the same number from each side of an inequality does not affect the inequality sign. When multiplying or dividing each side of an inequality by the same positive number, the inequality remains true. In such cases, the inequality symbol does not change. When multiplying or dividing each side of an inequality by a negative number, the inequality symbol must be reversed. For example, when dividing each side of the inequality $-4x \geq -8$ by -2, the inequality sign must be changed to $\leq$ for the resulting inequality, $2x \leq 4$, to be true. Since the solutions to an inequality include all rational numbers satisfying it, inequalities have an infinite number of solutions.

Representing Inequalities on a Number Line

The solutions of inequalities can be graphed on a number line. For example, if the solution of an inequality is $x < 5$, start an arrow at 5 on the number line, and continue the arrow to the left to show all values less than 5 as the solution. Put an open circle at 5 to show that the point 5 is *not* included in the graph. Use a closed circle when graphing solutions that are greater than or equal to, or less than or equal to, a number.

Order of Operations

Solving a problem may involve using more than one operation. The answer can depend on the order in which you do the operations. To make sure that there is just one answer to a series of computations, mathematicians have agreed upon an order in which to do the operations. First simplify within the parentheses, often called graphing symbols, and then evaluate any exponents. Then multiply and divide from left to right, and finally add and subtract from left to right.

Parametric Equations

Given an equation with more than one unknown, a statistician can draw conclusions about those unknown quantities through the use of parameters, independent variables that the statistician already knows something about. For example, you can find the velocity of an object if you make some assumptions about distance and time parameters.

Recursive Equations

In recursive equations, every value is determined by the previous value. You must first plug an initial value into the equation to get the first value, and then you can use the first value to determine the next one, and so on. For example, in order to determine what the population of pigeons will be in New York City in three years, you can use an equation with the birth, death, immigration, and emigration rates of the birds. Input the current population size into the equation to determine next year's population size, then repeat until you have calculated the value for which you are looking.

▶ *Use mathematical models to represent and understand quantitative relationships*

Solving Systems of Equations

Two or more equations together are called a system of equations. A system of equations can have one solution, no solution, or infinitely many solutions. One method for solving a system of equations is to graph the equations on the same coordinate plane. The coordinates of the point where the graphs intersect is the solution. In other words, the solution of a system is the ordered pair that is a solution of all equations.

A more accurate way to solve a system of two equations is by using a method called substitution. Write both equations in terms of y. Replace y in the first equation with the right side of the second equation. Check the solution by graphing. You can solve a system of three equations using matrix algebra.

Graphing Inequalities

To graph an inequality, first graph the related equation, which is the boundary. All points in the shaded region are solutions of the inequality. If an inequality contains the symbol $\leq$ or $\geq$, then use a solid line to indicate that the boundary is included in the graph. If an inequality contains the symbol $<$ or $>$, then use a dashed line to indicate that the boundary is not included in the graph.

▶ Analyze change in various contexts

Rate of Change

A change in one quantity with respect to another quantity is called the rate of change. Rates of change can be described using slope:

$$\text{slope} = \frac{\text{change in } y}{\text{change in } x}$$

You can find rates of change from an equation, a table, or a graph. A special type of linear equation that describes rate of change is called a direct variation. The graph of a direct variation always passes through the origin and represents a proportional situation. In the equation $y = kx$, k is called the constant of variation. It is the slope, or rate of change. As x increases in value, y increases or decreases at a constant rate k, or y varies directly with x. Another way to say this is that y is directly proportional to x. The direct variation $y = kx$ also can be written as $k = \frac{y}{x}$. In this form, you can see that the ratio of y to x is the same for any corresponding values of y and x.

Slope-Intercept Form

Equations written as $y = mx + b$, where m is the slope and b is the y-intercept, are linear equations in slope-intercept form. For example, the graph of $y = 5x - 6$ is a line that has a slope of 5 and crosses the y-axis at $(0, -6)$. Sometimes you must first write an equation in slope-intercept form before finding the slope and y-intercept. For example, the equation $2x + 3y = 15$ can be expressed in slope-intercept form by subtracting $2x$ from each side and then dividing by 3: $y = -\frac{2}{3}x + 5$, revealing a slope of $-\frac{2}{3}$ and a y-intercept of 5. You can use the slope-intercept form of an equation to graph a line easily. Graph the y-intercept and use the slope to find another point on the line, then connect the two points with a line.

MATH APPENDIX

Geometry

▶ *Analyze characteristics and properties of two- and three-dimensional geometric shapes and develop mathematical arguments about geometric relationships*

Angles

Two rays that have the same endpoint form an angle. The common endpoint is called the vertex, and the two rays that make up the angle are called the sides of the angle. The most common unit of measure for angles is the degree. Protractors can be used to measure angles or to draw an angle of a given measure. Angles can be classified by their degree measure. Acute angles have measures less than 90° but greater than 0°. Obtuse angles have measures greater than 90° but less than 180°. Right angles have measures of 90°.

Triangles

A triangle is a figure formed by three line segments that intersect only at their endpoints. The sum of the measures of the angles of a triangle is 180°. Triangles can be classified by their angles. An acute triangle contains all acute angles. An obtuse triangle has one obtuse angle. A right triangle has one right angle. Triangles can also be classified by their sides. A scalene triangle has no congruent sides. An isosceles triangle has at least two congruent sides. In an equilateral triangle all sides are congruent.

Quadrilaterals

A quadrilateral is a closed figure with four sides and four vertices. The segments of a quadrilateral intersect only at their endpoints. Quadrilaterals can be separated into two triangles. Since the sum of the interior angles of all triangles totals 180°, the measures of the interior angles of a quadrilateral equal 360°. Quadrilaterals are classified according to their characteristics, and include trapezoids, parallelograms, rectangles, squares, and rhombuses.

Two-Dimensional Figures

A two-dimensional figure exists within a plane and has only the dimensions of length and width. Examples of two-dimensional figures include circles and polygons. Polygons are figures that have three or more angles, including triangles, quadrilaterals, pentagons, hexagons, and many more. The sum of the angles of any polygon totals at least 180° (triangle), and each additional side adds 180° to the measure of the first three angles. The sum of the angles of a quadrilateral, for example, is 360°. The sum of the angles of a pentagon is 540°.

Three-Dimensional Figures

A plane is a two-dimensional flat surface that extends in all directions. Intersecting planes can form the edges and vertices of three-dimensional figures or solids. A polyhedron is a solid with flat surfaces that are polygons.

Polyhedrons are composed of faces, edges, and vertices and are differentiated by their shape and by their number of bases. Skew lines are lines that lie in different planes. They are neither intersecting nor parallel.

Congruence

Figures that have the same size and shape are congruent. The parts of congruent triangles that match are called corresponding parts. Congruence statements are used to identify corresponding parts of congruent triangles. When writing a congruence statement, the letters must be written so that corresponding vertices appear in the same order. Corresponding parts can be used to find the measures of angles and sides in a figure that is congruent to a figure with known measures.

Similarity

If two figures have the same shape but not the same size they are called similar figures. For example, the triangles below are similar, so angles A, B, and C have the same measurements as angles D, E, and F, respectively. However, segments AB, BC, and CA do not have the same measurements as segments DE, EF, and FD, but the measures of the sides are proportional.

For example, $\frac{\overline{AB}}{\overline{DE}} = \frac{\overline{BC}}{\overline{EF}} = \frac{\overline{CA}}{\overline{FD}}$.

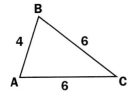

Solid figures are considered to be similar if they have the same shape and their corresponding linear measures are proportional. As with two-dimensional figures, they can be tested for similarity by comparing corresponding measures. If the compared ratios are proportional, then the figures are similar solids. Missing measures of similar solids can also be determined by using proportions.

The Pythagorean Theorem

The sides that are adjacent to a right angle are called legs. The side opposite the right angle is the hypotenuse.

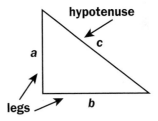

The Pythagorean Theorem describes the relationship between the lengths of the legs a and b and the hypotenuse c. It states that if a triangle is a right triangle, then the square of the length of the hypotenuse is equal to the sum of the squares of the lengths of the legs. In symbols, $c^2 = a^2 + b^2$.

Sine, Cosine, and Tangent Ratios

Trigonometry is the study of the properties of triangles. A trigonometric ratio is a ratio of the lengths of two sides of a right triangle. The most common trigonometric ratios are the sine, cosine, and tangent ratios. These ratios are abbreviated as *sin*, *cos*, and *tan*, respectively.

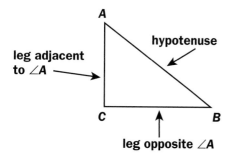

If ∠A is an acute angle of a right triangle, then

$$\sin \angle A = \frac{\text{measure of leg opposite } \angle A}{\text{measure of hypotenuse}},$$

$$\cos \angle A = \frac{\text{measure of leg adjacent to } \angle A}{\text{measure of hypotenuse}}, \text{ and}$$

$$\tan \angle A = \frac{\text{measure of leg opposite } \angle A}{\text{measure of leg adjacent to } \angle A}.$$

▶ *Specify locations and describe spatial relationships using coordinate geometry and other representational systems*

Polygons
A polygon is a simple, closed figure formed by three or more line segments. The line segments meet only at their endpoints. The points of intersection are called vertices, and the line segments are called sides. Polygons are classified by the number if sides they have. The diagonals of a polygon divide the polygon into triangles. The number of triangles formed is two less than the number of sides. To find the sum of the measures of the interior angles of any polygon, multiply the number of triangles within the polygon by 180. That is, if *n* equals the number of

sides, then (*n* − 2) 180 gives the sum of the measures of the polygon's interior angles.

Cartesian Coordinates
In the Cartesian coordinate system, the *y*-axis extends above and below the origin and the *x*-axis extends to the right and left of the origin, which is the point at which the *x*- and *y*-axes intersect. Numbers below and to the left of the origin are negative. A point graphed on the coordinate grid is said to have an *x*-coordinate and a *y*-coordinate. For example, the point (1,−2) has as its *x*-coordinate the number 1, and has as its *y*-coordinate the number −2. This point is graphed by locating the position on the grid that is 1 unit to the right of the origin and 2 units below the origin.

The *x*-axis and the *y*-axis separate the coordinate plane into four regions, called quadrants. The axes and points located on the axes themselves are not located in any of the quadrants. The quadrants are labeled I to IV, starting in the upper right and proceeding counterclockwise. In quadrant I, both coordinates are positive. In quadrant II, the *x*-coordinate is negative and the *y*-coordinate is positive. In quadrant III, both coordinates are negative. In quadrant IV, the *x*-coordinate is positive and the *y*-coordinate is negative. A coordinate graph can be used to show algebraic relationships among numbers.

▶ *Apply transformations and use symmetry to analyze mathematical situations*

Similar Triangles and Indirect Measurement
Triangles that have the same shape but not necessarily the same dimensions are called similar triangles. Similar triangles

have corresponding angles and corresponding sides. Arcs are used to show congruent angles. If two triangles are similar, then the corresponding angles have the same measure, and the corresponding sides are proportional. Therefore, to determine the measures of the sides of similar triangles when some measures are known, proportions can be used.

Transformations

A transformation is a movement of a geometric figure. There are several types of transformations. In a translation, also called a slide, a figure is slid from one position to another without turning it. Every point of the original figure is moved the same distance and in the same direction. In a reflection, also called a flip, a figure is flipped over a line to form a mirror image. Every point of the original figure has a corresponding point on the other side of the line of symmetry. In a rotation, also called a turn, a figure is turned around a fixed point. A figure can be rotated 0°–360° clockwise or counterclockwise. A dilation transforms each line to a parallel line whose length is a fixed multiple of the length of the original line to create a similar figure that will be either larger or smaller.

▶ *Use visualizations, spatial reasoning, and geometric modeling to solve problems*

Two-Dimensional Representations of Three-Dimensional Objects

Three-dimensional objects can be represented in a two-dimensional drawing in order to more easily determine properties such as surface area and volume. When you look at the triangular prism, you can see the orientation of its three dimensions, length, width, and height. Using the drawing and the formulas for surface area and volume, you can easily calculate these properties.

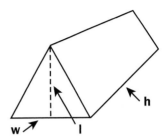

Another way to represent a three-dimensional object in a two-dimensional plane is by using a net, which is the unfolded representation. Imagine cutting the vertices of a box until it is flat then drawing an outline of it. That's a net. Most objects have more than one net, but any one can be measured to determine surface area. Below is a cube and one of its nets.

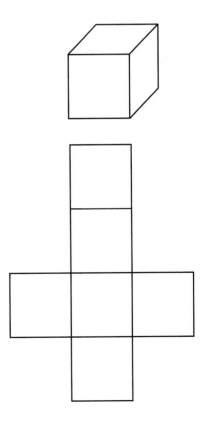

MATH APPENDIX

Measurement

▶ **Understand measurable attributes of objects and the units, systems, and processes of measurement**

Customary System

The customary system is the system of weights and measures used in the United States. The main units of weight are ounces, pounds (1 equal to 16 ounces), and tons (1 equal to 2,000 pounds). Length is typically measured in inches, feet (1 equal to 12 inches), yards (1 equal to 3 feet), and miles (1 equal to 5,280 feet), while area is measured in square feet and acres (1 equal to 43,560 square feet). Liquid is measured in cups, pints (1 equal to 2 cups), quarts (1 equal to 2 pints), and gallons (1 equal to 4 quarts). Finally, temperature is measured in degrees Fahrenheit.

Metric System

The metric system is a decimal system of weights and measurements in which the prefixes of the words for the units of measure indicate the relationships between the different measurements. In this system, the main units of weight, or mass, are grams and kilograms. Length is measured in millimeters, centimeters, meters, and kilometers, and the units of area are square millimeters, centimeters, meters, and kilometers. Liquid is typically measured in milliliters and liters, while temperature is in degrees Celsius.

Selecting Units of Measure

When measuring something, it is important to select the appropriate type and size of unit. For example, in the United States it would be appropriate when describing someone's height to use feet and inches. These units of height or length are good to use because they are in the customary system, and they are of appropriate size. In the customary system, use inches, feet, and miles for lengths and perimeters; square inches, feet, and miles for area and surface area; and cups, pints, quarts, gallons or cubic inches and feet (and less commonly miles) for volume. In the metric system use millimeters, centimeters, meters, and kilometers for lengths and perimeters; square units millimeters, centimeters, meters, and kilometers for area and surface area; and milliliters and liters for volume. Finally, always use degrees to measure angles.

▶ **Apply appropriate techniques, tools, and formulas to determine measurements**

Precision and Significant Digits

The precision of measurement is the exactness to which a measurement is made. Precision depends on the smallest unit of measure being used, or the precision unit. One way to record a measure is to estimate to the nearest precision unit. A more precise method is to include all of the digits that are actually measured, plus one estimated digit. The digits recorded, called significant digits, indicate the precision of the measurement. There are special rules for determining significant digits. If a number contains a decimal point, the number of significant digits is found by counting from left to right, starting with the first nonzero digit.

If the number does not contain a decimal point, the number of significant digits is found by counting the digits from left to right, starting with the first digit and ending with the last nonzero digit.

Surface Area

The amount of material needed to cover the surface of a figure is called the surface area. It can be calculated by finding the area of each face and adding them together. To find the surface area of a rectangular prism, for example, the formula $S = 2lw + 2lh + 2wh$ applies. A cylinder, on the other hand, may be unrolled to reveal two circles and a rectangle. Its surface area can be determined by finding the area of the two circles, $2\pi r^2$, and adding it to the area of the rectangle, $2\pi rh$ (the length of the rectangle is the circumference of one of the circles), or $S = 2\pi r^2 + 2\pi rh$. The surface area of a pyramid is measured in a slightly different way because the sides of a pyramid are triangles that intersect at the vertex. These sides are called lateral faces and the height of each is called the slant height. The sum of their areas is the lateral area of a pyramid. The surface area of a square pyramid is the lateral area $\frac{1}{2}bh$ (area of a lateral face) times 4 (number of lateral faces), plus the area of the base. The surface area of a cone is the area of its circular base (πr^2) plus its lateral area (πrl, where l is the slant height).

Volume

Volume is the measure of space occupied by a solid region. To find the volume of a prism, the area of the base is multiplied by the measure of the height, $V = Bh$. A solid containing several prisms can be broken down into its component prisms. Then the volume of each component can be found and the volumes added. The volume of a cylinder can be determined by finding the area of its circular base, πr^2, and then multiplying by the height of the cylinder. A pyramid has one-third the volume of a prism with the same base and height. To find the volume of a pyramid, multiply the area of the base by the pyramid's height, and then divide by 3. Simply stated, the formula for the volume of a pyramid is $V = \frac{1}{3}bh$. A cone is a three-dimensional figure with one circular base and a curved surface connecting the base and the vertex. The volume of a cone is one-third the volume of a cylinder with the same base area and height. Like a pyramid, the formula for the volume of a cone is $V = \frac{1}{3}bh$. More specifically, the formula is $V = \frac{1}{3}\pi r^2 h$.

Upper and Lower Bounds

Upper and lower bounds have to do with the accuracy of a measurement. When a measurement is given, the degree of accuracy is also stated to tell you what the upper and lower bounds of the measurement are. The upper bound is the largest possible value that a measurement could have had before being rounded down, and the lower bound is the lowest possible value it could have had before being rounded up.

Data Analysis and Probability

▶ *Formulate questions that can be addressed with data and collect, organize, and display relevant data to answer them*

Histograms

A histogram displays numerical data that have been organized into equal intervals using bars that have the same width and no space between them. While a histogram does not give exact data points, its shape shows the distribution of the data. Histograms also can be used to compare data.

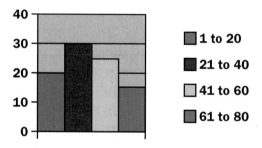

- ▨ 1 to 20
- ▪ 21 to 40
- ▢ 41 to 60
- ▨ 61 to 80

Box-and-Whisker Plot

A box-and-whisker plot displays the measures of central tendency and variation. A box is drawn around the quartile values, and whiskers extend from each quartile to the extreme data points. To make a box plot for a set of data, draw a number line that covers the range of data. Find the median, the extremes, and the upper and lower quartiles. Mark these points on the number line with bullets, then draw a box and the whiskers. The length of a whisker or box shows whether the values of the data in that part are concentrated or spread out.

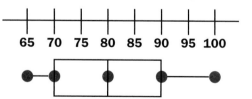

Scatter Plots

A scatter plot is a graph that shows the relationship between two sets of data. In a scatter plot, two sets of data are graphed as ordered pairs on a coordinate system. Two sets of data can have a positive correlation (as x increases, y increases), a negative correlation (as x increases, y decreases), or no correlation (no obvious pattern is shown). Scatter plots can be used to spot trends, draw conclusions, and make predictions about data.

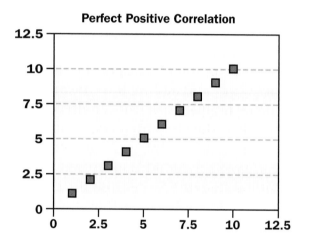

Randomization

The idea of randomization is a very important principle of statistics and the design of experiments. Data must be selected randomly to prevent bias from influencing the results. For example, you want to know the average income of people in your town but you can only use a sample of 100 individuals to make determinations about everyone. If you select 100 individuals who are all doctors, you will have a biased sample. However, if you chose a random sample of 100 people out of the phone book, you are much more likely to accurately represent average income in the town.

MATH APPENDIX

Statistics and Parameters

Statistics is a science that involves collecting, analyzing, and presenting data. The data can be collected in various ways—for example through a census or by making physical measurements. The data can then be analyzed by creating summary statistics, which have to do with the distribution of the data sample, including the mean, range, and standard error. They can also be illustrated in tables and graphs, like box-plots, scatter plots, and histograms. The presentation of the data typically involves describing the strength or validity of the data and what they show. For example, an analysis of ancestry of people in a city might tell you something about immigration patterns, unless the data set is very small or biased in some way, in which case it is not likely to be very accurate or useful.

Categorical and Measurement Data

When analyzing data, it is important to understand if the data is qualitative or quantitative. Categorical data is qualitative and measurement, or numerical, data is quantitative. Categorical data describes a quality of something and can be placed into different categories. For example, if you are analyzing the number of students in different grades in a school, each grade is a category. On the other hand, measurement data is continuous, like height, weight, or any other measurable variable. Measurement data can be converted into categorical data if you decide to group the data. Using height as an example, you can group the continuous data set into categories like under 5 feet, 5 feet to 5 feet 5 inches, over 5 feet 5 inches to 6 feet, and so on.

Univariate and Bivariate Data

In data analysis, a researcher can analyze one variable at a time or look at how multiple variables behave together. Univariate data involves only one variable, for example height in humans. You can measure the height in a population of people then plot the results in a histogram to look at how height is distributed in humans. To summarize univariate data, you can use statistics like the mean, mode, median, range, and standard deviation, which is a measure of variation. When looking at more than one variable at once, you use multivariate data. Bivariate data involves two variables. For example, you can look at height and age in humans together by gathering information on both variables from individuals in a population. You can then plot both variables in a scatter plot, look at how the variables behave in relation to each other, and create an equation that represents the relationship, also called a regression. These equations could help answer questions such as, for example, does height increase with age in humans?

▶ Select and use appropriate statistical methods to analyze data

Measures of Central Tendency

When you have a list of numerical data, it is often helpful to use one or more numbers to represent the whole set. These numbers are called measures of central tendency. Three measures of central tendency are mean, median, and mode. The mean is the sum of the data divided by the number of items in the data set. The median is the middle number of the ordered data (or the mean of the two middle numbers). The mode is the number or numbers that occur most often. These measures of central tendency allow data to be analyzed and better understood.

Measures of Spread

In statistics, measures of spread or variation are used to describe how data are distributed. The range of a set of data is the difference between the greatest and the least values of the data set. The quartiles are the values that divide the data into four equal parts. The median of data separates the set in half. Similarly, the median of the lower half of a set of data is the lower quartile. The median of the upper half of a set of data is the upper quartile. The interquartile range is the difference between the upper quartile and the lower quartile.

Line of Best Fit

When real-life data are collected, the points graphed usually do not form a straight line, but they may approximate a linear relationship. A line of best fit is a line that lies very close to most of the data points. It can be used to predict data. You also can use the equation of the best-fit line to make predictions.

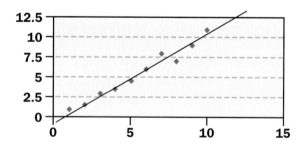

Stem and Leaf Plots

In a stem and leaf plot, numerical data are listed in ascending or descending order. The greatest place value of the data is used for the stems. The next greatest place value forms the leaves.

For example, if the least number in a set of data is 8 and the greatest number is 95, draw a vertical line and write the stems from 0 to 9 to the left of the line. Write the leaves from to the right of the line, with the corresponding stem. Next, rearrange the leaves so they are ordered from least to greatest. Then include a key or explanation, such as 1|3 = 13. Notice that the stem-and-leaf plot below is like a histogram turned on its side.

```
0|8
1|3 6
2|5 6 9
3|0 2 7 8
4|0 1 4 7 9
5|1 4 5 8
6|1 3 7
7|5 8
8|2 6
9|5
```
                        Key: **1|3 = 13**

▶ ***Develop and evaluate inferences and predictions that are based on data***

Sampling Distribution

The sampling distribution of a population is the distribution that would result if you could take an infinite number of samples from the population, average each, and then average the averages. The more normal the distribution of the population, that is, how closely the distribution follows a bell curve, the more likely the sampling distribution will also follow a normal distribution. Furthermore, the larger the sample, the more likely it will accurately represent the entire population. For instance, you are more likely to gain more representative results from a population of 1,000 with a sample of 100 than with a sample of 2.

Validity

In statistics, validity refers to acquiring results that accurately reflect that which is being measured. In other words, it is important when performing statistical analyses, to ensure that the data are valid in that the sample being analyzed represents the population to the best extent possible. Randomization of data and using appropriate sample sizes are two important aspects of making valid inferences about a population.

▶ *Understand and apply basic concepts of probability*

Complementary, Mutually Exclusive Events

To understand probability theory, it is important to know if two events are mutually exclusive, or complementary: the occurrence of one event automatically implies the non-occurrence of the other. That is, two complementary events cannot both occur. If you roll a pair of dice, the event of rolling 6 and rolling doubles have an outcome in common (3, 3), so they are not mutually exclusive. If you roll (3, 3), you also roll doubles. However, the events of rolling a 9 and rolling doubles are mutually exclusive because they have no outcomes in common. If you roll a 9, you will not also roll doubles.

Independent and Dependent Events

Determining the probability of a series of events requires that you know whether the events are independent or dependent. An independent event has no influence on the occurrence of subsequent events, whereas, a dependent event does influence subsequent events. The chances that a woman's first child will be a girl are $\frac{1}{2}$, and the chances that her second child will be a girl are also $\frac{1}{2}$ because the two events are independent of each other. However, if there are 7 red marbles in a bag of 15 marbles, the chances that the first marble you pick will be red are $\frac{7}{15}$ and if you indeed pick a red marble and remove it, you have reduced the chances of picking another red marble to $\frac{6}{14}$.

Sample Space

The sample space is the group of all possible outcomes for an event. For example, if you are tossing a single six-sided die, the sample space is {1, 2, 3, 4, 5, 6}. Similarly, you can determine the sample space for the possible outcomes of two events. If you are going to toss a coin twice, the sample space is {(heads, heads), (heads, tails), (tails, heads), (tails, tails)}.

Computing the Probability of a Compound Event

If two events are independent, the outcome of one event does not influence the outcome of the second. For example, if a bag contains 2 blue and 3 red marbles, then the probability of selecting a blue marble, replacing it, and then selecting a red marble is $P(A) \times P(B) = \frac{2}{5} \times \frac{3}{5}$ or $\frac{6}{25}$.

If two events are dependent, the outcome of one event affects the outcome of the second. For example, if a bag contains 2 blue and 3 red marbles, then the probability of selecting a blue and then a red marble without replacing the first marble is $P(A) \times P(B$ following $A) = \frac{2}{5} \times \frac{3}{4}$ or $\frac{3}{10}$. Two events that cannot happen at the same time are mutually exclusive. For example, when you roll two number cubes, you cannot roll a sum that is both 5 and even. So, $P(A$ or $B) = \frac{4}{36} + \frac{18}{36}$ or $\frac{11}{18}$.

◐ MAKING CAREER CHOICES

A career differs from a job in that it is a series of progressively more responsible jobs in one field or a related field. You will need to learn some special skills to choose a career and to help you in your job search. Choosing a career and identifying career opportunities require careful thought and preparation. To aid you in making important career choices, follow these steps:

STEPS TO MAKING A CAREER DECISION

1. Conduct a self-assessment to determine your:
   - values
   - lifestyle goals
   - interests
   - skills and aptitudes
   - personality
   - work environment preferences
   - relationship preferences

2. Identify possible career choices based on your self-assessment.

3. Gather information on each choice, including future trends.

4. Evaluate your choices based on your self-assessment.

5. Make your decision.

After you make your decision, plan how you will reach your goal. It is best to have short-term, medium-term, and long-term goals. In making your choices, explore the future opportunities in this field or fields over the next several years. What impact will new technology and automation have on job opportunities in the next few years? Remember, if you plan, you make your own career opportunities.

◐ PERSONAL CAREER PORTFOLIO

You will want to create and maintain a personal career portfolio. In it you will keep all the documents you create and receive in your job search:

- Contact list
- Résumé
- Letters of recommendation
- Employer evaluations
- Awards
- Evidence of participation in school, community, and volunteer activities
- Notes about your job search
- Notes made after your interviews

CAREER RESEARCH RESOURCES

In order to gather information on various career opportunities, there are a variety of sources to research:

- **Libraries.** Your school or public library offers good career information resources. Here you will find books, magazines, pamphlets, films, videos, and special reference materials on careers. In particular, the U.S. Department of Labor publishes three reference books that are especially helpful: the *Dictionary of Occupational Titles (DOT),* which describes about 20,000 jobs and their relationships with data, people, and things; the *Occupational Outlook Handbook (OOH),* with information on more than 200 occupations; and the *Guide for Occupational Exploration (GOE),* a reference that organizes the world of work into 12 interest areas that are subdivided into work groups and subgroups.

- **The Internet.** The Internet is becoming a primary source of research on any topic. It is especially helpful in researching careers.

- **Career Consultations.** Career consultation, an informational interview with a professional who works in a career that interests you, provides an opportunity to learn about the day-to-day realities of a career.

- **On-the-Job Experience.** On-the-job experience can be valuable in learning firsthand about a job or career. You can find out if your school has a work-experience program, or look into a company or organization's internship opportunities. Interning gives you direct work experience and often allows you to make valuable contacts for future full-time employment.

THE JOB SEARCH

To aid you in your actual job search, there are various sources to explore. You should contact and research all the sources that might produce a job lead, or information about a job. Keep a contact list as you proceed with your search. Some of these resources include:

- **Networking with family, friends, and acquaintances.** This means contacting people you know personally, including school counselors, former employers, and professional people.

- **Cooperative education and work-experience programs.** Many schools have such programs in which students work part-time on a job related to one of their classes. Many also offer work-experience programs that are not limited to just one career area, such as marketing.

- **Newspaper ads.** Reading the Help Wanted advertisements in your local papers will provide a source of job leads, as well as teach you about the local job market.

- **Employment agencies.** Most cities have two types of employment agencies, public and private. These employment agencies match workers with jobs. Some private agencies may charge a fee, so be sure to know who is expected to pay the fee and what the fee is.

- **Company personnel offices.** Large and medium-sized companies have personnel offices to handle employment matters, including the hiring of new workers. You can check on job openings by contacting the office by telephone or by scheduling a personal visit.

- **Searching the Internet.** Cyberspace offers multiple opportunities for your job search. Web sites, such as Hotjobs.com or Monster.com, provide lists of companies offering employment. There are tens of thousands of career-related Web sites, so the challenge is finding those that have jobs that interest you and that are up-to-date in their listings. Companies that interest you may have a Web site, which will provide valuable information on their benefits and opportunities for employment.

APPLYING FOR A JOB

When you have contacted the sources of job leads and found some jobs that interest you, the next step is to apply for them. You will need to complete application forms, write letters of application, and prepare your own résumé. Before you apply for a job, you will need to have a work permit if you are under the age of 18 in most states. Some state and federal labor laws designate certain jobs as too dangerous for young workers. Laws also limit the number of hours of work allowed during a day, a week, or the school year. You will also need to have proper documentation, such as a green card if you are not a U.S. citizen.

JOB APPLICATION

You can obtain the job application form directly at the place of business, by requesting it in writing, or over the Internet. It is best if you can fill the form out at home, but some businesses require that you fill it out at the place of work.

Fill out the job application forms neatly and accurately, using standard English, the formal style of speaking and writing you learned in school. You must be truthful and pay attention to detail in filling out the form.

PERSONAL FACT SHEET

To be sure that the answers you write on a job application form are accurate, make a personal fact sheet before filling out the application:

- Your name, home address, and phone number
- Your Social Security number
- The job you are applying for
- The date you can begin work
- The days and hours you can work
- The pay you want
- Whether or not you have been convicted of a crime
- Your education
- Your previous work experience
- Your birth date
- Your driver's license number if you have one
- Your interests and hobbies, and awards you have won
- Your previous work experience, including dates
- Schools you have attended
- Places you have lived
- Accommodations you may need from the employer
- A list of references—people who will tell an employer that you will do a good job, such as relatives, students, former employers, and the like

LETTERS OF RECOMMENDATION

Letters of recommendation are helpful. You can request teachers, counselors, relatives, and other acquaintances who know you well to write these letters. They should be short, to the point, and give a brief overview of your assets. A brief description of any of your important accomplishments or projects should follow. The letter should end with a brief description of your character and work ethic.

LETTER OF APPLICATION

Some employees prefer a letter of application, rather than an application form. This letter is like writing a sales pitch about yourself. You need to tell why you are the best person for the job, what special qualifications you have, and include all the information usually found on an application form. Write the letter in standard English, making certain that it is neat, accurate, and correct.

RÉSUMÉ

The purpose of a résumé is to make an employer want to interview you. A résumé tells prospective employers what you are like and what you can do for them. A good résumé summarizes you at your best in a one- or two-page outline. It should include the following information:

1. **Identification.** Include your name, address, telephone number, and e-mail address.

2. **Objective.** Indicate the type of job you are looking for.

3. **Experience.** List experience related to the specific job for which you are applying. List other work if you have not worked in a related field.

4. **Education.** Include schools attended from high school on, the dates of attendance, and diplomas or degrees earned. You may also include courses related to the job you are applying for.

5. **References.** Include up to three references or indicate that they are available. Always ask people ahead of time if they are willing to be listed as references for you.

A résumé that you put online or send by e-mail is called an *electronic résumé*. Some Web sites allow you to post them on their sites without charge. Employers access these sites to find new employees. Your electronic résumé should follow the guidelines for a regular one. It needs to be accurate. Stress your skills and sell yourself to prospective employers.

COVER LETTER

If you are going to get the job you want, you need to write a great cover letter to accompany your résumé. Think of a cover letter as an introduction: a piece of paper that conveys a smile, a confident hello, and a nice, firm handshake. The cover letter is the first thing a potential employer sees, and it can make a powerful impression. The following are some tips for creating a cover letter that is professional and gets the attention you want:

- **Keep it short.** Your cover letter should be one page, no more.
- **Make it look professional.** These days, you need to type your letter on a computer and print it on a laser printer. Do not use an inkjet printer unless it produces extremely crisp type. Use white or buff-colored paper; anything else will draw the wrong kind of attention. Type your name, address, phone number, and e-mail address at the top of the page.
- **Explain why you are writing.** Start your letter with one sentence describing where you heard of the opening. "Joan Wright suggested I contact you regarding a position in your marketing department," or "I am writing to apply for the position you advertised in the Sun City Journal."
- **Introduce yourself.** Give a short description of your professional abilities and background. Refer to your attached résumé: "As you will see in the attached résumé, I am an experienced editor with a background in newspapers, magazines, and textbooks." Then highlight one or two specific accomplishments.

- **Sell yourself.** Your cover letter should leave the reader thinking, "This person is exactly what we are looking for." Focus on what you can do for the company. Relate your skills to the skills and responsibilities mentioned in the job listing. If the ad mentions solving problems, relate a problem you solved at school or work. If the ad mentions specific skills or knowledge required, mention your mastery of these in your letter. (Also be sure these skills are included on your résumé.)

- **Provide all requested information.** If the Help Wanted ad asked for "salary requirements" or "salary history," include this information in your cover letter. However, you do not have to give specific numbers. It is okay to say, "My wage is in the range of $10 to $15 per hour." If the employer does not ask for salary information, do not offer any.

- **Ask for an interview.** You have sold yourself, now wrap it up. Be confident, but not pushy. "If you agree that I would be an asset to your company, please call me at [insert your phone number]. I am available for an interview at your convenience." Finally, thank the person. "Thank you for your consideration. I look forward to hearing from you soon." Always close with a "Sincerely," followed by your full name and signature.

- **Check for errors.** Read and re-read your letter to make sure each sentence is correctly worded and there are no errors in spelling, punctuation, or grammar. Do not rely on your computer's spell checker or grammar checker. A spell check will not detect if you typed "tot he" instead of "to the." It is a good idea to have someone else read your letter, too. He or she might notice an error you overlooked.

INTERVIEW

Understanding how to best prepare for and follow up on interviews is critical to your career success. At different times in your life, you may interview with a teacher or professor, a prospective employer, a supervisor, or a promotion or tenure committee. Just as having an excellent résumé is vital for opening the door, interview skills are critical for putting your best foot forward and seizing the opportunity to clearly articulate why you are the best person for the job.

RESEARCH THE COMPANY

Your ability to convince an employer that you understand and are interested in the field you are interviewing to enter is important. Show that you have knowledge about the company and the industry. What products or services does the company offer? How is it doing? What is the competition? Use your research to demonstrate your understanding of the company.

PREPARE QUESTIONS FOR THE INTERVIEWER

Prepare interview questions to ask the interviewer. Some examples include:

- "What would my responsibilities be?"
- "Could you describe my work environment?"
- "What are the chances to move up in the company?"
- "Do you offer training?"
- "What can you tell me about the people who work here?"

DRESS APPROPRIATELY

You will never get a second chance to make a good first impression. Nonverbal communication is 90 percent of communication, so dressing appropriately is of the utmost importance. Every job is different, and you should wear clothing that is appropriate for the job for which you are applying. In most situations, you will be safe if you wear clean, pressed, conservative business clothes in neutral colors. Pay special attention to grooming. Keep makeup light and wear very little jewelry.

Make certain your nails and hair are clean, trimmed, and neat. Do not carry a large purse, backpack, books, or coat. Simply carry a pad of paper, a pen, and extra copies of your résumé and letters of reference in a small folder.

EXHIBIT GOOD BEHAVIOR

Conduct yourself properly during an interview. Go alone; be courteous and polite to everyone you meet. Relax and focus on your purpose: to make the best possible impression.

- Be on time.
- Be poised and relaxed.
- Avoid nervous habits.
- Avoid littering your speech with verbal clutter such as "you know," "um," and "like."
- Look your interviewer in the eye and speak with confidence.
- Use nonverbal techniques to reinforce your confidence, such as a firm handshake and poised demeanor.
- Convey maturity by exhibiting the ability to tolerate differences of opinion.
- Never call anyone by a first name unless you are asked to do so.
- Know the name, title, and the pronunciation of the interviewer's name.
- Do not sit down until the interviewer does.
- Do not talk too much about your personal life.
- Never bad-mouth your former employers.

BE PREPARED FOR COMMON INTERVIEW QUESTIONS

You can never be sure exactly what will happen at an interview, but you can be prepared for common interview questions. There are some interview questions that are illegal. Interviewers should not ask you about your age, gender, color, race, or religion. Employers should not ask whether you are married or pregnant, or question your health or disabilities.

Take time to think about your answers now. You might even write them down to clarify your thinking. The key to all interview questions is to be honest, and to be positive. Focus your answers on skills and abilities that apply to the job you are seeking. Practice answering the following questions with a friend:

- "Tell me about yourself."
- "Why do you want to work at this company?"
- "What did you like/dislike about your last job?"
- "What is your biggest accomplishment?"
- "What is your greatest strength?"
- "What is your greatest weakness?"
- "Do you prefer to work with others or on your own?"
- "What are your career goals?" or "Where do you see yourself in five years?"
- "Tell me about a time that you had a lot of work to do in a short time. How did you manage the situation?"
- "Have you ever had to work closely with a person you didn't get along with? How did you handle the situation?"

AFTER THE INTERVIEW

Be sure to thank the interviewer after the interview for his or her time and effort. Do not forget to follow up after the interview. Ask, "What is the next step?" If you are told to call in a few days, wait two or three days before calling back.

If the interview went well, the employer may call you to offer you the job. Find out the terms of the job offer, including job title and pay. Decide whether you want the job. If you decide not to accept the job, write a letter of rejection. Be courteous and thank the person for the opportunity and the offer. You may wish to give a brief general reason for not accepting the job. Leave the door open for possible employment in the future.

FOLLOW UP WITH A LETTER

Write a thank-you letter as soon as the interview is over. This shows your good manners, interest, and enthusiasm for the job. It also shows that you are organized. Make the letter neat and courteous. Thank the interviewer. Sell yourself again.

ACCEPTING A NEW JOB

If you decide to take the job, write a letter of acceptance. The letter should include some words of appreciation for the opportunity, written acceptance of the job offer, the terms of employment (salary, hours, benefits), and the starting date. Make sure the letter is neat and correct.

 STARTING A NEW JOB

Your first day of work will be busy. Determine what the dress code is and dress appropriately. Learn to do each task assigned properly. Ask for help when you need it. Learn the rules and regulations of the workplace.

You will do some paperwork on your first day. Bring your personal fact sheet with you. You will need to fill out some forms. Form W-4 tells your employer how much money to withhold for taxes. You may also need to fill out Form I-9. This shows that you are allowed to work in the United States. You will need your Social Security number and proof that you are allowed to work in the United States. You can bring your U.S. passport, your Certificate of Naturalization, or your Certificate of U.S. Citizenship. If you are not a permanent resident of the United States, bring your green card. If you are a resident of the United States, you will need to bring your work permit on your first day. If you are under the age of 16 in some states, you need a different kind of work permit.

You might be requested to take a drug test as a requirement for employment in some states. This could be for the safety of you and your coworkers, especially when working with machinery or other equipment.

IMPORTANT SKILLS AND QUALITIES

You will not work alone on a job. You will need to learn skills for getting along and being a team player. There are many good qualities necessary to get along in the workplace. They include being positive, showing sympathy, taking an interest in others, tolerating differences, laughing a little, and showing respect. Your employer may promote you or give you a raise if you show good employability skills.

There are several qualities necessary to be a good employee and get ahead in your job:

- be cooperative
- possess good character
- be responsible
- finish what you start
- work fast but do a good job
- have a strong work ethic
- work well without supervision
- work well with others
- possess initiative
- show enthusiasm for what you do
- be on time
- make the best of your time
- obey company laws and rules
- be honest
- be loyal
- exhibit good health habits

LEAVING A JOB

If you are considering leaving your job or are being laid off, you are facing one of the most difficult aspects in your career. The first step in resigning is to prepare a short resignation letter to offer your supervisor at the conclusion of the meeting you set up with him or her. Keep the letter short and to the point. Express your appreciation for the opportunity you had with the company. Do not try to list all that was wrong with the job.

You want to leave on good terms. Do not forget to ask for a reference. Do not talk about your employer or any of your coworkers. Do not talk negatively about your employer when you apply for a new job.

If you are being laid off or face downsizing, it can make you feel angry or depressed. Try to view it as a career-change opportunity. If possible, negotiate a good severance package. Find out about any benefits you may be entitled to. Perhaps the company will offer job-search services or consultation for finding new employment.

TAKE ACTION!

It is time for action. Remember the networking and contact lists you created when you searched for this job. Reach out for support from friends, family, and other acquaintances. Consider joining a job-search club. Assess your skills. Upgrade them if necessary. Examine your attitude and your vocational choices. Decide the direction you wish to take and move on!

Glossary

How to Use This Glossary

- Content vocabulary terms in this glossary are words that relate to this book's content. They are **highlighted yellow** in your text.

- Words in this glossary that have an asterisk (*) are academic vocabulary terms. They help you understand your school subjects and are used on tests. They are **boldfaced blue** in your text.

- Some of the vocabulary words in this book include pronunciation symbols to help you sound out the words. Use the pronunciation key to help you pronounce the words.

Pronunciation Key		
a . . . . at	ô . . . . fork, all	th . . . thin
ā . . . . ape	oo . . . wood, put	th . . . this
ä . . . . father	o͞o . . . fool	zh . . . treasure
e . . . . end	oi . . . oil	ə . . . . ago, taken, pencil, lemon, circus
ē . . . . me	ou . . . out	
i . . . . it	u . . . . up	ˈ . . . . indicates primary stress (symbol in front of and *above* letter)
ī . . . . ice	ū . . . . use	
o . . . . hot	ü . . . . rule	ˌ . . . . indicates secondary stress (symbol in front of and *below* letter)
ō . . . . hope	u̇ . . . . pull	
ȯ . . . . saw	ŋ . . . . sing	

absorb • adoptive family

---

* **absorb** To take in; retain; soak up. (p. 529)

abstinence (ˈab-stə-nən(t)s) A deliberate decision to avoid high-risk behaviors, including sexual activity and the use of tobacco, alcohol, and other drugs. (p. 533)

* **abuse** Bad or improper treatment. (p. 517)

* **access** The ability, right, or permission to approach, enter, speak with, or use; admittance. (p. 209)

* **accountability** The state of being accountable, responsible, liable, or answerable. (p. 194)

acquaintance A person known to one, but usually not a close friend. (p. 87)

active listening A style of listening in which the listener works to understand the speaker's feelings and the message's true meaning. (p. 111)

adaptation (ˌa-ˌdap-ˈtā-shən) The means by which people make and adjust to changes. (p. 311)

addiction (ə-ˈdik-shən) A dependence on a particular substance or action. (p. 314)

adjustment The act of changing routines and feelings to function in a new setting. (p. 276)

adolescence (ˌa-də-ˈle-sᵊn(t)s) The time of life between childhood and adulthood. (p. 360)

adoption The legal process of taking a child of other parents as one's own. (p. 611)

adoptive family A family with a child or children who are made part of the family through legal action. (p. 45)

aerobic (ˌer-ˈō-bik) **exercise** Strenuous activity that raises the heart rate. (p. 437)

* **affect** To influence or alter; produce an effect or change in. (p. 569)

affirmation (ˌa-fər-ˈmā-shən) Positive input that helps others feel appreciated and supported. (p. 140)

ageism (ˈā-(ˌ)ji-zəm) The belief that older people are not as alert, intelligent, or capable as young people. (p. 292)

* **aggression** Hostile or destructive behavior or actions. (p. 112)

alcoholism An addiction to alcohol. (p. 314)

alimony (ˈa-lə-ˌmō-nē) Financial support of an ex-spouse. (p. 273)

altruism (ˈal-trü-ˌi-zəm) An unselfish concern for the welfare of others. (p. 398)

Alzheimer's disease A degenerative brain disease that causes memory loss, impaired thinking, and the inability to carry out daily activities. (p. 297)

* **analyze** To examine carefully and in detail so as to identify causes, key factors, and possible results. (p. 421)

annulment (a-ˈnəl-mənt) The legal dissolution of a marriage that declares the marriage never took place due to some prior condition. (p. 271)

anorexia nervosa (ˌa-nə-ˈrek-sē-ə -(ˌ)nər-ˈvō-sə) A disorder that shows itself in a fear of being overweight. (p. 436)

antibiotic A special medicine that destroys disease-causing bacteria. (p. 429)

* **anticipate** To expect; look forward to; be sure of. (p. 96)

application form A form that gives employers basic data about job candidates. (p. 494)

apprentice One who receives training from a skilled worker in a trade. (p. 488)

* **appropriate** Suitable for a particular purpose, person, or occasion. (p. 227)

aptitude A natural talent and capacity for learning a certain skill. (p. 486)

* **array** A large group, number, or quantity of people or things. (p. 9)

* **aspect** A part, feature, or phase. (p. 358)

assertive (ə-ˈsər-tiv) Firm; positive. (p. 112)

* **assess** To charge; to determine the value, significance, or extent of. (p. 450)

* **asset** Resource. (p. 344)

asset Something of value. (p. 456)

* **assume** To take for granted or suppose without proof. (p. 122)

attitude A person's state of mind or feeling. (p. 340)

auditory learning Learning by listening. (p. 353)

authoritarian style A parenting style in which parents expect children to trust and obey without question. (p. 640)

authoritative style A parenting style in which parents consider a child's desires, abilities, and ideas. (p. 640)

authority The right to give orders, make decisions, and enforce rules. (p. 161)

* **autocratic** Having absolute power. (p. 48)

autonomy The ability to direct one's life independently. (p. 417)

B

bankruptcy (ˈbaŋk-(ˌ)rəp(t)-sē) A legal process that declares a person unable to pay debts. (p. 253)

bargain A good buy. (p. 470)

* **barrier** Anything that restrains or obstructs progress; a limit or boundary of any kind. (p. 112)

* **belittle** To treat or speak of a person as small or unimportant; insult. (p. 317)

bereaved The condition of having lost a loved one. (p. 319)

betrayal The act of breaking another's trust; the feeling that trust has been broken. (p. 270)

Better Business Bureau An independent group sponsored by businesses in a community to watch over advertising, keep information about companies on file, and record consumers' complaints about businesses. (p. 478)

* **bias** A preference, especially one that prevents impartial judgment. (p. 338)

* **biology** The science of life and of living organisms, including their structure, function, growth, origin, evolution, and distribution. (p. 607)

birth defect A problem that happens when a baby is developing in the mother's body. (p. 620)

birth order The order in which each child in a family is born. (p. 150)

blended family A husband and wife, at least one of whom has children from a former relationship. (p. 44)

body image One's perception of one's physical self. (p. 352)

* **bolster** To boost up; increase. (p. 511)

bulimia (bü-'lē-mē-ə) An eating disorder that involves binge eating. (p. 436)

C

cardiovascular (ˌkär-dē-ō-'vas-kyə-lər) **disease** A heart-related disease. (p. 430)

career A series of related jobs or occupations done over a period of years. (p. 485)

career cluster A group of occupations and broad industries that have something in common. (p. 486)

career counselor A person who helps people choose and succeed in their work. (p. 486)

career path The connections existing between one job and another. (p. 490)

caregiver A person who provides direct care, usually for a child, older adult, or someone who is ill. (p. 289)

* **category** A specifically defined division in a system of classification; a class. (p. 459)

* **chagrin** Embarrassment. (p. 643)

* **channel** A course into which something may be directed. (p. 193)

character Moral strength. (p. 371)

* **characteristic** A distinguishing feature or quality. (p. 26)

* **check** To inspect so as to determine accuracy, quality, or other condition; to verify. (p. 493)

check A written document that transfers money from a bank account to a person or business. (p. 450)

child development How children grow and change at each stage from birth through the teen years. (p. 618)

chosen role A role that is deliberately selected. (p. 95)

chronic disease An illness or condition that occurs repeatedly or never goes away. (p. 290)

* **circumstance** An incident, event, situation, or occurrence. (p. 55)

citizenship Membership in a community that guarantees certain rights. (p. 389)

clarification To make clear; to understand or express a message clearly. (p. 127)

code of ethics A clear set of rules or principles that guide actions and decisions. (p. 374)

commitment A pledge to support something of value. (p. 141)

communication The process of sending and receiving messages. (p. 13)

communication channel A way in which a message is passed. (p. 106)

community A common area where different people live. (p. 8)

* **compare** To examine in order to note the similarities or differences of. (p. 453)

comparison shopping To look at the same item in several stores and compare quality and price before purchasing. (p. 470)

compatible Capable of existing or living together in harmony. (p. 515)

* **competent** Having suitable or sufficient skill, knowledge, or experience for some purpose; properly qualified. (p. 170)

competition A contest between rivals. (p. 129)

complementary needs The theory that people select partners who complete, or complement, their personality needs. (p. 548)

* **compress** To condense, shorten, or abbreviate. (p. 232)

compromise A settlement of differences in which each side makes concessions or sacrifices. (p. 124)

compulsion A behavior addiction. (p. 314)

compulsive eating A disorder in which people are unable to resist food. (p. 436)

conception The union of a sperm and egg. (p. 619)

confidential Done or communicated privately or secretly. (p. 105)

conflict A disagreement or struggle between two or more people. (p. 121)

conflict resolution A way to solve disagreements. (p. 13)

conform To follow the customs, rules, or standards of a group. (p. 377)

* **confront** To come face to face with. (p. 14)

conscience ('kän(t)-shən(t)s) A person's inner sense of what is right and wrong. (p. 371)

consequence ('kän(t)-sə-ˌkwen(t)s) The result of an action. (p. 186)

* **constructive** Serving to improve or advance; helpful. (p.129)

consumer A person who purchases goods and services. (p. 469)

Consumer Action and Advisory Panel Organizations formed by specific industries to help solve consumer problems. (p. 478)

* **contagious** Capable of being transmitted by bodily contact with an infected person or object. (p. 432)

contract A binding agreement between two or more people. (p. 575)

* **contradict** To assert the contrary or opposite of; deny. (p. 530)

control The action of directing another person's behavior. (p. 122)

* **controversy** A dispute, especially a public one, between sides holding opposing views. (p. 33)

conventional level A level of development of the moral self in which the rules, expectations, and judgment of the group surrounding a person become the standard for behavior. (p. 372)

cooperation The ability to work with others toward a common goal. (p. 160)

cope To deal with and overcome problems and difficulties. (p. 307)

cost Physical, mental, and emotional contributions made to a relationship. (p. 90)

* **create** To cause to exist; bring into being. (p. 420)

credit Money that is borrowed or used with the intention to repay later. (p. 452)

creditor Someone to whom debt is owed. (p. 253)

crisis ('krī-səs) A situation that has reached a critical phase. (p. 307)

* **criterion** A standard of judgment or criticism; a rule or principle for evaluating or testing something. (p. 550)

cross-contamination Moving disease causing organisms from one food to another. (p. 419)

cultural heritage The beliefs, customs, and traditions of an ethnic group. (p. 75)

culture Everything that defines the identity of a specific group of people, including beliefs, traits, customs, geography, knowledge, art, and technology. (p. 73)

custody The legal right to make decisions that affect children. (p. 272)

custom A common practice among many people that has been handed down from the past. (p. 575)

* **cycle** Any long period of years. (p. 53)

D

date rape Rape that takes place in a dating situation. (p. 538)

dating Shared social activity, usually involving two people going out together. (p. 516)

* **daunting** Discouraging or intimidating. (p. 277)

debit card A plastic card used to buy goods and services without cash. (p. 451)

debt Something that is owed. (p. 253)

* **deception** The act of deceiving; the state of being deceived. (p. 476)

~ **decision** A choice that is made. (p. 183)

~ **decision-making process** A series of steps to identify and evaluate possibilities and make a good choice. (p. 183)

* **décor** Style or mode of decoration, as of a room or building. (p. 413)

deductible On an insurance policy, the amount the policyholder pays when a loss occurs. (p. 454)

* **degrade** To lower in dignity; dishonor or disgrace. (p. 316)

dementia A progressive decline in cognitive function due to damage or disease in the brain. (p. 297)

denial (di-'nī-(-ə)l) Disbelief in the existence or reality of a thing. (p. 190, p. 320)

dependent Relying on something or someone else for aid or support. (p. 49)

* **determine** To decide or settle conclusively. (p. 458)

Glossary

development The process of growth and change over the course of life. (p. 53)

* **diet** The usual food or drink of a person or animal. (p. 434)

diplomacy The ability to handle situations without upsetting the people involved. (p. 171)

directive leadership A style of leadership in which a leader sets a group's goals. (p. 170)

* **disastrous** Causing great distress or injury; ruinous; very unfortunate. (p. 392)

discipline The process of helping children behave in acceptable ways. (p. 641)

disengagement Withdrawal from others and from activity. (p. 294)

* **distinguish** To recognize as distinct or different. (p. 24)

diversity The state or fact of being varied or different. (p. 74)

divorce A legal action that ends a marriage. (p. 269)

divorce mediation When a couple meets with a neutral third person to negotiate the terms of their divorce. (p. 271)

* **dominate** To rule over, govern, or control. (p. 107)

down payment An initial amount paid in cash during installment buying. (p. 453)

dysfunctional Impaired in function, especially of a family. (p. 7)

E

ecology The relationship of living things and their environment. (p. 392)

* **economic** Of or relating to the production, development, and management of material wealth, as of a country, household, or business enterprise. (p. 214)

economy The ways in which a group produces, distributes, and consumes its goods and service. (p. 71)

* **effect** A result or cause. (p. 95)

* **efficiency** Accomplishment of or ability to accomplish a job with a minimum amount of time and effort. (p. 68)

egocentrism Seeing life only from one's own point of view. (p. 379)

elder abuse Physical abuse of aging people. (p. 291)

electronic funds transfer To move money from one account to another by electronic means. (p. 451)

emotion A feeling experienced in response to thoughts, remarks, and events. (p. 24)

emotional abuse The wrong or harmful treatment of someone's emotional health. (p. 317)

emotional support The actions people take to meet the emotional needs of others. (p. 24)

empathy The ability to put oneself in another's situation. (p. 74)

empty nest A situation experienced by a couple whose children have become adults and moved out of the family home. (p. 57)

endurance The length of time one is able to work or exercise. (p. 437)

engagement A promise or intention to marry; the period of time after making this promise and before the wedding. (p. 569)

* **entice** To attract by arousing hope or desire; lure. (p. 469)

entrepreneur Someone who organizes and runs a business. (p. 213)

environment Surrounding conditions or circumstances. (p. 67)

epinephrine (ˌe-pə-ˈne-frən) The human hormone that causes physical reactions to stress. (p. 262)

* **esteem** To regard with respect. (p. 515)

estranged Alienated; distant; apart. (p. 596)

ethics The principles of conduct that govern a group or society. (p. 105)

ethnic group People of the same race or nationality who share a culture. (p. 74)

etiquette Manners; the rules of appropriate behavior. (p. 160)

* **evaluate** To examine and judge carefully; appraise. (p. 355)

* **exchange** To give in return for something received; trade. (p. 549)

expectation A belief about or a mental picture of the future. (p. 588)

* **explain** To make plain, clear, or comprehensible. (p. 476)

exploitation The act of using a person or thing unfairly for personal benefit. (p. 91)

extended family Relatives other than parents and their children, such as grandparents, aunts, uncles, and cousins. (p. 44)

extrovert A person who is focused outward on others. (p. 337)

F

* **facet** An aspect or phase. (p. 361)

family A group of two or more people who live together. (p. 7)

family bond A strong feeling of connection that unites a family in a committed relationship. (p. 25)

family system A system in which family members, with their various roles and personalities, act together. (p. 146)

favoritism When a parent favors one child over another. (p. 278)

feedback A response to a message that indicates whether or not the message was understood. (p. 111)

fertility The ability to have children. (p. 611)

fidelity Faithfulness to an obligation, duty or trust (p. 539)

financial plan A plan, or budget, that guides spending and saving. (p. 458)

fixed expense A regular expense. (p. 458)

fixed income A set amount that does not change. (p. 287)

flexibility The ability to move one's limbs to a great extent, sometimes to their fullest extent. (p. 437)

flexible expense An expense that does not occur regularly. (p. 459)

flextime A style of scheduling in which workers construct their schedules to suit their lives. (p. 232)

* **foresight** Perception of the significance and nature of events before they have occurred. (p. 165)

* **forethought** Deliberation, consideration, or planning beforehand. (p. 607)

foster family A family that takes care of children on a short-term basis. (p. 45)

* **frail** Weak; delicate; having delicate health. (p. 290)

free-rein leadership A style of leadership in which group members are allowed to plan and complete their work on their own. (p. 170)

* **frugal** Economical; prudently saving or sparing; not wasteful. (p. 287)

* **frustration** A feeling of dissatisfaction, often accompanied by anxiety or depression, resulting from unfulfilled needs or unresolved problems. (p. 128)

function A purpose, action, or role. (p. 7)

futurist A person who studies and predicts what may happen in the future. (p. 207)

G

* **gain** To acquire an increase or addition. (p. 9)

gender role The behavior and traits expected of a male or female. (p. 527)

* **generosity** Willingness to give. (p. 395)

genetic disease A disease that is passed from parent to child. (p. 608)

gerontology (ˌjer-ən-ˈtä-lə-jē) The study of the aging process. (p. 294)

given role A role that is automatically acquired, such as that of son or daughter. (p. 95)

global economy The ways in which the world's economics are linked. (p. 71)

goal Something one plans to achieve. (p. 50)

* **grant** To give, agree, or permit. (p. 232)

grief Painful emotions and physical feelings resulting from the death of a loved one. (p. 319)

H

* **hallmark** Any distinguishing feature or characteristic. (p. 168)

harassment Behavior that is threatening or disturbing. (p. 316)

heredity (hə-ˈre-də-tē) Genetic traits received from parents at birth. (p. 150)

homogamy (hō-ˈmä-gə-mē) Sameness. (p. 547)

hormone A chemical substance that regulates the activity of cells in the body. (p. 352)

household work The work a family does in the home to keep up with day-to-day living. (p. 225)

* hygiene Conditions and practices that serve to promote or preserve health or cleanliness. (p. 492)

I-message A message that begins with the word "I" and accurately reflects what the speaker thinks, believes, and feels. (p.111)

identity One's view of oneself as a person. (p. 253)

identity theft Using another person's personal information to steal money or credit. (p. 215)

immunity The condition of being able to resist a particular disease. (p. 437)

* impact To have an effect. (p. 67)

impulse buying The purchase of items without previous thought. (p. 471)

income-producing work Work that provides money for needs and wants. (p. 226)

independence The ability to take care of oneself. (p. 28)

* individuality The qualities and characteristics that distinguish one person or thing from others; character. (p. 377)

* induce To bring about, produce, or cause. (p. 436)

infatuation (in-ˌfa-chə-ˈwā-shən) An intense, emotional involvement that begins with a sudden, strong attraction. (p. 517)

infertility The inability to have children. (p. 611)

* influence A power affecting a person, thing, or course of events. (p. 74)

information society A society in which the main economic activity is creating and distributing knowledge. (p. 214)

* initiative The power or ability to begin or to follow through energetically with a plan or task. (p. 159)

institution of marriage Marriage as a way of living. (p. 557)

insurance A promise of payment in the case of loss. (p. 454)

* intensive Of, relating to, or characterized by intensity. (p. 599)

* interaction A mutual or reciprocal action; interacting. (p. 89)

interdependence A feeling among people, including family members, that they can rely on each other. (p. 48)

interest The extra money that is paid when a spender uses credit to make purchases. (p. 452)

interpersonal Occurring between people. (p. 13)

* interpret To understand, give or provide the meaning of; explain. (p. 486)

interrelate To link in a mutual relationship. (p. 356)

intervention Taking direct action to cause change when someone else is in a crisis. (p. 322)

interview A face-to-face meeting between an employer and a potential employee. (p. 494)

intimacy A closeness that develops from a personal relationship. (p. 595)

* intrigued To have aroused curiosity or interest. (p. 149)

introvert A person focused inward, on himself or herself. (p. 337)

intrusive (in-ˈtrü-siv, -ziv) Entering or interrupting without invitation. (p. 215)

invalidation ((ˌ)in-ˈva-lə-ˌdā-shən) When partners respond negatively to, make judgements about, or blame each other. (p. 270)

investment The purchase of an asset to make money. (p. 456)

isolation (ˌī-sə-ˈlā-shən) To feel set apart from others and completely alone. (p. 310)

jealousy Watchfulness in guarding a relationship with a loved one. (p. 557)

kinesthetic learning Learning by doing. (p. 353)

labor A series of contractions of the uterus. (p. 620)

landlord A property owner. (p. 413)

Glossary

laparoscope A tiny telescope that lets a surgeon see inside a patient's body. (p. 429)

latch-key child A child who is home alone after school. (p. 633)

launching The process in families during which children are sent away from the family home to live on their own, physically and financially. (p. 57)

leader A person who guides or influences others. (p. 169)

lease A written agreement between a landlord and a tenant. (p. 413)

leave of absence Time off from work to use for a purpose, such as after the birth of a child or during illness. (p. 232)

legal guardian A person who has financial and legal duties relating to the care of a child. (p. 45)

* **leisure** Freedom from the demands of work or duty. (p. 208)

life-span development The growth and change that occurs throughout a person's life. (p. 358)

life task A challenge to be met at each stage of growth. (p. 360)

listening A mental activity that allows one to receive messages accurately. (p. 110)

loan An agreement to borrow money and to pay back more than the borrowed amount. (p. 453)

long-term goal A goal that takes months or years to achieve. (p. 194)

management Using one's resources to obtain one's wants. (p. 13)

marriage commitment The desire to make a marriage work. (p. 587)

mature (mə-'tür, -'tyür) The state of having completed natural growth and development. (p. 376)

mature love Love that is shared between people at the highest level of emotional development. (p. 514)

maturity The state of being mature. (p. 376)

mediator A person who leads those in conflict to a solution. (p. 124)

* **merit** Superior quality or worth; excellence. (p. 185)

* **mingle** To associate or take part with others; participate. (p. 509)

* **minor** A person under the legal age of full responsibility. (p. 44)

miscarriage The birth of a fetus before it is able to live outside the mother's body. (p. 620)

monitor To keep close watch over. (p. 632)

moral code Personal beliefs about what is right and wrong. (p. 32)

moral reasoning Dealing with moral issues by using logic and critical thinking. (p. 373)

morality A system of conduct based on what is right and wrong. (p. 371)

motivate To make others want to work, try, act, or achieve. (p. 169)

motor skill An ability or skill that depends on the use and control of muscles. (p. 631)

mutual Agreed to by both partners, as in a marriage. (p. 597)

mutual fund An investment company. (p. 456)

mutuality (ˌmyü-chə-'wa-lə-tē) A condition in which both people in a relationship contribute to the feelings and actions that support the relationship. (p. 88)

need Something required for a person's survival or growth. (p. 23)

negotiate To deal or bargain with another person. (p. 123)

nonverbal communication Communication without words. (p. 106)

notice An official statement of resignation presented by an employee to an employer. (p. 495)

* **novice** A person who is new to the circumstances, situation, or work in which he or she is placed. (p. 150)

nuclear family A family consisting of a mother, a father, and their children. (p. 44)

nurture To help growth or development in person or thing. (p. 146)

Glossary

obesity The condition of being more than 30 percent over the ideal body weight. (p. 430)

* **obligation** A binding contract, promise, or sense of duty. (p. 399)

optimist Someone with a positive point of view. (p. 340)

* **optimistic** Expecting the best; having a positive outlook. (p. 262)

option A possible course of action that one might choose. (p. 184)

* **ordeal** A difficult or painful experience, especially one that tests character or endurance. (p. 308)

* **organize** To put together into an orderly, functional, structured whole. (p. 431)

* **overwhelm** To overcome completely in mind or feeling. (p. 307)

parenting The process of caring for children and helping them grow and learn. (p. 607)

parenting readiness A couple's level of preparation for having and raising a child. (p. 615)

participatory leadership A style of leadership in which the leader and group members work together to make plans and decisions. (p. 170)

passive listening A response to communication that invites the speaker to share feelings and ideas. (p. 111)

pathogen A disease-causing organism. (p. 419)

* **pattern** A consistent, characteristic form, style, method, or set of actions. (p. 591)

peer pressure Social pressure on a person to adopt a type of behavior, dress, or attitude in order to be accepted as part of a group. (p. 510)

permissive style A parenting style in which parents use minimal authority. (p. 641)

personality The characteristics that make a person unique. (p. 26)

* **perspective** A mental view or outlook. (p. 355)

pessimist Someone with a negative point of view. (p. 340)

philosophy of life The sum of one's beliefs, attitudes, values, and priorities. (p. 381)

placenta The life-support system for a fetus during pregnancy. (p. 619)

* **plan** A scheme, program, or method worked out beforehand for the accomplishment of an objective or goal. (p. 250)

pollutant An impurity in the environment. (p. 393)

positive reinforcement Something that acts to encourage a specific behavior. (p. 642)

post-conventional level The level of moral development in which a person begins to evaluate customs, rules, and laws in terms of personal standards. (p. 372)

postpartum The period of time after a baby's birth. (p. 620)

* **potential** Capable of being but not yet in existence; possible. (p. 553)

power The ability to influence another person or thing. (p. 122)

pre-conventional level The first level of moral reasoning in which a person's thinking focuses on the outcome of behavior. (p. 372)

prejudice ('pre-jə-dəs) An unfair or biased opinion. (p. 379)

premarital counseling When couples get advice from trained professionals before marriage. (p. 572)

premium A periodic payment made to an insurance company. (p. 454)

prenatal The time from conception to birth. (p. 619)

prenuptial agreement (ˌprē-'nəp-shəl) An agreement made between partners before a wedding, usually pertaining to property, ownership, or roles. (p. 576)

* **prevalent** Widespread; common; in general use or acceptance. (p. 532)

preventive medicine Behavior that serves to deter or avoid disease or an averse condition. (p. 429)

* **principle** A rule of action or conduct. (p. 31)

prioritize To order things from first to last or from most important to least important. (p. 186)

* **privilege** A right. (p. 643)

problem A dilemma that must be solved or worked out. (p. 183)

* **process** A series of actions, changes, or functions bringing about a result. (p. 105)

procrastination (prə-ˌkras-tə-ˈnā-shən) The act of putting something off; delaying work on a task or project. (p. 189)

* **produce** To bring into existence; make or manufacture. (p. 393)

professionalism A positive attitude exhibited by workers. (p. 492)

* **prone** Having a natural inclination or tendency to do something. (p. 258)

propinquity (prə-ˈpiŋ-kwə-tē) Nearness in time or place. (p. 549)

Q

* **qualify** To provide with or have proper or necessary skills, knowledge, or credentials. (p. 488)

* **quirk** A peculiarity of action, behavior, or personality. (p. 631)

R

rape Forced sexual intercourse. (p. 538)

rapport (ra-ˈpȯr) A feeling of ease with another person. (p. 89)

readiness Traits and conditions that show whether a person is prepared for marriage. (p. 553)

* **recall** To bring back from memory; recollect; remember. (p. 594)

reciprocation (ri-ˌsi-prə-ˈkā-shən) Giving and receiving in return. (p. 160)

reciprocity (ˌre-sə-ˈprä-s(ə-)tē) Mutual exchange. (p. 510)

* **recognize** To know or identify, especially from past experience or knowledge. (p. 341)

reference A person who will recommend a job applicant's ability and character. (p. 494)

* **refuse** To show or express unwillingness. (p. 534)

reimbursement (ˌrē-əm-ˈbərs-mənt) Money paid back to a person to compensate for expenses they have incurred. (p. 236)

* **relate** To establish or demonstrate a connection between. (p. 617)

relationship A connection with another person. (p. 87)

* **remember** To recall to the mind with effort; think of again. (p. 380)

* **reminisce** To recall or tell of past experiences and events. (p. 294)

* **require** To have need of; need. (p. 576)

resilient (ri-ˈzil-yənt) To be able to recover from or adjust easily to misfortune or change. (p. 250)

* **resolution** A solution, accommodation, or settling of a problem. (p. 557)

resource Something that may be used to reach goals and solve problems. (p. 185)

resourceful To recognize and make good use of resources. (p. 197)

respite care Temporary care of a person so that his or her main caregiver can have a break. (p. 289)

* **restriction** A limitation. (p. 616)

résumé A written account of one's qualifications for a job, including education, training, experience, skills, and activities. (p. 494)

reward A benefit that brings pleasure and satisfaction in a relationship. (p. 90)

* **rigid** Inflexible; unyielding; stiff. (p. 278)

risk The possibility of loss or injury. (p. 186)

role An expected pattern of behavior. (p. 95)

role conflict Differing views of role expectations. (p. 98)

role expectation The behavior that is expected and anticipated from those who fill certain roles. (p. 96)

role model A person from whom one learns behavior and attitudes. (p. 96)

S

sacrifice To give something up. (p. 252)

* **satisfaction** The fulfillment or gratification of a desire, need, or appetite. (p. 225)

security deposit A one-time payment made to a property owner when renting a place to live, often equal to one month's rent. (p. 412)

self-discipline The ability to direct one's own behavior in a responsible way. (p. 378)

self-disclosure The willingness to share personal matters pertaining to oneself with others. (p. 89)

Glossary

self-esteem The way one feels about oneself. (p. 342)

serotonin (ˌsir-ə-ˈtō-nən) A brain chemical that affects mood and attitude. (p. 340)

service industry An industry in which careers are geared toward providing assistance to others for a fee. (p. 70)

sexual identity The way people see themselves as males and females. (p. 529)

sexuality One's beliefs and values about sexual behavior. (p. 532)

sexually transmitted infection (STI) An illness that is spread through sexual contact. (p. 535)

share An ownership position, or indicator of investment, in a company. (p. 456)

short-term goal A goal that requires a short period of time to achieve. (p. 194)

sibling A brother or sister. (p. 149)

single-parent family A family consisting of one parent and his or her children. (p. 44)

sleep deprivation (ˌde-prə-ˈvā-shən) Not getting enough sleep. (p. 438)

small claims court A court that handles cases that do not exceed a money limit set by the state. (p. 478)

socialization The process of learning social skills. (p. 28)

society A group of people who have determined patterns of relationships from being around one another. (p. 8)

* **source** Any thing or place from which something comes or is obtained; origin. (p. 75)

stability The quality of being firm and steadfast. (p. 269)

* **stable** Resistant to change of position or condition; not easily moved or disturbed. (p. 139)

standard A rule or principle that is used as a basis for judgment or comparison. (p. 199)

* **steadfast** Firmly loyal or constant; unwavering. (p. 269)

stereotype An idea about the qualities or behavior of a certain group of people. (p. 97)

sterility (stə-ˈri-lə-tē) The inability to have children. (p. 536)

* **stimulation** Excitement; invigoration. (p. 630)

stock Shares, or investment, in a company. (p. 456)

* **strategy** A plan, method, or series of maneuvers for obtaining a specific goal or result. (p. 183)

strength The ability to apply force. (p. 437)

stress Physical, mental, or emotional strain or tension. (p. 257)

stress management The application of strategies to cope with the demands of life. (p. 258)

subjective Based on one's personal feelings and opinions. (p. 150)

* **subtle** So slight or delicate as to be difficult to detect or describe. (p. 472)

* **sufficient** Enough; as much as is needed. (p. 215)

support system A group of family and friends who are available to provide support when needed. (p. 24, 195)

T

* **tact** A sense of what to say or do to avoid giving offense; skill in dealing with difficult or delicate situations. (p. 140)

* **tactic** A plan for attaining a particular goal. (p. 122)

teamwork Cooperating to achieve a common purpose. (p. 167)

technology The use of science to do practical things. (p. 207)

telecommute Using telephones, faxes, and computers to do the same work at home that one would do at a workplace. (p. 213)

temperament A person's inborn style of reacting to the world and relating to others. (p. 355)

tenant A person who rents and lives in another's property, such as a house or apartment. (p. 413)

* **thrive** To grow, develop, prosper; be fortunate or successful. (p. 371)

time-out A short time during which a child is removed from the presence of others or from an activity. (p. 643)

* **tolerant** Accepting of the beliefs, practices, actions, or traits of others. (p. 270)

tradition A custom that is followed over time. (p. 143)

* **trait** A distinguishing characteristic or quality. (p. 572)

* **transition** Passage from one form, state, style, or place to another. (p. 250)

trend A noticeable change that takes place over time. (p. 67)

trimester Each of the three time periods into which a pregnancy is divided. (p. 620)

trust The belief that others will not reject, betray, or hurt one. (p. 89)

U-shaped curve Something that starts at a high level, drops as time goes on, and then rises again, in a pattern that visually forms the letter U. (p. 591)

* **underlie** To be at the basis of; form a foundation of. (p. 587)

* **understand** To perceive and comprehend the nature and significance of; grasp. (p. 371)

unemployment The condition of not having a job. (p. 253)

* **unique** Being one of a kind. (p. 335)

* **valid** Sound; just; well founded. (p. 576)

values Beliefs and principles. (p. 31)

value system The set of values that one has. (p. 31)

* **venture** An undertaking that is dangerous, daring, or of uncertain outcome. (p. 412)

verbal communication Spoken words. (p. 106)

* **vibrant** Vigorous; lively; energetic. (p. 295)

violence When physical force is used to harm someone or something. (p. 317)

visual learning Learning by seeing. (p. 353)

* **vital** Of critical importance. (p. 15)

* **voluntary** Done willingly; using one's free will. (p. 87)

volunteer A person who performs or offers to perform a service voluntarily. (p. 395)

vulnerable Able to be wounded. (p. 131)

want Something that is desired but not essential. (p. 23)

warranty A written guarantee that often comes with newly purchased merchandise. (p. 471)

wellness A positive state of physical and mental health. (p. 429)

work ethic A set of values based on the moral virtues of hard work and diligence. (p. 225)

working relationship A relationship that exists to accomplish a task or goal. (p. 159)

Glossary

Index

Index

Y

Cover: (l) Radius Images, **(tr)** Jose Luis Pelaez, Inc./Corbis, **(cr)** Paul Barton/Corbis, **(br)** Jack Hollingsworth/Getty Images, **iv** (t) Stockbyte/Getty Images, **iv** (l) Corbis, **v** (b) Polka Dot Images/Jupiterimages, **vi** (b) Rob Gage/Getty Images, **vii** (t) Chris Ryan/Getty Images, **viii** (b) SW Productions/Real Latino Images, **ix** (t) Gary Salter/Zefa/Corbis, **x** (t) Ken Reid/Getty Images, **xi** (b) Kelly Redinger/Design Pics/Corbis, **xii** (t) Trinette Reed/Brand X Pictures/Jupiter Images. **xiv** (b), Jack Hollingsworth/Real Latino Images, **xviii** (c) Ariel Skelley/Getty Images, **xix** (b) Alex Mares-Manton/Getty Images, **xx** (c), Brand X Pictures/PunchStock, **xxiv** (c), Martyn Vickery/Alamy, **xxiv** (b) Ariel Skelley/Corbis, **xxvi** (b) Getty Images/SW Productions, **xxvii** (c) Creatas/PunchStock, **xliii** (cr), Arthur Tilley/Photodisc/Getty Images, **xliv** (t) Royalty-free/Photodisc/Getty Images, **2-3** Jupiter Images; 4-5 Jupiter Images; **7** Jupiterimages; **9** Mary Kate Denny/Photo Edit; **10** Corbis; **13** Donna Coleman; **14** Getty Images/Jack Hollingsworth; **20-21** Corbis; **23** David Perez Shadi; **24** Dylan Ellis; **26** Real Latino Images, LLC; **27** SW Productions/Getty Images; **28** Zen Shui/Tips Images; **31** Real Latino Images, LLC; **33** Ronnie Kaufman; **34** (bl) David Hiller/Getty Images; (br) Getty Images/Digital Vision;. **35** Creatas Images/JupiterImages; (bc) Adrian Sherratt/Alamy; (bl) Jeff Greenberg/Alamy; **40-41** Comstock Select/Corbis; **43** Botanica/Jupiter Images; **45** Time & Life Pictures/Getty Images/Rich Frishman; **47** Brand X/Corbis; **48** Thinkstock/Jupiter Images; **49** Brand X Pictures/PunchStock; **50** Jack Hollingsworth/Real Latino Images; **53** Steve Mason/Getty Images; **54** Ariel Skelley/Corbis; **56** (bc) Jason Lugo; (bl) Tim Pannell/Corbis; (br) Paul Kline; **57** (bc) Jupiter Images/Corbis; (bl) Jack Hollingsworth/Real Latino Images; (br) Corbis; **60** Brand X Pictures/PunchStock; **64-65** Harris Brown/Corbis; **67** Blend Images/Jupiter Images; **69** Patagonik Works/Real Latino Images; **70** Getty Images; **74** Cliff Parnell/iStockphoto; **76** Robin Ryan; **81** Real Latino Images; **82-83** Dex Images/Corbis; **84** Terry Halsey/Real Latino Images; **87** Rob Gage/Getty Images; **88** (bc) Image Source/Getty Images; (bl) Creatas/PunchStock; (br) Christian Hoehn/Getty Images; **89** (bc) Inspirestock Inc./Alamy; (bl) Digital Vision/Getty Images; (br) Andrew Hetherington/Getty Images; **90** McGraw-Hill Companies/Kefover/Opatrany; **92** Image Source; **95** Liquidlibrary/Jupiterimages; **102-103** Comstock Images/Jupiter Images; **105** Image 100/Jupiter Images; **107** Artemis Gordon; **110** Getty Images/SW Productions; **114** Ginger Burr; **118-119** Bonnie Kamin/PhotoEdit; **121** Robert Llewellyn/Corbis; **123** Corbis; **124** Jupiter Images; **127** SuperStock/Jupiter Images; **129** Ron Chapple/Thinkstock/Jupiter Images; **130** Robert Llewellyn/ImageState/Alamy; **132** Creatas/PunchStock; **136-137** Jim Arbogast/Getty Images; **139** BananaStock/PunchStock; **140** Brand X Pictures/Jupiter Images; **142** (bc) Ken Seet/Corbis; (bl) Corbis; (br) Ariel Skelley/Corbis; **143** (bc) Rosanne Olson; (bl) Ron Chapple/Thinkstock/Getty Images; (br) Jupiter Images/Tetra Images; **146** Simon Marcus/Corbis; **148** BananaStock/PunchStock; **149** Yellow Dog Productions/Getty; **150** Radius Images/Jupiterimages; **156** Chris Ryan/Getty Images; **159** Superstudio/Getty Images; **161** Amana Productions Inc./Getty Images; **162** Nick White/Getty Images; **164** Inti St. Clair/Getty Images; **167** Royalty-Free/Jupiterimages; **168** Vicky Kasala/Photodisc; **169** Jupiter Images/Thinkstock/Alamy; **171** Jonathan Daniel/Getty; **177** BananaStock/PunchStock **178-179** Somos Images/Corbis; **180-181** Jaubert Bernard/Alamy; **183** Image100/Jupiter Images; **184** Image100, Ltd; **187** (b) Bonnie Kamin/PhotoEdit; (tl) Jose Luis Pelaez/Blend Images RF/Getty Images; (tr) Corbis Royalty-free; **188** Don Mason/Corbis; **190** Ausloeser/Zefa/Corbis; **193** Image Source Pink/Getty Images; **194** C Squared Studios/Getty Images; **195** Tony Freeman/PhotoEdit; **197** Michael Keller/Corbis; **199** Score By Aflo/Jupiter; **204-205** Jose Luis Pelaez Inc./Getty Images; **207** Moodboard/Corbis; **209** Getty Images; **213** Keith Brofsky/Getty Images; **214** BananaStock/PictureQuest; **215** Getty Images; **216** Comstock Images/PictureQuest; **218** John A. Rizzo/Getty Images; **222-223** Asia Images/Jupiter Images; **225** Jeff Cadge/Getty Images; **227** Yellow Dog Productions/Getty Images; **228** Workbook Stock/Jupiterimages; **231** Corbis/Jupiterimages; **233** Brand X Pictures/PunchStock; **234** (bc) Comstock/PunchStock; (bl) Comstock/Jupiter Images; (br) Jim Arbogast/Getty Images; **235** (bc) BananaStock/PunchStock; (bl) White Rock/Getty Images; (br) Corbis; **236** Picture Partners/Alamy; **238** Digital Vision/Getty Images; **243** Image Source Pink/Getty Images **244-245** SW Productions/Real Latino Images; **246** Lisa B./Corbis; **249** Tetra Images/Alamy; **250** Somos/Veer/Getty Images; **253** Digital Vision; **254** Onoky-Photononstop/Alamy; **257** Digital Vision/Getty Images; 258 Getty Images/SW Productions; **260** (bc) Ryan McVay/Getty Images; (bl) Purestock/PunchStock; (br)) Charlie Drevstam/Getty Images; **261** (bc) Terry Halsey/Real Latino Images; (bl) Altrendo Images/Getty Images; (br) Paul Barton/Corbis; **266-267** Jupiter Images; **269** Andrea Morini/Getty Images; **272** Corbis/Jupiterimages; **275** BananaStock/PunchStock; **276** Corbis; **277** Kristy-Anne Glubish/Design Pics/Corbis; **278** Digital Vision; **280** Corbis; **284-285** Stockbyte/Getty Images; **287** Jupiter Images; **289** Jose Luis Pelaez, Inc./CORBIS; **291** Gabe Palmer/Corbis; **294** Jupiter Images; **295** Photodisc Collection/Getty Images; **296** (bc) Anderson Ross/Blend Images/Alamy; (bl) Bob Rowan/Corbis; (br) Stockbyte/Punch-Stock; **297** (bc) Tim Pannell/Corbis; (bl) Jupiter Images; (br) Stockbyte/PunchStock; **298** Jack Hollingsworth/Real Latino Images; **300** D. Allen; **304-305** BananaStock/PunchStock; **307** Bruce Chambers/Orange County Register/Corbis; **308** (bc) Manchan/Digital Vision/Alamy; (bl) William Gottlieb/Corbis; (br) Milk Photographie/Corbis; **309** (bc) Zigy Kaluzny/Getty Images; (bl) Reza Estakhrian/Getty Images; (br) Seth Wenig/Star Ledger/Corbis; **310** Jupiter Images; **313** Image Source Black/Jupiter Images; **315** Lisa Peardon/Getty Images; **317** STOCK4B/Getty Images; **318** Corbis; **319** Owen Franken/Corbis; **321** Kevin R. Morris/Bohemian Nomad Picturemakers/Corbis; **322** Sean Justice/Getty Images; **324** Corbis; **329** Digital Vision/Getty Images; **330-331** Rick Gomez/Corbis; **332-333** Moodboard/Corbis; **335** Gary Salter/Zefa/Corbis; **336** Brand X Pictures/PunchStock; **337** Thomas Northcut/Getty Images; **340** SW Productions/Getty Images; **343** Jupiter Images/Corbis; **348-349** Purestock/PunchStock; **351** Simon Marcus/Corbis; **352** Images Source Pink/Alamy; **354** Digital Vision; **355** Andy Cox/Getty Images; **358** Purestock/Getty Images; **360** Graeme Harris/Getty Images; **362** (bl) Ken Seet/Corbis; (br) Tetra Images/Getty Images; **363** (bc) Sam Diephuis/Zefa/Corbis; (bl) Rick Gomez/Corbis; (br) Alan Powdrill/Getty Images; **368-369** Thinkstock/Corbis; **371** David Young-Wolff/Alamy; **372** Helen King/Corbis; **376** Getty Images/Real Latino Images; **377** Corbis; **379** Arthur Tilley/Getty Images; **380** Stock4B/Getty Images; **382** Unknown; **386-387** Jim West/PhotoEdit; **389** Powered by Light/Alan Spencer/Alamy; **390** Corbis; **392** Jim West/Alamy; **396** (bc) Marc Romanielli/Getty Images; (bl) Blend Images/Jupiter Images; (br) Jeff Greenberg/Alamy; **397** (bc) David Young-Wolff/Alamy; (bl) David Grossman/Alamy; (br) Bob Daemmrich/PhotoEdit, Inc.; **398** James Shaffer/PhotoEdit, Inc.; **400** Corbis; **405** David Young-Wolff/Alamy **406-407** Adam Gault/Getty Images; **408-409** Image Source Pink/Getty Images; **412** James Woodson/Getty Images; **414** Janis Christie/Getty Images; **417** Reggie Casagrande/Getty Images; **419** Stockbyte/Real Latino Images; **420** Clarissa Leahy/Zefa/Corbis; **426-427** Jamie Grill/Getty Images; **429** BananaStock/Jupiter Images; **430** Wesley Hitt/Getty Images; **434** Jack Hollingsworth/Getty Images; **436** Keith Ovregaard/Cole Group/Getty Images; **438** GoGo Images/Jupiter Images; **440** Kelly Redinger/Design Pics/Corbis; **442** Brand X Pictures/PunchStock; **446-447** Jack Hollingsworth/Alamy; **449** Kevin Dodge/Corbis; **450** Corbis; **451** Tom Stewart/Corbis; **452** Flying Colours Ltd/Getty Images; **454** Stewart Cohen/Getty Images; **458** Jupiter Images; **460** David Stuart/Getty Images; **462** Sean Justice/Corbis; **466-477** Plush Studios/Blend Images/Corbis; **469** Comstock Select/Corbis; **472** McGraw-Hill Companies, Inc./Gary He, Photographer; **475** Corbis; **477** Brand X Pictures/Punch-Stock; **482-483** Peter Dazeley/Getty Images; **485** DreamPictures/Getty Images; **486** Corbis; **489** Comstock/PictureQuest; **492** Image Source Black/Getty Images; **494** (bl) Jose Luis Pelaez, Inc./Getty Images; (br) Koki Lino/Getty Images; (cr) James Woodson/Getty Images; **495** (bc) Image100/Corbis; (bl) Ken Reid/Getty Images; (br) Digital Vision/Getty Images; **501** Corbis **502-503** Yang Liu/CORBIS; **504-505** Jack Hollingsworth/Corbis; **507** Ryan McVay/Getty Images; **508** PhotoAlto; **513** Greatstock Photographic Library/Alamy; **514** Comstock Images/Jupiter Images; **517** Digital Vision/Alamy; **518** Corbis; **524-525** Digital Vision/Getty Images; **527** Gary Salter/Zefa/Corbis; **528** ColorBlind Images/Getty Images; **529** Monika Bender/Getty Images; **532** Kelly Redinger/Design Pics/Corbis; **533** Toshio Hoshi/Jupiter Images; **534** Digital Vision/PunchStock; **540** Image100 Ltd.; **544-545** George Doyle/Real Latino Images; **547** George Doyle/Real Latino Images; **548** Rolf Bruderer/Corbis; **550** Images Source Black/Alamy; **553** Images Source Pink/Getty Images; **554** Digital Vision/Getty Images; **555** IT Stock/PunchStock; **557** Somos/Veer/Getty Images; **563** Kelly Redinger/Design Pics/Corbis **564-565** Ariel Skelley/Getty Images; **566-567** Brand X Pictures/PunchStock; **569** Martyn Vickery/Alamy; **571** Sean Justice/Corbis; **572** Ariel Skelley/CORBIS; **575** Janis Christie/Getty Images; **577** CBP Photo/Alamy; **578** Buccina Studios/Getty Images; **579** OJO Images Ltd/Alamy; **584-585** Digital Vision/Real Latino Images; **587** Kevin Dodge/Corbis; **588** Somos Images/Corbis; **589** Kirk Weddle/Getty Images; **593** Eric Audras/Alamy; **594** (bc) Tom Merton/Getty Images; (bl) Allison Michael Orenstein/Getty Images; (br) Blue Jean Images/Getty Images; **595** (bc) Christopher Robbins; (bl) John Henley/Getty Images; (br) Dan Tong/Real Latino Images; **598** Mark Karrass/Corbis; **600** Russell Bickers; **604-605** Larry Williams/Zefa/Corbis; **607** E. Dygas/Getty Images; **608** Images Source/Jupiter Images; **609** Simon Marcus/Corbis; **610** Artiga Photo/Corbis; **615** BananaStock/Alamy; **616** Digital Vision/Getty Images; **617** Dex Image/Jupiter Images; **619** BananaStock/Jupiter Images; **620** Trinette Reed/Brand X Pictures/Jupiter Images; **622** Thinkstock Images/JupiterImages; **626-627** Jupiter Images/Comstock Images/Alamy; **629** Digital Archive Japan/Punchstock; **631** Don and Liysa King/Getty Images; **632** Radius Images/Jupiter Images; **634** (bc) Gareth Brown/Corbis; (bl) Andersen Ross/Getty Images; (br) JGI/Getty Images; **635** (bc) Bruno Morandi/Robert Harding World Imagery/Corbis; (bl) Brand X Pictures/Jupiter Images; (br) Rick Gomez/Corbis; **636** Tom Grill/Corbis; **637** Thinkstock Images/Jupiter Images; **640** Photodisc Collection/Getty Images; **641** Patrik Giardino/Corbis; **642** Dex Images/Corbis; **643** JUPITERIMAGES/Brand X/Alamy; **649** Alex Mares-Manton/Getty Images